A CALENDAR OF THE CARTULARIES
OF JOHN PYEL AND ADAM FRAUNCEYS

A CALENDAR OF THE CARTULARIES OF JOHN PYEL AND ADAM FRAUNCEYS

edited by

S. J. O'Connor

CAMDEN FIFTH SERIES
VOLUME 2 (1993)

LONDON
OFFICES OF THE ROYAL HISTORICAL SOCIETY
UNIVERSITY COLLEGE LONDON
GOWER STREET WC1
1993

British Library Cataloguing in Publication Data

Cartularies of John Pyel and Adam Fraunceys.—
  (Camden fifth series; v. 2).
  1. History—Periodicals
  I. Royal Historical Society   II. Series
ISBN 0-86193-137-8

Printed and bound in Great Britain by
Butler & Tanner Ltd, Frome and London

CONTENTS

ACKNOWLEDGEMENTS

The publication of this volume is due in no small measure to the help and generosity of many people. In particular I should like to thank the Marquess of Salisbury for allowing me to work on the Fraunceys cartulary for such a lengthy period, and the archivist at Hatfield House, Robin Harcourt Williams, for depositing the manuscript at Senate House Library for my convenience. Equally, I should like to thank the College of Arms for allowing me unlimited access to the Pyel cartulary, and Robert Yorke, the College archivist, for all his kindness and assistance during the time that I worked at the College. I would also like to express my gratitude to Helen Young and the staff at the Palaeography Room, Senate House Library, who willingly took responsibility for the Hatfield manuscript while I transcribed it, and to the staff of the Corporation of London Record Office, where I worked regularly for some months. My debts to individuals for their help and advice are many, but I would like to offer special thanks to Barbara Harvey and Vanessa Harding for their constructive comments, and to the present editor of the Series, Michael Jones, for his editorial advice and not least his patience. Finally I wish to acknowledge the support of the History Department at Bedford and Royal Holloway Colleges, London, during my years as an undergraduate and postgraduate there, and I am especially indebted to Caroline Barron, who first encouraged me to embark on research and whose enthusiasm, guidance and boundless faith sustained me through long periods of doubt.

ABBREVIATIONS

Abbrev. Rot. Orig.	*Rotulorum Originalium in Curia Scaccarii Abbrevatio*, 2 vols., ii (London, 1810)
Beaven	*Aldermen of the City of London, temp. Henry III–1908*, ed. A.B. Beaven, 2 vols. (London, 1908)
BL	British Library
CCR	*Calendar of Close Rolls 1227–* (HMSO, 1902–)
CFR	*Calendar of Fine Rolls 1272–* (HMSO, 1911–)
Cheapside	D. Keene and V. Harding, *Historical Gazeteer of London before the Fire* (SESML): *Cheapside* (Cambridge, 1987), (microfiches)
CIMisc.	*Calendar of Inquisitions Miscellaneous 1219–1422*, 7 vols. (HMSO, 1916–68)
CIPM	*Calendar of Inquisitions Post Mortem* (HMSO, 1904–)
CLRO	Corporation of London Record Office
CPL	*Calendar of Papal Letters* (HMSO, 1893–)
CPP	*Calendar of Papal Petitions* (HMSO, 1896–)
CPR	Calendar of Patent Rolls 1216– (HMSO, 1901–)
CWCH	*Calendar of Wills enrolled in the Court of Husting, London 1258–1688*, ed. R.R. Sharpe, 2 vols. (London, 1889)
EconHR	*Economic History Review*
EHR	*English Historical Review*
Feet of Fines, Essex	*Feet of Fines for Essex*, ii (Colchester, 1928)
Feet of Fines Lond. & Middx.	*Calendar of Feet of Fines for London and Middlesex*, ed. W. J. Hardy and W. Page (London, 1892–3)
Foedera	*Foedera, Conventiones, Litterae et Acta Publica*, ed. T. Rymer, iii parts 1–2 (London, 1825–30)
LB	*Calendar of London Letter Books* A–L, ed. R.R. Sharpe (London, 1899–1912)
LPA	*London Possessory Assizes, a Calendar*, ed. H.M. Chew (London Record Society, i, 1965)
NRO	Northamptonshire Record Office
PRO	Public Record Office
SESML	Social and Economic Study of Medieval London
VCH	Victoria History of the Counties of England
Walbrook	D. Keene, *The Walbrook Study: Summary Report and Appendix* (SESML, 1987)
WAM	Westminster Abbey Muniments

INTRODUCTION

The manuscripts calendared in this volume, Hatfield CP 291.1 and College of Arms Vincent 64, are lay cartularies compiled for two London merchants, Adam Fraunceys (*ob.* 1375) and John Pyel (*ob.* 1382), men who emerged from shadowy beginnings to become wealthy members of London's mercantile élite and who purchased for themselves substantial estates outside the city. Fraunceys's cartulary is an abstract of the charters in his possession relating to his manors in Essex and Middlesex, while Pyel's deals mostly, though not exclusively, with his lands in Northamptonshire. Both supply detailed evidence of the way in which the manors were acquired and these methods will be examined more closely later.[1] The cartularies are also of intrinsic interest, in view of the rarity of lay cartularies in general, and a detailed description and analysis of their arrangement and purpose will be given in part 3 of this introduction. But more broadly they draw together two contemporary Londoners of substance who might not otherwise have been identified so closely with each other, and so provide a basis for a comparative study of their lives, careers and social aspirations which makes an important contribution to our all too limited knowledge of the personalities behind a burgeoning and increasingly influential urban middle class.[2]

---

1 See below pp. 37–74.

2 Among the few fourteenth-century merchants for whom biographies have already been attempted are Richer de Refham: B. Breslow, 'The Social Status and Economic Interests of Richer de Refham, Lord Mayor of London', *Journal of Medieval History* iii (1977), 135–45 and 'Ambiguities of Political Loyalties in Edwardian England: the Case of Richer de Refham', *Medieval Prosopography* vi (1985), 47–68; Gilbert Maghfeld: M. K. James, 'A London Merchant of the Fourteenth Century', *EconHR*, 2nd Ser., viii (1956), 364–76; Richard Lyons: A.R. Myers, 'The Wealth of Richard Lyons' in T.A. Sandquist and M.R. Powicke, eds., *Essays in Medieval History presented to Bertie Wilkinson* (Toronto, 1969), 301–29; William de la Pole: E.B. Fryde, *William de la Pole, Merchant and King's Banker* (London, 1988); Richard Whittington: C.M. Barron, 'Richard Whittington: the Man behind the Myth' in A.E. Hollander and William Kellaway, eds., *Studies in London History presented to P.E. Jones* (London, 1969), 197–248. There is also the rather older account of the life of John Lovekyn by A. Heale, 'Some Account of John Lovekyn', *Transactions of the London and Middlesex Archaeological Society* vi (1890), 341–70, besides those biographies of London merchants contained in *The House of Commons 1386–1421*, ed. J.S. Roskell, Linda Clark and Carole Rawcliffe, 4 vols. (History of Parliament Trust, 1992).

1. BIOGRAPHICAL BACKGROUND

i. Adam Fraunceys

Adam Fraunceys rose to become one of the wealthiest and most influential members of the London merchant class of his generation, yet of his background we know virtually nothing. He was born, probably in the first decade of the fourteenth century, in the obscurity of a provincial town or village, perhaps in the north of England, of parents whose names alone we know. His patronymic is of little help in locating his origins. The name, which simply means Frenchman, was common enough throughout England, and there were many men of that name engaged in trade in London itself at this time who were not necessarily of the same family. Indeed, not a few of the Fraunceys living in England in the fourteenth century were also called Adam, a fact which not only adds to our problems of identification but was to cause some embarrassment to the London mercer himself in later life.

From the survival of a single charter,[3] we learn that Fraunceys's father's name was also Adam and his mother's Constance, but no further acknowledgement of his parents occurs, beyond a cursory item in his will ordaining chantry masses to be said for their souls.[4] Some time before May 1359 he married Agnes, probably a London girl, though not before she had borne him at least two sons, Robert and Adam.[5] A third son, Thomas, died in infancy, and Robert, too, predeceased his father between 1362 and 1368. Fraunceys also had three daughters, Joan and Maud, who seem to have died in early life, and another Maud, who survived her father and went on to make a succession of good marriages.[6] A string of Christian names which follows the dedication to Adam's parents in his will may also refer to members of the family. Among these are Adam, perhaps an older brother, and Thomas and Maud, possibly his dead children (although there is no mention of Robert and Joan), the others being Simon, Peter, Roger, Richard, John, Sarah, Margaret and Juliana. Some of these may also have been dead children or siblings, or other members of the household. Simon Fraunceys, however, was the name of an eminent London mercer and former mayor, who died in 1358, with whom Adam was closely associated and for whom he had acted as executor. It is possible that this name refers to him.

3 BL Harl(eian) Ch(arters) 79.G.38.
4 CLRO Will of Adam Fraunceys enrolled in Hustings HR 103/79.
5 Below, Fraunceys Cartulary (hereafter F) 60.
6 BL Harl. Ch. 79.G.38, dated 21 March 1368, mentions Robert, Thomas, Joan and Maud as deceased children of Adam. Robert was mentioned as his father's heir in charters until July 1362 (*CCR 1360–4*, 411), and presumably died between these dates. No other mention is made of Thomas or his two sisters, who may all have died very young.

The whereabouts of the ancestral home presents a deeper problem. It is more than likely that the family were immigrants to the city.[7] If Adam was a newcomer to London, there is a large number of possible places from which he might have travelled. There were Fraunceys in most counties of England in the early fourteenth century, and even if we take those bearing familiar Christian names the choice is wide.[8] One such family, living in Lincolnshire, numbered among its members at least one citizen of London. These were the sons of William Fraunceys of Tathewell, John, Ellis and Richard. Ellis and Richard had both seen service with the duke of Lancaster in Brittany, at whose instigation they escaped outlawry for murder in 1358,[9] and at the same time Ellis received exemption from civic and civil duties at the behest of John, duke of Brittany.[10] It is quite possible that he was the same man as Ellis Fraunceys of London, mercer, associate of both Simon and Adam Fraunceys. His brother Richard was indeed a London citizen, and perhaps also a mercer, who died in 1374 and was buried at St Botolph's, Aldgate.[11]

Perhaps the strongest of these circumstantial connections links Adam Fraunceys with the county of Yorkshire. As elsewhere, charters in the county make frequent isolated references to men with his surname, but

7 There is a reference to an Adam Fraunceys who was master of a leper hospital at Eye in Westminster in 1337, and a passing reference to a man of that name accused of affray in London in 1305, but neither can be said with much conviction to be connected with the merchant's family (*CPR 1334–8*, 474, *Calendar of Trailbaston Trials under Commissions of 1305 and 1306*, ed. R.B. Pugh (London, 1975); no. 193.) Given the high death rate among children even of the greater citizens, the city was dependent on large numbers of immigrants to support the population levels, many of whom were children sent away from home to apprenticeships in London, (S.L. Thrupp, *The Merchant Class of Medieval London* (Chicago, 1948), 200, 206–7).

8 There was, for example, a tenant of the manor of Buckenham in Norfolk in 1306 named Adam Fraunceys, and references follow in 1308 to Robert and Juliana Fraunceys, the former described as a free tenant, the latter as villein of the same manor (*CCR 1302–7*, 475; *1307–13*, 61). Isolated references to men called Adam Fraunceys occur in a variety of locations. In 1318 John and Adam Fraunceys were among several men, including William, abbot of Malmesbury and one of his monks, accused of robbing Humphrey de Bohun, earl of Hereford, and assaulting his men at Lechlade, on the borders of Gloucester, Oxford and Wiltshire (*CPR 1317–21*, 295). In the same part of the country, the abbot of Cirencester received a pardon from the king in October 1315 for acquiring from Richard de Mynty and Adam Fraunceys certain lands and tenements in Minety, Wiltshire (*CPR 1313–7*, 364). And earlier, on 2 June 1302, Adam, son of Thomas Fraunceys, was pardoned for his part in causing the death of William Pyncheron in Markfield, Leicestershire (*CPR 1301–7*, 37).

9 *CPR 1358–61*, 35, 472.

10 Ibid., 35.

11 Will enrolled in Commissary Court of London, Reg. 1, f. 1. It is possible that Richard Fraunceys of Tathewell was the mercer of the same name to whom Adam Fraunceys granted the reversion of tenements of Simon Fraunceys in 1371 (CLRO Husting Rolls HR 99/154). See below.

it is his close relations with Simon Fraunceys, together with other factors, which make Yorkshire a more probable birthplace than elsewhere.

Simon Fraunceys was a generation older than Adam, but like him was mercer, alderman and mayor, and became a wealthy financier.[12] He first appears in the London records in 1311 at the time of his son John's apprenticeship.[13] Simon was described on that occasion as coming from Pontefract, and Professor Gwyn Williams has suggested that he came south with a number of his family in tow.[14] Adam's recorded associations with Simon are not frequent but are cumulatively significant. In the late summer of 1349 Simon Fraunceys and Thomas Leggy were besieged in a house in Puckeridge in Hertfordshire by a mob of locals and were rescued by mainprise of Adam Fraunceys and some other London citizens.[15] Two years later a storm at sea provides evidence of a joint business venture. During the winter of 1350–1 the two men had sent a shipload of merchandise north to Newcastle upon Tyne under the supervision of John Salman and Thomas de Eston, described as serjeants and merchants, when a gale blew the ship off course and John and Thomas were forced to put in at the port of Orwell in Suffolk, where the subsidy collectors impounded the ship pending payment of a levy on their goods.[16] In November 1352, Simon and Adam joined John Malwayn, alderman, in advancing £8,000 to the Exchequer.[17] Simon is also a witness to certain property deals of Adam and John Pyel, and himself had lands in Essex adjoining Adam's own manor at Leyton.[18] Finally, Adam was one of the executors of Simon's will in 1358, with Ellis Fraunceys, mercer, both men granting Simon's heir, Thomas, a loan of 2,000 marks on his father's death.[19] None of this is proof of a family relationship, but it does indicate a close association and raises the possibility that, if not a blood relative, Adam may at least have come from the same part of the country as Simon and may even, perhaps, have been apprenticed to him, adopting his surname.

There is further evidence which links Adam with Yorkshire, although it is equally circumstantial. Inserted into the Fraunceys cartulary is a copy of the proceedings of a court of King's Bench in 1369 which rehearses the details of a previous case held in York in 1350. This

12 For his civic career, see Beaven, i, 385.

13 *LBD*, 150.

14 G. Williams, *Medieval London: From Commune to Capital* (Oxford, 1963), 140. It is not quite clear what the evidence is for this assumption.

15 *CPR 1348–50*, 388.

16 *CCR 1349–54*, 348.

17 PRO Receipt Rolls E401/416, 19 Nov.-3 Dec. 1352.

18 *VCH Essex* vi, ed. R.B. Pugh (London, 1973), 256, 260.

19 CLRO Husting Rolls, HR 86/87; *CCR 1354–60*, 519.

concerned two felons named Adam Fraunceys, one of whom came from Ribchester in Lancashire, who in 1342 had perpetrated a number of crimes in the region of Hothersall, near Ribchester, and in Airedale and Bradley near Huddersfield in West Yorkshire.[20] It seems that neither of the accused appeared in court at the time and both were subsequently outlawed. This coincidence of name was causing Adam Fraunceys of London no little trouble and inconvenience, to the extent, apparently, that legal proceedings had been taken up against him.[21] He therefore took the initiative of going to court at Westminster, in November 1369, armed with a writ from the king which established that he was neither of the above outlaws, notwithstanding their common name. That Adam should have felt himself obliged to take such action to clear his name nineteen years after the original hearing suggests perhaps that suspicion attached to him not only because of his name, but also because of his earlier connections with that part of the country.

If Adam did originate from Yorkshire, he clearly severed all ties with his native region. He made no bequests there and seems to have had no intention of returning. Londoners who came from nearer parts, East Anglia, for example, or the East Midlands, seem more likely to have maintained links with their past, if not actually to have returned there in glory.[22]

Adam had moved to London and become a citizen before December 1339, when he first appears in the records responding to an appeal from the king for money.[23] His loan of £100 was significantly large and suggests that he had become a well-established and moderately wealthy merchant by that date. Fraunceys was in Bruges in late 1339, where he perhaps spent much of his time in the next few years, building up a commercial network. Bruges was a thriving town thronged with alien merchants, 'perhaps the greatest market of Christendom in the fourteenth century'.[24] It was not only a receptacle for English merchandise

20 F1286.
21 This suggests that outlawry had been proclaimed against the accused in London, although no record of this has come to light.
22 John Curteys of Higham Ferrers, a neighbour and partner of John Pyel, who had established himself in London later left the city to settle himself in grand style at Wemington on the Bedfordshire/Northamptonshire borders. And as we shall see, Pyel himself bought up land in and around his home village in Northamptonshire in anticipation of his retirement there. Michael Bennett notes, by contrast, how few Cheshire careerists, merchants or otherwise, returned to their native shire, but preferred to settle in other counties, closer to London. Edmund Shaa, for example, bought lands in Essex (M. Bennett, 'Sources and Problems in the Study of Social Mobility: Cheshire in the Middle Ages', *Transactions of the Historic Society of Lancashire and Cheshire for 1978* cxxviii (Liverpool, 1979), 84–5; Thrupp, *Merchant Class*, 366.)
23 *CPR 1338–40*, 405.
24 J.A. Van Houtte, 'The rise and decline of the market of Bruges', *EconHR*, 2nd Ser., xix (1966), 37.

to be distributed to other parts of the Low Countries, it also attracted a wide variety of goods from elsewhere, especially the Hanseatic towns and Italy, providing a ready import market for English merchants, and was for most of the 1340s the staple town for English wool.[25] There is unfortunately very little information regarding Fraunceys's mercantile career, but we know that his business was extensive and diverse and he derived sufficient wealth from his operations to be a financial supporter of the customs farmers in the late 1340s.[26]

Adam Fraunceys was a mercer and one of the four wardens recorded in the account book of 1347, yet surprisingly there is no trace of his dealing in mercery.[27] It was Richard Whittington's lucrative contracts to supply luxury cloths to the royal household which helped to further his career at the end of the century, and we might have expected Adam Fraunceys to have established himself in a similar way, but on supplies of such goods to the Crown or, indeed, to aristocratic households the records are silent.[28] Fraunceys was supplying the royal household with wine in 1347, but this seems to be an isolated occurrence for which there were probably special reasons.[29] Like most merchants, however, he was certainly dealing in wool, and this throughout his career.

Evidence of Fraunceys's wool trading, as with all his commercial activities, is patchy. To have lent money to the Crown at all during the 1340s, and especially to have been a financial backer of the customs farmers, a merchant must have been exporting some wool at least, so that he might be assured of a return on the loan. We know for certain that Fraunceys was exporting wool for the seventeen-month period between 21 April 1349 and 29 September 1350, although we do not know in what quantity. From the account book of John Malwayn, receiver of the customs and subsidy, we learn that Adam Fraunceys was in receipt of customs relief (*mitigacione*), amounting to £166 13s 4d, for exporting wool from several ports in England, according to the terms of an earlier agreement.[30] Adam and his partner John Pyel were possibly buying wool from Sulby abbey in Northamptonshire in the early 1350s, as well as entering into other financial arrangements there.[31]

25 Ibid., 34–6; D. Nicholas, 'The English Trade at Bruges in the Last Years of Edward III', *Journal of Medieval History* v (1979), 45.

26 E.B. Fryde 'The English Farmers of the Customs, 1343–51' in his *Studies in Medieval Trade and Finance* (London, 1983), X 5.

27 Heather Creaton, 'The Wardens' Accounts of the Mercers' Company of London, 1347, 1391–1464', (unpublished M.Phil. thesis, University of London, 1977), 2 vols., i, 148.

28 Barron, 'Richard Whittington', in *Studies in London History*, 199–202.

29 PRO Butlerage Accounts E101/79/17. See Stephen O'Connor, 'Finance, Diplomacy and Politics: royal service by two London merchants in the reign of Edward III' in *Historical Research* lxvii (1994), 18–39.

30 PRO E122/158/37.

31 Pyel Cartulary (hereafter P) 35–6.

Fraunceys was mayor of the Staple of Westminster in 1357,[32] and was appointed collector of the customs himself on several occasions in the late 1350s and 1360s, including 1365–6, which is the only year in which a detailed record of his wool exports survives. Fraunceys's total exports for that year amounted to 524 sacks, $11\frac{1}{2}$ cloves at a value of £1,217 19s $1\frac{1}{2}$d.[33] That wool was a major part of Fraunceys's trading operations can be seen further from a letter written to the treasurer Thomas Brantingham, bishop of Exeter, by Adam de Bury, mayor of Calais, on 9 September 1370, in which he speaks of a meeting at the Austin Friars in London of leading merchants of the Staple, including Adam Fraunceys, at which concerns were raised regarding the charges made at the Staple of Westminster on wool and woolfells due to be shipped to Calais.[34]

Details of Adam Fraunceys's other commercial ventures are virtually non-existent. As we have already seen, he had a business association with Simon Fraunceys, who had his fingers in a number of mercantile pies besides mercery, and who had been supplying the royal household with a wide variety of goods, especially between the years 1325 and 1332.[35] In April 1354, towards the end of his second term as mayor, Adam Fraunceys took the opportunity to write an official letter to the mayor and bailiffs of Huntingdon, complaining of a distraint made of his merchandise while it was being transported through their 'country', in default of a custom which they had demanded and which Adam reminded them was 'contrary to the franchise of the city of London'.[36] In 1368, Sir Henry Beaumont carried abroad with him a letter of exchange of Adam Fraunceys for £1,000, which would bring him an equivalent amount in foreign currency at his destination. This letter provides some evidence, at least, of commercial contact with the provincial gentry, otherwise remarkably absent.[37]

32 *CCR 1354–60*, 387.

33 PRO Customs Accounts E122/70/18 mm.6–9d. He was also appointed customs collector in April 1361, February 1363 and August 1368 (*CFR 1356–68*, 158, 250, 386), presumably coinciding with an increase in the financial support he was lending the Crown at this time. See O'Connor, 'Finance, Diplomacy and Politics'.

34 PRO Ancient Correspondence, SC1/41/200. The exact number of merchants at this meeting was not given, but apart from Fraunceys and Bury four were named, Simon Mordon, stockfishmonger, William Walworth, fishmonger, Richard Preston, grocer and John Philpot, grocer.

35 PRO Wardrobe Accounts, E101/381/9 m.2; E101/382/2 mm.6–8; E 101/383/9 mm.1–2; E101/383/6 mm.1–2; E101/385/1 mm.3, 5–6; E101/385/8 mm.3–5; E101/385/11 m. 2; E101/386/5 mm.4–6, 9–12. I am most grateful to Anne Sutton of the Mercers' Company for these references and for allowing me to see her research notes on these and other topics relating to her work on the early history of the company.

36 *Calendar of the Letters of the Mayor and Corporation of the City of London, 1350–70*, ed. R.R. Sharpe (London, 1885), 61.

37 *CPR 1367–70*, 132. Beaumont was a knight from the East Midlands who possessed

The surviving records, which give so little information on Adam Fraunceys's commercial activities, are less reticent about his two other principal business concerns, namely the extention of financial credit and the acquisition of land. The two were very often linked, as will be seen in the section on Fraunceys's and Pyel's landed estates, and Fraunceys seems to have been active in these pursuits from early in his career. A civil case recorded among the year books of Edward III for 1344–5 recounts the dealings of Adam and his partner of the day, Thomas de Brandon, with a Cornish knight named John Petit. Apparently Sir John and two colleagues had in 1343 borrowed £240 from the two London merchants for which they were both collectively and individually responsible. When repayment was not forthcoming, the Londoners sued for the Cornish lands of Sir John Petit on which the loan had been secured, and the sheriff of Cornwall duly delivered seisin to them. What no-one seems to have realised was that Petit had some years previously borrowed £1,600 from William Montagu, first earl of Salisbury, on which loan he had also defaulted, and on the earl's death in 1344 his executors had been granted seisin of Petit's Cornish lands, so that by the sheriff's subsequent actions the executors had effectively been disseised of those lands.[38] The details of the case are not of immediate concern. What is of interest is the fact that Fraunceys is making relatively large loans, other than to the king, in the early 1340s and thereby acquiring lands in counties as far distant as Cornwall. It is also Fraunceys's first recorded joint venture with Thomas de Brandon, and, somewhat ironically in view of his daughter's later marriage into the family, provides the first evidence of any contact with the Montagus.[39]

The Petit family continued to deal with London merchants. Michael Petit, Sir John's son, and William Waryn of Cornwall acknowledged a debt of £45 to Simon Fraunceys on 17 June 1345.[40] Both Adam and Simon Fraunceys were active in Cornwall in the 1340s and 1350s, as the Black Prince's Register testifies, advancing loans not only to the prince himself but to his tenants as well.[41] Dr Hatcher has pointed out that by and large the land market in Cornwall remained fairly buoyant

substantial and widely scattered lands mainly in the counties of Leicester and Lincoln (*CIPM* xii, no. 321).

38 *The Year Books of the Reign of Edward III 18–19*, ed. L. O. Pike, (London 1905), 364, 442–53.

39 See below and Stephen O'Connor 'Adam Fraunceys and John Pyel: perceptions of status among merchants in fourteenth-century London' in D.J. Clayton, R.G. Davies and P. McNiven eds., *Trade, Devotion and Governance: papers in later medieval history* (Gloucester, 1993).

40 CLRO Recognizance Rolls 10, m.3r.

41 *Calendar of the Register of Edward the Black Prince*, 4 vols. (London, 1930–3) i, 65; ii, 79, 58; iv, 284, 327, 402.

throughout the fourteenth century, partly through the stimulus of the
tin trade, but also because of the the system of 'assessionable' manors,
where leases were reassessed at regular intervals, which allowed for
adjustments to be made in rents.[42] This created a virtual free market
in land, which may have tempted London merchants to invest there.[43]

After 1343 recognizances recording debts to Fraunceys, on his own
or with a fellow merchant, occur quite frequently (see table below).
Apart from the Cornish and Brittany loans, all were made to Londoners
or men from the home counties, East Anglia or the East Midlands,
and all fall within the periods 1343–54 and 1366–75, with the greatest
number made between 1350 and 1354. A comparison with those loans
which were made specifically to the Crown, reveals that for the most
part there is almost no overlap with royal loans, which tend to cover
the period of the late 1350s and 1360s, with a short extension in 1370–
1, perhaps indicating a concentration of resources in a particular
direction at particular times.[44]

Another feature of the list is the number of recognizances made by
religious houses, especially in the years following the Black Death.
Recognizances, of course, reveal nothing more than indebtedness, and
there is no means of telling whether it was the result of a loan or simply
failure to pay in whole or in part for goods supplied. In either case,
however, some extension of credit was involved, and Adam Fraunceys
was evidently doing a sizeable amount of business with the Church.
The Pyel cartulary records one of these transactions. On 23 November
1353, the Premonstratensians of Sulby appointed three canons as
proctors to act on the convent's behalf in negotiations with merchants
on the sale of wool, rents or other commodities belonging to the abbey.
A copy of the procuration was then given to Adam Fraunceys and
John Pyel. On 3 December 1353 Pyel and Fraunceys accepted an
annuity of £40 from the convent for a down payment of £200 which
they had made on 28 November. The annuity was reduced two days
later to £20 to be paid to the merchants for life.[45] There is nothing in
these documents to confirm the purchase or provision of goods, although
it is conceivable that Fraunceys and his partner were also buying wool
from the abbey.[46]

The only reason given for the original payment of £200 was that it
was made at the abbey's 'great request and in relief of all their estate'.
This may be a form of words, but it may also be an accurate enough

42 J. Hatcher, 'A Diversified Economy: Later Medieval Cornwall', *EconHR*, 2nd Ser.,
xxii (1969), 208–27.
43 Ibid., 214.
44 See O'Connor, 'Finance, Diplomacy and Politics', Table I.
45 P32, 35–6. See also *CCR 1349–54*, 617.
46 See below, 1 (ii).

reflection of the hardship that many monastic houses, in common with other landlords, were experiencing in adjusting to the changed economic conditions following the Black Death. If the larger houses were finding it difficult either to enforce labour services or to commute the works owed by tenants in return for an economic rent, the same problems would have hit smaller houses with if anything greater force, since they lacked the resources to support them during the move towards all-rent tenancies.[47] It would not be surprising if certain abbeys looked to merchants to help tide them over a difficult period. We should be careful, however, not to over-emphasise the point. Financial assistance, whether it be in terms of credit for goods or in the form of loans, had been extended to religious houses, as elsewhere, before the Black Death. The abbot of Cleeve, Somerset, acknowledged a debt of £100 to Simon Frounceys in April 1343, and the abbot of Beaulieu, Hants., made a series of recognizances to him between between June 1344 and October 1346, totalling £513 6s 8d.[48] And Adam Frounceys's first purchase of an annuity occurred in February 1348, some months before the plague reached England, when the prior and brothers of the Hospitallers undertook to pay the enormous rent of £100 each year for life to Adam Frounceys and Simon Symeon, an East Midlands landowner, in repayment for an unspecified cash deposit.[49]

For the merchants themselves, these payments proved a sound investment. The annuity from Sulby abbey lasted, as far as Frounceys was concerned, for over 20 years, and in the case of John Pyel for nearly 30 years, virtually trebling the initial capital deposit.[50] Quite apart from any attendant spiritual benefits they may have been able to

47 For examples of the impact of the Black Death on the provision of labour services and the economic effects suffered by the larger abbeys, see Mavis Mate, 'Agrarian Economy after the Black Death: the Manors of Canterbury Cathedral Priory 1348–1391', *EconHR*, 2nd Ser., xxxvii (1984), 341–54, esp. 347, 351, Barbara Harvey, *Westminster Abbey and Its Estates in the Middle Ages* (Oxford, 1977), esp. 257–60, J.A. Raftis, *The Estates of Ramsey Abbey* (Toronto, 1957), 251, 257, and F.M. Page, *The Estates of Crowland Abbey* (Cambridge, 1934), 127.

48 *CCR 1343–6*, 108, 377, 655; *1346–9*, 147, 158.

49 Ibid., 495. Simon Symeon held extensive lands in Northamptonshire and Lincolnshire, as well as manors and small parcels of land in Huntingdonshire, Yorkshire, Wiltshire and Hampshire (*CIPM*, xvi, nos. 630–7). He was known to both Adam Frounceys and John Pyel. Symeon had lands in Irthlingborough, Cranford and Finedon, Northants., all places where Pyel himself had property, and in 1381 he granted the manor of Cransley, which Pyel had held until 1371, to the dean and chapter of St Mary's Leicester (A. Gibbons, *Early Lincoln Wills 1280–1547* (Lincoln, 1888), 78). It was Symeon who, with John Curteys, granted 50m to Pyel's wife, Joan, which had been bequeathed in Pyel's will. See below, 32 n. 162.

50 It was formally renounced in the codicil to Pyel's will, enrolled in the register of John Buckingham, bishop of Lincoln, Lincoln Archive Office, Episcopal Register xii, fo. 245r.

bestow upon benefactors, religious houses must have represented a reasonably secure risk for the investor and a steady source of income over a long period. For loans to laymen the security lay more squarely on their lands. The reasons behind lay indebtedness to merchants, as with the Church, were probably various. As well as the supply of merchandise and economic difficulties encountered in the aftermath of the plague, the demands of the Hundred Years' War must have caused many of those setting off on campaign to seek financial assistance in the costly business of equipping themselves. The Recognizance Rolls of the city of London for 1345 contain a number of acknowledgements of debt, possibly due to the preparations for the campaign in France which took place in 1346–7. Such may well have been the reason behind Sir Thomas Wake of Blisworth's debt to John Pyel.[51] There is less certainty regarding the recognizances to Adam Fraunceys. Some were made jointly, one or more of the partners themselves being London citizens.[52] So William Tudenham, mercer, and Thomas Bacwell joined Guy de Brian of Devon in acknowledging a debt of £200 to Adam Fraunceys and Nicholas de Causton, mercer. Similarly John Engayne of Teversham, Cambs., and Alexander de Gonardeston of Nottinghamshire were bracketed with John le Bele, skinner, as owing £300 to Adam Fraunceys and Thomas de Brandon on 13 May 1345. Engayne and Gonardeston were also in debt to the wealthy German merchant Tiddemann de Limbergh at about the same time.[53] Guy de Brian announced himself in debt to several substantial creditors, including the Black Prince in May 1344, and Elizabeth de Burgh in 1346. He was at Calais with the king in 1347, from where he brought back the captured Irish knight, Walter Mandeville, and delivered him to the Tower.[54] Brian was later to be associated with Fraunceys as assayer of the king's money in 1361, and as feoffee and executor of the will of Humphrey de Bohun, earl of Hereford, Essex and Northampton.[55] The war with France evidently provided business potential for merchant financiers, bringing them into close contact with members of the gentry and aristocracy, and in some instances, with their lands.[56]

51 See 2 (i) below.

52 See table below.

53 22 May 1345 (*CCR 1343–6*, 580). Later Engayne, a prominent member of the Cambridgeshire gentry, J.P. for the county and sheriff and escheator for Cambridge and Huntingdon, was assessed to provide ten men at arms and ten archers for the king's service in August 1346 (*CFR 1337–47*, 498).

54 *CCR 1343–6*, 366; *1346–9*, 150, 246.

55 *CPR 1358–61*, 582. For Fraunceys's relations with Bohun, see O'Connor, 'Fraunceys and Pyel: perceptions of status'. Brian was very much a household knight, and a useful contact at court for Fraunceys. See C. Given-Wilson, *The Royal Household and the King's Affinity* (Yale, 1986), 156–8.

56 See 2 (i).

Adam's civic career began rather precipitately in 1352, when he was elected alderman of Queenhithe ward in July and mayor the following October. It was uncommon, while not unprecedented, for an alderman to succeed to the mayoralty without holding the shrievalty, and Adam's sudden acceptance of high civic office was doubtless due, in part at least, to the ravages of the Black Death among London's population.[57] He was probably one of the few surviving citizens wealthy enough to sustain the dignity so speedily thrust upon him. It would, however, have been possible for him to refuse, or at least to defer the honour, as others seem to have done. John Pyel, for example, was amply suited at this time to have become alderman, sheriff and in due course mayor, and yet, as we shall see, he avoided those duties for almost another two decades.[58] Adam Frauncessnevertheless showed a willingness to accept his civic responsibilities, and we may discern even at this stage in his career a hint of pride in his association with London which does not seem to have been shared by Pyel. It is quite likely that Frauncesregarded his election to office as an honour as much as a burden, and his re-election in 1353 cannot simply have been because there was no one to replace him.

This early identification of Adam Frauncesswith London seems to be further borne out by his regular attendance in parliament. In the years in which Frauncess's civic career flourished, from 1352 until his death in 1375, he represented London in parliament at least six times, more than any other citizen at the time except Simon de Benington. The advantages to provincial burgesses of attending parliament, granting them a proximity to the king and court which they would not otherwise have, were not necessarily so great to Londoners, who lived close to the centre of power and had other opportunities of access to royal authority and patronage. No doubt there was a degree of status and prestige in representing the city at Westminster, and several prominent citizens were prepared to serve, including William Walworth, John Pecche, John Philpot. Yet attendance was time-consuming and if parliament were held elsewhere than in Westminster, the additional problems of travel would have made election an unenviable prospect for an enterprising merchant. While Frauncessonly attended at Westminster, the fact that he was willing to serve so often is an indication that he regarded such representation as an important civic

57 Between July 1348 and the end of 1349 alone at least thirteen aldermen are known to have died (Beaven, i, 380–6).
58 Pamela Nightingale has suggested that Nicholas Brembre and John Philpot, both men of sufficient means and standing to have been elected aldermen in the 1360s, were too preoccupied with their own affairs to become involved in city government, at least until it suited them ('Capitalists, Crafts and Constitutional Change in Late Fourteenth-Century London' in *Past and Present*, no. 124 (1989), 14).

function that men of his standing should be prepared to undertake. Again, by contrast, John Pyel seems to have been little interested in parliament, and sat only twice, in 1361 as a commoner M.P. and in 1376 as alderman, when his membership of the commons may well have saved him from impeachment.[59]

Following his election as alderman in 1352, Fraunceys acted on commissions and inquests in the city, or witnessed civic appointments and transactions at Guildhall in his official capacity. By the late 1360s he was the longest-serving and presumably the most senior of the aldermen. At delegations of citizens to attend upon the king or other dignitaries, Fraunceys's name often heads the list of aldermen, after the mayor and sheriffs. So in May 1367, Fraunceys headed a party of seven aldermen and six commoners elected to discuss matters of concern to the city with the archbishop of Canterbury and the bishop of London, and his name is prominent among the list of aldermen and representatives of the guilds, who were summoned to appear before the king at Guildford on 6 May 1371 to explain serious disturbances which had recently broken out in the city.[60] By this time Fraunceys's position as an elder statesman and city father for almost twenty years would have ensured respect for his counsel and judgment on issues of the day both from the court and the city.

Adam Fraunceys's close association with, and one might even say affection for, London will become clearer later when other aspects of his career and life are considered. There were of course other citizens who were associated in London government for long periods and evidently identified their interests with those of the city. Yet by contrast there emerged in the later part of the fourteenth century a group of citizens who were less scrupulous about manipulating power for their own ends, to the eventual detriment of civic harmony.[61] Several were charged with peculation in the Good Parliament of 1376 and the repercussions of their impeachment led to the implementation of a series of constitutional changes in the city.[62] It is by contrast with that

59 It is even conceivable that Pyel foresaw trouble and had himself elected in an attempt to deflect it. See O'Connor, 'Finance, Diplomacy and Politics'.

60 *LBG*, 216, 281. For the background to these disturbances see Nightingale, 'Capitalists, Crafts and Constitutional Change', 5–6.

61 The most famous example being the factional disputes between John of Northampton and Nicholas Brembre in the early part of Richard II's reign. There have been several attempts to explain the increase in civil disturbance in London in the 1370s and 1380s, notably by G. Unwin, *The Gilds and Companies of London*, new edn. (London, 1963), Ruth Bird, *The Turbulent London of Richard II* (London, 1949) and most recently by Pamela Nightingale, 'Capitalists, Crafts and Constitutional Change', which contains a brief summary of the historiography of urban conflict in England in the fourteenth century.

62 See G.A. Holmes, *The Good Parliament* (Oxford, 1975), 108–26, and Bird, *Turbulent London*, 30–43. See also C. M. Barron, *Revolt in London: 11th to 15th June 1381* (Museum of London, 1981).

overt struggle for personal or factional ascendancy, and perhaps with Pyel's more self-regarding concerns, that Fraunceys's career appears to be relatively disinterested, although that view may, at least in part, be coloured by the fact that Fraunceys died in 1375, before the most serious disturbances of that decade had erupted.

Adam Fraunceys, then, was an alderman for twenty-three years, was twice mayor of London, sat in parliament six times as well as attending other councils of the king, including merchant assemblies, and undertook routine administrative tasks for the city as well working on royal commissions.[63] He was, besides, an energetic and successful merchant, exporter of wool, importer, most likely, of luxury goods, one of the first four recorded wardens of the Mercers' Company in 1347, a supporter of the customs farmers and a source of financial aid to the Crown, religious houses and gentlemen in need. Without even mentioning his property acquisitions, his acts of charity and piety and his social aggrandizement, we are already aware of an impressive list of achievements attained by a man who started life in obscurity, and certainly with none of the advantages that accrued to men of gentle or aristocratic birth. Who, then, formed Fraunceys's social circle, the men with whom he did business, whom he patronized, and with whom he consorted as equals and perhaps friends?

Among his business colleagues, one man, apart from John Pyel, stands out, namely the mercer Simon Fraunceys, if for no other reason than that it is with Simon Fraunceys that we catch that rare glimpse of Adam Fraunceys's engagement in commercial activity.[64] There was undoubtedly a close association between the men but its exact nature can only be guessed. There is the possibility of kinship, as has been suggested above, and although there is no conclusive evidence to support this, the fact that Adam acted as executor to Simon certainly implies more than a formal business relationship, and Simon's wife, Maud, most likely accompanied Adam and Ellis Fraunceys, mercer and fellow executor of Simon Fraunceys, on pilgrimage to Rome in late summer 1350, which seems to have been an occasion for family or close friends.[65]

Adam Fraunceys's first regular business partner, however, associated with him in the granting of loans, making gifts to the Crown and the acquisition of property, was Thomas de Brandon. Fraunceys and Brandon first acted together in 1343, when they made the loan which eventually led to their prosecution for depriving the earl of Salisbury

---

63 See O'Connor, 'Finance, Diplomacy and Politics'.
64 See above.
65 *CPR 1348–50*, 560. Two other mercers also went with them, William Causton and Thomas de Langeton.

of his lands,[66] and for the next ten years or so they are quite closely connected, not only in business but appearing on witness lists together and in other demonstrations of mutual support. The association seems to have become looser by the late 1350s and to have been non-existent in the next decade, although Brandon survived until at least 1368.[67] Thomas Brandon was a woolmonger and mercer of moderate means, assessed in 1340 for a contribution of £10 to a corporate loan to the king.[68] He had a modest civic career, being a common councilman by 1350 and sheriff in 1355–6, when he served under Simon Fraunceys during his third and last mayoralty, although he never became an alderman.[69] He made joint loans with Adam Fraunceys in 1345, as we have seen, and also with him made loans to the Crown in 1346.[70] In March 1348 Brandon was Adam's partner in his first recorded property acquisition in London, a tenement of houses, shops and solars in Crooked Lane, Candlewick Street ward, and in 1349 Adam Fraunceys stood surety for him when he was granted custody of Thomas, son of the Londoner Roger Carpenter, which he held until 1363.[71] Their names were often linked in witness lists, and indeed appear together in the first book of Warden's Accounts for the Mercers' Company in 1347, in the list of members who paid the entry fine.[72]

Brandon was also prominent in his own right among the circles in which Adam Fraunceys moved. With John Pyel, John Philpot, pepperer and Walter Forster, skinner and Brandon's colleague in the shrievalty for 1355–6, he received £800 from the Exchequer in February 1358.[73] As early as April 1340, even before Brandon is known to have acted with Adam Fraunceys, he joined the Bohun earls of Hereford and Northampton and the mercers William Causton, Simon Fraunceys and Nicholas atte Merssh in attesting the lease of some land in Enfield to a fellow mercer, John de Garton, and so anticipated Adam's own links with the Bohun family.[74]

We may wonder, therefore, why such a close relationship cooled. Part of the reason may have been that whereas both men probably

66 See above.

67 *CCR 1364–8*, 408.

68 *LBF*, 48. He was a representative of the 'laners' or woolmongers at an assembly of guilds at Guildhall in 1351 (ibid., 239).

69 *LBF*, 286.

70 CLRO Letter Book F, fos. cxxi-cxxii; PRO Issue Rolls, E403/338, 339. See 3 below.

71 CLRO Husting Rolls HR 75/51, 52; *LBF*, 200.

72 Creaton, 'Mercers' Wardens' Accounts', i, 149.

73 PRO Issue Rolls, E403/388, 8 and 19 February. For further discussion of this spate of credit extension on the part of the Crown to a small group of London merchants, see O'Connor, 'Finance, Diplomacy and Politics'.

74 *CCR 1339–41*, 469.

began their careers on an equal footing as relatively humble outsiders, Brandon perhaps from East Anglia, Fraunceys from even further afield, Adam seems to have been more successful commercially than his former partner. It is true that in 1350 Brandon was associated in the colossal loan of 35,000 marks advanced to the king, which was recouped by exporting large quantities of wool through a number of English ports.[75] He was, however, at the same time acting as attorney for other royal creditors, and it is questionable how much of Brandon's own substance was invested in that sum.[76] It is likely, therefore, that Adam Fraunceys quite simply outgrew Thomas de Brandon in ambition and achievement, and began to find new business partners among people more in keeping with his new-found wealth and status.

We should perhaps try to distinguish between those with whom Fraunceys dealt simply at a business or official level, and those to whom he felt a more personal commitment. Some, like John Pyel and Simon Fraunceys, clearly belonged to both categories. With others it is less easy to tell. By the late 1360s Fraunceys, as a senior alderman, could count among his peers the wealthiest and most eminent of the city élite. He associated quite naturally with men like William Walworth, John Philpot and John Pecche, all wealthy and influential aldermen, and even with the more notorious members of the court clique like Richard Lyons and Thomas Latimer, yet it is doubtful whether all or indeed any of these could be described as personal friends. Even Thomas de Brandon, while he was clearly more than a mere business acquaintance, nevertheless cannot quite be considered a member of Fraunceys's inner circle.

There was also a group of citizens upon whom Fraunceys called to witness legal documents, who may have been neighbours, or fellow mercers, or even members of his household, who could be relied upon to give support to his legal transactions. The man who features most prominently among these was John Lovekyn. He was a stockfishmonger, had been sheriff as early as 1342, during Simon Fraunceys's second term as mayor, was elected alderman for Bridge ward in 1347, where he served until his death in 1368, and was three times mayor of London.[77] Lovekyn was a man whose career Adam Fraunceys might well have sought to emulate. He came from the Surrey town of Kingston where his father, Edward, had founded a chapel, which John later refounded.[78] He was a great property owner in the city, disposing

---

75 CCR 1349–54, 180–1, 186, 197, 256, 289 etc.
76 His partners in the loan were the wealthy German merchant Tiddemann de Limbergh, Richard Causton, London citizen and mercer, and Thomas de Notingham, another Londoner.
77 1348, 1358, 1366 (Beaven i, 386).
78 Thrupp, *Merchant Class*, 354.

in his will of tenements in the parishes of St Mary at Hill, Thames Street, and St Martin, Vintry, a tenement on the corner of Crooked Lane, purchased from Thomas de Brandon, and others in Candlewick Street.[79] Lovekyn's decision to rebuild and renew his father's religious foundation coincided with Adam Fraunceys's mayoralty and it was Fraunceys, as escheator, who in 1353 made inquisition into the properties in London with which Lovekyn was proposing to endow the chapel prior to the grant of a licence in mortmain.[80] Fraunceys and Lovekyn were M.P.s for London in 1365, but their primary association was as customs collectors in the 1360s. Lovekyn was collector of customs for the port of London for most of that decade, and Fraunceys joined him as collector in 1361, 1363–6, and replaced him on his death in August 1368.[81] John Lovekyn was certainly a man of wide civic experience, was favoured by the king, pious and wealthy. His apprentice, William Walworth, succeeded him as alderman of Bridge ward, joined Fraunceys shortly afterwards in making loans, and also founded a college.[82] At the time of his death, Lovekyn had been the most senior alderman for ten years, and his place was taken by Adam Fraunceys.[83] John Lovekyn may not have been the closest of Fraunceys's friends, but he was a man whom Fraunceys, as his own career progressed, would have wished to cultivate, and Lovekyn perhaps played a part in shaping Adam's attitude towards London and fostering his sense of civic pride.

Adam's growing reputation within the city led to his receiving guardianships of orphaned London children and to his appointment as an executor of wills, of which he was also often a beneficiary. His first recorded guardianship came in June 1346 when he was granted custody of Thomas, the seven-year old son of Thomas de Garton, on the death of the boy's mother Idonia. John de Causton and Geoffrey de Wychyngham, mercers, stood surety for Adam.[84] The other guardianships, all granted in wills, were Thomas Coterel, the son of John,

79 *CWCH*, ii, 117–8; A. Heales, 'Some Account of John Lovekyn', *Trans. of the London and Middlesex Arch. Soc.* vi (1890), 362.

80 *CPR 1350–54*, 362, 435–6. Fraunceys himself was preparing to found his own chantry college in the city at this time.

81 *CFR 1356–68*, 158, 250, 386; PRO Customs Accounts E122/70/18 m.6.

82 Beaven, i, 389; *VCH London* i, ed. W. Page (1909), 577. The college of St Michael's, Crooked Lane, was really a joint effort between Lovekyn, who rebuilt the church, and Walworth, who added the choir and side chapels.

83 Beaven, i, 250.

84 *LBF*, 142. Thomas Garton the elder, who had died *c.* 1340, was the son of the alderman, Hugh Garton (d. 1327), and the brother of John Garton, both mercers, and was almost certainly a mercer himself (*ibid.*, 45; *CWCH*, i, 326; Thrupp, *Merchant Class*, 345). His wife Idonia died six years later, and this guardianship seems to be an example of the mercers' stepping in to act on behalf of one of their number. One Thomas Garton, possibly the son of the orphan Thomas, became apprenticed to the mercer Robert Haryngeye in 1391 (Creaton, 'Mercers' Wardens' Accounts', i, 155).

another mercer, in April 1349, Simon son of Thomas Leggy, skinner and mayor, in July 1357 and the children of John de Bovyndon, apothecary, in April 1361.[85] Fraunceys did not formally take up custody of Simon Leggy until March 1365, by which time the boy was 13, and he claimed his inheritance in November 1371.[86] On 1 December 1371, Adam as executor of Simon Fraunceys, granted the reversion of several tenements in the parish of St Mary Woolchurch, which had belonged to the late mercer and mayor, to Simon Leggy, Richard Fraunceys, mercer, and Thomas Pateshull, chaplain.[87] The Bovyndon children were all dead by August 1372, and beyond further help, but Adam Fraunceys bought their father's property in Honey Lane, and granted it back to his widow Katherine and her new husband, John Furneys, draper, in June 1373.[88] Adam had also been granted custody of Paul Salesbury, the son of Sir Thomas Salesbury, a Londoner, who was a near neighbour of Fraunceys at his manor in Leyton, and who also held land in Edmonton, which was to become Fraunceys's principal manor. Adam died before Paul attained his age of majority, and it was left to his widow, Agnes, to render account of her guardianship, 29 May 1381.[89]

Adam Fraunceys was also granted wardships outside London, although these were less a guide to his reliability and respectability than to his ability to pay for them. He was one of a group of trustees to whom the wardship of John Hastings, second earl of Pembroke, had been awarded, which he surrendered when the earl came of age in 1364.[90] Later, in 1373, the king granted him 15 acres of land in Kent which had escheated to the Crown on the death of the countess of Huntingdon, Pembroke's grandmother, at a rent of £10 per annum.[91]

Others with whom Adam formed close links were members of the various branches of the Causton family. There were several sets of Caustons living in London during the fourteenth century, and as with

---

85 *CWCH*, i, 599, 699, ii, 40.
86 *LBG*, 185, 289.
87 CLRO, Husting Rolls, HR 99/154.
88 Ibid., HR 100/38, 100/119, 102/3. See 2 (iii) below.
89 *LBH*, 170. *VCH Essex* vi, 262. Paul Salesbury nursed a bitter grievance that some of his father's London property and his own inheritance had been unlawfully appropriated during his minority. Accordingly, on Friday 14 June 1381, just two weeks after his guardian had relinquished her responsibility for him, he seized the opportunity provided by the insurrection in London to repossess two of his father's houses in the city which had been leased to two aldermen, William Baret and Hugh Fastolf, grocers, forcing them to transfer seisin to him and acknowledge him as their lord. Salesbury was pardoned for his offences on 22 July. (Patent Roll 5 Richard II, part i, m. 31, printed in translation in *The Peasants' Revolt of 1381*, ed. R.B. Dobson (London, 1983), 228–30.) He died in 1400.
90 *CCR 1364–8*, 127.
91 *Abbrev. Rot. Orig.*, 325.

the Fraunceys, it is impossible to tell whether all were related or how closely. Those with whom Adam was friendly were all mercers. He was a beneficiary and also one of the executors of Henry Causton's will, dated 13 December 1348.[92] John Causton sold the manor of Wyke in Hackney to Fraunceys in 1349, and in July 1353 appointed him to be supervisor of his will.[93] William Causton also alienated property ultimately to Adam Fraunceys at the hands of two of his apprentices, although he had died before the final transaction was completed.[94] William Causton had been one of those accompanying the Fraunceys party on pilgrimage in 1350.

As executor of the will of John de Oxenford, skinner, in 1361, Adam was granted certain tenements in Finch Lane in the parish of St Michael Cornhill and charged with distributing £100 in specified sums among various of the testator's relatives with the residue to be devoted to 'pious uses'.[95] In July 1368 he was appointed executor of the will of Robert de Charwelton, rector of Ivychurch, Kent, from whom he received a gilt cruet with lid, and the will of John Andrew in October 1371, may perhaps be that of a former apprentice, since he describes Adam Fraunceys as 'his lord' and leaves bequests to him and his children, Adam and Maud.[96]

This somewhat unsatisfactory documentary evidence for establishing relationships between people inevitably provides only a sample of what must have been a network of personal ties based on craft and fraternity membership, trade and financial partnerships, neighbourhoods and parishes, and a series of hierarchical links embracing master and apprentice and other forms of patronage and service. From this evidence, however, one can at least begin to sketch in the background of Adam Fraunceys's social world, and identify those men who were closest to him and by whom he was especially trusted. To the names of John Pyel, Simon and Ellis Fraunceys, John and William Causton, and for a time at least, Thomas Brandon, all mercers, we may add others, John Malwayn and William Halden, Thomas de Langeton,

92 *CWCH* i, 638.
93 F130; *CWCH* i, 673.
94 F994.
95 *CWCH* ii, 53. This residue, amounting at least to £44 13s 4d, caused Fraunceys some trouble, but he repaid the confidence shown in appointing him executor. Since the regulations stipulated that no priest could be paid more than 5 marks *pa* for saying masses for a deceased person's soul, Fraunceys found it impossible to find anyone to do so for Oxenford. In the end he distributed the sum among among a number of religious houses in London deputing them to have masses celebrated and prayers said for Oxenford's soul (H.T. Riley, *Memorials of London and London Life in the Thirteenth, Fourteenth and Fifteenth Centuries* (London, 1868), 310–2).
96 *Register of Simon Langham, Archbishop of Canterbury* (Canterbury and York Society, 1956), 340–1; *CWCH* ii, 143.

mercer and clerk, and Peter Favelor, who was the only individual outside Adam's family and the convent of St Helen's to receive a bequest in his will.[97] What we may conclude about Adam's more intimate associates is that by far the greater number of them were mercers, that they were generally men who formed part of the city oligarchy, and that they were often substantial landholders, whether in London or elsewhere. The connections within his craft were evidently important in many ways. Two of the substantial landholders in Hackney and Edmonton who sold out to Fraunceys, John and William de Causton, were London mercers, and a third, Roger Depham, while not necessarily a mercer himself, may have had close connections with them.[98] Fraunceys's acts of piety and business transactions were also often shared with men of the same company. But he did not exclusively associate with mercers. Peter Favelor, as we shall see, was a close friend, but not a mercer, and members of other crafts remembered him in their wills, and entrusted their children's estates to his care. He seems to have been a man who inspired widespread respect and confidence in London, which can only have increased his reputation beyond the city. His relations with the Crown reveal a high regard at court for his professional ability and personal integrity.[99] He also moved with relative ease in aristocratic circles. We have already noted his appointment as trustee for the young earl of Pembroke. Later we shall observe his services for and personal friendship with Humphrey de Bohun, earl of Hereford and Essex, and his daughter Maud was to take as her third husband John Montagu, third earl of Salisbury. Adam Fraunceys, with his extensive estates in Middlesex and Essex was poised as much as any Londoner could be to make the transition from city merchant to landed gentleman. Yet important though this may have been to his sense of family honour and dignity, it seems to have mattered less to him personally. He never left London and continued to act on the city's behalf until his death, and even after. In November 1378 in fulfilment of what must have been the terms of another will, or possibly verbal instruction, Adam Fraunceys' executors offered 500 marks to assist in the repair of a conduit in Cheap.[100]

Fraunceys died on 4 May 1375, and was buried in the church of the convent of St Helen's Bishopsgate. In a lengthy will he established two chantries for the benefit of his soul and those of his family and provided in great detail for the appointment and endowment of chantry priests

---

97 For Malwayn and Halden see 1 (ii) below. For Langeton and Favelor, see 2 (ii).
98 Three Dephams, William, Raulyn and John were mentioned as members of the Mercers' Company in 1347 (Creaton, 'Mercers' Wardens' Accounts', i, 148–9).
99 O'Connor, 'Finance, Diplomacy and Politics'.
100 *LBH*, 108.

and the role of the nuns in assisting the priests.[101] He also left property and rents to the nuns themselves and in particular to a named sister, Katherine Wolf. He completed another chantry in the parish church at Edmonton which had been begun by his friend Peter Favelor, but made no other bequests.

Adam was succeeded by his only surviving son, Adam junior.[102] The younger Adam was married to Margaret, the widow of Thomas Tudenham, and came into possession not only of his father's London properties but also those which his wife had inherited through her first husband.[103] He seems to have played little part in London life, remaining mostly on his Edmonton estates and living the life of a country gentleman. Fraunceys's daughter Maud, as we have noted, married John Montagu and ended her days as dowager Countess of Salisbury.

If Adam Fraunceys senior did not turn his back on London, his children certainly did, but that was what Adam had provided for. As we shall see, all the evidence of social mobility in the Fraunceys family points to the elevation of future generations, while the focus of Adam's own vision remained with London. Unlike Pyel, he apparently made no contributions to his home village and if he built up a grand estate in Middlesex worthy to support a gentleman in dignity, it seems not to have been for his immediate benefit.

ii. John Pyel

John Pyel was a Northamptonshire man from the village of Irthling-borough, lying on the upper bank of the River Nene four miles north-east of Wellingborough. Situated on the principal trade route from Northampton to Peterborough, and indeed to the port of King's Lynn, the village was well-placed to transport commercial produce, which in the fourteenth century consisted principally of hides for the leather industry and wool. The surrounding area was also likely to have been rich in cereals and other arable crops. John Pyel inherited a plot of land in the village from his father, John senior, in 1348, and, although by now settled in London, he began from about this date to build up an extensive estate in this part of Northamptonshire.[104] He certainly showed special concern for Irthlingborough. It was at his prompting

101 CLRO Husting Rolls, HR 103/79.

102 *CFR 1369-77*, 323. For a biography of Sir Adam Fraunceys, see *The House of Commons 1386–1421* iii, 118–20. I am most grateful to Dr Carole Rawcliffe for allowing me to see a copy in advance.

103 Thomas Tudenham was the son of William Tudenham, mercer, one of the wardens named with Adam Fraunceys in the account book of 1347. He predeceased his father in 1372, and Adam junior married his widow, Margaret, shortly afterwards (ibid.).

104 P103.

that Peterborough abbey was granted a licence in 1375 to establish the parish church of St Peter as a college and it was to St Peter's that he granted the remainder of his estate and in its porch that he was to be buried. He also made bequests in his will to both parish churches in the village and provided for thirteen crosses to be set up there and for repairs to the bridge and highways.[105]

The family background is obscure, but some of it can be pieced together. John Pyel senior had two sons, his heir and namesake, the future London merchant, and a younger son, Henry, who became a cleric. John Pyel junior also had two sons, John and Nicholas, who were both under twenty-one in June 1379, and of whom the elder must have died not long after, since the estate eventually passed to Nicholas.[106] Here, then, are three generations of the Pyel family holding land in Irthlingborough in the fourteenth century, but their connection with the village goes back much further. There are references to Pyels of Irthlingborough in the last decades of the thirteenth century. The *Carte Nativorum* of Peterborough Abbey mentions Nicholas, son of John Pyel of Irthlingborough, actively engaged in property dealing. In September 1285 Nicholas bought a messuage with buildings in Peterborough from a certain William Marshal, and immediately leased it back to him. In 1289 he bought a windmill and its tackle from a neighbour in Irthlingborough, and in 1296 he is again to be found buying property in Peterborough.[107] Given the nature of the *Carte Nativorum*, that is, a cartulary relating to the properties of tenants, mostly villeins or holders of bond land of the abbot of Peterborough, we may suppose that the Pyels were or had been servile tenants of the abbey. Professor Postan in his analysis of the *Carte* discovered that most of the buyers of land who could be traced were unfree tenants and generally men of humble rank, either smallholders or wholly landless persons.[108] But despite their lowly origins, the Pyels were clearly bettering themselves by the end of the thirteenth century. If Nicholas was acquiring and leasing tenements in Peterborough, and could afford to invest in as costly an item as a

---

105 *CPR 1374–7*, 72; Pyel's will, Register of John Buckingham, fos. 244r-245v. See also the earlier and much shorter will enrolled in the Court of Husting, CLRO HR 110/117. The second parish in Irthlingborough was that of All Saints, considerably smaller than St Peters's, with a dwindling number of parishioners to support it. The church, which was in ruins by the middle of the sixteenth century, was situated next to the manor house of Bataille fee, one of the two fees of Irthlingborough manor held by John Pyel, which was probably his residence there (*VCH Northampton* iii, ed. William Page (London, 1930), 207).

106 Register of John Buckingham fo. 245r; *VCH Northampton* iii, 208.

107 *Carte Nativorum: A Peterborough Abbey Cartulary*, ed. C.N.L. Brooke and M.M. Postan (Northants. Record Society xx, 1969), nos. 65–68, 389.

108 Ibid., xxxvi.

windmill and reap the profits it brought, he can hardly be said to have been impoverished.[109]

Peterborough abbey held the manor of Irthlingborough, although the size of its demesne holdings was subject to wide variation in the early fourteenth century. A rental of the demesne manors of the abbey at the beginning of Geoffrey de Croyland's abbacy (c.1299–1300) reveals that Irthlingborough yielded an income of £37 16s 4¾d, while a more detailed extent made at the time of Abbot Geoffrey's death in 1321, lists one chief messuage and a windmill, and demesne lands of 70 acres of arable, 21 acres of meadow and some pasture. There were seven free tenants, twenty-three customary tenants and fifteen cottars, and the total annual income was given as £18 12s 0d, almost exactly half the yield of twenty years earlier.[110] A number of factors may have contributed to this decline, but the lean years of the opening decades of the fourteenth century, especially the famine following the 1315–17 crop failures and the consequent fall in population, may have forced the abbey to reduce its stock of demesne land.[111] Indeed two account rolls of Peterborough Abbey from the first decade of the century imply that the trend towards leasing out land was already in progress by 1309–10.[112] It is possible that the Pyels were among those to have benefited from these farms allowing them to increase piecemeal their holdings in Irthlingborough.[113] In the fourteenth century Irthlingborough was composed of three manorial fees. In 1317 Simon de Drayton, a member of an old county family, received one of these, the Bataille fee, from Henry de Drayton, possibly a relative, which he held until

109 See Richard Holt, *The Mills of Medieval England* (Oxford, 1988), 77–8. Pyel must either have farmed the mill from Peterborough abbey, or have been an independent mill-owner (ibid., 54–69). In the latter case, the abbey evidently regained control of the mill by 1321.

110 Register of Geoffrey of Crowland, abbot 1299–1321, 'The White Book', BL Cotton Ms. Vespasian E xxii, fo. 70; the Book of Walter of Whittlesey, BL Add. Ms. 39758, fos 123v-124.

111 J.L. Bolton, *The Medieval English Economy 1150–1500* (London, 1980), 58, 182–3; Edmund King, *Peterborough Abbey 1086–1310: A Study in the Land Market* (Cambridge, 1973), 120–1.

112 NRO Fitzwilliam Misc. 2388, 2389. These are account rolls for the years 1300–1 and 1309–10. The first shows manorial revenues for Irthlingborough at £29 19s 7d, the second at the much lower level of £13 7s 6d, but additionally shows a substantial farm of £15 4s 8d, making a total of £28 12s 2d. This suggests that as much as half the demesne or more of a decade earlier had been farmed out.

113 Edmund King observes the growth of entrepreneurship among abbey tenants at the end of the thirteenth and in the early fourteenth centuries, and cites two examples of tenants of abbey land in Irthlingborough at this time increasing their holdings and building on land probably for the purposes of leasing on the village land market. These men were likely to have been substantial freeholders or already possessed of customary land, a category of tenant the Pyels might well have belonged to (*Peterborough Abbey*, 119–21).

1353, when he sold his interest to John Pyel for £200 and a tun of wine, so marking the culmination of Pyel family fortunes in the village.[114]

To balance this account of the family's rise in Northamptonshire society, there were other Pyels living in this part of the county whose activities were less than exemplary. Commissions of oyer and terminer were established in 1316 and 1317 to inquire into a complaint by Ralph de Drayton, parson of the church of Lowick, some five or six miles north of Irthlingborough, that a group of malefactors including one Robert Pyel, had held him prisoner and carried away his goods.[115] And earlier, in August 1314, a jury of presentment at Northampton submitted that Robert Pyel of Rushton, near Kettering, stole a horse belonging to William Page at Desborough 'and is a common thief'. The sheriff reported that Pyel had disappeared and confirmed that he was 'of ill repute'.[116] Of more elevated status was that branch of the family holding land at Isham in the thirteenth century, who eventually became burgesses of Bristol while retaining their Isham lands until 1398–9, when Elizabeth, daughter of Henry Pyel of Bristol settled them on her cousin.[117]

John's brother, Henry Pyel, pursued a successful career in the Church. He was rector of the parish of Warkton, near Kettering and also clerk to Bartholomew de Burghersh, the king's chamberlain, who in 1353 petitioned successfully on his behalf for a canonry in Southwell, with expectation of a prebend.[118] He had been educated at Oxford, was a licenciate in canon and civil law and in December 1367 was appointed archdeacon of Buckingham.[119] He was transferred to the archdeaconry of Northampton in 1374 and by the time of his death in April 1379 was possessed of a substantial household and sufficient wealth to make sizeable bequests in his will.[120] He elected, like John, to be buried at Irthlingborough, though he left to his brother the choice of church.[121] Henry was occasionally associated with his brother and Adam Fr[a]unceys in property acquisitions, and with Fraunceys and William Braybrook,

---

114 *VCH Northampton* iii, 208; PRO Feet of Fines CP25(1) 176/687 no. 169; P111, 112.

115 *CPR 1313–7*, 582; *1317–21*, 82.

116 *Northamptonshire Sessions Rolls 1314–16, 1320* (Northants. Record Society, xi, 1940), 13.

117 *VCH Northampton* iv, ed. L.F. Salzman (London, 1937), 192.

118 *CPP* i, 253; *CPL* iii, 499. A list of the prebends of Southwell and their assessments for tax was given in the Pyel cartulary (fo. 116v).

119 A.B. Emden, *Biographical Register of the University of Oxford to A.D. 1500*, 3 vols. (Oxford 1957–9) iii, 1481; *CPL* iv, 72, 77.

120 John Le Neve, *Fasti Ecclesiae Anglicanae 1300–1541*, i (Lincoln Diocese), compiled by H.P.F. King (London, 1962), 11; Register of John Buckingham, f. 179.

121 Either St Peter's, where Pyel himself was to be buried, or All Saints, adjacent to the manor house.

rector of Cransley, he was deputed to take charge of John's affairs during his absence in Galicia in 1363.[122]

Henry's successful career in the Church, however, was eclipsed by that of his brother in London. John Pyel had become well-established in the capital by the mid-1340s, and so had presumably moved from Irthlingborough at some time in the previous decade. It is quite likely that, with Henry, he had received at least some elementary education. His will shows that he took a keen interest in his own sons' education, and the large number of books at his disposal suggests at least that he was literate beyond the average and had a respect for learning.[123] It is possible that one of the functions of Irthlingborough College was to provide elementary education for local children.

Pyel's first appearance in the records is in June 1345, when a creditor acknowledged a debt to him of £40.[124] On 1 April 1346 he was appointed one of three commissioners to enter all the benefices of non-resident alien clergy in the diocese of London to bring them under royal control and then lease or sell them at farm. The profits were to come to Pyel, who was to account for them to the king.[125] In the same year he was assessed for a corporate gift and loan to the king, having movables to the value of £10 or more. His contribution was £2, compared with Adam Fraunceys's joint loan with Thomas de Brandon of £19, and Simon Fraunceys's and William Causton's offerings of £100 each.[126] He was a mercer although he is not mentioned in the first wardens' account book of 1347, and he was at this time involved in exports with the wealthy Lynn merchant John de Wesenham.[127] Both

---

122 PIII, 152, 62.

123 In his will Pyel left liturgical texts, mostly breviaries, missals and psalters, and a bible to both parish churches and to the college when it was completed. He left his other books of an unspecified nature to the college. Nicholas Orme believes that the merchant class was being drawn towards works of literature in leisure hours. The commonest books to survive in townsmen's wills were, however, liturgical or other devotional works and of the twenty-three books which William Walworth bequeathed in his will, most were works of theology or canon law (*English Schools in the Middle Ages* (London, 1973), 46).

124 Sir Thomas Wake of Blisworth. See below, 2(i).

125 *CFR 1337–47*, 464.

126 CLRO Letter Book F, fo. cxxi–cxxii.

127 John de Wesenham, merchant of King's Lynn, had moved the base of his operations from Norfolk, where, in 1339, he was bailiff of three hundreds, to London, probably in the early 1340s, where he became a citizen and worked closely with the royal household (*CFR 1337–47*, 123). He held the farm of the customs from March to October 1346, was king's butler 1346–9 and collector of the customs on cloth and wine (E.B. Fryde, *Studies in Medieval Trade and Finance* , X 3–4, PRO Butlerage Accounts, *CFR 1347–56*, 28, 30). He was described as the king's merchant and appointed to take delivery of wool granted to the king by the county of Suffolk in 1347 (ibid., 12). In 1351 he was warden of the king's exchanges and was appointed keeper of the temporalities of Ely in 1358 (*CCR 1349–54*, 378; *1354–60*, 392). In 1364 he was arrested in Calais, where he had been mayor, had all his goods there confiscated and was taken back to England as

men were sued for negligence in two separate cases in November 1346 concerning the loss of goods at sea.[128] Wesenham remained a close friend, and when Pyel was gaoled in 1349 after the collapse of the customs farming syndicate with which he was involved, Wesenham and Adam Fraunceys stood bail for him, an act of friendship which Pyel never forgot and both men were singled out in his will for special prayers.[129]

Pyel's business activities are little better documented than those of Adam Fraunceys, and a picture has to be drawn from a few scanty references. We have already noted the joint contract which he and Fraunceys made with the abbey of Sulby and which was recorded in Pyel's cartulary.[130] The implication from the documents is that part at least of the annuity of £20 could be paid in goods, probably wool, and that the recognizance of £200 registered by the abbot represented an advance payment to earmark a quantity of wool each year, and was in effect a loan made to the abbey on the strength of future wool sales. Such contracts were not uncommon, and had been a method of buying wool favoured by Italian merchants, at least until the earlier years of the fourteenth century.[131] It was also a particularly lucrative operation and contained a useful means of concealing hidden interest in kind, in the shape of an extra sack or two of wool.[132]

In 1354 or 1355, John Garlekmongere, a Northampton merchant, was outlawed in London for not answering charges that he had failed to render an account to John Pyel and John Curteys of Higham Ferrers

mainpernor to Henry Brusele and John Chichester, assayers of the king's money, who had failed to carry out their duties satisfactorily. He was released in 1365 and probably died shortly afterwards (*CFR 1356–68*, 287; *CCR 1364–8*, 128).

128 *CCR 1346–9*, 166, 173. It seems that the losses occurred when Wesenham had control of the customs, and that he had allegedly misspent the proceeds from a tax of 1s a sack, which was granted to pay for the protection of shipping (T.H. Lloyd, *The English Wool Trade in the Middle Ages* (Cambridge, 1977), 202). In the event the Crown absolved Wesenham from liability, but the fact that Pyel was also sued shows how closely he was working with Wesenham's company.

129 For the account of Pyel's engagement with the customs farmers and his subsequent difficulties see O'Connor, 'Finance, Diplomacy and Politics'.

130 Above, 1 (i). Sulby abbey lay on the western boundaries of Northamptonshire, near the border with Leicestershire. In the thirteenth century it was granted the church and manor of Sulby, which comprised more than 1,500 acres of land. Sulby abbey also possessed some land in Irthlingborough and held the advowsons of several churches in the county, including Little Addington, one of the churches later patronised by John Pyel, of which the canons also acquired the manor from Peterborough abbey in 1300. At the dissolution the gross annual value of the abbey was £305 8s 5d (*VCH Northampton* ii, ed. R.M. Serjeantson and W. Ryland D. Adkins (London, 1906), 138–9; *Henry Pytchley's Book of Fees*, ed., W.T. Mellows (Northamptonshire Record Society, ii, 1927), 75).

131 Lloyd, *English Wool Trade*, 289–93.

132 Eileen Power, *The Wool Trade in Medieval English History* (Oxford, 1941), 43.

when he was their receiver.[133] The Garlekmongeres were a prominent
Northampton family. Adam Garlekmongere was mayor of the town in
1348 and Richard Garlekmongere held the same office in 1353.[134] John
was clerk of recognizances of debt at Northampton, but he also had
dealings with other London merchants and was himself a non-resident
freeman of the city of London and supplier of cloth to the royal
household.[135] It is possible that Garlekmongere was acting with Pyel
and Curteys in what Postan called a 'service partnership', and that he
was handling his associates' goods in Northampton for a percentage of
the profits.[136] Both Pyel and Curteys had moved to London, but still
retained interests in their home region, and Garlekmongere may have
been dealing with produce from Pyel's new manors there.[137]

There is no doubt that Pyel was concerned with regional trade in
the East Midlands. In November 1370 he was part of a commission
which included Sir Robert de Thorpe, chief justice of Common Pleas,
and John Cavendish, also a justice of Common Pleas, to inquire into
the number of new mills and ponds which had been erected in
Huntingdonshire. The commission was established in response to the
complaints of merchants from the surrounding counties that the River
Ouse between Huntingdon and St Ives was totally obstructed, pre-
venting the passage of foodstuffs and other merchandise.[138] Earlier in
the same year Pyel had been granted a licence to buy and ship to
London quantities of cereals and pulses from the East Midlands and
from Sussex, presumably to provide cheap food for the city.[139] Pyel had
been engaged in importing food into London since at least 1352, and
it is possible that this was one outlet for the produce of his own lands.[140]

In 1366 another of Pyel's agents, Walter Persone, while on business
in Chester, had his goods seized, which prompted a letter on his behalf
from the Corporation to the mayor and citizens of Chester, while in
1372 Pyel was shipping cloths and other merchandise to Bordeaux and
Lisbon.[141] Pyel may have been quite active in trade with the Iberian
peninsula. In 1363 he made preparations for a long voyage to St James
de Compostella, presumably on pilgrimage, though that was never
stated as the purpose for the visit. It is quite possible that he had
commercial reasons for going as well. Trade with Castile was buoyant,

133 *CPR 1354–8*, 205.

134 P82, 116.

135 *LBF*, 149; P7; PRO Wardrobe Accounts E101/390/9.

136 M.M. Postan, 'Partnership in English Medieval Commerce' in *Medieval Trade and
Finance* (Cambridge, 1973), 65–91.

137 For John Curteys see above, n.22.

138 *CPR 1370–74*, 35.

139 *CPR 1367–70*, 363, 369.

140 *CPR 1350–54*, 353.

141 *Letters of the Mayors of London, 1350–70*, 127, *CPR 1370–74*, 200.

at this time, and an alliance between Edward III and Pedro I in 1362 might have been expected to boost the confidence of English merchants in travelling to Spain.[142] These rather disparate and isolated examples of John Pyel's commercial activities at least point to his widespread and varied participation in national and international markets. As with Adam Fraunceys, however, it was Pyel's involvement in financial credit that brought him the greatest rewards.

John Pyel does not seem to have advanced credit to the same extent as Adam Fraunceys, and his largest loans were made to the Crown towards the end of his career.[143] Nevertheless they seem to follow the same pattern, that is, a mixture of loans to religious houses, to fellow Londoners, and to members of the gentry in straitened circumstances. Some of these transactions, like the contract with Sulby abbey, were copied into Pyel's cartulary. In October 1352 Edward Chamberleyn, parson of the church of Portland, Dorset, purchased with Pyel a farm worth £50 plus *pa* from William Swyft, prior of St Mary's Hospital, Bishopsgate, for a down payment of £300.[144] This may have been a similar arrangement to that made with Sulby, whereby much-needed cash at a time of economic difficulty was repaid by a package of rents and goods.[145] In January 1349 a Buckinghamshire woman, Agnes Brok, acknowledged herself in debt to Pyel and Henry and John Brusele for £100, while in November the London goldsmith William de Hatfeld, who held lands in Kent, borrowed 100 marks from Pyel alone.[146] Allowing for the smallness of the sample, it seems that a shortage of money both at the time of and in the aftermath of the pestilence of 1348–9 was attracting investment by London merchants with spare cash, and as we shall see when we look at Pyel's property acquisitions, it was the inability of some landowners to cope with the economic effects of the sudden and catastrophic decline in population which enabled him to buy up landed estates quickly and relatively inexpensively.[147]

It is noteworthy that Pyel never lost contact with his birthplace, which he continued to regard as his home. He seems to have had business operations in the region, and was beginning to buy up land there from early on. He also maintained an association with men from

142 Wendy Childs, *Anglo-Castilian Trade in the Later Middle Ages* (Manchester, 1978), 30–2.
143 O'Connor, 'Finance, Diplomacy and Politics', Table 2.
144 P27; *CCR 1349–54*, 505.
145 The hospital continued to suffer economic depression for the duration of the century and, in 1400, the chapter granted quit-rents in return for a payment of 300 marks 'for the relief of their house, heavily burdened with debt' (*VCH London* i, 532).
146 *CCR 1346–49*, 615; *1349–54*, 144. Henry Brusele was John Pyel's successor at the king's exchanges in May 1355.
147 Below, 2 (i).

his locality who like him moved to or spent much time in London, John Curteys and John Garlekmongere, for example, and several of his property deals in London were concluded with Northamptonshire men. He probably spent a good deal of his time away from London, and this physical distance seems to have bred a rather detached view of the city which contrasts sharply with the attitude of Adam Fraunceys. Although he had undertaken commissions for the Crown since 1346 and was wealthy enough to hold civic office by the 1350s, Pyel seems to have been reluctant to become involved in city government. In June 1360 he was granted immunity from any royal or civic duty against his will.[148] He was a member of common council in 1361, when he also represented London in parliament, but he was not elected alderman until 1369, serving as sheriff in 1370–1 and mayor for the year 1372–3, exactly twenty years after Adam Fraunceys's first mayoralty.[149] It is from this time that Pyel began to be more involved with affairs in London. He bought a house in Broad Street from Adam Fraunceys in 1374, which had been Pyel's residence in the city possibly since 1369,[150] and it is at this time that he began associating with members of the court party, especially the vintner Richard Lyons, and making large loans to the Crown. He also resumed his diplomatic activities, taking part in trade negotiations with Flemish merchants. But Pyel never seems to have identified with London in the way that Fraunceys evidently did, and his ties with the city loosened considerably after the Good Parliament. As a result of the new regulations governing the election of London aldermen and councillors, Pyel resigned his alder-manry of Castle Baynard in 1377. He was re-elected for one year in 1378, but thereafter seems to have taken less part in civic business. In 1379 he made the relatively small contribution of £5 to a city gift and this represents his last grant to corporate fund-raising. Thoughts of mortality may also have been influencing him in this year. On 28 February 1379 he drew up the second and longer version of his will, and by 16 April his brother Henry, whom he had named as executor in his first will, was dead. This second will was more attuned to Irthlingborough and local concerns there than towards London, and it may have been that by this time Pyel was spending more time on his Northamptonshire estates than in the city.

Pyel's will gives us a good impression of those people with whom he had come into contact during his daily life, both in London and in Northamptonshire, and who were of special concern to him. In an

148 *CPR 1358–61*, 433.

149 Beaven, i, 389.

150 CLRO Husting Rolls HR 102/190. Adam Fraunceys acquired this property before 30 July 1369 and may have leased it to Pyel shortly afterwards (HR 97/109).

interesting and illuminating section, Pyel devised the proceeds of a fifth share of his movables to endow priests to pray for his soul in death and the souls of his parents, brothers and relatives, and of Adam Fraunceys, John de Wesenham, William Halden and John Holt, all, barring the last, his colleagues in London.[151] Halden was an alderman and recorder of London 1365–76. He had strong connections with the county of Sussex where he acted as feoffee for one of the local gentry, Sir Andrew Sackville, acquired an estate of his own, and was of sufficient local standing to be appointed justice of the peace.[152] He had been executor with Pyel of Adam Fraunceys's will and had appeared twice as a witness to Pyel's property deeds. John Holt was a lawyer and an estate official of John of Gaunt at Higham Ferrers. He was also one of the supervisors of Pyel's second will. These four men can be identified as among John Pyel's closest friends, not merely business acquaintances or colleagues in city government, but men in whom he could place complete trust, and, presumably, whose company he enjoyed.

Another man with whom he was on intimate terms was also a Londoner, Nicholas Brembre, grocer and mayor of the city in 1383–5. Brembre, who was already godfather to Pyel's younger son, Nicholas, was appointed guardian of both boys and was to be responsible for their general welfare and education until they attained their majority. The will goes on to express explicitly Brembre's trustworthiness.[153] Pyel, a mercer, closely connected with the court party of the early 1370s, and enjoying, as we shall see, the support of John of Gaunt, might have been expected to be politically opposed to that faction led by Brembre.[154] But while it may be true, as we saw with Adam Fraunceys, that craft loyalties forged strong links between members, nevertheless friendships can arise for a variety of reasons and often transcend simple political or commercial interest. In 1374 Brembre and Pyel together held property that had originally passed to Pyel and John Stodeye, Brembre's father-in-law.[155] Stodeye was a wealthy vintner, originating from Norfolk, and alderman for Vintry ward,[156] who apparently also held lands in Northamptonshire. In December 1361 he and Pyel had mainperned for the debts incurred by the Italian merchant Bartholomew Changeour and Thomas de Notyngham, of whom the latter died and the former

---

151 Register of John Buckingham, fo. 244v.
152 N. E. Saul, *Scenes from Provincial Life: Knightly Families in Sussex 1280–1400* (Oxford, 1986), 63, 184 and n.
153 'ie maffie en lui et en son loiautee de foy devant touz autres.'
154 On Gaunt's relations with London see Nightingale, 'Capitalists, Crafts and Constitutional Change', esp. 20–24.
155 CLRO Husting Rolls, HR 103/24, 97; 101/67.
156 Beaven, i, 387; Thrupp, *Merchant Class*, 367.

left London, leaving the mainpernors to pay the £2,000 pledged to the king.[157] Eventually they received the London property of Changeour in compensation, and when Stodeye released his interest in the tenements in 1373 his place was taken by Brembre.[158] It is possible that Brembre's friendship with Pyel arose through their common connections with the Stodeye family, but whatever the origins there is no question about the strength of the attachment.[159]

The supervisors of the will were John Holt and John Hadley. The duty of supervisor was a position of honour and the appointment indicates a firm friendship and respect for both men.[160] The executors were different from those appointed in the first will. This very short document was drawn up on 23 June 1377 and bequeathed all Pyel's London lands held on lease to his wife, Joan, and if she died within the period of the lease, to the dean and college of Irthlingborough.[161] Joan and John's brother, Henry, were to be executors of the London will, but to execute and supervise his second will, Pyel appointed professionals, including two lawyers, William Thirning and John Holt, and a friar, Thomas Assheburn. His treatment of his wife in the second will is interesting. Joan Pyel who was to survive her husband by thirty years was a strong and determined woman as can be seen from her tireless efforts to complete the foundation of Irthlingborough College. In a codicil to the will, however, added 25 June 1379, Pyel introduces two rather curious clauses. First, to a hitherto unknown woman called Margaret Joye, he bequeathes some personal items of value, including a bed, a vessel (pecè) with silver lid, a goblet, a table-cloth, a towel, basin and water-jug and ten pounds, besides all lands tenements and rents in 'Thyndes' (?Finedon) for life. Next he requires all his feoffees in Northamptonshire to enfeoff his wife, Joan, and to ensure that she receives from those lands a pension of 50 marks pa, to take effect from seven years after his death.[162] He then adds, somewhat baldly, that if Joan does not agree to this arrangement, which the will makes clear is to supersede her rights of dower, she will receive nothing at all out of the bequests. The rest of the profits of his lands were to go towards the

157 CCR 1360–64, 302, 322.

158 HR 101/67.

159 Pyel also joined John Stodeye's brother, William, in standing surety for Henry Brusele and Thomas Ferrers in January 1362 (CCR 1360–64, 301).

160 Holt was steward of John of Gaunt's manor of Higham Ferrers and an eminent lawyer. John Hadley originated from the village of Hadleigh in Suffolk, where he endowed a chantry for his parents and relatives and, like Pyel, bequeathed money for poor relations in the locality although he seems to have left no lands there (Thrupp, 347).

161 CLRO HR 110/117.

162 These terms were fulfilled rather earlier than stipulated when Simon Symeon and John Curteys of Wemington granted to Joan 50 marks annual rental from lands which they held of Henry Pyel (CCR 1385–9, 143).

schooling and maintenance of his sons until they were of age. This stark contrast in tone between the rather intimate concern revealed by the donation of private effects to someone who was probably a local widow,[163] and the formal, almost grudging, performance of a duty to see that his wife was provided for, is surprising and not a little puzzling. It is almost as though Pyel had decided that his wife, who was almost certainly a Londoner, was already in receipt of rents from his London properties, and that was sufficient. His Northamptonshire properties were to provide sustenance for his sons and bequests to his friends, neighbours and dependants there.

Pyel's will, however, despite its overt partiality towards Northamptonshire, nevertheless shows that Pyel had developed close friendships with Londoners during the years he spent in the city. And if we look at those men lending their names to Pyel's charters and deeds, we find a similar group of people to that surrounding Adam Frounceys. An analysis of witnesses to John Pyel's property deeds in London reveals that the most frequent appearances were by Walter Southous (six times), an enigmatic figure, possibly a clerk and member of Pyel's household, John Lovekyn (five times), Henry Pycard, vintner, and Simon Frounceys (four times), and Thomas de Brandon, John de Chichestre, John Malwayn, John Wroth and Thomas Mildenhale (three times). Brandon's partnership with Adam Frounceys has already been discussed.[164] Thomas de Mildenhale was a London ironmonger.[165] The others, with the exception of Southous, were all aldermen and prominent merchant-financiers.[166] Pyel like Frounceys could take his place among the higher echelons of London society, while not losing touch with his fellow countrymen from the East Midlands who had also made the transition. But his closest relationships were formed with men he had met in the city.

In Northamptonshire the position is less clear. Certain names are prominent, in Pyel's will, in attestations and in business dealings, but it is less clear who these men were or to what social status they might have laid claim. In the codicil to his will, Pyel makes some individual bequests, one of which has already been described. Among the beneficiaries here were John Campion and Robert Molkous with their wives, who received 5 marks and 40s respectively. Molkous was an

163 Henry Pyel also left her £10 in his will. There is no other reference to Margaret Joye.

164 Above 1 (i).

165 *Letters of the Mayors of London 1350–70*, 107.

166 Malwayn was well-known to Frounceys, since they had made joint loans, and Frounceys acted as surety for Malwayn when he was granted the guardianship of Nicholas Mokkynge in 1354, and to secure his release from prison in 1357 (*CCR 1349–54*, 504; *1354–60*, 389; *LBG*, 52).

Irthlingborough man, who with Pyel had been a victim of harrassment by unknown persons in 1364.[167] John Campion appears most frequently in the charters recorded in Pyel's cartulary and was probably a close neighbour, and friend from the days before Pyel moved to London.[168] The families were evidently well-known to each other, and Henry Pyel granted Campion and his sons £5 in his will. The witness lists show quite clearly the local folk of Irthlingborough who were among Pyel's supporters. Next to Campion, who appears in these lists as many as twenty-nine times, comes John Stevens, who appears twenty-four times, and then in descending order John and Thomas Miriden, Robert Hardy, William Lord and John Ward, Robert Pu and John Body. All are described as 'of Irthlingborough' and form the nucleus of Irthlingborough society with whom Pyel had dealings, and were probably mostly minor landowners in the area, though some may have been members of Pyel's Northamptonshire household.

None of these men, however, appears to have been of any consequence outside the immediate locality, and one wonders whether Pyel kept company with them when he was in residence on his manor. Campion and Molkous may have been men whom he would have entertained on a social level, but Pyel would have aspired to count among his social connections men of more standing than these. As the study of Pyel's land acquisition in the county will show, there was a policy behind his purchases which was not simply determined by financial expediency, but was directed towards the formation of a unified manorial estate. But his neighbouring lords, men from whom in some instances he bought land, seem remarkably distant. Simon de Drayton of Lowick, the Wakes of Blisworth, the Mallorys at Sudborough, and the Seymour family, from whom Pyel bought one of the Irthlingborough fees, rarely if at all appear as attestors to his deeds. In some cases, like the Seymours, this may have been because those families themselves no longer lived on their lands in the area. But this was not the case with Simon de Drayton, and deeper reasons may have been in play. At county level, the families and men who dominated local society, like the Zouches of Harringworth, seem to have had little to do with Pyel, and Pyel himself held no important local office in the county. It appears, perhaps, that Pyel had some difficulty in finding

---

167 *CPR 1361–64*, 544. The main target for these attacks seems to have been John of Gaunt. See O'Connor, 'Finance, Diplomacy and Politics', and Anthony Goodman, *John of Gaunt: the Exercise of Princely Power in Fourteenth-Century Europe*, (London, 1992), 330.

168 The Campions were an old Irthlingborough family (*Carte Nativorum*, no. 555). John Campion was associated in the purchase of some land in and around the Addingtons, Northants., in 1351, for which Pyel alone paid (P107).

acceptance among the upper levels of Northamptonshire society.[169]

It is doubtful whether Joan Pyel ever moved to Northamptonshire. She may have accompanied her husband there on occasion, but while John will have begun to spend more of his time on his country estates in the last years of his life, she probably continued to live in their house in Broad Street in London. Pyel was married by 1349, presumably to Joan, who is first named as his wife in 1355.[170] She was probably a London girl and was associated with her husband in many of his property deeds there, but otherwise only takes on a personality of her own after his death. Her fight to establish Irthlingborough College is a tribute to her energy and tenacity, and not a little to her ingenuity, and she finally received a licence to proceed with the project in March 1388.[171] She supported other religious houses, including the nuns at Cheshunt, Herts.,[172] and appears herself to have retired to the convent of St Helen's, Bishopsgate, possibly as a vowess. She died towards the end of January 1412, at what must have been a venerable age, and after setting out the details of her funeral, devotes most of her will to charitable bequests to the poor and to religious houses in London, especially to the convent and nuns of St Helen's, where she was to be buried.[173] There is scant acknowledgement of her husband John, except to say that she had been his wife, and barely a reference to Northamptonshire, apart from bequests to a certain Thomas Kent of 'Shudborgh', which may be Sudborough, and to a priest called William of Northampton, whose name may be significant. She had outlived both her husband and her sons, and possibly her grandson, yet there was no provision for prayers for her family; on entering the convent she seems to have turned her back completely on her former life.[174]

Of Pyel's sons, John was dead by 1385, and Nicholas was in sole control of his father's lands.[175] Shortly before 1394, as part of a marriage settlement, Nicholas enfeoffed his prospective brother-in-law, Roger Lychefeld, possibly a London skinner, of all his Northamptonshire manors, including Irthlingborough, and Lychefeld re-enfeoffed him and

169 For fuller discussion of this point, see O'Connor, 'Fr... ...ceys and Pyel: perceptions of status'.

170 *CPP* i, 152; *CPL* iii, 559.

171 W. Dugdale, *Monasticon Anglicanum*, ed. J. Caley, H. Ellis and B. Bandinel, 6 vols. (London, 1815–30), vi, 1384–5.

172 A.K. McHardy, *The Church in London 1375–1392* (London Record Society, xiii, 1977), 74.

173 Lambeth Palace, Episcopal Register of Thomas Arundel ii, f. 161.

174 For a fuller description of the life of Joan Pyel, see C.M. Barron and Anne Sutton, eds., *Widows of Medieval London c.1300–c.1500* (forthcoming).

175 *CCR 1385–9*, 144.

his new wife, Elizabeth.[176] Part of the settlement was not paid by Roger, however, and Pyel re-entered his estates in 1400 paying homage to the abbot of Peterborough for them.[177] Lychefeld seems to have regained both Irthlingborough and Cranford by 1407.[178] Nicholas Pyel died (of poison according to one account), before 29 March 1406, leaving a son in nonage, John, who seems to have died shortly afterwards.[179] His inheritance passed immediately to his wife and her second husband, and then to Elizabeth Pyel, presumably his daughter, and her two husbands, first Sir William Hoddleston, and second Sir William Braunspath. The later descent of the lands appears to have been first with the Hoddlestons and then with the Cheyneys, into whose family Elizabeth Hoddleston, granddaughter of Elizabeth Pyel, married.[180] As with the Fraunceys, the estates moved out of the Pyel family through failure of the male line, although the name, at least, survived in one of the Woodford fees called Piell's.[181]

176 *VCH Northampton* iii, 256. Register of William Genge, abbot of Peterborough, BL Add. Ms. 25288, fo. 44d.

177 Reg. William Genge, fo. 8v.

178 Pyel Cartulary, fo. 3v. John Hadley, Thomas Rede and Roger Lychefeld were granted the farm of Cranford manor March 1405, by letter patent dated Michaelmas 1404 (*CPR 1405–8*, 121). Roger Lychefeld held court there in May 1405 and November 1407, although by 1409 the court at Cranford was held by William Hoddleston, first husband of Elizabeth Pyel, Nicholas's daughter (NRO Court Rolls for Cranford BQ 13.61).

179 *CIMisc.*, vii, 179; Reg. William Genge, fos. 10r, 44v. John Pyel was a minor in 1406, according to the register, but does not reappear after that date.

180 *VCH Northants* iii, 208–9, 256.

181 Ibid., 256.

2. LANDED ESTATES

The existence of cartularies for John Pyel and Adam Fraunceys, whatever else they might reveal about their career and aspirations, provide an unparalleled source for the study of merchants' property holdings in the later fourteenth century, telling us not only what they purchased and when, but to some extent how and why these transactions were achieved. There is no other London merchant of this period for whose property-dealing such a wealth of information is available and yet our enthusiasm for a unique source should not blind us to the difficulties and problems inherent in its use. Pyel's cartulary was not compiled systematically; the documents relating to each manor were not specifically grouped together, entries were made haphazardly and only in roughly chronological order, and the cartulary is by no means comprehensive. It is not possible, therefore, to trace the descent of a manor or parcel of land in the detail that the Fraunceys cartulary provides. For its part, the cartulary of Adam Fraunceys gives copies of charters as early as the twelfth century, and sometimes gives a detailed outline of the descent of a particular manor, but the transcriptions are only abstracts, no witnesses were included, and the incidental and often personal information which is to be found in the Pyel cartulary is lacking. There is, however, sufficient material in both documents to attempt an analysis of each man's land-holdings, and to give a good impression of the scope of their efforts and the extent of their achievements.

i. *Northamptonshire*

Pyel's first acquisitions in his native county took place in 1348. It was in this year that his father, John senior, died, and left to his son a plot of land in Irthlingborough.[1] The details of this and of other purchases in the village were apparently recorded elsewhere, possibly in another register, and so, unfortunately, the cartulary gives no further account of them. In the same year John Pyel junior also began making small purchases in the neighbouring parishes. He bought some nine acres of arable land, meadow, a dovecote and some land held in dower in Little Addington, a settlement lying barely two miles north and east of Irthlingborough. These he increased in desultory fashion over the next few years, as opportunity arose, adding $2\frac{1}{2}$ virgates in 1351, $7\frac{1}{2}$ acres in 1352 and a messuage with a further virgate of land in 1354. He also bought small plots of land in Great Addington and, a little further

1 P103.

afield, in the hamlets of Slipton and Twywell.[2] Yet although he continued to buy land in the Addingtons and became a respected patron of Little Addington church, he never acquired the manor itself, content to remain a substantial landholder and rentier. Pyel's piecemeal acquisitions here, however, contrast with his principal purchase of 1348, the manor of Cransley.

Cransley stands at some distance from the nucleus of Pyel's lands, which were mostly clustered around Irthlingborough, and the compiler of the cartulary evidently thought the purchase deserving of some explanation. The manor was held by Sir Thomas Wake of Blisworth, by virtue of his marriage to Elizabeth, daughter of Hugh of Cransley. Sir Thomas was chief falconer to the king, and was due to serve in the Crécy campaign, during which, or shortly before, he died, probably between 15 March and 23 October 1346.[3] Two years later, according to the cartulary, plague struck down the four direct heirs to the manor, which then reverted to Elizabeth Wake herself. Elizabeth thereupon granted the manor to John Pyel, which was confirmed by two charters dated 26 June and 1 July 1348.[4] Agnes, daughter of Elizabeth by an earlier marriage, and one of those who succumbed to the Black Death, had already sold to Pyel a rent of £3 pa issuing from lands in Orlingbury, roughly midway between Cransley and Irthlingborough, and the heirs to Elizabeth, her sons, Thomas Wake junior and his brother, Hugh, both issued releases to Pyel.[5]

The real reason behind the sale of the manor is not given in the cartulary. Even if the Cransley heirs had fallen victim to the Black Death, which does not appear to have reached the East Midlands in force before spring 1349, this does not explain why Elizabeth was so eager to alienate her sons' inheritance.[6] What is more likely to have prompted the sale was borrowing on the part of Sir Thomas senior in anticipation of his campaign in France. Even if he died before setting out, we know that preparations were under way, and that they were

2 P104–107. Pyel was also augmenting his holdings in Irthlingborough at this time (P108–110).

3 O. Barron, ed., *Northamptonshire Families* (London, 1906), 319. There is some confusion concerning the date of Wake's death. The queen granted Giles Beauchamp the office of falconer which had been held by Thomas Wake, 'deceased', in March 1346 (*CPR 1345–8*, 60). In April 1346 Sir Thomas was given leave not to go north, because he was too ill to move, a condition perhaps consistent with his being dead (ibid., 71), but on 7 July he was recorded in the French Rolls as being ready to embark for France in the service of Robert Ferrars (G. Wrottesley, *Crécy and Calais* (London, 1898), 114). In October 1346 it was again asserted that he was dead when Robert Seymour was appointed keeper of the forest of 'Whitlewode', a post formerly held by Wake.

4 P81–3.

5 P84, 87–8.

6 P. Ziegler, *The Black Death* (London, 1969), 174–80.

certain to have been costly. In the absence of account rolls, of course, it is impossible to tell how healthy the economy of Cransley was at the time. The decade or so before the Black Death, however, has been characterised as a period of deflation, low prices and low wages, and it would not be unreasonable to suppose that certain lesser landowners, like Sir Thomas, in minor household office, would have found equipping themselves for campaign a heavy and potentially disastrous drain on their resources, which booty and prizes of war would mitigate only very occasionally.[7] The consequences of prolonged absence for these lesser knights who, as Professor Postan argues, probably managed their own demesnes and were directly dependent on demesne produce for their livelihood, could be equally damaging.[8] In Sir Thomas's case, if, as seems likely, he died at the beginning of the campaign, then the costs which he had incurred had no chance of being defrayed by ransoms or spoils. It is also probable that he was forced to borrow money on the security of his lands, and that the alienation of Cransley by his dependants was an unavoidable consequence of his death. Although there is no direct evidence that Wake was deeply in debt to Pyel, he had acknowledged a debt to him of £40 in June 1345, and from what we shall see of Pyel's method of purchasing manors, we may be justified in suspecting that his acquisition of Cransley was at least partially connected with loans.[9] In 1349 Pyel bought Newmanor from Hugh Cransley, son of Sir Thomas, land which had been specifically excluded by the previous charter, and in 1354 he bought a further virgate of land from a Cransley landowner.[10] In March 1355, he settled the estate upon three local clerks, who re-enfeoffed Pyel in partnership with Adam Fraunceys, the latter paying £200 for his share of the manor.[11] The two surviving Wake sons, Thomas and Hugh, had already issued quitclaims to Pyel in 1350, yet the family still apparently retained an interest in the manor, as Sir Thomas is recorded as holding a fee in Cransley in 1363.[12] The two mercers, however, sold the manor to Sir Thomas de Melbourne in 1371.[13]

Meanwhile Pyel continued to buy up land around his home village. In August 1350 he purchased for himself and Adam Fraunceys lands and tenements, including a water-mill, belonging to Sir Robert Morley,

7 A.R. Bridbury, 'The Black Death', *EconHR*, 2nd Ser., xxiv (1973), 578; M.M. Postan, 'The Costs of the Hundred Years' War', *Past and Present*, no. 27 (1964), 42–4.

8 Ibid., 38.

9 CLRO Recognizance Rolls, 10, f. 3r.

10 P85; *Catalogue of Ancient Deeds*, 6 vols., (London, 1890–1915), iii, C3417, from Sir Walter Dalderby, lord of Loddington, Northants.

11 P131–3.

12 *VCH Northants* iii, 164.

13 PRO Chancery Ancient Deeds C46/10040.

marshal of Ireland, in Wellingborough, which lies four miles to the south-west of Irthlingborough.[14] In September 1350 he and a local minor clerk, John de Keteringge, bought a large area of lands and reversions in Irthlingborough and the adjacent parish of Finedon, comprising in all sixteen messuages, two tofts, 224 acres of arable, meadow and pasture, and 30s in rent.[15] In the same year Pyel and William Freman bought eighty acres of land at Astwick in the furthest corner of the county, near the borders with Oxfordshire and Buckinghamshire.[16] Pyel's practice of acting in partnership with others is interesting. When Adam Fraunceys is involved, the cartulary often specifies, as in the case of Wellingborough and Cransley, that Pyel paid the whole sum initially, and that his partner paid for his share only at a later date. This would suggest that these purchases fulfilled some prior financial arrangement agreed between the two merchants, whereby Pyel held the lands and received the benefits of lordship, while Fraunceys received a percentage of the income.[17] The purchase in 1350 of Astwick on the south-eastern borders of the county, completely isolated from any of Pyel's other lands, may simply have been a speculative investment for a cash return.

In 1353 Pyel acquired his second manor, that of Irthlingborough itself. The manor was held of the abbey of Peterborough by Sir Simon de Drayton, a member of an old Northamptonshire knightly family, who held one of three fees there. Simon had purchased the fee in 1317 for £100 and he sold it on 10 February 1353 jointly to John Pyel, Adam Fraunceys and Pyel's brother, Henry, although he issued a release to John Pyel alone on 24 February, and Pyel it was who paid the £200 and tun of wine valued at £5.[18] Drayton enfeoffed Pyel and his co-feoffees in the Bataille fee, which in the mid-twelfth century had amounted to $3\frac{1}{2}$ hides, and was $1\frac{1}{2}$ knights' fees in the thirteenth century. A second fee, which originated in the twelfth century, was held by the Seymour family in the fourteenth century.[19] In 1359 Nicholas Seymour granted to John Pyel for life his interest in the lands, including a two-thirds share in a 'wasted and poorly roofed old messuage' and three plots which had previously been built on but now stood vacant.[20] Evidently a sizeable proportion of the fee had been allowed to become derelict, and Seymour, who was lord

---

14 P93.

15 P180–1. Keteringge's son later released his rights in the property to Pyel in exchange for tenements in Northampton (ibid., 119, 17 February 1367).

16 P92.

17 A copy of the rental for 1358 of their joint holdings in the county is contained in the cartulary (P247).

18 PRO Feet of Fines CP25(1) 176/68 no. 169; P111–2.

19 *VCH Northampton* iii, 209.

20 P186.

of Castle Cary in Somerset, decided that it would be more advantageous to lease the land to Pyel. Infilling at Irthlingborough occupied Pyel most during his years of land purchase. His acquisitions there are the most frequent and evenly distributed of his purchases between 1348 and 1374, the years covered by the cartulary, with the greatest concentration of activity in the years 1357–60, at a time when he was not much taken up with civic affairs in London.[21]

The conveyance to Pyel of the manors of Woodford, Cranford and Sudborough followed in 1354, 1360 and 1361 respectively. The lordship of Woodford was apparently divided into four. On 22 April 1354 John de Boys granted the manor, except the advowson of Woodford church, to John Pyel for life. Within ten days, on 1 May, he had granted Pyel and Adam Fraunceys a £20 annuity, later reduced to 16 marks, on his lands in Lincolnshire in return for a £200 loan from Pyel. In November 1363, Pyel received part of the advowson of Woodford church along with a further half acre of land from de Boys.[22] Meanwhile, in November 1359, Sir Thomas Bosoun of Woodford granted an annual rent of £20 to Adam Fraunceys and John Pyel, later commuted to an annual payment of £5 or a lump sum of 50 marks, plus the wardship and marriage of Thomas's son and heir, Henry. These were provisions to satisfy £100 in which Thomas was bound to Adam Fraunceys. Sir Thomas was also preparing to go on pilgrimage to Jerusalem, which in part explains the timing of the settlement.[23] On 4 December Pyel was granted all Bosoun's goods in the county, as well as the procuracy of his half of the advowson of Woodford church in case a vacancy should occur in his absence.[24] Then in 1365, Pyel bought the wardship and marriage of John de la Hay, to whom belonged another quarter of the lordship of Woodford and who was barely one month old when his father died in 1361. The abbacy of Peterborough was at the time vacant, and the king took the de la Hay rights into his own hands and

21 See above, 1 (i).

22 P122, 124. The Woodford lordship was divided between de Boys, Thomas Bosoun and John de la Hay, and the advowson seems to have been shared on a rotational basis. See *VCH Northants* iii 256–7.

23 P213–4; *CCR 1354–60*, 659. A household account of Thomas Bosoun survives, recently redated by Christopher Woolgar (*Household Accounts from Medieval England*, ii (Oxford, 1993), 695) to 1348, which gives an interesting glimpse of the expenditure and life-style of a minor country landowner of this period. Domestic consumption was remarkably high, suggesting a substantial household to be supported. Sir Thomas was also fond of travelling, making journeys to Northampton for the jousting, to London, to visit his mother-in-law in Bedfordshire, and to Windsor, all within the space of eight weeks. It is hardly surprising that economic conditions after the Black Death made it difficult to sustain such a standard of living without recourse to credit. See G.H. Fowler 'A Household Expense Account, 1328', *EHR* lv (1940), 630–4.

24 P177–8.

granted them in May 1365 to John FitzEustace, who transferred them
to John Pyel in November. John found the manor 'utterly ruined'
(*oltrement destrut*) except for the hall and dovecote which were in great
need of repair.[25] The manor included two carucates of land and what
was described as a quarter part of the moiety of Woodford church.[26]
Quite what this means is unclear. As we have seen, Thomas de Bosoun
granted Pyel the proxy of half the advowson during his absence in
Jerusalem, and John de Boys the advowson which was in his gift in
1363. It would appear that the advowson was shared by all the lords
of Woodford, and that Pyel was gathering these disparate rights into
his own hands.

The description of the de la Hay properties, presumably following
four years of neglect, accords with that of the Seymour holdings in
Irthlingborough, which were also in a state of semi-dereliction. These
lands had been granted to Thomas Seymour and Laurence Seymour,
parson of Higham Ferrers, together with a quarter of the manor of
nearby Finedon and the manor of Eaton in Wiltshire, by Warin
Seymour in 1329.[27] Thomas died without heir and the land reverted
first to Alan Seymour and then to his brother, Nicholas. It seems likely
that these latter were rarely, if ever, resident in Irthlingborough and
had allowed the property to fall into decay. It was probably a conscious
policy on Pyel's part to choose lands, where they became available,
that were of little or no use to their owners, and could therefore be
purchased at a comparatively low price. His other principal ploy was
to make loans to indebted landowners.

On 20 October 1357, John, son of John Daundelyn, granted to John
Pyel and his wife Joan an annual rent for life of £10, to be raised from
lands in Cranford and Lyveden in Northamptonshire. The next day,
he and his father made a recognizance in the Staple of Westminster
that they were bound to John Pyel in 100 marks. In November 1357
John Daundelyn senior granted to Adam Fraunceys and Henry Pyel
various rents issuing from lands and cottages in the parishes of Cranford
St Andrew and Little Addington together with ten acres of meadow
and pasture. In July 1360, after a long and somewhat involved procedure
of multiple transfers, John Pyel was enfeoffed of the manor of Cranford
itself.[28] Whatever the reason for the complicated nature of the transaction, it seems clear that the sale, first of the lands and rents, and
then of the manor itself, was provoked by debt. On the same day as
the feoffment, 25 July 1360, Richard Bryan, one of the original feoffees

25 P68.
26 *la quarte partie del moite del eglise de Wodeford.*
27 P185.
28 P147, 149, 151, 198–202.

of John Daundelyn, and William Freman, also a feoffee, granted further lands in Cranford and in Ringstead to John Pyel. In September 1360, Pyel leased the manor back to John Daundelyn and his wife at a rent of £18 in the first year and £5 *pa* thereafter.[29]

It appears from a note in the cartulary that John Daundelyn was amerced in £100 in 1352 for a crime for which he had been indicted. He had been given leave to pay at the rate of 10 marks a year and by 1358 he was still in arrears. He had also failed to pay fully his contribution to the three-year subsidy granted in 1348 and that granted in 1352. Moreover, Daundelyn owed £20 to the abbot of Peterborough, who had paid the 10 mark fine on his behalf for three years. Pyel returned to the Exchequer two acquittances of £20 each on 2 December 1359, reducing Daundelyn's outstanding fine for his felony from £73 6s 8d to £33 6s 8d. The abbot of Peterborough sent to Pyel at Christmas 1359 an account of Daundelyn's debts to him, and at Easter 1360 Pyel paid £10 to the abbot on Daundelyn's behalf.[30] By July Pyel had received the manor into his own hands.

A pattern seems to be emerging, and one that is not altogether surprising, that Pyel and his agents were seeking out lands and manors whose lords were either absentee with major interests or preoccupations elsewhere and had allowed their estates to decline physically and economically, or were in some way impoverished and in debt and were only too willing to borrow heavily on the security of their lands. This we may surmise was not an isolated phenomenon. Such was the case at Edmonton, as we shall see, and the practice was no doubt widespread. Pyel's cartulary, however, shows in some detail the systematic nature of this policy, and underlines the continuing importance of the city merchant in influencing the direction and nature of the land market in fourteenth-century England.

Pyel acquired his last manor, Sudborough, shortly afterwards, in 1361. By contrast with his other manors, which were, with the exception of Cransley, in the fee of Peterborough, Sudborough was held of the abbey of Westminster, to whom it had been granted by Edward the Confessor.[31] In common with most of the other manors we have been considering, Sudborough was composed of a number of fees. In the late thirteenth century the manor had been held by Sir Reginald Watermill, who divided it among his three daughters, but two parts of the manor were reunited in the mid-fourteenth century by Simon de Drayton, who settled it on trustees in 1350.[32]

29 P219–20.
30 P248–52.
31 Barbara Harvey, *Westminster Abbey and its Estates*, 27n.
32 P45.

Simon de Drayton, who had held Irthlingborough since 1317, was one of the more substantial members of the Northamptonshire gentry. He was descended from a branch of the de Vere family, which had adopted the name Drayton in the early thirteenth century after the manor which had been with the de Veres since the eleventh century. Simon was born c.1282 and inherited Drayton on his father's death in early January 1292. He went on to acquire a number of holdings in Northamptonshire including lands in Brigstock, Great Addington and Twywell, the manors of Islip, Irthlingborough and Sudborough, and a joint holding of the manor of Lowick. Maud Simkins, writing in the *Victoria County History*, traces a distinguished career for him. He was employed as a royal envoy, served with the king against Roger Mortimer and the rebels in 1326 (as indeed did Sir Thomas Wake), and he served the king on an expedition in Gascony.[33] His standing was clearly high in the county. Between 1321 and 1337 he represented Northamptonshire in parliament fourteen times, and in the 1340s he was appointed to a number of legal commissions in the county.[34] By the 1350s, however, he seems to have retired from public affairs and he divested himself of a number of lands, including Irthlingborough in 1353 and Sudborough, which he granted to trustees in 1350.[35] He died on 31 May 1357 seised of the manor of Drayton, lands in Brigstock and Lowick, and two manors in Huntingdonshire which he held jointly with his wife Margaret.[36] Sir Simon represents the solid tradition of a Northamptonshire gentle family, settled on their lands for generations, and it would be interesting to know his reaction to the appearance of John Pyel in the county. From the evidence, slight as it is, their relations do not appear to have been close. Drayton witnessed only two of Pyel's charters, both of which concerned grants of land in Wellingborough by Robert Morley, marshal of Ireland, in August 1350, and are probably more indicative of his relations with the marshal than with Pyel.[37] Other witnesses on those charters included Sir John de Ashton, Henry Grene, Nicholas Grene, Simon Symeon and John Knyvet, all representatives of the greater men in the region. Pyel is supported by his Irthlingborough neighbours, who in various permutations appear on virtually all his deeds. Failure to appear as a witness on documents hardly proves cool relations, but it strengthens the suspicion that the Northamptonshire grandees, while making use of mercantile capital, kept their distance

---

33 *VCH Northants.* iii, 237.
34 *Return of the Members of Parliament*, part 1(i) (London 1878, reprinted Munich, 1980).
35 P49.
36 *CIPM*, x, no. 369.
37 P93, 95.

from the incarnation of that wealth.[38] This must have been especially marked in the case of Drayton, whose family's presence in the county dated almost to the conquest. Pyel had been a neighbour of Drayton but his forebears, even at the time of Simon's birth, were probably no more than relatively well-to-do villeins.[39] The reasons why a man like Simon de Drayton should sell out to Pyel can only be guessed. There is no suggestion of debt, as there is with Sir Thomas Wake at Cransley, or indeed William Malory, Drayton's immediate successor at Sudborough, as we shall see. He also had an heir, John, and so would have had every incentive to retain his lands. Given the diversity of his holdings, and noting the example of the Seymours, it may have been that with severe shortage of labour after the Black Death, resources were too stretched to keep all the land in hand, and leasing or selling some parts was inevitable. Nevertheless the feelings of Sir Simon, who had held Irthlingborough of Peterborough abbey since 1316, in selling to the descendant of an abbey bondman might well have been, at the very least, mixed. A man by then in his seventies, he is unlikely to have regarded Pyel as in any respect his social equal, whatever his wealth.

Sudborough, then, was settled on trustees in 1350, and in January 1358 the manor, or the two-thirds which Drayton held, were transferred to William Malory.[40] The Malorys seem to have been another well-established family in Northamptonshire, and were apparently related to the Zouches. Various members of the family appear on occasion among the witness lists in the cartulary. The Malorys were seen to have been in financial difficulties. In June 1358 William and Anketil, or Anketin, Malory acknowledged a debt to Pyel of £200, for which William was to pay an annuity of £20, reduced to 20 marks, based on his lands in Sudborough and elsewhere in Northamptonshire.[41] Meanwhile the third part of the manor which was not held by Simon de Drayton descended to William la Zouche, archbishop of York, and from him to Anketil Malory, referred to in the cartulary as Zouche's brother.[42] Pyel seems to have had no interest in this part of the manor. Whether or not William Malory was able to maintain the payments, in April 1361 he granted Sudborough to John Pyel, who added further lands and rents there in 1362.[43]

With the exception of small purchases and additions of land, mostly in Irthlingborough, the last of which was in 1374, the acquisition of

38 For further discussion on Pyel's place in Northamptonshire society, see O'Connor, 'Fraunceys and Pyel: perceptions of status'.

39 See above, 1 (ii).

40 P49–50.

41 P157–9.

42 P45.

43 P53, 74–6.

Sudborough manor completed the basic framework of Pyel's estates. From a fine levied in 1376, we can tell that he also acquired tenements in Higham Ferrers, and the cartulary records lands in Ringstead and a reversion purchased in Raunds.[44] All three parishes lay close to Irthlingborough, and Raunds and Higham formed part of the honor of the duke of Lancaster. Pyel also bought property in Northampton. In March 1353 he purchased several tenements from Simon de Launshull which were all leased out at rent.[45] One of these Pyel sold in 1358, but the rest he granted to John Keteringge, the son of the clerk mentioned earlier, in exchange for lands in Irthlingborough.[46] In 1357, he and John Curteys of Higham Ferrers bought a malting and wheat mill in the town which they leased back to the donor for an annual rent of 100s.[47]

It is quite likely that these Northampton properties were bought purely for their rental value, which prompts the question why was Pyel buying lands in Northamptonshire at all? It has sometimes been suggested that land was the only asset into which a successful merchant could sink his wealth. It is certainly true that investment in land was one option, but it was not the only one, nor was it necessarily the most beneficial in economic terms. Sir John Fastolf, for example, had a steadier and more secure return for his spoils of war by depositing them with merchants. These were short- or sometimes medium-term cash investments in mercantile trade and provided interest at a rate of 5%, similar to the average rate of return from land, but not subject to deductions.[48] Profits of trade were admittedly unpredictable, but so were the profits from land. Besides fluctuations in crop yields, harvest failure and livestock diseases, there was the necessity to collect rents, combat arrears, deal with inefficient or corrupt servants and worst, and most costly of all, fight off legal challenges to title.[49] The expenses involved in maintaining an estate could easily absorb all and more of the income it generated. Pyel might have done better to have ploughed his profits back into his own commercial enterprises, or invest with other merchants. Yet Fastolf also, like many of his contemporaries, chose above all to invest in land. One reason for this was the constant compulsion to exhibit outward and visible signs of wealth. Land, like

44 CP25(1) 178/85 no. 696; P219, 154–6.

45 P114–6. Launshull, the son of a wealthy burgess of the town who had sat as MP for the borough in 1324 and 1330, had inherited his father's Northampton properties in 1346 (P116).

46 P119.

47 P143–4

48 K.B. McFarlane, 'The Investment of Sir John Fastolf's Profits of War' in *England in the Fifteenth Century*, (London, 1981), 178–83.

49 Ibid., 192–5.

plate, jewellery, furniture and building, attracted large sums of surplus cash because it satisfied the aspiring gentleman's desire for display, what McFarlane called 'a passion for conspicuous waste'.[50] But more importantly land, or some land, conveyed lordship, and was therefore the means by which the door to social advancement could be opened still wider.

It was the attempt to acquire good manorial land which motivated ambitious merchants like Pyel.[51] Such land was not in abundance in the later fourteenth century and the avenues open to the gentry and aristocracy to acquire it, inheritance and marriage, were not open to townsmen. While a merchant's daughter might marry into a landed family, bringing with her a welcome cash dowry, it was rare for a merchant to marry an aristocratic heiress or widow.[52] So the socially-conscious merchant not only had to be selective in his choice of land, but he was also forced to acquire that land either through direct purchase or as a result of the owners' failure to repay loans raised against the security of their property. Both cases required cash investment.

While Pyel is likely to have bought land more for the social rewards it could bestow than for its financial yields, this does not mean that economic considerations were unimportant. It seems to be generally held that the concept of land acquisition as an 'investment', in the modern, economic, sense of the word is an anachronism.[53] As we have seen, the value of land lay in lordship, as a means of display and a mark of social status. This may well have been true for the gentry and the nobility, but they came by their lands through inheritance, marriage or by conquest; the last thing they did was buy land. Merchants had no alternative, and given their commercial frame of mind, it is unlikely that financial return played no part in their calculations. Adam Fraunceys, as we shall see, chose to buy manors among the rich soils of the Lea Valley,[54] and Pyel himself seemed quite concerned with aspects of trade in the East Midlands.[55] There is also a whiff of the account book about Pyel's cartulary. Frequent notes and memoranda record how much was paid for a particular deal and, more importantly, who paid.

50 Ibid., 191.
51 On the distinction between peasant holdings, which decreased in value after the Black Death, and manorial land which remained in demand see C. Carpenter, 'The Fifteenth-Century English Gentry and their Estates' in M. Jones, ed., *Gentry and Lesser Nobility in Late Medieval Europe* (Gloucester, 1986), 38, and S. Raban, *Mortmain Legislation and the English Church 1279–1500* (Cambridge, 1982), 179.
52 Thrupp, *Merchant Class*, 263–5.
53 Sandra Raban, 'The Land Market and the Aristocracy in the Thirteenth Century', in D.E. Greenway, C. Holdsworth and J. Sayers, eds., *Tradition and Change: Essays in Honour of Marjorie Chibnall* (Cambridge, 1985), 260.
54 Below, 2 (ii).
55 1 (ii) above.

The cartulary also contains a copy of a rental, for Michaelmas 1358, showing an income from the Northamptonshire property which he shared with Adam Fraunceys, of £110 1s 1½d.[56] Clearly Fraunceys, for his part, must have been interested in the monetary rewards from his investment, although we do not know what percentage of the profits accrued to him. Moreover, the tenements which Pyel purchased in urban areas, like Northampton, were evidently bought for their rental value, or to be used as units of exchange for more productive land.[57] His desire to obtain property for rent can also be seen in his acquisition of tenements in Bedford, which he proceeded to lease at a yearly rent of 2 marks.[58]

The acquisition of land outside London therefore served a dual purpose. All purchase was a means of investing surplus wealth, and all provided to a greater or lesser extent a return on that investment. But a distinction may be made between the social value of those lands purchased at Irthlingborough and in the adjacent parishes and manors, which were to form a long-term estate and a landed seat for the Pyel dynasty, and the value in cash and economic terms of those more isolated properties which he subsequently sold, including the manor of Cransley, the rents in Orlingbury and tenements in urban areas like Northampton and Bedford and, of course, London. If Pyel were to attempt to emulate a man like Simon de Drayton, it was essential for him to have land of economic quantity and social quality, which in itself formed a coherent estate.

ii. Essex and Middlesex

The first purchases made by Fraunceys outside the city came, as with Pyel, at the time of the Black Death. Unlike Pyel, however, he seems not to have returned to his native county, wherever it may have been, to buy land, but stayed quite close to the city. Fraunceys was associated with Pyel in a number of property transactions in and near London, certainly from the late 1340s to the early 1360s. He was also nominally involved with Pyel's dealings in Northamptonshire, as joint purchaser or trustee. His purchases in his own right, however, focus on north Middlesex and the south-western fringes of Essex, within striking distance of London. On 1 February 1349 Fraunceys bought, jointly with Thomas de Langeton, the manor of Wyke from John Causton and his wife, Eve.[59] This manor, which included Hackney Wick, and

56 P247.
57 As in the case of the exchange of land with John de Keteringge; see above.
58 P63-4.
59 F130.

parts of Old Ford and Stepney, had been consolidated by a London draper, Simon de Abyndon, mostly in the second decade of the fourteenth century.[60] After Simon's death in 1322, his widow, Eve, married John de Causton, a London mercer, who thereby received the estate. Causton made his own additions to the manor, which comprised at the time of the sale to Fraunceys at least two messuages and 114 acres of land, with possibly a further thirty-five acres of meadowland and a water-mill.[61] Fraunceys himself increased his holding by the addition of small parcels of land. In June 1349 Nicholas atte Wyke, clerk, conveyed a smallholding in Old Ford to Adam, and in 1350 and 1351 Simon de Hampton, apparently another clerical agent, gathered together small plots of land on Fraunceys' behalf.[62] In August 1352 Adam acquired further lands in Hackney, Stepney and Tottenham from Walter Turk, fishmonger and former mayor of London, and he continued to expand the estate over the next ten years by purchasing directly or through agents like Nicholas atte Wyke.[63]

From Hackney Wick Fraunceys moved eastwards, across the River Lea, to West Ham and Leyton. It is noteworthy that all four of Fraunceys' principal holdings, including those in Edmonton and Enfield, lay in or near the fertile marshland of the Lea Valley. The desirability of this area and its importance as a source of foodstuffs to the city suggest that Fraunceys's purchases outside London were not wholly unrelated to the quality and profitability of the land he was buying.[64] In 1357 he bought the manor known as 'Chabhames' or Chobhams after its occupier of the time, Sir Thomas de Chobham. Chobhams was composed of lands in East Ham, West Ham and Barking, with a small piece of meadowland in Stratford. Two years later Fraunceys settled the manor on trustees, Thomas de Langeton and Henry Burford, who granted the lands back to him for life with reversion to his eldest son Robert.[65] In 1359 he purchased the manor of Ruckholt Hall in Leyton from Nicholas atte Wyke and Thomas de Pateshull, both clerks who had acted before on Adam's behalf. They had been enfeoffed in 1355 by Richard la Vache and were probably holding the manor for Fraunceys for that time rather than acting on their own initiative.[66]

60 F88–101, 108–113.
61 F99, 109, 111–2, 123–5, 128. The thirty-five acres of land with water-mill were leased for ten years in 1319 (F112), but there is no record of their subsequently being granted in perpetuity or of the lease being renewed.
62 F170, 140–44.
63 F158–9.
64 See Paul Glennie, 'In Search of Agrarian Capitalism: Manorial Land Markets and the Acquisition of Land in the Lea Valley c.1450–c.1560', *Continuity and Change*, iii (1988), 11–40, esp. 14–15.
65 F55–6, 59–60.
66 F22, 16.

Like Wyke, Chobhams had been consolidated by a Londoner earlier in the century, John Preston, a wealthy corder, whose granddaughter later married John of Northampton.[67]

These transactions introduce several points of interest, not least Fraunceys's use of clerks as trustees, joint purchasers or agents. The foremost of these was Thomas de Langeton, who was frequently associated with Fraunceys, and occasionally with John Pyel, as co-feoffee in property deals and, as we have seen, was enfeoffed several times with land which Fraunceys had purchased to be held in trust for his heirs. He may well have had some legal training, and possibly acted in an advisory capacity to his patron. He remains, however, a shadowy figure. In his list of the monuments of St Helen's Bishopsgate, John Stow mentions that of 'Thomas Langton, chaplain', who, he says, was buried in the choir in 1350. He then goes on to record the monument of Adam Fraunceys himself, presumably close by.[68] If this is Fraunceys's clerk, his burial in St Helen's, and proximity to Fraunceys in death, reflects the closeness of their ties in life.[69] His career, however, is slightly puzzling. The first set of wardens' accounts for the Mercers' Company in 1347 mentions among its members a Thomas de Langeton, and there is a reference among the letters patent for merchants to a man of the same name who was owed £93 for wool sales in 1344.[70] Langeton features quite prominently in the will of John Causton, dated 30 July 1353, who with his wife Eve, we may recall, granted the manor of Wyke jointly to Langeton and Fraunceys in 1349. Thomas was to have the right of presentation to a chantry set up by Causton in the church of St Pancras, and he was to receive tenements and rents in several city parishes. He was appointed principal executor of the will, while Adam Fraunceys was one of the supervisors.[71] In 1350 the prior of the hospital of St Mary without Bishopsgate acknowledged a debt of £100 to Adam Fraunceys and Thomas de Langeton, both described as citizens and mercers of London. Later that year both men were granted licences to go on pilgrimage, in company with two other mercers, Ellis Fraunceys and William Causton, who was later to sell land to Fraunceys in Edmonton.[72] Thomas de Langeton accordingly appears as a reasonably successful mercer, to be numbered among the close associates of Adam Fraunceys. From the mid-1350s, however, his designation

67 Bird, *Turbulent London*, 8.

68 John Stow, *A Survey of London*, ed. C.L. Kingsford, 2 vols. (Oxford, 1908), i, 172.

69 The nearness of the memorials strongly suggests that this was the clerk associated with Adam Fraunceys, but if so the date of his death is incorrect, as Langeton was still alive in 1359.

70 Creaton, 'Mercers' Wardens' Accounts', i, 148; PRO C67/21.

71 *CWCH* i, 672–3.

72 *CPR 1348–50*, 560. See below.

changes. In 1355, a debt of £1,100 due to Thomas de Langeton, clerk of London, from John de L'Isle was to be paid at Adam Fraunceys's house.[73] And as we have seen, in his property transactions in the late 1350s Langeton was described as a clerk or chaplain. It is barely conceivable that there could be two men named Thomas de Langeton who were on such intimate terms with Adam Fraunceys at about the same time, and we can only conclude that the mercer and the clerk were the same man. Sylvia Thrupp writes that it was unknown for a London merchant to be so filled with religious zeal that he abandoned commerce for the church; perhaps Langeton is the exception.[74] Certainly merchants from other cities have been known to enter the church in their later years.[75] Since his clerical status only appears from 1355, we may infer that Thomas, too, took orders late in life and possibly ceased his mercantile activities, though clearly not his financial services.[76]

Langeton, a former colleague and friend of his patron, is evidently a special case. Other clerks who are known to have acted for Fraunceys include Nicholas atte Wyke, Thomas Pateshull[77] and John Pitee of Chishill, Cambs. It was not unusual for clerks to be called upon to convey property and to act as trustees, being generally men of reliable reputation who commanded positions of trust.[78] They were also men who were often without immediate heirs themselves, which made them additionally trustworthy. It is interesting that some, like Simon de Hampton, collected together small parcels of land before transferring them to Fraunceys, presumably acting upon instruction rather than engaged in their own speculative dealing.[79]

Fraunceys's acquisitions also highlight the prevalence of Londoners

---

73 *CCR 1354–60*, 109.

74 Thrupp, *Merchant Class*, 188.

75 William Canynges, the great fifteenth-century Bristol merchant, for example. See J. Sherborne, *William Canynges 1402–1474* (Bristol Historical Association Pamphlet, 1985).

76 There is a reference to a canon of Sulby abbey by the name of Thomas de Langeton, whose chest at Little Addington was burgled, for which crime the perpetrator was pardoned in September 1360 (*CPR 1358–61*, 397). The association of Thomas de Langeton, canon of Sulby, a house which, as we have seen, had financial links with both Pyel and Fraunceys, and Little Addington, where Pyel had substantial land-holdings and whose church sported the Pyel arms is interesting. One of the canons appointed in 1353 to deal with Pyel and Fraunceys was named Thomas de Langeton (P35). Could it be that he retired to end his days as a Premonstratensian canon?

77 Pateshull, like Fraunceys, was well-connected with the priory of St Helen's, Bishopsgate. He was rector of St John Walbrook, a church in the gift of the priory. In his will of 1394 (Guildhall MS 171/1 f. 33v.) he left 10 marks to the house, 1 mark to Dame Margaret Morey and £2 to Dame Margery Buntyng, nuns of St Helen's, and asked to be buried in the convent cemetery. He also seems to have acted as feoffee for the priory (*CPR 1391–6*, 156). I am most grateful to Dr Catherine Paxton for this information.

78 See, for example, Derek Keene, *Survey of Medieval Winchester*, 2 vols. (Oxford, 1985), i, 190.

79 F143–4.

who held land in the city's hinterland. He is hardly treading where no
Londoner had trod before. With the exception of Ruckholts, these
estates had been established by citizens long before Adam Fraunceys
bought them and they were transferred as compact parcels of land
which he consolidated further. Names of London citizens are com-
monplace among the previous landholders. The home counties in
general, and Middlesex in particular, were favourite places for Londoners to settle themselves, affording convenient places of refuge while
merchants remained in business in London, as well as providing for
future retirement.[80] And as land in Middlesex had been bought and
sold by Londoners for some time, a land market had grown up in the
county among the wealthier merchants, making it increasingly the
preserve of the London citizenry. We should not, therefore, be surprised
to find Adam Fraunceys creating his manorial base at Edmonton, partly
out of lands held by London merchants and partly from the manor of
Edmonton itself. The first gave him extensive real estate, the second
that which was even more highly prized, lordship.

Adam Fraunceys's first acquisition in Edmonton was made as early
as 1351, when he bought $13\frac{1}{2}$ acres of meadow and 13 acres of wood in
Edmonton and Enfield from Sir James de Bereford.[81] Fraunceys purchased the land jointly with Peter Favelor, and this is the first evidence
of their association.[82] Thereafter all lands purchased in Edmonton,
Tottenham and Enfield were bought in partnership with Favelor until
the latter's death in October 1360. In March 1355 the pair bought their
first substantial piece of land. This was the holding in Edmonton carved
out by the mercer William de Causton. Causton died in October 1354,
without heir, having entrusted his lands to two of his former apprentices,
John atte Berne and John Organ.[83] William Causton was one of the
most prolific purchasers of land in the district. Of the 1,088 charters in
the Fraunceys cartulary which relate to land sales in Edmonton since
the twelfth century, 276, just over a quarter, concern purchases by
Causton, made between 1307 and 1356. He bought land, often in very
small plots, from a variety of people, but principally from old local
families, like the Ansteys, the Marshes and the Fords. These charters
reveal interesting insights into Causton's methods of acquisition. Besides
straightforward grants and releases, much of the property seems to
have been transferred as a result of loans made to the holders by
Causton on the security of their lands, as John Pyel was doing in
Northamptonshire. John Patryk of Enfield, for example, leased and

80 Thrupp, *Merchant Class*, 284.
81 F1270.
82 For Favelor see below.
83 F989.

sold quantities of land to Causton over a period of thirteen years (1310–23). It seems that at least some of this land was alienated as a result of loans, since in December 1320, Patryk leased a parcel of land to Causton for one year, at the end of which he had to pay Causton £6 10s to recover it, or else grant it to him in fee for 10s. In 1315 Patryk had agreed to underwrite arrears of rent from land which he had granted to Causton, and in the same year was due to repay £10, borrowed on the security of a wood in Edmonton which he had inherited.[84] In March 1338 John de Chilterne granted all the lands which he had inherited from his uncle in Edmonton, as well as others he had bought, as security for a loan of £100. In August that year, Causton was again in receipt of a bond, this time of £200, due to mature at Christmas, and in November 1341 Chilterne acknowledged receipt of 200 marks 'with which to trade to the profit of William [Causton]', for which he had to render account with interest at Christmas.[85] Chilterne's position deteriorated so rapidly that in October 1343 he sold to Causton by fine 233 acres of arable, meadow and woodland, plus a messuage and three tofts.[86] Other examples of mortgages for land abound. Often the areas involved are very small, one or two acres, sometimes less, but the impression is that such transactions were being concluded on a large scale. The Chilterne sale represents perhaps the largest block of land to be transferred, but other well-established families sold out to Causton, the Marsh family, for example, and, to a lesser extent, William Ford.[87]

Finally there are several instances, recorded in the cartulary where Causton provided landholders with money, supposedly for trading purposes, and to make a return to him with interest. In June 1322 Reginald Fox was given 100s in return for which Causton was granted a wood and some adjacent arable land for twenty years.[88] This method of loan was employed regularly in the case of John le Venour. In May 1331, Venour leased pasture to Causton for three years in return for £8 'ad marchandisandum inde ad comodum ... Willelmi [de Causton]'. In the following October he acknowledged receipt of a further £10, and in consequence increased the lease of the pasture to six years and added a 17 acre meadow for a term of two or four years. In March 1333 he received £20 and in August 1334 a further £40. Finally on 5 September 1341, le Venour was again in receipt of £40 and on the

84 F822, 826, 843.
85 F862, 864, 868, 876–7, 880.
86 F980.
87 Some members of the Marsh family seem to have moved to London, like Nicholas, son of John Marsh, who was probably a mercer. (See, for example, his appearance on a witness list with other prominent mercers in 1340, *CCR 1339–41*, 469.)
88 F763–4.

same day granted a parcel of lands to William Causton.[89]

The second principal landowner from whom Fraunceys bought land in Edmonton, Roger Depham, seems to have acquired much of his estate in the same way.[90] An indenture of 1329 records the mortgage of a croft held by Thomas de Acton, and the reversion of part of it, for £10 until 1336. By 1334 Thomas had released his interest in the land to Depham.[91] In 1345 two bonds were granted to Depham by John le Venour, already in debt to William Causton, one of £40 and the other of £20, and in September 1346 all le Venour's land in Edmonton was assessed and delivered to Roger.[92] In a similar fashion, a recognizance of £40 made by Thomas le Rowe to Depham in May 1331 was followed one month later by a grant of land.[93] Depham's land-dealings, stretching from 1316 until 1355, do not appear to have been as extensive as William Causton's, but, like Causton's, the purchases often consisted of very small pieces of land, and in some cases both men were buying from the same landholders.[94] In December 1358 he sold all his lands in Edmonton to Thomas de Langeton and John Pitee, who transferred them to Fraunceys and Favelor for life in May and June 1359.[95] Roger Depham, like William Causton, had no direct heir and settled his lands during the last year of his life upon trustees or agents, by whom Adam Fraunceys and his partner were later enfeoffed. It is likely that Fraunceys had struck deals with both men some time before their final settlements.

Fraunceys's partner, Peter Favelor, was a retainer of William de Bohun, earl of Northampton, for whom he acted as attorney and later executor, and was rewarded for his services by grants of lands in Dorset, Oxfordshire, Essex and Kent.[96] Like Thomas de Langeton, he is an obscure but intriguing character. He was for a time a merchant operating out of Newcastle upon Tyne, although it is not known whether he originated there. He first appears in 1330, lending money or supplying goods in London, and thereafter is regularly lending or

---

89 F899–904, 920, 927, 974–5.

90 Depham was alderman for Candlewick ward, 1338–59, M.P. for London in 1334, Common Clerk in 1335 and Recorder from 1338 until his death in 1359 (Beaven, i, 385).

91 F1016–7.

92 F1068–72.

93 F1166, 1249–50.

94 Both Causton and Depham acquired land from John le Venour. Depham also received a substantial amount of land from John Marsh in compact parcels over a period of years, leased land from John de Chilterne and bought up plots of land from the widow of Thomas de Anesty.

95 F1264, 1271.

96 G.A. Holmes, *The Estates of the Higher Nobility in Fourteenth-Century England* (Cambridge, 1957), 69–70.

providing credit often for quite large sums.[97] In 1339 he and some other Newcastle merchants advanced £4,000 to the king, for which they received his protection and assignments on customs and subsidy, and in the same year Waltham Abbey recognized a debt to Favelor of £1,000.[98] He was an active participant in the wool export schemes of the late 1330s, shipping wool from Ipswich and London to Antwerp.[99] His association with William de Bohun, earl of Northampton dates from at least 1337, when he accompanied the earl on royal service overseas.[100] Favelor's lands in London, and possibly elsewhere, may have come through defaulting debts; most of the recognizances to him offered security on lands in London and Essex. Fraunceys probably met Favelor in London, or perhaps through trading connections in the country. In addition to their joint purchases in Edmonton, Favelor helped to establish a college of chantry priests in the chapel at Guildhall in 1356, and he had received a licence to go abroad, presumably on pilgrimage, in 1350, shortly before Adam and Ellis Frauncey and their friends, and perhaps intended to accompany them.[101] Frauncey also left instructions in his will to complete a chantry at Edmonton church which Favelor had founded for himself but had been unable to complete. Peter Favelor died in October 1360, and his share of the Edmonton manor reverted to Adam. His son and heir, Gregory, may have been a clerk.[102]

Part of the manor of Edmonton had been put in the hands of trustees some time before the death of its lord, Geoffrey de Say, in June 1359. On 31 May 1359 those trustees, Thomas de Langeton and John Pitee, granted the lands, which amounted to two messuages, 320 acres and some rents, to Adam Frauncey for life with reversion to his sons, first Adam, then Robert.[103] The grant was confirmed by Geoffrey's heir, William de Say, when he came of age in 1361. On 2 October 1361, William mortgaged the manor to Adam for a term of 22 years in return for a sum of £1,000, and at some time between 1362 and 1369, the manor with its lordship was transferred to Adam in perpetuity.[104]

The manor of Edmonton, whose acquisition prompted the compilation of the cartulary, was evidently intended to be the centrepiece of Frauncey' landed estates. He went on to consolidate the holdings, again through the agency of the clerks Thomas de Langeton and John

97 *CCR 1330–3*, 120, 169.
98 *CPR 1338–40*, 324; *CCR 1339–41*, 465.
99 Ibid., *1337–9*, 562; *1339–41*, 188.
100 *CPR 1334–8*, 531.
101 *CPR 1348–50*, 560.
102 *CPR 1343–5*, 374.
103 F1271.
104 F1279–80; PRO Inquisition Ad Quod Dampnum C143/367/17.

Pitee. In July 1362, Richard de Plesyngton granted to Fraunceys his lands in Edmonton, which were lands originally belonging to John le Venour, some of which, as we have seen, had been purchased by Roger de Depham and conveyed to Fraunceys in 1359.[105] By October 1369, Adam had acquired the manor in fee, and with it the right to firewood in the earl of Hereford's park at Enfield.[106] He granted the manor to Robert de Belknap, the lawyer and later chief justice of common pleas, and John Wroth, fishmonger and alderman of London, who granted it back to him for life, with remainder to his surviving children, Adam and Maud.[107] In March 1371, William Pymme granted to Fraunceys all his lands in the town and parish of Edmonton, which he and John de Clavering, clerk, had received from William Vikere, a member of another of the old landowning families there.[108] Later that year, 8 July 1371, Belknap and Wroth settled the manor, with its appurtenances of brushwood, on Adam to hold in chief of the king.[109]

Meanwhile Fraunceys was continuing to acquire parcels of land elsewhere. In addition to his interest in Pyel's lands in Northamptonshire, and his properties in the city and Southwark, Fraunceys bought or leased lands in Kent, Middlesex and Bedfordshire. In 1373 he is found to be holding half a knight's fee in Northolt and Ickenham of Humphrey, earl of Hereford, and some time before January 1372 he received the manor of Eyworth in Bedfordshire, which was still held by Adam Fraunceys junior at his death in 1417 and valued at that time at £20 pa.[110] This manor passed down with the other Fraunceys holdings until their forfeiture in 1486 as a result of Richard Charlton's treason. It may seem odd that Fraunceys should procure an isolated manor in Bedfordshire, but there were certain familiar features in the Eyworth environment.[111] A second part of the manor was held by St Helen's Priory, Bishopsgate, which had been granted all the lands belonging to Maud, daughter of William Bussy in the late twelfth or early thirteenth century. The priory increased the original grant and held on to the land until the Dissolution.[112] It may be noted that St

105 *CCR 1360–4*, 411.
106 Humphrey de Bohun, earl of Hereford, Essex and Northampton. The proximity of Edmonton manor to Bohun's own manor at Enfield probably encouraged his friendship with Fraunceys, who may have already been known to the family through Peter Favelor, steward to Humphrey's father, William, earl of Northampton. See O'Connor, 'Fraunceys and Pyel: perceptions of status'.
107 *CPR 1367–70*, 312–3.
108 *CCR 1369–74*, 292.
109 Ibid., 309.
110 *CIPM* xiii, nos. 167 (p. 142), 105. The fee in Middlesex was also close to Simon Fraunceys's manors of Northolt and Down.
111 A possible explanation of the acquisition of this manor is given in 3 below.
112 *VCH Bedford* ii, ed. W. Page (1908), 231–2.

Helen's also held land in Edmonton from about 1274. Although most
of its later landholdings there may, as Diane Bolton suggests, have been
granted out of the estates of its benefactor, Adam Fraunceys, yet St
Helen's evidently preceded Fraunceys as a landowner at Edmonton, as
it had at Eyworth.[113]

iii. London

Both Adam Fraunceys and John Pyel amassed a large stock of tenements
and rents in London, although Fraunceys seems to have been the more
assiduous and consistent in property dealing in the city. It is indeed
quite likely that buying and selling real estate formed a major part of
Fraunceys's business in London, and that medium- and long-term
investment in these assets provided him with a not insignificant income.
We may be led to such a conclusion, of course, because there is much
more information concerning the property deals of both Fraunceys and
Pyel than there is about their other entrepreneurial ventures, but the
scale and frequency of these transactions, certainly in the case of Adam
Fraunceys, are evidence that he attached considerable importance to
them. Here, too, there was a divergence between Fraunceys and Pyel.
Although from early on Pyel was ready to co-operate with Fraunceys
in the acquisition of property in London, he only came later in life to
purchase property there on his own account. This is consistent with
the generally detached attitude he seems to have assumed towards the
city, until political commitment and financial involvement made his
regular presence in the capital unavoidable.

The principal source for the London purchases of both men are the
deeds which were registered and enrolled each week in the court of
Hustings.[114] Fraunceys's cartulary contains no London deeds, but the
early folios of Pyel's cartulary yield some information on his joint
acquisitions with Fraunceys of properties in London and Southwark.

---

113 *VCH Middlesex* v, ed. R.B. Pugh (1976), 155. Simon Fraunceys also held lands in
South Bedfordshire some seven or eight miles distant at Holwell, whose manor he held
of John Malory (*VCH Bedford* ii, 286). In Essex, St Helen's held the manors of Mark, in
Leyton, and Walthamstow, while Simon Fraunceys had the adjoining manor of Low
Hall, and Adam Fraunceys the nearby manor of Ruckholts. It is uncertain whether the
convent had held the manor since the thirteenth century, or was endowed with the land
later by the Fraunceys family (*VCH Essex* vi, ed. R.B. Pugh (1973), 260).

114 Other sources include Fraunceys's will, also enrolled in Hustings, some entries in
the Close and Patent Rolls and a few charters in the British Library and Public Record
Office. For a general guide to records of London property see D. Keene and V. Harding
'Sources for Property Holdings in London before the Great Fire' (*London Record Society*,
xxii, 1985). For the properties in Cheapside and Poultry I have been able to make
extensive use of the work produced by the Museum of London Social and Economic
Survey of London under the direction of Dr Derek Keene.

From the spread of Fraunceys's and Pyel's lands and rents which these sources reveal, certain concentrations of property appear, notably for Fraunceys in the wards of Cheap, Broad Street, Cornhill and Bishopsgate, and for Pyel in Coleman Street and Broad Street. The greatest concentration of Fraunceys's holdings lay in the area of Cheapside and Poultry, particularly in the parishes of St Mildred and St Lawrence Jewry. In Poultry Fraunceys acquired a set of tenements, consisting of houses, shops and rents, on the south side of the thoroughfare, fronting the street. Two shops and the quit-rent from a third were acquired from William Tythynglomb, a poulterer, by Pyel and Fraunceys in November 1349.[115] A fourth tenement was added soon afterwards, in 1350 or 1351, from the executors of the woolmonger John Anketil, and a fifth in 1363.[116] All five, including the tenement from which the quit-rent was due, were contiguous, and a further tenement had been acquired from John Anketil's estate in the same parish in 1351, although its precise location is not known.[117] In the purchase of all but one of these properties, John Pyel was associated with Fraunceys, yet he seems to have had little to do with them. Of the properties whose descent can be traced, one was sold by Fraunceys alone, and the others found their way into the hands of his heirs.[118] As we have noted earlier, Pyel and Fraunceys often acted nominally or legally together in acquiring property in which one or other had the greater interest.

To the south of these properties, in Pancras Lane, lay a row of tenements stretching from Sise Lane in the east to Bucklersbury in the west. These had originally belonged to a merchant of Lucca and apothecary named Nicholas Guillem, and the end of his holding at Bucklersbury lay virtually opposite a large tenement, known since the early fourteenth century as Servat's Tower.[119] This building had once been occupied by merchants of the society of the Riccardi of Lucca, and was later used as the wardrobe of Edward III's mother, Queen Isabella. The king, who had taken control of Servat's Tower, leased it again to two merchants of Lucca in 1355, by which time the building and the street in which it stood, Bucklersbury, had become closely associated with financial operations. In 1344 the public exchange was established in Bucklersbury and from 1367 all exchanges of gold and

---

115 CLRO HR 77/260, 252, 264.

116 HR 80/7; 91/114.

117 P23. The five which can be located correspond to SESML tenements 132/15, 17–20 (*Walbrook*, iv, fig. A, and pp. 89–92, 103–28).

118 SESML 132/20 was sold by Fraunceys in June 1370 (HR 98/67); the rent from 132/18 and the tenements 132/17, 19 were bequeathed in Fraunceys's will to Agnes his widow, with reversion to his son, Adam junior (HR 103/79).

119 HR 83/98.

silver were to take place here.[120] Adam Fraunceys and one of his associates, the merchant Hugh de Wychyngham, acquired the premises in Pancras Lane from Nicholas's son, John William, in December 1355, possibly seeing the advantages of securing a base in this rapidly developing financial quarter.

At the western end of Cheapside was a further collection of tenements and rents which Fraunceys accumulated in the parishes of St Lawrence Jewry and All Hallows, Honey Lane. The first of these, two tenements in St Lawrence Jewry, were acquired in December 1349, about the same time as the shops in Poultry, from Hugh de Wychyngham. They were leased back to the vendor within a year, which was the pattern for most of the acquisitions made by Fraunceys in this area.[121] The properties in Honey Lane consisted of a quit-rent and a group of houses surrounded by a stone wall.[122] They were part of the estate of the merchant John de Bovyndon, who had given instructions in his will that these assets should remain to his children, under the guardianship of Adam Fraunceys, and thereafter be sold in trust and the proceeds put towards work on the church of South Mimms, Middlesex, and repair of the roads there.[123] Bovyndon's three children had all died by September 1368, when his widow and executrix, Katherine, sold the quit-rent to Fraunceys, who immediately granted it back to her for life.[124] Katherine Bovyndon later married John Furneys, a draper and friend of Fraunceys, and in July 1371 the couple granted the houses, which lay next to the precinct of All Hallows, Honey Lane, to Adam, John Osekyn, vintner and John Maryns, grocer. These houses were eventually resold to the Furneys in perpetuity in June 1373.[125]

Several other tenements which Fraunceys received in Cheapside were also part of a testamentary bequest, sold by executors. In May 1368 Anne Leyre, widow of William Leyre, probably the son of the alderman and pepperer of the same name,[126] sold the reversions of tenements and rents in St Lawrence Lane, Milk Street and Ironmonger Lane in Cheap ward, as well as in Thames Street in the parish of All Hallows the Less to Adam Fraunceys and John Osekyn, who were to make an annual payment of £18 13s 4d to Anne for life.[127]

Apart from these purchases, individual transactions brought Fraunceys houses, shops, cellars and solars in St Lawrence Lane in 1361 and

---

120 *Walbrook*, 10.
121 BL Harl. Chs. 58.C.31, 50.D.53, 50.D.52.
122 HR 96/137; 100/38 (see SESML 11/1a, 11/3 in *Cheapside*, 19–23, 47–8, fig.L).
123 *CWCH* ii, 40.
124 HR 96/137–9.
125 HR 100/38; 102/3.
126 Thrupp, *Merchant Class*, 353.
127 HR 96/60, 69.

1367, a further tenement in the parish of St Mary Magdalene, Milk Street at an unknown date, and a shop in Soper Lane, just off Cheapside, some time after 1366. The first two were leased back to the donors, in the fashion we have seen above, which may also have been the case with both the latter, but there is no confirmation of this.[128]

It may not seem altogether surprising that Fraunceys was concentrating his resources in the Cheapside district. Here was the commercial heart of the city, one of the main London thoroughfares where retail outlets lined the street, and trading stalls and manufacturing and processing premises lay behind, or in the side lanes leading off the main highway. The association of the crafts of mercery and drapery with Westcheap is well known. Silkmen, drapers and especially mercers congregated towards the eastern end of Cheapside, formerly known as Mercers' Row, and since at least the end of the thirteenth century mercers had gathered at the church of St Thomas Acon, where the company eventually established its hall. There was a group of mercers' residences in the vicinity of All Hallows, Honey Lane, and mercers had also held tenements in Soper Lane.[129] Fraunceys could scarcely have felt out of place in this locality although there is no evidence that he lived in Cheapside or indeed operated commercially from any of the shops he bought. Most of the tenements were either reversions or were immediately leased out, and none seems to have been in a prime retail site. Only one of the Bovyndon properties in Honey Lane faced Cheapside itself, and of this Fraunceys held only the quit-rent derived from it.[130]

If Fraunceys was buying up land principally to avail himself of its rental value, is there any reason why he should particularly have settled on Cheapside? An obvious incentive for concentrating a stock of property in any district was surely that it made supervision, collection of rents and general maintenance easier to undertake than for a number of isolated plots scattered over a large area. If Fraunceys began buying property in Poultry and Cheapside in the late 1340s, he would certainly have been interested in taking up any further land that became available in the district. But perhaps the foremost factor in Cheapside's favour was its success as a thriving commercial district and its comparatively high rents. Details of purchase price or rents, other than quit-rents, are seldom given, but Fraunceys and Osekyn were prepared to pay £18 13s 4d *pa* to widow Leyre for life for the reversion of her husband's

---

128 HR 89/69, 71; 95/40–1; will of Adam Fraunceys, HR 103/79. See also *Cheapside*, 255–6 and fig. L (SESML 145/20).

129 Ibid., liv, lvii.

130 SESML 11/1a (*Cheapside*, 19).

properties, which may have been something of a gamble on their part but is indicative of the value of these premises.

The attraction of Poultry was probably much the same. Of the properties known to have been acquired by Fraunceys here, at least five in a row occupied street frontage. One was a quit-rent of 12s, and one of the shops, which had been leased back to William Tythynglomb in 1349, was sold by Fraunceys when it reverted to him in 1364.[131] A third, described as a messuage, was a particularly large building and may have been a stone house. It was granted by John Scot, a poulterer, in or before July 1363, and was certainly large enough for Fraunceys to use as a residence had he chosen to do so. This messuage, the quit-rent and the second of the shops acquired from Tythynglomb seem to have been retained, while the last tenement in the row, which had belonged to John Anketil the woolmonger and consisted of a messuage, brewhouse and shops, was sold in 1370.[132] It is conceivable, although unlikely, that Fraunceys intended to operate more directly in Poultry. Poulterers were still much in evidence in this part of the street, and although we know little of Fraunceys's commercial activities, it is improbable that he would have concerned himself to any great extent in controlling small outlets for the benefit of retailing his own merchandise.[133] He presumably let the property for rent, no doubt to another poulterer.

To the east of Poultry was another cluster of properties acquired by Fraunceys, lying to the south and east of the Stocks Market. In August 1368 he received, with William Halden and John Maryns, an unspecified number of houses, shops and gardens, which had belonged to the vintner John Osekyn and his wife, in Lombard Street, Bearbinder Lane and the parish of St Ethelburga's, Bishopsgate.[134] Then in January 1372, Fraunceys, Halden and John Furneys bought the remainder of a twenty year lease on tenements in Bearbinder Lane and St Swithin's Lane in the parish of St Mary Wolnoth.[135] Fraunceys also bought, in June 1368, a £10 quit rent levied on tenements in the parish of St Christopher, just to the north-east of the Stocks Market, and earlier, in June 1361, he had bought two tenements with houses on the corner of Walbrook and Candlewick Street, on the very edge of the Stocks/Poultry area.[136] As Dr Keene has shown in the Walbrook survey, the covered market to the east of Cheapside, which became known as the Stocks and which had replaced an earlier market on the site in the thirteenth century,

131 SESML 132/15 (*Walbrook*, 89–91).
132 HR 98/67.
133 *Walbrook*, 15.
134 HR 96/170. For Halden, city recorder and Sussex gentleman, see 1 (ii).
135 HR 100/6.
136 HR 96/76–8; 89/130.

was an important feature and focal point of the area.[137] It offered expansive accommodation for stallholders and attracted a large number of traders from Cheapside in the late thirteenth and fourteenth centuries.[138] It is quite likely that such a thriving district would prove a good investment for property purchasers, with a high demand for accommodation stimulating high rents.[139]

The third group of properties, less densely packed than those previously mentioned, was situated in the wards of Cornhill, Broad Street and Bishopsgate. Part of this group is accounted for in the purchase of a number of properties which had belonged to John de Vere, earl of Oxford. Some time before June 1358, Adam Fraunceys and his clerk, Thomas de Langeton, bought a collection of lands, tenements and rents from de Vere in the parishes of St Martin Outwich, St Helen's and St Ethelburga's, Bishopsgate, and St Peter, Broad Street.[140] The parcel was kept remarkably intact, no part of it being leased or sold, until eventually it was used to endow the two chantries in St Helen's, which Fraunceys established in his will, proved in May 1375. In Bishopsgate, too, was the row of houses and shops which Fraunceys and Pyel built on land leased to them by the convent of St Helen's. This project, which is recorded in Pyel's cartulary, is the earliest documented real estate transaction undertaken by either merchant. In July 1348 the nuns of St Helen's leased to Fraunceys and Pyel some derelict land in their precinct consisting of houses, vacant plots and a lane which the merchants were to clear of their existing buildings and redevelop with a house and five two-storey shops. They were to pay £10 annually in rent in return for which they could hold the lands and the new buildings for life, with a remainder for a further twenty years to their heirs. By December 1349 the redevelopment was complete. Fraunceys and Pyel had in fact constructed at least eight shops and two houses and they were able to redeem their £10 annual rent by granting seven of the shops to the convent, while retaining a third house together with the eighth shop and the rooms above it.[141] We know from other sources that Fraunceys had a house in the close of St

---

137 *Walbrook*, 6.

138 Mainly butchers and fishmongers who occupied most of the seventy-one spaces for stalls in 1358–9 (ibid.).

139 Dr Keene has observed that despite a general long-term reduction in the demand for land in London as elsewhere after the Black Death, the short-term prospects for the property market in the city, especially in an area like Walbrook, were not so gloomy. While a number of houses and shops fell into disuse, demand for those remaining habitable increased, and there is evidence that the rental values of some properties in the Poultry area actually rose between c.1360 and c.1380, roughly the period when Fraunceys and Pyel were active in the land market (ibid., 20).

140 HR 87/101.

141 P1, 3.

Helen's, and it is possible that he retained this house for his residence, at least for a while. Evidently the convent had insufficient resources to maintain all its properties even before the Black Death, and would most certainly not have been in a position to do so afterwards. Fraunceys and his partner were therefore able to take advantage of the situation to invest some of their money and to assist a religious house simultaneously. Adam's close connections with St Helen's may well have begun at this time.

Another row of at least six shops, probably more, had been built by Adam Fraunceys to the east of the Austin Friars, lying at the northern end of Broad Street. The shops, which were built before 1373, were equipped with chimneys and were separated from the friary by a stone wall.[142] It would appear that this 'rent', like the one in Bishopsgate, had been, as it were, purpose-built by Fraunceys, whereas that in Poultry was purchased in stages from premises that were already in existence. Nevertheless, the Poultry tenement of John Anketil alone contained six shops, and it seems that Adam Fraunceys was ready to invest substantial sums in such developments for rent.

In the parish of St Bartholomew the Less, in Broad Street ward, Fraunceys held, or at least had an interest in, two sets of tenements. One of these he sold to Pyel in 1374, while at some point he also relinquished his interest in the other, a joint holding with Pyel.[143]

Finally, Fraunceys held some tenements in Gracechurch Street, which had been mortgaged in August 1368 to Fraunceys and two close associates, John Ussher, citizen, and the clerk, Thomas de Pateshull, for the sum of £200, and another tenement in the same street, which he sold in January 1374.[144] Adam also held a 4s rent from a tenement adjoining the west end of the church of St Michael le Querne, part of the Anketil parcel, which he and Pyel had acquired in 1349.[145]

The remaining London properties of which we have detailed records were tenements isolated from these main groupings. Among these was one of Fraunceys's earliest acquisitions, a collection of houses, shops and solars in Crooked Lane, Candlewick Street ward, which he bought in 1348 with the mercer Thomas Brandon.[146] Another consisted of a dwelling (habitacionem) with shops and houses on the corner of Mincing Lane and Fenchurch Street, which Fraunceys, Thomas de Langeton and John Pyel had originally acquired from William Credil in August

142 D. Harrison, 'The Surrey Portion of the Lewes Cartulary', *Trans. Surrey Archaeological Collections*, xliii (1935), 97.

143 See below.

144 HR 96/123; 101/81.

145 HR 102/53. Pyel and Fraunceys had received a second quit-rent of 4s in this parish from the Anketil estate (P9). For the Anketil properties, see below.

146 HR 75/51–2.

1349, but which Fraunceys alone sold in October 1371.[147] He also held a tenement and half share in a well in the parish of St Martin without Ludgate. Some tenements were received as part of a larger group, such as those in Beech Lane, Cripplegate, which were conveyed along with the Honey Lane properties by the executors of John de Bovyndon.[148] In the same way, the Leyre legacy, which contained the Cheapside properties whose reversions Fraunceys bought, also included houses and a quit rent in Thames Street.[149] Fraunceys held a few other waterside tenements, one such consisting of houses with an adjacent quay in St Dunstan, Tower ward, which he bought from John de Bovyndon when he was executor to Joan, widow of Henry Cros, in 1353. He also bought the reversion of a tenement and quay called Fresh Wharf in 1360, and in 1371 received a 40s rent from a quay with houses and shops belonging to a fishmonger as security for a debt of £25.[150] He seems, however, to have had no serious policy of buying property in the vicinity of the river for his commercial business.

John Pyel's properties in London are less extensive than those of Adam Fraunceys. Several were bought in partnership with Fraunceys, in which it is apparent from the descent of the properties that Pyel's interest was little more than formal or legal, in the way that Fraunceys was associated with Pyel's properties in Northamptonshire, and others feature Pyel as a member of a consortium of substantial merchants acting as trustees. The lands Pyel bought on his own account lay mostly to the north and east of the city. The greatest concentration was in the former, where Pyel had an interest in at least seven tenements, four on Coleman Street itself, two along Lothbury and one in Old Jewry. The first of these was purchased in March 1371. There is no description of the tenements, but they were sold with others in the parish of St Andrew's Holborn and were immediately leased back to the donors at a rent of £5 pa.[151] John was already in possession of a tenement in the parish of St Stephen, Coleman Street which had a number of charges attached to it. This he leased at farm to a city draper in April 1373 for a period of twenty years, with conditions relating to the charges incumbent on the property.[152] In July of the same year Pyel bought further tenements in Coleman Street, Soper Lane and Lothbury from

147 HR 99/127, P20.
148 HR 100/38, 119.
149 HR 96/69.
150 HR 81/72; 99/87; HPL 20 July 1360; HR 99/165–6.
151 HR 99/33, 42.
152 HR 101/119.

a group of agents acting on his behalf.[153] In February 1376 John and
his wife Joan, who was also associated with John in the two previous
acquisitions, were granted yet more lands in the area, namely in the
parish of St Stephen's, St Margaret Lothbury and St Olave Jewry.[154]

To the south of this nucleus of property lay the Poultry tenements
which Pyel shared with Fraunceys, and to the west of these the tenement
in Soper Lane referred to above. This was a small shop with solar or
solars above, which was located among a dozen or so similar shops at
the northern end of Soper Lane, near Cheapside.[155] Given the popularity
of this area among mercers, it might be expected that Pyel, like
Fraunceys, would have obtained more properties in this district.

To the east of Coleman Street Pyel had a more scattered collection of
tenements, principally in Broad Street, but spilling over into Bishops-
gate. Among these was Pyel's own residence in Broad Street (modern
Throgmorton Street) in which he had apparently been living for some
time, but which was only granted to him by Adam Fraunceys in
June 1374.[156] Pyel also shared with Fraunceys in the same parish, St
Bartholomew the Less, tenements which had been forfeited by Walter
Chiriton. In June 1350, at the time of the Chiriton company's fall from
grace and subsequent prosecution, the lands of the principal partners,
Chiriton himself, Thomas Swanlond and Gilbert de Wendlingburgh,
had been taken into the king's hands and granted to John de Wesenham.
In November 1362 Wesenham granted those lands to Pyel and Fraunceys, and they in turn granted them, in January 1371, to Alice Perrers,
who put them into the hands of clerical feoffees.[157] At some point they
were returned to the grantors, probably after the confiscation of Perrers'
lands in 1377, since they were confirmed in November 1383 as belonging
to Pyel, his heirs and executors, and to the executors of Adam Fraunceys
and they were eventually used by Pyel's executors to form part of the
endowment of Irthlingborough college.[158] Interestingly, four years
earlier, in 1367, Pyel had granted to Alice Perrers two other tenements

153 HR 101/99. Two of these came from Northamptonshire, John Molkous, son of
Robert Molkous, one of Pyel's neighbours in Irthlingborough, and Richard Cros of
Cransley. It is possible that these men had come to London under his patronage. The
third was John Watlyngton, the city's common crier (see Betty R. Masters, 'The Mayor's
Household before 1600' in *Studies in London History*, 104). There was evidently some dispute
concerning the conveyance of part of this property, which was eventually resolved in
Pyel's favour (HR 102/61, *LPA* 135, p. 50).
154 HR 104/1.
155 HR 101/99; 102/61 (SESML 145/6, see *Cheapside*, 75–6).
156 HR 97/109; 102/190 (SESML 32/10a); SESML *Interim Report on the Study of the
Bank of England Area* (July, 1988), 5–8. I am most grateful to Dr Derek Keene for allowing
me to see a copy of this report.
157 PRO Ancient Charters E210/1712, *CPR 1370–4*, 49–50.
158 HR 112/66. See below n.191.

in the parish, lying side by side in Bartholomew Lane.[159] These may also have been part of the Chiriton estate, although Adam Fraunceys is not mentioned in the grant. It may be that Pyel was by this time beginning to associate himself with the court party in London, with whom he was to have more extensive dealings in the next decade. In the nearby parish of St Martin Outwich, Pyel and three others acquired in December 1375 a 7s quit rent arising from buildings over an entrance or gateway adjacent to the parish church itself, and four shops with a small garden lying next to this same entrance.[160]

Outside these two main districts, Pyel had properties in Bread Street, where he held one of the Anketil tenements, in St James Garlickhithe, and further afield in St Andrew's Holborn and St Bride's Fleet Street.[161] He also held for a time the lands of Bartholomew Changeour for which he had sued, although details of their location are lacking, and with Nicholas Brembre, a close friend, he bought tenements in Lombard Street in September 1375.[162] As a member of a consortium he received lands and tenements in Gracechurch Street in February 1376, which had once been held by Adam Fraunceys and John Ussher, and tenements in All Hallows the Less, St Nicholas Acon and St Mary Abchurch in November 1377.[163]

The means by which the properties were conveyed to either merchant are not always clear. It is often very difficult to tell what is really going on as sums of money are rarely mentioned and the neutral word 'grant' used in the charter gives no idea of the reality behind the transaction. Some of these must have been direct purchases, whereby a sum of money changed hands and the vendor relinquished his title to the lands. Others were a temporary holding as security for a loan. For example in November 1371 Richard Turk, fishmonger, granted a 40s annual rent from some quayside properties in the parish of All Hallows Barking to Adam Fraunceys as security for a £25 loan which was to be repaid over ten years.[164] A similar arrangement had been made with John Bergholt, carpenter, in November 1368 concerning a £5 rent from houses in Cornhill, to be cancelled on payment of £20 at Christmas 1369.[165] Nothing further was heard of either of these contracts,

159 HR 95/130–1.
160 HR 103/299, 300. Both were sold on 16 April 1380, the lands to John Aubrey, grocer and son-in-law of Adam Fraunceys, and the quit rent to another grocer, John Chircheman (HR 108/122–3). Pyel's three associates were John Ussher, chaplain and fellow executor of Adam Fraunceys, Thomas de Santon, probably also a clerk, and William Hildeslee.
161 HR 80/7; 99/81; 99/33, 42; 102/136–7.
162 HR 103/205.
163 HR 104/39; 107/89.
164 HR 99/165–7.
165 HR 96/212–3.

and it might be assumed that the debts were repaid. In June 1368, the chandler Geoffrey de Westwyk granted Fraunceys an annuity of £10 based on tenements in the wards of Cornhill and Broad Street as security for the repayment of a debt of £40 within two years. When he had failed to repay the debt by July 1369, Fraunceys purchased the rent in perpetuity and cancelled the debt. Later Fraunceys released his interest in the rent, selling it to Richard Willesden, chandler.[166] Again, in 1368, tenements in Gracechurch Street were granted to Fraunceys and John Ussher by two property agents as security for a loan of £200. This loan was repaid by the end of the year and control of the property resumed, but in October 1369 the tenements were remortgaged to Ussher and Fraunceys for £347 10s.[167]

One of the largest parcels of city lands and rents which passed to Pyel and Fraunceys also came to them as the result of debt, but not through loans which they had themselves advanced. John Anketil, a city woolmerchant, and a man actively engaged in business at the time of Edward III's intervention in the woolmarket in the late 1330s, had incurred a debt of 100m in 1341 which he had failed to repay by June 1349 when his creditor, John Oweyn, also called Pulteney, died.[168] Anketil's London properties were assessed on 20 June 1349 at £18, half of which was granted to Pulteney's executors until their debt should be recovered.[169] Fraunceys and Pyel bought this half share in Anketil's tenements and rents shortly afterwards and probably at about the same time bought a statute merchant of 200 marks which had been made by Anketil to two other creditors, Roger Chauntecler and Nicholas Lolymer, in January 1348 but had not been redeemed.[170] On the strength of this bond, Pyel and Fraunceys then sued for the remaining half of Anketil's London holdings which were awarded to them on 31 October 1349.[171] The properties included part of a house and brewhouse, with two adjoining shops and four other shops in Poultry, one of the plots described above.[172] It is not known how long Fraunceys and Pyel held these tenements, possibly longer than the prescribed limit to recoup the debts, which was probably about 10 years. They were certainly still in possession in November 1356 when they found themselves liable to pay outstanding debts to the Exchequer on Anketil's behalf as holders of his property.[173]

166 HR 96/76–8; 97/88; 101/27, 40.
167 HR 97/130.
168 Not Sir John Poultney, the former mayor, who also died at about this time.
169 P4–5.
170 P6.
171 P7.
172 SESML 132/20.
173 P43.

These transactions suggest that after their association with the customs farmers in the 1340s Pyel and Fraunceys were looking for a way into the property market as a means of investing their surplus cash. The dates of 1348 and 1349 are significant not only because they mark the collapse of the custom-farming syndicates, but also because the initial impact of the Black Death was probably to depress the land market and allow much property to be bought up cheaply. Pulteney's executors were probably only too happy to sell their interest for a cash sum, and, as we have noted, the deal with St Helen's priory shows that even by June 1348 there was a certain amount of derelict building and waste land available for redevelopment which the arrival of plague in London can only have increased. The heading of Pyel's cartulary, 'the joint purchases of properties in London ... by Fraunceys and Pyel since Easter 1348,' indicates that this was the beginning of a major investment policy in London buildings and rents, and that they decided to do jointly in London what they were eventually to do as individuals in Middlesex and Northamptonshire.

There are, moreover, examples of tenements being acquired instead or in default of cash payments, as also happened in both these rural areas. In December 1361 John Pyel and John Stodeye mainperned for the payment of £2,000 due from Thomas de Notyngham and Bartholomew Changeour to the king. By the following year Notyngham was dead and Changeour had quit London leaving the sureties liable for the sum, which they eventually raised in 1364.[174] They successfully sued for the lands of the defaulters and in 1373 Stodeye renounced his title to these lands, leaving Pyel in sole possession.[175] There seems to have been a sizeable market in the properties which Changeour released for his bad debts, and in 1373 and 1374 Pyel and Nicholas Brembre bought up further tenements and rents which had originally belonged to Changeour and had subsequently passed to his creditors. The total sum invested by the pair in these properties was said to have been £400, and when Pyel sold his share to Brembre in December 1374, he received back half the purchase price and an additional 50 marks.[176]

Such brisk trading seems to suggest that one reason for buying up lands in London was to provide short- or medium-term returns, which as we have seen from Dr Keene's study of Walbrook may well have been a shrewd investment in the mid-fourteenth century. Tenements and rents were treated as commodities in which cash was held for a limited period and then released. They were also acquired to provide a steady income. This conclusion seems to run counter to the view that

174 *CCR 1360–4*, 302, 322; *1364–8*, 12–13.
175 *CPR 1370–4*, 281–3; HR 101/67.
176 HR 103/24, 26, 97–8.

urban property was hardly an ideal investment since the returns were so poor and was therefore seldom bought by individuals in large quantities.[177]

Pyel and Fr, Fraunceys often purchased tenements which they immediately leased back to the vendors, usually for life. This indicates a longer-term perspective, that the property was in effect being acquired for some future purpose or simply for rent or to provide income for their descendants. In one case, the shop and solar in the Poultry, which had been leased back to William Tythynglomb in November 1349, was sold in August 1364 after it had reverted to Fraunceys.[178] This was the exception, however. If we take the ward of Cheap, where many of the lease-back or reversion purchases occur, it is possible to trace the descent of most of the tenements. In the parish of St Lawrence Jewry, the quit rents and rents of the tenements which had formed part of the Leyre reversions to Adam Fraunceys were bequeathed by him in his will to the Favelor chantry in All Hallows, Edmonton.[179] The lands themselves passed to Adam Fraunceys junior, as did two other sets of houses and shops in St Lawrence Lane which had originally been leased back to their owners.[180] The two tenements granted by Hugh de Wychyngham were resold to him in 1351.[181] One further tenement in the parish, a house and garden adjacent to Guildhall, formed part of the endowment of Guildhall college in 1356.[182] A similar pattern exists for the other London properties, most of which were bequeathed to Adam's surviving son. The remaining Poultry tenements, namely the shop, stone house and 12s quit rent, were granted to his widow, Agnes, with reversion to Adam junior.[183] The parcel of lands belonging to the earl of Oxford, as we have seen, was used to endow the two St Helen's chantries dedicated to the Blessed Mary and the Holy Ghost, and the shop in Soper Lane and some tenements in Monkwell Street, Cripplegate, which Fraunceys had bought from the executor of John de

177 R.H. Hilton, for example, found from a sample of towns in the Midlands from the thirteenth to the fifteenth centuries that there were few individual accumulations of urban land and that those which existed seldom yielded sufficient income to provide adequate financial support for the purchasers. It was the large institutions, religious guilds, chantry foundations, monasteries, which tended to own the larger blocks of urban property ('Some Problems of Urban Real Property in the Middle Ages' in *Class Conflict and the Crisis of Feudalism* (London, 1985), 165–74).

178 HR 92/192.

179 This also includes the rents in Dowgate ward (Fraunceys's will, HR 103/79).

180 PRO Inquisitions Post Mortem C138/29.

181 BL Harl. Ch. 50.D.52.

182 Riley, *Memorials of London*, 289.

183 Fraunceys's will, HR 103/79.

Ecton, parson of Great Missenden, were later granted to the priory of St Helen's itself.[184]

It can be seen on this evidence that the lands which Fraunceys did not alienate in his lifetime were used in one of two ways, either to be settled upon his widow and heir, or else used to support religious foundations which would provide for his soul after death. There were certain advantages attaching to London property which made it an attractive asset when considering the requirements of the after-life. City custom allowed the privilege of transferring land or rents in mortmain without licence even after the statute *De viris religiosis* of 1279, although attempts were made during the fourteenth century to limit the scope of the privilege.[185] Nevertheless, the right to devise land to religious institutions without purchasing a licence encouraged many non-citizens to buy property in London for that purpose. Between 1300 and 1402 an average of 28 perpetual chantries per decade was founded in England, and it is hardly surprising that London citizens availed themselves of this advantage by buying parcels of land which they later used to endow chapels or chantries in their wills. Indeed, after 1364 only freemen of the city were legally qualified to devise freely in mortmain, although this seems to have done little to deter abuse.[186] Of course, determining which land was bought with the express intention of helping to establish a chantry, and which was simply bequeathed for the purpose out of an existing stock, is difficult. Occasionally there is some suggestive evidence. Reference has already been made to the college of priests set up in the Guildhall chapel by Adam Fraunceys and two of his friends, Henry Frowyk and Peter Favelor.[187] The lands given to endow the college are cited in the foundation documents, but no record has survived of the date of their acquisition. One of these properties, however, consisted of a messuage with a garden lying to the south of the chapel, and was later to provide accommodation for the chantry priests of the college.[188] Fraunceys and Favelor, who made the grant, may already have had the forthcoming foundation in mind when they bought the property, attracted by its proximity to the college.

It is possible that this was also true of the properties acquired from the earl of Oxford before 1358. It happened that the lands were kept intact, and all were used to endow Fraunceys's chantries in St Helen's, in the same way that the rents from the Leyre reversions were used for the establishment of the Favelor chantry at Edmonton, but this does not prove in either case that the properties were originally purchased

184 Ibid.
185 H.M. Chew, 'Mortmain in Medieval London', *EHR* lx (1945), 1–15
186 S. Raban, *Mortmain Legislation*, 103–4.
187 Above, 2 (ii).
188 Riley, *Memorials of London*, 289.

for this reason. Nevertheless, the endowment of chapels and chantries as a private and personal response to the soul's salvation was increasing during the fourteenth century, and Fraunceys probably reckoned that at least some of the property which he was collecting would be put to such use.

Adam Fraunceys, therefore, seems to have been buying land for the rents they produced, and to create a stock of property which could be used to endow charitable foundations and to provide for his widow and descendants after his death. It remains a matter of speculation to what extent Fraunceys made use of these buildings as residences or shops for his own goods. Given Fraunceys's elevated status as a merchant and financier he is probably more likely to have used the shops as sources of rent rather than retail outlets. It should also be remembered that Fraunceys's properties were likely to have been even more extensive than the records reveal. The inquisition post mortem of Adam Fraunceys junior includes among the property which he inherited from his father tenements in parishes other than those which can be found in the surviving sources available to us.[189] The value of the father's legacy at the time of his son's death, excluding the Leyre properties, was given as £45 10s 4d, which, allowing for alienations during the lifetimes of both men, represents probably no more than a fraction of the total value of the city properties which passed through Adam senior's hands. Whatever the many and varied reasons Fraunceys had for purchasing lands and rents in London, they clearly accounted for a large part of his financial investment.

While acknowledging the same gaps in the sources for Pyel's London property, it is still evident that his London holdings were less extensive than those of his partner. Like Fraunceys, Pyel often bought in association with others, but frequently these were syndicates or groups of trustees rather than Pyel acting as the principal purchaser with a partner or clerical assistant.[190]

It has already been remarked that in the joint acquisitions of Pyel and Fraunceys, one or other was the dominant partner. So, in the joint feoffments of the Poultry tenements, it was Fraunceys who sold or bequeathed those they did not otherwise lease out. Conversely, in the case of the Chiriton properties which Pyel and Fraunceys received at the hands of John de Wesenham, it was Pyel who disposed of two of the Broad Street tenements to Alice Perrers, and it was to him that all

189 C138/29.
190 Hence the enfeoffment of Pyel, William Walworth, Nicholas Brembre, John Ussher and others in the lands of Walter Tudenham by his executors, which were leased back to his widow for a rose in August 1375. By December Joan Tudenham had evidently died and the lands were sold off or else new trustees were enfeoffed (HR 103/200–1, 302).

the lands were returned after Perrers' disgrace and banishment. Fraunceys, of course, was dead by this time, but his heirs do not seem to have received a share.[191] Pyel and Fraunceys apparently divided the Anketil properties, or at least certain of them, between them. Fraunceys disposed of the Poultry holding in June 1370, while Pyel sold the Bread Street holding a mere three days later.[192] The Mincing Lane collection of shops and houses had been granted jointly to Fraunceys, Pyel and Thomas de Langeton in August 1349, but at some point Pyel and Langeton must have released their interest, since it was Fraunceys who alienated the tenement on his own terms in 1371.[193]

Pyel concentrated the properties he bought on his own account mainly along Coleman Street and Lothbury and into Broad Street, where his own house stood. The location of Pyel's residence here is a little surprising. The area around Lothbury, to the north of Broad Street (Threadneedle Street) contained a variety of manufacturing crafts, including those concerned with leather-making, metal working and some textile manufacture. Brewers and carpenters were two other trades represented in Lothbury and Broad Street (Throgmorton Street), and Pyel's residence itself adjoined a brewer's tenement. There were larger residences which housed the wealthier merchants, like those of Thomas Leggy, skinner and mayor, and Bartolomeo Bosano, a Lucca merchant who lived in Bartholomew Lane, but this was not a financial quarter in the late medieval period, and with the noise of metal working and the smells attendant upon leather processing, it cannot have been a very attractive or wholesome part of the city in which to live.[194]

It is interesting that John Pyel did not begin to purchase real estate in London on any scale until the 1370s. All that he had received of any substance before that date were the Anketil and Chiriton tenements, in both of which he was associated with Adam Fraunceys. This fact contrasts with Pyel's avid land purchasing in Northamptonshire during the 1350s and 1360s, and may partly be explained by Pyel's closer association with that county than with London in those years. It is likely that he spent a good deal of time there, and certainly spent long periods away from the capital, from which he had also made conscious efforts to distance himself politically and administratively. Pyel's aloofness from London came to an end in the late 1360s with his eventual acceptance of civic office, which seems to have coincided with a more marked interest in acquiring property in the capital. Moreover, as Pyel's

191 HR 95/130–1; 112/66. Although the quitclaim was made to Joan Pyel and the executors of Adam Fraunceys, the properties eventually went to endow Irthlingborough college.
192 HR 98/67, 69.
193 P20; HR 99/127.
194 SESML *Bank of England Report*, 5–8.

dabbling in the London property market became more serious, so his purchases in Northamptonshire declined. Apart from one set of lands which he acquired in January 1374, his acquisitions in the county seem to stop quite abruptly in 1369, the year of his elevation into the political life of London.[195] It has already been remarked that he bought his house in the parish of St Bartholomew the Less only in 1374, although he may have been living there since 1369, when Adam Frauceys secured title to it. His wife Joan may have continued to live there for a while after his death, and she evidently maintained an attachment to the parish church.[196] Pyel's more consistent presence in London will have fostered the growth of his business interests there, no doubt in trade, certainly in finance, and also in property investment. And Pyel could also endow his college, a project which he would almost certainly have had in mind by now, more easily with London properties than with other lands. In the London version of his will, he leaves the reversion of his city properties after his widow's death to the college of St Peter's. By the sixteenth century those properties lay in the parishes of St Bartholomew the Less, St Bride's Fleet Street and St Clement, Eastcheap,[197] and we can see John's widow, Joan, at work, marshalling these territorial resources in preparation for her renewed attempt to complete the foundation of the college. In 1383 she secured a quitclaim from the son of Walter Chiriton for the lands in the parish of St Bartholomew, and in 1386 from John Celer for the lands he had granted in St Bride's in 1374.[198] Otherwise Pyel bought, leased and sold lands and rents for financial gain in much the same way as Frauceys had.

We may conclude that property purchases at the time of and shortly after the Black Death could turn out to have been relatively lucrative investments. Despite the fall in population, rents, at least in certain parts of London, maintained their levels or even rose, and this may have been true in other towns. At the same time socially-conscious citizens who had aspirations to move away from their urban environment were also attracted by lands in rural areas, which was probably acquired more for reasons of social mobility than for economic investment. Many of the lands in both town and country seem to have been conveyed as a means of settling debts, and the impact of the Hundred Years' War was no doubt as much a factor in this as the arrival of the

195 Isolated acquisitions continue, such as a grant of sixty acres of land in Irthlingborough in Easter 1376 by Ralph de Hale (CP25(1) 178/85 no. 691), but the main body of the estate was formed by 1369.
196 Joan Pyel's will: Lambeth Palace, Episcopal Register of Thomas Arundel ii, f. 161v.
197 PRO SC12/37/13.
198 HR 112/66; 116/68.

plague in 1348–9 and its subsequent manifestations. Lastly, Pyel and Fraunceys had a practical regard for the future, both for the worldly maintenance of the dependants they left behind and for the spiritual sustenance of their souls after death. Real property was therefore acquired for the endowment of charitable and ecclesiastical institutions prepared to pray for their souls in perpetuity. Whether properties were earmarked for this purpose from their date of purchase is impossible to determine, but that this was an important function of land, especially in London, seems certain.

3. THE CARTULARIES

(i) The Cartulary Tradition

A cartulary (Latin: *chartularium*) is a compilation of deeds and charters, mostly relating to land rights and other privileges and franchises which an individual or corporate body possessed. Its purpose was to gather together for ease of reference copies of these important muniments, so that the originals might be located at a time of legal dispute, or evidence to title be supplied should those charters have been lost or destroyed.

Yet, common though disputes of land title were, the use of cartularies to defend such rights and liberties does not wholly explain why they were compiled. Ecclesiastical cartularies, for example, overwhelmingly outnumber those of laymen.[1] Monasteries, to be sure, will have boasted numbers of men who possessed the secretarial skills necessary to compose such documents, and are likely to have kept more systematic archives than all but the largest lay landowners. Moreover, religious houses were often in receipt of lands scattered over a wide area and so needed to be more scrupulous in keeping a record of their holdings and the means by which they were conveyed, and to insure against loss of the original deeds.[2] For laymen with smaller, more compact estates, there may have been less incentive to embark on the often quite laborious task of assembling charters and title-deeds in sufficient order to be transcribed into a register. Nevertheless, even allowing for the vagaries of survival, and the possibility of other lay cartularies coming to light, the imbalance between ecclesiastical and secular is so pronounced that, among laymen at least, the requirements of legal title cannot have been the only, or even the major reason for having these documents drawn up.

Cartularies were used as evidence of privilege in cases where the original documents had disappeared, but there do not appear to be many instances of their production in court, at least before the dissolution of the monasteries.[3] Indeed, if cartularies had been used regularly in this way, we might expect men like Sir John Fastolf or families like the Pastons, who suffered so much litigation and worse in defence of their lands, to have taken the precaution of drawing them

1 G.R. Davis in *Medieval Cartularies of Great Britain* (London, 1958) notes 1185 belonging to religious houses as opposed to 169 compiled for laymen.

2 The preface to the cartulary of Dover Priory of 1372, for example, gives the loss of documents in the past and the threat of future damage as the main reason for the compilation of the volume. See Trevor Foulds, 'Medieval Cartularies', *Archives* xviii (1987), 23.

3 Davis, *Medieval Cartularies*, xiv; Foulds 'Medieval Cartularies', 32–3.

up.[4] And since so few lay landlords considered the production of these manuscripts worth the effort, we may wonder what were the motives of those laymen, other than the great magnates, who did go to the trouble of compiling them.

Some were clearly inspired by a sense of family tradition and honour. In the fifteenth century, John Langley, a Gloucestershire esquire, endeavoured, with partial success, to recover the patrimony lost since his ancestor, Sir Geoffrey de Langley, had begun to build up the family estates in the thirteenth century.[5] John died childless in 1459, possessed of widely scattered lands worth about £100 pa, leaving as his heir Isabel de la Pole, his niece, whom he had married into an unrelated family, also called Langley. Isabel's son, William, had a cartulary compiled in order that, as Coss says, 'he might know his midland estates better and—more important—his title to them'.[6] But young William, in his enthusiasm, had transcribed into the manuscript every charter which survived, whether of lands still among the Langley inheritance or of others long since lost. William may have had designs on recovering more of his great-uncle's patrimony, but he certainly wanted to know what was and had been part of it, and to this extent the cartulary is as much a product of an interest and pride in family history as it is a collection of dry legal documents.[7]

Other fifteenth-century cartularies reinforce this sense of a desire to celebrate former glories. The Anlaby cartulary, for example, complete with original bindings and carrying case, was embellished with miniatures, marginal drawings of seals, tombs, and shields of arms.[8] The Clervaux cartulary includes family wills among its contents, and that of the Scropes of Castle Combe has copies of heraldic devices and family correspondence.[9] Dr Vale compares such documents, in terms

4 K.B. McFarlane, 'The Investment of Sir John Fastolf's Profits of War', reprinted in *England in the Fifteenth Century*, 194; Anthony Smith, 'Litigation and Politics: Sir John Fastolf's defence of his English property' in A.J. Pollard, ed., *Property and Politics* (Gloucester, 1984), 59–75; N. Davis (ed.), *Paston Letters and Papers of the Fifteenth Century* (Oxford, 1971), xl–lii. Clearly Fastolf was not uninterested in tracing manorial descents and establishing the legal status of his lands, as his employment of William of Worcester shows, yet he seems not to have thought it necessary to have a cartulary compiled.

5 P.R. Coss, *The Langley Family and its Cartulary: a Study in Late Medieval 'Gentry'* (Dugdale Society Occasional Papers, 22, 1974), 20.

6 Ibid., 3–4.

7 P.R. Coss, ed., *The Langley Cartulary*, Dugdale Society, xxxii (Stratford-upon-Avon, 1980).

8 M.R. James, 'The Anlaby Chartulary', *Yorkshire Archaeological Journal* xxxi (1934), 337–47.

9 Brigette Vale, 'The Scropes of Bolton and Masham, c.1300–c.1450: a Study of a Northern Noble Family with a Calendar of the Scrope of Bolton Cartulary' (unpublished D.Phil. thesis, University of York, 1987), 2 vols., ii, iv. For the Clervaux cartulary, see below.

of the value and esteem attached to them by their owners, with the family bibles of later generations. In the same vein, certain cartularies were drawn up to mark an important event or turning-point in an individual's life which was thought to have a lasting effect upon the family fortunes. The Percy cartulary, a large volume containing 1,100 charters of property which directly or ultimately descended to him, was drawn up to commemorate Henry Percy's creation as earl of Northumberland on the day of Richard II's coronation, 16 July 1377.[10] The monumental nature of the manuscript is underlined by the fact that no additions were made after its completion and that it contains no document of a date later than the charter of creation. In this respect it resembles the Fraunceys cartulary, which contains abstracts from a similar number of charters tracing property descent from as early as the twelfth century, and, as we shall see, was also compiled to mark an occasion.

Cartularies seem to have found favour among a number of the socially-conscious middle classes and careerists who acquired land and status in the later middle ages, and they often reveal the priorities and preoccupations of their owners. Robert Hylle was a lawyer's son who became a kind of medieval estate agent, managing the lands of the bishop of Bath and Wells, those of Joan, Lady Mohun, owner of the Dunster estates, and possibly also the Devon lands of Thomas, lord Despenser.[11] Robert secured through his wife, Isabel Fitchet, a collection of lands in the west country, mostly in Somerset, whose deeds he decided to record in a cartulary. It was begun by 1409 and was completed about 1416. It seems that Hylle had experienced a number of legal wrangles concerning his rights and was anticipating more, and his motivation in compiling the cartulary was to facilitate access to his muniments, should the need arise.[12] Hylle was a lawyer and land-manager, and so it may not be surprising that he organised his records in this way. Each section of the cartulary begins with an explanatory note setting out how the title had descended to him, and he includes extracts from court rolls where they support his claim to manorial rights. Dr Dunning remarks that there is much about the cartulary which reflects the personality of its owner. Besides the matter-of-fact collection of title deeds, which betrays the legal mind at work, memoranda often convey details of an intimate nature and record a highly personal reaction to events.[13]

An even more interesting point of comparison with the cartularies

10 M.T. Martin, ed., *The Percy Chartulary* (Surtees Society, cxvii, 1911), v.
11 R.W. Dunning, *The Hylle Cartulary* (Somerset Record Society, lxiv, 1968), xviii.
12 Ibid., xx.
13 Ibid., xv.

of Pyel and Fraunceys is the muniment of the Bromleys of Bromley-
in-Whitmore in Staffordshire.[14] The Bromleys, who compiled their
cartulary some time after 1348, were a merchant family, probably
timber-merchants from Newcastle-under-Lyme. They were also wealthy
money-lenders who expanded their holdings by advancing sums to
indigent landowners on the security of their mortgaged property.[15] The
parallels with Pyel and Fraunceys are obvious, but an interesting
contrast is the physical appearance of the cartulary itself. It was a roll
consisting of five skins sewn together, measuring 7ft 2ins in length and
9ins in breadth, containing copies of sixty-three deeds.[16] It was clearly
a working document, rather than a monument to social aggrandizement,
and the family never seems to have aspired to be anything more than
petty landowners.[17] Why, then, should this family, seemingly without
pretensions and remaining in relative obscurity, have drawn up such a
document? The Bromleys, like other families in their position, had their
fair share of litigation concerning their lands, and the cartulary may
have been of assistance in this. Another unusual factor is that several
members of the family were clerks in minor orders.[18] Clerical influence
and legal prudence may therefore have combined to produce this
interesting manuscript.

A more substantial volume which is both a record of burgeoning
lands and a reflection of family pride is the Clervaux cartulary. The
Clervaux family were originally merchants from York, whose cadet
branches continued their commercial pursuits in that city, while the
senior branch accumulated lands in the north of the county and married
into the Lumley family, themselves related by marriage to the Neville
earls of Westmorland.[19] The cartulary was apparently made for Richard
Clervaux about 1450, some seven years after he came into his inheritance
and at a time when the family fortunes were at their height.[20] It has
retained its original binding,[21] but in presentation and accuracy does
not approach the Fraunceys manuscript. Dates of charters were omitted
and the scribe betrays certain deficiencies in his knowledge of Latin

14 Charles Swynnerton, 'A Domestic Cartulary of the Early Fourteenth Century' in
Collections for a History of Staffordshire (William Salt Archaeological Society, 1913), 217–76.
  15 Ibid., 227.
  16 The original document was not traced by Davis (*Medieval Cartularies*, 142).
  17 Swynnerton, 'Domestic Cartulary', 260.
  18 Ibid., 227, 259.
  19 A. Hamilton Thompson, 'The Clervaux Cartulary', *Archaeologia Aeliana*, 3rd Ser.,
xvii (1920), 195.
  20 Ibid., 190. For the career of Richard Clervaux and an interesting account of the
consolidation and expansion of his estates, see A.J. Pollard, 'Richard Clervaux of Croft:
North Riding Squire in the Fifteenth Century', *Yorkshire Archaeological Journal*, 50 (1978),
151–169.
  21 *Proceedings of the Society of Antiquaries of Newcastle-upon-Tyne*, 3rd Ser., ix (1919–20), 98.

and in his familiarity with local topography.[22] Nevertheless, the cartulary seems to have been prompted by the desire to record the successful establishment of a Yorkshire gentry family.

Apart from their legal and administrative uses, therefore, lay cartularies can document a family's sense of its own history and importance, and were often drawn up at a high point or watershed in social achievement. Their arrangement varies considerably, but by and large they do not display the sophistication of style evident in their ecclesiastical counterparts. In this respect the cartulary of Adam Fraunceys, which is a masterpiece of organisation and clarity, differs from other lay cartularies. It is composed of 112 vellum folios, of which 106 carry abstracts of deeds relating to Fraunceys's lands in Middlesex and Essex. The deeds, some 1,234 in all, are arranged by manor into four sections, of which by far the largest is Edmonton, containing 1,088 abstracts, over 80% of the total. Each entry carries in one margin a brief note of the grantor and recipient of the transaction, and in the other a press mark, consisting usually of a number or letter and number. The original charters were kept in boxes or 'coffins', up to sixty per box, and on the dorse each carried the pressmark assigned to it in the cartulary together with the name of the manor to which it related. The boxes were labelled with the name of the manor and where there was more than one box of deeds, a number. This information was recorded in the cartulary in red ink at the beginning of each batch of sixty charters. After consulting the cartulary, therefore, it was possible in this well-organised muniment room to find an original charter, identified by its press mark, with the minimum of difficulty. Even so, to eliminate any possible confusion, the first folio of the cartulary contains a prologue, written in French, which describes at some length the system employed for finding documents.

Such a sophisticated arrangement, with detailed instructions, is quite rare even among ecclesiastical cartularies.[23] There are probably few parallels among those cartularies held by laymen, but at least one other example is to be found in the Mortimer Cartulary, of which two versions are extant.[24] Both manuscripts are of the late fourteenth-century and concern the inheritance of Philippa, daughter of the duke of Clarence and wife of Edmund Mortimer, earl of March and, by his

22 Thompson, 'Clervaux Cartulary', 190–1.

23 See David Walker, 'Organisation of Material in Medieval Cartularies', in D. Bullough and R.L. Storey, eds., *The Study of Medieval Lands. Essays in honour of Kathleen Major* (Oxford, 1971), 132–50.

24 BL Add. Ms. 6041, Harl. Ms. 1240.

marriage, earl of Ulster.[25] The first is a calendar of the muniments kept in the treasury at Wigmore which relate to Philippa's estates. The second manuscript, the cartulary itself, reproduces the calendar of the first manuscript and in a second section contains a detailed description of the cataloguing system and how the original deeds might be located. These were kept in boxes with their own titles, which were listed in the cartulary against the names of the manors whose charters they contained. A third section carries full transcriptions of every deed, identified by the catalogue numbers recorded earlier in the cartulary. The system is similar to that employed by Adam Fraunceys'ss scribe, if a little more complicated and unwieldy.

An example of an ecclesiastical register which closely approaches the Fraunceys system, and the Mortimer arrangement even more closely, is the Great Cartulary of the canons of Lanthony priory in Gloucestershire, written c. 1350.[26] Here a prologue in red ink describes the process of cataloguing. Each manor was allotted a numerical mark or *signum*, I-XXVIII. All the muniments were kept in wallets (*scrinia*), and each charter was marked with its *signum* plus another number, I i, I ii, I iii etc., which were so inscribed in the register. Since one *signum* could serve for several manors, a list of all the Lanthony manors grouped according to their *signum* was included after the prologue. Below this came a brief description of all the charters listed in numerical order *signum* by *signum*, to be followed finally by a full transcription, to each of which was attached a rubric which included each charter's identifying mark. This was a lengthy process, and necessitated a certain amount of duplication. Dr Walker notes that the scribe eventually began to weary of his task and became more laconic in the detail he recorded. Nevertheless, while Lanthony's, like Mortimer's, may have been more laboured than the Fraunceys system, the principle was the same. It differed only in that the form of the cartulary was determined by the arrangement of the Lanthony archive. The system of *signum* and number had evidently been devised for archival convenience, and the compiler of the cartulary was most reluctant to break the sequence even where violence might be done to topographical continuity. The cartulary of Canterbury priory has a similar arrangement based on archive organisation, although this, unlike the Lanthony register, is a composite volume, with sections drawn up by different scribes in the thirteenth century.[27]

25 Davis, *Medieval Cartularies*, 150; H. Wood, 'The Muniments of Edmund de Mortimer, Third Earl of March, concerning his Liberty of Trim', *Proceedings of the Royal Irish Academy* xl C, no. 7 (1932).
26 PRO C115/K2/6683 (continuation 6681). See also Walker, 'Organization of Medieval Cartularies', 140–2.
27 Ibid., 141–4.

Such systems, in which the scribe subordinates his arrangement to the demands of the muniment room, are likely to have been less rigidly followed in private cartularies, partly because it was often the scribe himself who had to organise the archival material, hitherto haphazardly stored, before beginning the work of transcription. This certainly seems to have been the case with the Fraunceys cartulary, where the original charters were apparently grouped and divided at the time it was drawn up in 1362. The process can be seen most clearly from the sections which deal with the smaller manors. In the part which concerns Ruckholts in Essex, the compiler first gives a synopsis of the descent of the manor from the late thirteenth century to the time when it was received by Adam and Agnes Fraunceys.[28] He then records the charters, duly numbered, in the order which makes the descent clearest, and it is evident that his account is based for the most part on the information contained in the charters rather than on external sources.

The manor of Chobhams was less straightforward in its descent than Ruckholts, but the scribe collected into separate groups charters relating to each parcel of land which made up the manor, labelling each group with the name of the principal owner of that parcel. Individual charters were then numbered chronologically within the group, e.g. Bryan i, Bryan ii, Bryan iii, Wyndesouere i, etc. All these parcels were eventually bought up by the London merchant, John Preston, and thereafter descended as a block of land, whereupon each charter now referring to the manor as a whole, was given a letter and number in chronological order, A i, B ii, C iii down to O xv, which includes the sale of Chobhams to Adam Fraunceys and his enfeoffment of two trustees. There remained, however, seven charters dealing with small parcels of land in Stratford, West Ham and Aldgate which do not appear to be part of the main body of lands comprising Chobhams, and which presented the compiler with the problem of where to include them. He eventually by-passed the difficulty by inserting them at the end and labelling them P i-vii. A similar thoughtful arrangement of charters, interspersed with explanatory memoranda in French, is to be found in the section concerning Wyke. Such is the care displayed both in labelling the charters and in organising them into a logical and clear sequence, that we must conclude that the compiler was not simply following a pre-ordained archival order, but had himself catalogued each document and attempted to trace the descent of the properties so far as he could.

The task of compiling the cartulary seems to have been shared by two men, though where the break came is not quite clear. The second scribe checked the work of his predecessor quite thoroughly and noted

28 F1.

in the margin errors where they occurred, such as the omission of number *li* in the Edmonton series of charters, which he attributed '*per negligenciam scriptoris*'.[29] He also came upon a group of six charters which he considered to have been entered in the wrong place and which he cancelled, leaving an instruction that they were to be found later in the manuscript.[30] He did not, however, make corresponding changes in the numbering system, which would have involved unsightly erasures not to mention much tedious effort.

No alterations were made to the text which reflect changes in the circumstances of the holdings. Some restore omissions made by the first scribe, such as copying in sections left out of the original transcriptions, but this is very rare. There were, however, some additional copies made at a later date on the blank folios at the end of the cartulary. They include a plea by William de Say, great-grandfather of the William who sold Edmonton to Adam Fraunceys, before the justices in eyre to seek compensation for certain rights which had been infringed, among which were those of free warren and view of frankpledge. Below this is a copy of the charter whereby Henry III granted free warren to de Say's father on his manors of Sawbridgeworth (Herts) and Edmonton.[31] The writing of these copies appears to be late fourteenth-century, and they may well have been commissioned by Adam Fraunceys junior as confirmation of rights to which he felt himself entitled, having settled into the lordship of Edmonton.

Two further copies appear on later folios which present a problem of interpretation but which might throw some light on the descent of the cartulary, and will be considered below. Finally, inserted at the end, possibly when the cartulary came to be bound, was a copy of a case heard in King's Bench in 1369, in which Adam Fraunceys sought to deny that he was either of two notorious villains of the same name, who had been committing crimes in the areas of Hothersall, near Ribchester, Bradley upon Colne and Airedale, in Lancashire and West Yorkshire nearly two decades earlier. It is possible that there is a clue here to the birth-place of Adam Fraunceys, but if so, it is the only one we have and remains uncorroborated.[32]

Fraunceys'ss cartulary was regarded therefore as a register of legal title and right, and was very occasionally used after its completion to record documents of some legal significance. Two of these, however, seem to have been written down much later and only make sense when considered in the context of the descent of the cartulary itself. The

29 F225.
30 F424–5.
31 F1282–3.
32 F1286. See 1 (i).

most obvious explanation is that the cartulary followed the descent of the Edmonton lands. These were passed down through the daughter of Adam Fraunceys junior, Agnes, to her grandson, Richard Charlton, the son of Speaker Sir Thomas Charlton, who died fighting for Richard III at Bosworth and so forfeited his inheritance for future generations. The lands were then divided and passed through several hands, mostly royal retainers, until they were reunited between 1571 and 1588 by William Cecil, Lord Burghley.[33] By 1588 Burghley had acquired nearly 2,000 acres of land in Edmonton,[34] a substantial holding centred on his Hertfordshire house Theobalds. It would thus seem a fair assumption that the cartulary descended from lord to lord as evidence of title to the lands, until it came to rest with the Cecils, who by 1607 were settled in their new seat at Hatfield.[35]

The existence, however, of two apparently unconnected charters, copied onto the dorse of folios 109 and 112, the final folio of the cartulary, raises some interesting questions. The first (F1284), written in a late fifteenth- or conceivably sixteenth-century hand, concerns an assize of novel disseisin in 1447 brought against a certain John Virly by several freeholders of Harefield, Middlesex, whose lands he was alleged to have appropriated. The second (F1285), written in the same hand as the first, is the copy of a fine, dated 1341, recording the sale of a messuage, 118 acres of land and 10s rent in Eyworth, Bedfordshire, by John and Joan Purley to Edward and Anne Despenser, son and daughter-in-law of the notorious younger Hugh. Below the copy, also in the same hand, is written 'Lambart of Weston made exchaunge of Eyworth for other lyvelode that was steward of Londe with Edward Spenser', and in the margin, in a late sixteenth- or seventeenth-century hand, is the note 'Eyworth/nowe my Lo[rd] Andersons'.

What are we to make of these additions? The only connection between Harefield and Eyworth that is at all apparent is that in the late sixteenth century both manors came into the hands of Sir Edmund Anderson, Lord Chief Justice of Common Pleas, a fact attested, in the case of Eyworth, by the marginalia quoted above.[36] What the significance of this might be is not immediately obvious, and why these charters should have been copied into the cartulary is even more

33 *VCH Middlesex* v, ed. T.F.T. Baker (London, 1976), 149, 150, 156–7; Glennie 'In Search of Agrarian Capitalism', 15.

34 *VCH Middlesex* v, 163.

35 Lawrence Stone, 'The Fruits of Office: The Case of Robert Cecil, First Earl of Salisbury, 1596–1612' in F.J. Fisher, ed., *Essays in the Social and Economic History of Tudor England in honour of R.H. Tawney* (Cambridge, 1961), 108.

36 He received Harefield in 1586 in exchange for a Warwickshire manor (*VCH Middlesex* iii, ed. Susan Reynolds (London 1962), 241), and Eyworth in 1594–5 (*VCH Bedford* ii, 231, 232).

puzzling. Did Anderson come into possession of the manuscript for a time, and if so, why? We know that the Fraunceys family held one of the fees of Eyworth in the late fourteenth and early fifteenth centuries, although it was never a central part of their estates. It is presumably possible that when Anderson took over the fee in 1595 that he somehow acquired the cartulary which he later passed on to the Cecils but it seems unlikely. That the Despenser steward, Lambert de Weston, held one of the Eyworth fees is of interest, however, and may explain when and how that manor passed to Adam Fraunceys. Weston was a Lincolnshire knight who held lands as a feoffee for his master in a number of counties.[37] By 1369 he seems to have been seriously short of money and in February of that year he borrowed heavily from Adam Fraunceys and three of his colleagues, offering his lands in Lincolnshire as security.[38] If Weston defaulted on the loan, even in part, it is quite likely that he would have sought to exchange a manor in Bedfordshire in order to regain his demesne. It is possible, therefore, that Fraunceys came by Eyworth, in 1369 or 1370, through Despenser's own 'steward of londe'.

By whatever route, however, Fraunceys's cartulary became part of the Cecil archive by the early seventeenth century, and Robert Cecil, first earl of Salisbury, commissioned a survey of his own lands in Edmonton, undertaken by Israel Amice in 1606, which was subsequently bound in with the cartulary.

To gauge the accuracy of the cartulary, and how much detail was included in the extracts, some at least of the original documents need to be consulted for comparison. Here the nature of the cataloguing system is invaluable. As we have seen, the land market close to London was buoyant, with a frequent turnover of tenements especially among Londoners themselves, and the number of charters surviving from the Edmonton, Enfield and Tottenham areas runs into thousands.[39] A glance at the dorse of any deed, however, is sufficient to identify whether a charter was part of the Fraunceys archive or not. Even so, despite the large numbers of surviving Edmonton deeds, very few belonging to the original Fraunceys archive have come to light. Nineteen are to be found at Hatfield, two at the Public Record Office, and just

37 *CIPM*, xiii, no. 193 p. 162; *CIMisc.* vii, no. 489.

38 *CCR 1369–74*, 74. The three colleagues are all Fraunceys familiars, the lawyer and recorder of London, William Halden, John Oskyn, vintner and John Ussher, clerk. Lambert acknowledged a debt of 800m.

39 Mr D.O. Pam notes that there survive over 1,600 charters recording the sale of land in Edmonton between 1200 and 1400 (*The Hungry Years: The Struggle for Survival in Edmonton and Enfield before 1400*, Edmonton Hundred Historical Society Occasional Papers, New Series, 42 (1980), 14).

one, the only non-Edmonton original, at the British Library.[40] By far
the largest collection, however, is kept at Westminster Abbey, namely
332, of which two are duplicate charters, which gives a total, excluding
the duplicates, of 352 surviving original deeds out of a total of 1,238,
or roughly 28%.[41] This represents a good enough sample to allow some
comment. Judging by the evidence of these charters, Fraunceys's scribe
performed his task with efficiency and competence. The essential details
of each deed were included with admirable conciseness. Standard
clauses of distraint or exclusion were omitted, except in special circumstances, but warranty, or the lack of it, was always mentioned.
Place names and patronymics often differ in spelling from their originals,
and occasionally, in very long charters, details of location were over-
looked, whether by accident or by design. The fines, too, which
were paid for property conveyance were not considered of sufficient
importance to be recorded. Substantial errors or omissions, however,
are few. In isolated instances a date was excluded, or the wrong year
given, but in view of the number of deeds with which the compiler was
dealing, such lapses in accuracy were remarkably rare. No witness lists
were included, of course, which were of little interest to contemporaries
and whose absence made a great saving in time and space. The
cartulary served a two-fold function in providing a catalogue to the
muniments with a guide to their location, and a collection of abstracts
which contained sufficient information to mitigate the effects of damage
or loss. Viewed in this light the quality of the work is impressive.

Finally we might consider the circumstances in which Adam Fraunceys commissioned his cartulary and his reasons for so doing. According
to the heading on the first folio, it was written in 1362, although much
time would already have been spent in arranging and cataloguing the
charters before the transcription began and the work itself would
have taken many months. Fraunceys had been engaged in property
acquisition in London since the late 1340s, and outside the city from
the early 1350s, he purchased substantial lands in Edmonton from the
estates of fellow Londoners as early as 1355, and he continued to
consolidate this his main holding for some years after 1362. Why, then,
did he decide to have a cartulary of his properties drawn up, and why
in 1362? Certainly the practical aspect was important. The introduction,
which explains the system, makes it clear that the cartulary was not
merely of ornamental value but was intended to be used. Given the
sheer number of charters, abstracts rather than full descriptions were

40 Hatfield Deeds; PRO Ancient Deeds E40/4401, 2038; BL Add. Charters 40513.
41 Why so many of the original charters were acquired by Westminster abbey is a
matter for speculation. Perhaps the documents were deposited there for safe-keeping at
some time.

more practicable, yet, as we have seen, sufficient detail was included in each copy to give the full force of the original, rather than simply a catalogue entry of donor and recipient. The care taken with presentation, however, combined with the overall aesthetic appearance of the manuscript suggests that this was more than a working document. Nor was the date 1362 wholly arbitrary. No charters were added after completion, at least during the lifetime of Adam himself. The last entry dates from 1361, and concerns the conveyance of the manor of Edmonton by William de Say to Adam Fraunceys. Although Adam had purchased the minor holdings of Caustons and Dephams in the 1350s, it was de Say's lands which carried with them lordship of the manor and eventually a tenancy-in-chief. While, therefore, a number of factors may have influenced Frauncey's's decision to compile a cartulary, his immediate concern, confirmed by the timing, was that he was about to create his own seat of lordship at Edmonton, where he was to settle his family, and that a suitably impressive document should be drawn up to mark the occasion.

Frauncey's'ss cartulary was compiled both topographically and by press-mark, an unusually sophisticated arrangement. The overall impression is of an intelligently conceived and professionally executed piece of work, a document of which the owner could be justly proud. Pyel's cartulary, by contrast, was put together in a more haphazard way. Its dating, conception and compilation, including the number of scribes, is far less certain. Indeed, the reasons which lay behind the transcription of Pyel's muniments may well have altered while the work was in progress.

The first seventeen folios were concerned with properties in or close to the city of London which were all joint purchases with Adam Fraunceys. The first heading of the cartulary proclaims not an exclusive register of Pyel's deeds, but 'tenements and rents purchased jointly by Adam Fraunceys and John Pyel since Easter 1348'. The original intention therefore seems to have been a record of a commercial partnership, where details not only of real property but of loans and a business contract were set down. The rather complicated history of the Anketil properties with copies of the relevant documentary material is included at length, presumably as these tenements constituted a sizeable proportion of both men's holdings in London.[42] After folio 17, however, following several blank folios, the cartulary resumes, but with a geographical shift to Northamptonshire, and with the focus now firmly on Pyel's own properties.

In the absence of any firm declaration in the titles, the dating of the cartulary has to be deduced from internal evidence. There is a distinct

42 P4–8.

impression from the manuscript that it was compiled over a period of time. Changes of hand, cancellations of entries and apparently random jumps in topography, combined with the general lack of a recognizable system reinforce the belief that the cartulary was composed in fits and starts. It may have been begun as early as 1349, almost certainly by the end of 1351. Three or four different hands can be identified in the first seventeen folios, suggesting that at intervals evidences of new holdings were recorded in the register as they were acquired. This first section was probably completed in 1357.

There is only one clue to authorship of the cartulary, which occurs in this first part. It consists of a stray signature on folio 10r, 'Shirbourne'. In Pyel's will, there is an isolated bequest of 20s to a friar named 'Souebourne', an unusual name, but perhaps not sufficiently close to suggest a connection with the signatory in the cartulary. There is no other clue to the identity of the man.

Work was started on the second section, dealing with Pyel's own Northamptonshire estates, possibly in 1363, prompted, perhaps, by Adam Fraunceys's own cartulary, which would have been well advanced by this stage, and by Pyel's forthcoming journey to Galicia, when he entrusted all his lands in the county to Fraunceys, his own brother, Henry Pyel, and William Braybrook, rector of Cransley.[43] The date of Christmas 1360 in the heading meant that of those lands previously acquired, only charters concerned with the manor of Sudborough, received in April 1361, were to be included. Thereafter, as new lands fell into Pyel's hands, their documents were copied into the cartulary, giving a chronological sequence until February 1366, when the process seems to have been discontinued. There follows a break of some eight years until 1374, when work recommences, possibly by the same scribe who had begun the Northamptonshire section. It is at this point that charters relating to the earlier acquisitions in the county are included, but the variety of hands and the somewhat jumbled sequence of the muniments renders any more precise dating after 1374 impossible.

In appearance and conception, therefore, the cartulary of John Pyel is the complete antithesis of his partner's. There is neither chronological nor topographical consistency; at times charters seem to be entered as they come to hand. Often, it is true, charters relating to one manor, or to transactions with one person or family, are grouped together, giving the semblance of a scheme, but this may have been because they were stored together in the Pyel archive, and additional muniments which refer to one or other of these groups frequently appear later. The inclusion of material is therefore not entirely at random, and the compiler has made some effort to organise his material within small

43 P59.

sections, but there does not seem to have been any referencing system. Occasionally he attempts to clarify the descent of a particular manor or the significance of a transaction by explanatory memoranda. For example, at the opening of the section on the Northampton estates there is a long prologue relating the history of Sudborough manor, and how it came into the hands of the men who eventually enfeoffed John Pyel. A similar prologue is to be found introducing charters which chronicle the transference to Pyel of the manor of Cransley, giving a simplified and not altogether convincing account of the reasons behind the sale.[44] As with the compiler of the Fraunceys cartulary, Pyel's scribe was able to base most of his analysis on a careful reading of the documents themselves, but from time to time he shows that he is possessed of further information which we are unable to verify from the cartulary.[45] These lengthy memoranda were confined mainly to the Northamptonshire section, compiled up to 1366, and therefore presumably the work of one man. Thereafter there does not seem to have been any one guiding hand at work, and the cartulary becomes a composite production, employing the talents of several scribes, and gradually loses its sense of purpose and direction. Towards the end the records of land acquisitions give way to the recording of general miscellanea; transcripts of court proceedings, the history of a debt repayment which Pyel made on behalf of a neighbour, a complete rental of the Northamptonshire lands for one year (1358), even a list of the bad debts which Pyel bought up in 1352–4 to exonerate himself from his own debt to the Crown. All these were written up after 1374 in no chronological order and for no apparent reason. It may have been that, after the traumatic events of 1376, when a number of his associates and fellow citizens were successfully impeached in parliament and he had felt the hand of retribution uncomfortably close to his own collar, Pyel became obsessed with having what he considered the important details of his earlier life put down in writing. But even if this were the case, the items included are highly selective and conform to no logical pattern.

After Pyel's death the cartulary ceased to be used with any regularity. It remained in the family under Pyel's second son Nicholas, and Nicholas's daughter, Elizabeth, in use mainly as an occasional account book of rents due and wages paid. There is also a list of the prebendaries of Southwell in 1396, compiled for tax assessment, and other odd writings, including a piece of prophetic doggerel written in Latin.[46]

44 P81. See above, 2 (i).

45 For example, the interest which William la Zouche, archbishop of York had in part of the manor of Sudborough, which he granted to Anketil Malore, apparently his brother (P45).

46 John Pyel's brother, Henry, had been a canon of Southwell (CPL, iv, 72).

The fact that the cartulary could have been used by Pyel's descendants for such ephemera might suggest that the manuscript failed to inspire much sense of family pride or tradition. One cannot imagine Sir Adam Fraunceys, for example, lord of Edmonton, allowing his clerk to work out the wages on a blank folio of his father's cartulary. For, in effect, that was what happened to Pyel's manuscript. It was not intended as a record of accounts, but used merely for the paper on which they could be written, which was then either torn out or left in. The Pyel cartulary had started out as a working record of joint holdings, principally in London. Whatever Pyel may have intended in the meantime, it ended as a working record of miscellaneous facts, degenerating into a source of scrap paper.

And yet, the contrasts between these two mercantile cartularies, in purpose, treatment and content, may be more apparent than real and should not be exaggerated. There was undoubtedly a connection between them, and they are no doubt the product to some extent of mutual influences. The register of London properties was probably started by Pyel, which Fraunceys decided, as we have seen, to develop into something more significant than a record of business transactions, a departure which Pyel followed shortly afterwards. That Fraunceys'ss efforts were far grander in design and more ambitious in execution than Pyel's does not necessarily mean that their intentions were at variance. It may simply have been a difference of degree. For all Pyel's apparent desire to be a man of consequence in Irthlingborough and to emulate the greater county gentry, he perhaps lacked that breadth of vision and consciousness of style which might have come from a greater intimacy with the class to which he aspired. Fraunceys'ss association and friendship with men like Humphrey de Bohun gave him a more instinctive appreciation of how a man of that standing would expect to draw up a document of family importance. In essence, however, the cartularies shared a common purpose, both as legal record and mark of social transition, and the fact that the younger Pyels did not consider the appearance of the cartulary to be of great significance does not mean that they did not value its existence. On the contrary, its very survival proves that they did.

(ii) The Manuscripts

College of Arms Ms Vincent 64

The manuscript of John Pyel's cartulary is part of the great collection of manuscripts which belonged to Augustine Vincent, Rouge Rose pursuivant in 1616 and Windsor herald by his death in 1626. The collection was bequeathed to Ralph Sheldon of Beoley, Worcestershire, by Vincent's son, John, in 1671 and was presented by Sheldon to the College of Arms in 1684, a fact confirmed in the case of the Pyel cartulary by an inscription inside the front cover.[47] The manuscript was bound by Augustine Vincent in a fashion similar to others in his collection, in reverse calf binding with leather clasps, later reinforced with brass strips.[48] The outer cover is tooled with the motif 'ZZ' and inside is inscribed 'Vincent 64'. It contains 120 folios of paper composed in nine quires of which none bears a number or identifying mark. The folios measure 270 x 202mm and the text varies between 196 x 115mm and 205 x 155mm. There are six fly leaves at the beginning and two at the end. The collation is as follows:

1^8 (2,3,5,6 missing); 2^7 (12–14 missing); 3^8; 4^8; 5^{7+1}; 6^{7+1}; 7^8 (3,5,14 missing); 8^7 (8–12 missing); 9^6 (5 strip c.4cm wide, 7,8 missing).

The manuscript was unfoliated, but for the purposes of the calendar it has been foliated by the editor with the approval of the archivist of the College of Arms, beginning with the folio which bears the title of the cartulary. This gives 118 folios, with two folios preceding the cartulary proper. Of these, eight are wholly blank, ten are blank verso only, seven recto only. There are no catchwords. Seventeenth-century marginalia appear on many of the folios and two pedigrees executed by Vincent himself, one of the Fraunceys family, the other of the lords of Sudborough, were inserted at binding.

The cartulary was composed by several scribes at different times and there seems to have been no attempt to organize the material chronologically, topographically or according to archival arrangement. It was certainly not intended to serve as a guide or catalogue to a muniment room. There are no press marks, nor is there any obvious indication of the location of the originals, beyond the occasional vague reference to a charter remaining, for example, *en les mayns le dit Adam Fraunceys*. Many of the entries are copied in the form of memoranda rather than as direct transcriptions, especially in the opening section on London, which suggests that this part of the cartulary functioned as an *aide-mémoire*. There are several occasions, for example, when the person who actually paid for the purchase of a joint acquisition is named (mostly, but not always, Pyel), and sometimes the sum paid is noted. On the folio facing folio 1r of the cartulary there is a note which records that a copy of the cartulary, or at least part of it, was kept in London, perhaps by Adam Fraunceys?[49]

Some comment has already been made on the date and method of

47 L. Campbell and F. Steer, eds., *A Catalogue of Manuscripts in the College of Arms Collections* i (London, 1988), 233.

48 Ibid., 293.

49 *Memorandum qe la copie de ceste papir est escript en une tiele papir demurant a Londres.* Is this perhaps the 'white paper' referred to in P66, 69?

compilation.[50] The last, and longest, section, begun c.1374, contains much earlier material that was previously unrecorded, including, for example, the acquisition of Cransley manor in 1348. It seems that a decision was made to turn this register of selected transactions into a full-blown cartulary containing details of all acquisitions and purchases made in Northamptonshire and such a change was signalled by the rubric at the top of folio 38r which announces the lands, tenements and rents purchased by John Pyel for himself and Adam Fraunceys jointly and for himself alone in the county of Northampton and elsewhere.[51] Notice the reappearance of Adam Fraunceys and the stress on exactly who was making the purchases. This emphasis was repeated among the charters, as they had been in the earlier London section.[52] Following this latest change an attempt was made to keep some kind of topographical integrity. So the memoranda and charters which deal with Cransley cover folios 38r-42v and provide a reasonably coherent, if not altogether forthcoming, account of the conveyance of the manor.[53] Unfortunately such standards were not always maintained and the topography becomes scattered and less coherent as the manuscript proceeds.

After folio 96 the character of the cartulary alters yet again. Deeds cease and the entries now relate wholly to financial affairs, from which, it seems, Pyel's thoughts were never far away. It is here that the case of Pyel and the customs farmers, which had taken place in 1349, was recorded, together with details of the bonds which Pyel returned to the Exchequer in 1354 to satisfy his debts. Pyel's short-lived appointment to the royal exchange and purchases of statutes merchant also find a place here, while on folios 103-4 there is a copy of a complete rental of the income for Pyel and Fraunceys arising from their lands in Northamptonshire for the year 1358.[54] After an account of Pyel's financial support for John Daundelyn of Cranford, the cartulary ends, rather curiously, with a charter and an indenture concerning further lands in Bedford which Pyel acquired in 1369. Thereafter the remaining blank folios were used by Pyel's descendants to record miscellaneous accounts and other ephemera. None of the original charters has been located, apart from some of the fines in the Public Record Office, and enrolments in the Close and Patent rolls.

The following is a broad outline of the main sections:

1r-17v   London, Southwark and Kent

50 Above, 3 (i).
51 Preceding P79.
52 E.g. P99 and the note preceding P93.
53 P71-91.
54 P247.

22r–27v	Sudborough and grant of lands to trustees
29r–37v	Bedford, Irthlingborough, Woodford, Addington
38r–96v	Various lands in Northants. acquired since 1346, in Cransley, Cranford, Irthlingborough, Addington, Northampton, Wellingborough, Woodford and Finedon
99r–103r	Customs case and debt to the Crown; appointment to royal exchange
103v–104v	Rental of 1358
105r–v	John Daundelyn
108r–v	Bedford
109v–118v	Miscellanea

Hatfield Ms CP 291

The cartulary of Adam Fraunceys consists of abstracts of 1,283 deeds and charters relating to the manors of Ruckholts and Chobhams in Leyton and West Ham, Wyke in Hackney, and Edmonton. It is contained on 112 folios of vellum, made up of fifteen quires, the first thirteen of eight folios, the last two of four, all complete. Quire signatures of arabic numerals appear at the foot of the first folio of each quire. The folios measure 360 x 270mm and the size of the text is 228 x 142mm. The main part of the cartulary covers 106 folios, and the remainder was originally left blank, although copies of other muniments were subsequently added. The plan is as follows:

1r–3r	Ruckholts
3r–5v	Chobhams
6r–14v	Wyke
14v–106r	Edmonton
106v	Copy of a plea of William de Say in King's Bench and charter of Henry III granting him free warren
107r–108v	Blank
109r	Copy of 15c charter
110–111	Blank
112v	Copy of 14c fine

Inserted into binding, a copy of a suit in King's Bench

The present binding is eighteenth-century, and the cartulary was bound with a seventeenth-century survey of the manor of Edmonton, with plans and maps, executed by Israel Amice for Robert Cecil, first earl of Salisbury, in 1606.

The work was begun in 1362, when Adam Fraunceys purchased the manor of Edmonton, and seems to have been undertaken by two scribes. Great care was taken with the presentation of the manuscript, and the first folio contains a lengthy memorandum outlining the scope of the work and the method behind its compilation. The purpose, according to this memorandum, was to record the essence of the legal transactions contained in each of the documents held by Adam Fraunceys relating to his lands in Essex and Middlesex. It was also to show where each charter was located should the need arise to consult the original. Some 354 of the original charters survive, most among the muniments of Westminster abbey.

The manuscript has been in the hands of the Cecil family probably since at least the early seventeenth century. The most likely explanation of its descent is that it passed with the manor of Edmonton, which was confiscated by the Crown after Bosworth in 1485, and later acquired by William Cecil, Lord Burghley some time in the late sixteenth century, although the cartulary itself seems to have been kept for a time by Sir Edmund Anderson, lord chief justice of Common Pleas.[55] The cartulary is an impressively executed and monumental piece of work. The initial letter on the title folio, R for Registrum, was omitted, possibly because it was originally to have been a decorated capital. No charters were cancelled, apart from six which were judged to have been in the wrong place, none was added after completion and no annotations or textual alterations were made, except for the additional entries added on the blank folios at the end, presumably after Fraunceys's death. While it is likely that Pyel's cartulary was to some extent a working document, there is no evidence that Fraunceys's cartulary was ever used as such, and its primary function seems to have been to mark the purchase of Edmonton manor as an event of some moment in the history of the Fraunceys family.

(iii) Editorial Method

It seemed that the most useful treatment of both manuscripts was to produce a calendar in English rather than a full edition. Certain words or phrases in the original languages have been included in italics and in round brackets where the meaning may be obscure or to indicate variant spellings, and I have left wholly in the original the preface to the Fraunceys cartulary, where the scribe has given an account of his own editorial method and how it related to the archival system. Each item, whether charter or memorandum, has been numbered separately and the original language noted at the end. In the case of the Fraunceys cartulary, in which the details of each charter were written in Latin and all memoranda and scribal comments written in French, language has only been noted where an original charter was found to be in

55 See above, 3 (i).

French. Where the documents from which the cartularies were compiled have been located, references are given below the respective entries.

Since the Fraunceys cartulary was, in effect, a calendar itself, I have largely retained the form in which entries were made there, but where a surviving original charter provides useful additional information this has been incorporated into the text. Where discrepancies occur between the cartulary and its original, the detail from the latter will appear in the text, and the cartulary variation, if it is thought necessary to record, will appear as a footnote prefixed by MS. With the Pyel cartulary lengthy charters have been abbreviated to contain only the essential details. Unhelpful repetition or duplication has been avoided and standard clauses of distraint, arrears, exclusion and sealing omitted, unless of particular interest, but warranty clauses have been noted. 'Etc.' is used in the text only where it appears in the original, unless enclosed in square brackets. All other editorial insertions, whether for an uncertain reading or to make the text clearer, are likewise enclosed in square brackets, as are all editorial comments which are not in the footnotes.

Rubrics occur in the Fraunceys cartulary at intervals of roughly sixty charters, indicating in which coffin each batch is kept. I have thought it necessary only to include the first rubric of each manorial collection in order to illustrate the archival arrangement. I have not noted the pressmarks, except where these are at variance with those on the original charter or where mistakes in the numbering have occurred.

Place-names are given their modern equivalents where these can be identified, but have otherwise been left in the original in inverted commas. Where a place-name is part of a personal name, the original spelling is retained. Christian names are modernised in line with common practice but not surnames, which appear as in the manuscript. The exceptions to this are some names which are frequently repeated, most notably Pyel and Fraunceys, where these spellings are kept throughout, and names appearing in French or Latin. These I have rendered in modern English followed by the original in italics and round brackets. Where such forms recur regularly I have omitted the Latin after the first couple of occasions for reasons of space. Thus the original for the name Marsh as it appears in the calendar is invariably *de Marisco* and for Castle *de Castello*, unless otherwise indicated. *Filius* I have translated as 'son of', even where it may sound a little laboured, except where there is reasonable certainty that it formed part of the surname, as with the FitzJohn family and Sir John FitzEustace.

Dates have been modernised. Where internal evidence allows, or where an original charter survives, approximate dates have been suggested for undated entries, but not otherwise.

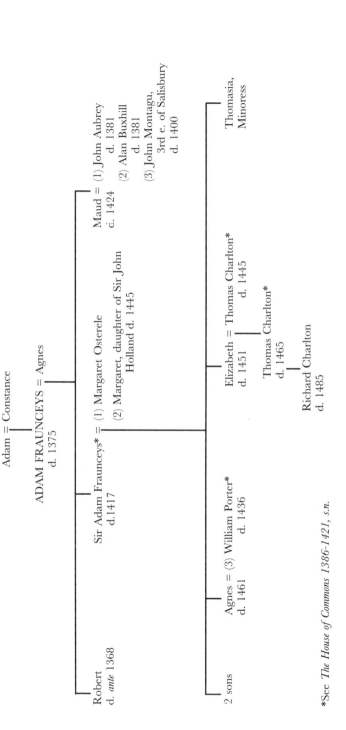

Adam = Constance

ADAM FRAUNCEYS = Agnes
d. 1375

Robert
d. *ante* 1368

Sir Adam Fraunceys* = (1) Margaret Osterele
d.1417   (2) Margaret, daughter of Sir John
                              Holland d. 1445

Maud = (1) John Aubrey
d. 1424   d. 1381
          (2) Alan Buxhill
               d. 1381
          (3) John Montagu,
               3rd e. of Salisbury
               d. 1400

Agnes = (3) William Porter*
d. 1461   d. 1436

2 sons

Elizabeth = Thomas Charlton*
d. 1451   d. 1445

Thomas Charlton*
d. 1465

Richard Charlton
d. 1485

Thomasia,
Minoress

*See *The House of Commons 1386-1421, s.n.*

2. THE PYEL FAMILY

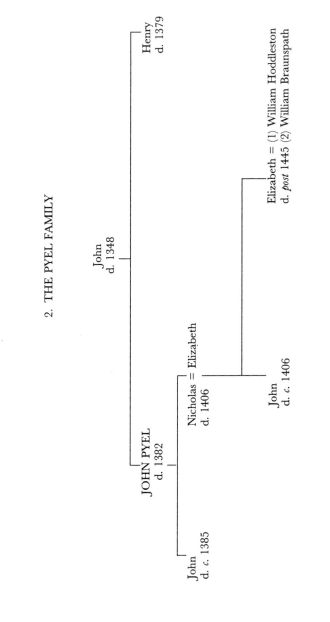

John
d. 1348

Henry
d. 1379

JOHN PYEL
d. 1382

John
d. c. 1385

Nicholas = Elizabeth
d. 1406

John
d. c. 1406

Elizabeth = (1) William Hoddleston
d. post 1445 (2) William Braunspath

TABLE

Recognizances of Debt to Adam Fraunceys

Date	Debtors	Creditors	Sum	Source
1343	John Petit, kt Michael de Trenewythe Robert Duraunt	AF/Thomas de Brandon	£240	YB[1] 444–445n.
21 Feb 1345	Guy de Bryan, kt Thomas Bacwell, c.Lond. William Tudenham, c.Lond.	AF/Nicholas de Causton	£40	CLRO RR[2] 10 m.1
13 May 1345	John Engayne, kt Alexander of Gonardeston John le Bele, c.Lond.	AF/Thomas de Brandon	£300	Ibid., m.2d
26 Nov. 1345	John de Evesham, kt Thomas de Baa, kt	AF/Thomas de Brandon	£40	Ibid., m.5
12 Feb. 1348	Bro. Philip de Thame, prior St John's Hosp.	AF/Simon Simeon	[£100 p.a.][3]	CCR 1346–9, 495
21 Sept. 1350	Nicholas, prior Holy Trinity, London	Adam Fraunceys	£100	CCR 1349–54, 243
26 Dec. 1350	James, prior St Mary without Bishopsgate	AF/Thomas de Langeton	£100	Ibid., 278
17 Dec. 1351	Bro. John, abbot Stratford atte Bow	Adam Fraunceys	£200	Ibid., 406
5 Sept. 1352	John de L'Isle of Rougemont	AF/John Malwayn	£400	Ibid., 504
20 Oct. 1352	William, s. John de Northtoft, [?kt]	AF/John Pyel	£40	Ibid., 508
13 April 1353	Nicholas Shordych of Hackney	Adam Fraunceys	32m	Ibid., 592
18 June 1353	Richard Lacer, c.Lond., and John his son	Adam Fraunceys	£100	Ibid., 601
28 Nov. 1353	Prior and convent Sulby abbey	AF/John Pyel	£200	Pyel Cart. no.34
18 Feb. 1354	Richard, abbot Lesnes, Kent	AF/Thomas de Langeton	£100	CCR 1354–60, 57
1 Feb 1366	John IV d. of Brittany	Adam Fraunceys	500m	DB,[4] 217
? 1366	John IV d. of Brittany	Adam Fraunceys	1500 écus	DB,[4] 218
11 May 1367	William de Morle, kt	Adam Fraunceys	£200	CCR 1364–8, 377
22 Feb. 1369	Lambert de Weston	AF/William Halden/ John Oskyn/John Ussher	800m	CCR 1369–74, 74
1 May 1373	William de Skipwyth	Adam Fraunceys	£100	Ibid., 554
24 July 1374	Elizabeth, widow William Daunvers	Adam Fraunceys	£20	CCR 1374–7, 81

1 *The Year Books of Edward III 18–19.*
2 Recognizance Rolls.
3 Annuity of £100 paid in return for an unspecified loan.
4 Michael Jones, *Ducal Brittany 1364–1399* (Oxford, 1970).

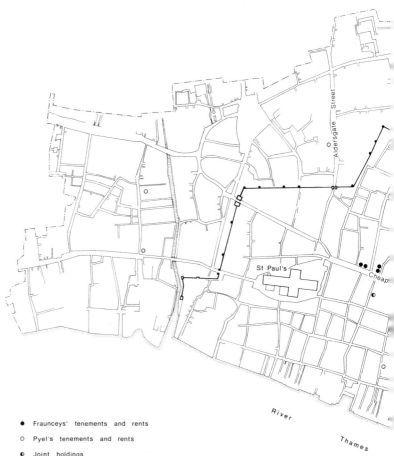

St Paul's

Aldersgate Street

Cheap

River

Thames

- ● Fraunceys' tenements and rents
- ○ Pyel's tenements and rents
- ◑ Joint holdings
- ■ □ Properties mortgaged for debts to Fraunceys / Pyel

0   2000 ft

0   500 m

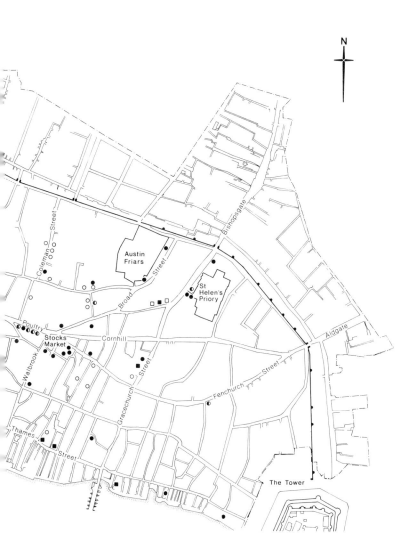

N

Coleman Street

Austin
Friars

Broad Street

Bishopsgate

St Helen's
Priory

Poultry

Stocks
Market

Cornhill

Walbrook

Gracechurch Street

Aldgate

Fenchurch Street

Thames

Street

The Tower

THE CARTULARY OF JOHN PYEL

[*f. 1r*] CEUX SONT LES TENEMENTZ ET RENTES JOYNTE-
MENT PURCHASEZ PAR ADAM FRAUNCEYS ET JOHN PYEL
SIBIEN EN LONDRES COME AILLOURS PUIS LE FESTE DE
PASK LAN DU ROI E.TIERS XXII A EUX ET AS HEIRS DE
CELUY QI SURVESQIT EN MANERE COME ENSIEUT

First a copy of a charter of the house of St Helen.

1 Chirograph of Eleanor de Wynton, prioress, and convent of St
Helen within Bishopsgate, London, leasing to Adam Fraunceys
and John Pyel, citizens of London, all houses with adjacent
gardens and vacant plots in the parish of St Helen's situated
between the convent's new rent (*novum redditum*) and the tenement
of Simon Broune to the south, the tenement formerly of Roger
Trug and the corner shop called 'atte Stone' to the north, the
royal highway to the west, and the tenement of Alice de Amerose,
the cemetery and the convent's large garden to the east, also one
vacant lane extending from the said garden westwards to the
royal highway, [between] the convent's plot on the north side
and the tenement of the prior of St Bartholomew's to the south,
to be held by Adam and John for the term of their lives at a
rent of £10 *pa*. Distraint clause. [*f. 1v*] Meanwhile the lessees will
demolish (*prosternent*) the houses, the lane and the plots on which
old houses now stand and will rebuild one house and five two-
storey shops next to the house, facing the street, with reversion
to the convent on the death of the lessees. The house with
adjacent garden is to remain to the heirs, executors or assigns of
Adam for a further term of twenty years at an annual rent of
one double rose to be paid at midsummer. [*f. 2r*] Warranty.
Witnesses: [Not transcribed.]
London, 24 July 1348.
[Latin]

2 Memorandum that four copies of this indenture were made, of
which two parts were sealed with the common seal of the prioress
and convent and are in the keeping of Adam and John, and the
other two parts were sealed with the seals of Adam and John
and remain with the prioress and convent.
[Latin]

3 Memorandum that on 10 December 1349 Adam Fraunceys and
John Pyel purchased of Margery, prioress of St Helen's, with the
assent of the whole convent as appears by their indenture, the

annuity of £10 which Adam and John were paying for the tenements which they had recently built in the parish of St Helen's. In return Adam and John granted to the prioress and convent the seven shops newly built by them by the highway to the north together with the two houses made by the [f. 2r] said Adam and John which John Frost, carpenter, now holds next to the tenement of St Bartholomew's, reserving to themselves all their house together with the eighth shop built by them to the south, including the rooms above the shop and free entrance and exit from the convent garden or elsewhere, for the term of their two lives plus twenty years. In addition the purchasers gave to the prioress and convent by way of charity 50 marks and four quarters of wheat for the relief of their house, as appears in the charter which is in the keeping of Adam.
[French]

3a [f. 3. Blank folio on the verso of which the following memoranda were later recorded in Latin by separate hands:]

(i) that Nicholas Pyel received of William de Weldon, his collector, for the term of Michaelmas 1404: £5 6s 8d.

(ii) that William de Weldon, collector of rents for Roger Lychefeld and his associates in Irthlingborough, delivered to the same at Irthlingborough at Michaelmas and Christmas 1405: 57s 2d.

4 [f. 4r] John Pyel and Adam Fraunceys purchased of Robert de Pulteney and others, executors of John de Pulteney,[1] one half of all the tenements and rents which John Anketil held in the city of London on 19 July 1341 and which the said executors now held by execution of debt made Saturday before the Nativity of St John the Baptist[2] by force of a recognizance which Anketil had made to Pulteney on the above date [19 July 1341]. The tenements and rents were assessed at £9 *pa* for each half and delivered to the executors until they should raise the 100 marks written below, which will be around seven and a half years. The interest of Adam and John is set out below.
[Latin]

1 Not the former mayor of London.
2 20 June 1349 (regnal year not given). See **5**.

5 Inquisition held before John Lovekyn, mayor, and Thomas de

Walden, chamberlain, at Guildhall, 20 June 1349, to inquire into
the lands, tenements and rents which John Anketil, citizen and
woolmonger, held within the liberty of the city on 19 July
1341, on which day Anketil in the presence of Roger Depham,
alderman, and Thomas de Mayne, chamberlain, acknowledged
that he owed John Oweyn called de Pulteneye 100 marks due to
be paid on 29 September following. William de St Albans (*Sancto
Albano*), Roger atte Brok, William de Newcastle (*Novo Castro*),
John Joye, cordwainer, William Algard, shearman, Roger atte
Tour, John Sprot, John de Donmowe, John de Bulkern, Robert
Sproun, [*f. 4v*] John atte Wade and John Pulder say on oath
that on the day on which the debt was due, John Anketil had 5
marks annual quit rent issuing from the tenement held by Agnes
widow of John Scot in the parish of St Mildred, Poultry, which
rent Nicholas Anketil, kinsman and heir of John, now receives;
also in the same parish a messuage, a brewhouse with two shops
adjoining and another four shops, worth in all £14 13s 4d *pa*
from which should be deducted £4 for a chantry in St Mildred's
church and a further 70s for repairs to tenements, and so the
aforesaid tenements are worth 10 marks *pa* quit; in the parish of
All Hallows Bread Street, a brewhouse and shop which Agnes
widow of John Anketil holds, worth annually £4 16s 8d, which
with deductions of 6s 8d *pa* quit rent to the prioress of Kilburn
and 40s *pa* for repairs is valued at 50s net; in the parish of St
Mary Magdalene Milk Street, two selds, four solars, one small
shop which Agnes Anketil now holds, in all worth £9 10s gross
pa, giving a net income of 110s after allowing for 20s annual quit
rent to be paid to the *conversi* residing [*f. 5r*] in Chancellor's Lane
[and 60s for repairs].[1] Total value of all tenements and rents:
£18.
[Latin]
[Cf. *CPMR* 224–5]

1 See **7**.

6 Adam Fraunceys and John Pyel purchased of Roger Chauntecler
and Nicholas Lolymer a letter of statute merchant for £200
made to Roger and Nicholas by John Anketil on 5 January 1348
to be paid on 2 February following whereby John and Adam
pursued execution of all tenements and rents which Anketil had
in the city of London on the day on which the statute was made.
By force of this execution the other half of all the rents and
tenements belonging to John Anketil, plus other tenements and
rents not assessed in the previous extent [**5**], were delivered to

Roger and Nicholas at £11 10s 8d net, to be held until they had levied the £200 contained in the statute. Roger and Nicholas granted their interest in this statute to Adam and John until the £200 should be paid.
[French]

7 The extent of the above tenements and rents made on the recognizance of the said statute.

Inquisition made before Ralph de Lenn and Adam de Bury, sheriffs of London, 31 October 1349, into the lands and tenements held by John Anketil in London on 5 January 1348, on which day Anketil appeared before Adam Garlekmongere, lately mayor of Northampton, and John Garlekmongere, clerk [*f. 5v*] for the recognizance of debt in Northampton, and acknowledged a debt of £200 to Roger Chauntecler and Nicholas Lolymer of Attleborough to be repaid 2 February 1348. William de Okham, cordwainer, William Algard, shearman, John Lorchoun, armourer, John Joye, cordwainer, John Scot, helmet-maker (*heaum'*), Salamon le Coffrer, John Sprot, salter, Henry Pouchemakere, John de Walden, tailor, and Thomas Malvel say on oath that on 5 January 1348 John Anketil held the following: in the parish of St Mildred Poultry, the moiety of one messuage, one brewhouse with two adjoining shops and four other shops, to the value of £7 1s 8d *pa*, with annual deductions of 40s for maintaining part of a perpetual chantry in the church of St Mildred and 35s for repairs to the above tenements, which Nicholas Anketil now holds, leaving a net total of 5 marks for the moiety; in the parish of All Hallows Bread Street, the moiety of one brewhouse and one shop worth 48s 4d *pa*, from which should be deducted 3s 4d in part payment of an annual quit rent to the prioress of Kilburn, and 20s *pa* for repairs, and so the moiety of the aforesaid tenements which are now held by Agnes, late the wife of John Anketil,[1] is worth 25s *pa* net; [*f. 6r*] in the parish of St Mary Magdalene Milk Street, a moiety of two selds, four solars and one small shop, worth in all £4 15s annually from which should be deducted 10s in part payment of an annual quit rent to the *conversi* in Chancellor's Lane, and 30s for repairs, leaving the net value of the moiety of the above tenements at 55s. Agnes Anketil now holds these tenements; in the parish of All Hallows Barking, one tenement with appurtenances in a lane called 'Berewards Lane' which is worth 40s *pa*, from which is to be deducted 13s 4d *pa* for repairs, and so the net value of the tenement which Nicholas Anketel now holds is 26s 8d; in the

parish of St Michael le Querne, 4s annual quit rent issuing from a tenement which was formerly of Hugh le Marberer, which rent Nicholas Anketil now receives; in the parish of St Mildred Poultry, a moiety of 5 marks annual quit rent issuing from a tenement which Agnes, who was the wife of John Scot, now holds, which moiety, viz. 33s 4d, Nicholas Anketil now receives; in the parish of St Michael le Querne, 4s annual quit rent issuing from a tenement formerly of Richard le Cook which Nicholas Anketil now receives, and in the same parish [f. 6v] 4s annual quit rent issuing from a tenement of Thomas Leggy, which the same Nicholas also receives; in the parish of St Giles without Cripplegate, 6s annual quit rent issuing from a tenement held by Philip de Aylesby and 6s annual quit rent issuing from a tenement which John Knyght holds in the same parish, both of which Nicholas Anketil now receives.
[Latin]

1 John Anketil died before May 1349, (*CPMR* 224) although his will, dated October 1348, was not proved until 19 April 1350 (*CWCH* i, 632).

8 Memorandum that Adam Fraunceys and John Pyel have between them a statute of £500 made to them by John Anketil which has not so far been mentioned (*attamee*), with a certificate dated 31 March 1348 attached to it, in the keeping of Pyel, about which nothing has been done (*quele certificat est takke al dit estatut en la garde Pyel et rienz a ceo nest fait*).
[French]

9 Memorandum that when these two extents were completed, William Tythynglomb, poulterer of London, shortly after Michaelmas 1349 produced two letters of statute made to him by Robert Tolosan on certain conditions as appears by two evidences made between Robert and William. These conditions were entirely fulfilled on the part of Robert, as is contained by a copy of them (*exemplicacion*) sealed with the great seal of Chancery. This copy remains in the possession of Adam Fraunceys and John Pyel. And without contesting the said conditions, William purchased writs and had an extent made of all the tenements and rents which Adam and John held in Poultry, [f. 7r] London and in the parishes of St Mary Magdalene Milk Street and All Hallows Bread Street by a false inquisition (*fauce enqueste*), which said that these tenements and rents and certain other tenements belonged to Robert in 1336 and 1337, and they were delivered to Tythynglomb on the basis of the said extent,

namely (*en noum de*) 20 marks *pa* until he should raise the £120 contained in the two statutes.
[French]
[Cf. *LPA* no. 70]

10 [Margin.] Memorandum of the assize on the said tenements. Whereupon Adam Fraunceys and John Pyel purchased at that time, in 1349, an assize against the same William Tythynglomb that he and Roger atte Tour, John Nasard and Roger Tyly had wrongly disseised them of a brewhouse, six shops and of six marks rent in Poultry, London, and of a brewhouse in Bread Street with a shop and two selds, with four solars built above and a small shop in front of the selds. And the assize said that William had disseised Adam and John of all the above tenements to the loss of £20 and more, and that the aforesaid Roger atte Tour, John Nasard were accessories [*caidantz*] to this. Thereupon the foregoing tenements and rents were redelivered to Adam and John by Ralph de Lenn, sheriff of London, to hold as their free tenements.
[French]
[Cf. *LPA* no. 70.]

11 Memorandum that Adam and John have a release and quitclaim made to them by William Tythynglomb at that time, in 1349, of all the tenements and rents they hold in the city of London which formerly belonged to John Anketil.
[French]

12 [*f. 7v*] Adam Fraunceys and John Pyel purchased in 1349 from William Tythynglomb a shop in Poultry, London, to them, their heirs and assigns in perpetuity, by enrolled charter, and they also purchased of William 12s annual quit rent issuing from tenements which were formerly of Ralph de Braghynge in Poultry, which tenements are situated etc. as appears in the said charter.[1] And at the same time Adam and John enfeoffed William and his wife Joan of the shop for the term of their two lives at an annual rent of four capons.[2] After the death of the feoffees, the shop will return to Adam and John.
[French]

1 CLRO HR 77/260.
2 HR 77/252.

13 John Pyel and Richard atte Dich' purchased on 11 September

1349, from Joan Joye who was the wife of Robert de Keteryngham a messuage with three small houses and all appurtenances in St Clement's Lane, near Candlewick Street in London, which messuage descended to Joan after the death of John Joye her brother. And Richard atte Dych' made a release to John Pyel, 30 November 1351, of all his right in perpetuity.
[French]

14 [*f. 8r*] Adam Frounceys and John Pyel purchased, 31 May 1349, from John Lucas son and heir of Adam Lucas of London, as appears in an indenture made on that date, all lands, tenements and rents, with appurtenances which he had in Lesnes and Plumstead, Kent, together with the reversion which will descend to him in the said vills after the death of his mother, Maud. Whereupon Maud in pure widowhood made a release to Adam and John, on 18 June 1349, of all her rights in the vills of Lesnes and Plumstead as appears in her deed. And Juliana, who was wife to John [Lucas], then made another release. And Adam and John granted to Maud in return for her release £3 annual rent for the term of her life as appears by their indenture made on 25 June 1349. These tenements were then leased to William Hatfeld, goldsmith, for five years for an annual quit rent of £10.
[French]
[This entry was subsequently cancelled.]

15 Adam Frounceys, John Pyel and Thomas de Langeton bought, 4 June 1349, from Ralph de Lenn, Simon de Mordon, merchants of London, and William de Newerk, clerk, all tenements and rents in Southwark with their gardens and all other appurtenances, which the vendors had purchased of John Lucas son and heir of Adam Lucas, 31 May 1349.
[French]

16 Adam, John and Thomas bought of the said Ralph, Simon and William, on the same day, as appears by their indenture, 20 acres of land in Newington at 'Hasardesmerssh' near London, lying in a place called 'la Hyde', enclosed with hedges and ditches, which these same vendors had also purchased of John Lucas, 31 May 1349.
[French]

17 [*f. 8v*] Juliana late the wife of John Lucas made a release in pure widowhood to Ralph, Simon and William, their heirs etc., 13 June 1349. And Idonia sister of John Lucas in pure virginity made a release to Adam, John and Thomas etc., 13 June 1349. And Maud Lucas mother of the said John made a release in her pure widowhood to Adam, John and Thomas etc., 13 June 1349. [French]

18 On 20 June 1349 Adam, John and Thomas enfeoffed the said Maud of the above tenements and rents in Southwark with the 20 acres of land for the term of her life at a rent of one rose each year. And after her death the tenements, rents and 20 acres were to return to Adam, John and Thomas and their heirs etc. [French]

19 John Pyel purchased and paid for all the tenements and rents in Lesnes, Plumstead and Southwark together with the said 20 acres of land. [French]

20 [f. 9r] Memorandum that Adam Fraunceys, John Pyel and Thomas de Langeton purchased of William Crydel, clerk, within fifteen days of 1 August 1349, a brewhouse, shops and other appurtenances on the corner of Mincing Lane near Fenchurch in London, to be held by them, their heirs and assigns in perpetuity. Which tenement and shops William had of the gift and feoffment of Esmon de Hardyngham, parson of the church of All Hallows Staining, and John Bullok, executors of the will of William Palmere, formerly citizen and tapicer of London, around 24 June 1349. The charters were enrolled in the Guildhall, London, at about the same time and in the same year, and also remain in the hands of Adam Fraunceys, and the said tenements, shops and appurtenances, are worth 13 marks *pa* quit, and Adam Fraunceys paid for them himself.
[French]   [fo. 9r]
[The property was sold by Adam Fraunceys 24 October 1371, (HR 99/127).]

21 [f. 9v] Notification that whereas John Anketil, lately citizen and woolmonger of London, enfeoffed Hugh de Lemynstre in a tenement with appurtenances in Cheap, London, and in another tenement with all appurtenances which Robert de Newent holds for a term of years in Bread Street next Cheap, Hugh then enfeoffed John and his wife Agnes in the above tenements, to be held by them and their heirs, and if John and Agnes died without heirs the tenements would revert to the right heirs of John Anketil. And John died without heir begotten of himself and

Agnes, and in his will he bequeathed all the above tenements after the death of Agnes, and all other tenements and appurtenances and all remaining terms in tenements and rents he held at farm in the city of London and the suburbs, to be sold by his executors and by two good and lawful men of that ward in which the tenements were situated. And the tenements were delivered to Adam Frounceys and John Pyel by Ralph de Lenn and Adam de Bury, sheriffs of London, by virtue of a recognizance and statute made by John Anketil before he enfeoffed Hugh de Lemynstre in the above tenements. Nicholas Anketil, heir and executor of John Anketil, Simon Frounceys, citizen and alderman of Cheap, John Alban, merchant of the same ward, John Terry, citizen and fishmonger of Bread Street ward, and Robert Newent, citizen of the same ward, by virtue and authority of the will of the same John Anketil proved and enrolled in the Court of Husting, London, held on 19 April 1350,[1] sold, granted and quitclaimed to Adam Frounceys and John Pyel, [f. 10r] their heirs and assigns, all the tenements and rents which Anketil had in the parish of St Mildred, Poultry, and all the tenements and rents which he had lately acquired of Hugh de Lemynstre in London and the suburbs, to be held in perpetuity by Adam and John [etc.] after the death of Agnes freely, quitly, in peace and by hereditary right. Andrew Aubrey, mayor, John Wroth and Gilbert Steyndrop, sheriffs.

Witnesses: Richard Lacer, Simon de Benyngton, William atte Welde, John Lovekyn, Thomas Dolselny, Thomas de Brandon, Richard de Causton, John de Chichestre, goldsmith, William de Epegrave, goldsmith, Robert de Norwicz, goldsmith, John atte Welle, vintner, Richard Toky, woolmonger, Thomas Same, and others.

London, 16 November 1351.

[Scribal note.] This charter was read and enrolled in the court of Husting, Pleas of Land, held 5 February 1352.

Shirbourne.

[Latin]

[HR 80/7]

1 *CWCH* i, 632.

22 [f. 10v] Notification that Robert le Hore, formerly salter of London, 12 April 1340, enfeoffed John de Thurston, poulterer of London, and William Bray, skinner of London, in all the tenements with appurtenances which Robert had of the bequest of John le Hore, lately citizen and corn-dealer of London, in Poultry

as appears in the will, proved and enrolled in the court of
Husting, 12 May 1337,[1] to be held by John Thurston and William
Bray, their heirs and assigns, in perpetuity. And these tenements
were divided equally between John and William. Later, on 23
May 1348, John de Thurston enfeoffed John Scot, citizen and
poulterer, in his tenement in perpetuity, and the said John Scot
bequeathed that tenement to Agnes his wife and executrix to be
sold as appears in his will.[2] Agnes by virtue and authority of the
same will granted to Adam Fraunceys and John Pyel the whole
of the above tenement with appurtenances in Poultry situated
between the tenement of the same Adam and John in the west
and the tenement formerly of John Russel in the east and
extending from the tenement of John de Enefeld in the south to
the street of Poultry in the north, to be held by Adam and John,
their heirs and assigns, [*f. 111*] in perpetuity of the chief lords of
the fee for due service and by customary right. Warranty. Andrew
Aubrey, mayor, John Wroth and Gilbert de Steyndrop, sheriffs,
Simon Fraunceys, alderman of that ward.
Witnesses: John de Seint Alban, Henry Ware, John Deyne,
Adam Leche, William Tythinglomb, William Laurence, Roger
de Depham and others.
London, 27 January 1352.
[Latin]

1 *CWCH* i, 420.
2 Modification made here by the scribe to his original transcription of the
document, which does not alter the force of the charter.

[*f. 111v*] Touching the tenements purchased by William Northtoft
in Lesnes, Plumstead and Erith, with 22 acres of land.

[The following entries, **23–26**, were all subsequently cancelled
by a line drawn diagonally across them.]

23 Charter of William, son of John de Northtoft, knight, granting
in perpetuity to Adam Fraunceys and John Pyel, citizens and
merchants of London, all lands, rents and tenements with appur-
tenances which he had of the gift and feoffment of Thomas son
of John Cros in Erith, Lesnes and Plumstead, Kent. Warranty.
Witnesses: Simon Fraunceys, John Lovekyn, Henry Picard, John
Wroth, John Malwayn, citizens of London, Robert Bradefeld,
Henry Katour, Henry atte Freth, John Otewy of Lesnes, John
Squyer, Thomas de Fulham, Robert de Hereth and others.
London, 17 October 1352.
[Scribal note.] Enrolled on the dorse of the Close Roll in the

king's Chancery in the month of October in the same year.
[Latin]
[*CCR 1349–54*, 508]

24 William Northtoft made a letter of attorney to Peter atte Cokke
of Lesnes on the same date as the above charter to put Adam
and John in seisin of the said lands and tenements, which he
then did.
[French]

25 [*f. 12r*] The said William made a recognizance in Chancery of
£40 to Adam Fraunceys and John Pyel in October 1352 to be
paid at Christmas next, on condition that if Adam and John
were disturbed from the above lands in any way then William
should pay the said £40 as appears plainly in an indenture.
[French]
[*CCR 1349–54*, 508]

26 Pyel purchased these lands himself and paid £40 for them. These
lands etc. with other lands in Lesnes etc. purchased of J[ohn]
Lucas were sold by Adam Fraunceys and John Pyel to John
Chichestre by charter with warranty 25 July 1353 for £200, as
appears above.¹
[French]

    1 Presumably an omission.

27 [*f. 12v*] Memorandum of a farm purchased of the prior, William
Swyft, and convent of St Mary without Bishopsgate by Edward
Chamberlyn, parson of the church of Portland, and John Pyel
as appears by the copy of an indenture written in another red
paper of the fashion of this paper (*escripte dune autr' rouge papir del
fassoun' de ceste papir*),¹ which farm is worth £50 *pa* quit.
[French]
[*CCR 1349–54*, 505, dated 13 October 1352]
[This entry is cancelled.]

    1 Perhaps another version of the cartulary, like the white paper referred to
later. Cf. **66**.

28 [*f. 13r*] Memorandum that Adam Fraunceys and John Pyel
purchased, 3 December 1353, of the abbot and convent of Sulby,
an annual rent of £20 for their two lives. Pyel himself purchased
this annuity for Adam and himself and he alone paid 200 marks.
[French]

29 Charter of Walter, abbot, and the convent of Sulby in the diocese of Lincoln granting to Adam Fraunceys and John Pyel, citizens of London, for their lives and the life of the one who lived longer an annual rent of £40 in return for a sum of money which Adam and John granted in hand (*devant les mayns*) at the convent's great request in relief of all their estate. The rent was to be taken and received of all the convent's manors of Sulby, Little Addington and Welford in Northamptonshire and paid to Adam and John, and the one who lived longer, each year at Easter for life in the church of St Helen within Bishopsgate, London. Distraint clause in the event of arrears. [*f. 13v*] Warranty. And abbot Walter and the convent put Adam and John in peaceful seisin by the payment of 100s. Chapterhouse of Sulby, 3 December, 1353.
[Latin]

30 Memorandum that the said abbot and convent, for the greater surety of Adam and John, made another letter of annuity of £40 sealed with their common seal, of the same tenor as the above.
[No date.]
[French]

31 [*f. 14r*] And memorandum that the said abbot and convent for the greater surety of [Pyel's and Fraunceys'ss] annual rent of £20, made a bond of £100, sealed with their common seal, as appears by the copy written below [**34**].
[French]

32 The said abbot, for himself and the said convent made a recognizance in chancery, 28 November 1353, of £200 to be paid to Adam and John at Easter next following [**36**].
[French]
[*CCR 1349–54*, 617]

33 The said abbot and three canons of his convent left a letter of proxy with Adam and John on the above date, sealed with the common seal of their convent, by virtue of which they had power to bind their convent, as appears by the copy written below [**35**].
[French]

34 Recognizance of Walter, abbot of Sulby, and the convent of the same place acknowledging that they are bound by this letter for themselves and their successors to Adam Fraunceys and John

Pyel, citizens of London, in £100 to be paid to Adam and John
or to one of them, their heirs, executors or attorney presenting
this letter, at the house of the said Adam in St Helen's in London
on the feast of Easter next. For payment of which £100 the
abbot and convent bind themselves and their successors in all
their goods, movable and immovable, spiritual and temporal,
whether they be distrained by the justice of Holy Church or by
a lay court.
Sulby, 3 December 1353.
[French]

35 [f. 14v] Letter of the convent of the monastery of the Blessed
Mary of Sulby, of the Premonstratensian order in the diocese of
Lincoln, appointing their venerable father, brother Walter, abbot,
and their brothers in Christ and fellow canons Richard Burston,
William de Suleby, and Thomas de Langhton true and lawful
nuncios and procurators to treat, agree and determine on the
convent's behalf with whatsoever merchant or merchants on the
sale of wool, possessions or rents or any other thing pertaining
to the convent for a term of life or of years, as will seem more
suitable to the said father and brothers, granting to the same by
these letters patent sealed with the common seal full power of
binding the monastery to the said merchants up to the sum of
£300 and on the aforesaid sale, should any be made by the
same, and of receiving money from the said merchants and
making acquittance of receipt to the same.
Chapterhouse of Sulby, 23 November 1353.
[Latin]

36 Indenture made between brother Walter, abbot, and the convent
of Sulby in the diocese of Lincoln of the one part, and Adam
Fraunceys and John Pyel, citizens of London of the other part,
that whereas the abbot and convent, for a sum of money in
relief of their house and at their great request, granted to Adam
and John an annuity of rent of £40 to be taken from all lands
and tenements belonging to the abbot and convent in the manors
of Sulby, Little Addington and Welford in co. Northampton, and
whereas the abbot by assent of the whole convent made a
recognizance in Chancery, 28 November 1353, of £200 to be
paid to Adam and John at Easter next following and the said
abbot and convent are held for themselves and their successors
by a bond sealed with their common seal in full chapter to Adam
and John in £100, to be paid at Easter, notwithstanding these
Adam and John grant that if abbot Walter and the convent and

their successors pay to Adam and John or to one of them in the
church of St Helen within Bishopsgate, London, annually for
the whole of their lives and of the one of them living longer £20
at four terms in equal portions, then the said annuity [of £40],
recognizance [of £200] and bond [of £100] will be held null.
And if the said manors, lands and tenements relating to the
above annuities be discharged by [*f. 15v*] recovery of law (*deschargez
par recoverir de iugement*) or for any other cause, or if insufficient
distress be found on the manors, lands and tenements for either
the annuity of £40 or the annuity of £20 to be paid to Adam
and John in the manner abovesaid for all their lives, then the
recognizance of £200, the annuity of £40 and the bond of £100
will stay in force, notwithstanding this indenture. And the abbot
and convent grant for themselves and their successors that they
will not lease at farm or grant any other interest to anyone in
the manor of Addington without leave of Adam and John. And
the abbot and convent bind themselves and their successors to
pay the said annuity of £20 and to keep all the above agreements
and to hold their whole abbey and all their other lands and
tenements with appurtenances, and their goods and chattels,
both spiritual and temporal, to the distraint of the said Adam
and John. And for greater surety in keeping these agreements
the abbot and convent made two letters patent, sealed with their
common seal, to Adam and John, of one tenor with the said
annuity of £40. And Adam and John grant by these presents
that the letter of the annuity of £40 will not take effect.
Chapterhouse of Sulby, 5 December 1353.
[French]
[A confusing set of charters, not helped by the fact that they are
copied out of sequence. Pyel and Fraunceys seem to have bought
two annuities, one at £40 (**29**), and the other at £20 for which
Pyel paid 200m (**28**), both on 3 December. The abbey had
already acknowledged a debt of £200 on 28 November (**32**) and
a further bond of £100 to support, according to the scribe, the
£20 annuity, on 3 December (**31, 34**). On 5 December all these
debts were cancelled, it seems, except for the annuity of £20
which was payable for life (**36**). Pyel later confirmed the cancellation of this annuity in his will.]

[A seventeenth-century genealogy of the Fraunceys family is
inserted between fos. 15 and 16.]

37 [*f. 16r*] Memorandum that in 1356 a writ of *scire facias* was sent
to the sheriffs of London to summon Adam Fraunceys and John

Pyel as holders of the land of John Anketil in London and Thomas Chauntecler as heir and executor of the will of Roger Chauntecler [regarding] his tenements in London. And a writ of the same tenor was sent to the sheriff of Norfolk to summon those holding land of John Tuwe of Deddington for debt due to the king of wool shipped from England to Dordrecht in 1337, namely £59 11s 1¼d for 7 sacks, 5½ stones and three pounds of surplus wool, shipped in the names of John Anketil, John Tewe and Roger Chauntecler, as appears hereafter.
[French]

38 Memorandum that William atte Pole and Reginald del Conduyt loaded 18 sacks, 10 stones, 2 pounds of wool, price £159 9s 8d, received of John Anketil and John de Tewe of Deddington, and afterwards paid them at Dordrecht £34 19s in two parts, and of the remaining £124 8s 8d letters patent were made to John Anketil and John Tewe.
[Latin]

39 The same William de la Pole and Reginald del Conduyt loaded 12½ sacks, 9½ stones and 5 pounds of wool, price £171 9s, received of John Anketil and Roger Chauntecler, of which £34 19s was paid at Dordrecht and of the remaining £136 10s letters patent were made to John and Roger. And afterwards allowances were made of the same £136 10s as of the above £124 10s [*sic*], and £120 8s 4½d was due by the two aforesaid patents, which was allowed to the same John Anketil, Roger Chauntecler and John Tewe in common, and the two patents were restored as is contained in the customs account roll, viz. of the account of Thomas de Melchebourne and associates, lately farmers of the customs in England for the years 1343 and 1344, as appears in the Recorda for Trinity term 1355.
[Latin]
[cf. PRO E368/127 Trinity Recorda rot. 36]

40 Memorandum that £59 11s 1¾d is demanded at the Exchequer as the price of 7 sacks, 5½ stones and 3 pounds of wool transported under the names of John Anketil, John de Tewe of Deddington and Roger Chauntecler in 1337 and not assessed for customs and so made forfeit by the king, for which £59 11s 1¾d the sheriffs of London and Middlesex were ordered to inform John, John and Roger or their heirs and executors or those now holding the lands and tenements which were theirs in fee in the year 1337 and after, that they should be at the Exchequer on the

octave of Michaelmas 1355 to show etc. And on that day the
sheriffs returned that they had informed Adam Fraunceys, who
holds one messuage in Bread Street ward, one messuage in
Cheap ward, and one messuage in Poultry, which were of the
aforesaid John Anketil, [f. 16v] also Thomas de Chauntecler, heir
and executor of the will of Roger Chauntecler, holding two
messuages in Fleet Street and one messuage in Holborn in the
ward of Farringdon-without, and on the morrow of Hilary 1356
John Pyel, who holds one messuage in the ward of Cheap and one
messuage in Bread Street ward which belonged to John Anketil.
[Latin]

41 And Adam Fraunceys, John Pyel and Thomas Chauntecler
acknowledged that they held all the aforesaid tenements and
severally replied through the sheriffs to the Exchequer that they
were willing and ought to be charged by the king with respect
to the £59 11s 1¾d, being the price of the said wool, insofar as
the said tenements which each held were sufficient. It was
therefore decided that Adam, Thomas and John should be
charged by the king with the above sum by reason of their own
acknowledgement.
[Latin]

42 Memorandum that in view of the legal proceedings against
Adam Fraunceys and John Pyel as holders of land of John
Anketil, Thomas Chauntecler as holding land of Roger Chauntecler, and those holding land of John Tewe, John Pyel sued in
court with the agreement of these landholders that the tenements
which belonged to John Anketil should be assessed and taken
into the king's hands for the whole sum of £59 11s 1¾d, as appears
by the commission below [**43**] and the extent made subsequently
[**44**]. And the landholders agreed that Thomas Chauntecler for
his part should pay to Adam Fraunceys £24, those holding land
of John Tewe £8, and that Adam Fraunceys would pay the
remaining £27 11s 1¾d. And a tally was levied in October 1355
in the Exchequer of Receipt containing the said sum plus 8s 10d
which had been paid to Adam Fraunceys to round up the tally
to £60, and this sum was assigned by the court to Henry Grene,
whom Adam paid. And Adam and John Pyel will receive the
tally and deliver it to the Exchequer in the above month (October
1355), and they are quit of the above sum, as appears in the pipe
roll.
[French]
[Pro E372/201 Pipe Roll rot.15 m.1]

43 [*f. 17r*] Commission by the king to Henry de Greystoke, baron of the Exchequer, and Henry Pycard, mayor and escheator of London. Whereas the sum of £59 11s 1¾d, being the price of wools forfeited by John Anketil and others, was demanded from Adam Fraunceys, John Pyel and Thomas Chauntecler, and the aforesaid Adam and John severally acknowledged that they held certain tenements which belonged to John Anketil in fee in the year 1337 and afterwards, namely one messuage each in the wards of Bread Street and Cheap and a third messuage in Poultry held by Adam Fraunceys, and one messuage in Cheap and another in Bread Street held by John Pyel, and that they wished to make satisfaction of the debt according to the true value of the above tenements, the commissioners were to determine what other tenements belonging to John Anketil in 1337 in addition to those acknowledged above are now held by Adam Fraunceys and John Pyel and divers others, and for what reasons, so that the debt might be the more speedily satisfied, and also what other tenements and rents of this kind John Anketil had in fee in London in that year, who now held them, and the total value of all the said tenements and rents. The commissioners were assigned to inquire by the oath of good and lawful men of the city who had no connection of any kind with Adam [Fraunceys] and John Pyel, or any other holders of the said tenements, more fully the truth concerning each of the aforesaid articles and their details, and also to survey all other tenements, in whose hands they were and their annual value.
Witness G. de Welforde, 12 November 1356.
[Latin]
[Scribal note.] By the Recorda of the Memoranda Roll, Trinity 1355. [See above, **39**.]

44 [*f. 17v*] Inquisition and extent of the lands and tenements which were held by John Anketil made before Henry de Greystoke, baron of the Exchequer, and Henry Pycard, mayor and escheator in the city of London, at St Martin le Grand on 24 February 1357, in the presence of Adam Fraunceys, John Pyel and Nicholas Anketil, kinsman and heir of John Anketil, deceased, and executor of his will. By authority of the king's commission directed to this inquisition, Henry de Ware, John Deyns, William atte Castell, Robert Norwich, Adam Carlel, Simon Rasyn, William Okham, John de Ditton, William Senescerre, John atte Noke, Thomas de Staundon and William Sherman say on oath that Adam Fraunceys and John [Pyel] hold jointly the rents and tenements which were of John Anketil in fee in 1337 and

afterwards in the city, as follows. Bread Street: one brewhouse
with shop attached, value £4 16s 8d *pa*, less annual payment to
the nuns of Kilburn, 6s 8d, and necessary deductions, £2. Net
value of brewhouse and shop, £2 10s *pa*. Cheap: two messuages,
value £9 10s *pa*, less annual payment to the house of the *conversi*,
Chancellor's Lane, £1, and necessary deductions £3. Net value,
£5 10s *pa*. Poultry: four shops, value £5 8s *pa*, two further shops,
value £2 8s *pa*, a brewhouse with shop attached, value £6 *pa*,
another shop which John Pople holds, value £3 6s 8d *pa*, a quit
rent issuing from the tenement which was held by John Scot,
£3 6s 8d *pa*, less payments to two chaplains celebrating divine
service, £7, and to two men overseeing that the chantries are
well maintained, 6s 8d, for keeping one lamp in the church of
Wolchirche, 4s, and for rent to the abbot of Westminster, 6s,
and for necessary deductions of all tenements in Poultry £3 10s.
Net annual value, £9 2s 8d. And the total net value of all rents
and tenements of John Anketil in the city of London in 1337 is
£17 2s 8d *pa*.
[Latin]

[Folios 18, 19, 20, 21 blank. Three subsequent folios excised and
an insertion adjoined to the stub of the third of these showing a
genealogy (a seventeenth-century compilation) of the lords of
Sudborough.]

LANDS PURCHASED BY JOHN PYEL IN THE COUNTY OF NORTHAMPTON SINCE CHRISTMAS 1360

45 [*f. 22r*] Memorandum that Sir Reginald Watermill was lord of
all Sudborough, and that when he died the lordship was divided
between his three daughters, the eldest Joan, the second Petronilla, and the third, Margaret. Joan was married to Sir Robert de
Veer, and they had a son called Robert. The second Sir Robert
had a son, also called Robert, who sold all his part [of the
manor] to Sir Nicholas de Beech, who in turn sold it to William
de la Zouche, archbishop of York. The archbishop granted it to
his brother, Anketil Malore, and Anketil granted it to William Braybrook and Nicholas Rose of Isham, chaplains, who then re-
enfeoffed Anketil by fine for the term of his life with remainder
to Thomas Grene and Hale his wife, who was the daughter of
Anketil, and to their heirs, with remainder to the heirs of the
said Anketil. And memorandum that Petronilla, the second sister,
was married to Sir John Wykham, and Sir John sold all his part
to Sir Robert de Arderne, whose son Giles sold all his part to

Sir Simon de Drayton. And memorandum that Margaret, the
third sister, was married to Sir Henry Techemerssh, and they
had a son called Sir John, whose son, also called Henry, sold all
his right to Sir Simon de Drayton. So Simon de Drayton
purchased for himself and his heirs two parts [of the manor],
which he then granted to William de Lofwyk, William de
Isslep', parson of Conington, John de Reyngsted and John de
Harwedon'. These enfeoffed William Malore and his heirs in the
said two parts, whereupon John de Harwedon and Sir John de
Drayton, heir of Simon, made a release with warranty to William
of the same. And William enfeoffed John Pyel and his heirs as
appears later by copies of the feoffments.
[French]

46 [f. 22v] Final concord made at Westminster on the quindene of
Easter 1358 between Simon de Drayton, plaintiff, and John de
Wykham and Petronilla his wife, defendants, concerning a third
part of the manor of Sudborough with appurtenances for which
Simon paid John and Petronilla 20 marks.
[Latin]

47 Release by Giles, son and heir of Sir Robert de Arderne, knight,
to Sir Simon de Drayton, knight, and his heirs, of all right
and claim in the lands and tenements which Simon holds in
Sudborough, near Lowick, of the lease and grant of Sir Thomas
Wake, knight, for the term of the life of Nichola, Sir Thomas's
wife. Grant to Simon and his heirs of the reversion of all lands and
tenements which John de Berughby and Isabel, his wife, hold in
Sudborough, for the term of the life of Isabel, which were of
Giles's inheritance and were to revert to him and his heirs; these
to remain wholly to Simon and his heirs in perpetuity. Warranty.
Witnesses: Thomas de Verdon, Robert Pavely, Thomas de Bulton,
Robert de Daventre, knights, Nicholas de Vyeleston, John de
Craneslee, William Seymour of Boughton.
Sudborough, 7 April 1345.
[Latin]

48 [f. 23r] Release of Henry de Tychemerssch, son and heir of John
de Tychemerssch to Sir Simon de Drayton, knight, of the third
part of the manor of Sudborough, namely his chief messuage
with all appurtenances, lands, rents, services, meadows, pastures,
woods, vineyards (*vineres*), ponds, mills, view of frankpledge, and
all his free tenants, wardships, marriages, reliefs and escheats

and all his villeins (*neyfs*) with their dependants, service, goods and chattels, and all reversions, to be held of the chief lord of the fee for due services and customs. Warranty.

Witnesses: William de Lyvedene, William de Nouwers, John de Aylyngton, John, son of John de Lufwyk, William de Wanton of Sudborough, who for greater surety have appended their seals. Drayton, 6 September 1349.
[French]

49 Indenture witnessing that Sir Simon de Drayton, knight, granted and demised to William de Lufwyk, parson of the church of Aldwinkle, William de Islep, parson of the church of Conington, John de Harwedon of 'Sibeston',[1] and John de Ryngstede, vicar of the church of Brigstock, his manor of Sudborough with appurtenances together with all other lands and tenements which he holds in the same vill, with meadows, grazing-land, pastures, woods, mills, rents, services of free and bond tenants, view of frankpledge, suit of court and all other easements, liberties and appurtenances within the vill and without, to be held of Simon by the feoffees for their lives by paying to the grantor for life £60 *pa*, and after his death one rose to his heirs at midsummer for all services and demands. Licence to re-enter in the event of arrears. [*f. 23v*] Moreover, the said feoffees will, grant and bind themselves jointly and severally by oath on the holy gospels that after the death of Simon all profit of the manor and other tenements will be used for the benefit of his soul and that of Margaret his wife by the celebration of masses and the payment of alms. Warranty.

Witnesses: Robert de Holand, John de Verdon, knights, John Daundelyn, Anketil Malore, William de Nouwers and others. Drayton, 19 September 1350.
[Latin]

1 Probably Sibson, Hunts.

50 Charter of William [de Islep], parson of the church of Conington, and John de Ryngsted, parson of the church of Lowick, granting to William Malore of Sudborough, his heirs and assigns, the manor of Sudborough, with all appurtenances together with all lands, meadows, grazing-land, pastures, woods, hedges, millponds, rivers, rents, services of free and bond tenants, view of frankpledge, suit of court, reversions, escheats, wardships and reliefs within the vill, to be held by the grantee of the chief lords of the fee by rendering due service and custom.

Witnesses: Sir William la Zouche, Sir John Doyle, knights, Robert Veer, John Barkervile (*recte* Baskervile), William de Nowers and others.
Sudborough, 18 January 1358.
[Latin]

51 Release by John de Harwedon to William Malore of all right and claim in the manor of Sudborough with all appurtenances which he had of the gift and feoffment [*f. 24r*] of Simon de Drayton, knight.
Sudborough, 29 January 1358.
[Latin]

52 Release of John son of Simon de Drayton of all right and claim in the manor of Sudborough and all other lands and tenements named and unnamed in the said vill, and in all lands and tenements which Robert le Walshe formerly held in villeinage, and in the suits and dependants (*sequelis*) of the said Robert, and also in the reversion of all lands and tenements which William de Wanton holds for the term of his life of the lease of Simon de Drayton, late father of John, and in all other reversions and rights pertaining to him by inheritance after the death of his father. Warranty.
Witnesses: Simon le Warde, Anketil Malore, Thomas Grene, John Chaumberleyn, Richard de Goldryng and others.
Sudborough, 21 June 1359.
[Latin]

53 Charter of William Malore of Sudborough granting to John Pyel of Irthlingborough the manor of Sudborough, and all other tenements with appurtenances which he had in the same vill of the gift and feoffment of John de Harwedon, William de Islep, parson of Conington church, and John de Ryngested, clerk, which manor, lands and tenements these men had of the gift and feoffment of Simon de Drayton, knight, to be held by John Pyel, his heirs and assigns, of the chief lords of those fees for due service and by customary right in perpetuity. Warranty.
Witnesses: John de Drayton, knight, John Chaumberleyn of Lowick, John Baskervill of the same, [*f. 24v*] Gilbert Loord of the same, Thomas Pavely of Slipton, Richard Goldryng of Sudborough, Richard Caunteleve of the same, Robert Veer of Addington, John Lenton of Woodford, John Schakyl of the same, Robert Greylond of Islip, William Lord of Irthlingborough,

Thomas Miriden of the same, William Clerk of Rothwell and others.
Sudborough, 7 April 1361
[Latin]

54 Release of William Bonge, parson of the church of Sudborough, William Hereman and William in ye Greyne of 'Henele', chaplains, to John Pyel of the manor of Sudborough and all lands and tenements in the same vill, which they lately had of the gift and feoffment of William Malore. Warranty.
Witnesses: [As in **53**.]
Sudborough, 9 April 1361.
[Latin]

55 [*f. 25r*] Final concord made at Westminster, three weeks of Easter 1360, between William de Braybrook, parson of the church of Rushden, and Nicholas Rose, chaplain, plaintiffs, and Anketil Malore, defendant, concerning the manor of Sudborough with appurtenances, except two messuages, 1 carucate and 40 acres of land, 12 acres of meadow, 42 acres of wood and 5 marks of rent in the same manor. And the defendant acknowledged the right of the plaintiffs in the manor which they had of his gift, and for this acknowledgement, fine and concord, William and Nicholas granted the said manor to Anketil for life, with remainder to Thomas Grene, Hale his wife and their heirs and thereafter to the right heirs of Anketil.
[Latin]
[PRO CP25(1)/177/81 no. 491]

56 [*f. 25v*] Release of Robert Reynaldyn of Sudborough to John Pyel of one messuage, $25\frac{1}{2}$ acres of land in Sudborough, which were formerly of Robert de Wanton and Helen his wife. Warranty.
Witnesses: Anthony Malore, John Malore, Richard Goldryng, Hugh Mounfort, Richard Malyn and others.
Sudborough, 14 April 1363.
[Latin]

57 Charter of Richard Milnere, vicar of Brigstock, granting to John Pyel of Irthlingborough, an assart of wood to be held separately throughout the year (*unum assartum bosci separale omnibus temporibus anni*) called 'Cattesheed' within the bounds of Brigstock, comprising 8 acres and 3 roods lying between the field of Sudborough in the east and the field of Brigstock in the west, and from [the land of] Walter Weyate in the south to the wood of John Pyel, called 'Middelhawe', in the north, to be held by John, his heirs

and assigns, of the chief lords of the fee by due service and right
customs. [*f. 26r*] Warranty.
Witnesses: Anthony Malore of Sudborough, John Malore of the
same, Richard Goldryng of the same, Peter Werketon of Brigstock, Robert [E]tebreed of the same and others.
Brigstock, 24 April 1353.
[Latin]

[Folio 26v blank.]

58 [*f. 27r*] Memorandum that John Pyel granted tenements in
Irthlingborough and elsewhere in the county of Northampton as
follows, on 1 May 1363, at which time Pyel left Irthlingborough
for Santiago in Galicia.
[French]

59 Charter of John Pyel of Irthlingborough granting to Adam
Fraunceys, citizen and merchant of London, Henry Pyel, rector
of the church of Warkton, and William Braibrok, rector of the
church of Cransley, all lands and tenements with appurtenances
and all goods and chattels in Irthlingborough, Wellingborough,
Northampton, Orlingbury, Finedon, Cranford, Sudborough,
Brigstock, Woodford, Little Addington, Great Addington,
Ringstead and Higham Ferrers in the county of Northampton,
to be held by the feoffees, their heirs and assigns, of the chief
lords of those fees by due service and right customs. Warranty.
Witnesses: John Campioun, John Stevenes, Ralph Golde, John
Warde, Robert Peu and others.
Irthlingborough, 1 May 1363.
[Latin]
[Scribal note in French.] This charter is enrolled in Chancery
and in the common bench for the above month of May.
[*CCR 1360–64*, 523]

60 Notification that John Pyel ordained and appointed in his place
Robert, rector of All Saints, Irthlingborough, John Cartere,
chaplain, John Campioun, William Freman, as his attorneys
jointly and severally to deliver to Henry Pyel, clerk, Adam
Fraunceys, citizen and merchant of London, and William Braibrok, rector of Cransley church, full and peaceful seisin of the
above lands and tenements.
Irthlingborough, 1 May 1363.
[Latin]

61 [*f. 27v*] Charter of John Pyel granting to Adam Fraunceys, Henry Pyel and William Braibrok, all goods and chattels existing in the above vills in the county of Northampton.
Irthlingborough, 1 May 1363.
[Latin]

62 Acknowledgement by Henry Pyel, parson of Warkton, and William Braibrok, parson of Cransley, that whereas John Pyel of Irthlingborough had granted and by his charter enfeoffed Adam Fraunceys and themselves in all lands, tenements, rents and all other appurtenances in Irthlingborough, Wellingborough, Northampton, Orlingbury, Finedon, Cranford, Sudborough, Brigstock, Woodford, Great Addington, Little Addington, Ringstead and Higham Ferrers in the county of Northampton, with all goods and chattels on the said lands or elsewhere in the county, [to be held] by Adam and themselves, their heirs and executors in perpetuity as appears in the said charter, on condition that they act in accordance with the ordinance and will of the donor concerning the lands [etc.], [*f. 28r*] they bind themselves, their heirs and executors, and each one for all, to John Pyel, his heirs and executors in £2,000, to be paid should they fail to implement his will. And they further grant that in the event of such failure, it is permitted to the said John to re-enter the lands and tenements, to be held by him, his son John, and the heirs and assigns of John senior in perpetuity. And for greater surety the feoffees took an oath on the Holy Gospels. In witness etc.
Irthlingborough, 1 May 1363.
[French]

[Folio 28v blank]

63 [*f. 29r*] Writ of the king to the sheriff of Bedford instructing him to arrest Helen, wife of the late William Rothewell of Bedford, who acknowledged, 15 March 1362, before John Pyel, lately mayor of the Staple of Westminster, that she owed to Henry Pyel, clerk, and Thomas Smyth £10 which was to have been paid to them within a month of Easter then following, and to imprison her until she has made full satisfaction of the debt, and to make an extent of all her lands and chattels in his bailiwick by the oath of good and lawful men by whom the truth might be better known, and to take them into the king's hands so that they might be delivered to Henry and Thomas until the debt be satisfied. And the sheriff was to inform the king by sealed letters

in Chancery on the quindene of Easter how he had executed
the writ. He returned that Helen had at Bedford one messuage
with wine-shop adjoining, which was [formerly] of William
Crowe and was worth 8s *pa* net, 8 acres of arable land worth 4s
pa net, and one shop in 'Bocheria' worth 2s *pa* net. The sheriff
was ordered to deliver the messuage, tavern, shop and land to
Henry and Thomas, if they were willing to receive them, to be
held as their free tenement until they should be satisfied of the
said debt, together with losses and expenses sustained. And the
sheriff was to inform the king by sealed letters in chancery on
the octave of Michaelmas how he had executed this writ. [*f. 29v*]
Witness the king himself, Westminster, 3 July 1363.
[Latin]

64 And memorandum that Henry and Thomas granted all their
interest in the above lands and tenements to John Pyel at
Michaelmas 1363, and at the same time John leased the tenement
with tavern to William Crowe for an annual quit rent of 13s 4d.
And John leased the shop in 'la Boucherie' and 8 acres of land
to John Schepherd for 6s [?8d].
[Addition in different hand.] And at Michaelmas 1365 John Pyel
leased to Roger Levy all his interest in the above plot and tavern
for a quit rent of 20s. Thus Pyel received annually 2 marks [?*recte*
3 marks] quit.
[French]

[*f. 30r*] Lands purchased by John Pyel from Ralph Hale and
Joan Miriden his wife at Michaelmas 1365.

Ralph had enfeoffed master Richard Brother in these lands some
two years earlier, whereupon Richard re-enfeoffed Ralph in the
said lands in Irthlingborough and Ralph and Joan, his wife,
enfeoffed John Pyel and Joan, his wife.

65 Charter of Richard Brother of 'Staverne',[1] chaplain, granting to
Ralph Hale of Irthlingborough all his right and claim in all
lands, tenements, and rents with appurtenances, which he had
in Irthlingborough of the gift of Ralph, to be held by the feoffee,
his heirs and assigns, by due services and customs.
Witnesses: John Campyoun, John Stevene, Simon Hencok, John
Body, Robert Pu of Irthlingborough and others.
Irthlingborough, 10 August 1365.
[Latin]

1 (?) Staverton, Northants.

66 Indenture whereby Ralph de Hale and Joan his wife of Irthlingborough grant to John Pyel and Joan, John's wife, all their lands,
tenements, rents, services, reversions, meadows, pastures with
appurtenances in Irthlingborough, to be held by John Pyel, his
wife and heirs in perpetuity for twelve years by paying 46s 8d
each year, [*f. 30v*] with liberty to the grantors to make distraint
on all the feoffee's lands and tenements in Irthlingborough, if he
should be in arrears at any time within the said twelve years.
And after the completion of twelve years, the feoffees are to pay
£20 annually. Warranty. And in witness of this the above parties
attached their seals to the indentures. And Joan, wife of Ralph,
of her own free will promised to fulfil and perform everything
contained in these indentures in the event of her husband's
death, for which she made an oath on the Holy Gospels and
pledged her faith to John Pyel and Joan his wife and attached
her own seal to these charters.
Witnesses: Thomas de Navenby, John Campyoun, John Stevene,
Robert Pu, John Body, John Ward, Hugh Chaundeler, and
others. Irthlingborough, 30 September, 1365.
[Scribal note] And memorandum that the parcels of lands and
tenements purchased by Ralph Hale are written in the white
paper (*en la blank papier*).[1]
[French]

1 This 'white paper' is mentioned several times in the course of the cartulary
and may refer to another copy of the document, possibly that in the keeping of
Adam Fraunceys.

67 [*f. 31r*] Charter of Richard Brother of 'Staverne', chaplain,
granting to John Pyel of Irthlingborough and Joan his wife all
lands, tenements, rents and appurtenances which he had in
Irthlingborough of the gift of Ralph Hale, to be held by John,
his wife and heirs, of the chief lords of the fee by due service
and right customs in perpetuity. Also release and quitclaim to
John and Joan of all the above lands and tenements. Warranty.
Witnesses: John Campyoun, John Stevene, Simon Hencok, John
Body, Robert Pu of Irthlingborough and others.
Irthlingborough, 3 August 1365.
[Latin]
[Scribal note in French.] By this charter Pyel took seisin, and
the previous charter of Ralph Hale was made for greater surety.
[A confusing transaction. The deeds may be masking some other
deal which had been struck between the parties.]

[Folio 31v blank.]

[*f. 32r*] The lands purchased by John Pyel belonging to the manor of Woodford which were of John de la Hay.

68 Memorandum that John de la Hay had a manor in Woodford, which held a fourth part of the lordship of Woodford. This manor had belonged to William de la Hay, father of John, and had descended to him after the death of Henry Trayly, son of Geoffrey Trayly. Henry Trayly granted the manor to Adam Bloundel, parson of the church of Woodford, and Ralph de Horton in fee. On 26 July 1331, Adam and Ralph re-enfeoffed Henry and Aubrey his wife in the manor with all its appurtenances for life, to be held after their deaths by William, son of Miles de la Hay, and Emma his wife and their heirs, and if they had no heirs, by the heirs of Miles de la Hay and Alice his wife, and if they died without heir, by the heirs of Henry son of Geoffrey Trayly in perpetuity as appears by a charter of the above date. And William, son of Miles, and Emma his wife had a son, John de la Hay, who died in seisin on 1 November 1361. And John and his wife Agnes, daughter of Sir John de Drayton, had a son John, who was born 29 September 1361. And the said manor was held of the abbot of Peterborough by knight's service at an annual rent of one pair of gold spurs or 6d. And when John son of William died, the abbot of Peterborough was also dead, whereupon the king granted possession to John son of John de la Hay and held his wardship and marriage because of the vacancy caused by the death of the said abbot. And memorandum that [*f. 32v*] the king granted the wardship and marriage to John FitzEustace, esquire, residing with Lady Isabel daughter of the king, as appears by a letter patent made in Chancery 3 May 1365.[1] And John FitzEustace granted all his interest in the wardship and marriage to John Pyel on 20 November 1365, as appears by two deeds sealed by John Fitz-Eustace to John Pyel. On the same day FitzEustace delivered the king's patent to Pyel together with the son of John de la Hay. And when the manor came into the hands of John Pyel, it was utterly ruined (*oltrement destrut*), except for the hall and a dovecote which were in a state of much disrepair. And the manor contained 2 carucates of land in demesne and tenancy, and a quarter of the moiety of the church of Woodford, with rents, services, meadows and pastures, and whatever belonged to the fourth part of the lordship of the vill.
[French]

1 *CPR 1364–7*, 124.

69 [*f. 337*] Charter of John FitzEustace, esquire, containing the letters patent of the king granting him wardship of the lands held by John de la Hay, deceased, in the county of Northampton of the abbey of Peterborough, lately vacant, which were in the king's hands by reason of the death of John de la Hay and the minority of his heir, and were leased at farm of 6 marks *pa* to the Royal Exchequer, to be held until the heir attained his majority, together with his marriage, without disparagement or payment to the king. Witness the king himself, Westminster, 3 May 1365. Also a declaration that John FitzEustace granted the above wardship and marriage to John Pyel to be held according to the tenor of the letters patent. And whereas Agnes, who was wife of John de la Hay, granted and leased for the term of her life a third part of all the lands, tenements, rents and services with appurtenances which belonged to John de la Hay in Woodford, which she held as dower as can be seen in an indenture made 15 October 1365, John FitzEustace granted to John Pyel all his interest in that third part, as well as in the other two parts, to be held by Pyel, his heirs and assigns according to the content and tenor of the said letters patent and indenture. London, 27 November 1365.
[French and Latin]
[Scribal note in French.] Memorandum that the parcels belonging to the said manor are written in the white paper.

70 Charter of Adam Bloundel, rector of a moiety of Woodford church, and Ralph de Horton, chaplain, granting to Henry, son of Geoffrey Trailly and Aubrey his wife, a messuage with appurtenances in Woodford and 2 carucates of land with appurtenances in the same vill and in Great Addington, and 40 acres of land held in Woodford and Twywell. Also one pair of gilt spurs or 6d in rent issuing from a messuage and a carucate of land in Woodford, formerly of Bartholomew de Lutyngham, which tenement John de Lenton holds, together with the services of the same John de Lenton; 2s rent issuing from one messuage and 2 virgates of land which Luke Manse once held, with homage and services of the tenants; 5s 2d rent issuing from a communal oven in Woodford which Henry son of Philip Traylly holds for life, with reversion of the said oven after his death; 7s rent issuing from a messuage which William son of Roger le Walker holds for ten years, with reversion of the messuage after the said term; 7s rent issuing from a fourth part of the tenement formerly of Roger Abraham, with homage and services of the tenants; 6d rent issuing from a messuage which John son of Peter holds,

with homage and services; 7d rent issuing from a messuage formerly of Anthony Butcher (*Carnificiis*), with homage and services of the tenants; 3d rent issuing from a messuage which Geoffrey atte Grene and Agnes White (*Dalbe*) hold, with homage and services; [*f. 34r*] 1d rent issuing [from a messuage] which Maud Bayl[l]y holds, with homage and services; 6d rent issuing from a messuage which Thomas Domcesby and Alice his wife hold by right of Alice, with homage and services; 30s rent issuing from a messuage and a virgate of land which William Shakell holds for life, with reversion of the tenements after his death; 30s rent issuing from a messuage and a virgate of land which Hugh Gumfray and Juliana his wife and Roger their son hold for the term of their lives, with reversion of the tenements after their deaths; 6s 3½d rent issuing from a messuage and two virgates of land formerly belonging to Robert de Twywell, which rent is apportioned among the tenants, with homage and services; 3s rent issuing from a messuage and 4 acres and 3 roods of land which John Trailly once held, with homage and services; 12d rent issuing from a messuage with croft which Isolde Herbert, Richard Simon and Ismania their daughter hold for the term of their lives, and 2s after the death of Isolde, with reversion of the tenements after their deaths; ¼ pound of cumin as rent from a meadow called 'Wodefordholm', with homage and services of William de Craneford, who holds the meadow; 3s 4d rent issuing from a messuage which Robert Herberd and Alice his wife hold for their lives and that of one of their sons; a cottage which Hugh le Taillour holds at will; a moiety of a messuage which Simon le Sekeston lately held; a fourth part of water for fishing (*piscar' aque*) on the Nene; a fourth part of the advowson of a moiety of Woodford church, and the presentation when it falls due, and all tithes and profits which the donors have in the vill of Woodford pertaining to the fourth part of the manor of Woodford; to be held by Henry and Aubrey his wife for their lives of the said Adam and his heirs. And after the death of Henry and Aubrey, all the aforesaid tenements will remain to William, son of Miles de la Hay, and Emma his wife, to be held of the said Adam and his heirs by services of one clove of garlic. And if William and Emma die without heir, all the tenements will remain to Miles de la Hay and Alice his wife and their heirs, to be held of the chief lords of the fee by due services and right customs. And if Miles and Alice die without heir, [*f. 34v*] all the tenements will remain to the right heirs of Henry son of Geoffrey in perpetuity. Woodford, 26 July 1331.
[Latin]

[*f. 35r*] The lands purchased by John Pyel from John Waryn of 'Tonoworth' in Irthlingborough on 2 February 1366, which he purchased from John Ferthelord. And Ferthelord purchased them from John Lord and his wife by a fine in Common Pleas (*comun banke*) and by charter, and from others, as appears by the charters. [French]

71 Charter of John Waryn of 'Tonoworth', granting to John Pyel of Irthlingborough a messuage, a headland and two curtilages in Irthlingborough, which messuage lies between the tenement of the feoffee on one side and the croft formerly of Thomas Miriden on the other and extends from the royal highway to the tenement formerly of William Eire, and the headland lies in the field of Irthlingborough at 'le Milneweye' by the common road which leads to Upwell, and one curtilage lies between the tenement of John Pyel and the land of Agnes, lately wife of Thomas Henry, and the second curtilage lies between the tenement of Henry le Grene and the land of the said Agnes, extending from the royal highway to 'le Hay', according to the boundaries and divisions made there, to be held by John Pyel, his heirs and assigns, of the chief lords of the fee by due services and right customs. Warranty.
Witnesses: John Campyoun, John Steven, John Ward, John Body, John Golde, Ralph Golde and others.
Irthlingborough, 4 February 1366.
[Latin]

72 [*f. 35v*] Memorandum that Simon Goldesburgh of Irthling-borough enfeoffed Richard Sauce and Agnes his wife of the same vill, on 26 December 1334, in one messuage and $1\frac{1}{2}$ roods of land in Irthlingborough lying at the west end of Irthlingborough next to the tenement once held by John Keteryng, clerk, son of Hugh de Keterynge. And on 2 January 1346 Richard and Agnes enfeoffed John their son and Sarah their daughter, their heirs and assigns, in the messuage and land which, since John was a friar, descended by inheritance to Sarah, who was then married to John Dru. And John Dru and Sarah had a son, John Dru, who inherited the messuage and land after the death of his parents. And John Dru the son enfeoffed John Pyel, citizen and merchant of London, on 8 January 1374, in perpetuity as appears below.
[French]

73 [*f. 36r*] Charter of John Dru granting to John Pyel, citizen and merchant of London, one messuage and $1\frac{1}{2}$ roods of land in Irthlingborough, which he inherited of his mother, Sarah, daughter of Richard Sauce, which messuage and land lie at the west end of Irthlingborough next to the tenement which was lately of John Keterynge, clerk, son of Hugh de Keterynge, extending from the street called 'Hamptoneweye' to the street called 'Mersshweye', to be held with all appurtenences by John Pyel, his heirs and assigns of the chief lords of the fee by due services and right customs. Warranty.
Witnesses: John Campioun, John Stevene, John Body, John Warde, Robert Pu, all of Irthlingborough, and others.
Irthlingborough, 8 January 1374.
[Latin]

[*f. 36v*] Sudborough and Addington. Touching the tenements which belonged to Gilbert Tolthorpe purchased by John Pyel from Amice Tolthorpe and John Chamberleyn.

74 Charter of Amice daughter of Sir John de Tolthorpe, knight, granting to John Pyel of Irthlingborough his heirs and assigns, all her lands and tenements with appurtenances in the vill and field of Sudborough, to be held of the chief [lords]. Warranty.
Witnesses: Anketil Mallore of Sudborough, Oliver Duffyn of Lowick, Gilbert Lord of the same, Robert Hardy of Irthlingborough, William de Cotene of the same, Roger Daundelyn of Addington, John atte Cros of Woodford and others.
Sudborough, 2 May 1362.
[Latin]

75 Lease by the same Amice Tolthorpe to John Pyel of Irthlingborough of all lands and tenements with all appurtenances which she had in the vill and field of Sudborough, to be held by John Pyel, his heirs and assigns in perpetuity, by paying to the lessor and her assigns an annual rent of 26s 8d for fifteen years, and 40s each year for five years thereafter, and thus for the whole life of John Pyel plus one year. And if he should die within the term of twenty years, the lessor grants that the lands and tenements will remain to his heirs and assigns for the same rent until the end of that term. And after twenty years, or the life of the lessee plus one year, his heirs and assigns will henceforth pay to the lessor and her heirs each year 100s. [*f. 37r*] Warranty.
Witnesses: Anketil Mallore of Sudborough, Oliver Duffyn of Lowick, Gilbert Lord of the same, Robert Hardy of Irthling-

borough, Roger Daundelyn of Little Addington and others.
Sudborough, 14 September 1362.
[Latin]

76 Indenture made between John Chamberleyn of 'Catesdene' and
John Pyel of Irthlingborough witnessing that whereas Amice
Tolthorpe leased to John Pyel in fee all her lands and tenements
in Sudborough [continues as **75**], and because Amice died 27
February 1365, the said tenements remained to Katherine her
sister, wife of John Chamberleyn. And by this indenture John
Chamberleyn granted to John Pyel and Henry Pyel his brother,
to have and to hold the above tenements for the life of John
Pyel, for the rent of one rose at midsummer, paying to the chief
lords of the fee the rents and services due to them. And if John
Pyel should die within sixteen years of the date of these [presents],
his heirs are to hold the tenements in the above manner for
those sixteen years, [*f. 37v*] and if they hold them beyond that
term, John Pyel grants that they should make payment for them
according to the indenture made between himself and Amice.
Warranty of John Chamberleyn and his heirs for the above
tenements to John Pyel and Henry, their heirs and assigns.
Witnesses: Anketil Mallore, Richard Goldryng, Richard Canteleve
of Sudborough, Gilbert Lord, Oliver Duffyn of Lowick and
others.
Sudborough, 24 June 1365.
[French]

77 Charter of John Chamberleyn of 'Catesdene', Herefs., brother
of Sir Richard Chamberleyn, knight, granting to John Pyel of
Irthlingborough all his lands, tenements, rents and services,
together with villeins and their households, reversions, fishponds
and all other appurtenances in Little Addington, Northants., to
be held by John Pyel, his heirs and assigns, in perpetuity.
Warranty.
Witnesses: Roger Daundelyn, Nicholas Pygot, John Colyn,
Thomas Daundelyn, William Beeby of Little Addington, John
Stevene, John Body, Robert Pu of Irthlingborough, and others.
Irthlingborough, 10 March 1368.
[Latin]

78 Lease of John Chamberleyn of 'Catesdene', Herefs., brother of Sir
Richard Chamberleyn, knight, to John Pyel of Irthlingborough of
all lands, tenements, rents and services, together with villeins
and their households, reversions, fishponds and all other...

[unfinished].
[Latin]

[*f. 38r*] The lands, tenements and rents purchased by John Pyel for himself and Adam Fraunceys jointly and for John Pyel individually in Northamptonshire and elsewhere since 1346.

79 Final concord made at Westminster, 16 April 1340, between Thomas Wake of Deeping, knight, and Elizabeth his wife, plaintiffs, and Simon de Braibrok, parson of the church of Cransley, and William, son of William de Upton, chaplain, defendants, by which eight messuages, one toft, 2 virgates and 84 acres of land, 7 acres of meadow, 6 acres of pasture, 12 acres of wood and 23s 10d rent with appurtenances, in Cransley, were acknowledged to be the right of Simon, of which the defendants hold two messuages, 62 acres of land and half the aforesaid meadow, pasture, wood and rent of the gift of the plaintiffs. And Simon and William granted to Thomas and Elizabeth the same tenements for life, to be held of the chief lords of the fee. Moreover, Simon and William granted for themselves and the heirs of Simon the reversion of the following lands which were all held for life: one messuage and 1 virgate of land held by Alice de Wilughby, one messuage and 1 virgate of land held by Simon de Craneslee, parson of Great Oxendon [Northants.] [*f. 38v*] and Hugh his brother, one messuage held by Robert le Forester and Margery his wife, Hugh and Thomas their sons with their sister Juliana, one messuage held by Elias Roke, one messuage held by Roger le Thacher and Isabel his wife, one messuage held by Ralph le Treschere and Margery his wife, the aforesaid toft held by John Elys, 15 acres of land held by John le Mareschal and Agnes his wife for the life of Agnes, 5 acres of land held by Ralph Erle, 1½ acres of land held by Margery Aleyn of the inheritance of Simon de Braibrok in Cransley, all of which were due to revert, after the deaths of the above tenants, to Simon de Braibrok and William and the heirs of Simon. It was granted that these lands should wholly remain, after the deaths of the said tenants, to Thomas Wake and Elizabeth, to be held for life together with the other tenements which remain to them by this fine. And after their deaths all the aforesaid tenements will remain to Agnes and Elizabeth, daughters of Elizabeth, for life. And after their deaths the tenements will remain wholly to [*f. 39r*] Hugh son of Thomas and Elizabeth, and afterwards to Thomas Wake, knight, brother of Hugh, and the heirs of his

body with remainder to the right heirs of Elizabeth wife of Thomas.
[Latin]
[PRO CP25(1) 177/76 no. 202]

80 Final concord made at Westminster, octave of Trinity 1312, between Hugh de Cransley, plaintiff, and Reginald, parson of the church of Cransley, defendant, by which the advowson of Cransley church and the manor of Cransley with appurtenances except 80 acres of wood in the same manor were acknowledged to be the right of the defendant, who, in return for this fine, granted them to the Hugh Cransley [*f. 39v*] to be held for life of the chief lords of the fee. And after the death of Hugh, the advowson and manor were to remain to John son of Roger de Heigham and Elizabeth his wife and the heirs of their bodies in perpetuity, with remainder to the right heirs of Hugh.
[Latin]
[PRO CP25(1) 175/64 no. 138]

81 [*f. 40r*] Memorandum that the said Elizabeth was daughter and heir to Hugh de Cransley and married to John son of Roger de Heigham. And John and Elizabeth had a son John and a daughter Agnes, and their son married the daughter of Sir Robert de Thorpe, sister to Sir William and Robert de Thorpe, and they had a son and a daughter. And the son married the niece of Sir William de Shardeshull, and when his father died his mother, the daughter of Sir Robert de Thorpe, thereafter married John de Gayton, esquire. And in 1348 the said son and daughter and their mother, whom John Gayton had married, and Agnes, mentioned above, all died in the plague, so that the inheritance of Cransley descended to Elizabeth as right heir of her father, Hugh Cransley. And Elizabeth, after the death of her husband, John son of Roger de Heigham, had married Sir Thomas Wake of Blisworth a long time before the plague and they had two children, Sir Thomas Wake, the heir, and Hugh his brother, and a daughter Elizabeth, whom Richard Maundeville had married and who died in the plague of 1348. And the said Sir Thomas, husband to Elizabeth, died a full three years before the plague,[1] and after his death Elizabeth as right heir of Hugh Cransley made over her interest in the manor of Cransley with appurtenances to John Pyel in the following manner.
[French]

1 He died in 1346, probably before embarking on campaign in France. See Introduction 2 (i).

82 Charter of Elizabeth lately the wife of Thomas Wake of Blisworth, knight, granting to John Pyel junior, citizen and merchant of London, [*f. 40v*] the whole manor of Cransley with the homage and services and of all tenants, both free and villein, the reversion of all tenancies together with the advowson of the church of Cransley and all rights and appurtenances, as fully and wholly as Hugh de Cransley her father held it by inheritance from Simon de Cransley his father, to be held by John, his heirs and assigns, in perpetuity of the chief lords of the fee by due services and right customs. Warranty.
Witnesses: Adam Garlekmongere, mayor of Northampton, Richard Bede and John Goos, bailiffs of the same town, John de Longuevill, John Garlekmongere, Richard Garlekmongere, Adam de Catworth of Northampton, John de Craneslee and John his son.
Northampton, 1 July 1348.
[Latin]

83 The aforesaid Elizabeth enfeoffed John Pyel junior, citizen and merchant of London, in all those tenements, lands, wood, rents, with meadows, feedings, pastures and all other appurtenances which Thomas Wake, her late husband, and herself had of the gift and feoffment of Simon de Braibrok, [*f. 41r*] parson of the church of Cransley, which lands and tenements Elizabeth inherited after the death of Hugh her father, except the tenement called 'Neuwemanere' in the said vill, to be held by John for life with warranty. Aforesaid witnesses.
Northampton, 26 June 1348, as appears more fully in the said indenture.
[Latin]

84 Memorandum that the said Agnes, daughter of John de Hegham, purchased in Orlingbury £3 annual rent issuing from 3 virgates of land which, if Agnes died without heir, would descend to Hugh Wake her half-brother. Agnes by her charter enfeoffed John Pyel in this rent, to be held by him and his heirs in perpetuity (*as touz iours*).
[French]

85 Hugh Wake enfeoffed by charter, dated 2 August 1349, for the term of his life, John Pyel and his heirs in the place called

'Neuwemanere' excluded in the above charter. [French]

86 And Sir Thomas Wake, son and heir of Elizabeth, made a
release enrolled in Chancery in April 1350, together with two
other releases of the same tenor, one sealed with the seal of the
mayoralty of London to witness his deed, of all the above
tenements as appears below.
[French]

87 [f. 41v] Release of Thomas son of Sir Thomas Wake, knight, to
John Pyel, citizen and merchant of London, his heirs and assigns,
of the manor of Cransley with advowson of the church there,
and a mill, and all other appurtenances which John first had of
the gift and feoffment of Elizabeth, mother of Thomas. Also of
a certain plot called 'la Neuwemanere' with woods [etc.] and all
appurtenances which John had of the grant of the said Elizabeth
and Hugh, brother of Thomas, in Cransley and Broughton, and
of all lands and tenements which the same John had of the gift
and feoffment of Agnes, sister of Thomas, in Orlingbury. [f. 42r]
Warranty.
Witnesses: Walter Turk, mayor of the city of London, Adam de
Bury and Ralph de Lenne, sheriffs, John de Wesenham, Simon
Fraunceys, Thomas Leggy, John Lovekyn, Adam Fraunceys,
Thomas de Brandon, Thomas de Langeton, Hugh de
Wichyngham, Robert Neuwent and others.
London, 21 April 1350.
Enrolled on dorse of Chancery Close Roll, April 1350.
[Latin]
[*CCR 1349–54*, 212.]

88 Hugh Wake, brother of Sir Thomas, made a release in London
of the same tenor as the release made by Sir Thomas to John
Pyel, and of the same date, and the release was enrolled in
Chancery in April 1350.
[French]
[*CCR 1349–54*, 216.]

89 And for all the time after Pyel was enfeoffed he was in full
possession of all the lands as written.
[French]

90 Simon de Braibrok, parson of the church of Cransley, who
claimed to be the nearest heir to the manor since the entailed
issue was extinct, made a release, 6 January 1353, to John Pyel.

And Braibrok took nothing in return for this release, which was
unnecessary (*de quelle reles' nestoit nul mestier*).
[French]

91 [*f. 42v*] Memorandum that Sir Thomas Wake, brother of Hugh,
in 1353 enfeoffed John de Langeton, parson of Blisworth, and
his heirs in perpetuity in the manor of Blisworth, Northants.,
with appurtenances, in which the said John re-enfeoffed Sir
Thomas and Alice his wife and their heirs, with remainder to
the right heirs of Thomas. The manor had descended to the said
Thomas after the death of Lady Elizabeth by the right of Sir
Thomas his father, with whom Elizabeth was joint feoffee for
life with remainder to the heirs of Sir Thomas senior.
[French]

92 John Pyel purchased for himself and his heirs and for William
Freman a tenement in Astwick near Brackley in 1350, with more
than 80 acres of land, with meadow and pasture and all other
appurtenances, from William Burgh of Brackley, which he had
purchased from Richard Dykons of Brackley, and which had
descended to the said Richard after the death of his father. And
William Freman made a release of these tenements to John Pyel.
[French]
[This entry cancelled.]

[*f. 43r*] The lands, tenements and rents purchased by John Pyel
in Wellingborough from Sir Robert de Morlee and Sir William
his son, for John Pyel and Adam Fraunceys jointly as appears
below. For which tenements, although Adam was joint feoffee,
the said John paid himself without any payment from Adam.

93 Charter of Robert de Morlee, knight and marshal of Ireland,
granting to Adam Fraunceys and John Pyel, citizens and merchants of London, a water-mill and all lands, tenements, rents
and services of both free and bond tenants in the vill of
Wellingborough with all appurtenances, wholly accruing by right
of inheritance to Robert after the death of William de Morlee
his father, to be held by Adam and John, their heirs and assigns
in perpetuity, of the chief lords of the fee by due services and
right customs. Warranty.
Witnesses: Simon de Drayton, John Daschton, knights, Henry
Grene junior, Nicholas Grene of Isham, Simon Simeon, John
Knyvet, Thomas de Byfeld, Simon de Rislee and Henry
Chepman of Finedon, Hugh Curteys, John Curteys and Adam

Bodeweye of Higham Ferrers, William le Lord, John Campeon, Thomas de Merden and Nicholas de Addington of Irthlingborough, Robert Colynessone, William Millere of Wellingborough and others.
Wellingborough, 1 August 1350.
Enrolled on dorse of Chancery Close Roll, May 1352.
[Latin]
[*CCR 1349–54*, 493]

94 [*f. 43v*] Letter of Robert de Morlee, knight and marshal of Ireland, appointing in his place Aubrey Rose of Irthlingborough, chaplain, John Campeon of the same and William Millere of Wellingborough his attorneys, jointly and severally to deliver to Adam Fraunceys and John Pyel, citizens and merchants of London, full and peaceful seisin of one water-mill and all lands, tenements, rents and services in Wellingborough which he granted by charter to the same Adam and John.
Wellingborough, 1 August, 1350.
[Latin]

95 Release of William de Morlee son and heir of Sir Robert de Morlee to Adam Fraunceys and John Pyel of all right in one mill and all rents and services of free and bond tenants, with suits of court, wardships, marriages, reliefs, escheats and all other appurtenances which the same Adam and John had of the gift and feoffment of Sir Robert in Wellingborough, which the said William should inherit after Robert's death. [*f. 44r*] Warranty.
Witnesses: Simon de Drayton, John Daschton, knights, Henry Grene, Nicholas Grene, John Campeoun, Thomas de Merden and others.
Wellingborough, 10 August 1350.
[Latin]

96 Memorandum that further to the above charter, letter of attorney and release, an indenture was made between the said Sir Robert of the one part and the said Adam and John of the other, that if Adam and John hold the above tenements for fifteen years after the date of the charter quitly and peacefully, and at the end of the term return them to Sir Robert ...[1] Whereupon it was agreed by the two parties, 15 May 1352, that the indentures had been broken, and for the sum of 100 marks, a tun of wine priced £7 0s 11d, and other expenses amounting to 10 marks, Sir Robert made a release to Adam and John of all the above tenements on the same day and had it enrolled in Chancery in

May 1352 as appears below, and at the same time he had enrolled there the charter made by him above.

[French]

1 Clause omitted.

[This memorandum was subsequently cancelled.]

97 [*f. 44v*] Release by Robert de Morlee, knight and marshal of Ireland, to Adam Fraunceys and John Pyel, citizens and merchants of London, their heirs and assigns of all right in one mill and all lands, tenements, rents and services [etc.] which Adam and John recently had of Robert's gift and feoffment in Wellingborough. Warranty.

Witnesses: Simon Fraunceys, Richard Lacer, John Lovekyn, Ralph de Lenne, John de Stodeye, Simon de Bedyngton, Adam de Acres, Thomas de Brandon, John de Horsford, John Albon, Thomas de Langeton, Richard de Causton, John de Chichestre, goldsmith, William de Hatfeld, goldsmith, Walter de Harwedon, currier, and others.

London, 15 May 1352.

Enrolled on dorse of Chancery Close Roll, May 1352.

[Latin]

[*CCR 1349–54*, 494]

98 [*f. 45r*] And memorandum that the said tenements in Wellingborough with all appurtenances descended to Sir William de Morlee as his right inheritance, and after his death they descended to Sir Robert de Morlee, knight, son and heir of Sir William. And when Robert's own son and heir William married Cecily, the daughter of Sir Thomas Bardolf, he promised to grant to William his son and Cecily for their sustenance, for the term of the life of Cecily, land totalling £100 *pa*, to revert after her death to Robert and his heirs, and by way of surety Sir Robert made a bond to Sir Thomas Bardolf, father of Cecily, of £2,000. And it was agreed between them that the tenements in Wellingborough should be a parcel of the £100 *pa*. But Sir Robert had not at any time enfeoffed Sir William or Cecily his wife in anything before the date of the above charter and release, nor had Sir Robert ever been out of possession of the said tenements in Wellingborough before he enfeoffed Adam Fraunceys and John Pyel.

[French]

99 John Pyel himself purchased these tenements etc. both in

Cransley and in Wellingborough and he alone paid all the money, but then John Pyel enfeoffed the parson of Cransley and others in the manor of Cransley with appurtenances and the feoffees re-enfeoffed Adam Fraunceys and John Pyel in the said manor as appears below, and Adam paid to John Pyel for his part in the manor £200 etc.
[French]

[Folio 45v blank.]

[f. 46r]   Irthlingborough and Finedon

100 On 26 January 1351 John de Keteringge enfeoffed John his son, and John Pyel in all his lands and tenements in Irthlingborough with appurtenances, [with reversion] to the heirs of his son, and if he should die without heir to the said John [Pyel] and his heirs, and should Pyel die without heir, to the heirs of John Keteringge [senior], paying to the said John Keteringge a rent of £3 for the term of his life as appears by an indenture made between them. And then, on 17 February 1367, John son of John de Keterynge enfeoffed by charter the said John Pyel, his heirs and assigns in all the lands and tenements that he held of his father in Irthlingborough and Finedon in exchange for certain tenements in Northampton. And on 1 June 1368 the said John Keteryng junior made a release with warranty to Pyel of all the lands and tenements, as appears below.
[French]

101 Memorandum that Simon Herleys of Finedon leased in 1351 (*lan xxv*^{te})^1 to William Colyns and his wife all tenements in Finedon with all appurtenances in fee at a rent for the first six years of 40s *pa*, and afterwards £20. And Simon granted this rent with the reversion of all the aforesaid lands and tenements in the same year to John Pyel and John Keteringge as appears by his deed, and the said William attorned to them.
[French]

    1 Cf. **181** where the date is given as 1350.

102 John Pyel purchased for himself and John Keteringge in fee in 1351 from William Roo a vacant plot, a large part of which lay next to the plot which belonged to the said Simon [Herleys], and on which the gates belonging to the above plot are fixed (*sur quelle place les portz sont assiz partenant al place susdit*). And the deed

of William Roo was enrolled in the court of Simon Symeon in
Finedon, 20 September 1321.
[French]

103 One plot with lands and appurtenances descended to the said
John Pyel after the death of his father in Irthlingborough in 1348
(*lan xxij*^{e}), of which the parcels of this and all other purchases etc.
are written more fully in another paper.
[French]
[This entry cancelled by light pen strokes.]

104 [*f. 46v*] First Pyel purchased in 1348 around 9 acres of land with
meadow, and a plot with dovecote and appurtenances, and
dowerland (*une douwere*) which Miriele, widow of Asceleyn le
Ferthelord, held of William Freman in Little Addington.
[French]

105 Item Pyel purchased in fee of Robert Cake in 1352 (*lan xxvj*^{e}) $2\frac{1}{2}$
acres of land with appurtenances in Little Addington.
[French]

106 Item Pyel purchased of Emma, who was the wife of Simon le
Cartere, in 1352, for the term of her life, 5 acres of land in Little
Addington.
[French]

107 Item Pyel purchased in 1351 (*lan xxv*^{e}) for himself and for John
Campion of John Dengayne of Stilton a plot and around $2\frac{1}{2}$ virgates of land with other plots, meadows and all other appurtenances in Little Addington and with $1\frac{1}{2}$ virgates of land in demesne
and one virgate of land with services and all other appurtenances in Great Addington, Twywell and Slipton. For which lands
Pyel alone paid.[1] And John Campioun made a full release to
John Pyel on 1 June 1354 of the above lands and tenements.
[French]

    1 Added later.

108 [*f. 47r*] Item Pyel purchased in fee from Thomas Miriden and
Nicholas Addington on 24 September 1352 all lands and tenements which they had of the feoffment of John, son of Henry
de Haddone, in Irthlingborough at an annual rent to one or
both of them of 40s for twenty-five years, and thereafter £20 *pa*
as appears by the indentures made between them. And[1] Nicholas

died about Michaelmas 1353 and Thomas made a release, about 27 April 1354, to John Pyel in perpetuity of a moiety of the said lands and tenements, and Margaret who was the daughter of John de Haddon in her virginity made another release to the said Pyel. Item[2] the said Thomas made a release of the remainder of the said lands and tenements on 30 September 1354 with warranty.
[French]

1 This sentence added by a new hand.
2 The final sentence added, possibly by a third hand, and subsequently cancelled by light pen strokes.

109 Item Pyel purchased in fee in 1349 (*lan xiij*[r]) of William Brabasoun of Rushden 6 acres of meadow in 'Longdole' and 'Thurgersholm' for £5 5s on condition that payment be made within three weeks of Easter 1349.
[French]

110 And memorandum that on 1 March 1369 Isabel, the other daughter of John de Haddone, twenty-three years of age and in her pure virginity, made two releases to John Pyel in fee of the tenements which belonged to her father in Irthlingborough, with warranty. And Pyel gave £20 at the marriage of Isabel by reason of the said releases, and of his bounty gave a further 20 marks.
[French]

[*f. 47v*] Tenements purchased by John Pyel from Sir Simon de Drayton in Irthlingborough

111 Charter of Simon de Drayton, knight, granting to John Pyel of Irthlingborough, Adam Fraunceys of London and Henry Pyel, brother of John, his manor in Irthlingborough with the reversions of all his tenancies for life, homages, wardships, reliefs, escheats when they occur, suits of court and all other rights and appurtenances belonging to the said manor, and all his other lands and tenements in Irthlingborough except those lands and tenements which were formerly of Henry le Bakere, which tenements the grantor had by right of his wife, to be held in perpetuity by John, Adam and Henry, and the heirs and assigns of John, of the chief lords of the fee by due services and right customs. Warranty.
Witnesses: Henry Grene junior, John de Ashtone, Thomas Miriden of Irthlingborough, John Campion of the same, Nicholas Ading-

ton of Irthlingborough, John Curteys of Higham, and others.
Irthlingborough, 10 February 1353.
[Latin]

112 [*f. 48r*] Sir Simon made a release with warranty to John Pyel
alone, 24 February 1353, and he made another charter to the
said John alone of the same tenor and date as the charter written
above. For which tenements Pyel himself paid £200 and a tun
of wine priced 100s to Sir Simon.
[French]

113 John de Drayton, son and heir of Sir Simon, made a release
with warranty to John Pyel on 1 August 1358 as appears below.[1]
[French]

    [1] The release was not transcribed.

[*f. 48v*] The tenements purchased by John Pyel in Northampton
in 1353 and after.

114 First [John Pyel] purchased, on 3 March 1353, from Simon
Launshull (MS:Lampthull) of Finedon the tenements and rents
written below as appears by his charter written hereafter [**116**].
First a tenement with appurtenances in 'Goldstret', Northampton,
between the tenement of John Plomer on one side and that of
Simon de Grafton on the other, which Simon Averai and Alice
his wife hold of the grant of the said Simon [Launshull] for the
term of their two lives at an annual rent of 14s, and they maintain
the tenements at their own cost.[1] Sold to Robert Stowe 1358.
Item a tenement in the narrow lane called 'Lariestwychyne' with
a garden which lies near the tenement of William Durnasal and
the tenement of Richard de Stratford, together with a shop near
William Wythemale on the north side, which tenement, garden
and shop Philip Pifford and Margery his wife hold for life by
indented charter of the grant of the said Simon, at an annual
rent of 20s for the first twenty years beginning 1351 and thereafter
40s each year, and they maintain the houses at their own cost.
Item a curtilage in 'Bocheresrowe' next to the tenement of Simon
Lorifer to the west, which Thomas Campion, butcher, and Joan
his wife hold for life, by indented charter of the grant of Simon
[Launshull] at a rent of 3s *pa* and their maintenance. And Pyel
has these indentures in his possession.
[French]

    1 This section cancelled. In margin: *Vendu ceste tenement al Paske anno xxxij° a
Robert Stowe draper.*

115 [*f. 49r*] Item[1] the said Pyel purchased of the said Simon [Launshull] a shop in the Poultry at Northampton next to the tenement of John de Staunforde, which shop Nicholas Trank holds of John Pyel at will paying a yearly rent of 12s, of which 4s to be paid at the house of Dingley.[2]
[French]

   1 Margin: *vacat quia venditur.*
   2 The preceptory of the Knights Hospitallers. See *VCH Northants* ii, 142–4.

116 Charter[1] of Simon son of Simon de Launshull of Finedon granting to John Pyel, citizen of London, all his tenements with rents and services and reversions with appurtenances, which were bequeathed to him by Simon his father in his will, proved and enrolled in the court at Northampton, 12 June 1346, before Peter de Boys, mayor of that town, to be held by John Pyel, his heirs and assigns, of the chief lords of the fee by due services and right customs in perpetuity. Warranty. And Amice wife of Simon of her own will and without compulsion, being duly examined in full pleas of husting at Northampton, ratified this recognizance and deed and released and forfeited all her right and claim in the said tenements by reason of dowry, purchase or other title whatsoever, to John Pyel, his heirs and assigns. [*f. 49v*] And because his seal is unknown, the donor caused the seal of the mayoralty of Northampton to be appended.
Witnesses: Richard Garlekmongere, mayor of Northampton, Robert Spicer and Alan de Wakerle, bailiffs of the same, Philip de Pifforde, John de Strattone, ?Honorius [*onorio*] of St Jean de la Porte, Nicholas Trank, coroner of Northampton, John Garlekmongere, William Wyne, Laurence de Stratton, Thomas Tylly, Simon de Houghton, John Molyner, clerk, and others. Northampton, 3 March 1353.
This charter was enrolled 6 May [1353] in full husting at Northampton before Richard Garlekmongere, mayor, and the coroner etc.
[Latin]

   1 Margin: *vacat*

117 And memorandum[1] that the tenements purchased of Simon Launshull in Northampton were claimed by the collectors of fifteenths, when they were granted to the king, to be worth 8s *pa*, because all the tenements which belonged to Simon his father were charged to pay to the fifteenth, when it was granted, 8s *pa*, and because the collectors found these tenements nearer than

others they distrain in that place at about 8s for the fifteenth (*les coilleurs troevent celes tenementz plus pres qe autres ils destreynent illoeques pour les viij s. enturs pur la dite xv^e*).
[French]

1 Margin (bracketed with **118** and **119**): *vacat.*

118 And memorandum that of the tenements which belonged to the said Simon which will be charged to pay 8s, William Smyth de Hardingstone held in Hardingstone, Preston and Hackleton, Northants., tenements which are worth 40s *pa*. Item John Burles held with his wife divers lands and tenements in Finedon and Benefield which will be charged. Item Simon Launshull and William Colyn, who married the daughter of Simon, held in Finedon divers lands and tenements which will be charged.
[French]

119 [*f. 50r*] And memorandum that John Pyel enfeoffed John Keteryng of Irthlingborough in the abovesaid tenements, curtilage and two shops with appurtenances in Northampton in exchange for certain lands and tenements in Irthlingborough and Finedon, 17 February 1367, to be held in perpetuity by the feoffee and the heirs of his body, namely the tenement with garden lying in the narrow lane called 'Laurencetwychen' in Northampton near the tenement of William Durnesale and that of Richard de Stratford, together with one shop near William Wythemale on the north side, which tenement, garden and shop Philip Pyfford and Margery his wife held and which Robert Golofre now holds, and the curtilage lying in 'Bocheresrowe' in Northampton next to the tenement of Simon Lorifer to the west, which curtilage Thomas Campyoun, butcher, and Joan his wife hold, and the other shop is in the Poultry at Northampton next to the tenement of John de Staunfford, which shop Nicholas Trank holds. And the said Keterynge will pay an annual rent of 5s for these tenements, and should he die without heir they will return to the said Pyel and his heirs in perpetuity as appears in an indenture made between Pyel and Keterynge on 17 February 1367.
[French]

120 [*f. 50v*] Memorandum that John Pyel enfeoffed Robert, parson of the church of All Saints in Irthlingborough and William de Lubbenham, chaplain, and their heirs, 20 May 1353, in a messuage, cottages and a croft with appurtenances which belonged to Sir Nicholas de Addington, and then to Simon de

Drayton, knight, in which messuage etc. the said Simon enfeoffed
John Pyel and his heirs.
[French]

121 And memorandum that the said Robert and William enfeoffed
Aubrey Rose, chaplain, and Henry son of Simon and their heirs
in perpetuity with warranty in the said messuage, cottages, garden
and croft, 11 June 1353.
[French]

[*f. 51r*] The lands purchased of Sir John du Boys in Woodford in
the county of Northampton in 1354, as appears by the copy of
an indenture written below.

122 Indenture made between Sir John du Boys and John Pyel of
Irthlingborough witnessing that Sir John du Boys granted to John
Pyel his manor of Woodford with all rights and appurtenances,
messuages, lands, meadows, grazing-land, pastures, rents, reversions, wardships, reliefs, homages, escheats, suits of court and all
other rights and easements pertaining to the said manor, except
the advowson of Woodford church, to be held by John Pyel and
his assigns of Sir John de Boys and his heirs for life plus one
year by paying to them as chief lords of the fee due services and
customs. And if John Pyel should die within ten years of the date
of these presents then the donor wills and grants that the
executors or assigns of John Pyel may hold the said manor until
the completion of the term of ten years for the said services. [*f.
51v*] Warranty. And John de Boys wills and grants for himself
and his heirs that John Pyel, his executors or assigns are not
responsible for waste or distraint made on the said manor,
except in the following buildings, namely in the principal
chamber, the sheep-house, grange, stable, the cattle-shed with
old hay-barn adjoining, granary and kitchen, which buildings
the lessee will maintain in the condition or better in which
he received them. These buildings, on the day on which he
received them, were old, ruinous, weak and poorly roofed and
were valued at £10. And the donor granted that [the lessees]
were in no way liable for any waste or distraint in the
aforesaid buildings, or in others existing within the manor,
beyond the sum of £10, but were only liable for the value of
waste up to the sum of £10.
Witnesses: Thomas Bosoun, John Shakel, John de Lenton of
Woodford, William le Lord, Thomas Miriden, John Campioun,

John Miriden, Robert Hardy, John Stephenes, William Freman of Irthlingborough and others.
Woodford, 22 April 1354.
[Latin]

123 [*f. 52r*] Release by John de Boys, knight, lord of Coningsby, co. Lincoln, to John Pyel of Irthlingborough his heirs and assigns of the manor of Woodford with all appurtenances and easements as fully as the same John Pyel now has and holds the manor of his grant and demise. Warranty.
Witnesses: Simon Fraunceys, John Malwayn, John Lovekyn, John Wroth, Thomas de Langeton, Thomas de Santon, clerk, and others.
London, 1 May 1354.

124 Charter of John de Boys, knight, of Coningsby granting to Adam Fraunceys and John Pyel, citizens of London, an annual rent of £20 sterling to be received of the grantor's manor of Coningsby and of all his other lands in the said county, to be held by Adam and John, their heirs and assigns in perpetuity. Licence granted [*f. 52v*] to enter the said manor and lands and distrain the goods and chattels found there whenever the said rent fell into arrears. And the grantor has placed the said Adam and John Pyel in full seisin of the annual rent by payment of 20s.
Witnesses: [As in **123**.]
London, 1 May 1354.
[Latin]

125 Notification that John de Boys, knight, lord of Coningsby is bound to John Pyel, merchant, in £200 for merchandise bought from him, to be paid to the same John Pyel or his attorney showing this letter or his executors at the Nativity of St John the Baptist next after the date of these presents. And if he does not do this, de Boys grants that he, his heirs and executors will incur the distraint and damages provided in the statute at Westminster for merchants issued in the time of Edward I.
London, 1 May 1354.
[Latin]

126 [*f. 53r*] Indenture made between Sir John du Boys, knight, lord of Coningsby, of the one part, and Adam Fraunceys and John Pyel, citizens of London, of the other part, witnessing that whereas the said Sir John du Boys had by charter of feoffment granted to the said Adam and John Pyel an annual rent of £20 from his manor of Coningsby and all his other lands and

tenements with appurtenances in the said county as appears
more fully in the said annuity, notwithstanding this Adam and
John Pyel grant that if Sir John, his heirs or executors or anyone
else acting in their name, pay or cause to be paid to Adam and
John, or to one of them, for life and to their executors one year
after the death of the one who lives longer, in the close of St
Helen's London, or in the town of Irthlingborough, 16 marks
annually, then the said annuity of £20 will lose its force for ever.
And also, whereas the said Sir John had leased the manor of
Woodford in the county of Northampton entirely with all its
appurtenances to John Pyel for life, and to his executors one
year after his death as is more fully contained in an indenture
made between them, and the same Sir John had released and
quitclaimed to John Pyel all his right and claim in that manor
as is more fully contained in the release made thereof, and
whereas he is also bound to John Pyel by a statute merchant in
£200 to be paid according to the tenor of the same statute,
notwithstanding this, the said John Pyel grants that if Sir John
[du Boys], his heirs and executors pay annually to the said Adam
and John Pyel [f. 53v] for life and to their executors one year
after the death of the one who survives 16 marks in the aforesaid
manner, then the release made to John Pyel of the manor of
Woodford will be held null. And John Pyel also grants that if he
might enjoy freely the said manor of Woodford for life plus one
year as appears in the said indenture, then the said statute of
£200 will lose its force in perpetuity. And Sir John du Boys
grants that if he or any other in his name fail in any payment
of the above 16 marks *pa* in part or in whole contrary to the
above form, then the said release will remain in full force. And
if the said John Pyel, his heirs and assigns, are disturbed in any
way in future of the fee of the said manor or of any part of it
by the said Sir John or by any other, Sir John grants that the
statute of £200 will remain in force. And the said Sir John wills
and grants that no acquittance made by him elsewhere than in
the close of St Helen's, London, or in the town of Irthlingborough
and [otherwise than] indented might have any value or be a
substitute.
London, 3 May 1354.
[French]
[The above indenture was cancelled with light pen strokes.]

127 Memorandum that the above were purchased from Sir John de
Boys by Pyel himself, and he alone paid all the money.
[French]

128 [*f. 54r*] Charter of John Boys, knight, granting to John Pyel of Irthlingborough $\frac{1}{2}$ acre of land with appurtenances in Woodford, of which one side abuts on the tenement of Richard de la Souche, knight, to the south, which the same Richard purchased of Thomas Tychemersch, together with the advowson of the church of Woodford, these lands and advowson with all their appurtenances and rights to be held by John Pyel, his heirs and assigns, of the chief lords of the fee by services due thereof and right customs in perpetuity. Also release and quitclaim by the grantor of all right and claim in the manor of Woodford with all appurtenances and in the said lands and advowson. Warranty. *Witnesses*: Richard la Souche, knight, John Lenton, Roger Leycestre, John Shakel, Roger Herberd, Richard Norreys, Robert Veer and others.
4 November 1363.
Enrolled on the dorse of the Close Roll in the month of November of the above year.
[Latin]
[*CCR 1360–4*, 554]

129 [*f. 54v*] Charter of Thomas son and heir of John Tichemersch of Woodford near Thrapston granting to John Pyel of Irthlingborough one messuage and 1 virgate of arable land with meadows, grazing-land, pastures and all other appurtenances, which William Barkere lately held of the grantor in Little Addington, to be held by the said John, his heirs and assigns in perpetuity of the chief lord of the fee by due services and right customs. Warranty.
Witnesses: John Campioun, Robert Hardy, John Miriden of Irthlingborough, Walter Daundelyn, Nicholas Pygot, Thomas Daundelyn of Addington, Thomas Beson, John Lenton and John Schakele of Woodford and others.
Little Addington, 11 June 1354.
[Latin]

130 [*f. 55r*] Letter patent that whereas John Druel of Newington leased to Thomas Maister of Ringstead and Elizabeth his wife for the term of their lives 20 acres of land and 2 acres of meadow in Great Addington which John Geffrey held, and Thomas died and Michael de Staunford married the aforesaid Elizabeth, and John Druel quitclaimed to Michael and Elizabeth, their heirs and assigns, all his right and claim which he had in the said tenements with their appurtenances, Michael and Elizabeth his wife granted to John Pyel of Irthlingborough, his heirs and

assigns the aforesaid 20 acres and 2 acres of meadow with appurtenances, to be held by John Pyel, his heirs and assigns of the chief lords. And because the said Elizabeth on the day these presents were made was married to Michael, she pledged her faith of her own free will and without compulsion, and touching the Holy Gospels she took the corporal oath that she would not press any right or claim in the said land or tenements in future. *Witnesses*: Robert Veer, Henry atte Welle, John Bone Kyrke of Addington, William Lord, John Campion etc.
Irthlingborough, 15 January 1355.
[Latin]

[*f. 55v*] Memorandum how John Pyel granted the manor of Cransley etc. and Adam Fraunceys and Pyel were re-enfeoffed as appears below.

131 Charter of John Pyel of Irthlingborough, citizen and merchant of London, granting to Simon de Braibrok, rector of the church of Cransley, John Preest of Higham Ferrers, chaplain and Richard Brian, chaplain, the manor of Cransley with all rights and appurtenances, together with the advowson of Cransley church and all other lands and tenements, rents and services with appurtenances which the grantor had in the same vill, and all goods and chattels on the said manor and tenements, to be held by the said Simon, John and Richard, their heirs and assigns, of the chief lords of the fee by the services due thereof. Warranty.
Witnesses: [Walter Dalderby, lord of Loddington], John de Cranes-lee, Simon Welewes of Cransley, Thomas of St Germans (*de Sancto Germano*), [John Campioun, John Miriden, John Keteringge of Irthlingborough].
Cransley, 9 March 1355.
Enrolled on the dorse of the Close Roll in the month of April 1355.
[Latin]
[*CCR 1354–60*, 190]

132 [*f. 56r*] Charter of Simon de Braibrok, John Preest of Higham Ferrers, chaplain, and Richard Brian, chaplain, granting to Adam Fraunceys, citizen of London, and John Pyel of Irthlingborough the manor of Cransley which the grantors had of the feoffment of the aforesaid John Pyel, with all rights and appurtenances, together with the advowson of Cransley church and all lands and tenements, rents and services which they had of the feoffment of John Pyel, and all goods and chattels thereon, to be held of

the chief lords of the fee by due services. Warranty.
Witnesses: [Walter Dalderby, knight, Thomas of St Germans (*de Sancto Germano*), John de Craneslee, John de Waldegrave, William de Harwedone, John Leukenore.]
Cransley, 21 March 1355.
Enrolled on the dorse of the Close Roll in the month of April 1355.
[Latin]
[*CCR 1354–60*, 191]

133 And memorandum that the said Adam Fraunceys paid on the above date [21 March 1355] to John Pyel £200 for his part of the purchase of the said manor.
[French]

134 [*f. 56v*] John Pyel purchased on 21 March 1355 from the abbey and convent of Peterborough for 60 years a plot in Irthlingborough which lies on a corner of a little lane near the church of St Peter in Irthlingborough on one side and the tenement of the said John on the other and to the west next to the lane called 'Heireslane', and the whole plot comprises in width next to the said lane, 51½ feet, and in length next to the said church, 76 feet, as appears in an indenture sealed both with the seals of the abbot and the seal of the convent. And John Pyel was to pay to the abbot and convent 8d *pa* for all services until the end of the term of 60 years.
[French]

135 [*f. 57r*] Pyel purchased on 19 December 1355 from Robert Hardy two pieces of land of which one is called 'la Redewong' in East Field and comprises 3½ acres in 14 selions, and is held of the king's fee in Finedon, and the other piece [is] in 'Holbusk' on 'Longlondes' between two hedges, which contains 5 acres and is of the same fee. Pyel was enfeoffed in these two pieces on this day as appears by the copy of the charter written below, and the inspections (*veuwes*) written then were delivered to the said John Pyel.
[French]

136 Charter of Robert Hardi of Irthlingborough to John Pyel, citizen of London, granting two pieces of arable land in the field of Irthlingborough, of which one is called 'la Redwong' in 'Crakestonefeld' and lies between two boundary markers there and abuts on 'le Chirchehaflond' on the north side and on the

land of John Pyel and the land formerly of John Collessone
on the south side, and the other lies in 'Holwbuskfeld' near
'Thingdenecros' in 'le Longewing' between one boundary mark
to the south and the land of William le Eir to the north and
abuts on the headland of William le Lord to the west and on
the land of John Stevenes to the east, to be held of the chief
[lords]. Warranty.
Witnesses: [Not recorded.]
Irthlingborough, 19 December 1355.
[Latin]

137 [*f. 57v*] Memorandum that John Pyel purchased on 15 August
1357 of Robert Hardi ½ acre of land in 'Holbosk' next to the land
of John Pyel on both sides by a charter made at the time.
[French]

138 Memorandum that John Pyel held there of John Stevene 3 roods
of land which Pyel had bought from Robert Hardi in exchange
for 3 roods of his own land on 'Brookfurlong' near 'Helewys
Haddon'.
[French]

139 [*f. 58r*] Memorandum that whereas John Collesone enfeoffed
Emma, his wife, for life in his messuage in Irthlingborough, in 3
acres of land, one piece of meadow and [another piece called]
'Fordole' in the fields and meadows of Irthlingborough, of which
the messuage lies in width between the tenements of the abbey
of Peterborough on both sides and in length from the highway
of Irthlingborough to the narrow lane which looks onto the
church of All Saints, and of the 3 acres, 3 roods lie in a selion
below 'Knythlondhavedone' and extend as far as 'Wak-
kemedesyk', ½ acre lies on 'Aprillesakyr' next to the land of John
Pyel, ½ acre on 'Clerkeswelle' next to the land of John Whitelok,
1 rood at 'Brokkesdalehavedon' and extends onto 'le Kyke-
havedon', 1½ roods on 'le Hangendhull' next to the land of Alice
le Milnere, 1¼ roods at 'Wakkemede' next to the land of John
Pyel, and 1 rood on 'Sharpewelle' next to the land of William
Lord, and one piece of meadow called 'Fordole' lies in 'Tounholm' at 'Stennyng', and the other lies in 'Tounholm' near the
River Nene to the east and the meadow of Sir John Semor to
the west and comprises 30 perches in length and 11 perches in
width. And whereas the messuage, lands and meadows should
revert after the death of the said Emma to John son of the
aforesaid John Collesone as his rightful inheritance, this said

John broke out of the prison of Peterborough and seized the land and was later arrested and died in Leicester prison in 1355, and by way of forfeiture the said tenements, lands and meadows fell to the chief lords of the fees and the said messuage and meadows to John Pyel as of his fee. And inquisition should be made [to ascertain] of what fees the land is composed and if he [?John Collesone] has more (*et del terre soit enquis de quelle fees il est et sil ad plus*).
[French]

140 [*f. 58v*] Memorandum that on 8 May 1356 in the church of All Saints, Irthlingborough, in the presence of Robert, parson of the said church, John Keterynge, John Campioun, William Freman, son of the said Emma [wife of John Collesone], and others, John Pyel stated that Emma had surrendered to him her interest in the aforesaid messuage, lands and meadows, of her own free will, and a deed to this effect was made on the advice of John Campion and William Freman. And when the deed was due to have been sealed the said Emma was informed of a deed whereby the said John, son of John [Collesone] was supposed to have enfeoffed Margaret his wife and her heirs, at which [those present] were astonished, and John Pyel complained that this had been done to remove him from his right. Whereupon Emma, in the presence of the said parson, Keteringge, Pyel, Campioun and Freman and others, was asked whether she or anyone in her place had ever attorned to Margaret or any other in the aforesaid messuage, lands and meadows in which she was enfeoffed for life by virtue of the said deed or by other means, and she said and swore that she had never attorned to anyone in anything. For which reason among others it seemed to John Pyel that the said deed[1] was without force.
[French]

1 I.e. the deed between John Collesone and his wife Margaret.

[An intriguing incident. It seems that the information about the earlier deed was revealed in the church, presumably by someone present to witness the sealing of the first deed and acting in the interests of Margaret Collesone.]

141 And memorandum that soon after the above forfeiture a parcel of the aforesaid messuage which Thomas Freman holds reverted to Pyel, and $1\frac{1}{2}$ roods on the 'Brendelondes' which was purchased from Robert Hardy, and 1 rood on 'Bradeburk' which the said

John son of John [Collesone] had in his possession.
[French]

142 [*f. 59r*] Memorandum that John Pyel purchased of Sir Walter
Dalderbi, 17 November 1354, 1 virgate of land which Simon de
Craneslee, parson of Great Oxendon, held of Sir Walter, together
with all the other lands, tenements and rents which the said
Walter had in Cransley, to be held by the said John and his
assigns, for life and two years after his death at an annual rent
of 20s payable to the said Walter. Warranty as appears by an
indenture made on the above date between the said Walter and
the said John.
[French]
[Very faint pen stroke crossing text as if in cancellation.]

143 [*f. 59v*] Memorandum that John Pyel and John Curteys of
Higham Ferrers purchased from John de la Parte (?Paste) of
Northampton and Isabel his wife a malting (*un molyn a brees*) and
a wheat mill situated in a house in Northampton, to be held by
the purchasers, their heirs and assigns in perpetuity as appears
by a charter sealed with the seal of the mayoralty of Northampton
enrolled in the memoranda of the husting of Northampton in
the time of John Goos, mayor of that town, 17 April 1357.
[French]

144 Item John Pyel and John Curteys re-enfeoffed the said John and
Isabel and John Wayn their son of the said mills for the term of
their three lives at a rent of 100s *pa*, by surety of a bond of £100
by statute merchant made in London to the said John Pyel alone,
and the re-enfeoffment was made 9 April 1357.
[French]

145 [*f. 60r*] Item John Pyel purchased from William Eyr of Irthlingborough 3 roods of land in Upwell in fee simple. Item Pyel
purchased a piece of a garden on the edge of Irthlingborough,
in the direction of Higham Ferrers, from John Bothewey and
Agnes his wife, paying them 6d *pa*. Item [Pyel purchased] from
Thomas Shadewe a piece of a garden in the same place, for
which Pyel granted two ponds (*estanks*), which Margery (*Magge*)
Parys once held for 2s *pa*, [and Shadewe] paid to the said Pyel
18d for the ponds. Item Pyel purchased in the same place of
John Makeseye a plot of ground and a garden in return for
which Pyel granted him a cottage next to the gate of Helewys
Haddon.
[French]

[The above entries cancelled]

146. Item the said Pyel purchased from Henry son of Simon by charter 6 roods of land above 'le Belf'' in Irthlingborough, on which John Pyel has put a mill.
[French]

[Folio 60v blank.]

147 [*f. 61r*] Charter of John Daundelyn senior of Cranford, Northants., granting to John Pyel, citizen and merchant of London, and Joan his wife an annual rent of £10 for life to be raised from all the donor's lands, tenements and rents with appurtenances in Cranford and Lyveden, Northants., and elsewhere in the county. And the donor put John Pyel and Joan in seisin of the rent by payment of 10s.
Witnesses: William Lord of Irthlingborough, Thomas Miriden, John Miriden, John Campion, John Stevene of the same, Richard de Hoo of Cranford, John de May of the same, and others.
Cranford, 20 October 1357.
[Latin]
Text cancelled by two faint diagonal cross-strokes of the pen.

148 Charter of John son of John Daundelyn of Cranford that whereas John Daundelyn senior enfeoffed for life John Pyel and Joan his wife of the above rent issuing from all lands, tenements and rents in Cranford and Lyveden and elsewhere in co. Northampton, [*f. 61v*] which after the death of his father should revert to himself, he has granted and confirmed (*ratificasse*) for himself and his heirs, with warranty, the interest and right which John Pyel and Joan have in the said rent. And because his seal is unknown he had the seal of office of Adam Fraunceys, mayor of the Staple of Westminster, and that of John Daundelyn his father appended to these presents at his instance and personal request.
Witnesses: Fulk de Horwod, Nicholas Punge, Robert de Lychefeld, Nicholas Anketil, John de Rounhale and others.
London, 20 October 1357.
[Latin]

149 Recognizance by John Daundelyn senior of Cranford and John his son, that they are bound, jointly and wholly, to John Pyel, citizen and merchant of London, in 100 marks for merchandise

purchased of him in the Staple of Westminster, to be paid to the same John Pyel or his attorney, heirs or 'executors in London, 2 February next [1358]. And unless they pay what is incurred by them the penalty ordained in the statute of the Staple for the recovery of these debts [will be exacted].
Staple of Westminster, 21 October 1357.
[Latin]

150 [*f. 62r*] Indenture witnessing that whereas John Daundelyn senior of Cranford enfeoffed John Pyel and Joan his wife for life in a rent of £10 [**147**], and whereas John son of John Daundelyn confirmed their right and interest in the said rent [**148**], and whereas John Daundelyn senior and John his son are bound by statute merchant to John Pyel in 100 marks [**149**], the said John Pyel and Joan his wife will and grant jointly and severally for themselves, their heirs and executors, that if John Daundelyn and John his son or either of them, their heirs or executors, pay to John and Joan Pyel or their executors at Irthlingborough for the term of their lives, or of the one who survives, £4 annually, then all the aforesaid writings and statutes will be cancelled and held null in future. And if John Daundelyn and his son neglect to pay the sum for one month beyond the term due, then all the above writings will remain in force, and that no acquittance for payment may take place or effect unless it has been made at Irthlingborough.[1] Moreover [*f. 62v*] John Daundelyn senior affirmed to John Pyel on oath that 2 carucates of his land at Cranford which are of the fee of the earl of Gloucester on the day this present indenture was made were not entailed.
London, 21 October 1357.
[Latin]

    1 The text to this point cancelled.

151 Charter of John Daundelyn senior of Cranford, granting to Adam Fraunceys, citizen of London, and Henry Pyel, clerk, 4s and one capon annual rent issuing from 8 acres of land with appurtenances which William Nichol holds of the grantor for life in Cranford, together with the reversion of the same 8 acres. Also 8s 8d and four capons annual rent issuing from two cottages and 12 acres of land with appurtenances which William de Arderne holds for life in Cranford, together with the reversion of the same after his death. Likewise 2s and two capons issuing from a cottage with appurtenances which Richard Lomb and Agnes his wife hold for life in the parish of Cranford St Andrew, with reversion of the same cottage, 20d and two capons issuing from a plot of land which Richard Adam holds in the same parish, 8d and five capons and a hen from three cottages with appurtenances which Nicholas Gykke holds for life in Cranford St Andrew, with reversion of the three cottages. Also six barbed arrows which the grantor used to receive from the lands and tenements of Walter, John and Thomas Daundelyn of [f. 63r] Little Addington, with wardships, marriages, reliefs, escheats and scutages when they occur. Moreover, 10 acres of meadow and pasture in Cranford, of which 8 acres lie on 'Coswayneswong' and 2 acres called 'Hordesholm' lie next to the river there, one croft of land called Barton Orchard lying in Cranford. All the above lands, tenements, rents, meadows and pastures, with all appurtenances are held of the fee of the earl of Gloucester. John Daundelyn also granted to Adam Fraunceys and Henry Pyel all his tenements, rents, meadows, pastures with reversions which he had jointly or separately in Cranford, Little Addington and Barton, which are held of the fee of the said earl of Gloucester, with 13s 4d annual rent raised from the tenement, and $\frac{1}{2}$ virgate of land held for life by William Gotherde in Cranford with reversion after his death, and one pair of gloves price 1 [?shilling][1] sterling annual rent issuing from the lands and tenements of John Pyel in Great and Little Addington, to be held by Adam and Henry, their heirs and assigns of the chief lords of the fee by due service and right customs. Warranty.

Witnesses: Richard de Hoo, John May, Robert de Starton of Cranford, John Saveraye of Barton, John Ranlyn, junior, of the same, Roger his brother, Walter Daundelyn of Little Addington, John Daundelyn of the same, Thomas Daundelyn of the same and others.

Cranford, 22 November, 1357.
[Latin]
[*CCR 1354–60*, 428]

1 Word omitted.

152 [f. 63v] Memorandum that whereas the feoffment was made to Adam Fraunceys and Henry Pyel, the said tenements were annually charged to John Pyel etc. And the said John Pyel purchased them and he alone paid all the money.
[French]
[Cancelled.]

153 Memorandum that Adam Fraunceys and John Pyel re-enfeoffed the said John Daundelyn and Avice his wife for life in all the

said lands, tenements and rents with appurtenances contained in
the above charter in Cranford only, at a rent to Adam Fraunceys
and Henry Pyel of 20s *pa* as [appears] by the indented charter
made at Christmas 1357.
[French]
[Cancelled.]

154 [*f. 64r*] Charter of Edmund Rose of Norfolk (*sic*) that whereas
Roger Portreve, chaplain, son and heir of John Portreve of
Raunds, Northants., by a certain deed granted the reversion of
all lands, rents and tenements with appurtenances which John
Portreve holds for life in Raunds and which after his death, by
grant of the said Roger, were to remain to Edmund or his heirs,
should now remain to John Pyel, citizen and merchant of London,
his heirs and assigns in perpetuity, to be held of the chief lords
of the fee by due services and right customs. Warranty.
Witnesses: Thomas de Myryden, John Permont, William Lord,
John Campion, John Stevenes, Robert Hardy of Irthlingborough
and others.
Raunds, 18 December 1357.
[Latin]

155 Charter of John Portreve of Raunds that whereas Edmund Rose
lately purchased from Roger Portreve, chaplain, son and heir of
John, the reversion of all lands, rents and tenements which he
holds for life in Raunds, which reversion the said Edmund
granted by his deed to John Pyel, citizen and merchant of
London, his heirs and assigns, the said John Portreve upon the
grant made by Edmund to John Pyel has attorned and paid
service (*attendenciam fecimus*) to John Pyel in respect of the reversion
by payment of 40d.
Witnesses as above (*T. ut supra*)[**154**].
Raunds, 21 December 1357.
[Latin]

156 Memorandum that John Pyel paid for the above reversion to Sir
Roger de Clove in the name of the said Edmund £20.
[French]
[**154–156** cancelled.]

[Folio 64v blank.]

157 [*f. 65r*] Charter of William Malorre of Sudborough, Northants.,
granting to John Pyel, citzen and merchant of London, and Joan

his wife an annual rent of £20 to be received each year for their lives from his manor of Sudborough and all his other lands and tenements in the said vill and elsewhere in the said county. And William put the said John and Joan in full and peaceful seisin of the rent by payment of 40d.

Witnesses: Baldwin de Drayton, John Daundelyn of Cranford, William Nowers, John Lofwyk, John Campioun, John Miriden, John Stevene of Irthlingborough, and others.

Irthlingborough, 15 June 1358.

[Latin]

[Cancelled.]

158 Recognizance by William Molorre (*sic*) of Sudborough, Northants., and Anketil Malorre of the same that they are bound to John Pyel, citizen of London, in £200 for merchandise purchased from him in the Staple of Westminster, to be paid to the same John or his attorney showing this letter, his heirs or executors in London at Christmas next. And if the recognizors do not make or grant what is owed, the penalty ordained in the statute of the Staple for the recovery of debts [will be exacted].

Staple of Westminster, 15 June 1358.

[Latin]

[Cancelled.]

159 [*f. 65v*] Indenture that whereas William Mallorre of Sudborough granted to John Pyel and Joan, his wife, the above rent of £20, and whereas the said William and Anketil his brother are bound to John Pyel in £200 by a statute merchant made before Adam Fraunceys, mayor of the Staple of Westminster, the aforesaid John and Joan will and grant for themselves, their heirs and executors that if William, his heirs or executors, pay or cause to be paid to the said John and Joan or their assigns for their lives and that of the one who lives longer 20 marks each year in Irthlingborough then the said annuity of £20 and the said statute merchant of £200 will be cancelled and of no force. And if William, his heirs and executors, default in this payment then the annuity and statute will retain their force. And William and Anketil grant that no acquittance made to them should be effective unless it has been made at Irthlingborough.

London, 16 June 1358.

Moreover, whereas the above deed of annuity is enrolled in Chancery for June of the said year, the said William wills and grants by these presents that if the same deed of annuity is lost that the aforesaid John and Joan may have and receive the said

annual rent and distrain for arrears, both by virtue of the enrolment and by virtue of the said deed of annuity. And William and Anketil took corporal oaths faithfully to observe and fulfil all these agreements.
[Latin]
[*CCR 1354–60*, 521]
[Cancelled.]

160 [*f. 66r*] Tripartite indenture of Hugh Wake of Clifton, knight, granting to Adam Fraunceys and John Pyel, citizens of London, and Joan the wife of John all lands, tenements and rents with services, meadows, pastures, commons, demesnes, suits of court, wardships, marriages, reliefs, escheats, together with villeins (*nativi*) and their dependants, waifs and strays, hundreds and leets, and all other appurtenances which should accrue to the donor in Irthlingborough after the death of lady Isabel de Asschton his mother, and also after the death of John de Keteringge, chaplain, and John his son, and John the son of William Gobert of Irthlingborough, to be held by the feoffees, their heirs and assigns of the chief lords of the fee for due services and right customs in perpetuity at an annual rent for the term of their lives of one rose at midsummer for all services, and after the deaths of Adam, John and Joan, £100 annually. And if the annual rent of £100 is wholly or partly in arrears for seven months beyond any term, then the donor, his heirs or assigns, might take seisin of the said lands, rents and tenements and hold them peacefully in perpetuity. Warranty.
Witnesses: John de Knyghton, William Harwedon, Thomas Miriden, John Campioun, William le Lord, John Miriden, John Stevene and others.
Irthlingborough, 20 June 1358.
[Latin]

161 [*f. 66v*] Notification of Isabel de Asschton, John de Keteryngg, chaplain, John his son, and John son of William Gobert of Irthlingborough that whereas Hugh Wake of Clifton, knight, son of the said Isabel granted to Adam Fraunceys, John Pyel, citizens of London, and Joan, wife of the same John Pyel, all lands, tenements, rents in Irthlingborough which should accrue to the said Hugh after their deaths, they have attorned to the said Adam, John and Joan [in the above lands] and paid service (*attendenciam fecisse*) by reason of the aforesaid grant.
Irthlingborough, 26 June 1358.
[Latin]

162 Charter of John de Keterynge of Irthlingborough that whereas Elizabeth de Ashton granted to him all her lands and tenements, rents and services, villeins and their dependants, leets and courts, with all other appurtenances in Irthlingborough as appears by the deeds of Elizabeth to John, the aforesaid John has granted to John Pyel of Irthlingborough all his interest in all the lands and tenements, rents [etc.] and all other appurtenances, to be held by John Pyel and his assigns as fully as he had them of the gift and grant of the said Elizabeth.
Irthlingborough, 5 April 1357.
[Margin.] Memorandum that John Keteringe, John his son, [John] the son of William Gobert and Henry Overton were granted an interest in these tenements by the said Elizabeth for forty years after Michaelmas 1357 as appears by indenture.
[French]

163 Memorandum that John Pyel granted to John de Keterynge, 24 September 1359, by his deed that all the profits of the above tenements for the life of the said Elizabeth or, if she dies, for a term of four years after this date should remain in his name. Memorandum of a release of all the above tenements etc.
[French]

164 [*f. 67r*] Notification that whereas Simon de Drayton, knight, granted to John his son, his heirs and assigns all those lands and tenements with appurtenances which Henry Baker lately purchased in Irthlingborough, and afterwards Margaret who was the wife of the said Simon in her pure widowhood released all her right and claim in the said lands and tenements, the said John gave, granted and for himself and his heirs quitclaimed to John Pyel all the aforesaid lands and tenements and all other lands, tenements, rents and services, together with all reversions and rights pertaining to him in the same vill, to be held by John Pyel, his heirs and assigns of the chief lords of the fee by due services and right customs in perpetuity. Warranty.
Irthlingborough, 3 August 1358.
Witnesses: John Keteryng, clerk, John Campeon, John Miriden, Robert Hardi, John Stevenes and others.
[Latin]

165 And memorandum that John Pyel leased the same lands and tenements to Robert Puwe and his wife for the term of their lives, paying each year to John Pyel 13s 4d and also making the suits of court and services which pertain to the said John Pyel.

And if the rent is wholly or partly in arrears for one month after any term then John Pyel might enter the lands and retain them with all goods found thereon in perpetuity as appears by an indented charter dated 10 August 1358.
[French]

166 [f. 67v] And John Pyel enfeoffed William Braibrok, chaplain, Henry Pyel and William Freman in all the aforesaid lands and tenements with appurtenances, 24 April 1359, as appears by sealed deed.
[French]

167 And the aforesaid William Braibrok, Henry Pyel and William Freman enfeoffed, 31 May 1359, Richard Brian, chaplain, and Robert Peu in all aforesaid lands and tenements as appears by the sealed deed.
[French]

168 And the said Richard [Brian] and Robert Peu enfeoffed, 29 September 1359, Aubrey Rose, William Eir and John Miriden in the said tenements as appears by their charter.
[French]

169 Item the said Aubrey Rose, John Miriden and John Stevene enfeoffed John Pyel, for himself and his heirs, of the said tenements, 22 November 1360.
[French]

170 [f. 68r] John Portreve of Raunds enfeoffed Roger his son, chaplain, in all the lands and tenements which he had in Raunds with appurtenances for him and his heirs in perpetuity, and Roger re-enfeoffed his father in the same lands and tenements for life with remainder after his death to Edmund Rose and his heirs in perpetuity. And John Portreve granted his interest to John de Sutton and the said Edmund granted his interest to John Pyel and his heirs in perpetuity as appears by the deed written hereafter, whereupon the said John Sutton as tenant of the said lands for life acknowledged John Pyel in due form on 8 October 1358 by his sealed deed as appears below.
[French]
[Cancelled.]

171 Charter of Edmund Rose of co. Northampton [granting] that whereas Roger Portreve, chaplain, son and heir of John Portreve of Raunds gave and granted to him by his deed reversion of all lands, rents and tenements with appurtenances which the said John Portreve held for life in Raunds and which ought therefore to remain to him, Edmund, or his heirs after the death of the same John, these should now remain to John Pyel, citizen and merchant of London in perpetuity, to be held of the chief lords of the fee by due services and right customs. Warranty.

Witnesses: Thomas de Miriden, John Permont, William Lord, John Campion, John Stevenes, Robert Hardy of Irthlingborough and others.

Raunds, 18 December 1357.

[Latin]

[Cancelled.]

172 [*f. 68v*] Charter of John de Sutton of Berkshire that he attorned to John Pyel in due form in accordance with the grant of the said Edmund of all the aforesaid lands and tenements.

Irthlingborough, 8 October 1358.

[French]

[Cancelled.]

173 [*f. 69r*] Charter of Roger Levy and Agnes his wife of Irthlingborough granting to John Pyel of Irthlingborough six pieces of arable land lying in the fields of Irthlingborough, of which 1 acre lies on 'Bleschowe' between the land of the abbot of Peterborough to the north and the land of the same John which Margery Parys holds to the west, and another piece lies on 'Lirtepoke' next to the land of the same John which William son of Henry holds, and one piece lies on 'Longelondes' between the land of the same John on either side, and one piece lies in 'Overthwertforghes' next to the land of the same John in the west which John Basse holds, and two pieces of land, namely a headland and a selion adjacent in the same furlong next to the land of John Miriden to the east, to be held by John Pyel, his heirs and assigns of the chief lords of the fee by due services and right customs, with warranty. And because on the day these presents were made Agnes was married to Roger, she took, of her own free will and without compulsion, a corporal oath that she would not claim any right in the six pieces of land.

Witnesses: John Miriden, John Campeon, John Stephenes, William Cotes, John Ankus and others.

Irthlingborough, 29 September 1358.

[Latin]

174 [*f. 69v*] Charter of William Eyer and Agnes his wife granting John Pyel and Joan his wife one messuage, 24 acres of land and 4 acres of meadow with all appurtenances in Irthlingborough which accrued to the donors for life by right of the said Agnes by reason of a certain feoffment lately made by John Martyn, to be held by John Pyel, his wife Joan and the heirs of John of the chief lords of the fee by due services and right customs. Warranty. *Witnesses*: John de Keteryng, clerk, John Campion, John Miriden, John Stephenes, Robert Hardy, W[illiam] Coton, John Ward and others.
Irthlingborough, 5 November 1358.
[Latin]

175 Charter of Nicholas Herveys of Irthlingborough granting to John Pyel and Joan his wife and the heirs of John all lands and tenements with all their appurtenances which the donor inherited after the death of John Martyn his uncle. He also released to John Pyel and Joan and the heirs of John all his right and claim in a messuage, 24 acres of land and 4 acres of meadow which the said John and Joan had of the gift and feoffment of William Eyer of Irthlingborough and Agnes his wife, to be held [*f. 70r*] of the chief lords of the fee for due services and right customs. Warranty.
Witnesses: [As **174**.]
Irthlingborough, 12 November 1358.
[Latin]

176 [*f. 70v*] Final concord made at Westminster on the octave of St Hilary 1318 between Hugh Wake and Isabel his wife, plaintiffs, represented by John de Sandford, and William Lengleys, defendant, whereby Hugh acknowledged the defendant's right to ten messuages, 2 virgates, $4\frac{1}{2}$ bovates and 5 acres of land, 3s rent and further rent of four capons and pasture sufficient for one ox with appurtenances in Irthlingborough, which he had of Hugh's own gift. And for this acknowledgement, fine and concord, the same William granted to Hugh and Isabel the aforesaid tenements and pasture, and in the same court granted him four messuages, 1 virgate, $2\frac{1}{2}$ bovates, 1 acre and $3\frac{1}{2}$ roods of land, and the aforesaid rent and pasture, to be held by Hugh and Isabel and their heirs of the chief lords of the fee by due services. And moreover the said William granted for himself and his heirs the reversion of the following to Hugh and Isabel and their heirs in perpetuity: one messuage which Simon Paston held for life, one messuage and 1 bovate of land which Robert Trewe held for life, one messuage, 1 bovate and 3 acres of land which Roger de Parys held for life, one messuage and ½ rood of land which Ascelm de Romeneye held for life, [f. 71r] one messuage which William Dalle held for life, one messuage which Nicholas de Paston held for life, and 1 virgate of land which Gilbert Belle and Margery his wife held for life, of the inheritance of the aforesaid William Lengleys in the said vill on the day on which this concord was made, all of which, after the death of the above tenants, were to revert to William Lengleys and his heirs. And if Hugh and Isabel die without heir the said tenements and pasture will remain to the right heirs of the same Hugh.

[Latin]

[PRO CP25(1) 176/68 no. 332]

177 Charter of Thomas Bosoun of Woodford granting to John Pyel, citizen of London, all his goods, movable and immovable, wherever they exist in co. Northampton.

London, 4 December 1359.

[Latin]

178 [f. 71v] Letter patent of Thomas Bosoun of Woodford, Northants., stating that because he is going to Jerusalem, from where there is no certainty of return, and whereas a moiety of the church of Woodford at the first vacancy is in his gift and presentment, Thomas has granted to his dear and beloved [friend] John Pyel, citizen of London, his heirs and assigns, at the first vacancy permission to present whichever suitable parson he chooses to the moiety of the said church which belongs to the donor and his heirs. And the said Thomas wills and grants that if John Pyel is hindered by himself or his heirs, then he, his heirs and assigns will have to account for a statute merchant of £200 made by the said Thomas before the mayor of the Staple of London, to John Pyel his heirs and assigns.

London, 4 December 1359.

[French]

[Cf. **218**.]

179 [f. 72r] Indenture made between John Pyel of the one part and John de Keteringge of the other part witnessing that John de Keteringge granted and leased to John Pyel the court and leet of the king's fee in Irthlingborough with all the profits issuing from these, which the said John de Keteringge had by a lease from Isabel de Ashton. And John de Keteringge granted and leased to John Pyel all the free rents of the fee as entirely as he had them of the said Isabel, with all arrears and appurtenances, to be held by John Pyel and his assigns for a term of twenty years beginning at Easter 1359 at a rent of 20s *pa* to John de Keteringge and paying due [service] to the chief lord of the fee. And John de Keteringge granted and leased to John Pyel a piece of meadow in Irthlingborough lying in 'Ulnesdole' which John Pyel formerly held of Isabel de Asshton, to be held for three years by paying to John de Keteringge 40s, and by paying due services on his behalf to the chief lord of the fee. And John Pyel granted to John de Keteringge a plot of pasture in Irthlingborough called 'Thursqueche', to be held for the whole term for which John Pyel held the tenements of the abbey of Peterborough which were of the said John de Keteringge for no payment.

Witnesses: Thomas de Miriden, John de Miriden, William Freman, William Braibrok, chaplain, and Richard Brian, chaplain, and others.

And the value of the rents[1] to be paid to John Pyel: 12s 9d *pa*.

Irthlingborough, 21 April 1359.

[French]

1 Mentioned in the first part of the indenture.

[Cancelled.]

[fo. 72v blank]

180 [*f. 73r*] Final concord made at Westminster, 30 May 1332, and afterwards on the octave of Michaelmas [6 October] 1332 between Adam de Welughby of Finedon and Isabel his wife, plaintiffs, and John Byweston of Finedon, chaplain, defendant, whereby Adam acknowledged the defendant's right to sixteen messuages, two tofts, 200 acres of land, 17 acres of meadow, 7 acres of pasture and 30s rent with appurtenances, in Finedon and Irthlingborough. Of these the said John had thirteen messuages, the aforesaid tofts, 194 acres of land, $16\frac{1}{2}$ acres of meadow and the aforesaid pasture and rent of the gift of Adam. And for this recognizance, fine and concord, John granted to the said Adam and Isabel the same tenements with appurtenances in the same court, to be held in perpetuity of the chief lords of the fee by due service. And moreover, John granted the reversion of the following lands to Adam and Isabel and the heirs of Adam: two messuages and $3\frac{1}{2}$ acres of land which Henry Ailvie held for life, and one messuage and 1 rood of meadow which Robert le Leche held for life, and 1 acre of land which Alice Macurneys held for life, and $\frac{1}{2}$ acre of land which John Rose held for life, and 1 rood

of meadow which Juliana Gerard held for life, of the inheritance of the said John on the day on which this concord was made, and which after the death of the said tenants were to revert to John Byweston and his heirs, to be held of the chief lords of the fee by due service. And if Adam die without heir [*f. 73v*] the tenements will remain to William son of Simon Harleys of Riseley, and his heirs, and if William die without heir, to Simon his brother, then to John brother of Simon and to the right heirs of Adam.
[Latin]
[PRO CP25(1) 177/74 no. 111]

181 Charter of Simon Harleys of Finedon granting to John Pyel and John Keteringge of Irthlingborough all his lands and tenements, rents and services which he had on this day in the vill and fields of Finedon by hereditary right without purchase. Also the reversion of all those lands and tenements, rents and services with appurtenances which Simon recently granted to William Colyns of 'Gleve' and Elizabeth his wife in Finedon and Irthling-borough, to be held [*f. 74r*] by John Pyel and John de Keteringge, their heirs and assigns in perpetuity of the chief lords of the fee for due services and right customs. Warranty.
Witnesses: Thomas de Bifeld, John Giles, Henry Chapman of Finedon, William le Lord, Thomas Miriden, John Campioun, John de Miriden, Nicholas de Adington and John Stevenes of Irthlingborough and others.
Finedon, 24 September 1350.
[Latin]

182 Release of John Harleys of Riseley, chaplain, to John Pyel and John Keteringge, chaplain, their heirs and assigns of all the lands and tenements, rents and services which John Pyel and John Keteringge had in Finedon of the gift and feoffment of Simon Harleys of Riseley. Warranty.
Witnesses: John Campioun, John Miriden, Robert Hardy of Irthlingborough, Thomas Bifeld, Henry Chapman of Finedon, Henry Pepir of the same, and others.
Irthlingborough, 22 March 1358.
[Latin]

183 Charter of William le Roo of Willoughby granting to John Pyel and John Keteringge of Irthlingborough all his lands and tenements, rents and services, and the reversions of all his tenancies in Finedon, to be held in perpetuity of the chief lords

of the fee for due service. Also release to John Pyel and John de
Keteringge [f. 75r] of all those lands and tenements which were
once of Adam de Wyluby in Finedon. Warranty.
Witnesses: John Campioun, Thomas Miriden, Henry son of
Simon, Nicholas de Adington and John Miriden of Irthling-
borough, Thomas de Bifield, Henry Chapman, Henry le Eir,
Thomas de Overton of Finedon, and others.
Finedon, 10 May 1351.
[Latin]

184 Release of John Keteringge of Irthlingborough, clerk, to John
Pyel of Irthlingborough of all lands, tenements, rents and services,
with all their appurtenances which Pyel and Keteringge held
jointly of the gift and feoffment of Simon Harleys in Finedon.
Witnesses: Thomas Miriden, John Campioun, John Miriden,
Robert Hardy of Irthlingborough, Robert Harwedon, Richard
de Bonyngton, Henry Eir of Finedon, and many others.
Irthlingborough, 13 June 1359.
[Latin]

[Folio 75v blank]

185 [f.76r] Final concord made at Westminster on the octave of
Michaelmas 1329 between Thomas de Seymour (*de Sancto Mauro*)
and Laurence de Seymour, parson of the church of Higham
Ferrers, plaintiffs, and Warin de Seymour, defendant, whereby
Thomas acknowledged the manor of 'Eton' [?Eaton], Wilts., and
three messuages, $3\frac{1}{2}$ virgates of land, 2 acres of meadow and 30
shillings in rent with appurtenances in Irthlingborough, and a
fourth part of the manor of Finedon Northants., to belong to
Warin, since he had granted them to the defendant himself. And
for this recognizance, fine and concord Warin granted to Thomas
and Laurence the said manors and land in the same court, to
be held by Thomas and Laurence, and the heirs of Thomas, of
the chief lords of the fee in perpetuity with remainder, if Thomas
die without heir, to Alan his brother and his heirs. And if Alan
die without heirs then the manors and lands would remain to
Nicholas brother of Alan, and his heirs, then to Laurence de
Sancto Martino (*sic*) and his heirs, [f. 76v] and then to the right
heirs of Thomas.
[Latin]

186 Indenture made 13 June 1359 between Sir Nicholas Seymour (*de
Sancto Mauro*), knight, lord of Castle Cary, Somerset, of the one
part and John Pyel of the other, witnessing that the said Sir

Nicholas granted to the said John two-thirds of an old messuage, wasted (*debilis*) and poorly roofed, and of three plots of vacant land, formerly built on, and of all other lands and tenements with crofts, meadows, grazing-land, pastures, rents, services and all other appurtenances which were once of Thomas de Seymour, knight, brother of Nicholas in the said vill of Irthlingborough, together with the reversion of the third part of the said messuage, three plots of land, the tenements and rents with appurtenances which Alice lately wife of Sir Thomas holds for life as dower. The messuage is situated between the tenement of John de Haddon on the east side and a brook called Westbrook on the west and the royal highway to the south and the field of the said vill to the north, to be held by John Pyel, his heirs and assigns for his life plus one year of the aforesaid Sir Nicholas and his heirs, by performing due service and right customs to the chief lords of the fee on behalf of Nicholas and his heirs for the said term, at a rent of one rose annually at midsummer. And if John Pyel should die within twelve years then Sir Nicholas grants that the heirs and assigns of the same John might have and hold the said two-thirds of the messuage, plots and tenements with appurtenances and reversion up to the end of the twelve years. [*f.77r*] Warranty.
Witnesses: Thomas Miriden, John Campion, John Stevene, Robert Hardy, William Eir, John Ward and Henry son of Simon of Irthlingborough.
Irthlingborough, 13 June 1359.
[Latin]

187 Letter patent of Nicholas Seymour [*de Sancto Mauro*], knight, lord of Castle Cary, Somerset, appointing William de Bradeleye, William de Braibrok, chaplains, and John Miriden of Irthlingborough as his attorneys to deliver in his name to John Pyel of Irthlingborough full and peaceful seisin of the above.
Irthlingborough, 14 June 1359.
[Latin]

188 [*f. 77v*] 1359.[1] Item purchased of Robert Hardy, 23 July, by charter in fee 5 roods of land in a selion in 'Knyghtlond' between [the lands of] John Keteringge and William Whitelok.
[French]

1 33 Edward III.

189 [*f. 78r*] Indenture witnessing that Isabel de Asshton of Stanwick

leased and granted at farm to John de Keterynge of Irthlingborough, John his son, John Goberd and Henry de Everdon all
her lands and tenements, rents and services in Irthlingborough,
and John Royle, her villein (*nativus*) with all his dependants, and
all his goods and chattels, and all her villeins with their dependants, with reversions, wardships, escheats, reliefs, heriots, courts,
views of frankpledge with their profits, and with all other profits
accruing to her in Irthlingborough, and all her meadow lying in
'Estmersche' in Irthlingborough with all their appurtenances, to
be held by the feoffees for a term of forty years commencing 29
September 1357, by paying each year to the said Isabella for the
next four years one rose at midsummer for all services, and for
the following three years 13s 4d, and from then until the end of
the term $8\frac{1}{2}$ marks. Warranty. [*f. 78v*]
Witnesses: Sir Hugh de la Wake, knight, John Hammond of
Stanwick, John Pyel, William le Loord, John Campeoun, John
Miryden, Robert Hardy of Irthlingborough and others.
Irthlingborough, 29 September 1357.
[Latin]

190 Memorandum that the said Elizabeth two or three years after
this indenture made two releases to the said John [de Keteringge]
of all her right in perpetuity with warranty in all the tenements
contained in the indenture as appears below.

191 Release of Isabel lately wife of John de Asshton of Stanwick,
knight, to John de Keteryng of Irthlingborough of all her right
and interest in John Royle, her villein, with all his dependants,
and in all lands and tenements, goods and chattels which the
same John Royle held in Irthlingborough, and also in all other
rents, suit of court, view [of frankpledge] and services, and in all
other lands and tenements which the said John de Keteringge
held of her in the said vill. Warranty.
Stanwick, 5 November 1357.
[Latin]

[*f. 79r*] Touching the purchase by John Pyel of the manor of
Cranford, and the copies of old charters touching the said manor
written hereafter.

192 Charter of John Daundelyn, knight, granting to William de
Whatton, parson of the church of Stoke Doyle, and John Benet,
parson of the church of 'Doneheved',[1] the manor of Cranford
with appurtenances, except the lands and tenements which are

of the fee of the honor of Gloucester, and one messuage and 1
virgate of land which William son of Agnes held of him for life
in the same manor, to be held of the chief lords of the fee by
due services and right customs. Warranty.
Witnesses: Sir Humphrey de Bassingbourne, Sir Simon de
Drayton, knights, Ranulph de Veer, Henry Traili, William de
Seymour (*Sancto Mauro*) junior, Richard de Islepe, Thomas
Curzon of Cranford, Thomas Henefrei and Richard Power of
the same, and others.
Cranford, 25 October 1339.
[Latin]

1 (?)Downhead, Somerset.

193 [*f. 79v*] Charter of William Whatton, parson of the church of
Stoke Doyle, and John Benet, parson of 'Donheved', granting to
Sir John Daundelyn son of Sir Hugh Daundelyn, knight, the
manor of Cranford with appurtenances which they recently had
of the gift and feoffment of the same John son of Hugh, to be
held by John and his heirs of the chief lords of the fee by due services and customs. And if he should die without heir of his body
then the manor will remain to John his son and the heirs of his
body, and if the said John son of John Daundelyn die without
heir, the manor will remain in turn to his brothers, Henry,
[*f. 80r*] Robert, Thomas and Ralph and their heirs, and to the
right heirs of John, son of Hugh Daundelyn. Warranty. [*f.80v*]
Witnesses: [As **192**.]
Cranford, 28 January 1340.
[Latin]

194 Charter of John Daundelyn of Cranford granting to William
Lenneysy of Hemel Hempstead and William Daundelyn his
manor of Cranford with appurtenances, except those lands and
tenements of the fee of the earl of Gloucester and the wood
called 'le Shorte', to be held of the chief lord of the fee by due
services and customs in perpetuity. Warranty. [*f.81r*]
Witnesses: Henry Daundelyn, Robert Elys, John Mey of the Hoo,
William Nicholl and others.
Cranford, 13 March 1353.
[Latin]

195 Charter of William Lenneyse of Hemel Hempstead and William
Daundelyn of Cranford granting to John Daundelyn of Cranford
and Amice his wife an annual rent of 100 marks to be raised

from the manor of Cranford, and if the rent should be in arrears by fifteen days then the said John and Amice and the heirs or assigns of John may enter and hold [the manor] without objection by the grantors.
Witnesses: Oliver Duffyn, John Mey, Robert Elys, [*f. 81v*] Richard of the Hoo, John Lenneyse and others.
Cranford, 13 April 1349.
[Latin]

196 Charter of William Lenneyse of Hemel Hempstead and William Daundelyn granting to John Daundelyn and Amice his wife all lands and tenements, rents and services, with all appurtenances in the vill of Cranford which the grantors had of the gift and feoffment of John son of John Daundelyn, knight, to be held by John and Amice and the heirs and assigns of the said John of the chief lords of the fee by due services and right customs in perpetuity. Warranty.
Witnesses: Richard de Hoo, Robert Eliz, John Mey, Thomas Lomb, John Lenneyse, John Sterne of West Addington, Oliver de Lufwyk and others.
Cranford, 23 May 1353.
[Latin]

197 [*f. 82*] Charter of John son and heir of John Daundelyn of Cranford, being of full age, ratifying and confirming the grant of John his father to William Lenneyse and William Daundelyn of the manor of Cranford with appurtenances, except the lands held of the fee of the earl of Gloucester and the wood called 'le Shorte', and also the grant made by the same William and William of the said manor to the said John Daundelyn senior and Amice his wife.
Witnesses: Simon de Drayton, knight, Richard la Souche, Geoffrey, rector of the church of Cranford St Andrew, Thomas de Byfelde, Richard atte Hoo and others.
Cranford, 27 November 1356.
[Latin]

198 [*f. 83r*] Final concord made at Westminster on the octave of Michaelmas 1359 between Henry Pyel, parson of the church of Warkton, and Richard Bryan, chaplain, plaintiffs, and John Daundelyn and Avice (*sic*) his wife, defendants, whereby John and Avice acknowledged the manor of Cranfordto belong to Henry Pyel, and conveyed it to Henry and Richard in the same court, to be held in perpetuity of the chief lords of the fee by

due services, with warranty. And for this fine and concord Henry and Richard paid 100 marks.
[Latin]
[PRO CP25(1) 177/81 no. 69]

[Memoranda relating to Cranford.]

199 On 16 October 1359 Henry Pyel of Irthlingborough and Richard Bryan of Denford, chaplains, enfeoffed Geoffrey, parson of the church of Cranford St Andrew, Aubrey Rose of Irthlingborough, chaplains, and William Freman of the same vill in the manor of Cranford as fully as they held it of the grant of John Daundelyn and Avice his wife.
[French]

200 [*f. 83v*] On 7 December 1359 the said Geoffrey, Aubrey and William Freman enfeoffed Richard, parson of Barton Seagrave, William Clerk of Rothwell and Robert, parson of the church of All Saints, Irthlingborough, in the said manor as appears by the charters made thereof.
[French]

201 Robert, Richard and William enfeoffed William Braybrok, clerk and John de Keteryngge, clerk, in the whole manor of Cranford with appurtenances by the charter dated 5 February 1360.
[French]

202 William Braibrok and John Keteringge on 25 July 1360 enfeoffed John Pyel and his heirs in the said manor of Cranford in perpetuity.
[French]

203 On 11 September 1360 John Pyel enfeoffed John Daundelyn and Avice his wife for the term of their two lives in the manor at an annual rent of 100s with reversion to John Pyel as appears by the copy of the said charter written below [**220**].
[French]

204 Item, at the same time John Pyel granted to John Daundelyn that he might lease a parcel of the said manor for life or a term of years to a tenant then living in Cranford by one deed and no other, and this by reason that by the terms of the said charter [**220**] no one may lease without leave of John Pyel.
[French]

205 [*f. 84r*] Charter of John Lord of Irthlingborough, rector of the church of Harpole, William Lord, Aubrey Rose, chaplain, and John Miriden of Irthlingborough granting to John Pyel a plot of land in Irthlingborough with all appurtenances situated between the croft of the donors called 'le Newechorcherd' and the wharf (*ripam*) of Irthlingborough to the south, the tenement of John Miriden to the west and the tenement of John Pyel to the east, together with all walls, hedges and ditches surrounding the plot, to be held by John Pyel, his heirs and assigns of the chief lords of the fee by due services and right customs in perpetuity. Warranty.
Witnesses: Henry son of Simon, Robert Hardy, John Stevenes, William Cotene, William Campioun and others.
Irthlingborough, 12 January 1360.
[Latin]

206 [*f. 84v*] Charter of William Lord of Irthlingborough granting to John Pyel of the same vill 10 feet of assize land with appurtenances for the whole width of the donor's croft called New Garden, next to the wall of the said John between his enclosures (*pondes*) and the said croft to the north, to be held of the chief lords of the fee by due service in perpetuity. Warranty.
Witnesses: Thomas Miriden, John Miriden, John Campioun, Henry son of Simon, William le Heir and others.
Irthlingborough, 2 October 1360.
[French]

207 [*f. 85r*] Final concord held at Westminster on the quindene of St Martin 1310 between John Spigurnel and Alice his wife, plaintiffs, and Hugh Spigurnel, clerk, defendant, whereby the plaintiffs acknowledge two messuages, three mills, 4 carucates of land and £20 in rent with appurtenances in Woodford, Thrapston and Denford, to belong to the defendant, as he had received them of the plaintiff's own gift. And for this fine and concord, the same Hugh granted and conveyed the said tenements to John and Alice in the same court, to be held by them and their heirs of the chief lords of the fee by due service in perpetuity, with remainder to John son of Roger Bosoun, and thereafter to the right heirs of John Spigurnel.
[Latin]
[Cancelled.]

208 [*f. 85v*] Memorandum that the manor of Woodford formerly belonged to Sir Richard Traylly, who had a daughter Alice, heir

to the manor after the death of her father. Alice married Sir
Roger Bosoun and had issue, John Bosoun. When Roger, the
father of John, died, his wife, Alice, married Sir John Spigurnel,
knight. And afterwards at Westminster, on the quindene of St
Martin 1310, a fine was made on behalf of themselves and the
heirs that John Spigurnel might have by the said Alice, and if
he died without heir by the same Alice, then the aforesaid
tenements would wholly remain, after the deaths of John and
Alice, to John, son of Roger Bosoun, and his heirs. And John
Spigurnel died without heir so that the said manor passed to
John Bosoun, and after his death to Thomas Bosoun his son
and heir.
[French]

209 And memorandum that of the manor of Cranford, half of one
knight's fee is held in chief by John Traylly, and a quarter of
one knight's fee by the abbey of Peterborough, and the lands of
Thrapston and Denford by one knight's service, and the mill of
Sir Richard Chaumbirleyn for 2d *pa* for wardship, marriage,
reliefs and all other services.
[French]

210 Memorandum that Thomas Bosoun has 2 virgates of land in
Woodford which are not entailed, of which Thomas Wright
holds one and Henry de Aldwynkle holds the other. These details
were written in London on 7 December 1359 by the said Thomas
Bosoun, on the day he set off for Jerusalem in company with
master Henry la Zouche.
[French]

211 [*f. 86r*] Duplicate of **199**.

212 Duplicate of **200**.
[Both cancelled.]

213 [*f. 86v*] Enrolled on the dorse of the Chancery letters close for
the month and year written below.
Charter of Thomas Bosoun of Woodford granting to Adam
Fraunceys and John [Pyel], citizens of London, an annual rent
of £20 to be raised annually and in perpetuity of all lands and
tenements in Woodford, Thrapston and Denford, Northants.,
with permission to distrain all goods and chattels in the event of
arrears. And the said Adam and John were put in seisin by
payment of 6s 8d. *Witnesses*: Sir Richard la Zouche, Sir Richard

Chaumbirleyn, knights, John Drayton, Robert Veer, Roger Ley-
cestre, Roger Herberd of Woodford, William Lord, John
Campeon, John Miriden, John Stevene, Robert Hardy of Irthling-
borough and others.
Irthlingborough, 3 November 1359.
[Latin]
[*CCR 1354–60*, 659.]
[Margin.] Void because Alice Bozoun paid 40 marks 21 July
1360 in respect of the grant of John Pyel.
[But cf. *CIPM* xi, 237 (p. 197), where on Alice's death in 1361 the
lands were given as chargeable to Fraunceys and Pyel at £20
pa.]
[Cancelled.]

214 Indenture bearing witness that whereas Thomas Bosoun of
Woodford enfeoffed Adam Fraunceys and John Pyel, citizens of
London, of an annual rent of £20 sterling to be taken from all
the lands and tenements of the said Thomas in Woodford,
Thrapston and Denford, as is contained in a writing [*f. 87r*]
made by Thomas to Adam and John, and whereas the said
Thomas is bound by a statute merchant to the said Adam in
£100 as is contained in the same statute, notwithstanding this
the said Adam and John will and grant that if Thomas, his heirs
or assigns, pay to them or their attorney at Irthlingborough each
year for the term of their lives 100s, or if he pay to them 50
marks within the first year of his return from Jerusalem where
he is going on this day in company with Henry la Zouche, clerk,
and if the said Adam and John hold peacefully the wardship and
marriage of Henry son and heir of Thomas and, if Henry should
die under age, the wardship and marriage of Elizabeth and Alice
daughters of Thomas without hindrance or disturbance, then the
aforesaid bonds of £20 annual rent and the statute merchant of
£100 will lose their force and be held null in perpetuity, and the
payment of 100s *pa* will cease after the said payment of 50 marks,
provided Adam and John have the wardship and marriage of
the children in the aforesaid manner. Otherwise this indenture
remains in force notwithstanding. [*f. 87v*]
Witnesses: Sir Richard de la Zouche, Sir Richard Chambirleyn,
knights, John de Drayton, Robert Vere, Roger Leycestre, Roger
Herberd of Woodford, William Loord, John Campeon, John
Miriden, John Stevenes, Robert Hardi of Irthlingborough, and
others.
Irthlingborough, 9 December 1359.

And John and Thomas have pledged their faith to each other to keep these covenants.
[French]
[Cancelled.]

215 Charter by which Thomas Bosoun of Woodford sold to Adam Fraunceys and John Pyel, citizens of London, the wardship and marriage of Henry his son and heir and if Henry should die under age, the wardship and marriage of Elizabeth and Alice his daughters without contradiction or hindrance on his part or by any other in the future.
London, 4 December 1359.
[Latin]
[Cancelled.]

216 [*f. 88r*] Charter of Thomas Bosoun of Woodford granting to Henry his son for the term of his life for his sustenance an annual rent of 40s, to be raised from all the donor's lands and tenements in Woodford, Thrapston and Denford, and if payment of the rent fall into arrears, then it is permitted to Henry and to John Pyel, citizen of London, and their assigns to distrain for all goods and chattels in the said lands and tenements until the arrears of the annual rent be fully satisfied. And if Henry die under age, then the said rent will remain to Elizabeth and Alice, Thomas's daughters, for the term of their lives in the above form.
Witnesses: As **214**.
Irthlingborough, 3 December 1359.
[Latin]

217 [*f. 88v*] As **177**.

218 Letter of Thomas Bosoun of Woodford notifying that because he is going to Jerusalem and there is no certainty of his return and since the moiety of the church of Woodford at the first vacancy belongs to his gift and presentation, he assigns and ordains his dear and beloved [friend] John Pyel, citizen of London, his attorney and procurator, to present the moiety of the said church to whichever suitable person he chooses if a vacancy should occur during his absence.
London, 4 December 1359.
[French]
[Cf. **178**]

219 [*f. 89r*] Charter of Richard Brian of Denford, chaplain, granting to John Pyel of Irthlingborough and William Freman of the same

all his lands and tenements in Cranford and Ringstead together
with all reversions there belonging to the donor for life or a term
of years, to be held by the said John and William, their heirs
and assigns, of the chief lords of those fees for due services and
right customs in perpetuity. Warranty.
Witnesses: Gilbert Lord, Baldwin de Drayton, William Nicol of
Cranford, Roger atte Welle, John Thingden, Thomas atte Watir
and others of Ringstead.
Cranford, 25 July 1360.
[Latin]
[Added later in French.] Item purchased on the same day from
Christine Fox 1 rood of land lying at the 'wyndmylne' [?windmill]
next to [the land of] John Pyel.

220 Notification by John Pyel that whereas John son of John Daundelyn of Cranford, knight, enfeoffed William Lennyssy and
William Daundelyn of the manor of Cranford [**194**], and they
enfeoffed John son of John and Avice his wife of the said manor
[**196**], which feoffment was ratified and confirmed by John, son
of the same John son of John, when he was of full age [**197**],
and whereas John and Avice granted the manor by fine to Henry
Pyel and Richard Brian [**198**], who enfeoffed Geoffrey, rector
of Cranford St Andrew, Aubrey Rose of Irthlingborough and
William Freman of the said manor [**199**], [*f. 90r*] and Geoffrey,
Aubrey and William enfeoffed Richard, rector of Barton Seagrave, William Clerk of Rothwell and Robert, rector of All
Saints, Irthlingborough [**200**], from whom William Braybrook
and John Keteryng purchased the said manor [**201**], which John
Pyel had of their gift and feoffment [**202**], as is more fully
contained in the aforesaid charters, John Pyel leased to John
Daundelyn, son of John and Avice the said manor, to be held
of the lessor, his heirs and assigns for the term of all their lives
at a rent for the first year of £18, [*f. 90v*] and thereafter 100s
each year, and by payment to the chief lords of the fee, and any
other lords, rents and due services and right customs. And if the
said John and Avice, or either of them, demise the manor to
anyone without the lessor's assent or will, or that of his heirs or
assigns, then he may enter, take possession of and peacefully
hold the tenements without contradiction of the said John and
Avice and raise the said 100s each year from the residue of the
manor. And John Pyel grants for himself, his heirs and assigns
that the lessees will not be disturbed, harried or sued during
their lives for any waste that has been or might in future be
made on the said manor. And if the lessees are impleaded by

Joan his wife so that they lose one third of the manor by reason of dower, then they will be discharged for life from the 100 [*f. 91r*] shillings for all the time that the third part of the manor stands in Joan's hands. Warranty.
Witnesses: William Lord of Irthlingborough, Thomas Miriden, John Miriden, William Nicol, John Mei, Richard of the Hoo, Richard Adam and others.
Irthlingborough, 11 September 1360.
[Latin]

221 Memorandum that John Daundelyn enfeoffed John Doylly, William Lennesy and Sir William of Knyghtle, parson of Stoke Doyle, and their heirs in his manor of Cranford but the feoffment was not put into effect as the said John was never out of possession, since at the time of the transaction and subsequently the manor was seised in the hands of the king and in the hands of the abbot of Peterborough, as the manor of John Daundelyn was forfeit to the king, and the said John held it as his own. Nevertheless the said feoffees made a release to John Daundelyn of the manor, which is in the keeping of John Daundelyn's wife. And when John [Doylly] and William Lenneysy died, William [Knyghtle] made a release as appears below.
[French]
[It seems that Daundelyn had intended to settle the manor on trustees who were presumably to re-enfeoff him for life, but that at the time the settlement was made the manor was forfeit to the Crown through debt (see below) and therefore Daundelyn was not in a legal position to convey it. The feoffees, therefore, issued releases of their right in the manor, one of which is reproduced below.]

222 [*f. 91v*] Release of William Knyghtle, rector of the church of Stoke Doyle, to John Daundelyn of Cranford, his heirs and assigns, of the manor of Cranford with all appurtenances. Warranty.
Witnesses: Geoffrey, rector of the church of Cranford St Andrew, Richard Adam of the same, John Mey of the same, Richard atte Hoo of the same, Robert Starton and others.
Cranford, 15 September 1359.
[Latin]

223 [*f. 92r*] Release of Hugh Wake of Clifton to John Pyel, his heirs and assigns of all lands tenements and rents with services, meadows, pastures, commons, demesnes, suits of court, ward-

ships, marriages, reliefs, escheats together with villeins and their dependants, waifs, strays, hundreds and leets, and all other appurtenances, which he granted to Adam Fraunceys and John Pyel, citizens of London. Warranty.
Witnesses: Henry Pycard, John Malewayn, John Pecche, John Wroth, John Litle, Richard Smelt, Richard Double and others.
London, 16 October 1358.
[Latin]

224 Memorandum that John Wake son of the said Sir Hugh made a release in fee with warranty to John Pyel of all the said lands and tenements on 29 September 1365.
[French]

225 [*f. 92v*] Charter of Simon Henkok of Irthlingborough granting to John Pyel $8\frac{1}{2}$ acres of land with appurtenances lying between two boundary marks (*divisiones*) on 'Longelondes', which John Haddon once held, to be held of the chief lords of the fee by due services and right customs in perpetuity. Warranty.
Witnesses: John Campioun, John Stevene, Robert Hardy, John Warde, Robert Peu and others.
Irthlingborough, 10 January 1362.
[Latin]

226 Pyel purchased on 5 October 1362 of Robert Hardy 1 acre and 1 rood of land lying adjacent to his [land] at 'Longelondes'.
[French]

227 Memorandum that John Pyel received at Michaelmas 1362 11 acres 3 roods of land in Irthlingborough and a large piece of meadow in 'Stakeford' which belonged to Ralph Stevene, since Ralph was a bastard and died without heir and the lands and meadow reverted to Pyel as chief lord as appears more fully in the white paper.
[French]

228 [*f. 93r*] Memorandum that John Pyel purchased from John Campioun at Christmas 1362 two separate acres of land at Upwell in the 'Wong' belonging to John Pyel, and an acre of meadow at 'Bartholotesford' in 'Tounholm', for which land and meadow Pyel granted to Campioun 5 roods of land in 'Hoggeswell' next to Campioun's own land which abuts on the 'Wong' at Upwell, and a cottage by the church of All Saints which

belonged to John Spayne. Pyel also released to him suit at his court in Irthlingborough and 5s annual rent issuing from a croft adjacent to the land of the said Campioun called 'Westhorcher' for which he usually pays 8s *pa*.
[French]

229 [*f. 93v*] [Margin.] Assize between John le Loord of Irthlingborough, Alice who was the wife of John Miriden, and John Pyel.
An assize was held to declare whether John le Loord of Irthlingborough, parson of the church of Harpole, and Alice who was wife of John Miriden of Irthlingborough unjustly and without judgement disseised John Pyel of his freehold in Irthlingborough. It was alleged that they disseised him of a plot of land comprising 200 feet in length and 5 feet in width, with appurtenances. And John le Loord and Alice did not appear, but John Cook replied for them as their attorney and on their behalf said that the defendants had neither injured nor disseised the plaintiff and they submitted the issue to the assize. And John Pyel likewise took out a writ of assize against them. And the jurors said on oath that John Pyel was seised of the said plot of land with appurtenances as of his free tenement until the said John le Loord and Alice unjustly, without judgement and by force of arms, disseised him to the loss of £20. It was accordingly agreed that John Pyel should recover his seisin by view of the jurors of the assize and that his losses should be assessed by the said jurors. And John le Loord and Alice were taken before the justices for the said disseisin and John Pyel declared that he was satisfied as to the said losses. Whereupon John le Loord and Alice petitioned that they might be permitted to make fine with the king on this occasion, and they were granted permission as appears by the Rolls of the Exchequer of the aforesaid justices of the said time. [*f. 94r*]
Names of the jurors: Henry Chapman of Finedon, John Schakyl of Woodford, Hugh de la Hay of the same, William Cotyne of Irthlingborough, Robert Harwedon of Finedon, William atte Cros of Woodford, John Gyles of Finedon, Thomas Sompt[er] of Great Addington, Robert Kyng of Burton, William Joshu' of Islep, Thomas Tree of Irthlingborough, William Nicol of Cranford, Richard Warein of Aldwincle, Ralph Golde of Irthlingborough, Richard atte Hoo of Cranford, William Warde of Little Addington, Nicholas Pygot of the same, Hugh Chaundeler of Irthlingborough.

[Latin]
[PRO JUST1 1467 m.5d]

230 Letter of Richard Wydemill, sheriff of Northampton, requesting
Robert Pwe (*sic*) of Irthlingborough, his bailiff, to deliver full
seisin of the above plot of land to John Pyel.
[Latin]

[Folio 94v blank.]

231 [*f. 95r*] Release of John Wake son of Sir Hugh Wake to Adam
Fraunceys, John Pyel, Henry Pyel, clerk, and William de Braybrook, clerk, their heirs and assigns in all land and rents with
services, meadows, pastures, commons, demesnes, suits of court,
wardships, marriages, reliefs, escheats, reversions together with
villeins and their dependants, waifs, strays, hundreds, leets and
all other appurtenances in Irthlingborough which should pass to
him right of inheritance after the deaths of his father and of
Isabel de Assheton, mother of the said Hugh his father. Warranty.
Witnesses: John Stephene, John Campioun, Robert Pu, John
Ward, John de Heigham and others.
Irthlingborough, 28 September 1365.
[Latin]

[*f. 95v*] Touching the lands and tenements which John Pyel had
of John son of John de Keterynge of Irthlingborough, clerk, in
Irthlingborough and Finedon, by exchange for certain tenements
in Northampton on 17 February 1367 as appears by indented
charter.

232 Charter of John Keterynge of Irthlingborough granting to John
Pyel of the same all his lands and tenements in Irthlingborough
and Finedon, which he had of the gift of John Keterynge, clerk,
son of Hugh Keterynge of Irthlingborough, to be held by John
Pyel, his heirs and assigns, of the chief lords of the fee by due
services and right customs in perpetuity. Warranty.
Witnesses: John Campyoun, John Stevene, John Warde, John
Body, William Coton, Robert Pu, all of Irthlingborough, and
others.
Irthlingborough, 17 February 1367.
[Latin]

233 Indenture bearing witness that John Pyel of Irthlingborough granted to John Keterynge of the same, by way of exchange for certain lands and tenements in Irthlingborough and Finedon, one tenement in Northampton in a narrow lane called 'Laurencetwychen' with appurtenances between the tenement which was formerly of William Durnesale and the tenement which was formerly of Richard de Stratford, together with one shop adjacent to William Wythemale, which tenement and shop Philip Pyfford and Margery his wife once held of Simon Launcehull and which Robert Golofre now holds. Also a curtilage in Butchers' Street (*vico carnificum*), Northampton, next to the tenement which was formerly of Simon Lorifer to the west, which curtilage Thomas Campyoun and Joan his wife now hold. Also a shop in the Poultry [*vico pellipariorum*), Northampton, formerly of John de Staunfford, which Nicholas Trank held of the donor and which the said Robert [Golofre] now holds, which tenement, curtilage and shops [*f. 96r*] the donor had of the gift and feoffment of the said Simon Launshull, to be held by John de Keterynge and his heirs in perpetuity, at an annual rent to the donor of 5s and rendering to the chief lords of the fee due services and right customs. If John Keterynge die without legitimate heir, the properties will revert to John Pyel and his heirs, and if Pyel or his heirs is sued with regard to the lands and tenements in Irthlingborough and Finedon by John Keterynge, his heirs or assigns or anyone else in his name, then he may re-enter those tenements and occupy them peacefully in perpetuity, the present charter notwithstanding. Warranty.

Witnesses: William Wakeleyn, mayor of Northampton, Robert Spycer and John Geydyngton of the same, John Campyoun of Irthlingborough, John Stevene, John Warde and Robert Pu of the same and others.

Irthlingborough, 17 February 1367.

[Latin]

234 [*f. 96v*] Release of John Keterynge of Irthlingborough to John Pyel, his heirs and assigns of all his lands and tenements in Irthlingborough and Finedon which he had of the gift of John Keteryng clerk, son of Hugh Keterynge of Irthlingborough. Warranty.

Witnesses: John Campyoun of Irthlingborough, John Stevene, John Warde, John Body, William Coton and Robert Pu of the same.

Irthlingborough, 1 June 1368.

[Latin]

[Fos. 97 and 98 blank.]

235 [*f. 99r*] Memorandum that Walter de Chiriton, Thomas de
Swanlund and Gilbert de Wendlingburgh, farmers of the king's
customs, were bound to John Pyel and his associates in more
than £2,500, and the said Walter and his associates sent a letter
to their attorney Richard de Stourton, one of the customers at
the port of St Botolph, to pay the said John £1,000 in part
payment of the sum on 29 September 1349. Whereupon Stourton
delivered to him by indenture £926, for which Pyel was arrested
in London on 11 November 1349 at the suit of John Malwayn
and Hugh de Ulseby, mainpernors of the said Walter and his
associates, by reason that Walter and his associates were also in
debt to the king and that satisfaction should be made to the king
before any other. Pyel was accordingly adjudged in the court of
Exchequer to the Fleet until he should have made satisfaction of
the said sum, as appears in the memoranda of the year 1349–50
among the Recorda of the Michaelmas term before William
Peek.[1] And so for this reason Pyel remained in prison for about
half a year and was then mainperned. And at the same time he
worked as an agent for the king, who granted by letter patent
that he should be discharged of the sum of £926, restoring to
the Exchequer true debts owed by the king amounting to the
said sum within three years as appears by the copy of the said
patent written hereafter.
[French]

   1 PRO LTR E368/122 Michaelmas Recorda rot. 9.
[See introduction 1 (ii).]

236 [*f. 99r-v*] Transcription in full of letter patent dated 26 May 1352.
[*CPR 1350–1354*, 265–6.]
[Latin]

237 [*f. 99v*] And memorandum that John Pyel was granted a post-
ponement for the repayment of £300 of the said bills and patents
in the Exchequer for the first year by virtue of a writ addressed
to the treasurer and barons of the Exchequer as appears by the
copy written hereafter.
[French]

238 [*f. 100r*] Copy of a writ addressed to the treasurer and barons of
the Exchequer granting of the king's special grace a post-
ponement to John Pyel with respect to the restoration of letters
patent or bills of true debts owed by the king up to the sum of
£300 from before the quindene of Easter next until the quindene

of Michaelmas next, and then, by the king's further grace until
the quindene of Easter following [1355].
Witness the king himself.
Westminster, 10 October 1353.
[Latin]

239 And memorandum that John Pyel restored to the Exchequer on
20 February 1354 in five letters patent, tried (*triez*) in the Exchequer, of true debts owed by the king from Dordrecht to the
value of £325 9s 6¼d, namely:
A patent made to Hugh Curteys of Hicham of Higham Ferrers,
26 January 1351, containing £107 19s 10¼d.
[Margin.] Purchased of him.
A patent made to Peter a Besewyk of Beverley, 1 February 1351,
containing £33 10s 5d.
A patent made to John Jurdan of Retford, 15 May 1352 containing
£33 15s 1¼d.
[Margin for both the above patents.] Purchased of Walter Kolby.
A patent made to Henry Goldbetere of York and John Loc-
rington, 30 June 1352, containing £107 4s 9d.
A patent made to Roger Selyman of Stafford, 20 July 1352,
containing £35 19s 4¾d.
[Margin for both patents.] Purchased of William Melchebourne.
[French]

240 [*f. 100v*] Memorandum that John Pyel restored to the Exchequer
on 26 April 1354 a letter patent cleared in the Exchequer (*claree
en leschere*) made to John Baret containing the sum of £302 0s 9d
and dated 12 October 1353.[1]
By memoranda roll for 1353-4.
[French]

1 PRO LTR E368/126 Michaelmas Commissions rot. 1d.

241 Item a patent of John atte Holte of Birmingham, cleared in the
Exchequer (*clarifiee en lescheqer*), being part of the debt from
Dordrecht and bearing the Exchequer seal, of £398 5s 5d which
Pyel restored to Sir William Peek in the Exchequer on 9 February
1355 in full payment of the £926. And so John Pyel had a surplus
of £99 15s 8½d, and a patent to the value of that sum was made
in his favour, sealed by Sir William Peek as appears below. And
Pyel was quit.
[French]

242 Copy of a letter patent of the Exchequer notifying that before
the prescribed date of Easter, viz. 9 February 1355, John Pyel

restored there a letter patent under seal of the Exchequer dated
23 April 1353 among the commissions of the Easter term,[1] by
which letter the king was bound to John atte Holte of Birmingham
in £398 5s 5d for wool delivered by the said John at Dordrecht
to the use of the king, and that the same John Pyel petitions that
restitution of the said letter be allowed, [f. 101r] namely that
£298 9s 8[½]d be allowed from it in fulfilment of the total
amount which he had to restore in patents or bills of true debts
at Easter 1355 in complete restitution of the said £926, which
had been postponed in the Exchequer Rolls of William Peek,
and that a new letter patent of the remaining £99 15s 8½d should
be made to him under seal of the Exchequer. And this was
granted, and restitution of the said letter patent containing £398
5s 5d was allowed and allowance was also made to John Pyel
for £298 9s 8½d according to his request, and a new letter was
made to him under the seal of the Exchequer for the remaining
£99 15s 8½d, and the letter patent containing £398 5s 5d was
cancelled. And this patent was made in the middle of the year
1354-5 among the Commissions of the Hilary term.[2]
[Latin]

1 PRO LTR E368/125 Easter Commissions rot. 11d.
2 E368/127 Hilary Commissions.

243 And so the said John Pyel is quit in the Exchequer. And he has
a surplus of £99 15s 8½d of which he has a patent under seal of
the Exchequer under the name of John atte Holte.
[Latin]

[f. 101v. blank]

244 [f. 102r.] Touching the exchanges of the king in which Pyel was
involved as appears among the Recorda of the Michaelmas term
1353.[1]

Copy of an entry in the Originalia Rolls for 1352-3 that the king
by letters patent under the great seal, dated 3 September 1352,
appointed John Pyel to the office of changer (cambiatoris) of all
the king's moneys, both gold and silver, to hold and exercise for
himself and his deputies in any location within the kingdom of
England, in mints (cunagiis) and elsewhere as the king may please,
according to an indenture made between the king and the same
John who was summoned to appear in the Exchequer on 30
September [1354] to render account to the king of the issues and
profits for the time he was in office and for which he had not

rendered account. And the same John came and said that he was not due to make account for this since he had satisfied the king for the time he was in office, viz. from 1 August 1352 to the following Christmas, with respect to the farm of the exchanges and all the moneys received by him by virtue of the said office. Whereupon he delivered a writ of the king under great seal which is among the *communia* of this term concerning his acquittance as follows: Edward king of England and France and lord of Ireland to his Treasurer and barons of the Exchequer. Whereas John Pyel, lately farmer of our exchanges of coinage, delivered by our command to John de Wesenham all the moneys which he had received of our chamber for the better maintenance of this office and also £100 for the farm which pertains to this office of money-changer for all the time which the same John Pyel held this office, from 1 August 1352 to the following Christmas, to our beloved clerk William Rothewell, receiver of moneys of the Chamber, and to provide for the security of the same John Pyel, we have remitted and quitclaimed, as appears in our letters patent sealed with the griffon seal, to him, his heirs and executors all actions and suits which we and our heirs [might have] against him because of his involvement [*melluris*] in the said exchanges, we command that when you have seen these letters you cause the said John Pyel to be discharged from rendering such an account to you and to be quit thereof, according to the tenor of our letters abovesaid, charging the others who were responsible for the receipts from that Christmas [1352], [*f. 102v.*] and you must order all distraint you have made against the same John Pyel to be released. Witness the king, Westminster, 4 October 1353. And he showed the court two letters patent under griffon seal, one being an acquittance of £100 in these words:
[A French copy of the foregoing writ given under griffon seal and dated Westminster, 24 July 1353.]
And since in the said patents under great seal mention was made of an indenture made between the king and the same John concerning the office of changer, John Pyel was asked to show the indenture. And he said that no such indenture was made and that he had left office before such an indenture was made, as Henry de Greystoke, steward of the chamber estates, here present in court bears witness. And so it was considered that the same John should be discharged of the said account and that the account itself should be postponed indefinitely [*de reddicione inde eat sine die*]. And John returned the letters patent under great seal.

[Latin]
[*Abbrev. Rot. Orig.*, 222]

  1 PRO LTR E368/126 rot.7.

245 [*f. 103r.*] Memorandum that John Pyel, citizen of London, on 16
December 1353, made a recognizance of statute merchant before
Adam Fraunceys, mayor of London, to Thomas de Langeton
and Robert de Lichefeld, citizens of London of £1,097 13s 4d to
be paid at Easter next following. And John Pyel made the
recognizance without sealing the statute and was therefore not
bound to the said Thomas and Robert in anything. He did this
in order to safeguard his lands and rents in case any risk should
attend them (*en cas qe null' peril y avenist*).
[French]

246 Item Pyel made a similar statute of the same sum and date to
Robert de Lichefeld and Thomas de Langeton, but nothing is
owed and Pyel has the two said statutes with him.
[French]

247 [*f. 103v*] The income from rent etc. of John Pyel, Michaelmas
1358, and of Adam Fraunceys in the county of Northampton.

First of Sir John de Boys 16 marks for the term of the lives of
Adam and John and one year beyond, as appears before in this
paper: £10 13s 4d
Item of the abbot of Sulby £20 for the term of the lives of the
said Adam and John as appears before:[1] £20 0s 0d
Item of William Malore of Sudborough 20 marks for the lives of
the said John and Joan his wife as appears before: £13 6s 8d.
Item of John Daundelyn of Cranford 100s for the lives of the
said John and Joan as appears more fully before: £5 0s 0d
Rent from demesne holdings.
First in Irthlingborough by good estimation around £13 in fee
and 70 capons and 1 lb of cumin.
Item of John Trewe 20s.[2]
Item around 10 marks at the death of Lady Ashton [Dasshton]
of the tenements which she holds of the Wakes fee in Irthlingborough.[2]
Item his mill leased in Irthlingborough for 23 quarters of toll
corn each year. And John Pyel will be quit of all toll for the
whole of this year.
[*f. 104r*] Item in Great Addington: £2 1s 9½d and twenty capons.

Item in Little Addington: 18s od and three capons.
Item in Northampton: £4 5s od.
of which 4s to be paid to the master of Dingley.[3]
Item in Woodford: £10.
Item in Wellingborough: £13.
and will increase by sixteen parcels of 'bordlond' at the end of
six years after Michaelmas 1358, around 20s.[2]
Item the mill of John Pyel, worth *pa*: [Ms. blank].
[*f. 104v*] Item in Orlingbury: £2 8s od.
Item in Cransley, by estimation: £12.
Also 6 capons, 2lb cummin, 17 hens and 9 cocks.
Total: £106 7s 9d.
[French]

1 See above, **36**.
2 The total appears not to include the 10 marks accruing after the death of
Lady Ashton, nor the two additional rents of 20s.
3 The preceptory of the Knights Hospitallers at Dingley. See *VCH Northants* ii,
142–4.

248 [*f. 105r*] John Daundelyn acknowledged a debt to the king of
£100 on 30 March 1352,[1] of which £40 was to be paid at
midsummer 1352, and £60 at Michaelmas 1352 by mainprise of
William of Irthlingborough [and] William Lenneise of county
Bedford. And he received an account of £73 6s 8d as still
outstanding on this debt, of which £20 was restored to the king
in his chamber through the hands of Robert de Mildenhale,
clerk, receiver of moneys of the king's chamber, in the form of
letters patent of the king sealed with the griffon seal, dated 1352,
for which £20 the said Robert must make account (*debet respondere*),
and £20 was restored to the king in chamber through the hands
of William de Rothewelle, clerk, receiver of the same chamber,
in the form of letters patent sealed with the griffon seal, dated
1353, for which £20 William must make account.[2] And John
Daundelyn still owes £33 6s 8d in the great roll of the year 33
Edward III [1358–9] in Item Norht'.
[Latin]
[PRO Pipe Roll E372/204, Item Norht' m. 2.]

1 As a fine for felony, see below.
2 Both sums restored on Daundelyn's behalf by John Pyel in 1359, see below.

249 Memorandum that John Daundelyn was indicted of felony and
made satisfaction to the king for £100 and received his charter.
He was then given grace to pay 10 marks *pa*, of which 10 marks
was paid by himself, and £20 for three years by the abbot of

Peterborough, and John Pyel delivered two acquittances under
griffon seal to the Exchequer, as appears above, on 2 December
1359. And £33 6s 8d remained outstanding, as appears in the
Pipe Roll.¹ And the said John Daundelyn owed to the abbot of
Peterborough the amounts which follow, an account of which
the said abbot sent to John Pyel at Christmas 1359.
[French]

    1 See above, **248**.

250 [Margin.] De pipa anno xxxij.¹

From John Daundelyn: of the remainder of 42s for the first year
of the fifteenth and tenth granted to the king for three years by
the laity in 1348, 24s; for the second year of the subsidy, 47s;² for
the third year of the subsidy, 42s. From John Daundelyn, lately
collector of the fifteenth and tenth, for the same fifteenth for the
same year, 42s; for the tenth and fifteenth granted by the laity
for three years in 1352, 42s; assessed for one archer, 40s.
[Latin]
[PRO Pipe Roll E372/202 Norht' mm. 1d, 2d, Item Norht' m.
1.]

    1 *recte* 31 Edward III (1356–7).
    2 *recte* 42s.

251 Memorandum that Pyel paid in London at Easter 1360 for John
Daundelyn to the abbot of Peterborough £10.
[French]

252 [*f. 105v*] De pipa anno tricesimo tercio.¹

Of John Daundelyn of moneys which the said John [owed], 30
March 1352, by mainprise of William of Irthlingburgh and
William Lenneyse of county Bedford: £80.
Of the same John of issues and amercements: 9s.
[Latin]
[PRO Pipe Roll E372/203 Norht' m. 1d.]

    1 *recte* 32 Edward III (1357–8).

[Folios 106 and 107 blank.]

[*f. 108r*] The lands etc. purchased of William atte Walle of
Bedford.

253 Charter of William atte Walle, son of Geoffrey atte Walle of
Bedford, granting to John Pyel of Irthlingborough, John Clyve

and John Wendlyngburgh, a tenement in Bedford with appurtenances situated in 'Bryggestrete', Bedford, between the tenement lately of Robert Carbonel, carpenter, to the south, and
the tenement which Roger Levy holds of the master of St John
of Bedford to the north, 28 acres of arable land in the fields and
within the liberty of Bedford, and 2 acres of meadow lying in
'Kyngesmede' in the parish of Newnham next Bedford, to be
held by the feoffees and the heirs and assigns of John Pyel of the
chief lords etc. in perpetuity.
Witnesses: John Bozoun, mayor of Bedford, Thomas Jordon and
Roger Bartelos, bailiffs of the same town, Richard Frereman,
clerk of the same, William Kempeston, Simon Arnold, Roger
Salford, John Frereman of Bedford and others.
Bedford, 2 May 1369.
[Latin]   [fo. 108r]

254 Indenture made between John Pyel of Irthlingborough, John
Clyve and John Wendlyngburgh of the one part, and William
atte Walle son of Geoffrey atte Walle of Bedford and Isabel his
wife of the other, bear witness that whereas the said John Pyel,
John Clyve and John Wendlyngburgh leased to William and
Isabel for their lives the above tenement in Bedford at an annual
rent to the lessors of 60s and rendering to the chief lords of the
fee the charges and services due, [*f. 108v*] the lessors will and
grant that if the said William should pay to the said Pyel 40
marks within three years of the date of this [indenture], they will
re-enfeoff him in the said tenements, lands and meadows. And
the said William wills and grants that if he is re-enfeoffed he will
not sell or transfer his interest in the said tenement, lands and
meadows, or any parcel thereof, except to the said John Pyel, if
he is willing to pay as much as another, and if he does, Pyel is
permitted to re-enter the tenement. And to keep these covenants
the said parties bind themselves, their heirs, executors and all
their goods, and for greater surety the said parties have pledged
their faith to each other.
Bedford, 3 May 1369.
[French]

255 Memorandum that William atte Walle, at the time of this
indenture, made a bond to Pyel of £40 to be paid at Michaelmas
next, and the bond was put in the hand of Roger Levy, as in
neutral hand [*come en owele main*], to keep on condition that if the
said Pyel should be disturbed of the said lands or any covenant
written above by the said William or any other acting on his

behalf, that the said bond would be entrusted by the said Roger to John Pyel, his heirs or assigns, to be recovered from the said William.

[The remainder of the cartulary consists of miscellaneous lists, mostly accounts of labourers' wages, but also includes a list of the assessment for tax of the prebends of the canons of Southwell (undated)].

The Cartulary of Adam Fraunceys

[R]EGISTRUM CARTARUM FINIUM ET MUNI-
MENTORUM DE MANERIIS TERRIS ET TENEMENTIS ADE
FRAUNCEYS CIVIS LONDONIENSIS COMPILATUM ANNO
REGNI REGIS EDWARDI TERCII POST CONQUESTUM
TRICESIMO SEXTO

Et fait savoir qe par cest registre poet home conustre et clerement
entendre leffect et la force de touz les chartres, relees, fyns,
records, endentures de couenantes et autres escritz et munimentz
en la garde le dit Adam esteantz qi touchent les manoirs, terres
et tenementz susditz si avant come home les eust en present et
en paroles plus courtes.

Item en quel cophin chescun chartre ou autre fait sera pre-
stement et coment trove en cas qe home eit en affaire a monstrer
loriginal.

Item coment les ditz manoirs, terres et tenementz ont este
translatees par purchace, descent ou altrement dune persone en
altre tanqz a la fesance de cest registre, cestassavoir par lescriture
en latyn escrit owelement avant deinz le corps le dit registre
leffect et la force de chescune chartre et dautre muniment de la
terre contenue en meme la chartre.

Et par lescriture et nombres mises sur le margyn dune part
coment le cophin deinz quel chescune des chartres et munimentz
susditz sera trove.

Et coment la chartre et autre muniment contenuz en mesme le
cophin sera auxint trove, cestassavoir le cophin par le noun del
manoir et tenement ou ville escrit sur le dit cophin ensemblement
ove un title acordant a lescriture mis sur le dit margin fesant mencion de meisme le cophin et chescune des cartres et munimentz
en ycele par autiel noun del manoir, tenement ou ville escrit sur le
doos de meisme la chartre ou muniment ensemblement ove un
noumbre acordant al noumbre mis sur meisme le margyn owelement encontre la dite escriture de la force de meisme la chartre ou
muniment. Et lescriture mise sur le margyn dautrepart le noun de
celui qi fist la chartre ou autre muniment et le noun de celui a
qi ele feust faite. Et par lescriture en franceois escrit a comence-
ment courtement est declare coment les ditz manoirs et tenementz
feurent purchacez et translatees tanqz au dit Adam et par
lescriture en franceois ascune part entremedle coment la terre
dont la dite escriture fait mencion feust auxint translate plus
especialement par descent ou autrement a autre persone.

Et principalement fait assavoir qe lescriture en latyn qi recite la

force de chartre ou autre muniment est issint entenduz qe le fait
avynt tiel come est suppose par ycele si avant come si ouertement
escrit feusse qe celui qi fist une tiele chartre enfeoffa celui a qi la
chartre feust faite de tant de terre come est contenuz en yceste ou
celui qi fist un tiel relees relessa a celui a qi le relees est suppose
estre fait tout son droit de tant de terre come est contenuz en le dit
relees et issint de touz les fyns et altres munimentz.

[f. 1v]   MANOR OF RUCKHOLT HALL.

[Rubric] Quere omnia scripta tangentia manerium de Rok-
holteshall' in coffino titulato Rokholteshalle.

1 William son of Robert de Bumpstede was seised of the manor
of Ruckholt Hall in the time of Edward I, in which he enfeoffed
Richard la Vache, knight, who re-enfeoffed William in tail, with
reversion to the said Richard and his heirs. And William, son of
the said William de Bumpstede, enfeoffed Robert Bast, who
granted the manor to two chaplains [Nicholas de Staunton and
Geoffrey of Little Billing], and they in turn enfeoffed John
Shordych, knight, and Helen his wife and two others. And
William son of William made a release with warranty. The four
feoffees then enfeoffed two others, [Henry Casenel and Richard
le Moigne, chaplains,] who re-enfeoffed John Shordych and
Helen his wife. John outlived Helen and enfeoffed Nicholas de
Taunton, receiving back a life interest in the manor, with
remainder after his death to William de Bumpstede and Joan,
daughter of the said John Shordych, and their heirs, and thereafter, in default of issue, to the right heirs of William. And this
William is taken to be the son of William son of William son of
William[1] to whom the manor was first granted in tail. When
John Shordych died, William and Joan took possession [of the
manor] and died without issue. After their deaths Richard la
Vache, knight, being the cousin and heir of the said Richard,
donor [of the manor] in tail, took possession by reversion and
received a release with warranty from Robert de Bumpstede, son
of William de Bumpstede, heir collateral to the said William[2] who
had last died in seisin. And [Richard] enfeoffed two chaplains, of
whom one died and the other enfeoffed Adam Fraunceys, as is
contained in the following deeds.

    1 A curious multiplication of the generations (cf. below, 14). In fact this William
was the son of the first William de Bumpstede, son of Robert. For the descent of
this manor see *VCH Essex* vi, 194.
    2 Probably the brother of William junior.

2 Copy of a record made before the justices in eyre in Essex, 1285, containing the enrolment of a charter of William son of Robert de Bumpstede in fee simple with warranty made to Richard de la Vache of the above manor of Ruckholt Hall, and a plea concerning the *quo waranto* of warren and view of frankpledge and the liberties of the said manor.

3 Copy of a fine levied in 1286, containing that Richard la Vache granted the said manor to William son of Robert de Bumpstede and Maud his wife and the heirs of his body, with reversion to the said Richard and his heirs.
[*Feet of Fines, Essex* ii, 54]

4 Charter of William de Bumpstede, son of the above William, son of Robert, and Maud, in fee simple with warranty made at [MS blank], 10 September 1331, to Robert Bast of the same manor of Ruckholt Hall.

5 Release by the same William with warranty made at [MS blank], 3 October 1331, to the same Robert Bast of the aforesaid manor.

6 [*f. 21*] Then the said Robert Bast granted the said manor to Nicholas de Staunton, parson of the church of St Matthew Friday Street, London, and to Geoffrey of Little Billing (*de petit Belynges*) [Northants.], chaplain, who granted it further as appears by the following charter.

7 Charter of the aforesaid Nicholas de Staunton, parson of St Matthew Friday Street, and Geoffrey of Little Billing (*de parva Belynges*), chaplain, in fee simple with warranty made at [MS blank], 7 July 1332, to John Shordich and Helen his wife, Roger Bast, parson of the church of Trimley St Mary [Suffolk], and William Bast his brother of the same manor of Ruckholt Hall.

8 Release in perpetuity by William de Bumpstede son of William de Bumpstede, knight, with warranty made at Leyton, 25 July 1332, to the said John, Helen, Roger and William of the said manor.

9 Charter of John de Shordych and Helen his wife, Roger Bast and William his brother in fee simple with warranty made in London, 10 February 1333, to Henry Casenel of Peterborough, chaplain, and Richard le Moigne of Tadlow [Cambs.], chaplain, of the manor of Ruckholt Hall.

10 Then the said Henry Casenel and Richard le Moigne enfeoffed John Shordych and Helen in the said manor, to them and to the heirs of John.

11 Release in perpetuity by William de Bumpstede with warranty made in London, 15 October 1339, to John de Shordych and Helen his wife of the manor of Ruckholt Hall with appurtenances.

12 After the death of the said Helen, John de Shordych enfeoffed Nicholas de Taunton, parson of the church of Postwick [Norfolk], of the said manor in fee simple. And Nicholas made further feoffment thereof in the following manner.

13 Duplicate copy of a fine engrossed 17 June 1341 containing that Nicholas de Taunton, parson of the church of Postwick, granted the manor to John Shordych, knight, for life with remainder after his death to William de Bumpstede and Joan daughter of Nicholas Shordich and their heirs, and thereafter to the right heirs of William.
[*Feet of Fines, Essex* iii, 59.]

14 Then John de Shordich died and the said William de Bumpstede who was issue in tail of William son of Robert de Bumpstede, first named [*f. 2v*] above [**2**], and his wife Joan took possession [of the manor] and died without issue. Whereupon Richard la Vache, knight, cousin and heir of the abovesaid Richard la Vache, *viz.* son of Richard, son of Richard, son of the above Richard la Vache, took possession of the manor, and Robert de Bumpstede, heir collateral to the second William de Bumpstede, made a release with warranty in the following manner.

15 Release in perpetuity by Robert de Bumpstede son of William de Bumpstede, knight, with warranty made at Chalfont, 6 July 1349, to Richard la Vache, knight, of the said manor of Ruckholt Hall.

16 Charter of the same Richard la Vache, knight, in fee simple made at Leyton, 23 June 1355, to Thomas de Pateshull, chaplain, and Nicholas atte Wyk of the aforesaid manor of Ruckholt Hall.

17 Writing of the same Richard la Vache, of the same place and date, granting all chattels in the said manor to Thomas de Pateshull and Nicholas atte Wyk.

18 Letter of attorney, of the same place and date, made by the same Richard to deliver seisin of the said manor to Thomas de Pateshull and Nicholas atte Wyk.

19 Letter patent of the said Richard addressed to the said tenants of the said manor to attorn to the said Thomas and Nicholas following the said feoffment. [No date given].

20 Release in perpetuity by the said Richard made in London, 29 June 1355, to the same Thomas de Pateshull and Nicholas atte Wyk of the manor of Ruckholt Hall.

21 Then the said Nicholas died, whereupon the whole [manor] accrued to the said Thomas, who granted it by fine to Adam Fraunceys and Agnes his wife in the following manner.

22 Part of a fine levied at Westminster, 31 May 1359, containing that Thomas de Pateshull granted the aforesaid manor to Adam Fraunceys, citizen of London, and Agnes his wife for the whole of their lives, with remainder to Robert Fraunceys in fee tail and thereafter to Adam Fraunceys junior in fee tail and the right heirs of Adam Fraunceys, citizen of London.
[*Feet of Fines, Essex* iii, 124.]

23 Release in perpetuity by Philip de Bumpstede son and heir of Robert de Bumpstede of Stoke with warranty made in London, 11 April 1360, to Adam Fraunceys and Agnes, Robert, and Adam [*f. 31*] Fraunceys junior of the manor of Ruckholt Hall.
[*CCR 1360–4*, 108]

24 Release in perpetuity by Nicholas Shordych of Leytonstone and Alice his wife without warranty made at Leyton, 2 February 1357, to Adam Fraunceys and Thomas de Langeton, chaplain, of 3 acres of land with appurtenances in Leyton lying in 'Wachefeld'.

Tenements in the Vills of East Ham, West Ham, Barking and Stratford Called Chobhams

[Rubric] Quere omnia scripta tangentia tenementa vocata Chabhames in coffino titulato Chabhames.

25 Memorandum that these tenements were purchased from divers persons by parcels and were transferred from one person to another in parcels until they came into the possession of John de Preston, lately citizen and corder of London, who was the first to have the whole [manor], partly by purchase and partly by descent. And this John enfeoffed John de Sutton, knight, of Wivenhoe and Robert de Teye in fee simple, and Robert released his right to the said John de Sutton, who then enfeoffed Thomas de Chabham, and he in turn enfeoffed Adam Fraunceys as is contained in the following deeds.

26 Charter of Gilbert de Mountfichet in fee simple without date and warranty made to Ralph FitzUrry of half of one hide of land with buildings and pastures in Stratford which Walter de Stretford formerly held of the donor. These tenements by common knowledge (*par overte notice*) had not previously been conveyed by charter.

27 Charter of John de Malbesbury in fee simple with warranty made at West Ham, 15 April 1321, to Thomas Bryan of Southwark and Alice his wife and the heirs of the same Thomas of $\frac{1}{2}$ acre of land with windmill built on it and 7 acres of land with willows and ditches lying in a place called 'Westmerssh', and of 4 acres and 1 rood of arable land, 2 further acres of arable land, 2 acres and 1 rood of meadow, and another acre and a moiety of three hopes of meadow (*hoparum prati*) with appurtenances in West Ham, which the same John had previously acquired of several persons separately as his charter testifies. And the charters of these purchases cannot be found.

28 Thomas Bryan and Alice had issue, William and Richard. Thomas died and Alice outlived him and alienated [the tenements] in the following manner, and William and Richard made releases.

29 [*f. 3v*] Charter of Alice who was the wife of the said Thomas Bryan in fee simple with warranty made at West Ham, 25 June 1330, to John de Preston, citizen and corder of London, of the same tenements acquired by her and her husband, and of all other tenements which she held in West Ham as appears by her charter.

30 Release in perpetuity by William son and heir of Thomas Bryan with warranty made at West Ham, 29 June 1330, to John de

Preston, citizen and corder, of all tenements which were held by his father in West Ham.

31 Release in perpetuity of Richard, the second son of the said Thomas Bryan, without warranty made at West Ham on the same day to John de Preston of all the above lands and tenements.

32 Memorandum that John de Preston succeeded (*avynt*) to the above parcels in the manner abovesaid and to the parcels below in the following manner.

33 Charter of Walter de Wyndesouere in fee simple with warranty without date made to Adam son of William de Lincoln of Great Yarmouth and Joan his wife of all his lands and tenements in East Ham and West Ham.

34 And the said Adam and Joan had issue, Walter, who took possession of these tenements after their deaths and of other tenements which the said Adam and Joan held in their lifetime in East Ham and West Ham and purchased a release from the abbot of Peterborough.

35 Release in perpetuity of the abbot and convent of Peterborough made in chapter, 22 March 1318, to the same Walter son of Adam son of William de Lincoln etc., namely Walter son of Adam of Yarmouth, of the tenements which were held by John de Middleton in East Ham and West Ham.

36 Charter of Walter son of Adam of Yarmouth in fee simple with warranty made at West Ham, 26 June 1318, to Thomas son of Martin de Iseldon of all his tenements in West Ham, namely his capital messuage, 80 acres of land, 26 acres of meadow, 40 acres of pasture, 10s rent, together with other messuages in 'la Forde'.

37 Release in perpetuity by Beatrice, daughter and heir of the said Walter of Wyndesouere of the above charter [**33**] without warranty made at [*f. 4r*] West Ham, 30 May 1321, to Thomas, son of Martin de Iseldon of all the said lands and tenements which were held by her father.

38 Charter of Thomas son of Martin de Iseldon in fee simple with warranty made at West Ham, 13 August 1329, to John de Preston, citizen and corder of London, of all his lands, tenements, rents and reversions in West Ham, East Ham and Barking.

39 Release in perpetuity by William son of Martin de Iseldon, brother of the said Thomas, without warranty made at West Ham, 18 August 1329, to John de Preston, citizen, of all the said lands, tenements and rents.

40 Release in perpetuity by Walter Punchon of West Ham without warranty made at West Ham, 18 August 1329, to John de Preston, citizen, of $2\frac{1}{2}$ acres of land lying in a croft called 'Littlestanefeld', being parcels of tenements which the said John de Preston had acquired of Thomas, son of Martin de Iseldon.

41 Charter of Walter Punchon in fee simple with warranty made at West Ham, 16 June 1331, to John de Preston of two-thirds of a piece of land lying in 'Littlemede' in West Ham, and the reversion of the other third.

42 Charter of Walter Punchon in fee simple with warranty made at West Ham on the same day to John de Preston of 1 acre of land in West Ham in the field called 'Alvenefeld'.

43 Charter of John de Sutton of West Ham in fee simple with warranty made at West Ham, 9 January 1333, to John de Preston of 2s 6d rent from the tenements which were formerly of William Skynnere in West Ham.

44 Release in perpetuity by John de Sutton with warranty made in London on the same day to John de Preston of 2s 6d rent which the said John de Sutton used to receive of the tenement which was then held by the same John de Preston and which previously had been held by Roger le Bakere in West Ham.

45 [*f. 4v*] Release in perpetuity by John de Sutton with warranty made at West Ham, 17 January 1333, to John de Preston of the said 2s 6d rent from the tenement which appears in the above charter [**43**].

46 After the above tenements came into the possession of the said John de Preston they were transferred as follows until they came into the possession of Adam Fraunceys.

47 Charter of John de Preston, citizen and corder of London, in fee simple with warranty made at West Ham, 1 March 1335, to John de Sutton of Wivenhoe, knight, and Robert de Teye of all lands, tenements, rents and reversions which the grantor had in

East Ham, West Ham and Barking, together with the reversion of $4\frac{1}{2}$ acres of land lying in 'Couchecroft', which William Aleman then held for life of the demise of the said Thomas son of Martin [de Iseldon], and the reversion of a third of a piece of land in 'Littlemede' which Christine lately wife of Warin Ede held in dower.

48 Letter patent of John de Preston granting all his goods and chattels in the said lands and tenements, made on the same day, to the said John de Sutton of Wivenhoe and Robert de Teye.

49 Letter patent of the same John de Preston made on the same day and addressed to all his tenants in East Ham, West Ham and Barking, to attorn to the said John de Sutton and Robert de Teye in respect of their services.

50 Duplicate release in perpetuity by the said Robert de Teye without warranty made in the abbey of Barking, 4 June 1335, to John de Sutton of Wivenhoe of all the said lands, tenements, rents and reversions.

51 Charter of John de Sutton, knight, in fee simple with warranty made at Wivenhoe, 10 January 1343, to Thomas de Chabham of all the said lands, tenements, rents and reversions.

52 Letter patent of John de Sutton made at Wivenhoe on the same day appointing William de Teye and John, the donor's son, his attorneys to deliver seisin to the aforesaid Thomas of the said lands, tenements, rents and reversions.

53 [f. 51] Letter patent of John de Sutton of the same date addressed to all his tenants in those places to attorn to Thomas de Chabham.

54 Letter patent of John de Sutton of the same date granting to the same Thomas all goods and chattels on the said tenements.

55 Charter of Thomas de Chabham in fee simple with warranty made at West Ham, 1 August 1356, to Adam Fraunceys, citizen and mercer of London of all lands, tenements, rents and services which the donor had in East Ham, West Ham and Barking.

56 Another charter of Thomas de Chabham in fee simple with warranty made at West Ham, 5 May 1357, to Adam Fraunceys of all lands, tenements, rents and services which the donor then had in the above vills.

57 Letter patent of Thomas de Chabham made on the same day, granting to Adam Fraunceys all his goods and chattels in the said tenements.

58 Release in perpetuity by Thomas de Chabham with warranty made at West Ham, 21 May 1357, to Adam Fraunceys of all the above lands, tenements, rents and services.

59 Charter of Adam Fraunceys in fee simple with warranty made at West Ham, 15 September 1359, to Thomas de Langeton, chaplain, and Henry de Burford of all lands, tenements, rents and services which the grantor had of the gift and feoffment of Thomas de Chabham in East Ham, West Ham and Barking.

60 Charter of Thomas de Langeton and Henry de Burford with warranty made at West Ham, 1 November 1359, to Adam Fraunceys and Agnes his wife of all the said lands, tenements, rents and services, to be held by the grantees for life with remainder to Robert Fraunceys of London, their son born before marriage (*ante sponsalia*), in fee tail, and thereafter to Adam de Fraunceys of London junior, also the son of Adam and Agnes born before marriage, in fee tail, and to the right heirs of Adam Fraunceys, citizen.

61 [*f. 5v*] Release in perpetuity of Margaret who was the wife of Thomas de Chabham without warranty made in London, 24 February 1362, to Adam Fraunceys, citizen and mercer of London, of all lands, tenements, rents and services in East Ham, West Ham and Barking.

62 Charter of Thomas Brasour of West Ham and Ida his wife in fee simple with warranty without date made to Matthew le Chaundler, citizen of London, of $2\frac{1}{2}$ acres of meadow in Stratford, of which 2 acres lie in the 'Whetecroft' next to the meadow of Agnes Tropynel in the north and the meadow called 'Steremede' to the south, extending from the meadow of Adam Fulham to the east to the meadow of Warin Ode in the west, and $\frac{1}{2}$ acre lies in the 'Crokele' next to the meadow of Warin Ode in the north and the meadow of Agnes Tropynel in the south, extending to the River Lea leading to 'Claveresbrugge' in the east and the

meadow of Warin Ode to the west, to be held of the donor by
the service of 12d *pa* for all services.

63 Release in perpetuity of the aforesaid Ida, under the name of
Edith (*per nomen Edithe*), after the death of the said Thomas her
husband without warranty or date to the said Matthew of the
said meadow.

64 Charter of Nicholas Ode of West Ham in fee simple with
warranty without date to Matthew le Chaundeler of $\frac{1}{2}$ acre of
meadow in West Ham lying in the meadow called the 'Wylde'
between the meadow of St Thomas de Acon, London, in the
north and the meadow of Robert le Bret in the south, extending
from the meadow of Richard le Prat in the east to the landing-
stage (*ripam*) of the abbot of Stratford[1] in the west, to be held of
the donor by the service of 2d *pa*.

   1 Stratford Langthorne in West Ham, Essex.

65 Charter of Ellis, son and heir of Matthew le Chaundler, in fee
simple with warranty made at West Ham, 29 May 1315, to
Gilbert de Hardyngham, chaplain, of one messuage in the parish
of St Mary Matfelon without Aldgate, London, and of the said
3 acres of meadow.

66 Release in perpetuity of Thomas le Brasour made at Stratford,
29 May 1315, to Gilbert de Hardyngham of 12d rent contained
in the above charter [**62**].

67 Charter of Gilbert de Hardyngham in fee simple with warranty
made at West Ham, 1 April 1316, to Roger de Depham of the
same 3 acres of meadow.

68 A similar charter concerning the same land.

[*f. 6r*]   WYKE

[Rubric] Quere .l. scripta sequentia in coffino titulato coffinus
.j.

69 Memorandum that the manor of Wyke was purchased in separate
parcels before coming into the possession of Robert Belebarbe
as appears by the following charters. Robert was wholly seised
of the greater part of the manor and enfeoffed Simon de

Abyndon, who purchased several other parcels to the manor as will appear also by the following charters, and then enfeoffed John de Causton of the whole. He in turn purchased other lands as part of the manor and then enfeoffed Adam Fraunceys and Thomas de Langeton, who purchased from Walter Turk and others several parcels to the said manor. Then Thomas de Langeton died [and] after his death the said Adam was foremost in [possession of] the whole (*est einz en lentier*) by surviving, and purchased for himself alone further parcels both in the lifetime of the said Thomas and after his death, as will appear by the following charters.

70 Charter of brother Richard de Hastynge,[1] lately master of the military order of the Temple and head of the same order, in fee simple without date made to Robert de Wych of the whole land of the same master and brothers, which was of brother Aubrey (*Albrighti*), and of 4 acres of land which William de Hastyng had previously granted to the said master and brothers, to be held of the grantors by service of 2 marks *pa.*

> 1 Master of the Temple c.1160 (*VCH London* i, 490).

71 Charter of brother Geoffrey,[1] master of the military order of the Temple in England, and his bretheren in fee simple made without date to Edmund de Grava, son of the aforesaid Robert de Wych, of all that tenement which the said Robert previously held of the said master and brothers, to be held of the same by the same service.

> 1 Geoffrey FitzStephen, master of the Temple c. 1180–5 (*VCH London* i, 490).

72 Charter of confirmation of Fulk, lately bishop of London,[1] in fee simple without date made to Roger Cole of Stepney of all lands with appurtenances which the said Roger formerly held of the said bishop and his predecessors, to be held henceforth by rent of 6s 8d *pa.*

> 1 Fulk Basset, bishop of London 1244–59.

73 Charter of Walter Grumbald son of Richard Grumbald in fee simple with warranty without date made to Hugh son of Hugh Belebarbe of William de Aston his villein (*nativo*) and 13 acres of land, to be held of the donor by service of 8s *pa.*

74 Charter of Hugh son of Hugh Belebarbe in fee simple with warranty, acquittance and defence without date made to Robert le Marchaunt of Hackney of $2\frac{1}{2}$ acres and 1 perch of land in Hackney lying in a field called 'Blakheth', to be held of the donor by annual service of 12d.

75 [*f. 6v*] Memorandum that the above tenements except the said 2 $\frac{1}{2}$ acres and 1 perch descended to Robert de Belebarbe of Hackney, who leased the same tenements and others to Geoffrey Shyre for a term of years, and the same tenements were conveyed in divers ways until they came to Simon de Abyndon.

76 Indenture of Robert Belebarbe made on 29 September 1301 to Geoffrey de la Shire of all his land in Wyke in the parish of Hackney, to be held at farm for twelve years.

77 And the said Geoffrey appointed his executors and died within the said term, and the executors leased the remainder of the term to Richer de Refham of all the above lands.

78 Indenture of Simon de Norton, Andrew de Norton and Ralph Radespreye, executors of the will of the aforesaid Geoffrey de Shire made on 25 December 1302, of all their interest in the remainder of the term of twelve years to Richer de Refham, citizen and mercer of London, of the above tenements in Wyke.

79 Release in perpetuity by Robert de Belebarbe with warranty made in London, 31 October 1312, to Richer de Refham of the said tenements to be held in fee simple at an annual rent of £10 to Robert for life.

80 Memorandum that this release seems suspect (*suspecionous*) in that the seal does not accord with other seals of the said Robert, and defective (*defectif*) in that it appears that the above term of twelve years had ended before the release was made.

81 Another release by perpetuity of Robert de Belebarbe as above [**79**].

82 Indenture of Robert Belebarbe made in London, 29 September 1315, containing that whereas the same Robert formerly leased to Richer de Refham his tenements in the above form at an annual rent to him of £10 for life, and whereas the same Richer later granted the said tenements back to Robert for life in recompense for the said ten [*f. 7r*] pounds, the same Robert grants that as soon as Richer pays him 100 marks then he may take possession of the said tenements, to be held by him and his heirs in perpetuity.

83 And memorandum that the term of the first lease made to the said Geoffrey de Shire of the above tenements, which term, after the death of the said Geoffrey, was purchased by the said Richer as is written above, ended in the sixth or seventh year of the reign of King Edward II.[1] At the end of this term the said Robert took possession as upon his reversion, before which he had never released to Richer the above tenements as he himself testified in his letter patent following [**87**], so that the said Richer had no other interest in the above tenements except for that term, and the above release and indenture and another release following [**84**] were made when the said Robert was in possession after the end of the term of the first lease made to Geoffrey Shire.

    1 I.e. between 8 July 1312 and 7 July 1314.

84 Indenture of an agreement [made] between Robert Belebarbe and Richer de Refham, presumed to be counterfeit (*supposita fore facta*), 29 September 1313, whereby Robert granted the tenements of Wyke to the said Richer to be held until Christmas and that the same Richer of his grace granted that the said Robert might henceforth hold the tenements for life.

85 And memorandum that when the said Robert had entered upon his tenements at Wyke as in his reversion after the said term of twelve years, he leased the same tenements to Simon de Abyndon for a term of twelve years and then affirmed his interest by charters of release and by fine as will appear by the following evidences, and he leased other tenements in Stepney to John Tolymer and then released to him, and also entered negotiations (*bargaigna*) with John Prodehomme on the same tenements first leased to the said Simon, but finally Simon purchased the interest of each of them and secured release from them so that his interest was well affirmed by all parties.

86 Release in perpetuity by Robert Belebarbe made 22 January 1316 at Stepney to John Tolymer of a messuage and adjacent field called 'Northshote' in Stepney which the said Robert had previously granted to him by charter.

87 Letter patent of Robert Belebarbe, written in French in London, 20 November 1317, approved by the seals of nine other persons testifying that all agreements [made] by the said Robert [f. 7v] with the said Richer de Refham or John Prodhomme of the aforesaid lands or tenements were false and contrived (*coniecturate*) in order to defraud Simon de Abyndon of his title.

Here begin the deeds of purchase of Simon de Abyndon of the above tenements.

88 Release in perpetuity of Robert Belebarbe with warranty, made at Stepney, 5 January 1316, to Simon de Abyndon and Eve his wife and the heirs of Simon of the above messuage and field called 'Northshot' in Stepney which John Tolymer purchased of the said Robert and granted to Simon and Eve.

89 The charter of the messuage and field made by John Tolymer to Simon de Abyndon follows [**92**], and thus shows that this release is dated before the charter.

90 Confirmation and release in perpetuity of Robert Belebarbe made with warranty at Hackney, 9 January 1316, to Simon de Abyndon and Eve his wife and the heirs of Simon of the whole manor of Wyke in Hackney with a weir pertaining to the manor and $4\frac{1}{2}$ acres of meadow in a meadow called 'Bokemed', which the same Simon and Eve formerly held at farm of the demise of the said Robert for a term of years.

91 Charter of Robert Belebarbe in fee simple with warranty made at Hackney, 10 January 1316, to Simon de Abyndon and Eve and the heirs of Simon of all lands and tenements contained in the preceding confirmation.

92 Charter of John Tolymer in fee simple with warranty made at Stepney, 12 January 1316, to the said Simon and Eve and the heirs of Simon of one messuage and one adjacent field called 'Northshot' which he had of the gift and feoffment of Robert Belebarbe.

93 Another charter of Robert Belebarbe in fee simple with warranty made at Stepney, 12 January 1316, to Simon de Abyndon and Eve and the heirs of Simon of the above messuage and field.

94 [f. 8r] And memorandum that the said Robert released his right in these tenements as appears above [**88**].

95 Release in perpetuity by John de Leenham called Prodhomme, made in London, 13 January 1316, to Simon de Abyndon of 36 acres of land with appurtenances in the field called 'Northshote' in Stepney which Robert Belebarbe had granted by his charter to Simon.

96 Release in perpetuity by John Tolymer made at Hackney, 14 January 1316, to Simon de Abyndon and Eve of the whole manor of Wyke and all lands and tenements in Hackney in which Robert Belebarbe enfeoffed the said Simon and Eve.

97 Another release by John Tolymer made in London, 29 March 1316, to Simon and Eve of the messuage and field called 'Northshote' in Stepney.

98 Indenture of John Tolymer made to the said Simon and Eve in London, 15 January 1316, containing that if Simon and Eve were sued by Robert Belebarbe, by John de Leenham called Prodhomme or by Richard Poterel concerning the above messuage and field, then they should retain out of 140 marks which they owe to John Tolymer their expenses incurred by that suit.

99 Duplicate part of a fine made on 13 June 1316, whereby Robert Belebarbe acknowledged two messuages and 90 acres of land with appurtenances in Stepney and Hackney which comprise the manor of Wyke to be the right of the same Simon, to be held in fee simple with warranty by Simon and Eve and the heirs of Simon.
[*Feet of Fines, Lond. & Middx.* i, 92]

100 Release in perpetuity by Robert Belebarbe son and heir of the said Robert Belebarbe made in London, 21 November 1317, to Simon de Abyndon and Eve of all lands and tenements in Hackney and Stepney in which his father had enfeoffed Simon and Eve.

101 [*f. 8v*]Release in perpetuity by Basilia who was the wife of Robert Belebarbe senior made in London, 23 December 1321, to Simon and Eve of all the aforesaid lands and tenements.

102 Memorandum that in the above form the said Simon and Eve purchased the said manor of Wyke and the other lands and tenements mentioned above, and then by the charter below [**108**] and those which follow it [purchased] other lands and tenements. And now the next five deeds show how Adam Fraunceys bought certain tenements in Stepney which formerly belonged to Robert Barnard.

103 Charter of John Westheye and Aubrey his wife in fee simple with warranty, acquittance and defence without date made to Robert Barnard of 13 acres of land, 4 acres of meadow, part of a moiety of one messuage in Old Ford, and the reversion of a dower in the parish of Stepney of the inheritance of the said Aubrey.

104 Part of a fine levied 25 February 1294 whereby John de Westheye and Aubrey granted the moiety of one messuage, 80 acres of land and 28 acres of meadow in Stepney and other tenements in the same vill to Robert Barnard and his heirs in perpetuity. [*Feet of Fines, Lond. & Middx.* i, 65]

105 Indenture of Roger Osekyn and Isabel his wife, kinswoman and nearest blood heir to Robert Barnard, made 29 September 1346 to Thomas Peterfeld and Elizabeth his wife of one messuage with adjacent garden and a croft called 'Conyer', 8 acres of land and a moiety of a piece of meadow called 'Chalshope', 3 acres and 6 roods of meadow in 'Bryghtonesmersh' and 'Littlehamme', with ponds and ditches, a small garden [and] three shops with solars opposite the messuage in Old Ford, to be held for twelve years, which tenements are parcels of the said tenements contained in the fine [**104**].

106 Charter of Isabel lately wife of Roger Oskyn in fee simple with warranty made at Old Ford, 29 August 1359, to Adam Fraunceys and Thomas de Langeton, clerk, of the tenement contained in the preceding indenture.

107 Letter patent of the said Isabel of the same date addressed to Walter Hedecrone to deliver to the same Adam and Thomas seisin of the said tenements.

[*f. 91*] Here follow other deeds showing how the said Simon de Abyndon and Eve his wife purchased other tenements in Hackney and Stepney and how the tenements descended.

108 Release in perpetuity by Richard de Wretile of Chigwell with warranty, made at Old Ford, 29 September 1317 to Simon de Abyndon of all land in 'Calvercroft', 'Eldelonde' and 'Colleshache' in Stepney in which the said Richard formerly enfeoffed the said Simon.

109 Charter of Helen le Chapman of Hackney and Benedict la Chapman son and heir of Cecily le Chapman, sister of the said Helen, in fee simple with warranty, made at Hackney, 18 May 1319, to Simon de Abyndon of $2\frac{1}{2}$ acres and 1 rood of land lying in a field called 'Blackhathe' in Hackney.

110 Release in perpetuity by William Godyng of Hackney made at Hackney on the same day to Simon de Abyndon of the land last mentioned.

111 Charter of William Richecale of Stepney in fee simple with warranty made at Stepney, 29 April 1321, to Simon de Abyndon of 5 roods of land in a place called 'Colleshache' in Stepney.

112 Indenture of Sir John de Hastynges, lord of Abergavenny, made in London, 20 July 1319, to Simon de Abyndon of a water mill, 35 acres of meadow, lordship and service of all his tenants in Hackney, to be held at farm for a term of ten years from the said date.

113 Quitclaim of the said John de Hastynges made in London, 1 August 1319, to Simon de Abyndon of all the farm which Simon ought to pay him for the above tenements.

114 [f. 9v] Memorandum that the said Simon completed his term's interest in the above tenements, and then the said lord [Hastynges] entered them, whereby Simon had no further interest in them. And Simon had a son, Stephen, and Simon died seised of such interest as he had purchased in the above manner in all the tenements and manor of Wyke. After his death John de Causton, citizen and mercer of London, married Eve, who was Simon's wife, and with such title as he had (*de tiel estat come il poait*) he seized (*occupa*) all the manor, lands and tenements which Simon had purchased, until the said Stephen, his son and heir, made release to John and Eve and the heirs of John in the following manner.

115 Release in perpetuity by Stephen son of Simon de Abyndon with warranty made in London, 16 December 1327, to John de Causton, citizen and mercer of London, and Eve his wife, mother of the said Stephen, of all the manor, lands and tenements abovesaid, and all other tenements in Hackney and Stepney which should descend to Stephen after the deaths of the said Simon and Eve.

116 Memorandum that the said Stephen married a woman pregnant with a son, Adam, fathered by another person, and the same woman acknowledged before a notary that the said Adam was not the son of Stephen and the instrument of this recognizance follows.

117 Acknowledgement of Isabel, wife of Stephen de Abyndon son of Simon, made before a notary that Adam, son of the said Isabel and born within wedlock, was not the son of the said Stephen.

118 Memorandum that the said John de Causton purchased other lands and tenements in Hackney and Stepney to the aforesaid manors and other lands in the following manner.

119 Release in perpetuity by William de Athirby, made in London, 1 December 1345, to the said John de Causton and Eve his wife and the heirs of the same John of all lands and tenements which they then held in Hackney and Stepney.

120 [*f. 10r*] Release in perpetuity by John son of John de Refham made in London, 25 November 1348, to John de Causton and Eve his wife of all the aforesaid manor, lands and tenements.

121 Charter of Richard Trugge in fee simple with warranty without date made to William le Bakere of 1 acre of land lying in the field called 'Blakhath' in Stepney.

122 Charter of Robert Barnard of Stepney in fee simple with warranty made at Stepney, 12 March 1299, to John Colman of the said acre of land lying at 'Blackhath'.

123 Charter of Agnes Barnard daughter and heir of Robert Barnard in fee simple with warranty made at Stepney, 16 November 1323, to John de Causton and Eve and the heirs of John of $6\frac{1}{2}$ acres in Stepney of which the aforesaid acre lying in 'Blakhath' is one.

124 Another charter of the same grantor and grantees made on the same date of 8 acres and 3 roods of land in Stepney.

125 Charter of John May in fee simple with warranty made at

Stepney, 23 February 1327, to John de Causton and Eve and the heirs of John of 3 acres of meadow in Stepney called 'Langemede'.

126 Charter of Robert Aylmar in fee simple with warranty made at Stepney, 4 February 1321, to Richard atte Pyrye of 2 acres of land in Stepney lying in a place called 'Derwalles'.

127 Memorandum that the said Richard re-enfeoffed the said Robert of the above 2 acres of land.

128 [*f. 10v*] Charter of Robert Aylmar in fee simple with warranty made at Stepney, 15 March 1338, to John de Causton and Eve and the heirs of the same John of the said 2 acres of land lying in 'Derwalles'.

129 Memorandum that the said John de Causton, having such interest in the manor of Wyke and the other lands and tenements mentioned above, enfeoffed Adam Fraunceys and Thomas de Langeton as follows. And Adam and Thomas then purchased several other lands and tenements which lay around the same vills in the following manner.

130 Charter of John de Causton and Eve his wife in fee simple with warranty made at Hackney, 1 February 1349, to Adam Fraunceys and Thomas de Langeton, citizens of London, of the whole of the manor of Wyke and all other lands and tenements with appurtenances which the said John and Eve then held in Hackney and Stepney.

131 Letter patent of John de Causton and Eve made on the same day to William de Causton to deliver seisin to the said Adam and Thomas of the said manor, lands and tenements.

132 Letter patent of the same John and Eve made in London, 31 January 1349, to the same Adam and Thomas concerning chattels in the said lands and tenements.

133 Release in perpetuity by John and Eve with warranty made at Hackney, 6 February 1349, to the said Adam and Thomas of the above manor, lands and tenements.

134 Memorandum that the said manor, lands and tenements thus descended (*devyndrent*) to the said Adam, who outlived Thomas, together with other lands, several in the same vills, in the following manner.

135 [*f. 11r*] Charter of Richard Godyng in fee simple with warranty made at Hackney, 2 October 1323, to Viel Colman, with a garden at 'le Tumbe', $1\frac{1}{2}$ acres and $\frac{1}{2}$ rood of land in 'Sirmannescroft' and 'Sirmannesfeld' in Hackney.

136 Charter of John Brythmare son and heir of John Brythmare in fee simple with warranty made at Hackney, 14 October 1330, to Thomas Fauchon of one messuage with garden and land at 'Tumbestrate' in Hackney.

137 Charter of John Britham (Brithm̊) in fee simple with warranty made at Hackney, 26 October 1335, to Viel Colman and Christine his wife, John and Thomas his sons, and the heirs of John and Thomas of a garden in the same place.

138 Charter of Richard Godyng of Hackney and Alice his wife, called Alice atte Wyke, in fee simple with warranty made at Hackney, 19 March 1321, to Richard atte Pirie of 3 roods of land in Hackney in a place called 'Shortlande'.

139 Charter of Viel Colman in fee simple made at Hackney, 18 April 1350, to Simon de Hampton, chaplain, of a garden with 3 roods of meadow, 1 acre and 1 rood of land at 'Tumbestrete', and two pieces of land in a place called 'Shortlande'.

140 Charter of Roger Legat of Old Ford in fee simple with warranty made at 'Tumbestrete', 31 March 1350, to Simon de Hampton of 1 rood of land in Hackney next to the tenement formerly of Geoffrey le Dryvere.

141 Charter of Nicholas atte Wyke of Bramley in fee simple with warranty made at 'Tumbestrete', 9 May 1350, to Simon de Hampton of 3 roods of land in Hackney next to the garden of Nicholas atte Wyke.

142 [*f. 11v*] Charter of John Rutere in fee simple with warranty made at 'Tumbestrete', 2 May 1350, to Simon de Hampton of $1\frac{1}{2}$ roods of land with appurtenances in Hackney next to the land which he once held there.

143 Charter of Simon de Hampton in fee simple with warranty made at Hackney, 20 July 1350, to Adam Fraunceys and Thomas de Langeton of a garden, 3 roods of meadow, 1 acre and 1 rood of land and two other pieces of land lying in 'Shortelonde' and 'Tumbestrete' in Hackney, and of a further $5\frac{1}{2}$ roods of land in Hackney.

144 Another charter of Simon de Hampton in fee simple with warranty made at Stepney, 18 June 1351, to Adam Fraunceys and Thomas de Langeton of 1 acre in Stepney lying in a place called 'Derwalles', in which John son and heir of Geoffrey Smart of Old Ford, formerly enfeoffed the said Simon. Moreover the said Adam had other lands and tenements in Hackney and Stepney as follows.

145 Charter of Alban de Bevery in fee simple with warranty made at Hackney, 13 January (?)1318,[1] to Richard Pylk and Helen his wife of 11 acres of land and $\frac{2}{3}$ acre of meadow, two-thirds of a messuage and two gardens in Hackney, and the reversion of the land and tenements which Robert Clarel and Alice his wife then held in dower of the same Alice, and the homage and service of William Rolf, Richard Rolf, Benedict de Aston, John de Aston, William de Algate, William le Taillour, Hamo Goodchep, and William de Gerton.

1 The cartulary has Friday, the feast of St Hilary 11 Edward III (1338). In fact Hilary falls on a Tuesday in this year, which in any case must be wrong in view of the date of the following charter. This is evidently a scribal error, probably for 11 Edward II, when Hilary does fall on a Friday.

146 Charter of John de Pontoise and Helen his wife, who was formerly the wife of the said Richard Pilk, in fee simple with warranty made at Hackney, 8 December 1331, to Richard de Stondon, citizen of London, of all the above tenements and rents and divers other tenements and rents which Richard Pylk and Helen jointly [*f. 12r*] acquired in Hackney and Stepney.

147 And the said Richard de Stondon then enfeoffed Walter Turk of all the lands and tenements thus purchased by him, and Walter enfeoffed Adam Fraunceys and Thomas de Langeton as appears by the charter below [**158**].

148 Charter of Edmund Crepyn brother and heir of Ralph Crepyn, son of Walter Crepyn, in fee simple with warranty made at Stepney, 30 November 1331, to William Hannsard of 16 acres of land in a place called 'Collesfeld' with reversion of 2 acres in the same place which Joan, mother of the said Edmund, then held in dower in Stepney.

149 Charter of William Hannsard in fee simple with warranty made at Stepney, 16 July 1340, to John de Brendewode and Alice his wife and the heirs of John of a certain piece of land called 'Collesfeld' in which the said Edmund had enfeoffed him.

150 Release in perpetuity by Edmund Crepyn made in London, 2 February 1341, to John de Brentwode of 8s rent issuing from the tenements which the said John acquired of Robert atte Gate in Hackney.

151 Part of a fine made 13 October 1343[1] whereby John de Brentwode and Alice his wife granted two messuages, 60 acres of land and 3 acres of meadow with appurtenances in Hackney, Tottenham and Stepney, to Michael Mynot and his heirs in perpetuity with warranty, in which are contained the aforesaid 18 acres of land in 'Collesfeld'.
[PRO CP25(1) 150/59 no. 167]

1 MS: 1341.

152 Memorandum that the said Michael Mynot enfeoffed Walter Turk, citizen of London, of the tenements contained in the said fine and of all his other tenements which he had in Hackney, [f. 12v] Tottenham and Stepney, and the interest Walter had by the feoffment continued until John Minot, son and heir of the said Michael, made a release to Walter Turk by the following deed.

153 Release in perpetuity by John Mynot, goldsmith, son and heir of Michael Mynot, with warranty made in London, 10 June 1347, to Walter Turk of all lands, tenements and rents in Hackney, Tottenham and Stepney, in which the said Michael had formerly enfeoffed the said Walter.

154 Release in perpetuity by Mary, who was the wife of Edmund Crepyn, made in London, 19 April 1346, to Walter Turk of all lands and tenements in Stepney which were of the said Edmund as is stated above.

155 Release in perpetuity by Henry atte Broke of Leyton made at Stepney, 28 September 1347, to Walter Turk of $3\frac{1}{2}$ acres of meadow in Leyton.

156 Recovery of $3\frac{1}{2}$ acres of meadow with appurtenances in Leyton at the suit of John de Wrotham of London against Eleanor who was the wife of John Hunteman, who failed to appear (*per defaltam*) before the justices of the bench, 25 November 1347.
[PRO Common Pleas CP40/352 rot. 592.]

157 Charter of John de Wrotham in fee simple with warranty made at Leyton, 26 December 1347, to Walter Turk of the $3\frac{1}{2}$ acres recovered by the said John against the said Eleanor.

158 Charter of Walter Turk in fee simple with warranty made at Hackney, 5 August 1352, to Adam Fraunceys and Thomas de Langeton of all lands and tenements which were of Richard Pilk and Helen his wife in Hackney, of which mention was made in the charter above [**146**], and of 18 acres of land called 'Collesfeld' in Stepney, of which mention was made in the charter above [**151**], between the land of the bishop of London on the west side and the land formerly of John de Stebenhethe and now of the donor on the east side, abutting on the land of Adam Fraunceys and the land of Thomas Morice in the south and on the land formerly of John de Stebenhethe and now of the donor in the north, [*f. 13r*] and of 12 acres of land in Tottenham next to the road called 'Chichiblane' between the land of John Geffray to east and west, abutting on the highway called 'Chichelane' to the north and the land of Peter Adam to the south, and of $\frac{1}{2}$ acre of meadow in Hackney marsh at 'Adgorsoverwade' between the land formerly of John de Aston in the south and the land of William le Taillour which was formerly of John son of Ellis Oke (*de Quercu*) in the north, extending in length from the land of the heirs of Richard Alvard in the west to the River Lea in the east. *Witnesses*: John Galeys, Thomas Morice, Nicholas atte Wyke, John atte Pole, Nicholas Shordich, John de Tuwe, Nicholas Forester, Robert Spir, Hugh Lambyn and others.
[BL Add. Ch. 40513.]

159 Another charter of the same Walter in fee simple with warranty made at Leyton, 8 August 1352, to Adam Fraunceys and Thomas de Langeton of $3\frac{1}{2}$ acres of land in Leyton in which John de Wrotham enfeoffed the said Walter by the above charter [**158**].

160 Letter patent of the same Walter Turk addressed to Nicholas atte Wyke to deliver seisin to the said Adam and Thomas of the said meadow according to the form of the said charter.

161 Release in perpetuity by Nicholas de Silveston made 20 August 1352 to Adam Fraunceys and Thomas de Langeton of all lands and tenements with appurtenances in which Walter Turk enfeoffed the said Adam and Thomas by charter [**158**].

162 Part of a fine made 9 February 1352 whereby Henry Vanner and Joan his wife granted 22 acres of land with appurtenances in Stepney to Nicholas atte Wyke and John de Benyngfeld, chaplain, and the heirs of the said John with warranty.
[*Feet of Fines, Lond. & Middx.* i, 130]

163 Charter of the said Nicholas atte Wyke and John de Benyngfeld, chaplain, in fee simple with warranty made at Stepney, 11 June 1352, to Adam Fraunceys and Thomas de Langeton of 18 acres of land in Stepney lying in the field called 'Harinsardesfeld' next to 'Gyescrouche', which land is included in the preceding fine.

164 Release in perpetuity by John le Smyth of Leytonstone and Helen his wife made at Hackney, 28 June 1358, to Adam Fraunceys and Thomas de Langeton of all lands and tenements which were held by Viel Colman, of which mention was made in charter [**139**].

165 [*f. 13v*] Indenture of William de Gloucestre of London and Maud his wife, lately wife of Edmund Trentmarcz, and John son and heir of the said Edmund made in London, 1 June 1361, to Adam Fraunceys of 16 acres of land which were held by the said Edmund in separate strips (*divisim*) lying in Stepney, leased to the said Adam from that day for a term of seven years.

166 Release in perpetuity of John son and heir of Edmund Trentmarcz with warranty made in London, 1 September 1361, to Adam Fraunceys of the 16 acres of land contained in the preceding indenture.

167 Letter patent of Walter Turk made at Stepney, 5 August 1352, of an annual rent of £10 to the same Adam and his heirs in perpetuity, to be received each year from all the mills which the grantor then held in Stepney, with distraint clause.

168 Indented defeasance made 5 August [1352] containing that if the said Adam Fraunceys and Thomas de Langeton peacefully hold for themselves and their heirs all lands and tenements in which the said Walter had enfeoffed them in the counties of Essex and

Middlesex, then the said letter patent of the £10 annual rent will be be held null.

169 Charter of John Scut of Stepney in fee simple with warranty made at Old Ford, 13 July 1348, to Nicholas atte Wyke of all his tenement and 1 acre of land lying next to it in Old Ford, and of 4 acres of land also in Old Ford.

170 [*f. 14r*] Charter of Nicholas atte Wyke in fee simple with warranty made at Old Ford, 23 June 1349, to Adam Fraunceys and Thomas de Langeton of all the preceding lands and tenements.

171 Copy of the roll of a court held at Stepney, 4 February 1357, containing the surrender into the lord's hands, forfeited by Richard Andreu and Emma his wife, of 1 rood of meadow in Hackney to the use of the said Adam Fraunceys and Thomas, and the forfeiture of the grant thereof to the said Adam and Thomas.

172 Copy of the roll of a court held at Hackney, 28 October 1358, containing the surrender into the lord's hands, forfeited by Thomas and William Goldeston, of 1 acre and 1 rood of land in 'Moweresdoune' to the use of the said Adam and Thomas, and the forfeiture of the grant thereof to the same Adam and Thomas.

173 Charter of John Selverlok in fee simple with warranty made at Stepney, 18 December 1354, to Henry atte Welle of 'Broume', chaplain, of 1 acre of land with appurtenances in Stepney in the place defined (*limitato*) in the charter.

174 Part of a fine made 13 June 1316, whereby Simon de Abyndon and Eve his wife granted (*reddiderunt*) 4 acres of meadow in Hackney to Walter Morice in fee without warranty.
[*Feet of Fines, Lond. & Middx.* i, 92]

EDMONTON

175 Tenements in Edmonton.[1]
Memorandum that these lands and tenements were purchased in parcels by divers persons from others who acquired them by purchase made also in small parcels, and finally Roger de Depham acquired a large quantity of the above tenements by such collections (*par tiels quilettes*) and William de Causton another large quantity of the same [*f. 14v*] tenements also by collections

(*quyllettes*) as it appears. And Adam [Fraunceys] acquired the same quantities as appears towards the end of the muniments relating to the above tenements.

1 This memorandum is written by a different hand. What follows is written by the original scribe.

[Rubric.] Quere .lix. scripta proxima sequentia in coffino titulato Edel[meton] coffynus j[us].

176 Charter of Henry, son of Gerald the king's chamberlain, in fee simple without warranty and date made to Robert Blund of London of land which Leofwine the steward held in Sawbridgeworth [Herts.], and of $\frac{1}{2}$ virgate of [?the land once held by] Serle (*Serloni*) and $\frac{1}{2}$ virgate of [?the land once held by] Sigar with the beard, and the land of Saric, Gerald and Godwine Granere with their tenement, to be held of the donor by $\frac{1}{6}$ knight's fee.

177 Charter of confirmation of Geoffrey, earl of Essex,[1] in fee simple made without warranty and date to Robert Blund of London of lands which Warin, son of Gerald the king's chamberlain, and Henry his brother granted to him in Sawbridgeworth, which is in the fee of the earl.
[Date: 1156 x 1166.]

1 Geoffrey de Mandeville, second earl of Essex.

178 Charter of Hamelin in fee simple made without warranty and date to Robert Blund of London of 20 acres of land in Sawbridgeworth, namely 14 acres in a field called 'Legh' and 1 acre at 'Cumberwatere' near the land of Robert White (*Albi*) and 5 acres near the house of Maurice, retainer of the donor, to be held of the donor by service of 2s.

179 Charter of confirmation of William, earl of Essex,[1] in fee simple without warranty and date made to Robert Blund of the aforesaid 20 acres of land which Hamelin granted to him in Sawbridgeworth.
[Date: 1166 x 1189.]

1 William de Mandeville, third earl of Essex.

180 Charter of confirmation of William, earl of Essex, in fee simple without warranty and date made to Robert Blund of the security (*vadio*) which Hamelin pledged to him, namely of one marsh (*mare*), on security of which Robert lent to Hamelin 60s, and of

three parcels of land containing 16 acres, [*f. 151*] of which two
parcels lie next to the land of Robert at 'Cumberwatere' and the
third parcel consists of all the land which Hamelin had in the
field near the house of Maurice, on security of which Robert
lent to the same Hamelin 40s.

Witnesses: de (?)Pleistz, steward (*dap' meo*), Ralph de Bertures,
Hugh de Auco, John de Rothcale, Bernard Pine, Ralph Fitz-
Durant, Eustace, chamberlain, Heremerus, Alvredus Pie de
Vilem.

[Date: 1166 x 1189.]

[Hatfield Deeds, 56/8]

181 Charter of Geoffrey, earl of Essex, in fee simple without warranty
and date made to Robert Blund of London of 1 hide of land and
1 virgate in Edmonton and of one pasture which is called
'Rusfeld', which hide and virgate contain $1\frac{1}{2}$ virgates of land
which Ralph Gargate held, and a field called 'Stroda' and a field
called 'Horscroft', and a croft which Alfwine Blund held and a
field called 'Middelege', and 5 acres of land in villein tenure (*in
manum villani*) and a small croft before the gate of Ralph the
clerk, and 3 acres in 'Berfeld' and a part of the land of Dungel
and a small piece of land (*curtam terram*) by the side of 'Berfeld',
and 1 acre which Geri held and a small piece of land (*terriculam*)
in front of 'Horscroft', to be held of the donor by $\frac{1}{4}$ knight's fee.

[Date: 1156 x 1166]

182 Charter of confirmation of Henry II in fee simple without
warranty and date made to Robert Blund of land which he held
of Earl Geoffrey in Edmonton, and of land which he held of
Henry son of Gerald the chamberlain, in Sawbridgeworth, and
of land which he held of Maurice de 'Tileteia' in the manor of
Woodham, in the fee of the earl Ferrers, by charter of Earl
Robert of Ferrers and the charter of the said Maurice, and of
land which he held of the [convent] church of [St] Ethelburga
of Barking in the manor of Hockley by charter of the abbess
and convent.

183 Charter of confirmation of William, earl of Essex, in fee simple
without warranty and date made to Robert Blund of the grant
made to the same Robert by Geoffrey brother of the said William
in Edmonton, to be held of the earl by services reserved in the
charter of the grant.

[Date: 1166 x 1189]

184 Charter of confirmation of William de Mandeville, earl of Essex, in fee simple without warranty and date made to Robert son of Robert Blund of lands granted to Robert [Blund] the father in Edmonton by Geoffrey, brother of the earl, and by the same earl.
[Date: 1166 x 1189]

185 Charter of confirmation of William Mandeville, earl of Essex, in fee simple without warranty and date made to John son of Robert Blund of all lands in Edmonton which Geoffrey, brother of the said earl, granted to Robert, to be held of the earl by service of $\frac{1}{4}$ knight's fee.
[Date: 1166 x 1189]

186 [*f. 15v*] Charter of confirmation of Simon de Mathuem in fee simple without warranty and date made to John son of Robert Blund of London, of 20 acres of land in Sawbridgeworth which Hamelin, Simon's uncle, granted to Robert Blund as above [**180**], namely 14 acres in the field called 'Legh', 1 acre at 'Cumberwatere' and 5 acres next to the house of Maurice.

187 Charter of Michael de Hockele in fee simple without warranty and date made to James son of John Blund of Edmonton of land [?in Edmonton] lying between the land of Robert son of Philip and the land of St Peter of Hockley [Essex] and of a messuage by a drain (*ad hulvam*) which Batildis held, in exchange for land of the said James in Hockley granted to the said Michael for life, although Michael could continue to hold the whole of the aforesaid land for life (*dum tamen predictus Michaelus tenere possit totam terram predictam ad vitam suam*).

188 Charter of Geoffrey de Say[1] in fee simple with warranty without date made to Alice Blund of Edmonton of $\frac{1}{2}$ virgate of land which Reginald son of Ralph held in the manor of the same Geoffrey of Edmonton, to be held of the donor by service of 5s pa.
[Date: 1214 x 1230]

  1 Lord of Edmonton manor. See *VCH Middlesex* v, 149.

189 Charter of William[1] son of Geoffrey de Say, in fee tail with warranty and acquittance made without date to Ralph son of Peter de la Berge of Edmonton and Agnes la Filtere, of the whole tenement which Geoffrey Swonyld lately held of the donor

in Edmonton, to be held of the donor by suit of court and rent of $\frac{1}{2}$ mark.
[Date: 1230 x 1272]

1 Lord of Edmonton manor. See *VCH Middlesex* v, 149.

190 Confirmation of William de Mandeville, earl of Essex, in fee simple without warranty and date made to Picot son of Turstan of 8 acres of land in Edmonton which were of Wolwym le Hayward and 8 acres of land which were of Walter son of Brihtrich with meadows pertaining to the said lands, to be held of the earl by service of 5s *pa*.

191 Charter of William son of Fubert in fee simple without warranty and date made to Picot son of Turstan of land called Fubert's field (*campus Fuberti*) in Edmonton lying to the west of the High street, and of the rest of the land which the donor had in the west lying between the High street and the house which was once held by Turstan, to be held of the donor by service of 4s *pa*.

192 [*f. 16r*] Charter of Ralph Heyroun in fee simple with warranty without date made to Picot Marsh (*de Marisco*) of 3 acres of land and $2\frac{1}{2}$ acres of meadow, of which the land lies in the field called 'Langheg' between the land of Wolvena the widow and the land of Richard Gisors to the east, and the meadow lies in the long meadow next to the meadow of Denise the widow to the west, and of the whole land which Philip son of Britrich held of the donor with service of the same Philip, to be held of the donor by service of 2d *pa*, saving foreign service.

193 Charter of Amice daughter of Richard Burser in fee simple with warranty and acquittance without date made to Richard son of Picot of a croft of land in Edmonton which the said Richard called Burser gave to the donor in free marriage, lying between the highway in front of the messuage formerly of Roger del Heegate and the land of the feoffee, extending north to south, at one end to the road called 'Heghegatestrete', and at the other to the pasture of Roger le Burser, to be held of the donor by service of 4d *pa*.

194 Charter of William de Say son of Geoffrey de Say in fee simple with warranty without date made to Thomas Picot of $\frac{1}{2}$ virgate which Richard le Noble lately held of the donor by villein tenure

(*native*) in Edmonton, to be held of the donor by service of 3s *pa*.
[Date: 1230 x 1272]

195 Release in perpetuity of John FitzJohn of Edmonton without
warranty and date made to Thomas Picot of 3 acres of land for
which a plea had been made between them before the justices
in eyre at Westminster, 28 Henry III.[1]

> 1 14–20 January 1244. See D. Crook, *Records of the General Eyre* (HMSO, 1982),
> 104.

196 Charter of John son of Robert de Forde of Edmonton in fee
simple with warranty without date made to Thomas Picot of
Edmonton of 3 acres of meadow in Edmonton marsh lying
between the meadow of John Blund in the north and the meadow
of Geoffrey Sabern in the south, extending in length from the
River Lea in the east to the meadow called 'Manemade' in the
west, to be held of the donor by service of 1d *pa*.

197 [*f. 16v*] Charter of Cecily daughter of Hugh Peverel in fee simple
with warranty without date made to Thomas son of Picot of
Edmonton of 11 acres of land lying in the field called 'Berghfeld',[1]
from the land of Edmund Smith (*Fabri*) in the east, extending
from north to south, to be held of the donor by service of 3s *pa*
saving foreign service.

> 1 Details omitted here.

198 Confirmation of Robert le Marescall without warranty and date
made to Thomas Picot of 11 acres of land in 'Berghfeld' which
the feoffee had of the gift of Cecily wife of the confirmer.

199 Charter of Joan daughter of Ralph de Clare in fee simple with
warranty without date made to Thomas Picot of 4 acres of land
lying in the field called the Hyde, and of ½ acre in the field called
'Penyacre' in Edmonton, of which 2 acres lie between the land
of Maud, sister of the donor, to the west and the land of John
Gilbert to the east, extending in length from north to south, 1
acre lies between the land of the said Maud to the west and the
land of James Sone to the east, and 1 acre lies between the land
of Maud to the east and the road leading to London, and ½ acre
between the land of the said Maud and the land of William de
la Forde to the east, to be held of the donor by service of 16d
pa.

200 Release in perpetuity by Susan daughter of Robert Belhoft without warranty and date made to Thomas Picot of land called 'Belhoftsland' in Little Wrotham [?Kent].

201 Charter of Robert son of Richard de Strate in fee simple with warranty without date made to Thomas Picot of 2 acres of land in Edmonton lying in the field called 'Fotescroft' between the land of John Blund in the north and the land of Roger Burser in the south, extending eastwards to the land formerly of the said Roger, and westwards to the land called 'Spitelland', to be held of the donor by payment of one rose *pa* on his behalf at the altar of St Mary in Edmonton church, and to the chief lord 4d.

202 [*f. 17r*] Charter of Robert son of Richard de la Harestrate with warranty and acquittance without date made to Thomas Picot of ½ acre of land in Edmonton lying in the field called 'Langeheg' between the land of the said Thomas to the east and the land of Reginald le Dul to the west, extending in length from north to south, to be held of the donor by 1d *pa* for all services.

203 Surrender of Robert Taylor (*Cissor*) of Edmonton without warranty and date made to Thomas Picot of the messuage of the donor which he lately held of the said Thomas in Edmonton.

204 Charter of Godard Aubrey in fee simple with warranty and acquittance without date made to Thomas Picot of 1 acre of land in Edmonton lying in the field called Colewell, between the land of the donor in the north and the land of Ralph de Querndon in the south, extending from the east from the lane which leads to the Hale westwards to the land of Ralph de Querndon, to be held of the donor by 1d *pa* for all service.

205 Charter of William son of William Tannor of Edmonton leasing and granting in fee simple without warranty and date to Thomas Picot one messuage and 3 acres of land which were once held by Goshune, of which 1 acre lies next to the aforesaid messuage to the north, one end extending west to the royal highway and the other eastwards, and another acre lies in the field called 'Wychgrave' between the land of William de Forde to the east and the land of James le Sone to the west, and the third acre lies in the field called 'Tulbertesfeld'.

206 Charter of Thomas son of Picot in fee simple without warranty

and date made to Beatrice daughter of Ellis de Brykenden of 2
acres of land in Edmonton lying between the land which was of
Richard son of Philip and the land of the said Thomas Picot,
extending eastwards to the door (*ianuam*) of the said Richard and
westwards to the land of William son of Reymer, to be held of
the donor by service of 12d *pa.*

207 Charter of William son of Picot of Edmonton in fee simple with
warranty without date made to Geoffrey de la Forde of one
messuage and one croft of land in Edmonton lying between
the pasture of the said Geoffrey and the lane which leads to
'Scottescrouche', extending from the west from the pasture which
was of William de la Forde to the east, [*f. 17v*] to be held of the
donor by service of one peppercorn.

208 Charter of Reginald Kynot of Edmonton in fee simple without
warranty and date made to Geoffrey son of Robert de la Forde
of 1d rent from the tenement of Nicholas de Wynton, namely
an acre of meadow in Edmonton, in the marsh there, lying in
the place called 'Chipolshot' between the meadow of John del
Heg and that of Robert North (*Aguylon*).

209 Indenture of John le Brennere and Margery his wife, lately wife
of Henry son of William, of a lease made 18 April 1283 to
Geoffrey son of Robert de Forde of 1 acre of land lying in the
Hyde and 3 roods lying in 'Littelwys' which were of the dower
of his wife, to be held for nine months for 4s paid to the lessors
in advance (*per manibus*).

210 Charter of William Sperke of Edmonton in fee simple with
warranty and acquittance without date made to Geoffrey son of
Robert Ford (*de Forda*), of a plot of land in 'Tybournesfeld' lying
between that land and the highway leading to Enfield wood, to
be held of the donor by one rose *pa* for all service.

211 Charter of Thomas son of Robert atte Forde in fee simple with
warranty and acquittance without date made to Geoffrey atte
Forde his brother of 3 acres of meadow in Edmonton, of which
one lies in 'Holfletsot' next to the meadow of Agnes de Colewel
extending from north to south, another acre lies in 'Chipolshot'
next to the meadow of Eustace le Pilcard extending from east to
west, and $\frac{1}{2}$ acre of land in 'Esthale' between the meadow of
William de Say and the meadow of Peter Paterye and extends
from north to south.

[Later insertion.] And another ½ acre lies opposite the meadow [unclear] of the lord, of which the eastern edge abuts on 'Leymade', to be held of the donor for 1d annual service, saving foreign service. The first acre mentioned below [**1009**].

212 Release in perpetuity by John son of Thomas de la Forde with warranty and acquittance without date made to Geoffrey de la Forde his uncle of the 3 acres of meadow last mentioned, to be held by 1d reserved above in the charter of his father.

213 Charter of William de Say son of Geoffrey de Say in fee simple with warranty and acquittance without date made to Geoffrey de la Forde of the whole land and meadow which Richard Proudfot, his villein (*nativus*), held of the donor in his manor of Edmonton, to be held for 2s 6d annually for all service. [Date: 1230 x 1272]

214 [*f. 18r*] Charter of Richard Denys of Edmonton in fee simple with warranty and acquittance without date made to Geoffrey son of Robert de la Forde of a piece of land in Edmonton lying in the field called 'Wellefeld' between the dowerland of the donor's mother in the north and the road in the south, extending from the land of Richard Bolle from the west to the land of the donor in the east, to be held of the donor by 1d annually for all service.

215 Charter of Richard Denys of Edmonton in fee simple with warranty and acquittance without date made to Geoffrey Ford (*de Forda*) of Edmonton of 1½ acres of land lying in the field called 'Wellefeld' between the land of John Fountain (*de Fonte*) and the land of Philip Smith (*Fabri*), to be held of the donor by 2d *pa* for all service.

216 Charter of Richard Denys of Edmonton in fee simple with warranty and acquittance without date made to Geoffrey atte Forde of 1 acre of land in Edmonton lying in the field called 'Welfeld' between the land of William Frere in the north and the land of the donor in the south abutting on the land of Philip Smith (*Fabri*) in the east, to be held of the donor for 4d for all service.

217 Charter of Richard [Denys] of Edmonton with warranty and acquittance made without date to Geoffrey de la Forde, citizen of London, of a piece of land in Edmonton called 'Sonesland'

lying in a field called 'Wellefeld' between the land of William
Frere in the south and the land of Denise, mother of the donor,
in the north, extending to the land of Philip Smith (*Fabri*) in the
east and the land of William de Say in the west, to be held of
the donor for 4d *pa* for all service.

218 Charter of Alan Cole of Stepney in fee simple with warranty
and acquittance without date made to Geoffrey son of John
David of 1½ acres of meadow in Edmonton marsh lying in a
meadow called 'Leymade' next to the meadow formerly of Hugh
Bourser, to be held of the donor by one clove of garlic *pa* and
½d to the chief lord, namely Robert Gisors, for all service.

219 Charter of Geoffrey son of John Davyd of Enfield in fee simple
with warranty and acquittance without date made to Geoffrey
son of Robert atte Forde and Leven his wife of the aforesaid 1½
acres in Edmonton marsh lying in the meadow called [*f. 18v*]
'Leymade' next to the meadow formerly of Hugh le Bourser, to
be held of the donor by one clove of garlic and ½d to be paid to
the chief lord, Robert Gisors, for all service.

220 Charter of Walter Cullyng of Edmonton in fee simple with
warranty and acquittance and without date made to Geoffrey
Ford (*de Forda*) of the whole part of the donor's messuage lying
(*existentem*) between the messuage of the feoffee and the wall
(*parietem*) called 'Herwogh', and of the wall itself and a third part
of the garden of the said messuage, to be held of the donor for
4d *pa* for all service.

221 Charter and release of Walter Cullyng of Edmonton in fee simple
with warranty and acquittance without date made to Geoffrey
Ford (*de Forda*) of the aforesaid 4d annual rent from the said part
of the messuage conveyed by the donor to the said Geoffrey, to
be held of the donor by one clove of garlic annually for all
service.

222 Charter of John son of William de la Forde in fee simple without
warranty and date made to Geoffrey son of Robert atte Forde
and Emma his wife and the heirs of Geoffrey of all the tenement
in Edmonton in which the said Geoffrey previously enfeoffed
the donor, to be held of the donor by 1d *pa* for all service.

223 Charter of John son of William atte Forde in fee simple without
warranty and date made to Geoffrey son of Robert atte Forde

and Emma his wife and the heirs of Geoffrey of the whole tenement in Edmonton in which Geoffrey previously enfeoffed the donor, saving to the donor $12\frac{1}{2}$d rent issuing from the messuage of William Bridde, to be held of the donor for 1d *pa* for all service.

224 Charter of Richard de Anesty in fee simple with warranty and acquittance without date made to Geoffrey Ford (*de Forda*) of Edmonton of 2s rent to be raised annually from one messuage and $\frac{1}{2}$ acre of land which was formerly of Roger Oke (*de Quercu*) in Edmonton and which rent Agnes la Coupere used to pay to the donor, to be held of the donor by one grain of corn annually for all service.

225 Charter of Richard de Anesty of Edmonton in fee simple with warranty and acquittance without date made to Geoffrey son of Robert atte Forde of the whole land which the donor had in Edmonton in the field called 'Bedesfeld' extending from the land formerly of John FitzJohn in the south [*f. 19r*] to the road leading to Enfield park, to be held of the donor by 1d *pa* for all service.

[Margin.] Hic omittitur unus numerus per negligenciam scriptoris. [The following entry was given the press mark lij instead of lj.]

226 Release in perpetuity by Diamand who was wife of Richard de Anesty of Edmonton without warranty and date made to Geoffrey atte Forde of the whole field called 'Bedesfeld' and of 8d rent belonging to the dower of the said Diamand and of the land and rent in the two previous charters granted (*alienatas*) by Richard her husband.

227 Charter of Robert son of Richard de Strate of Edmonton in fee simple with warranty and acquittance without date made to Richard son of Robert Ford (*de Forda*) of $\frac{1}{2}$ acre of meadow in Edmonton marsh lying between the meadow of the abbot of Walden in the south and the meadow which was of Godfrey Puttok in the north, extending from the meadow of the said abbot in the east to the meadow of Tristram son of Salman in the west, to be held of the donor for 2d *pa* for all service.

228 Charter of Robert Gysors of Edmonton in fee simple with warranty and acquittance without date made to Richard son of

Robert Ford of $2\frac{1}{2}$ acres of land lying in a field called 'Stonefeld'',
to be held of the donor for 1d *pa* for all service.

229 Charter of Robert Gysors in fee simple with warranty without
date made to Richard son of Robert Ford of $2\frac{1}{2}$ acres of land in
Edmonton lying in the long field on the east side of the bridge
between the land formerly of William Woldyng in the west and
the high street in the east, extending from the 'Medesenge' from
south to north.

230 Charter of Neyre, widow of William son of Walter of Edmonton
in fee simple with warranty and acquittance without date made
to Thomas son of Robert Ford of 1 acre of land in Edmonton,
lying in a field called 'Haggefeld' between the land of Roger son
of Warin in the north and the land of Geoffrey Marsh (*de Marisco*)
in the south, extending from the land of the said Thomas, feoffee,
in the west to the land of John son of John Marsh in the east,
to be held of the donor for 1d *pa* for all service.

231 Charter of John FitzJohn of Edmonton with warranty and
acquittance without date made to Thomas son of Robert Ford
of 1 acre in Edmonton lying in the field called 'Haggefeld'
between the land of Henry son of William in the south and the
land of Geoffrey Marsh in the north, [*f. 19v*] extending from west
to east, to be held of the donor for 1d *pa* for all service.

232 Charter of Richard de la Forde in fee simple without warranty
and date made to Thomas de la Forde of the whole land which
the donor held in Edmonton, to be held of the chief lords of the
fee.

233 Charter of Roger Oke (*de Quercu*) of Edmonton in fee simple with
warranty without date made to Thomas son of Robert de Forde
of 2 acres of land in Edmonton, of which 1 [acre] lies in a field
called 'Truffionesfeld', extending from the messuage of Richard
le Lyf in the east to the messuage of Truffion in the west, and
another acre called 'Clayacre' extends from the messuage of the
said Truffion in the east as far as 'Hammyngesbourn' in the
west, to be held of the donor for 7d annually for all service.

234 Charter of Richard Cook (*Coci*) in fee simple with warranty and
acquittance without date made to Thomas son of Robert de
Forde of 1 acre of land in Edmonton lying in the field called
'Langeheg' between the land of William Water (*de Aqua*) in

the west and the land of the canons of Holy Trinity, London, in the west, and extending from the land of William Ford (*de Forda*) in the north to the boundary of Tottenham in the south, to be held of the donor for one clove of garlic and 4d *pa* to the chief lord for all service save foreign. Thomas paid $2\frac{1}{2}$ marks in fine.

Witnesses: John Blund, Thomas Pycot, William de Forda, Laurence de Ford, William Pycot, Richard Pycot, Geoffrey Cook (*Coco*), Hugh Peverell, John FitzJohn, Saher Clerk, and others.

[Date: *temp.* Henry III.]

[WAM 270]

235 Charter of Adam Taylor (*Cissoris*) of Edmonton in fee simple with warranty and acquittance made in 28 Henry III[1] to Thomas Ford (*de Forda*) of 1 acre of land in Edmonton lying between the land of Robert son of Richard in the west and the highway to the east, extending from the north from the street which leads through the gate (*portam*) of Robert son of Richard to the land called 'Lacedomesland' in the south, to be held of the donor for $\frac{1}{2}$d annually for all service.

    1 28 October 1253–27 October 1254.

236 Charter of Henry son of William of Edmonton in fee simple with warranty and acquittance made 19 January 1258 to Thomas son of Robert de Forde of 1 acre of meadow in Edmonton marsh lying between the meadow formerly of John Park (*de Parco*) in the east and the meadow which was of John Smith (*Fabri*) in the west, extending from the River Lea in the south to the meadow of the hospital of St Giles in the north, to be held of the donor for 4d *pa* for all service. Thomas paid 40s in fine.

Witnesses: William de la Forde, John Blund, Thomas Pycot, John FitzJohn, Laurence de la Forde, John de la Forde, Richard Pycot, William Pycot, Saher Clerk, and others.

[WAM 269]

237 Charter of Robert le Champioun of London in fee simple with warranty and acquittance made 25 June [*f. 20r*] 1257 to Thomas de la Forde of 28d rent in Edmonton, of which 16d comes from John Neuman and 12d from Richard Denys, to be held of the donor for one rose and due services to the chief lords of the fee, the nuns of Clerkenwell, namely 10d saving foreign service. Thomas paid 18s.

Witnesses: William de la Forde, Thomas Pycot, Peter Spirc, Saher Clerk.
[WAM 298]

238 Confirmation of Hugh Peverell of Edmonton with warranty and acquittance made 11 March 1257 to Thomas de la Forde of all the land with houses which the same Thomas had of the gift of William Peyntour in Edmonton, to be held of the confirmer for 5s 8d annually for all service save foreign. Thomas paid 40s in fine.
Witnesses: William de la Forde, Laurence de la Forde, John FitzJohn, Richard FitzJohn, Geoffrey Cook (*Coco*), Richard [?Cook], William ..., Richard Pycot, Richard de A[nesti], Saher Clerk, and others.
[WAM 274]

239 Assignment of the previous rent made by Hugh Peverell without date and warranty to the prior and brothers of the hospital of St John, containing that William de Benyton had been accustomed to hold the said tenement of the said Hugh.
Witnesses: William de la Forde, John FitzJohn, Richard FitzJohn, William Pycot, Geoffrey Cook [*Coco*], Saher, clerk, and others.
[WAM 282]

240 Charter of John le Croper of 'la Rugge' in fee simple with warranty and acquittance without date made to Thomas de la Forde, draper of London, of 1 acre of land in Enfield lying between the hedge of Enfield park and the land of Maud Cobbes, extending from east to west, to be held of the donor by a clove of garlic and due services to the chief lords.

241 Charter of Warin son of Ingulf with warranty and acquittance without date made to William de Holme of 1 acre of land in Edmonton lying between the highway and the land of the said Warin in the same field, extending from east to west, to be held of the donor for 4d *pa* for all service. William de Holme paid 8s.
Witnesses: Peter de Berga, William son of Geoffrey, Picot Marsh, William son of Walter, John FitzJohn, John White (*Albo*), Richard son of Hereward of Enfield and William his son, William Mot, Absalom de Enefeld, clerk, and others.
[Date: *temp.* Henry III.]
[WAM 267]

242 Charter of William de Say son of Geoffrey de Say with warranty without date made to Adam Cole son of William Cole of $\frac{1}{2}$

virgate of land in Edmonton comprising all the land which Geoffrey son of Baldwin held of the donor and all the land which Thomas Turkyl held of the same donor for 6d *pa* for all service.
[Date: 1230 x 1272.]

243 Charter of William son of Geoffrey de Say with warranty and acquittance without date made to Adam Cole, son of William Cole, of 8 acres of land in Edmonton which Robert [*f.20v*] le Smale formerly held of the donor, to be held of the donor for 1d *pa* for all service.
[Date: 1230 x 1272.]
Witnesses: Hamon de Gattone, Ralph Pessun, Walter de Keu, knights, William de Forda, Thomas Pycot, John le Faucon', Nicholas Ford (*de Forda*), John FitzJohn, Geoffrey Marsh.
[WAM 51]

244 Charter of Geoffrey le Rowe in fee simple with warranty and acquittance made without date to Adam Cole, draper of London, of $1\frac{1}{2}$ acres of land lying between the gate (*ianuam*) of Roger le Burser and the field which is called Job's field (*campus Job*), and of 12d rent which Jordan le Heldere held of the donor in Edmonton, to be held of the donor for 1d for all service.

245 Charter of Adam Cole, citizen of London, in fee simple with warranty and acquittance made 24 September 1257[1] to Thomas son of Robert de la Forde of all the land which the donor had in Edmonton of the gift of William de Say, except 2 acres of land lying together in the field called the Hyde, and of 1 acre of land in Edmonton with 12d rent which the donor bought and held of Geoffrey son of Henry of Edmonton, to be held of the donor for $\frac{1}{2}$ lb of pepper and due services to the chief lord, namely 7d to William de Say, and due services to Geoffrey son of Henry. Thomas paid 20m in fine.
Witnesses: Richard de Ewelle, sheriff of London, David de Enefeud, Richard Bonaventure, Richard de Enefeud, Roger de Bristowe, draper, John le Leyner of St Albans, John FitzJohn, Richard Picot, William Picot, Peter de Edelmetone, Walter le Blont and many others.
[WAM 252]

1 MS: without date.

246 Charter of William Pateryk in fee simple with warranty and acquittance without date made to Thomas son of Robert de Forde of 2 acres of land in Edmonton lying in a field called 'Thewenethe' or 'Yeweneye', of which 1 [acre] lies between the land of Reginald son of Warin in the south and the land of the aforesaid Thomas in the north, extending from the land of Henry son of William in the east to the land of Reginald son of Warin in the west, and another acre lies between the field called 'Aggefeld' in the east and the land of Reginald son of Warin in the west, extending from south to north, to be held of the donor for 8½d *pa* for all service.

247 Charter of James son of Hilda in fee simple with warranty without date made to William son of Stephen Bolle of 1 acre of land and 3 selions in Eastfield and of one messuage, the land extending northwards from the messuage to the 'Medesenge' alongside the road (*de longo in longum camini*), to be held of the donor for 9d *pa* for all service save foreign.

248 Charter of William son of Stephen Bolle in fee simple with warranty and acquittance without date made to Thomas de la Forde of one messuage and 1 acre of land in Edmonton lying between the land formerly of James son of Hilda in the east and the lane leading to the house of John Newman in the west, extending from the lane [*f. 21r*] leading to 'Beckestyghele' in the south to the river called 'Medesenge' in the north, to be held of the donor by payment of one rose annually and by 9d to the chief lord for all service, saving service to the king. Thomas paid 18s to William for the grant.
Witnesses: William de la Forde, Thomas Picot, Laurence de la Forde, John FitzJohn, Richard Picot, William Picot, Geoffrey Cook (*Coco*), Richard le Neuman, John le Neuman, Saher Clerk, and others.
[Date: *temp.* Henry III.]
[WAM 339]

249 Charter of Geoffrey son of William in fee simple with warranty and acquittance without date made to Geoffrey de la Forde of Edmonton of 3 roods of meadow in Edmonton marsh, lying between the meadow of Robert North (*Aquilon*') in the south and the meadow of William son of Geoffrey in the north, extending from the stream (*la laak*) in the east to the land of William Marsh in the west, to be held of the donor for 1d annually for all service. Geoffrey de la Forde paid the donor 30s in fine.
Witnesses: John le Blont, Thomas Picot, William Ford, John

Idoyne, Henry son of William, Reginald son of Warin, Maurice
Hayward (*Messor*), Saher Clerk, and others.
[Date: early 14th cent.]
[WAM 265]

250 Charter of Geoffrey de la Forde in fee simple with warranty and
acquittance without date made to Thomas de la Forde of 3 roods
of meadow in Edmonton marsh lying between the meadow of
Robert North (*Aquilon'*) in the south and the meadow of Henry
son of William in the north, extending from 'le Holteflet' in the
east to the land of William, son of Nicholas Marsh, to be held
of the donor for 1d *pa* for all service.

251 Charter of Reginald Nuncius[1] in fee simple with warranty without
date made to Agnes wife of Robert Hyrland of 2 acres of land
in Edmonton next to the house of Robert Hyrland in 'Honifeld',
of which one side of one acre extends eastward to the land of
William son of Walter and another westward to the messuage of
the said Robert Hyrland, and one side of the second acre extends
from the north to the land of Warin Ingulf, in the south to the
first acre and to a small hay meadow, to be held of the donor
by a pair of white gloves and 8d *pa* to the chief lords of the fee.
Agnes paid 21s in fine.
Witnesses: William Peverell, Peter de Berga, Richard ..., [John]
White (*Albo*), William son of Geoffrey, Walter son of Walter, John
Park (*de Parco*), John Desat..., [?Richard] son of Hereward,
William his son, Robert de Hyrland, Ralph Palmer and others.
[Date: early 13th cent.]
[WAM 272]

1 MS: Nomoi.

252 Charter of Warin Ingulf in fee simple with warranty and acquittance without date made to Geoffrey Pateryk of 2 acres of land
in Edmonton, namely all the land which Agnes who was the
wife of Robert Little (*Parvi*), sister of the same Geoffrey, held of
the donor, to be held for 8d *pa* for all service.

253 Charter of John son of Walter Hudi in fee simple with warranty
without date made to Richard son of Ralph of one messuage
which Walter Siccor held of the donor in Edmonton of the fee
of Godlyng next to the highway to the west, to be held of the
donor for 1d *pa* and 4d to the chief lord for all service. 3m paid
in fine.

Witnesses: Ralph de Heyrun, Geoffrey de Querndon, John White (*Albo*), William Peverell, Picot [Marsh], Thomas his son, Robert de Forde, Richard Harulf, William son of Geoffrey, Robert (?)Silvern, Robert Bursor, John son of Walter, William his brother, Peter de Burgha and others.
[Date: (?)early 13th cent.]
[WAM 255]

254 [*f. 21v*] Charter of John FitzJohn of Edmonton in fee simple with warranty and acquittance without date made to Stephen Bukerell, citizen of London, of all the land which the donor had in Edmonton, to be held of the donor by 1d *pa* for all service.
Witnesses: Richard de Coudres, sheriff of Middlesex,[1] Richard Bonaventure, Reginald de Suthfouk, John le Blund of Edmonton, Ralph de Querndon, Thomas Picot, William Marsh, Robert de Gisors, Richard Picot, William Picot, Laurence de la Forde, John la Cornere, Geoffrey [?Cook], John son of Idonia, William Clerk, and others.
[WAM 287]

1 No one of this name appears as sheriff of Middlesex in the *List of Sheriffs for England and Wales from the earliest times to 1831* (HMSO, 1896), although John de Codres was sheriff of Middlesex 1238–9.

255 Charter of Richard Wroth of Edmonton in fee simple with warranty and acquittance without date made to William Bukerell, citizen and draper of London, of all the land which the donor had of Vincent Fox lying between the land of Richard de Anesty in the south and the land of John Goldyng in the north, extending on the western side to the land formerly of Gilbert le Bourser and on the other side to the lane leading to the house of Reginald le Dessere, to be held of the donor by 4d *pa* to the chief lords and one clove of garlic to the donor for all service. And Bukerell paid 8s 4d.
Witnesses: Geoffrey Cook (*Coco*), Richard de Anesty, Roger Hillary, William Spirck, Richard Cook, Henry Tayl, Geoffrey de la Forde of Edmonton, William de Dunelm, Thomas de Basing, Richard Esswy, John Minor, citizens, William de Basevile, Ralph de Pelham, chaplain, and others.
[Date: *temp.* Henry III.]
[WAM 283]

256 Charter of John Goldyng of Edmonton in fee simple with warranty and acquittance without date made to William Bukerell, citizen of London, of an enclosed croft in which William de Say had enfeoffed Geoffrey Goldyng, father of the donor, lying between the land of the said feoffee which he had bought of Richard Wroth in the south and the lane leading to the house of Reginald Dessere in the north, extending on the western side to the land of Geoffrey Cook (*Coco*) and on the other side to the land of the feoffee, to be held of the donor for 6d *pa* for all service. The feoffee paid the donor 19s in fine.

Witnesses: John Blund, Geoffrey Cook, Richard de Anesty, Roger Hillary, Richard Cook, Geoffrey de la Forde of Edmonton, William de Dunelm, Thomas de Basing, Richard Esswy, John Minor, citizens of London, William de Basevile, Ralph de Pelham, chaplain, and others.

[Date: *temp.* Henry III.]

[WAM 247]

257 Release in perpetuity by William de Borham without warranty and date made to Denise, who was wife of William Bukerell, and Isolde, daughter and heir of the said William, of ½d rent issuing from tenements which were once held of Vincent Fox of which mention has been made above [**255**].

258 Indenture of Hugh son of William Peverel, made 24 June 1234, to Stephen Bokerel of 6 acres of meadow in Edmonton meadow, of which 2 acres lay between 'Chiphole' and the River Lea between part of the meadow of John Yarild in the north and that of Richard Deonys in the south, 2 acres lay between the meadows of Richard Cook (*Coci*) in the south and John de Trumpeton in the north, 1 acre lay between the meadows of Gilbert Prodhome in the south and Laurence de la Forde in the north, and 1 acre between the meadow of the donor in the south and that of Richard Gisors in the north, to be held for the twelve years with warranty.

Witnesses: Henry de Edelmeton, Eustace le Peverer, William le Lutre, Richard Cook, John Blund, William son of Geoffrey, Picot Marsh, John, servant of the prior of Holy Trinity, Geoffrey de Enefeld, Richard Clerk, and others.

[WAM 297]

259 [*f. 22r*] Charter of Simon de Molestuma in fee simple with warranty without date made to Lady Susan, who was the wife of Ralph de Pland, of the whole meadow called 'Stanmede' next to the bridge called 'Stokbrege' by the stream leading to the (?)footbridge (*scalariam*) which leads to the house of the donor, adjacent to the meadow of William Squytin, alongside (*de longo* *in longum*) arable land, to be held of the donor for 20d *pa* for all service.

260 Charter of John FitzJohn of Edmonton granting in mortgage to Henry le Wympler, citizen of London, 5 acres of meadow lying in Edmonton in the meadow called 'Stonygate', to be held by the feoffee from the feast of All Saints 46 Henry III [1 November 1261][1] for five years unless the donor pay the said Henry 5 marks on this date and notwithstanding any suit Henry might initiate to recover the 5 marks. And this deed is entrusted to Robert Hauteyn to hold impartially (*in equa manu*).
Witnesses: Thomas de Waltham, John Wisler, John Blund, Robert Hauteyn and others.
[WAM 264]

1 MS: 40 Henry III [1255].

261 Charter of John son of John Marsh of Edmonton, in fee simple with warranty and acquittance without date made to John le Claper of 1 acre of meadow in Edmonton lying between the meadow of Richard Anesty and the meadow of Thomas de la Forde, extending from east to west, to be held of the donor by 4d *pa* for all service. The feoffee paid 4 marks in fine.
Witnesses: William de la Forde, Thomas Picot, John FitzJohn, William Picot, Richard Picot, Laurence de la Forde, Ralph Paterick, Richard Claper, William Picot (*sic*), Geoffrey Cook (*Coco*), Saher Clerk, and others.
[Date: *temp.* Henry III.]
[WAM 312]

262 Charter of John le Claper in fee simple with warranty and acquittance without date made to John Marsh of 1 acre of land in Edmonton lying in the field called 'Pymor', between the land of Henry Church (*de Ecclesia*) and the land of Richard de la Strate, vicar of Edmonton, and the land of the feoffee, extending from the south from the land of William de la Forde in the north to the water called 'Stebbyng', to be held of the donor by a garland (*unam certam*) of roses and 4½d to the chief lord, Henry Church, for all service.
Witnesses: William de Forde, Thomas Picot, John FitzJohn, Richard Picot, Laurence de Forde, Ralph Paterick, William Picot, Richard Claper, Geoffrey Cook (*Coco*), Saher Clerk, and others.

[Date: *temp.* Henry III.]
[WAM 263]

263 Charter of Christine, daughter of Philip Marsh, in fee simple with warranty without date made to Roger[1] son of Philip of one messuage next to the high gate and 1 acre of land lying next to 'Hakebrok', to be held of the donor for 8d *pa* for all service, save foreign.
Witnesses: James Blund, Ralph de Heron, Walter son of William, Geoffrey his brother, Pycot Marsh, John Marsh, Geoffrey Ford (*de Forda*), Edward his brother, Robert Ford, William Peverell, Richard Harulf, Robert de Herun, John Park (*de Parko*).
[Date: *temp.* Henry III.]
[WAM 254]

    1 MS: Reginald.

264 Charter of Robert de Anesty in fee simple with warranty without date made to John, son of John Marsh, of 1 acre of land in Edmonton in the field called 'Bryfeld' lying between the land called 'Berghesacre' in the south and the land of Henry Monk (*de Monasterio*) in the north, extending from the land of John Smith (*Fabri*) in the west to the land of (*f. 22v*) John son of Agnes in the east, to be held of the donor by a garland (*certum*) of roses and due services to the chief lords. John Marsh paid 12s.
Witnesses: John Blund, Robert his son, William Ford (*de Forda*), Thomas Picot, Richard Picot, Hugh Peverel, Richard Cook (*Coco*), John son of Agnes.
[Date: *temp.* Henry III.]
[WAM 293]

265 Charter of Bartholomew de Brunne in fee simple with warranty and acquittance made without date to John Marsh of 2 acres of meadow in Enfield, of which one lay between the meadow formerly of Arnulf Maundevill and the meadow formerly of William Mot, being 40 perches in length and 4 in width, and the other lay between the meadow of the said Arnulf and the meadow of Robert le Prestre, being 20 perches in length and 8 in width, to be held of the donor by one garland (*sertum*) of roses and 8d to the chief lord for all service.

266 Charter of William de Say son of Geoffrey de Say in fee simple with warranty without date made to John son of John Marsh, of 6 acres of land in Edmonton which Godard Aldred, villein

(*nativus*) of the donor, held of Robert son of Acharius and Cecily his wife in the field called Berghfield, and of 1 acre of meadow lying in 'Manemade' between the meadow of the feoffee and the meadow of John Sawale which Philip son of Godard, villein, held of the donor, to be held for 1d *pa* saving services to the king and the chief lords. 4m paid in fine.
Witnesses: Robert de Chastelun, Thomas Picot, William Ford (*de Forda*), Roger Burser, Hugh Peverel, Geoffrey son of William, Robert Gysors, Geoffrey Marsh, Geoffrey Cook (*Coco*), Richard Picot, Alan de Waldene, Laurence de Forde and others.
[Date: 1230 x 1272]
[WAM 266]

267 Charter of William Cook (*Coci*) and Maud his wife in fee simple with warranty and acquittance without date made to John son of John Marsh, of 1 acre of meadow in Edmonton marsh lying in 4 acres called 'Holflet Manemade' in which the donors are partners (*participes*) with Geoffrey son of William, between the meadow of Richard Yarild and the ditch called 'Holflet' extending from the River Lea to the west, to be held of the donor for 1d *pa* for all service. And John paid 35s.
Witnesses: Thomas son of Picot, John FitzJohn, Laurence de Forde, Peter Spirc, William Picot, Geoffrey Cook, Richard son of Picot, Geoffrey Marsh, Robert Church (*de Ecclesia*), John Street (*de Strata*), Richard Cook, Alan de Waldene and others.
[Date: *temp.* Henry III.]
[WAM 294]

268 Writing of William Humphrey of Edmonton without warranty and date made to John Marsh whereby the said William surrendered to the said John 1 acre of land lying between the land of Ralph Picot and the land of Robert Gulle in the field called 'Berghfeld'.

269 Another writing of Geoffrey Humphrey surrendering to John Marsh 2 acres of land which he held of the same John in 'Berghfeld' between the land of Ralph Picot and the land of Philip le Neuman, and of 6d rent which he used to receive from Robert Gulle from 1 acre of land lying next to the said 2 acres.
Witnesses: Ralph de Berewe, William le Vikere, John Street (*de Strata*), John Sarp, William Ydeine, Stephen de Colewelle and others.
[Date: *temp.* Henry III.]
[WAM 296]

270 [*f. 23r*] Confirmation of William son of Geoffrey de Say with warranty without date made to John, son of John Marsh, of 1 croft of land called 'Rammescroft' and of 3 roods of meadow pertaining to the said croft and of $1\frac{1}{2}$ acres of meadow in Edmonton marsh which the said John acquired of Godard, the villein of the said William, to be held of the latter for 12d *pa* and by suit of court for all service. John paid 4m in fine.
Witnesses: John Blund of Edmonton, Richard Gysors, Roger le Burseyr, ... Picot, Thomas Picot, William de la Forde, Hugh Peverell, [John Fitz]John, Robert (?)Barfle, John Marsh of Enfield, John David of the same, ... of Tottenham and others.
[Date: 1230 x 1272]
[WAM 284]

271 Charter of William, son of Geoffrey de Say, and Avice (*Awisia*)[1] de Clare with warranty[2] and date made to John son of John Marsh (*de Mareys*), of the croft called 'Rammescroft' and of 3 perches of meadow in Edmonton lying in 'Middelmerssh' and pertaining to the said croft, to be held of William for 12d *pa* for all service. And the grantee paid 60s in fine.
Witnesses: Aunfrey de Fhering', seneschal, Stephen de Dunmowe, bailiff, John Blund, William de la Forde, Thomas Picot, Richard Harulf, Peter de la Berewe, Richard de Gysors, Nicholas Marsh, Geoffrey his brother, William son of Geoffrey, Laurence de la Forde.
[Date: 1230 x 1272]
[WAM 261]

1 MS: Aelesia.
2 MS: without warranty.

272 Charter of John son of Idonia of Edmonton in fee simple with warranty and acquittance without date made to William son of Richard, his brother, of all land, meadow and rent which the said John had in Edmonton, and of all the meadow which he had in Enfield, to be held of the donor by one garland of roses saving services to the chief lords.
Witnesses: William de la Forde, John FitzJohn, William Thurkil, Geoffrey son of Henry, Laurence de la Forde, Reginald son of Warin, John Bridge (*de Ponte*), Saher Clerk, and others.
[Date: *temp.* Henry III.]
[WAM 248]

273 Release in perpetuity of William Idoyne of Edmonton without

warranty and date made to John son of William Marsh of all
the land which the said William had of the feoffment of John
Idoyne in Edmonton. And John paid 4s.
Witnesses: John le Blund, William de la Forde, Richard de Anesty,
William de Kaen, Richard Picot, William Spirc, John . . ., Richard
Street, John Prodhumme, John Clerk, and others.
[Date: *temp.* Henry III.]
[WAM 277]

274 Charter of William Idoyne of Edmonton in fee simple with
warranty and acquittance without date made to John Marsh of
1 acre of land in Edmonton lying in the field called 'Langeheg'
between the land of Richard de Lodebury on either side,
extending from the east to the highway called 'la Herestrate'
and in the west to the lane (*semitam*) called 'le Garsonneswey', to
be held of the donor by payment of one clove of garlic for all
service.

275 Charter of William Ford (*de Forda*) in fee simple with warranty
and acquittance without date made to John Marsh of 2 acres of
land and one messuage in Edmonton which the donor acquired
of Robert North (*Aguilon*), of which 1 acre lies in the field called
Longacre between the land of Adam Cole, of which the northern
edge abuts on the water called 'Skynnespand' and the southern
part on the land of Hamekin Ingulf, and the other acre lies in
the field called 'Selwynesfeld' and is called 'Irynnesacre', to be
held of the donor by payment of 18d *pa* for all service.

276 [*f. 23v*] Release in pepetuity by John son and heir of Richard le
Carpenter of Tottenham without warranty made at Tottenham,
12 July 1332, to John atte Mersch of the whole piece of land called
'Squattokesland' and in the meadow called 'Squattokesmede' in
which the said Richard had enfeoffed the said John atte Mersch.
Witnesses: John le Venour, John atte Castel, Edmund Pymme,
John atte Strete of Edmonton, Roger atte Loffte, Ralph Dulay,
John le Keu, John le Notiere, John de Rudham, John Abraham,
clerk, of Tottenham, and others.
[WAM 286]

277 Charter of Walter Wroth in fee simple with warranty without
date made to John son of John Marsh of 1 acre of land in
'Honifeld' extending in length to 'le Estspitel' in the east and to
the house of Broun Stronge in the west, lying between the garden
of Richard Swenyld in the south and the land of the donor in

the north, to be held of the donor by payment of 1d for all service.

278 Charter of Walter Wroth in fee simple with warranty without date made to John son of John Marsh of 1 acre of land in 'Honifeld' [continues as **277**], and of 12d rent which Broun Stronge used to pay to the donor, to be held by payment of 2d *pa* for all service.

279 Charter of John Herbert with warranty and acquittance without date made to John son of John Marsh of 2 acres of land in Edmonton lying in the field called 'Churchefeld', of which 1½ acres lies between the water called Stebbyng in the south and the land of the abbot of Walden in the north, extending from east to west, and ½ acre lies between the land of the abbot of Walden in the north, extending from east to west, and the road called 'Garsoneswey' in the east, extending from north to south, to be held of the donor by payment of a garland of roses for all service.

280 Charter of Geoffrey son and heir of Maurice Hayward (*Messor*) of Edmonton with warranty and acquittance without date made to John Marsh, Edmund de Totenhale and Ralph de Brewe of the whole tenement which the donor had after the death of his father, to be held of the donor by payment of ½d for all service. And the feoffees paid 20m.
Witnesses: Richard de Anesty, Saer Clerk, Ralph Clerk, Robert Gizors, William Spirk, William Idoyne, ..., Walter Cook (*Coco*), William Ford, Geoffrey son of Laurence, Nicholas his brother, Roger Spirk, John ...
[Date: *temp.* Edward I.]
[WAM 289]

281 [*f. 24r*] Release in perpetuity by Richard de Wilehale made at Edmonton, 2 April 1317, to John son of John Marsh of an annual rent of 4d issuing from 1 acre which William de la Forde held in Edmonton.

282 Charter of Godard Aubert of Edmonton in fee simple without warranty and date made to Roger son of Benedict de Harleston of a piece of land in Edmonton adjacent to the messuage of the said Roger comprising 4 perches in length and 3 [perches] in width, extending from west to east to the street next to the messuage of the feoffee, to be held of the donor by payment of 4d *pa* for all service.

283 Charter of Thomas son of Godard of Edmonton in fee simple with warranty and acquittance without date made to Roger son of Benedict de Harleston of the aforesaid piece of land and of 3 roods of land lying between the land of the donor in the south and the land of Richard Picot in the north, extending on the eastern side to the pasture of Robert Gisors and in the west to the messuage of the feoffee, to be held of the donor by payment of 4d *pa* for all service.

284 Charter of Richard de Anesty and Diamand his wife in fee simple with warranty and acquittance without date made to William de Wynton, draper of London, Massenta his wife and John their son of all the land which the donor had in Edmonton which was once held by John le Bourser, and of 2s 5d rent, to be held of the donor by paying 1d *pa* and due services to the chief lords.

285 Charter of Richard de Anesty and Diamand his wife in fee simple with warranty and acquittance without date made to William de Wynton, citizen and draper of London, of a piece of land in Edmonton lying in the field called the Hyde between the land of Edmund de Totenhale and Margery his wife which they held in dower of the said Margery and the land of Maud Reyner, extending on the eastern side to the land of Denise Bukerel and in the west to the land of William de la Forde, to be held of the donor by paying 1d *pa* for all service.

286 Charter of Humphrey de Plechenden' in fee simple with warranty and acquittance without date made to William de Wynton, citizen and draper of London, Massenta his wife and John their son of all the land which the donor had in Edmonton which was formerly of John le Bourser, and of 2s 5d rent, to be held of the donor by payment of 1d *pa* and services due to the chief lords. Humphrey paid William and Massenta £60.
Witnesses: Richard Assewy, Geoffrey ..., Edmund de Totenhale, Ralph de Berwe, John Marsh, Ralph Clerk.
[Date: *temp*. Edward I.]
[WAM 300]

287 Release in perpetuity by Richard son and heir of Richard Rowe with warranty made in London, 13 April [*f. 24v*] 1295, to William de Wynton, citizen of London of all lands, tenements and rents which were of John Bourser in Edmonton.

288 Charter of William de Wynton, draper, and Massenta his wife in fee simple with warranty without date made to Robert le Despenser of Acton of one messuage, 50 acres of land, 6 acres of meadow [and] 10d of rent in Edmonton which were formerly of John le Bourser, in which Humphrey Waleden enfeoffed the donors, to be held of the chief lords of the fee for due services. *Witnesses*: William de la Forde, John de la Forde, John Marsh, Ralph de la Berwe, Ralph Clerk, William le Vikere, Nicholas Lauerens of Edmonton, Robert atte Fen, John Tebaud of Tottenham, Richard Duraunt, Saier Herberd, John Baldewine of Enfield, Richard Poterel senior, Richard Poterel junior, William Poterel, Peter de Edelmetone, Walter le Lord, John de Harewe, clerk.
[Date: 1295 x 1313]
[WAM 299]

289 Release in perpetuity of John son of William de Wynton, draper, with warranty made at Edmonton, 6 May 1313, to Robert le Despenser of Acton of all tenements in Edmonton which were formerly of John Bourser, in which William de Wynton, his father, and Massenta his wife, mother of the said John, enfeoffed the said Robert as above [**288**].
Witnesses: William de Forde, John de Forde, John Marsh, William le Fyker, Ralph Clerk, John atte Strate, Thomas le Rowe, William de Anesty, John Castle (*de Castello*), John Gysors, William Laur', Robert de Fen of Tottenham, John Tebaud, Richard Carpenter (*Carpentario*), John FitzJohn, John Stephen, Robert de Solio.
[WAM 246]

290 Charter of William le Vikere senior in fee simple with warranty made at Edmonton, 13 January 1349, to Robert le Vikere, son of the donor, of a plot of land with a house built on it and a garden called 'Shepcote' between the land formerly of William atte Forde in the east and the tenement of Henry Swyft in the west, extending from the land formerly of Hamo Fishmonger (*Piscenarii*) from the south to the lane called 'Haggesfeldeslane' in the north, and of 1 acre of land in Edmonton lying in the field called the Hyde between the land of Roger Depham in the north and the land formerly of William Smyth in the south, extending from the land of Richard Godhowe in the east and the land of

William de la Forde in the west.
Witnesses: John de Wilhale, John Castle, William atte Strate, Thomas de Fareindon, William Pymme, John Smith (*Fabro*), Robert le Taillour and others.
[WAM 273]

291 Charter of William son of William Vikere in fee simple with warranty made at Edmonton, 9 April 1349, to Roger de Depham and Margery his wife and the heirs of Roger of 1 acre of land in Edmonton lying in the Hyde, being the acre mentioned above [**290**].

292 Acquittance of Edmund de Neuyle made 13 January 1343 of 100s received from William Furneys in which William was bound to Edmund.

293 [*f. 25r*] Release in perpetuity by John Chyngford, clerk, without warranty made at Tottenham, 4 November 1296, to Richard Baldewyne senior of one messuage in Tottenham between the messuage of John Dymor and the messuage of Thomas Marsh, which John Chyngford held for life of the lease of Thomas Terry. *Witnesses*: John Tebaud, Walter le Bunde, William de Derneford, John Stephen, William le Notier, William Baker (*Pistor*), Nicholas de Solio, Robert le Cupere, John Vinch, Thomas Dine, Reginald Dine, John Dimor, Thomas Marsh, William de Halewys, John Abraam, John Belofte, John atte Stone and others [WAM 271]

294 Charter of William de Huntydon in fee simple with warranty without date made to Robert son of Edenarth of all the land which the donor had outside the gate of the bishop of London,[1] lying next to the land of Richard son of [omitted] before the gate of St Botolph,[2] to be held of the donor by payment of 8d and 16d to the bishop of London, the chief lord.

  1 Bishopsgate.
  2 Aldgate or Aldersgate.

295 Indenture of Walter Werth[1] made to John son of Idonia of the croft called 'Estspitell' comprising 2 acres enclosed, extending from the field called 'Swenild' in the south to the land of Richard Lif in the north, to be held from the current eleventh year of the cycle (*ab anno currente cycl' undecimo*)[2] for twelve years. And John paid 12s in fine.

Witnesses: William Ford, Thomas Pycott, Hugh Ford, Nicholas Ford, Hugh de Peverell, John FitzJohn, Geoffrey Marsh, William his brother and others.
[Date: (?)1254]
[WAM 268]

1 MS:Wroth.
2 MS:*anno currente currentecul' undecimo*. Presumably a reference to the indiction, although we have no means of telling in which cycle this charter was made. Possible dates might be 1239, 1254, 1269. See C.R. Cheney, *Handbook of Dates* (1945), 2–3.

296 Charter of John Hereward of Edmonton with warranty and acquittance without date made to William son of Idonia of 1 acre of land lying in 'Resfeldes' between the land of the donor and the pasture of the feoffee extending from east to west, to be held of the donor by paying 2½d *pa* for all service.

297 Charter of Geoffrey Cook (*Coci*) of Edmonton with warranty and acquittance without date made to William son of Idonia of 8d rent which the feoffee was accustomed to pay the donor for 1½ acres of land lying in Edmonton between the field called 'Longewelde' and the land of Richard la Rue, rendering to the donor one rose for all service.

298 Charter of John Hereward in fee simple with warranty and acquittance without date made to William Ydoyne of 8d rent which William Hereward used to pay the donor for 2 acres of land in Edmonton lying in the field called Westfield, and 4d rent which Geoffrey le Chivaler used to pay to the donor for 1 acre lying in the same field, and of 4d rent issuing from 1 acre in the same field which William Casiere holds, and of another 4d rent issuing from 1 acre of land which Walter Cook held in the same field, and of 4d rent issuing from another acre of land which Robert Godbywe held in the same field, and of 20d rent issuing from the land and pasture which the feoffee held of the donor, to be held of the same donor by one rose, and 4s to the chief lords.

299 [*f. 25v*] Charter of John Hereward in fee simple with warranty and acquittance without date made to the same William son of Idonia of 1 acre of land in Edmonton in the field called 'Risshefeld' or 'Reysfeld' between the land of Henry le Prechour, extending from the land of the feoffee in the south to the brook (*brocam*) called Hakebroc in the north, to be held of the donor by payment of 1d *pa* for all service.

300 Charter of John Hereward in fee simple with warranty and acquittance made without date to William Idoyne of all the pasture which the donor had in 'Resshefeld' next to the water called Hakebrok in the east, to be held of the donor by payment of $\frac{1}{2}$d for all service.

301 Charter of Edmund de Totenhale in fee simple with warranty and acquittance without date made to William Ydoyne of a piece of land in Edmonton between the land of the feoffee and the water of 'Medesenge', extending from the messuage of Richard Knotte in the east to the road called 'Garsoneswey' in the west, to be held of the donor by payment of 3d *pa* for all service.

302 Charter of Alice de la Slo in fee simple with warranty and acquittance without date made to William Idoyne and Elice (*Elicie*) his wife of 1 acre of meadow in Edmonton lying between the meadow of Richard le Rugh' and the meadow of the feoffee, extending in the east to 'la Rydelak' and in the west to the meadow of John Godeson, to be held of the donor by a rose and by 15$\frac{1}{2}$d to the chief lords.

303 Charter of Samuel Kalle in fee simple with warranty and acquittance without date made to William son of Idonia of one messuage and 3$\frac{1}{2}$ acres of land in Edmonton, of which 1$\frac{1}{2}$ acres lie between the land of Geoffrey son of Henry in the north and the land of William son of Reyner in the south, extending from east to west, and $\frac{1}{2}$ acre lies in the field called the Hyde between the land of William de Forde and the dyke called 'Newedych', and 1$\frac{1}{2}$ acres lie between the land of Reginald le Knyght and the land of Reyner the tailor (*sutoris*), to be held of the donor by one rose and by 15$\frac{1}{2}$d to the chief lords.

304 Charter of Jordan de Oxegate and Margery his wife with warranty and acquittance without date made to William son of Idonia of 5 roods of land in Edmonton lying in the field called 'Langeheg' between the land of William de la Forde and the land which (?)Fulk (*Folx*) Faulkner (*Falconarii*) holds in dower with Beatrice his wife, extending in the south to the land of Geoffrey Cook (*Coci*) and in the north to the land of Richard son of Geoffrey Rue, to be held of the donor by 1d for all service.

305 [*f. 26r*] Charter of William Dolphin in fee simple with warranty and acquittance without date made to Henry atte Berne of 4d rent which he was accustomed to receive from the tenement of the same William (*sic*) in Edmonton.

306 Charter of John Hereward of Edmonton in fee simple with warranty and acquittance made to William Ydoyne of 1 acre of land lying in Edmonton in the field called 'Resshefeld' between the land of the feoffee and the water called 'Cherchebrok', extending to the said water in the north and to the pasture of the feoffee and the lane called 'Resshefeldeslane' in the south, to be held of the donor by one rose and by 4d annual payment to the chief lords.

307 Charter of John Marsh in fee simple with warranty and acquittance without date made to Maurice Hayward (*Messor*) of 4 acres of land in the field called 'Gladewenesfeld' between the land of Ralph Gladewene and the land of Geoffrey Cake, extending from the field called 'Thareldefeld' in the north to the street called 'Cakestrate' in the south, to be held of the donor by one rose and by 14d annual payment to the chief lords.

308 Charter of John Goldyng in fee simple with warranty and acquittance without date made to Maurice Hayward of 1 acre of meadow in Edmonton marsh in the place called 'Chipolsot' between the meadow formerly of John FitzJohn and the meadow formerly of Christine Fountain (*de Fonte*), extending from the land of John Marsh in the west to the meadow called 'Rundmade' in the east, to be held of the donor by 4d *pa* for all service.

309 Charter of John Smith (*Fabri*) of Edmonton in fee simple with warranty and acquittance without date made to Maurice Hayward of $\frac{1}{2}$ acre of meadow in Edmonton lying between the meadow of the abbot of Walden and the meadow of John Street (*de Strata*) extending to the the meadow of the said abbot in the east to the meadow of Geoffrey Thurstan called 'Gore' in the west, to be held of the donor by one clove of garlic for all service.

310 Charter of John Goldyng of Edmonton in fee simple with warranty and acquittance without date made to Maurice Hayward of $\frac{1}{2}$ acre of meadow in Edmonton marsh between the meadow of Robert Houten and the meadow of the prior of Holy Trinity, extending to the River Lea in the east and to the meadow of John Marsh called 'Dykemad' in the west, to be held of the donor by 1d *pa* for all service.

311 Charter of Henry son of William of Edmonton in fee simple with warranty and acquittance without date made to Maurice de Eppyng of 1 acre in Edmonton (*Edelington*) in [*f. 26v*] the field called 'Haggefeld' between the land of the donor and the land of Geoffrey Pipard, extending from north to south, to be held of the donor by 12d for all service.

312 Charter of William de Wynchestre in fee simple with warranty and acquittance without date made to Maurice Hayward (*Messon*) of all the donor's land in Edmonton lying between 'Parkstrate' and the land of William de Forde, extending to the land of Agnes Colewell in the east and the land of Robert de Gledesey in the west, to be held of the donor by one clove of garlic and by 16d *pa* to the chief lords of the fee for all service.

313 Charter of Geoffrey de Querndon in fee simple with warranty and acquittance without date made to Ralph de la Berwe of Edmonton of 3 acres of land in Edmonton lying in the field called 'Nokhole', between the land which the donor's mother held in dower and the field called 'Wedenestrete', extending to the land of Robert Gisors and the land of Robert Blount to the south and north, to be held of the donor by one clove of garlic for all service.

314 Charter of Geoffrey de Querndon in fee simple with warranty and acquittance without date made to Ralph de la Berwe of all the land called 'Colewell' between the land of Richard Humfrey and the ditch called 'Grenedych', extending to the donor's land in the west and to the street called 'Holelane' in the east, to be held of the donor by one clove of garlic for all service.

315 Charter of Geoffrey de Querndon in fee simple with warranty and acquittance without date to Ralph de la Berwe of 10 acres of land in Edmonton in the field called Southfield, between the dowerland of the donor's mother and the street leading from the pasture called 'la Hope' to the bridge called 'Heyegatesbrugge', extending to the meadow of the donor called 'Dykemade' in the east and to the land of the donor called 'Hanedlond' in the west, to be held of the donor by one pair of spurs, price 3d, for all service.

316 Charter of Geoffrey de Querndon in fee simple with warranty and acquittance without date made to Ralph de la Berwe of Edmonton of 1 acre of meadow lying in Edmonton marsh between the meadow of Richard Humfrei and the meadow formerly of Richard de la Hale, extending in the east to the meadow called 'Halwacres' and in the west to 'Dykemade' of John le Blount, to be held of the donor by one rose for all service.

317 Release in perpetuity of John Denteyt without warranty made at Edmonton, 8 May 1314, to John Thebaud [*f. 27r*] of Tottenham of 1 acre of land in the field called 'Langeheg' in which John Marsh enfeoffed the said John Thebaud.

318 Indenture made at Edmonton, 13 May 1299, whereby John Denteyt and Thomas his father leased to Hamo le Palmer of London all the land which they had in 'Middeleresfeld' in Edmonton and two pieces of pasture lying next to the same land and 1 acre of meadow lying in Edmonton marsh, between the meadow of John Marsh and the meadow of Richard le Rowe, to be held for eight years.

319 Release in perpetuity by John Denteyt without warranty made at Edmonton, 5 May 1314, to William Godhowe of Edmonton of 1 acre in the field called the Hyde which the said William acquired of John de Luco.

320 Charter of William le Cook of Edmonton made at Edmonton, 3 July 1341, to Thomas son of Maud de Anesty and Isabel his wife of all lands and tenements in Edmonton which the said Thomas formerly granted to the donor, to be held for the life of the feoffees with remainder in turn to each of those written below, to be held in fee tail if the first die without issue, namely Thomas, Maud and Alice, children of the said Thomas and Isabel, and if all die without issue to remain to the right heirs of Thomas.

321 Charter of John Taylor (*Cissoris*) of Edmonton in fee simple with warranty and acquittance without date made to Hamo Fishmonger (*Piscatori*) of London of the land lying in 'Austynesfeld' between the land of William de la Forde in the north and the land of William de la Holme in the south, extending in the east to the land of John de la Forde and in the west to the highway

called 'Scotteslane', to be held of the chief lords of the fee by
due services.

322 Charter of William de la Forde in fee simple with warranty and
acquittance without date made to John le Taillor of 2 acres of
land lying between the donor's land in the north and the land
of William Holm (*de Hulmo*) in the south, extending in the east
to the land of John de la Forde and in the west to to the land
of the feoffee, to be held of the donor for 12d *pa* for all service.

323 [*f. 27v*] Release in perpetuity by John de la Forde of Edmonton
without warranty made in London, 5 March 1318, to Hamo le
Fishemongere of London of 12d rent which the releasor was
accustomed to receive of the croft called 'Scottescroft' which he
had previously granted to John le Taillour, lying in Edmonton
between the land of William de Holm (*de Hulmo*) in the south
and the land lately of John son of Hugh in the north, extending
in the east to the land formerly of the said John son of Hugh
and in the west to 'Scotteslane'.

324 [Change of hand.] Charter of John son of Idonia of Edmonton
in fee simple with warranty, acquittance and defence without
date made to William de la Forde of 1 acre of land in Edmonton
called 'Irchonesacre' lying in the field called 'Stonyfeld', to be
held of the donor by service of 2d *pa*.

325 Charter of Roger Sprik (*sic*) in fee simple with warranty and
acquittance without date made to William de la Forde of all the
land lying close by the messuage of John de la Hegh, except
dowerland (*excepta dote*) in Edmonton, and of a messuage which
John le Coupere held next to 'Blakemanneswell', to be held of
the chief lords of the fee by paying to the donor 1d *pa*.

326 Charter of William le Vikere of Edmonton in fee simple with
warranty without date made to William de la Forde of $1\frac{1}{2}$ acres
of land in the field called 'Westcolgrave' between the land
formerly of Katherine, widow, on either side, of which the
northern part abuts on the land of Katherine More, to be held
by service of 2d *pa*.

327 Charter of Saer Clerk of Edmonton in fee simple with warranty
and acquittance without date made to William de la Forde of
the pasture lying between the pasture of the same William and
the pasture called 'Potmor', extending in length from north to

south, to be held of the donor by service of $\frac{1}{2}$d *pa*.

328 Charter of Sabine who was the wife of William Patrik in fee simple with warranty made at Edmonton, 10 May 1318, to William de la Forde of 1 acre in Edmonton lying in the field called 'Haggefeld' in which the feoffee enfeoffed the donor.

329 Charter of John Patrik in fee simple with warranty made at Edmonton, 6 August 1316, to William atte Forde of all tenements of which Reginald Waryn died seised in [*f. 28r*] Edmonton, except the capital messuage which William Deonys holds.

330 Release in perpetuity by Gilbert son of Nicholas de Paris with warranty without date made to William atte Forde of 7 acres of land in Edmonton which Katherine daughter of William Frere had purchased from Walter le Moyne and in which she enfeoffed the said William.

331 Charter of Edmund de Totenhale in fee simple without warranty and date made to William de la Forde of a headland (*forera*) in Edmonton lying in the field called 'Langeheg' and a perch of pasture lying in 'Forecroft' on the southern side next to the stream (*cursum aque*) flowing between the pasture of the donor and the pasture of the feoffee.

332 Charter of William de la Forde of Edmonton in fee tail without date made to William son of William Pateryk and Sabine daughter of John Saleman of 1 acre of land in Edmonton lying in the field called 'Haggefeld' between the land of Agnes de Colewell in the north and the land of Reginald Waryn in the south, extending from east to west, at a rent to the donor of 1d *pa*.

333 Charter of Godard son of Philip of Edmonton in fee simple with warranty and acquittance without date made to William de la Forde of one messuage in Edmonton situated next to Southgate between Enfield park and the messuage of Thomas William, and of one croft of enclosed land in East Barnet, between the land of Adam Dylbarn and the road leading from the wood of 'Osseheg' to Enfield park, to be held of the donor by one clove of garlic annual rent for all service, and by paying 4d *pa* to Thomas William, the chief lord.

334 Release in perpetuity by Robert son of Alice, daughter of Robert

Salveyn, without warranty made 4 February 1294 to William son of William de la Forde of all the lands and tenements in Edmonton which were of Robert Salveyn, grandfather of the said Robert son of Alice.

335 Charter of William Winton, citizen and draper of London, in fee simple with warranty without date made to William de la Forde of $1\frac{1}{2}$ acres land in Edmonton, of which [1] acre lies in the field called the Hyde between the land of Edmund Totenhale which he holds by right of dower (*nomine dotis*) and the land of the feoffee, extending in length to the land of the said Edmund [*f. 28v*] in the south and north, and $\frac{1}{2}$ acre lies in the same field between the land of the said Edmund which he holds by right of dower on either side, extending to the south and north on the pasture of the said Edmund, to be held of the donor by $\frac{1}{4}$d for all service.

336 Charter of John son of William Ford (*de Forda*) in fee simple with warranty and acquittance without date made to Philip Smith (*Fabro*) of a certain messuage in Edmonton between the land of Roger le Pottere and 'Potterestrate', extending in length from the messuage of the said Roger in the west to the messuage formerly of Gilbert Belle in the east, to be held of the donor by service of 18d annually.

337 Charter of Robert de Gledeseye in fee simple with warranty without date made to William de la Forde of a certain piece of land called 'Hamekyneshawe' in Edmonton, to be held of the chief lords of the fee for 1d.

338 Charter of Thomas de la Forde, brother of William de la Forde in fee simple with warranty without date made to Denis le Avener, citizen of London, and Isabel his wife of 3 acres of meadow in Edmonton marsh, of which 1 acre 3 roods lie between the meadow of Robert Bate and the meadow of William Chicheley extending to 'Humberlond', and 1 acre and 1 rood lie in the place called 'Niewechepynge' between the meadow formerly of Diamand de Anesty and 'Shaddeshalacre', to be held of the chief lords of the fee.

339 Charter of Nicholas Laurence in fee simple with warranty and acquittance made at Edmonton 24 May 1299 to William de Forde of one piece of land in Edmonton lying in the field called 'Langheg' in a plot called called 'Longforlang', extending on one side to the land of Edmund de Totenhale and on the other side to 'le Stynkyndelond', in exchange for a piece of land lying in the same field between the land of the prior and convent of Holy Trinity and the land of Reginald Pymore.

340 Indented charter of the prior and convent of Holy Trinity London in fee simple with warranty and acquittance without date made to William de Forde of $\frac{1}{2}$ acre of arable land in Edmonton lying in the field called 'Yarledefeld' between the land of the same religious (*eorundem religiosorum*) and the land of the feoffee near Enfield wood, to be held of the donor by annual service of 4d.

341 Charter of William de la Forde in fee simple with warranty and acquittance without date made to William his son of the grove called 'Scottesgrove' in Edmonton [*f. 29r*] and of 4 acres of land in the same vill, of which 2 acres lie in the field called 'Estfeld' between the land of William le Frere on either side, and 2 acres lie in the field called 'Storkesnest' between the land of the said William and the land of Philip Smith (*Fabri*), and of 5 acres of pasture in 'la Dane' in the same vill lying next to the land of the said William Frere, to be held of the donor by service of $\frac{1}{2}$d and to the chief lords of the fee, namely to Hugh Peverel 3d and to Thomas lately vicar of Edmonton a garland of roses for all service.
[Cf. PRO Ancient Deeds E40/2038, which is almost identical in content but which bears no dorsal pressmark.]

342 Charter of Richard Denys of Edmonton in fee simple without warranty and date made to Geoffrey son of Robert de la Forde of $\frac{1}{2}$d annual rent to be received from the hands of Margery, formerly wife of Henry son of William, of the gift...', which the donor bought of John Fountain (*de Fonte*).

  1 Words omitted.

343 Charter of Stephen[1] prior of Holy Trinity, London, and of the convent of the same place in fee simple with warranty and without date made to William de Forde of 20 acres of land in Edmonton in the field called 'Heyfeld' between the street which leads from the house of John atte Welle as far as 'Sawalescrouche' in the south and the street leading from the house of John Baroun to the messuage of Richard le Pot' in the north and the street leading from the messuage of the said Richard le Pot' to

'Sawalescrouche' in the west, to be held of the donor by annual service of 10s, as security for which payment the feoffee pledged the other lands contained in the charter.

[Cf. PRO E40/1740, without dorsal pressmark.]

[Date: 1294 x 1303]

1 Stephen de Watton (*VCH London* i, 474).

344 Charter of John de la Forde in fee simple with warranty made at Edmonton, 12 November 1312, to Robert le Despenser of Acton of 1 acre of meadow in Edmonton between the meadow of William Vykere and the meadow of Robert Smith (*Fabri*), extending on one side to 'le Spitelmed' and on the other to the River Lea.

345 Indented charter of William son of William de Forde in fee tail with reversion preserved (*salvato*) in default of issue with warranty and acquittance without date made to Godard son of Philip of Edmonton and Alice his wife of all the land in which the said Godard enfeoffed the donor in Edmonton and East Barnet, to be held of the donor by service of 10d *pa*.

346 [*f. 29v*] Charter of Roger Spyrk in fee simple with warranty and acquittance without date made to William de la Forde of 1 acre of meadow in Edmonton marsh between the meadow of John Bonde in the north and the meadow of Richard le Spyrk in the south, extending from the River Lea in the east to the meadow of John Marsh in the west.

347 Charter of Thomas de la Forde in fee simple with warranty made in London, 31 October 1310, to John de la Forde brother of the donor of 2 acres and 3 roods of meadow in Edmonton, of which 1 acre and 3 roods lie between the meadow of the feoffee and the meadow of Robert Smith (*Fabri*), extending from 'Manemad' to the meadow called 'le Spitelmad', and 1 acre [lies] between the meadow of William le Vikere and the meadow of the said Robert Smith, extending from the River Lea to 'le Spitelmad', at a rent to the donor of 24s *pa* for life.

348 Charter of Henry le Prechour in fee simple without warranty and date made to William de Forde of 12d rent issuing from the messuage of Thomas Wyse in Edmonton.

349 Letter of Geoffrey de Say made at Sawbridgeworth, 7 April 1319, to Lorence, wife of William son of William de la Forde, of the body of Maud daughter of the said Lorence and heir of the said William and William, whose custody and upbringing pertained to the said Lorence (*cujus custodiam ad dictam Lorenc' pertinebat per viam nutriture*) for life since the said William held his land in socage.

350 Charter of Arnulph son of Samuel of Edmonton in fee simple with warranty and acquittance without date made to William de la Forde of 1 acre of land in Edmonton which Walter de Salern formerly granted to the said Arnulph, and of 4d rent issuing from the tenement of Godard the donor's brother, to be held of the donor by service of one clove of garlic for all service.

351 Release in perpetuity by Ralph of Edmonton, clerk, without date made to William de la Forde of 12d rent which the same William had paid to the said Ralph for his tenement, which [tenement] a certain Alan de Waleden had once granted to John Gilberd.

352 Charter of Geoffrey de la Forde in fee simple with warranty and acquittance without date made to William de la Forde of a moiety of 1 acre of meadow lying in Edmonton marsh next to the meadow of John de la Forde, of which the northern side extends [*f. 30r*] to the meadow lately of John le Blund called 'le Dykedemad' and the southern [side] to the meadow of Ralph de la Berewe called 'Querendoneshope', to be held of the donor by the service of 1d.

353 Release in perpetuity by Robert son of Maurice le Heyward with warranty made at Westminster, 3 January 1293, to William de la Forde of one messuage 6 acres of land and $\frac{1}{2}$ acre of meadow in Edmonton, which the said Robert formerly sued (*petebat*) against him before the justices of assize etc. by writ of *mort dancestor*, and of $\frac{1}{2}$ acre of meadow in Tottenham.

354 Indented charter of John Street (*de Strato*) and Alice his wife in fee simple with warranty made at Edmonton, 20 July 1318, to William de la Forde of 1 acre of land lying in 'Haggefeld' in exchange for 12d rent which the donor was accustomed to pay to the said William for one piece of land lying before the gate (*portam*) formerly of Richard Deonys, and the said acre of land lies between the land of the said William on either side, extending from the land formerly of Geoffrey Waryn in the east to the land lately of Reginald Waryn in the west.

355 Charter of Richard Spyrk in fee simple with warranty and acquittance without date made to William de la Forde of 9d rent to be received of Roger Spyrk from a tenement in a field called 'Deggles Aldwych'.

356 Charter of Thomas vicar of Edmonton in fee simple with warranty and acquittance without date made to William de la Forde of all the pasture which the donor had of Henry son of William in 'la Wedeidaire' in Edmonton lying between the field called the Hyde and the field called 'le Estfeld', extending from the east from the land of the prior of Holy Trinity, London, to the dower land of Alice lately wife of Geoffrey son of William in the west, and of 2 acres of land along the length of the said pasture, to be held of the donor by one garland of roses for all service.

357 Charter of William Carpenter (*Carpentarii*) in fee simple with warranty without date made to William de la Forde of 5s rent and of rent of $\frac{1}{2}$ lb of pepper to be received from land which the donor leased to Florence his sister in 'Godeleston'.

358 [*f. 30v*] Charter of Robert le Neuman with warranty and acquittance without date made to William de la Forde and Cecily his wife and the heirs of the same William of 1 acre of meadow in Edmonton marsh lying between the meadow of John Goddessone and the meadow of Katherine de la Hull, extending from the meadow formerly of John le Blund called 'Nyneacres' in the east to the meadow of Richard Swonyld in the west, to be held of the donor by service of 4d annual rent to John Marsh.

359 Charter of Richard Wylehale in fee simple with warranty without date made to William de la Forde of 3 acres of pasture lying in Edmonton at 'le Manmad' between the tenements of the said William, and of 6 acres of land in Edmonton, of which $2\frac{1}{2}$ acres lie at Chapel Hill, extending in the south to the land of the said William and in the north to the lane leading to the house of the nuns of Clerkenwell, and $1\frac{1}{2}$ acres of land lie between the land formerly of Edmund de Totenhale and the land of the said William, extending in the north to the land of the said William called 'Benepirtel', and 2 acres lie at Highbridge (*altum pontem*) between the highway in the west and the land of John Taylor (*Cissoris*) in the east, extending in the south to the water called 'Medesenge', to be held of the chief lords.

360 Release in perpetuity of Robert le Burser without warranty and
date made to William de Forde of 40 acres of land in Edmonton
of which a suit had been moved between them before the justices
of the bench, 27 January 1265.
[Cf. **367** below.]

361 Confirmation in fee simple with warranty and acquittance
without date made by Henry de Thakstede and Alice his wife to
William de la Forde of the gift, concession and quitclaim which
the said Alice [made] to the said William of the whole tenement
called the tenement of Basilia in Edmonton, to be held of Henry
and Alice and their heirs by service of $\frac{1}{2}$d, and 4d to the chief
lords for all service.

362 Charter of Richard Lyf in fee simple with warranty and acquittance without date made to John son of Robert de Forde of 3
roods of meadow in Edmonton marsh lying between the meadow
of Sir Robert de North (*Aquylon*) in the north and the meadow
of Elizabeth daughter of Roger Smith (*Fabri*) in the south,
extending from east to west, to be held of the donor by service
of $\frac{1}{2}$d.

363 [*f. 311*] Charter of Walter Gorge in fee simple with warranty and
acquittance without date made to William de la Forde of a croft
in Edmonton called 'Cockesfeld' lying between the field called
'Lynesfeld' and the field called 'Vykeresfeld', to be be held of
the donor by one clove of garlic and $\frac{1}{2}$d *pa* to Richard Anesty,
chief lord, for all service.

364 Release in perpetuity by Walter le Moyne without warranty and
date made to William de la Forde of 5 acres of meadow in
Edmonton marsh in which the said William had previously
enfeoffed him.

365 Letter made at Edmonton, 14 January 1307, whereby John Marsh
assigned in his place William le Frere and Roger Lofte to deliver
to Nicholas, William and Robert, his sons, seisin of three pieces
of land and of one piece of pasture in Edmonton by form of a
charter made to them in fee simple, and to deliver to Katherine
and Alice, his daughters, seisin of 6 acres of meadow in Edmonton
by form of a charter made to them.

366 Charter of John Wood (*de Bosco*) of Winchelsea in fee simple with
warranty without date made to William de Forde of 6d rent in

Edmonton rising from the tenement which the donor once held in Edmonton.

367 Release in perpetuity by Robert le Burser without warranty and date made to William de Forde of 40 acres of land in Edmonton of which a plea had been made between them at Westminster before the justices of the bench.
[Cf. **360** above.]

368 Charter of John Marsh (*del Mareis*) of Enfield with warranty without date made to Gamelian de Lugefare with Emma sister of the donor of 2 acres of meadow called 'Langemad' lying between the Hermit's Rood (*rodam Eremite*) and the half-acre of (?)Azon (*Azonis*), granted in free marriage (*in liberum maritagium*).

369 Release in perpetuity by Nicholas Laurence without warranty made at Edmonton, 12 March 1307, to William de la Forde of a hedge and ditch newly begun (*de novo tunc incepto*) between the tenement of the said Nicholas and the tenement of the said William at 'Westcolgrove' in Edmonton.

370 [*f. 31v*] Indented charter of Richard le Rowe in fee simple with warranty and acquittance without date made to William de la Forde of 3 roods of land in Edmonton lying in the field called 'Langeheg' between the land of the feoffee in the west and the land of the prior of Holy Trinity London in the east, extending from the land of the said prior from the south and the land of Geoffrey Laurence in the north, to be held of the donor in exchange for $5\frac{1}{2}$ roods of land lying in the field called the Hyde between the land of Ancellus Knotte in the east and the land of Roger atte Pole in west.

371 Charter of Edmund Pymme in fee simple with warranty without date made to William de la Forde, of 4d rent in Edmonton in which William Picot, uncle of the donor, enfeoffed him.

372 Charter of John Patryk of Edmonton in fee simple with warranty made at Edmonton, 10 April 1340, to Henry Lorymer of a croft of land enclosed in Edmonton lying in the place called 'Alvenebregge' between the land of Agnes le Hoppes in the east and the royal highway leading to Winchmore Hill in the west.

373 Acquittance of Gilbert le Mareschal, citizen of London, made in London, 30 June 1316, to John Patryk of Edmonton of £7[1]

received from the said Gilbert and acknowledged to be his in
the Exchequer on 27 April 1313[2] by the said John and by Robert
le Forester of Enfield.

[PRO KR Memoranda Rolls E159/86 rot. 6od.]

1 MS: £6.
2 MS: 26 April.

374 Release by John son of Philip Patryk with warranty made at
Edmonton, 27 May 1339, to Thomas Horn, chaplain, of all that
tenement in Edmonton lying between the wood of William de
Causton and the land formerly of Thomas William in the north
and the wood formerly of Philip Wileby and that of the prioress
of St Helen's, London, and the land of Ralph Cowe in the south,
extending from the street called South Street in the west to the
field called 'Taylesfeld' in the east, which tenement the said John
son of Philip lately granted to Robert Albon, and which John de
la Panetrye, mercer, afterwards granted to Thomas Horn.

375 Surrender and release in perpetuity of William de la Forde
without warranty and date made to Edmund de Totenhale of 3
roods of land called 'Joddes Hamstal'.

376 [f. 32r] Charter of William de Forde in fee tail without warranty
and date made to Edmund de Totenhale and Margery his wife
of all the land lying in Edmonton in the field called 'Panyacre'
between the land of the feoffee and the land of Alice, mother of
the donor, extending from the street called 'Wordestrate' in the
south to the water called 'Panyacrebeche' in the north, to be
held of the donor by annual service of $\frac{1}{2}$d.

377 Indented charter of William son of William de Forde in fee tail,
saving reversion to the donor, with warranty without date made
to Godard son of Philip of Edmonton and Alice his wife of all
that tenement in Edmonton and East Barnet of which the feoffee
enfeoffed the donor, to be held of the donor by service of 10d
annually.

378 Charter of John de la Forde, citizen of London, in fee simple
with warranty without date made to Thomas son of William de
la Forde of 13d rent, of which 12d issues from the whole tenement
of William Dolfyn son of Simon Dolfyn in Edmonton and 1d
issues from 'Waldyngemad' which Thomas Picot holds, to be

held of the donor in total lordship of the said tenements by service of one clove of garlic.

379 Charter of William de la Forde in fee simple with warranty and acquittance without date made to Thomas his son of all that tenement in the vill of Walthamstow in which Adam Cole enfeoffed the donor, to be held of the donor by service of $1\frac{1}{2}$d *pa.*

380 Charter of Richard Dyonys with warranty and acquittance without date made to William de la Forde and Cecily his wife and the heirs of William of 4d rent which Avice Kellynges used to pay for a small croft (*crofticula*) lying in Edmonton between the field of the donor and the street leading from 'la Pirieslo' to Palmer's Green.

381 Charter of Peter de la Flagge in fee simple without warranty and date made to Thomas Clerk of Malmesbury of the whole croft facing 'Pirie' and called 'Gulecroft' between the land of Richard Blund and the land of Thomas le Hope, to be held of the donor by annual service of 2s.

382 [*f. 32v*] Charter of John Patryk in fee simple with warranty without date made to William de la Forde of all tenements in Edmonton of which Alice who was wife of William Deonys died seised, except the chief messuage which the said William Deonys holds, and of 4s 4d rent belonging to the said tenement, of which 8d issued from the tenement formerly of Philip Smith (*Fabri*) in the field called 'Hagefeld', 4d from the tenement formerly Robert Bolle in the same field, 6d from the tenement of John Saleman, 4d from the tenement of William de Forde, 12d from the tenement formerly of Geoffrey Waryn, 2d from the tenement of Robert Burdeyn in the said field, and 2d from the tenement of Robert Burdeyn in the field called 'Storkesnest', 5d from two pieces of meadow which William de Causton holds, and 10d from the tenement lying next to 'Hemyngeswodegate' which John Hemyng holds by English law, to be held of the chief lords of the fee.

383 Charter of William de la Forde in fee simple with warranty and acquittance without date made to William his son of 60 acres of land in Edmonton, comprising 46 acres lying in parcels which the donor held of the fee formerly of Robert Saweyn, and 7 acres formerly of Clarice, lately wife of Geoffrey Goce, and 1 acre called 'Pintokespitel', formerly purchased from William de la Berghe, and 6 acres which the prior of Holy Trinity, London, once granted to the donor in exchange, of which 3 acres lie in 'Stonfeld' within the fee of Robert Saweyn and 3 acres were of Robert de Little, and of 16d rent, of which 12d issue from the messuage formerly of John Richer and 4d from 1 acre lying in the field of Arnulph Samuel which Godard Samuel once held, to be held of the donor by service of 20s 8d for his life, and of the donor's heir by service of 8d *pa*, saving foreign service.

384 Charter of William son of William de la Forde in fee simple with warranty and acquittance without date made to Richard son of William de la Berewe of all that messuage which Richard le Lyf once held in Edmonton, situated next to the highway leading from Enfield park to the place called 'le Park Crouche', to be held of the donor by service of 12d *pa* for all service saving heriot and relief.

385 Another charter of William de la Forde in fee simple with warranty and acquittance without date made to William his son of 65 acres of land and 16d rent, of which 60 acres and the rent are the same 60 acres and the same rent granted by the [*f. 33r*] previous charter [**383**], but of the remaining 5 acres 1 acre lies in 'Stonyfeld' and is called 'Irchonesacre' and the donor had another 4 acres therein by escheat of William Smalwode, to be held of the donor by service of 2s 4d *pa* for all service saving foreign.

386 Charter of William de Anesty in fee simple with warranty made at Edmonton, 6 March 1307, to William de la Forde of three pieces of land in Edmonton, of which one lies in the field of John son of Hugh and another in the field of John son of Gilbert and the third in the field called 'Hokfeld', with release of all his right in the land which Margery the donor's mother held as dower in the same fields.

387 Release in perpetuity by Maud who was wife of William Cook (*Coci*) without warranty and date made to William de la Forde of the whole of the tenement with land which the said William acquired of her husband in Edmonton, by paying to the said Maud for life 1d *pa*.

388 Charter of Geoffrey de la Forde in fee simple without date made to William de la Forde of 12½d rent which the said William was previously accustomed to pay to the donor for the messuage of William Brid.

389 Release in perpetuity by Alice daughter of William de la Forde made at Edmonton before the feast of Tiburcius and Valerian 5 Edward II[1] to her father of all the tenements in Edmonton which he had previously leased to her.

   1 14 April 1312; the day was presumably omitted by scribal error.

390 Charter of Robert Gege in fee simple with warranty without date made to Geoffrey FitzJohn of $1\frac{1}{2}$ acres of land and of one messuage lying between the house which was of William Casiere and the house which was of Geoffrey Ried extending from north to south in Edmonton, and of rent issuing from the house of Simon Crupho and from the house of Geoffrey Ried belonging to the same land, and of 2 acres of land in the Hyde lying between the land of Sir Richard Percy and the land of John son of Agnes, to be held of the donor by $1\frac{1}{2}$d *pa* and 5s 4d to the chief lords for all service.

391 [*f. 33v*] Release in perpetuity by Geoffrey de Querndon without warranty and date made to Robert son of Robert Deggel of Edmonton of the customs and services held [of] Hawys Cadbaken which the said Robert previously held of Geoffrey.

392 Letter of Richard atte Hulle without date by which he granted permission to Edmund de Chiltren to distrain in all his other lands whenever rent due from 1 acre of land leased to the same Richard for life by gift of Edmund was in arrears.

393 Release in perpetuity by Alice Gisors without warranty made at Edmonton, 18 Edward I,[1] to John de Gisors her brother of all land lying in Southfield between the land of Richard Neel in the south and the land formerly of Thomas Picot in the north, extending from the east from the land of William de Wynton to the west to the curtilage of William Godhowe.

   1 20 November 1289–19 November 1290. Date omitted.

394 Release in perpetuity by Agnes Beneytes without warranty made at Tottenham, 22 January 1292, of a ditch belonging to the land called 'Clobbersfeld', namely between the land of the said Agnes and 'Clobbersfeld'.

395 Release in perpetuity by Richard Spyrk of Edmonton without
warranty made at Edmonton, 17 February 1292, to Walter le
Bunde of Tottenham of that acre of meadow in Edmonton which
was formerly of Richard Denys lying between the meadow of
Roger Spyrk in the south and the meadow of Richard de Anesty
in the north, extending from the River Lea in the east to the
meadow of John Marsh in the west.

396 Charter of William Belofte of Tottenham in fee simple with
warranty made, 1 September 1296, to Fulk son of Hubert of 8s
5d rent in Tottenham to be received of the tenement which
Reginald le Chaundeler and Isabel his wife held, lying between
the donor's tenement in the south and the tenement of William
le Notyere in the north, to be held of the donor by 1d for all
services.
Witnesses: Laurence Duket, John FitzJohn, John Tebaud, Robert
de le Fen, Roger de Derneford, John atte Stone, Angel de
Hatfeld, Roger le Kyng, Walter le Bonde, Robert de Carshalton,
John atte Watere, John son of Stephen, Hugh de Heyden, clerk,
and others,
[PRO E40/4401]

397 Release in perpetuity of Margery, who was the wife of William
Belofte without warranty made at Tottenham, 17 April 1297, to
the same Fulk of the same rent and the tenement from which
the rent issued.

398 [*f. 34r*] Charter of John son and heir of Robert Gisors in fee
simple with warranty made in London, 28 March 1301, to
Richard Horn, citizen and fishmonger of London, of 1½ acres of
meadow in Edmonton marsh lying in 'le Esthale' between the
meadow of the abbot of Thorney in the east and the meadow
of Christine Sotiers in the west, extending from the River Lea
in the north to Tottenham 'marke' in the south.

399 Indenture made in London, 11 March 1302, whereby Ralph de
Honilane, citizen of London, leased to Richard de Haleford 6
acres of meadow in Enfield called 'Rondemede' lying in the
meadow called 'Mellemerssh' in which Walter Cellyng of
Cheshunt had enfeoffed the lessor, to be held from 25 March
following for the life of the said Richard.

400 Charter of Alexander de Chigewelle, citizen of London in fee
simple with warranty made at Edmonton, 19 February 1303, to

Richard Carpenter (*Carpentario*) of one piece of land in Edmonton lying in the field called 'Langheg' between the land of John Thobald in the south and the land formerly of Roger Aldred in the north, extending from the highway in the east to 'Garsoneswey' in the west.

401 Charter of William Vikere of Edmonton in fee simple with warranty made in London, 25 November 1304, to Robert de Upton, draper of London, of one piece of meadow in Edmonton marsh lying between the meadow of Geoffrey de la Berewe and the meadow of Hugh Skyn, extending from the pasture of the said Geoffrey to the meadow of Sir William de Gloucester (*Glovernia*).

402 Charter of Roger Spyrk of Edmonton in fee simple with warranty made at Tottenham, 27 June 1305, to Thomas le Rowe son of Richard le Rowe of $\frac{1}{2}$ acre of meadow in Edmonton lying between the donor's meadow and the meadow of the prior and convent of Holy Trinity, London, extending from the meadow of William le Vikere to the meadow called 'Roundemad'.

403 Release in perpetuity by Geoffrey Brose without warranty made 28 April 1306 to Ralph atte Park of a curtilage in Edmonton lying between the messuage of John Humfrey and Maud Humfrey next to the road leading to the Hale [*f. 34v*] for which he had sued the same [Ralph] by writ of *mort dancestor*.

404 Charter of John Pycok of Edmonton in fee simple with warranty made 22 December 1305 to Augustine Alewale of 4 acres of land in Edmonton in the field called 'Westberewefeld' lying between the land of Willam Amys and the land of William Smith (*Fabri*), extending from the tenement formerly of John le Blund in the south to the land of Ralph Park (*de Parco*) in the north.

405 Charter of Hugh le Knyght of Edmonton in fee simple with warranty made at Edmonton, 2 February 1307, to Walter Basse of 1 acre of land lying in the field called 'le Risshfeld' in Edmonton between the land of Philip de Neuman in the south and the land of the feoffee in the north, extending from the land of John Denteut in the east to the land of Nicholas Bruse in the west.

406 Charter of Thomas de Forde brother of William de Forde in fee simple with warranty made at Edmonton, 9 June 1309, to Denis le Avener, citizen of London, and Isabel his wife of 3 acres of meadow in Edmonton marsh, of which 1 acre and 3 roods lie between the meadow of Robert Bate and the meadow of Robert Kenere, extending from the pasture of William le Venour called 'Amberland', and 1 acre and 1 rood lie in the place called 'Newchepyng' between the meadow formerly of Diamand de Anesty and 'Shadeshalfacre', to be held of the chief lords by due services.

Witnesses: William de Forde, John Marsh (*de Marisco*), John de Ford, Ralph Clerk, Robert de Actone, William le Fiker, John Tebaud, Thomas de Anesty, John Gysors, John Castle (*de Castello*), William Clerk and others.

[PRO E40/12134]

407 Indenture made at Edmonton, 8 December 1308, containing that Geoffrey Thomas of Reading leased to Robert de Acton 4 acres of meadow in Edmonton of which $1\frac{1}{2}$ acres lie between the meadow of William de la Forde and the meadow of Richard de Wyldehale and 5 roods lie between the meadow of William le Vikere and the meadow called 'le Roundmade', and 3 roods lie between the meadow of Geoffrey de la Berewe and 'le Roundemad', and $\frac{1}{2}$ acre lies between meadow of the lessor and the meadow of Robert Gulle, to be held for eight years.

408 Charter of Michael le Bailiff, called le Armurer, of London in fee simple with warranty made in London, 2 February 1309, to William Casiere of one messuage in Edmonton lying between the messuage of William Smith (*Fabri*) in the south and the messuage of Christine Collyng in the north, extending from the land of William Amys in the east to the highway in the west.

409 [*f. 35r*] Letter of the same Michael le Bailiff made on the same day to Alan son of John de Westeleton to deliver seisin according to the above charter.

410 Charter of John le Carpenter in fee simple without warranty made at Edmonton, 3 February 1309, to John Marsh (*de Marisco*) of all that tenement in Edmonton in which the feoffee had previously enfeoffed the donor.

411 Release in pepetuity by John Marsh without warranty made at Edmonton, 15 July 1309, to Isabel and Maud his daughters of one piece of land in Edmonton called 'Foulberdesfeld'.

412 Release in perpetuity by John Marsh son and heir of John Marsh without warranty made at Edmonton, 30 April 1312, to Roger de Solio of Tottenham of 3s rent, being a portion of the 4s rent which the said Roger was accustomed to pay to the said John for his tenement in Tottenham, situated between the tenement of the same Roger and that once held by William Egepol.

413 Charter of Ralph son of Ellis de Honylane in fee simple with warranty made at Enfield, 23 June 1311, to John de la Chambre, clerk, of 6 acres of meadow in Enfield lying in 'le Melnemerssh' near 'Halveneye' in the north and 'Stodymad' in the south and the meadow formerly of Bartholomew Abselon in the west and the meadow formerly of Sir Henry de Enefeld in the east.

414 Letter of the same Ralph made 19 June 1311 to John de Waltham, clerk, and Robert le Planeter to deliver seisin according to the aforesaid charter.

415 Charter of John son of William Hereward in fee simple with warranty made at Edmonton, 17 February 1314, to John le Spenser of Acton of one piece of land in Edmonton lying in 'le Russhefeld' between the land of Oger le Casiere and the land of John Denteyt extending from the land of the same John Denteyt in the east to the land of Nicholas Brose in the west.

416 [f. 35v] Charter of Roger de Hakeneye in fee simple with warranty made, 1 November 1315, to Roger Kenere of Enfield of one piece of land containing 2 acres lying in Enfield in the field called 'Aydon' between the land of Margery Bradeleye on either side, extending from the land of John Castle (*de Castello*) to the land of Sir John de Enefeld.

417 Charter of Roger atte Lofte in fee simple with warranty made at Tottenham, 14 May 1317, to John Mountchaysi of Waltham of a messuage in Tottenham situated between the tenement of John Ekepol in the north and that of the donor in the south, extending from the highway in the west to the tenement of the said John Ekepol in the east.

418 Release by Agnes de Coventre without warranty made in London, 23 October 1317, to Reginald de Fox of the whole of the wood called 'Conneldeshegges' with arable land in Edmonton in which William le Keu son of Agnes enfeoffed the said Reginald, which wood lies between the highway called 'Armoltestrete' in the north and the wood of the nuns of Clerkenwell and the tenement of John Amys in the south, extending from the grove formerly of John Wyndesouere in the east and the said highway in the west.

419 Charter of John le Barkere in fee simple with warranty made at Tottenham, 30 August 1321, to Ralph de Lay of 1½ acres of meadow in Tottenham lying between the River Lea in the east and the meadow of Walter Thurtyl in the west, extending from 'Felicedych' in the north to 'Loundeuissedich' in the south.

420 Release in perpetuity by Thomas le Barkere son and heir of John le Barkere without warranty made at Tottenham, 20 September 1322, to the same Ralph de Lay of the same meadow.

421 Charter of Walter son and heir of Oliver Brounyng citizen of London in fee simple with warranty made at Enfield, 2 February 1329, to Roger Hakeneye and Alice his wife of one piece of meadow of 3½ acres in the meadow called 'le Wyldemerssh', between the meadow of the prioress of Cheshunt in the north and that of Thomas [*f. 36r*] Toky in the south in which the recipient had enfeoffed the donor's father.

422 Release in perpetuity by Margery who was the wife of Robert le Squyler without warranty made at Edmonton, 7 October 1330, to Thomas her son of the tenement formerly of Augustine Alewele, the tenement formerly of Richard Colewell, the tenement formerly of Julia de Whatteshacche, part of the garden lately of John Austyn, pasture once belonging to William Smith (*Fabri*), and 2 acres of meadow formerly of William de Forde, all of which her said husband acquired in severalty (*separatim*) in Edmonton.

423 Charter of William le Taillour in fee simple with warranty made at Edmonton, 9 July 1332, to Augustine de Woxebrugge and Maud his wife and the heirs of Augustine of 2 acres of land in Edmonton in a field called 'le Honifeld' between the land of William le Keu in the east and the land of John le Tailour in the west, extending from the land of Richard de Wyrehale in the north to the plot called 'Degleshache'.

424 Charter of John Janyn, cook of London, in fee simple with warranty made at Edmonton, 13 September 1332, to William le Vikere and Joan his wife and the heirs of William of one piece of land with a house built above lying in Edmonton between the

land formerly of William de la Forde in the east and the tenement of Henry Swyft in the west, extending from the land formerly of Hamo Fishmonger (*piscenarii*) of London in the south to the lane called 'Haggesfeldlane' in the north.
[The six entries which originally followed here were afterwards cancelled and included later in the text, nos. 1264–6, 1268–70].
[Margin:] Hic cancellantur sex carte quia scribuntur alibi maius ordinatim.

425 [*f. 36v*] Charter of William de Say in fee simple without warranty and date made to Thomas Romeyn and Julia his wife of 5 acres of meadow in Edmonton which were once of Roger son of William lying in 'Middlemerssh' next to the 'Wodehaghe' and next to the meadow of Robert Shyn, to be held of the donor by service of of $\frac{1}{2}$lb of pepper or by 4d for all service.
[Date: 1230 x 1272]

426 Charter of John son of William de la Forde in fee simple with warranty and acquittance without date made to Augustine Alwele of 1 acre of land lying in the field called the Hyde between the land of Oger le Casiere in the east and the land of William le Vikere in the west, extending in the south from the land of William de la Forde and William de Anesty to the demesne formerly of William de Say, to be held of the donor by 1d *pa* for all service.

427 [*f. 37r*] Charter William de Say son of Geoffrey de Say in fee simple with warranty and acquittance without date made to Ralph Patryk of all the land which Wolwrych once held of the donor in Edmonton by service of 9d *pa*.
[Date: 1230 x 1272]

428 Charter of Stephen Wroth son of Richard Wroth in fee simple with warranty and acquittance without date made to Henry Bolloc of an enclosed cottage (*cotagio incluso*) in Edmonton called 'le Sopereshawe' lying between the land formerly of Nicholas le Claper on two sides, namely to the north and east, and the land of the prior of Holy Trinity, London, in the south and the highway (*communem*) leading from the gate of Enfield park towards London, to be held of the chief lords.

429 Charter of John son of Adam de Enefeld in fee simple with warranty and acquittance without date made to Robert Asketyn of $1\frac{1}{2}$ acres of meadow in Enfield marsh called 'Melmerssh' lying

between the meadow of Pagan Mount (*de Monte*) and the meadow
of William de Ferynges, to be held of the donor by service of 2d
pa.

430 Charter of John le Blund son of Edward le Blund in fee simple
with warranty and acquittance without date made to John le
Longe and Idonia his wife, daughter of the donor, of 6 acres of
meadow in Edmonton which descended to him after the death
of his father, and of the whole of that meadow in which Ralph
atte Berewe enfeoffed him, to be held of the chief lords.

431 Charter of James White (*Albi*) in fee simple with warranty without
date made to Geoffrey de Colewell of 3 acres of land between
the land of Philip son of Godard, called Colewell, and the road
leading from east to west which belonged to Richard de Colewell,
and of 1 acre of meadow in Middlemerssh lying between the
meadow of William Smith (*Fabri*) and the meadow of James son
of Sabine.

432 Charter of Robert de Lodne in fee tail with warranty without
date made to Adam Mistiers, called Plastrer, of London and
Edith de Basynges of all lands and tenements in Edmonton in
which Isabel who was the wife of Robert Stouke enfeoffed the
donor. If the feoffees die without issue, the said tenements will
remain to the right heirs of Adam.

433 Charter of William le Vikere in fee simple with warranty and
acquittance without date made to John Broun of a curtilage and
pasture in which John le Blund had enfeoffed the donor, lying
between the pasture formerly of Ralph de Querndon [*f. 37v*] and
the messuage formerly of Geoffrey Preacher (*predicatoris*), to be
be held of the donor by service of three capons *pa* and due
services to the chief lords of the fee.

434 Charter of Roger son of Richard Blund in fee simple with
warranty and acquittance without date made to Ralph Asshewy
of 2 acres of meadow in Edmonton, of which 1½ acres lie between
the meadow of Richard Cook in the north and the meadow
[MS blank] in the south, extending from the meadow of Richard
Marsh (*de Marisco*) in the west to the River Lea in the east, and
½ acre lies between the meadow of John Blund in the south and
the meadow of Eustace Mercer in the north, and between the
meadow of Thomas Pycot in the west and the River Lea in the
east.

435 Grant of all interest of Christine who was wife of Stephen de Colewell without warranty and date made to John de Colewell and Hamo le Paulmer of all her dower in Edmonton in the field called the Hyde and in the ploughlands (*culturis*) called 'Coggescroft' and Great Colewell.

436 Charter of Richard Denys in fee simple with warranty and acquittance without date made to William Spyrk and Alice his wife of 1 acre of meadow in Edmonton marsh lying between the meadow of Nicholas son of Laurence in the north and the meadow of John son of Robert de la Forde in the south extending from the River Lea in the east to the meadow of John son of William Marsh in the west, to be held of the donor by service of 4d *pa*.

437 Charter of John le Blund of Edmonton in fee simple with warranty without date made to Walter le Vikere of the whole messuage which the donor bought of Richard son of Peter de Alwyne, and of 2 acres of pasture pertaining to the said messuage, to be held of the donor by annual service of 3 capons.

438 Charter of Robert Asketyn, citizen of London, in fee simple with warranty and acquittance without date made to Rigon de Cantebrugge, goldsmith, of 1½ acres of meadow lying in Enfield marsh called 'Melmersch' between the meadow of Pagan Mount (*de Monte*) and the meadow of William de Ferynges, in which John son of Ace de Enefelde enfeoffed the donor by charter titled [MS blank], to be held of the donor by service of 2d.

439 [*f. 38r*] Charter of Warin de Westwode in fee simple with warranty and acquittance without date made to Robert de Keveshale of all the donor's messuage in the vill of 'Balbyngworth' in the fee of Richard Pikerell, to be held of the donor by service of 2d *pa*.

440 Charter of Richard Picot in fee simple with warranty without date made to Maurice Hayward (*Messor*) of 2 acres of land in Edmonton lying between the land of Roger Barker (*Bercarius*) and the land of Richard Proutfot, extending from the land of Geoffrey de Forde in the south to the road leading the gate of Geoffrey Warin in the north, to be held of the donor by service of 4d.

441 Charter of Richard son of Peter Ailwyne in fee simple with

warranty and acquittance without date made to John le Blund
of Edmonton of the whole messuage situated next to the highway
called 'le Herestrat', and of 2 acres of pasture lying between the
pasture formerly of Adam Cole and the pasture of Geoffrey de
Querndon called 'Pymor', extending from the garden formerly
of Geoffrey Preacher (*predicatoris*) in the south to the pasture of
Geoffrey Querndon in the north, and the messuage is situated
between the messuage of Emma Tenant (*Tenatricis*) and the land
of William Pymor.

442 Charter of Roger Burser of Edmonton in fee simple with
warranty without date made to Geoffrey son of Henry of 1 acre
of meadow in Edmonton marsh lying between the meadow of
the donor in the north and the meadow of Ralph Weaver (*Textor*)
in the south, extending from the meadow called 'Querndones-
dykedemad' in the west to the meadow of Richard son of Picot
in the west (*sic*), to be held of the donor by service of 4d *pa.*

443 Indenture made 3 April 1306, whereby Richard Wynard leased
to Roger Doget 1 acre of meadow in Enfield lying between the
meadow of the same Roger and the ditch called 'Lithle-
stoneydych', to be held for five years.

444 Charter of Ralph de Herun in fee simple with warranty without
date made to William Stanhard of all the land which Golding
Stanhard the feoffee's father held of Ralph the donor's father in
Edmonton, and of one ditch extending between the donor's land
and the land of the feoffee, and of 1 acre of meadow in the
marsh lying between the meadow of Robert de Herun and the
meadow of Julia wife of John Bukehunte, to be held of the donor
by service of 2s 2d, saving foreign service.

445 [*f. 38v*] Charter of Robert Gysors in fee simple with warranty
and acquittance without date made to Richard Humfrey of $\frac{1}{2}$
acre of meadow in Edmonton marsh between the donor's
meadow and the meadow of Hugh le Burser, extending from
the meadow of the abbot of Walden in the east to the 'gore'
(*goram*) of the meadow of Geoffrey Swonyld, to be held of the
donor by service of $\frac{1}{2}$d *pa.*

446 Charter of Nicholas son of John Marsh in fee simple with
warranty and acquittance without date made to Geoffrey his
brother of all the land which Idonia the donor's mother held in

Edmonton in dower of the gift of John the donor's father, to be held of the donor by annual service of 3s.

447 Charter of Laurence de la Forde in fee simple with warranty and acquittance without date made to Alice his daughter of the whole enclosed croft in Edmonton called 'Aldewych', and of 6d rent which John Dogel was accustomed to pay the donor for his tenement in Edmonton, and of 2d rent which Peter Spyrk used to pay for 1 acre of land in Edmonton lying in the field called 'Langeheg', and of 5d rent which William son of Peter Spyrk used to pay him for a croft lying by the house of John Doggel in Edmonton and of an acre lying in 'Langehcg', to be held of the donor by annual service of $\frac{1}{2}$d.

448 Charter of Walter Sumery of Enfield in fee simple with warranty without date made to John le Chapeler, citizen of London, of 1 acre of meadow in Enfield in the marsh called 'Southmerssh' lying between the meadow of Thomas de Forde in the north and the meadow of William Putok in the south, extending from the ditch called 'Markedych' in the east to the meadow called 'Lemannemad', to be held of the donor by annual service of 4d.

449 Charter of William son of Reymer in fee simple with warranty and acquittance without date made to John son of Richard le Claper of $1\frac{1}{2}$ acres of meadow in Edmonton lying in the marsh between the meadow of Nicholas son of Joce in the north and the meadow of the hospital of St John, London, in the south, extending from the River Lea in the east to the stream leading from 'Holflet' to 'Chipol' in the west, to be held of the donor by service of 1lb of cumin.

450 [f. 39r] Charter of John son of Idonia in fee simple with warranty and acquittance without date made to John son of Thomas of 1 acre of land and 3 roods of meadow in Edmonton marsh lying between the meadow of lord de Say in the south and the meadow of Richard le Neweman in the north, to be held of the donor by service of 1d.

451 Charter of Hugh Peverel in fee simple without date made to Stephen Bukerel of 7d rent which Stephen was accustomed to pay to the donor from 6 acres of meadow in Edmonton, in which the donor had enfeoffed him according to his charter. And it was granted that the said Hugh should receive the eighth penny ıs contained in the said charter at the house of the said Stephen in London.

452 Charter of Richard Knotte with warranty and acquittance without date made to Anselm Quenteyn in free marriage with Maud, the donor's niece, of all the donor's lands and tenements in Edmonton, to be held in fee simple by paying ıd to the donor and due services to the chief lords.

453 Charter of William de Forde in fee simple with warranty and acquittance without date made to Benedict de Gyllingham of one field in Edmonton called 'Cockesfeld' lying between 'Haggesfeld' and the land of Agnes de Colewelle in length and between 'Linesfeld' and 'Vikeresfeld' in breadth, to be held of the donor by annual service of 2s.

454 Charter of Robert Albon in fee simple with warranty made at Edmonton, 20 March 1335, to Michael Humfrey of Sall, citizen of London, of the whole tenement in Edmonton in which John son of Philip Patryk had enfeoffed the donor, which is situated between the wood of William de Causton and the land formerly of Thomas William in the north, and the wood formerly of Philip Wileby, the wood of the prioress of St Helen's, London, and the land of Ralph Cowe in the south, extending from South Street to the field called 'Taillesfeld' and the street called 'Wopoleshull'.

455 Charter of Ralph de Mepirshale in fee simple with warranty made at Edmonton, after 3 July (*citra festum translacionis Sancte Thome*) 1335, to William de Brynkelee and Alice his wife of all lands and tenements in Edmonton in which the said William had enfeoffed the donor.

456 Charter of John son of Thomas Sabern and Custance his wife in fee simple with warranty made at Enfield, 30 September 1337, to Hervey (*Herveo*), vicar of Enfield, of $4\frac{1}{2}$ acres of land in the field called 'Folewell' in Enfield, of which 2 acres lie between the land of John Orpedo in the east and the land of John Castle (*de Castello*) in west, and another 2 lie between the land of John atte Castel in the south and the land of Walter Clay junior in the north, and $\frac{1}{2}$ acre lies between the land of John atte Castel in the north and the land which Joyce Brid holds in the south.

457 Charter of John Sabern and Custance his wife in fee simple with

THE CARTULARY OF ADAM FRAUNCEYS

warranty made at Enfield, 23 September 1339, to John de Bristowe, citizen of London, of $3\frac{1}{2}$ acres of land in Enfield lying in the field called 'Little Aydon' between the land of Martin le Ferour in the south and the land of Peter atte Lanende in the north, extending from the land of John de Garton in the east to the land of John Castle (*de Castello*).

458 Letter of Edmund Pymme made at Edmonton, 1 April 1341, to John Abraham to deliver seisin to Geoffrey son of the said Edmund of $\frac{1}{2}$ acre of meadow contained in the next charter.

459 Charter of Edmund Pymme in fee simple with warranty made at Edmonton, 2 April 1341, of $\frac{1}{2}$ acre of meadow in Edmonton marsh in the place called 'Langemed' between the meadow of William de Causton in the south and north, extending from the River Lea in the east and the meadow of John de Beaumont (*Bello Monte*) in the west.

460 Release in perpetuity by John Sabern, son and heir of John Sabern and Custance his wife, with warranty made at Enfield, 27 January 1348, to Hervey (*Hervico*), vicar of Enfield, of 4 acres in the field called 'Folewell' shown by boundary marks in which he [sc. John senior] had previously enfeoffed him.

461 Charter of Geoffrey Pymme son of Edmund Pymme in fee simple with warranty made at Tottenham, 28 April 1348, to Christine his sister of $\frac{1}{2}$ acre lying in 'Langeheg' between the land of John Goldyng in the north and the land of William Pymme in the south, extending from the land of Thomas le Rowe in the east [*f. 40r*] to the land of Roger Depham in the west and of $\frac{1}{2}$ acre of meadow between the meadow of William de Causton on either side, extending from the River Lea in the east to the meadow of lord de Beaumont in the west.

462 Letter of the same Geoffrey Pymme made at Tottenham on the same day to William son of William de Anesty to deliver seisin according to the aforesaid charter.

463 Charter of Henry de Braybrok of co. Hertford and Alice his wife in fee simple with warranty made at Enfield on Wednesday after the feast of St Mathias [24 February][1] to John de la Panetrie, citizen and mercer of London, of 4 acres and 3 roods of land, of which $1\frac{1}{2}$ acres lie in the field called 'Aydon' between the land of Peter Laneende and the land formerly of John le Fullere extending from the land of John atte Castel to 'Garsonesway', 2 acres lie in the field called 'Southberifeld' between the land of John de Enefeld and 'Boundeslane' extending from the road called 'Aylmesgrene' to the land formerly of Richard de Bradeleye, and 1 acre 1 rood lie in the field lately held by John Heyron next to the land of John Heyne extending from the royal highway to 'Plesaunces Well', and of $3\frac{1}{2}$ acres of meadow in 'Southmerssh' in a plot called 'le Brendrekhawe' between the meadow of the abbot of Walden and the meadow formerly of John Heron extending from the meadow formerly of Richard Durant to the meadow formerly of the said John Heyron, which land and meadow were lately held by John Underwode in Enfield.

1 Year omitted

464 Charter of William Saleman and Alice his wife in fee simple with warranty made at Edmonton, 6 May 1305, to Michael le Baillif, armourer of London, of all that tenement which the donors had in Edmonton between the tenement of John de la Gyhale and the tenement of Christine Cullyng, extending from the land of William Reyner to the highway.

465 Duplicate part of a fine levied at Westminster, September 1305, by which the same William Saleman and Alice his wife acknowledged the aforesaid tenement, namely one messuage in Tottenham, to be the right of the same Michael, to be held in fee simple with warranty of William and Alice and of the heirs of William.
[*Feet of Fines, Lond. & Middx.* i, 74]

466 Charter of John Marsh (*de Marisco*) in fee simple with warranty made at Edmonton, 14 January 1307, to Nicholas, William and Robert his sons of three pieces of land, of which one is called 'Stonyfeld' and another contains 4 acres lying between 'Stonyfeld' and the land formerly of Richard Hereward called 'Commeldefeld', [*f. 40v*] and another piece called 'Benecroft' lies between the said 4 acres and the lane leading to 'Russhfeldes', and of one piece of pasture called 'Trompetonemor'.

467 Charter of the same John Marsh in fee simple with warranty made at Edmonton, 15 July 1309, to Nicholas, William and Robert his sons of all the messuage in which John Carpenter enfeoffed the donor, situated between the tenement of William Godho and the tenement of Philip le Haver.

468 Release in perpetuity by the same John Marsh without warranty made at Edmonton, 15 July 1309, to the same sons of all land and pasture contained in the above charter.

469 Charter of John Marsh of Edmonton in fee simple with warranty made at Tottenham, 10 January 1305, to Roger atte Lofte of all the messuage situated between the feoffee's messuage and the messuage formerly of William Egepol, extending from the tenement formerly of the said William to the highway at an annual rent of 4s 4d.

470 Release in perpetuity by John son and heir of William Egepol made at Tottenham, 21 September 1309, to Roger atte Lofte of one piece of curtilage in Tottenham lying between the donor's land in the north and the land of the feoffee in the south, extending to the tenement formerly of Richard Bunde to the west containing in width 1½ perches and 4 feet, and to the donor's croft in the east containing in width 1 perch and 4 feet.

471 [*f. 41r*] Charter of Augustine Waleys of Uxbridge and Maud his wife in fee simple with warranty made at Edmonton, 9 April 1336, to Thomas le Bonde of Tottenham of 2 acres of land in Edmonton in the field called 'le Honifeld' between the land of William le Keu in the east and the land of John le Taillour in the west, extending from the land of Richard de Wyrhale in the north to the place called 'le Honifeld' between the land of William le Keu in the east and the land of John le Taillour in the west, extending from the land of Richard de Wyrhale in the north to the place called 'Deglesbeche' in the south.

472 Letter of the same Augustine and Maud made on the same day to Walter, vicar of Tottenham, to deliver seisin of the above land according to the charter.

473 Charter of John le Taillour of Edmonton in fee simple with warranty made at Edmonton, 4 April 1336, to Thomas le Bonde of 3 acres of land enclosed in Edmonton between the land of Malyne de Anesty in the east and the donor's land in the west, extending from the land of John Wyrehale in the north to the land of William de Causton in the south.

474 Indenture made in London, 27 March 1336, containing that if John le Taillour of Edmonton pay to Thomas Bonde in his house in London on 9 April next 38s and on 29 September next 11s 8d, then the said charter of 3 acres of land and a letter of receipt (*littera compoti*) of 50s made to the same Thomas le Bonde by the same John will be made null.

475 Release in perpetuity by John son of Ralph Patryk of Edmonton without warranty made at Edmonton, 24 June 1323, to Edmund de Chilterne and to John his son and Maud, John's wife, of all that tenement which Godard atte Wodegate once held of William atte Forde in Edmonton, and a croft lying in East Barnet between Enfield park in the north and the lane called 'Barnetteslane' in the south.

476 Indented charter of the same Edmund de Chilterne in fee tail made at 'Mukelfeld', 9 December 1323, to John son of Ralph Patryk of the same tenement and croft at a rent to the donor, to John his son and Maud, John's wife, of 5s *pa* and by paying heriot, relief and suit of court to the donor.

477 [*f. 41v*] Indented charter of John son of Edmund de Chilterne in fee tail made at Edmonton, 25 April 1335, to John son of Ralph Patryk of the same tenement and croft at a rent to the donor of 6s *pa* and by paying heriot, relief and suit of court.

478 Letter made 25 April 1335 whereby the same John Patryk granted that he would demise (*dimittere*) the said tenement in as good a state as that in which he received it, together with one lead vessel with handle (*uno plumbo et uno manuali*) valued at 6s, in the event that he should leave the tenement.

479 Charter of John atte Oke of Hanslope [Bucks.] and Joan his wife, daughter of Robert de Chilterne, in fee simple with warranty made at 'Mikelfeld', 27 October 1337, of all lands and tenements in Edmonton which descended to his wife after the death of John son of Adam de Chilterne.

480 Release in perpetuity of the same John atte Oke and Joan his wife without warranty made at 'Mikelfeld', 17 April 1338, to the same John son of Edmund de Chilterne of all lands which were once of Adam de Chilterne and Helen his wife in Edmonton.

481 Charter of John atte Castel of Edmonton in fee simple with

warranty made at Edmonton, 16 November 1348, to Walter
de Heremondesworth, vicar of Edmonton, and Robert Patryk,
chaplain, of all the donor's lands and tenements in Edmonton
and Enfield.

482 Letter of the same John atte Castel made at Edmonton, 16
November 1348, granting all his goods in the said vills to the
same vicar and chaplain.

483 Release in perpetuity by the same John atte Castel with warranty
made at Edmonton, 21 November 1348, to the same vicar and
chaplain of all the said lands and tenements.
Witnesses: Robert de Plesyngton, John atte Merssh, William
Vykere of Edmonton, Thomas Durant, Ralph Baldewyne,
Thomas de Norton and Richard Toky of Enfield.
[Hatfield Deeds, 129/14.]

484 Charter of Thomas de Anesty in fee simple with warranty made
at Edmonton, 10 February 1332, to John Duket of Tottenham of
12d rent in Edmonton which the donor [*f. 42r*] was accustomed
to receive from the house and adjacent curtilage which Augustine
Kernelitel holds in Southgate.

485 Charter of the same John Duket in fee simple with warranty
made at Edmonton, 20 March 1340, to Robert de Plesyngton of
the same 12d rent.

486 Letter of the same John Duket made at Westminster on the
same day to Thomas de Anesty to put the same Robert in seisin
of the said rent.

487 Charter of John Taillour of Edmonton in fee simple with warranty
made at Edmonton, 5 January 1340, to Henry Lorymer of 1 acre
of land in Edmonton lying in the field called 'Barresfeld' between
the land formerly of William Anesty in the south and the donor's
land in the north, extending from the donor's land in the east
to the tenement formerly of William de Anesty in the west.

488 Indenture made at Edmonton, 29 September 1342, containing
that if the same John Taillour pay to the same Henry Lorymer
16s 8d for three years the above charter will be cancelled.

489 Letter of the same Henry Lorymer made at Edmonton, 11 March
1347, in which Henry received from Robert de Plesyngton 2

marks, and for these 2 marks John Taillour of Edmonton mortgaged to Henry an acre of land lying in Edmonton next to the Anesty capital messuage, of which the same Henry, with the assent of the said John, granted $\frac{1}{2}$ acre to Robert, to be held in fee simple.

490 Charter of the same John le Taillour of Edmonton in fee simple with warranty made at Edmonton, 22 October 1346, to Robert de Plesyngton of 1 acre and 1 rood of land in Edmonton lying in length between the land of Maud de Anesty and 'Pirilane' and in width between the land of the same Maud and that of Robert de Hadham.

491 Charter of Ralph atte Noke, called le Couhurde, in fee simple with warranty made at Edmonton, 30 August 1325, to Geoffrey de Anesty of a messuage and adjacent grove lying in Edmonton between the highway called Southgate [*f. 42v*] in the west and the wood of William de Causton in the east, extending on either side to the wood of William de Causton, which messuage was formerly held by Richard le Lyf.

492 Release in perpetuity by Robert de Anesty son and heir of Thomas de Anesty with warranty without date made to Isabel, who was wife of the said Thomas, of all lands and tenements which were of the said Thomas his father which she holds for life in Edmonton.

493 Charter of Warin Ingulf with warranty and acquittance without date made to Geoffrey son of Turkil of 3 roods of meadow in Edmonton marsh called 'la Hoke' lying between the meadow formerly of Geoffrey de Querndon and the meadow of Renger, to be held of the donor by 1d *pa* for all service.

494 Charter of John Street (*de Strato*) in fee simple with warranty without date made to Geoffrey son of Turkil of 5 roods of meadow in Edmonton lying on 'le Holeflet' called the 'Gore', surrounded by the stream (*circumdatis per la lake*), to be held of the donor by 1d *pa* for all service.

495 Charter of John Park (*de Parco*) in fee simple with warranty without date made to Geoffrey son of Turkil of the same 5 roods of meadow, to be held of the donor by 1d *pa* for all service.

496 Charter of Stephen Asshewy son and heir of Stephen Asshewy and Isabel his wife in fee simple with warranty without date made to Geoffrey de Eyton, clerk, of 13 acres of meadow in Edmonton, of which 1 acre lies between the meadow of Isabel de Vesci in the north and that formerly of William Laurence in the south extending to the meadows of Richard Prichet in the west and of John le Doul in the east, and another acre lies between the meadows of the hospital of St John, London, in the north and of John le Doul in the south extending to the meadows of Richard Cook in the west and of Agnes le Holmes in the east, and $\frac{1}{2}$ acre lies between the meadows of Stephen de Abyndon in the north and of Richard de Wyrehale in the south extending to the meadow of Isabel de Vesci in the west and to 'Mymmemade' in the east, and another $1\frac{1}{2}$ acres lie between the meadows of the said Isabel de Vesci in the north and of Walter Crepyng in the south extending to the meadow of the said Isabel in the west and to the River Lea in the east, and $2\frac{1}{2}$ acres lie between the meadow of Thomas le Rowe in the south and that of William de Causton and Adam Yarild in the north extending to the meadow of John Marsh (*de Marisco*) in the west and to the River Lea in the east, and $1\frac{1}{2}$ acres lie between the meadows of the master of the hospital of St John, London, in the south and of Richard Wyrehale in the north extending to the meadow called 'Chipolshot' in the west and to the River Lea in the east, and 2 acres lie between the meadows of Robert de Acton in the south and of Edmund Pymme in the north [*f. 43r*] extending to the meadows of John Marsh in the west and of William de Anesty in the east, and 1 acre lies between the meadow of Richard Skyn in the south and that formerly of Edmund de Totenhale in the north extending to the meadows called 'Ley-emede' and 'Smalemede', to be held of the chief lords of the fee.

497 Letter of attorney of the same Stephen [de Asshewy], made in London, 21 June 1321, to deliver seisin according to the said charter.

498 Charter of the same Geoffrey de Eyton, canon of the church of St Paul's[1] in fee simple without date made to Thomas de Eyton his brother of the same 13 acres of meadow.
Witnesses: Walter Moys of Stepney, John de Mundene, John Mew, John de Pole, Henry atte Crosse.
[Date: 1325 x 1328]
[Hatfield Deeds 88/16]

1 Cf. John le Neve, *Fasti Ecclesiae Anglicae 1300–1541*, v (*St Paul's, London*), compiled by J. Horn (London, 1963), 21.

499 Charter of John atte Stone son of Gilbert atte Stone of Tottenham in fee simple with warranty without date made to Richard de Staundon and Maud, who was wife of Geoffrey le Mareschal of Sutton at Hone [Kent], and the heirs of Richard, of $\frac{1}{2}$ acre of meadow in Tottenham lying in the meadow called 'Yokford' between the meadows of William Terry in the north and of Laurence Egepol in the south, extending from the meadow of Ralph le Blund in the east to the stream called 'Medesenge' in the west, to be held of the chief lords of the fee.

500 Release in perpetuity by Geoffrey le Marchal without warranty made at Standon [Herts.], 28 May 1321, to Richard de Staundon of the said $\frac{1}{2}$ acre of land.

501 Charter of Maud who was wife of Hamo Fysshmongere of London in fee simple with warranty made at Edmonton, Wednesday following the feast of St Luke 6 Edward III [21 October 1332][1], to Roger de Depham and Margaret his wife of all the donor's lands and tenements in Edmonton.
Witnesses: William de Braghyng, William de Camerwell, John of St Edmunds (*de Sancto Edmundo*), Thomas of Canterbury (*de Cantuar'*), William de Walden, John de Hardyngham, John de Shireburne, Thomas de Morlee and others.
[Hatfield Deeds 76/11, but endorsed (Edmonton) cccxxxiij rather than cccxxxij as appears in the cartulary.]

1 MS: Sunday the feast of St Luke (18 October).

502 Release in perpetuity by the same Agnes (*sic*) made in London, 3 June 1332, to the same Roger and Margaret of the above lands and tenements.

503 Charter of Edmund Pymme in fee simple with warranty made at Edmonton, 24 October 1333, to Roger de Depham and Margaret his wife of one piece of land in Edmonton lying in the Hyde between the land of the said Roger on the south and north sides, extending from 'Garsoneswey' in the east to the land of the same Roger in the west.

504 [*f. 43v*] Charter of Geoffrey Marsh (*de Marisco*) son of John Marsh in fee simple with warranty and acquittance without date made to Ralph son of John Patryk of all the land which the said Ralph used to hold of lord de Say in Edmondton, to be held of the donor by service of 3s 1d *pa*.

505 Charter of Geoffrey de Say in fee simple with warranty and acquittance without date made to John Patryk of the tenement and wood which Gervase atte Wodegate held in Edmonton of William, the donor's father, to be held of the donor by service of 3s and 12d *pa*.
[Date: 1295 x 1322]

506 Release in perpetuity by John son of John Marsh without warranty made at Edmonton, 5 May 1333, to John Patryk of all that tenement in Edmonton in which John Denteyt enfeoffed the said John Patryk.

507 Charter of John Quoye and Joan his wife in fee simple with warranty and acquittance without date made to John Cokham of the whole portion (*perparte*) of meadow belonging to the said Joan after the death of John Renger her uncle, lying in Edmonton in the meadow called 'Rundmed' in which Thomas Bermund formerly enfeoffed Richard Renger, father of the said John, to be held of the husband and wife and the wife's heirs by rent of one clove of garlic.

508 Indented charter of Idonia daughter of Richard Renger in fee simple with warranty and acquittance made at Plumstead [Kent], 26 September 1272, to John de Cokham her son of all her portion of meadow accruing to her after the death of the John Renger her brother in Edmonton, at an annual rent of 8s for life and after her death one clove of garlic to her heirs for all service.

509 Charter of Maud who was wife of Walter de la More of London with warranty and acquittance made 9 November 1269 to Alan Castle (*de Castello*), citizen of London, her father, of all the land with house which Thomas Thurkyl held of William de Say in Edmonton lying in 'Beristrete', and of all the land which Geoffrey Baldewyne held of the same William in Edmonton lying in the place called 'la Hale', and of 5 acres of land in the field called 'Westcolegraf' between the land of Robert de la Forde on either side, [*f. 44r*] and of 3 acres of meadow in Edmonton marsh, of which 1½ acres lie between the meadow of Geoffrey Bedell in the north and the meadow of the prior of Holy Trinity in the south, and 1 acre lies between the meadow of the same prior in the north and that of Richard de la Hale in the south, and ½ acre lies between the meadow of the abbot of Walden in the north and the meadow of Walter de Wandlesworth in the south, to be held of the donor by one clove of garlic and 16d to Thomas de la Forde for all service.

510 Charter of Ralph de la Berewe in fee simple with warranty and acquittance without date made to Alan Castle, citizen of London, of 5 acres of land lying in Edmonton in [the field called] 'Hoetkholte' between the land formerly of John le Blund and the land formerly of William de Hales, and of 1 acre of land in 'Estfeld' between the land of Richard de Hale in the north and that of William de Hales in the south, and of 1 acre of land in the same field between the land of Richard atte Hale in the south and that once held by William de Hales in the north, and of ½ acre of land in the same field between the lands of Hugh Bedell in the north and Richard Swonyld in the south, and of all that piece of land in 'Stresfeld' between the lands of the same Hugh and Richard to the north and south, and of the whole piece of land in the same field between the land formerly of William de Hales in the south and the land of Hugh Bedell in the north, to be held of the donor by annual service of 2s.

511 Charter of Ralph de la Berewe of Edmonton in fee simple with warranty and acquittance without date made to the same Alan Castle of 2½ acres of land in Edmonton lying between the lands of Richard de Hales in the south and of Thomas le Couherde in the north, and of another ½ acre of land in Edmonton lying between the land formerly of Geoffrey le Bedel in the north and the land of John Saleman in the south, abutting on 'Herestreste', to be held of the donor by service of 12d *pa*.

512 Charter of Maud who was wife of Walter de la More in fee simple with warranty and acquittance without date made to Alan Castle (*de Castro*), citizen of London, her father, of 1½ acres of enclosure (*una acra et dimid' inclus'*) next to the street called 'Derlane' in the south, extending from east to west along the road towards Edmonton marsh, to be held of the donor by one clove of garlic *pa* for all service.

513 [*f. 44v*] Charter of John de Enefeld, son of Sir Henry de Enefeld, knight, in fee simple with warranty made at Enfield, 26 April 1312, to John Castle (*de Castello*) of 12 acres of land in Enfield, of which 6 acres lie in the croft called Little 'Aydon' between the land of Geoffrey de Say in the south and the field called 'Voulewell' in the north, and $\frac{1}{2}$ acre lies in the field called Great 'Aydon' between the land of the said Geoffrey de Say in the south and the land of Thomas Ivylane in the north, and $5\frac{1}{2}$ acres lie in 'Voulewell' between the land of the said Thomas Ivylane and that of Adam Orpede in the south and 'Bundyeslane' in the north.

514 Charter of Alan Castle (*de Castello*), son of Robert Castle, in fee simple with warranty without date made to John Castle of Edmonton of 2d rent to be received from the messuage which William de Panetria and John Cordel hold of the donor in Enfield.

515 Release in perpetuity of Alan son of Robert Castle without warranty, made in London, 7 December 1299, to John son of Alan Castle, lately citizen of London, of one messuage, 10 acres of land and 15 acres of meadow in Enfield, and of one messuage, 32 acres of land and pasture in Edmonton, and of 8s 11d rent and $\frac{1}{2}$d rent in Enfield in which the same Alan enfeoffed the said John.

516 Letter of John de Enefeld made at Enfield, 26 April 1312, to Richard de Stocton and John Ballard to deliver to John Castle seisin of the land in the above charter.

517 Charter of John le Chapeler son and heir of John le Chapeler, late citizen of London, in fee simple with warranty made at Enfield, 5 January 1309, to Robert de Pypehurst, citizen and goldbeater (*aurimalliatu[i]*)[1] of London, of one piece of meadow in Enfield lying between the meadow lately of Walter Thoky in the south and the water called 'le Elde' in the north in the marsh (*submarisco*) called 'Barfletesmerssh', extending from the meadow formerly of Richard Warflet called 'Chalveseyesacre' to the northeast

1 ~*u* written over ~*ori*.

518 [*f. 45r*] Charter of the same John le Chapeler in fee simple with warranty made at Enfield, 29 December 1308, to the same Robert de Pypehurst of 1 acre of meadow in Enfield in the marsh called 'le Southmerssh' between the meadow of Thomas de la Forde in the north and the meadow formerly of William Puttok in the south, extending from the ditch called 'le Markedych' in the east to the meadow called 'Lemmannesmade'.

519 Charter of Idonia de Cantebrugge who was wife of Reginald de Cantebregge in fee simple with warranty made in London, 30 June 1309, to the said Robert de Pypehurst of $\frac{1}{2}$ acre of meadow in Enfield lying in the meadow called 'Mellemerssh' in which John de Cantebregge, son of the said husband, enfeoffed her.

520 Letter of attorney of the same Idonia made in London on the same day to Walter de Kyngeshale to deliver seisin according to the aforesaid charter.

521 Release in perpetuity by Emma who was the wife of John le Chapeler son and heir of John le Chapeler, late citizen of London, without warranty made in London, 5 May 1311, to the same Robert de Pypehurst of all the meadow contained in the two charters above [**517, 518**].

522 Indenture made at Enfield, 20 January 1314, containing that the same Robert de Pypehurst granted to Roger de Hakeneye of Enfield $\frac{1}{2}$ acre of meadow in Enfield lying in the meadow called 'Mellemerssh' between the meadow of Sir John de Enefeld in the south and the meadow of the feoffee in the north in fee simple with warranty, in exchange for $\frac{1}{2}$ acre of meadow in Enfield lying in the meadow called 'le Southmerssh' between the meadow of the same Robert in the south and the meadow of the said Roger in the north, to be held by them in fee with warranty.

523 Release in perpetuity by Roger Spyrk of Edmonton without warranty made at Edmonton, 23 March 1303, to Roger le Kyng of Tottenham of one piece of land in Edmonton lying in the field called 'Langeheg' between the land of Richard le Rowe and the land of Julia daughter of Geoffrey Laurence, extending from the land of John Tebaud in the east.

524 [*f. 45v*] Charter of Alexander de Chygwelle, citizen of London, in fee simple with warranty made at Edmonton, 10 April 1303, to Roger le Kyng of a piece of land in Edmonton lying in the field called the Hyde between the lands of William de la Forde and of Augustine Alewell, extending from the land of the said William to the land of William Godhowe.

525 Release in perpetuity of Richard son of Richard de Lothebury without warranty made in London, 23 September 1304, to the same Roger le Kyng of the same acre of land in which the same Alexander Chygewell had enfeoffed him.

526 Charter of John Homund of Edmonton in fee simple with warranty made at Edmonton, 13 January 1299, to the same Roger le Kyng of 3 roods of meadow in Edmonton, lying between meadow of John le Burser in the east and west and the meadow of John Halstede in the north.

527 Charter of Maud who was wife of Geoffrey Bedell of Edmonton in fee simple with warranty without date made to Maurice de Eppynge of $\frac{1}{2}$ acre of meadow in Edmonton marsh lying from east to west between the meadow of the prior of Holy Trinity, London, and the meadow of Julia Stonhard, to be held of the donor by service of one peppercorn.

528 Charter of John Stone (*de Petra*) of Tottenham in fee simple with warranty and acquittance without date made to the same Maurice de Eppyng of $\frac{1}{2}$ acre of meadow in Tottenham marsh between the meadow of Absolom Marsh (*de Marisco*) and the meadow of Isabel who was the wife of Nicholas Miller (*Molendinarii*), extending from the meadow of Philip de Chesterhunte called 'Pyke-demad' in the west to the meadow of William de Derneford in the east, to be held of the donor by one rose annually for all service.

529 Charter of Richard son of Richard Denys in fee simple with warranty and acquittance without date made to the same Maurice de Eppynge of 1 acre of land in Edmonton lying in the field called 'Westcolegraf' between the land of William Idoyne and the donor's land, extending from the land of Nicholas de la Forde in the east to the land of William Pycot in the west, to be held of the donor by $\frac{1}{2}$d *pa* for all service.

530 Letter of Augustine de Alewelle without date whereby he bound over all his tenements in Edmonton to the distraint of Stephen de Colewell whenever rent of 18d due [*f. 46r*] for a piece of land lying in the field called 'Geggescroft', which the same Stephen holds, was in arrears.

531 Release in perpetuity by Roger Spyrc without warranty made, 24 August 1292, to Stephen de Colewelle of land lying in the

field called 'Newelond' and in the field called 'Fruffeld', and of
$1\frac{1}{2}$ acres and 1 rood of meadow lying in Edmonton marsh, next
to the meadow of Richard in le Hale, and of 3 roods of meadow
lying in 'Middelmerssh iuxta Pipelere', and of $\frac{1}{2}$ acre of meadow
held of Reginald Pymme.

532 Letter of attorney of the same Roger Spyrc to John Marsh (*de
Marisco*) to put Stephen de Colewelle in seisin of one messuage
in Fleet Street and 4s rent which Richard Marchal was accustomed to pay for a tenement outside Ludgate in London.

533 Release in perpetuity by the same Roger Spyrc without warranty
made 12 March 1292 to the same Stephen de Colewelle of a
portion of pasture in Edmonton, and of $\frac{1}{2}$d rent which William
Weaver (*Textor*) was accustomed to pay for another piece of
pasture lying next to the former in the place called 'Pymor' in
Edmonton.

534 Letter without date whereby John Cowherd (*Vaccarius*) surrendered to the same Stephen Colewelle in fee simple that which
he held of him, [namely] a messuage with curtilage in Edmonton
situated between the messuage of Reginald le Maltmakiere and
the messuage of Philip le Neuman.

535 Release and quitclaim of the same John Cowherd (*Vaccarii*)
without date made to the same Stephen of 6d rent which John,
as mesne tenant (*tanquam medius*), used to receive from Philip son
of Robert le Neuman, demesne tenant (*tenente in dominico*), for a
messuage in the fee of the same Stephen, his superior lord.

536 Grant and confirmation of William de Say without warranty and
date made to Robert Hauteyn, citizen of London, of 3 acres of
meadow in Edmonton marsh which Henry son of William of
Edmonton sold to the said Robert, and of $1\frac{1}{2}$ acres of meadow
which William Frere of Sawbridgeworth sold to him.
[Date: 1230 x 1272]

537 Charter of Geoffrey de Querndon in fee simple with warranty
without date made to Stephen de Colewell of that portion [of
land] in Edmonton, lying in the field called 'Mochelecolewell',
between the land of Ralph le Berewe and the land of Richard
Humfrey, [*f. 46v*] extending eastwards from the land of Ralph to
the lane called 'Halelane', to be held of the donor by one clove
of garlic for all service.

538 Letter without date containing that Roger Spyrc surrendered and remitted to John son of Stephen de Colewelle all his right in his tenement in 'le Hale', and likewise in 2 acres of meadow in Edmonton marsh formerly held by John le Blund and Ralph atte Berewe in the place called 'Blontesdykedemadesfoc', which tenement and meadow the said Roger held by English law.

539 Charter of Stephen de Colewelle in fee simple with warranty and acquittance without date made to Richard his brother of a messuage with curtilage in Edmonton which was formerly of John Shepherd (*Pastoris*),[1] situated between the messuage of Reginald le Maltmakiere and the messuage of Philip Neuman, whereof mention was made above [**535**], to be held of the donor by service of 7d *pa*.

    1 *alias* Cowherd.

540 Charter of Laurence de Hugate and Julia his wife, daughter and heir of John Slonhard, in fee simple with warranty and acquittance without date made to William de Hales, citizen of London, of all the donor's land in Edmonton lying between the land of Robert Sweyn in the south and the land of Nicholas Claper and William Bedel in the north, extending from the grove of the prior of Christchurch [Holy Trinity, London] in the east to the highway in the west, and of 1 acre of meadow in Edmonton marsh between the meadow called 'la Roundmade' in the south and the meadow of Maurice le Hayward in the north, [extending] from the meadow called 'la Clarycegore' in the east to 'la Roundemade' in the west, to be held of the donor by one clove of garlic and due services to the chief lords.

541 Charter of Ralph de la Berghe in fee simple with warranty and acquittance without date made to William de Hales of $5\frac{1}{2}$ roods of meadow in Edmonton marsh, of which 1 acre lies between the meadow of the nuns of Clerkenwell in the south and the meadow of Robert Gysors in the north, extending from the meadow of Robert Heyroun in the west to the meadow of the abbot of Walden and the vicar of Edmonton in the east, and $1\frac{1}{2}$ roods lie between the meadow of the feoffee in the north and the meadow of Maud la Bedel in the south, extending from the meadow of John le Blund in the west to the meadow of the said William in the east, to be held of the donor by service of 1d.

542 Charter of Sabine, daughter and heir of Alan de Waleden in fee simple with warranty and acquittance without date made to the same William de Hales, citizen of London, [*f. 47r*] of 1 acre of meadow in Edmonton marsh between the meadow of the hospital of St John, London, and the meadow of Alice de Forde, extending from 'la Holflete' in the east, to be held of the donor by one clove of garlic.

543 Release in perpetuity by Ralph de la Berewe of Edmonton without date made to Agnes and Christine, daughters of William de Hales, of all rent and all services which he claimed of the tenement called 'Pemor', formerly of Peter Aylwyne in Edmonton.

544 Charter of John Gilbert of Edmonton with warranty and acquittance without date made to William de Hales, citizen of London, of 2 acres of land, of which 1 acre lies in the field called 'Langeheg' between the land of Simon Picot in the south and the land of Reginald Pyrumc in the north, extending from the land of William Reyner in the east to 'Garsoneswey' in the west, and the other acre lies in the field called the Hyde between the land of Robert Godhowe in the south and the land of Roger de la Pole in the north, extending from the messuage of the latter in the east to the land of Henry le Prechour in the west, to be held of the donor by one clove of garlic.

545 Charter of John Broun of Edmonton in fee simple with warranty and acquittance without date made to William de Hales, citizen of London, of a messuage with curtilage and $12\frac{1}{2}$ acres of enclosed pasture in Edmonton in which Walter le Vykere had enfeoffed the donor, which lie between the road leading from Tottenham to Cheshunt in the east and the pasture of William de Forde in the west and between the pasture of Geoffrey de Querndon called 'Pymore' and the land of John Pymor in the north and the respective lands of Emma le Croyser, Richard atte Strate, Roger de Harleford and William le Teler in the south, to be held by one clove of garlic.

546 Charter of Alan Castle [*de Castello*], citizen of London, in fee simple with warranty and acquittance without date made to William de Hales, citizen of London, of one messuage formerly of Richard de Coudres in Edmonton and of 4 acres of land lying between the land of John le Blund in the north and the land of William de Say in the south, extending from the land of the said John le Blund in the east, and 5 acres of land in Edmonton lying

in the field called 'Colegrave' between the land of John de la
Forde son and heir of Robert de la Forde in the east and west,
extending from the land of William Spyrc in the north to the
land of Nicholas de la Forde and William Idoyne in the south,
to be held of the donor by [service of] 20d *pa.*

547 Charter of the same Alan Castle in fee simple with warranty and
acquittance without date made to the same William de Hales of
3 acres of meadow in Edmonton marsh, of which $1\frac{1}{2}$ acres lie
between the meadow of the prior of Holy Trinity, London, in
the south and the meadow of William le Keu in the north, and
1 acre lies between the meadow of the said prior in the north
and the meadow of Richard de la Hale in the south, and $\frac{1}{2}$ acre
lies between the meadow of the said prior in the south and the
meadow of John Smith (*Fabri*) in the north, to be held of the
donor by service of 6d *pa.*

548 Charter of Christine daughter of Thomas Picot and widow of
William Marsh (*de Marisco*) in fee simple with warranty and
acquittance without date made to William de Hales, citizen of
London, of 2 acres of meadow in Edmonton marsh, of which 5
roods lie between the meadow of Nicholas de Parys in the south
and the meadow of Robert North (*Aguilon*) in the north, extending
from the field called 'le Estfeld' in the west to the meadow of
Stacius le Baillif, and 3 roods lie in 'le Esthale' between the
meadow of the said Nicholas in the east and the meadow of
William de Say in the west, extending from the boundaries (*metis*)
of Tottenham in the south to the meadow of Margery de la
Forde, to be held of the donor by service of 1d for all service

549 Charter of Richard Denys in fee simple with warranty and
acquittance without date made to the same William de Hales of
$\frac{1}{2}$ acre of land in Edmonton lying between the land of Nicholas
de Forde in the south and the pasture of Alice de la Forde in
the north, extending from the land of William Spyrc in the east
to the land of Katherine Webbe in the west, to be held of the
donor by service of a 1d *pa.*

550 Charter of Sabine daughter and heir of Alan de Waleden in fee
simple with warranty and acquittance without date made to the
same William de Hales of $1\frac{1}{2}$ acres of meadow in Edmonton
marsh, of which 1 acre lies between the meadow of the hospital
of St John, London, in the south and the meadow of Alice de la
Forde in the north, extending from the River Lea in the east to

'la Holsflete' in the west, and $\frac{1}{2}$ acre lies between the meadow of Walter de Wandlesworthe in the south and the meadow called 'Spytelmad' in the north, extending from the River Lea in the east to 'la Chipole' in the west, to be held of the donor by 1 clove of garlic.

551 Charter of Richard Denys in fee simple with warranty and acquittance without date made to the same William de Hales of $\frac{1}{2}$ acre in Edmonton lying between the land of William Spyrc and Nicholas Laurence in the east and the land of Katherine le Webbe in the west, extending from the land of William Spyrc and William Ydoyne in the south to the land of the feoffee in the north, to be held of the donor by 1d *pa* for all service.

552 [*f. 48r*] Charter of Reginald son of Richard called Pymme in fee simple with warranty and acquittance without date made to the same William de Hales of $\frac{1}{2}$ acre of meadow in Edmonton lying between the meadow of St Bartholomew's hospital, London, in the south and the meadow of Godard Aubrey in the north, extending from the meadow of Geoffrey Thorsteyn in the east to the meadow of John le Blund called le 'Dykedemad' in the west, to be held of the donor by service of 2d *pa*.

553 Charter of William Ydoyny in fee simple with warranty and acquittance without date made to the same William de Hales of $\frac{1}{2}$ acre of land in Edmonton lying in the Hyde between the land of William de la Forde in the south and the land of William de Say in the north, extending from the land of William Frere and the land of the prior of Holy Trinity, London, in the west, to be held of the donor by service of 1d *pa* for all service.

554 Letter of assent by William Spyrc made in London, 29 September 1285, that Roger his first-born son might endow Agnes daughter of William de Hales at the church door at the time of their marriage with a third part of his lands and tenements in Edmonton, namely one third of 66 acres of meadow.

555 Release in perpetuity by John de Cantebrugge son of Reginald de Cantebrugge, late citizen of London, without warranty made 19 April 1282 to Idonia Esshwy widow of the said Reginald of $\frac{1}{2}$ acre of meadow in the marsh of Enfield called 'Melmerssh' lying next to the meadow which the same John sold to John Davy of Enfield, extending from the River Lea in the east, which the said Idonia previously held in dower.

556 Charter of John de Cantebregge son of Reginald de Cantebregge in fee simple with warranty and acquittance without date made to the same Idonia Esshewy of $\frac{1}{2}$ acre of meadow in the marsh of Enfield called 'Melmerssh' lying next to the meadow which the donor sold to John Davy, extending westwards from the River Lea, to be held of the donor by one rose.

557 Charter of Ralph de la Berewe in fee simple with warranty without date made to Edmund de Totenhale and Margery his wife and the heirs of Edmund of $\frac{1}{2}$ acre of land in Edmonton, lying in the Hyde between [the land of] Notekyn son of Katherine the widow and the feoffee's land, extending from the land of John Brice, villein (*nativus*) of lord de Say, in the west to the land of William de Patrykbourne in the east, to be held of the donor by one clove of garlic.

558 [*f. 48v*] Charter of Robert Gysors in fee simple with warranty and acquittance without date made to Edmund de Totenhale and Margery his wife and the heirs of Edmund of 2 acres [of land] in Edmonton lying in the field called 'Langeheg' between the land of William Bukerel and the land of the prior of Christchurch [Holy Trinity, London], extending from the land of Nicholas Laurence in the east to the land of Richard le Rugh', to be held of the donor by 1d *pa*.

559 Charter of Christine daughter of Stephen de Newhall (*de Nova Domo*) of Tottenham in fee simple with warranty without date made to the same Edmund de Totenhale and Margery and the heirs of Edmund of $\frac{1}{2}$ acre in Edmonton in the field called 'Langeheg' between the land of Nicholas Lorenz and the land of John le Dunle, extending from the land of the said Nicholas in the north to the land of John Tebaud in the south, to be held of the donor by one clove of garlic for all service.

560 Charter of William Ydoyne in fee simple with warranty and acquittance without date made to Edmund de Totenhale and Margery his wife and the heirs of Edmund of 1 acre of land in Edmonton between the land of Alice Ford (*de Forda*) and the land of John Ford, extending from the place called 'Penyacrebeche' in the north to the lane called 'Wordestrete' in the south, to be held of the donor by service of 4d *pa*.

561 Release in perpetuity by Sarah who was wife of Walter Castle (*de Castello*) without warranty made in March 1307 to Edmund de Totenhale of 1 acre of meadow in Edmonton in which the said Walter enfeoffed the same Edmund and Margery his wife.

562 Charter of Augustine Alewele in fee simple with warranty and acquittance without date made to William le Casiere of 1 acre of land in Edmonton lying in the Hyde between the land of Oger le Casiere in the east and the land of William le Vikere in the west, extending from the land of William de Forde and William de Anesty in the south to the demesne of lord de Say, to be held of the chief lords etc.

563 Charter of William le Vicaire of Edmonton in fee simple with warranty made at Edmonton, 5 February 1307, to William le Casiere of one piece of land in Edmonton lying in the field called 'Berghfeld' between the land of Alice atte Strate and the land of William Smith (*Fabri*), extending from the land of Sir Walter de Gloucestre to the land of Ralph atte Parc.

564 [*f. 49r*] Charter of Robert le Geg of Edmonton in fee simple with warranty and acquittance without date made to Geoffrey son of John Marsh (*de Marisco*) of $1\frac{1}{2}$ acres of land with a whole messuage in Edmonton lying between the house once held by William le Casiere and the house once held by Geoffrey Red, and of a rent issuing from the house of Simon de Croncheho and the house of Geoffrey Red, and of 2 acres of land lying in the Hyde between the land of Sir Richard Percy and the land of John son of Agnes Street (*de Strata*), to be held of the donor by $\frac{1}{2}$d, and 5s 4d to the chief lords of the fee.

565 And know that Hugh Peverel, the above lord, then confirmed the same grant by the following charter and released the said rent of 5s 4d as will appear.

566 Charter of confirmation of Hugh Peverel in fee simple with warranty without date made to Geoffrey son of John Marsh of all the land which Robert Geg held of the said Hugh in Edmonton in which Robert had enfeoffed Geoffrey, to be held of Hugh by 5s 4d *pa*.

567 Charter of Hugh Peverel in fee simple with warranty without date made to Geoffrey Marsh of 5s 4d rent which the same Geoffrey used to pay to the donor for the lands and tenements which Robert Geg lately held of the donor in Edmonton, at a rent of 2d *pa* to the donor and his heirs.

Witnesses: John Blund, Thomas Picot, William Ford (*de Forda*), John FitzJohn, Geoffrey Cook (*Coco*), Laurence Ford, Richard Cook, John de Tessunt, William Picot, Richard Picot and many others.
[Date: *temp.* Henry III.]
[Hatfield Deeds 56/30]

568 Charter of William de Say in fee simple with warranty without date made to Geoffrey Marsh of 4 acres of land which Samar once held lying in the assart next to Enfield park.

569 Release in perpetuity of Geoffrey Turkyl without warranty and date made to Geoffrey son of John Marsh of all the tenement which was lately of Geoffrey de Coleville in the fee of Ralph de Querndon except 4 acres of land on the west side of the same tenement, and the releasor granted to the tenant to make a moiety of the service due for the said tenement.

570 Charter of William dc Say in fee simple with warranty without date made to Geoffrey son of John Marsh of Geoffrey son of Turkel, villein of the donor, and of 4 acres of land which the said villein held in Edmonton lying in 'Coldehanesote' between the land of Richard Goding in the south and the land of Golding de Beristrate in the north, and of all the land which he held of the donor in 'Rudynge', to be held [*f. 49v*] of the donor by 16d *pa* and 3d to the nuns of Clerkenwell for all service

571 Idem supra titulo cccxix [487][1] de verbo in verbum et ideo non intratur hic

1 Curiously out of sequence. Perhaps an error for ccciiij^xx xix [569]

572 Charter of William de Say in fee simple with warranty without date made to Geoffrey son of John Marsh granting all the land which Ralph Patryk, his villein, previously held of the donor and granting the same Ralph himself with his dependants (*cum sequela sua*), to be held of the donor by service of 3s 4d *pa*. And Geoffrey paid 16 marks.
Witnesses: Richard de Plesseis, Robert Rarbefle, William de Unilade of (?)'Oumel', John le Blund, Thomas Picot, William Ford, Hugh Peverel, Roger Burser, Geoffrey Cook, Alan de Waledene, Gilbert Culling, John de Anesty, John FitzJohn, ... de Wiltone, William de (?)Berricone and others.
[Hatfield Deeds 224/30]

573 Eadem carta supra titulo cccxv [**482**]¹ et ideo non intratur hic

1 (?)For ccciiij^{xx}xv [**564**]

574 Charter of Christine daughter of John FitzJohn of Edmonton in fee simple with warranty and acquittance without date made to Richard son of Geoffrey Marsh of a piece of land lying in Edmonton in the field called 'Brodewelde', between the land of William Ford (*de Forda*) and the land of Alice, the donor's sister, extending from the land of John Saleman in the north to the lane called 'Parcstrete', to be held of the donor by service of 8d *pa*.

575 Charter of the same Christine daughter of John FitzJohn in fee simple with warranty and acquittance without date made to the same Richard son of Geoffrey Marsh of 1 acre of land in Edmonton in the field called 'Stonyfeld' which was formerly of John Park (*de Parco*) between the land of Agnes de Colewelle and the land of Alice, the donor's sister, to be held of the donor by service of 6d *pa*.

576 Charter of the same Christine FitzJohn in fee simple with warranty without date made to the same Richard son of Geoffrey of the piece of land in Edmonton which the donor had inherited in the field called 'Honifeld' and was formerly of John Park, to be held of the donor by service of 4d *pa*.

577 Charter of Ivo de Bedeford in fee simple with warranty and acquittance without date made to Emma daughter of Aillewe of Tottenham of the donor's messuage in Tottenham situated between the messuage formerly of Roger de Solio and the messuage of John Egepol, extending from the land of the said John Egepol in the east to the highway in the west to be held of the donor by rent of 12[d] to the lord of the fee.

578 [*f. 50r*] Charter of Richard Bunde and Helen his wife in fee simple with warranty and acquittance without date made to Walter Lippe of the donor's messuage in Tottenham situated between the messuage of Nicholas Salter (*de Salar'*) and the messuage of William Egepol, extending from the highway in the west to the land of the said William Egepol in the east, to be held of the donor by service of 12d to the chief lord of the fee, and ½d to the donor for all service.

579 Charter of Walter Lippe in fee simple with warranty and acquittance without date made to Maurice le Hayward of the same messuage, to be held of the donor by service of 12d *pa* to William Egepol, chief lord, and ½d to the donor and ½d to Richard Bund for all service.

580 Charter of William son of Geoffrey de Say in fee simple with warranty and acquittance without date made to William son of William de la Forde of all the land which John Smith (*Faber*), Robert le Filter and John le Filter formerly held in villeinage (*native*) of the donor in Edmonton, to be held by service of 4s *pa* for all service.
[Date: 1230 x 1272.]

581 Charter of Geoffrey de Say in fee simple with warranty and acquittance without date made to William de la Forde of the tenement which Roger le Porter formerly held of William de Say, the donor's father, and of 2½ acres of land which Richard le Hoppere held in villeinage lying in parcels between the lands of the same William, to be held of the donor by service of 2s 2d *pa*.
[Date: 1295 x 1322.]

582 Charter of William de Say in fee simple with warranty and acquittance made at Portsmouth, 24 August 1294, to William de la Forde of 2 acres and 3 roods of meadow in Edmonton marsh, of which 1½ acres were formerly of William le Keu extending eastwards to the pasture formerly of John le Blund, and ½ acre lies in 'Esthale' next to the meadow formerly of Robert Castle (*de Castello*), and 3 roods lie between the meadow called 'Smalemad' and 'Lovesdayacre', to be held of the donor by one rose for all service.

583 Release by William de Say made at Botley, 22 August 1294, to William de la Forde and Cecily his wife for their lives of a rent of 22s 4d which the same William and Cecily used to pay to the said lord for all their lands and tenements in Edmonton.

584 [*f. 50v*] Charter of William de Say son and heir of William de Say in fee simple with warranty and acquittance without date made to William de la Forde of all the tenement which Simon

Loveday once held of the donor in Edmonton, to be held of the donor by service of 5s 6d *pa.*
[Date: 1272 x 1295.]

585 Charter of William de Say[1] without date made to William Ford (*de Forda*) of $\frac{1}{2}$ virgate of land and $2\frac{1}{2}$ acres of meadow in Edmonton, namely of all the land which Godard Aldred used to hold of the donor in Edmonton, and of 1 acre of meadow formerly pertaining to the land which William Woldyng once held of the donor, and of 1 acre of meadow once pertaining to the land which Geoffrey Bryce held of the donor, and of $\frac{1}{2}$ acre of meadow which Geoffrey Water (*de Aqua*) likewise held of the donor, to be held in free marriage with Alice, the donor's sister.
[Date: *c.* 1265]

1 Probably granted in connection with the loan mentioned below. *VCH Middlesex* v, 163 gives the date of Ford's marriage to Alice de Say as 1264, citing this document.

586 Indenture agreeing that unless William de Say paid to William de la Forde on 8 July 1265 the 10 marks lent by the latter, a certain tenement granted by William de Say to William de la Forde would remain with him in perpetuity, reverting to the said William de Say only if he were to pay the said sum.

587 Indented charter of William de Say in fee simple with warranty and acquittance without date made to William Ford (*de Forda*) of 2 acres and 1 rood of land in Edmonton in the field of John Brice between the recipient's land and garden and the land of the said John Brice and extending from the recipient's garden to 'Steremannestile', in exchange for 2 acres and 1 rood of land in the Hyde in Edmonton.

588 Letter of William, son of William de Say, made in London, 21 October 1280, notifying that he had granted to William de la Forde, his tenant, to pay to William de Patrikbourne an annual rent of 20s for life, which he formerly paid to William de Say.

589 Charter of William son of Geoffrey de Say in fee simple with warranty and acquittance made to William Ford of 5 acres of land which Geoffrey Joce once held in villeinage (*native*) in Edmonton, saving to the donor the meadow which used to pertain to the said land, to be held of the donor by service of 1d *pa.*
[Date: 1230 x 1272.]

590 [*f. 51r*] Charter of Robert atte Grene in fee simple [with warranty] and acquittance without date made to William de la Forde of all the tenement in Edmonton which descended to Christine, the donor's wife, after the death of Richard le Chamberleyn her father and Julia her mother, to be held of the chief lords of the fee.

591 Charter of Augustine Alewelle in fee simple with warranty and acquittance without date made to William de la Forde of one piece of land lying in the place called 'Lyngeshawe' between the donor's and recipient's lands to the north and south and the land of the abbot of Walden in the west and the land of the same William de la Forde in the east, to be held of the donor by service of 1d.

592 Charter of Walter le Bunde of Tottenham in fee simple with warranty made in London, 30 May 1294, to Walter de Hernestede, draper of London, and Christine his wife of 1 acre of meadow in Edmonton which was formerly of Richard Denys and lies between the meadow of Roger Spirc in the south and the meadow of Richard [?Denys] in the north, extending from the River Lea in the east to the gate of John Marsh (*de Marisco*) in the west, to be held of the chief lords by due services.

593 Indenture made 22 February 1294 by which Roger son of William de Derneford leased to Walter de Hernestede 2 acres of meadow in Tottenham lying in the meadow called 'Yocford' between the meadow of Walter le Bunde in the north and the meadow of William Derneford, the lessor's father, in the south, extending from the the meadow of Robert le Brus[1] in the east to the meadow called 'Tounemannemede' in the west, to be held for thirteen years.

1 Probably the father of Robert I, king of Scotland

594 Release in perpetuity by Roger son of William de Derneford of Tottenham with warranty made 28 April 1294 to Walter de Hernestede, draper of London, of 2 acres of meadow in Tottenham lying in the meadow called 'Yocford', [continued as **563**], which the said Walter has of the lease of William Derneford.

595 Release in perpetuity by Richard Denys made in London, 15 March 1294, to Walter de Hernestede of 4d rent which he used to receive from the same Walter for 1 acre of meadow in

Edmonton which the said Walter had of the feoffment of Walter le Bunde of Tottenham.

596 [*f. 51v*] Letter of Christine who was wife of Walter de Hernestede made at Felsted [Essex], 12 January 1323, granting to Walter her son to sell 1 acre of meadow in Edmonton in which Walter Bounde, the father of Christine, enfeoffed her.

597 Charter of Walter de Hernestede, draper of London, in fee simple with warranty without date made to Walter his son of 2 acres of meadow in Tottenham lying in the meadow called 'Yocford' in which Roger son of William Derneford enfeoffed the donor, as above in charters [**593**] and [**594**].

598 Charter of the same Walter son of Walter de Hernestede in fee simple with warranty made at Tottenham, 10 February 1323, to John de Causton, citizen and mercer of London, of the same 2 acres of meadow.

599 Charter of Christine who was wife of Walter de Hernestede in fee simple with warranty made at Edmonton, 1 April 1323, to John de Causton of 1 acre of meadow in Edmonton which was once of William Spirc lying between the the meadow formerly of Roger Spirc in the south and the meadow of Richard de Anesty in the north.

600 Letter of the same Christine made at Felsted, 13 February 1323, to Walter de Hernestede her son to deliver seisin of the said acre of meadow to John Causton.

601 Charter of Robert son of William le Vicaire in fee simple with warranty made at Edmonton, 8 March 1349, to John atte Panetrye of one piece of land and one house with garden in Edmonton lying between the land formerly of William atte Forde in the east and the tenement formerly of Henry Swyft in the west, extending from the land formerly of Hamo Fishmonger (*Piscenarii*) from the south to the lane called 'Hoggefeldlane' in the north.

602 Charter of William Martyn son of Martin de Weldon in fee simple with warranty made at Enfield, 3 December 1348, to John de la Panetrye, citizen of London, of 7 roods of meadow, of which 3 roods lie in the meadow called 'Mellemerssh' and $2\frac{1}{2}$ roods in the place called 'le Scoche' in the same meadow, and

$2\frac{1}{2}$ roods in the meadow called 'Wyldemerssh' in Enfield.

603 [*f. 52r*] Charter of Geoffrey de Say, knight, in fee tail with warranty made at Edmonton, 4 June 1355, to John de la Panetrie, citizen of London, of $1\frac{1}{2}$ acres of land lying in a croft called 'Threacres' in Edmonton between the land of the feoffee in the south and his own garden (*gardinum suum*) in the north, extending from the lane leading to 'Estfeld' in the east to the lane called 'le Hale' in the west.

604 Charter of Henry, vicar of Enfield, in fee simple with warranty made at Enfield, 1 March 1349, to the same John atte Panetrye of $4\frac{1}{2}$ acres of land in Enfield in a field called 'Folewell', of which 2 acres lie between the land of Margery Orpede of 'Grenestrete' in the east and the land of John Castle (*de Castello*) in the west, and 2 acres lie between the land of John Castle in the south and that of Walter Clay junior in the north, and $\frac{1}{2}$ acre lies between the land of John Castle in the north and the land which John Brid holds in the south.

605 Letter of attorney of William Martyn of Islington made at Edmonton, 6 December 1346, to John Troc of Enfield to deliver seisin to John de la Panetrye of 7 roods of meadow according the charter above [**602**].

606 Charter of Walter de London, clerk, with warranty without date made to John Page, citizen of London, of all the tenement which was once held by Vincent Miller (*Molendinarii*) and Alice his daughter in Edmonton in which William le Vikere enfeoffed the donor, to be held of the chief lords by due services.

607 Charter of John Patrye in fee simple with warranty and acquittance without date made to John Page, citizen of London, of a messuage and crofts in which Geoffrey de Say enfeoffed the donor, to be held of the chief lords of the fee by due services.

608 Charter of Edon Ragonel in fee simple with warranty made at Tottenham, 8 December 1316, to the same John Page, citizen of London of $\frac{1}{2}$ acre of meadow in Tottenham marsh lying between the meadow of John atte Merssh in the north and the meadow of John de Laudesdale in the south, extending from the meadow of 'Yocfordelane' in the west to the lord's meadow in the east.

609 [*f. 52v*] Charter of Roger Kyng of Tottenham in fee simple with warranty made at Edmonton, 31 March 1317, to John Page, citizen of London of the piece of meadow in Edmonton which he had of the gift of John Aumond lying between the meadow of John le Bourser in the north and the meadow of Isabel de Vescy in the south, extending from the meadow of Stephen Asshewy and the meadow formerly of William Laurence in the west to the meadow called 'Holmesmade' in the east.

610 Charter of Edon Ragonel in fee simple with warranty made at Tottenham, 14 April 1316, to the same John Page of 1 acre of meadow in Tottenham marsh between the meadow of John Mire in the north and the meadow formerly of William Sproteman in the south, extending from the meadow of lady de Vescy in the west to the meadow called 'Yocford' in the east.

611 Charter of Michael Humfrey of Sall [Norfolk] in fee simple with warranty made at Edmonton, 10 August 1335, to John de Panetria, citizen of London, of the tenement in Edmonton in which Robert Albon enfeoffed the donor, which is situated between the wood of William de Causton and the land formerly of Thomas William in the north and the wood formerly of Philip Wileby and the wood of the prioress of St Helen's, London, and Ralph Cowe in the south, extending from the lane called Southgate to the field called 'Taillesfeld' and the lane called 'Wopeleshull'.

612 Charter of the same John de Panetrie in fee simple with warranty made at Edmonton, 10 January 1336, to Thomas Horn, chaplain, of all that tenement in Edmonton in which Michael Humfrey of Sall enfeoffed him by the preceding charter.

613 Charter of Geoffrey Querndon in fee simple with warranty and acquittance without date made to William Amys son of Geoffrey Marsh (*de Marisco*) of Edmonton of 2s rent which Stephen de Colewell used to pay to the donor for one messuage and 7 acres of land which the same Stephen held of the donor's father and afterwards of the donor himself.

614 Charter of Alice daughter of John FitzJohn of Edmonton in fee simple with warranty and acquittance without date made to the same William Amys of the tenement which the donor inherited after the death of Maud her mother in Edmonton, except $\frac{1}{2}$ acre of meadow in Edmonton marsh, and of the piece of land which the donor bought of Christine her sister, to be held of the donor by service of $\frac{1}{2}$d and 2s to the chief lord.

615 [*f. 53r*] Release in perpetuity of John Amys son of William Amys, citizen and fishmonger of London, without warranty made in London, 19 December 1302, to William Amys, citizen and fishmonger of London, and Julia his wife of all the tenements in Edmonton which were of Edmund Amys, brother of the said John, and of one messuage in the parish of St Benedict de Gracechurch, London, and of 2 acres of meadow in the parish of Rotherhithe in which William Amys enfeoffed Edmund.

616 Charter of John Gysors in fee simple with warranty made at Edmonton, 1 August 1305, to William Amys, citizen of London, of two pieces of land in Edmonton in the field called 'le Bernfeld', of which one piece lies between between the land of Ralph Picot in the east and the land of Robert Gulle in the west, extending from the land formerly of John le Blund in the south to the land of John atte Strate, and the other lies between the land formerly of John Sharp both east and west, extending from the land formerly of John le Blund in the south to the land once of John Goule in the north.

617 Charter of Reginald Fox in fee simple with warranty made at Edmonton, 1 August 1318, to John Amys of Haveringland [Norfolk], citizen of London, of the wood called 'Gonneldeshedges' with arable land in the same place in Edmonton in which Wiliam le Keu son of Henry le Keu, late painter (*pictoris*) of London, enfeoffed the donor, lying between the highway called 'Armoleststrete' in the north and the wood of the nuns of Clerkenwell and the tenement of the feoffee which was formerly held by Richard de Haverynge and Joan his wife in the south, extending from the grove formerly of John de Wyndesore in the east to 'Arnoltestrete' in the west.

618 Letter of William le Keu son and heir of Henry le Keu, late painter of London, John de Coventre and Thomas le Broun of Waltham made in London, 21 December 1321, containing that they had received of John Amys, citizen of London, 100s to trade with to the profit of the said John, and binding them and each one of them to render account and to pay the said 100s to John whenever he pleased.

619 Indenture made in London, 23 December 1321, between the said parties agreeing that for as long as the said John Amys shall peacefully hold the piece of land and wood called 'Gonneldeshegges' in which the said Reginald Fox enfeoffed him without disturbance by William le Keu the above letter of account will remain in abeyance, and [*f. 53v*] as soon as the said William releases to John Amys his right thereof with warranty the said letter will be completely void.

620 Release in perpetuity by the said William le Keu son and heir of Henry le Keu, late painter of London, with warranty made in London, 25 October 1321, to the same John Amys of Haveringland, citizen of London, of the same wood and land called 'Gonneldeshegges'.

621 Charter of John Lestrange (*Extranei*) the fifth, lord of Knockin [Salop], in fee simple with warranty and acquittance without date made to Walter le Venour of the whole land which Simon Wyot once held in Hunstanton and in which the donor's father later enfeoffed Roger, the donor's brother, to be held of the donor by service of one catapult bolt (*sagitte catapulte*) *pa.*

622 Charter of William de la Forde in fee simple with warranty and acquittance without date made to Thomas de la Forde his brother of 3 acres of meadow in Edmonton marsh, of which 1 acre and 3 roods lie between the meadow of Robert Bate and the meadow of William Chichele extending to 'Humberlond', and the other acre and rood lie in the place called 'Newechepynge' between the meadow of Diamand de Anesty and 'Shaddeshalfacre'.

623 Release in perpetuity by Robert son of Alice, daughter of Robert Selueyn, made in London, 28 March 1294, to William son of William de la Forde of all lands and tenements which Robert Selueyn, grandfather of the releasor, once held in Edmonton.

624 Charter of John le Sime in fee simple with warranty and acquittance without date made to John Patryk of 2 acres of land in Edmonton lying between the land of the feoffee and the land of Stephen son of William son of (?)Hildchime, to be held of the donor by service of 6d *pa.*

625 Charter of Bartinus de Chyngeford and John de Canne in fee simple with warranty and acquittance made at Hertford, 12 October 1262, to William le Frere of all the land in Edmonton in which Henry son of William enfeoffed the donors, to be held of the donor for 1d *pa* for all save foreign service and due services to the chief lord.

626 Charter of William le Frere in fee simple with warranty and acquittance without date made to Robert Hauteyn of 1½ acres of meadow in Edmonton marsh lying between the meadow of the feoffee and the meadow of the prior of Holy Trinity, London, extending from the River Lea to the meadow of William Marsh (*de Marisco*) called 'Donemed', to be held of the donor by 1d *pa* for all service.

627 Charter of John Marsh in fee simple with warranty and acquittance without date made to Robert Hauteyn of 2 acres of meadow lying in the parish of Enfield in the meadow called 'Stoneye' which Emma, the donor's sister, once held, to be held of the donor by 6d *pa* for all service.

628 Indenture made 29 September 1267 whereby Nicholas Miller (*Molendarius*) of 'Sewardeston' leased to Robert Hauteyn for 10 years 1½ acres in 'Sewardeston' lying in the meadow called 'Mademereye' between the meadow of Alexander the reeve (*prepositi*) and the meadow of Maud atte Melne, extending from the River Lea in the west to Miller's pond (*stagnum Molendini*) in the east.

629 Charter of Richard Wynard in fee simple with warranty and acquittance without date made to Robert Hauteyn of 5 roods of meadow in Enfield marsh in the meadow called 'Stoneheye' lying between the meadow of the new hospital in the south and the meadow of Roger Doget in the north, extending from the River Lea in the east to the water called 'la Ree' in the west, to be held of the donor by 1d *pa* to be paid for all service.

630 Charter of Henry son of William of Edmonton in fee simple with warranty and acquittance without date made to Robert Hauteyn of 3 acres of meadow in Edmonton marsh lying between the meadow formerly of Geoffrey Goldyng in the south and the meadow formerly of William Frere which Alice his wife held in dower, extending from the River Lea in the east to the meadow called 'Donmed' in the west, to be held of the donor by one pair of gloves or by 1d *pa* for all service.

631 Charter of John Laufare son and heir of Gamelian Laufare in fee simple with warranty and acquittance without date made to Robert Hauteyn of 2 acres of meadow lying in the meadow called 'Stoneye' in Enfield and [which] are called 'Longemed' and lie between Hermit's Rood (*rodam heremit*) and the halfacre [of meadow] formerly of Azon (*Azonis*), to be held of the donor by one clove of garlic for all service.

632 Release in perpetuity by Henry son of William of Edmonton without warranty and date made to Robert Hauteyn of 1½ acres of land in Edmonton marsh between [*f. 54v*] the meadow of the said Robert and the meadow of the prior of Holy Trinity, London, extending from the River Lea in the east to the meadow of William Marsh (*de Marisco*) in the west, in which William Frere had enfeoffed Robert.

633 Charter of William de Say in fee simple without warranty and date made to William son of Roger of 5 acres of meadow in Edmonton lying next to 'Wodenghe' and the meadow of Robert Skyn, which Matthew son of William son of Isabel leased to Martin son of William son of Isabel, to be held of the donor by 1lb of pepper.

634 Charter of Robert son of Roger de Doget in fee simple without warranty and acquittance and date made to Robert de Hauteyn of 1 acre of meadow in Enfield lying in the place called 'Stoneye' between the meadow of the said Robert and the meadow of John Marsh (*de Marisco*), extending from the River Lea in the east to 'la Ree' in the west, to be held of the donor by ½d *pa* for all service.

635 Release in perpetuity by Robert le Mareschal of Cheshunt [Herts.] without date made to Robert Hauteyn of 1d rent rising from 1 acre of meadow in Enfield lying in 'Stoneye' which he used to pay on behalf of the heir of Roger Doget.

636 Release in perpetuity by Robert Hauteyn of Royston [Herts.] with warranty without date made to Thomas Romeyn and Juliana his wife of a tenement with garden outside the bar (*barram*) of Southwark, and of one messuage in Waltham in Essex, and of 9 acres of meadow in the same parish of Waltham and in the parishes of Enfield and Edmonton, which tenements were formerly of Robert Hauteyn, citizen of London, and husband of the said Juliana.

637 Release in perpetuity by Philip Hauteyn son and heir of Robert Hauteyn with warranty made in London, 25 December 1301, to Thomas Romeyn and Juliana his wife and mother of the said Philip of 9 acres of meadow in Waltham, Enfield and Edmonton.

638 Indenture of Margery who was wife of Henry son of William made 25 December 1283 to Thomas Romeyn and Juliana his wife of 1 acre of meadow in Edmonton opposite 'Chinlesford' Hall, to be held of the same Margery for life at a rent of 2s *pa.*

639 Release in perpetuity by Margery de Caoun who was wife of Henry son of William without warranty and date made to Thomas Romeyn and Juliana his wife of the same acre of meadow.

640 [*f. 55r*] Release in perpetuity by Isabel de Cranestoke without warranty made in London, 24 June 1301, to Thomas Romeyn and Juliana his wife of 5 acres of meadow in Edmonton in which Roger son of William, late husband of Margery, enfeoffed them.

641 Indenture made 29 June 1301 of 3 acres of meadow in Enfield lying in the meadow called 'Rameye' between the meadow of Henry de Enefeld, knight, in the south and the meadow of Walter Humfray in the north, extending from 'Enfeldeslane' in the west to the River Lea in the east, leased by Walter Humfray to John Derby, chaplain, to be held for twelve years.

642 Indenture made 1 August 1304 of 3 acres of meadow in Enfield [continued as **641**] leased by Alice who was wife of Adam atte Merssh, Walter Humfray of Waltham her son and Amice, Walter's sister, to John Derby, chaplain, to be held for nine years.

643 Release and grant for the aforesaid term of three years made by the said John Derby to Thomas Romeyn and Juliana his wife of the above 3 acres.

644 Indenture made 11 June 1304 of 3 acres of meadow in Enfield in the meadow called 'Rameye' lying between the meadow of Geoffrey Marsh (*Mareys*) in the north and the meadow of Walter Humfray and Amice his sister in the south, extending from the River Lea to 'Enfeldeslake' in the west, leased by the same Walter and Amice to Thomas Romeyn and Juliana his wife, to be held for twenty years.

645 Indenture of Walter Humfray made, 11 June 1304, to the same Juliana of the same 3 acres of meadow, to be held for ten years.

646 Ratification and confirmation of the lease [**644**] made without date by Richard de Loketon and the aforesaid Amice, then his wife, to the aforesaid Thomas Romeyn and Juliana of the said 3 acres of meadow.

647 Charter of Roger son of William in fee simple with warranty without date made to Thomas Romeyn and Juliana his wife of 5 acres of meadow in Edmonton in 'Middelmerssh' [*f. 55v*] between the meadow of St Giles's hospital in the north and the ditch called 'Bluntesdych' in the south and the meadow of Robert Skyn in the west and the wall called 'le Burywal' in the east, to be held of the donor by 1d *pa* and ½lb of pepper to the chief lord for all service.

648 Charter of Alice daughter of William Picot in fee simple with warranty and acquittance without date made to Edmund de Totenhale of 1 acre of land in Edmonton in the field called 'Langheg' between the land of Richard de Anesty and the land of Henry Preacher (*Predicatoris*), extending from the field of William Reyner in the east to the road called 'Garsoneswey' in the west, to be held of the donor by 1d and 2d *pa* to the chief lord for all service.

649 Charter of William Ydoyne in fee simple with warranty and acquittance without date made to the same Edmund de Totenhale and Margery his wife and the heirs of Edmund of 1 acre of land in Edmonton lying in the Hyde between the land of John Marsh (*de Marisco*) and the land of Reginald Pymme extending from the land of William Ford (*de Forda*) to the land of Henry Preacher to be held of the donor by 3d *pa* for all service.

650 Charter of Arnulph de Mounte, knight, in fee simple with warranty and acquittance without date made to the same Edmund de Totenhale of 1 acre of meadow in Edmonton marsh in the meadow called 'Mymmemade' lying between the meadow of Peter Picot and Ranulph Munchanes and that of the same Edmund in width, extending from the meadow of Robert Hauteyn to 'Shadeshalfacre', to be held of the donor by 1d *pa*.

651 Charter of Walter Castlc (*de Castello*) in fee simple with warranty, made June 1296, to the same Edmund de Totenhale and Margery his wife and the heirs of Edmund of the whole meadow which the donor had in 'Mymmemade' in Edmonton marsh.

652 Charter of John son of John Hereward in fee simple with warranty and defence without date made to William son of John Hereward of 1 acre of land lying in the place called 'Rysshfeld' between the land of William Casiere and the land of William Ydoyne, extending from the donor's land in the east to the land of William Godho in the west, to be held of the donor by service of 4d or rent for all service (*aut redd' pro omni servicio*).

653 Release in perpetuity of Ralph son of Eustace Stourd without warranty made at Edmonton, 6 January 1318, to Alice daughter of William Hereward of one piece of land lying in 'Russhfeld' between the land of John Basse in the south [*f. 56r*] and the land of William de Causton in the north, extending from the land of the same William de Causton in the east to the land of Nicholas Brose in the west.

654 Indenture made at Edmonton, 10 May 1321, containing that if Thomas Rowe paid 20s to John Assherugge at his house in London on 29 September next, then the moiety of 1 acre of land lying between the meadow formerly of Roger Spyrk and the meadow of the prior of Holy Trinity, London, in which the said Thomas enfeoffed the said John will revert to the same Thomas notwithstanding the charter of this feoffment.

655 Charter of Richard Spyrk with warranty at Edmonton, 24 January 1322, to the same John de Asshrugge of 3 acres of land in Edmonton lying in the field called 'Aldewych' between the grove of Edmund Pymme in the south and the donor's land in the north, extending from east to west to the land formerly of Roger Spyrk.

656 Charter of Richard Spyrk in fee simple with warranty made at Edmonton, 16 May 1322, to the same John de Assherugge and Amice his wife of 1½ acres of meadow lying between the meadow of Thomas Wyliot in the north and the meadow of John Godwyne in the south, extending from the meadow of William Picard in the east to the meadow formerly of Richard Swanyld in the west.

657 Release in perpetuity of Richard de Marham, tanner, with warranty made in London on the same day to the same John Assherugge and Amice of the same meadow.

658 Charter of Ralph Englussh in fee simple with warranty made at Edmonton, 30 March 1323, to the same John Asshrugge and

Amice of 1d rent to be received from William Cook (*Coco*) and John de Notyngham from a croft in Edmonton lying 'atte Wykynlaneande' between the land of the same John Assherugge in the west and the same lane in the east and the grove of Edmund Pymme in the south and the road leading to 'Blakemanneswalle' in the north.

659 Charter of John de Notyngham, tawyer of London, and Joan his wife, daughter of Roger Spyrk, in fee simple with warranty made at Edmonton, 27 April 1323, to the same John Assherugge and Amice his wife and the heirs of John of all the donor's share of the same croft.

660 [*f. 56v*] Charter of William Cook (*Coci*) of Edmonton in fee simple with warranty made at Edmonton, 21 December 1328, to the same John de Assherugge of the remaining part of the same croft.

661 Charter of Richard Spyrk in fee simple with warranty made at Edmonton, 24 August 1331, to John de Assherugge of an enclosed croft called 'Aldewyk' in Edmonton lying between the lane called 'Wykelane' in the east and the land of William de Causton in the west, extending from the land of the feoffee in the south to the same lane in the north.

662 Indented charter with warranty without date containing that William de la Forde granted in fee simple to William de Wynton, citizen of London, the whole part of that grove called 'Patryksgrove' recently acquired of Walter le Moyne and Alice his wife in Edmonton, together with reversion of the whole of his share of the third part of the same grove, to be held after the death of Margery who was wife of Robert de la Forde and who holds it in dower in exchange for all the land which William Wynton held in 'Polgrof' and 'Sitheresgrof'.

663 Release in perpetuity by Diamand who was wife of Richard de Anesty with warranty made in London, 3 December 1293, to the same William de Wynton of all the lands of the inheritance of the said Diamand in which the said Richard enfeoffed William.

664 Charter of Beatrice daughter of William Spyrk in fee simple with warranty made at Edmonton, 12 October 1305, to Roger le Kyng of Tottenham and John his son of 1 acre of land lying in 'Langehegg' between the land lately of Richard de Anesty on both sides, and of 1 acre of land in the same field lying between the land of Edmund de Totenhale and the land of the prior of Holy Trinity, London.

665 Release in perpetuity of Richard Spyrk without warranty made at Edmonton, 18 January 1312, to the same Roger le Kyng and John his son of the same land in which the same Beatrice, sister of Richard, enfeoffed them.

666 Charter de Querndon in fee simple with warranty without date made to William Amys son of Geoffrey Marsh (*de Marisco*) of 2s to be received of Stephen de Colewell of one messuage and 7 acres of land in Edmonton between the field called called 'Querndonescolewell' and the street called 'Colewellestrete'.

667 [*f. 57r*] Charter of Alice daughter of John FitzJohn of Edmonton in fee simple with warranty and acquittance without date made to William Amys son of Geoffrey Marsh (*de Marischo*) of the whole of the donor's tenement descending to her by inheritance after the death of Maud her mother, except $\frac{1}{2}$ acre of meadow in Edmonton marsh and of all that piece of land in Edmonton marsh which the donor bought of Christine her sister.

668 Charter of Geoffrey Bruce in fee simple with warranty without date made to John Brun his brother of one messuage and garden in Edmonton which was once of Bruno Roger, the donor's father, and Isabel his mother, lying between [the land of] Richard Humfray in the east and 'le Halestrate' in the south and the messuage of William Barker (*Bercarii*) in the north.

669 Release in perpetuity by Geoffrey de Querndon made, 13 April 1278, to John le Brun of all services and customs due to him of a messuage with pasture which were formerly of Peter Eylwyne in Edmonton.

670 Charter of Robert Bourne of Mile End near London in fee simple with warranty made at Edmonton, 4 August 1310, to John de Wyndesore, citizen of London, of all the land and the wood growing on it which was formerly of Maurice[1] Smith (*Fabri*) in Edmonton, lying between the land and wood of Adam le Plastrer in the west and the wood of Robert le Webbe in the east, extending from the highway leading to 'Armhilte' to the wood of the prioress and convent of Clerkenwell in the south, to be held by annual rent of 6d to the prioress and convent of St

Helen, London, for all service and ½d to Vincent le Webbe and his heirs.
Witnesses: William atte Forde, Ralph Clerk, Alan Paterick, William Anesty, Richard Cook (*Coco*), William Neweman, John Page, John Bussel, Vincent le Webbe and others.
[Hatfield Deeds 129/13]

> 1 MS: Martin.

671 Release in perpetuity of Robert Forester of Mile End with warranty made at Edmonton on the same day to John de Wyndesore of the same land and wood.

672 Charter of Diamand de Anesty in fee simple with warranty without date made to Richard her son of 3 acres of land lying in the field called the Hyde next to the land of the recipient, to be held of the chief lords of the fee and by an annual rent to the same Diamand of 2s.

673 Part of a fine levied at Westminster, 19 June 1306, whereby Richard de Anesty and Robert de Alveto granted one messuage and 1 carucate of land in Edmonton to William de Anesty and Maud his wife and the heirs of William without warranty.
[*Feet of Fines, Lond.& Middx.* i, 78]

674 [*f. 57v*] Charter of Richard son of Richard de Anesty in fee simple with warranty made at Edmonton, 5 April 1312, to William son of William de Anasty of all the land in Edmonton lying in the Hyde, and of 2 acres of land lying in 'Colesgrove' between the land of William de la Forde on both sides which Margery atte Forde formerly held in dower and in which William, the donor's brother, enfeoffed him.

675 Charter of William son of William de Anesty in fee simple with warranty made at Edmonton, 15 September 1325, to Robert son of Richard de Anesty, Geoffrey his brother and Sybil, wife of Geoffrey, of ½ acre of land in Edmonton lying in the Hyde between the land of the said Geoffrey and the land formerly of William de la Forde, extending from the land of the same Geoffrey in the east to the pasture lately of William de la Forde in the west, and of half of a second acre of land in the same field between the grove formerly of William de la Forde in the west and the land formerly of the same William in the east, extending from 'Penyakerlane' in the south to the land formerly of William de la Forde in the north.

676 Charter of Walter le Venour in fee simple with warranty without date made to William de Causton, citizen of London, of three messuages and 8 acres of land in Hunstanton and of 2 acres of land in Great Ringstead [Norfolk] in which John Lestrange, lord of Knockin, enfeoffed the donor, to be held of the chief lords of the fee by due services.

677 Charter of Joan Basyng lately wife of Anselm Knotte, citizen and fishmonger of London, in fee simple with warranty made at Edmonton, 15 October 1307, to the same William, citizen and mercer of London, of all lands and tenements in Edmonton which the said Joan acquired jointly with her husband from Edith la Palmere formerly wife of Robert le Palmere, late citizen of London.

678 Letter of attorney of the same Joan made in London on the same day to Geoffrey le Palmere, citizen and mercer of London, to deliver seisin to the same William of the above tenements according to the said charter.

679 Release in perpetuity by John son and heir of the said Anselm Knotte without warranty made in London, 11 October 1307, to the same William de Causton of all lands and tenements in Edmonton which the said Anselm formerly acquired of Richard Cnotte.

680 [f. 58r] Charter of Robert le Despencer of Acton in fee simple with warranty made at Edmonton, 18 June 1310, to the same William de Causton of a grove in Edmonton called 'Patri-kesgrave' which the donor acquired of William de Wynton and which lies between Enfield wood in the north and the wood of Thomas William and the land of William Patrik in the south, extending from the tenement of John le Rede and the land of William Patrik in the east to the grove of Thomas William in the west.

681 Release in perpetuity by Massenta who was wife of William de Wynton, late citizen and draper of London, without warranty made in London, 26 July 1310, to Robert le Despencer of Acton of all right of the field in Edmonton called 'le Frenchefeld' which might belong to her by reason of dower or other means.

682 Release in perpetuity by the same Massenta without warranty made in London on the same day to the same Robert le Despencer of the whole of the above grove of which mention is made above in that she might have a claim to it by right of dowry or otherwise.

683 Release in perpetuity by the same Massenta made without warranty in London, 16 August 1310, to William de Causton of the above grove contained in the previous releases and above charter [**680**].

684 Charter of Ralph del Par in fee simple with warranty made at Edmonton, 18 February 1311, to William de Causton of a messuage with adjacent garden in Edmonton situated between the tenement of John Hunfray in the north and the tenement of Maud Hunfray in the east and between the highways to the south and west.

685 Charter of William Amys of Edmonton, citizen of London, in fee simple with warranty made at Edmonton, 25 April 1311, to William de Causton of one messuage and 11 acres of land in Edmonton, of which the messuage, which the donor acquired of Agnes his mother, lies between the land of John atte Strate in the east, north and west and the highway in the south, and 1 piece of land lies in the field called 'Pantfeld' between the land of the said John atte Strate in the west and the land of Richard Amys in the east, another lies in 'Stonifeld' between the land of William atte Forde in the east and the land of Richard Amys in the west, a third piece lies in 'le Felde atte gate' between the land [*f. 58v*] of William atte Forde in the south and the land of John atte Strate in the north, and a fourth lies in 'Brodefeld' between the land of Richard Amys in the east and the land of John atte Strate in the west, a fifth piece lies in the 'Berghfeld' between the land of Ralph Picot in the east and the land of Robert Gulle in the west extending from the land formerly of John le Blound in the south and the land of John atte Strate in the north, and a sixth piece lies in 'Berghfeld' between the land formerly of John Sharp in the east and west extending from the land formerly of John Blund in the south to the land formerly of John Goule in the north, and of 2s rent arising from one messuage and 7 acres of land lying in Edmonton between the field called 'Querndonescolewell' and the street called 'Colewellestrate', which rent the donor acquired of Geoffrey de Querndon.

686 Charter of the same William Amys in fee simple with warranty
made at Edmonton on the same day to William de Causton of
the same messuage [and] of 6 of the said 11 acres of land
contained in the previous charter, lying in the said fields of
'Pantfield', 'Stonyfeld', 'le Felde atte gate' and 'le Brodefeld', to
be held by rendering to the chief lords 18d of silver for all
services.
Witnesses: Robert le Sqyeler, John Gysors, William Vicayr, Ralph
called 'le Clerk', John atte Ford, John atte Strate, John son of
John atte Merhs', William le Casiere, William, son of John atte
Strate, Ralph de Ynilane, clerk, and others.
[Hatfield Deeds 29/15]

687 Another charter of the same William Amys in fee simple with
warranty made at Edmonton on the same day to the same
William de Causton of the remaining 5 acres contained in the
said charter [**685**] in the field of 'Berghfeld'.

688 Another charter of the same William Amys in fee simple with
warranty made at Edmonton on the same day to the said
William Causton of the said 2s rent likewise contained in the
first charter [**685**].
Witnesses: John atte Merhs', William Vicayr', Robert le Sqyeler,
John atte Strate, Ralph le Clerk, William le Smyth, Ralph Clerk
and others.
[Hatfield Deeds 58/16]

689 Charter of William le Casiere in fee simple with warranty made
at Edmonton, 29 April 1311, to the same William de Causton
[of] 1 acre of land in Edmonton which the donor acquired of
Augustine Alwele lying in the Hyde between the land of Giles
le Casiere in the east and the land of William de Anesty in the
west, extending from the land of [?William] de la Forde and the
land of William de Anesty in the south to the land of William
de Say.

690 Charter of William le Casiere in fee simple with warranty made
at Edmonton on the same day to William de Causton of one
messuage in Edmonton which the donor acquired of Michael le
Baillif, called 'le Armurer', of London, situated between the
messuage of William Smith (*Fabri*) in the south and the messuage
of Christine Cullyng in the north, extending from the land
formerly of William Amys in the east to the highway in the west.

691 [*f. 59*] Release in perpetuity by Margery who was wife of John
Broun of Edmonton without warranty made at Edmonton, 27
June 1311, to William de Causton of all lands and tenements
which were formerly of her husband in Edmonton.

692 Charter of John son of John atte Merssh in fee simple with
warranty made at Edmonton, 26 April 1313, to William de
Causton of a piece of land in Edmonton in the croft called
'Shortefeld' lying between the lane called 'Rowelane' in the east
and the land of Nicholas, William and Robert, the donor's
brothers, in the west, extending from the donor's land in the
north to the land of Maud and Isabel, the donor's sisters, in the
south, and of 2 acres and 3 roods of meadow in Edmonton
marsh, of which 1 acre lies in 'Dykedennadsshot' between the
meadow of William Pykard in the south and the meadow of
Thomas Sabyn in the north, extending from the meadow of
Robert de Wylughby from the east to the the meadow of William
Amys in the west, another acre lies in 'Chipolshot' between the
meadow of the feoffee in the south and the meadow of Isabel
Bardolf in the north, extending from the meadow of William
atte Forde in the east to the donor's land in the west, and 3
roods lie between the meadow called 'Holmesmad' in the east
and the feoffee's meadow in the west, extending from 'Tot-
enhammare' in the south.

693 Another charter of John atte Merssh made on the same day to
William de Causton of the same land and meadow.

694 Letter of the same John atte Merssh made at Edmonton, 27
April 1313, in which he bound himself and his heirs to acquit
the said William de Causton his heirs and assigns against the
chief lords of the fee of the said land by one rose each year.
Witnesses: William atte Ford, John atte Ford, William le Vykere,
Robert de Actone, John atte Strate, John Gesors, Walter Laurenz
and others.
[Hatfield Deeds 190/24]

695 Charter of William Amys, citizen of London, in fee simple with
warranty made at Edmonton, 2 November 1312, to William de
Causton of a grove in Edmonton, lying between the land of
Thomas William in the east and Southgate in the west, extending
from the grove of the nuns of St Helen's, London, in the north
to the land of Philip Patryk in the south, and of 6d rent to be
received of the messuage formerly of Richard Lyf.

696 Charter of Fulk son of Hubert in fee simple with warranty, made at Tottenham, 15 October 1312, to William de Causton of 8s 4d rent to be received of a tenement which Isabel who was wife of John le Chaundeler holds in Tottenham situated between the messuage of John le Notiere in the north and the messuage formerly of William Belofte in the south, extending from the land formerly of the same William from the east to the road in the west.

697 [*f. 59v*] Release by John Quyntyn of Newport made in London, 9 December 1312, to William de Causton of all services which the said William previously owed to him for the tenement which he purchased from William Amys in the field called 'Berghfeld' in the fee of the said John in Edmonton.

698 Charter of Roger atte Lofte of Tottenham in fee simple made at Tottenham, 11 [or 18] February (*die dominica proxima ante post festum Sancti Valentini*) 1313, to William de Causton of 12s rent to be received of all the donor's lands and tenements in Tottenham, making no mention of the length of term of the lease (*non faciens mencionem ad quos terminos*).

699 Charter of Denis le Avener, citizen of London, in fee simple with warranty made at Edmonton, 25 April 1313, to William Causton of 3 acres of meadow in Edmonton marsh, of which 1 acre and 3 roods lie between the meadow of Robert Bate in the north and the meadow of Robert Kenere in the south, extending from the pasture of William le Venour called 'Amberland' in the west to the meadow of the said William le Venour in the east, and 1 acre and 1 rood lie between the meadow of Robert de Anesty and William de Anesty and Stephen de Abyndon in the west, extending from the River Lea in the north to the feoffee's meadow in the south.

700 Charter of Robert le Despencer of Acton in fee simple with warranty made at Edmonton, 3 May 1313, to William de Causton of 1 acre of meadow in Edmonton lying between the meadow of William le Vikere and the meadow of Robert Smith (*Fabri*), extending from 'le Spitelmad' to the hithe of the River Lea (*riperiam de la Luye*).

701 Indenture made at Edmonton on the same day containing that if the same Robert le Despencer pay to William de Causton 40s at Edmonton at Michaelmas next, then the aforesaid acre of

meadow will revert to the said Robert and the charter made
thereof be held null.

702 Another part of the same indenture.

703 Release in perpetuity by Augustine Alewele without warranty
made in London, 31 October 1313, to William de Causton of all
lands and tenements which he once held in Edmonton.

704 Charter of Thomas Denteyt in fee simple with warranty made
at [*f. 60r*] Edmonton, 9 December 1313, to William Causton of
1 acre of land in Edmonton lying in the field called 'le Southland'
between the land of Thomas le Rowe on both sides, extending
from the land of Richard de Willughby in the east to the land
of John Castle (*de Castello*) in the West.

705 Charter of Amice de Thurkile in fee simple with warranty made
at Edmonton, 16 January 1314, to William de Causton of 1 acre
of land and 1 rood of meadow lying in the meadow of Edmonton
between the meadow of William Vicaire in the east and the
meadow 'le Roundemade' in the west.

706 Letter of the same Amice made at Edmonton on the same day
to Geoffrey Thomas her son to deliver seisin of the said meadow
to the same William.

707 Release in perpetuity of Geoffrey Thomas son of Amice Thurkyld
with warranty made at Edmonton, 20 January 1314, to William
de Causton of the above meadow in which the said Amice
enfeoffed him.

708 Charter of Katherine daughter of Robert atte Fen in fee simple
with warranty made at Edmonton, 14 January 1314, to William
de Causton of $1\frac{1}{2}$ acres of meadow in the meadow of Edmonton
between the meadows of John Denteyt in the south and John
Hammyng in the north, extending from the meadow of
[?Thomas] le Rowe and Robert de Acton in the west to the
meadow called 'Longemed' in the east, and [of] $\frac{1}{2}$ acre lying
between the meadows of Robert Gulle in the east and the
meadow of John Saleman in the west, extending from 'Blun-
tesdykdemad' in the north to the meadow of the said Robert de
Acton in the south.

709 Charter of Geoffrey Thomas son of John Thomas of Reading in fee simple with warranty made at Edmonton, 7 February 1314, to William de Causton of 3 acres of meadow in Edmonton marsh, of which 1 acre and 3 roods lie between the meadow of William de la Forde in the north and the meadow of Richard Wylehale in the south, and 3 roods lie between the meadow formerly of Geoffrey de la Bergh and the feoffee's meadow in the north and the meadow called 'Roundemad' in the south, and $\frac{1}{2}$ acre lies between the meadows of William Amys in the east and Robert Gulle in the west.

710 Release in perpetuity by the same Geoffrey [Thomas] without warranty made at Edmonton, 14 February 1314, to William de Causton for the same 3 acres (*eisdem tribus acris*) of meadow, and of 1 acre and 1 rood of meadow in which Amice, mother of the said Geoffrey, enfeoffed William by the charter above [**705**].

711 [*f. 60v*] Release in perpetuity by the aforesaid of Amice de Thurkild' who was wife of John Thomas of Reading without warranty made at Edmonton, 17 March 1314, to William de Causton of the same 3 acres of meadow in Edmonton in which Geoffrey Thomas her son enfeoffed the same William.

712 Release in perpetuity by Christine who was wife of Fulk Hubert, late citizen of London, without warranty made in London, 26 July 1314, of 8s 4d rent which the said Fulk granted to the said William, to be received from the tenement of John le Chaundeler in Tottenham.

713 Indenture made at Tottenham, 29 August 1314, agreeing that if Roger de Solio pay to William de Causton 50s at Whitsun next [7 July 1315], then 12s rent in Tottenham granted to the same William by charter of the said Roger will revert to the said Roger.

714 Another part of the same indenture.
Witnesses: John son of John Peter, Robert atte Fen, John Stephen, Richard Carpenter, Anselm de Hatfeld and others.
[Hatfield Deeds 88/3]

715 Acquittance of Isabel and Maud daughters of John Marsh made in London, 17 October 1325, whereby the said Isabel and Maud received arrears of 4s rent due to them for 8 acres of land lying in the field called 'Fulberadesfeld' in Edmonton.

716 Charter of Robert atte Hull in fee simple made at Edmonton, 9 February 1315, to William de Causton of 2s rent to be received of all the donor's lands in Edmonton.

717 Charter of John le Chaundeler of Tottenham made at Tottenham in fee simple to William de Causton of 4s rent issuing from his tenement in Tottenham situated between the tenement of William Beloft in the south and the tenement of John le Notiere in the north and extending from the tenement of the said William Beloft in the east to the highway in the west.

718 Charter of Thomas Dyne in fee simple made at Tottenham, 6 April 1316, to William de Causton of 2s rent to be received each year of all the donor's tenements in Tottenham situated between the tenement of John Baldewyne in the south and the tenement of Walter Swetewull in the north, extending from the pasture of John son of Peter in the east to the highway in the west.
Witnesses: Roger del Fen, John Tebaud, Roger atte Lofte, Anselm de Hatfeld, John le Mareschal, John le Notiere, John le Chaundler and others.
[Hatfield Deeds 162/16]

719 [*f. 61r*] Charter of Christine Colewell formerly wife of Stephen Colewell in fee simple made at Tottenham, 3 April 1316, to William de Causton of 3s annual rent from all the donor's tenements in Tottenham between 'Amberdenelane' in the south and the tenement formerly of John le Bakere in the north, extending from the tenement of Robert atte Fen in the east to the highway in the west.

720 Charter of Marcia Belofte in fee simple made at Tottenham, 13 April 1316, to William de Causton of 12d rent to be received annually of the donor's lands in Tottenham situated between the tenement of John le Chaundeler in the north and the tenement of Agnes Beloft in the south, extending from the land of Robert atte Fen in the east to the highway in the west.

721 Charter of Henry Bullok in fee simple made at Edmonton, 23 April 1316, to William de Causton of 2s rent to be received annually of the donor's tenements in Edmonton situated between the land of the prior of Holy Trinity, London, in the south and the land of John Feverel in the north, extending from the land of the same John Feverel in the east to the highway in the west.

722 Charter of John Reyner in fee simple made at Tottenham, 6 May 1316, to William de Causton of 2s annual rent from all the donor's tenements in Tottenham situated between the tenement formerly of Robert le Fulle in the north and the tenement of John le Notiere junior in the south, extending from the tenement of the said John le Notiere in the east to the highway in the west.

723 Charter of Alice Mariner in fee simple made at Tottenham, 6 May 1316, to William de Causton of 12d annual rent from all the donor's tenements in Tottenham situated between the tenement of Walter Meleward in the north and the tenement of John Abraham in the south, extending from the tenement of John son of Peter in the east to the highway in the west.

724 [*f. 61v*] Release in perpetuity by John son of John atte Merssh without warranty made at Edmonton, 8 September 1316, to William de Causton of all the lands and tenements in which Joan who was wife of Anselm Knotte enfeoffed William in Edmonton.

725 Charter of the same John son of John atte Merssh in fee simple with warranty made at Edmonton, 8 September 1316, of 1 acre of meadow in Edmonton marsh lying between the meadow of Richard de Wilehale in the east and the meadow of Lady de Bardolf in the west, and of 22d rent in Edmonton, of which 12d to be received of the tenement of Robert atte Hull, 4d of the tenement of Robert le Sheperde, and 6d of the tenement of Henry Swift.

726 Indenture made at Edmonton on the same day agreeing that if the said John son of John atte Merssh pay to the said William de Causton 6 marks from 1 November 1316 for one year in the church of St Matthew Friday Street, London, the said acre of land and rent will revert to the donor and the charter be held null.

727 Charter of William le Casiere in fee simple with warranty made at Edmonton, 16 December 1316, to William de Causton of 2½ acres of land in Edmonton lying in the field called 'Berghfeld' between the land of William le Smyth in the east, extending from the land of John le Blund in the south to the land of Richard Gisors in the north.

728 Charter of John son of John atte Merssh in fee simple with
warranty made at Edmonton, 22 March 1317, to William de
Causton of 1 acre of meadow in Edmonton marsh, of which $\frac{1}{2}$
acre of meadow lies in 'Chipolshot' between the meadow of
Edmund Pymme in the north and the meadow of William de
Causton in the south, extending from the donor's croft in the
west to the meadow called 'le Roundemade' in the east, and $\frac{1}{2}$
acre lies in 'Dunmadeplot' between the meadow of Richard
Spyrk in the north and the meadow of the prior of Holy Trinity,
London, in the south, extending from the donor's meadow called
'Dounemad' in the west to the meadow of Robert atte Fen in
the east.

729 Indenture made at Edmonton on the morrow of the same day
[23 March 1317] agreeing that [if] the same John atte Merssh
pay to the same William de Causton in the church of St Matthew
Friday Street, London, on 29 September 1317 4 marks, the said
acre of meadow will be returned to the donor and the said
charter be held null.
Witnesses: William atte Forde, John atte Forde, William de Anesty,
Robert Scuyler, William le Vykere, John Castel, John atte Strate
and others.
[Hatfield Deeds 129/9]

730 [*f. 62r*] Charter of John le Chaundeler of Tottenham in fee
simple with warranty made at Tottenham, 12 January 1318, to
William de Causton of the whole of the donor's tenement in
Tottenham situated between the tenement of John le Notiere in
the north and the tenement of Marcia Beloft in the south,
extending from the tenement of the said John le Notiere in the
east to the highway in the west.

731 Charter of Richard called le Carpenter of Tottenham in fee
simple with warranty made at Edmonton, 7 February 1318, to
William de Causton of one piece of land in Edmonton lying in
the field called 'Langheg' between the land of John Thebaud in
the south and the land formerly of Roger Aldred in the north,
extending from the donor's tenement in the east to 'Garsoneswey'
in the west.

732 Release in perpetuity by Isabel who was the wife of John atte
Merssh without warranty made at Edmonton, 29 January 1318,
to William de Causton of all the lands and tenements which
John had granted to the said William in Edmonton.

Witnesses: William atte Forde, John atte Forde, William de Anesty, Robert de Acton, John Castle (*de Castello*), John atte Strate, John Gysors and others.
[Hatfield Deeds 188/20]

733 Charter of Henry Bullok in fee simple with warranty made at Edmonton, 22 February 1318, to William de Causton of a house with adjacent enclosed curtilage in Edmonton called 'Sopereshawe' lying between the land formerly of Nicholas le Claper in the north and east and the land of the canons of Holy Trinity, London, in the south and the highway leading from the south gate of Enfield to London.

734 Release in perpetuity by Agnes who was wife of Geoffrey Thomas of Barnet without warranty made at Edmonton, 29 January 1318, to William de Causton of 4 acres of meadow in Edmonton which the said Geoffrey granted to the said William.

735 Release in perpetuity by Maud le Cokes formerly wife of Alexander Lorimare with warranty made at Edmonton, 26 June 1318, to William de Causton of one piece of land in Edmonton lying in the field called 'Longheg' between the land of John Tebaud in the south and the land formerly of Roger Aldred in the north, extending from the messuage of Richard le Carpenter in the east to the land of John Dul.

736 Indenture made at Edmonton, 17 January 1339, whereby Nicholas, William and Robert, sons of John Marsh (*de Marisco*), were at liberty to sell three pieces of land and one piece of pasture in Edmonton leased to William de Causton at a rent for the first 20 years of 17s *pa* and thereafter 30s to whomsoever they wished within that term of 20 years, unless the said William wished to give as much as another for the same land and meadow.
Witnesses: William atte Ford, John atte Ford, Robert de Acton, John de Marsh, John atte Strate, Thomas le Rouwe, Roger atte Sloth and others.
[Cf. **950**, (WAM 184)]

737 Indenture made at Edmonton on the same day containing that Isabel and Maud daughters of John Marsh were at liberty to sell 16 acres of land in Edmonton leased to William de Causton in fee simple by the same at an annual rent of 8s for the first 20 years and thereafter 16s to whomsoever they wished within the

term of 20 years, unless the said William wished to give as much
as another for the same land.

738 [*f. 62v*] Indented charter of Nicholas, William and Robert, sons
of John Marsh, in fee simple with warranty made at Edmonton,
14 January 1319, to William de Causton of their messuage and
of three pieces of land and one piece of pasture in Edmonton
which their father had granted to them and which he had
acquired from John Carpenter. And of these pieces of land one
is called 'Stonifeld' and another piece contains four acres of land
and lies between the first piece and the land formerly of Richard
Hereward called 'Gunildesfeld', and the third piece is called
'Benecroft' lying between the said second piece of land and the
lane leading to 'Russefeld', and the aforesaid pasture is called
'Trumpetonemor', [to be held] at a rent of 17s *pa* to the donors
for the first 20 years and thereafter 30s.

739 Another part of the same indenture.
Witnesses: William atte Ford, John atte Ford, Robert de Acton,
John Marsh (*de Marisco*), John atte Strate, Thomas le Rouwe,
Roger atte Sloth and others.
[Hatfield Deeds 57/18]

740 Indented charter of Isabel and Maud daughters of John atte
Merssh in fee simple with warranty made at Edmonton on the
same day to William de Causton of 16 acres of land in Edmonton
which their father had granted to them lying in the field called
'Fulbertesfeld' between the land of the said William in the north
and the highway and land of Richard de Wyrhale in the south,
[to be held] at a rent to the donors of 8s *pa* for the first 20 years
and thereafter 16s.

741 Another part of the same indenture.

742 Release in perpetuity of Robert son of John Marsh with warranty
made at Edmonton, 19 August 1319, [*f. 63r*] to Nicholas his
brother of his whole share of 17s rent and of the lands and
tenements contained in the above charter [**738**].

743 Charter of William de Causton made at Edmonton granting that
Nicholas son of John atte Merssh was at liberty to sell the whole
of that part of the aforesaid lands, tenements and rents acquired
of Robert his brother to whomsoever he wished, unless the said

William wished to give to him as much as another for the same part.

744 And memorandum that there ought here to be a release made to the said William on the part of Nicholas and it seems that enquiry should be made concerning this release (*et il semble qe lavaundit rel[es] de tut par quei soit enqis*).

745 Charter of John Mountchaysy in fee simple with warranty made in London to William de Causton of 1 acre of meadow in Edmonton marsh lying between the meadow of Thomas Wiliot of Mimms in the north and the meadow formerly of William atte Forde in the south.
Witnesses: John atte Forde, William de Anesty, John Marsh (*de Marisco*), John atte Strete, William le Vykere and others.
[Hatfield Deeds 56/14]

746 Release in perpetuity of John Marsh of Edmonton made at Edmonton, 7 March 1320, to William de Causton of 32d rent which the said John used to receive from William for a field called 'Berghfeld'.

[Here an error occurs in the numeration of the charters, subsequently noted in the margin: Hic omittuntur duo numeri per negligenciam scriptoris.]

747 Release in perpetuity by Isabel and Maud daughters of John Marsh without warranty made in London, 10 July 1320, to William de Causton of 8 acres out of those 16 acres of land contained in the charter above [**740**], which 8 acres lie in the southern part of the said piece.

748 Acquittance made by Maud daughter of John Marsh notifying that she received of William de Causton the whole of her share of the rent of 8s contained in the charter above [**740**] from 29 September 1319 for four years.

749 Charter of Robert de Pyphurst, citizen and goldbeater of London, with warranty made at Enfield, 21 July 1321, to William de Causton of 2 acres and 1 rood of meadow in Enfield lying in two pieces, of which one lies in the marsh between the meadow of Roger de Hakeneye in the north and the meadow of Richard de Bradele in the south, extending to 'le Markedych' in the east and to the meadow of Sir John de Enefeld in the west, and the other piece lies between the meadow of Walter Clay [*f. 63v*] in the south and the meadow of Roger de Hakeney in the north, extending to the meadows of the said Walter and Roger in the west and of William Durant in the east.

750 Charter of John le Spencer in fee simple with warranty made at Enfield, 4 September 1321, to William de Causton of a piece of enclosed land in Edmonton which the donor acquired of John son of William Hereward lying between the land of Giles le Casiere in the north and the land of the feoffee in the south, extending from the land of the feoffee in the east to the land of Nicholas de Bruse in the east (*sic*).

751 Charter of Ralph Hereward son of Helen Hereward in fee simple with warranty made at Edmonton, 15 September 1321, to William de Causton of 1 acre of land lying in the field called 'Lusshefeld' in Edmonton between the land of the feoffee in the north. . .¹, extending from the land of Nicholas Brese in the west to the land of the feoffee in the east.

    1 Omission.

752 Release of the same Ralph without warranty made at Edmonton, 8 November 1321, to William de Causton of the same acre of land.

753 Charter of Richard Amys son of Richard Amys, late fishmonger of London, in fee simple with warranty made at Edmonton, 1 February 1321, to William de Causton of $4\frac{1}{2}$ acres of land in Edmonton, of which one piece lies in 'le Brodefeld' between the feoffee's land in the west and the land of Richard Saleman in the east, extending from the pasture of John Saleman in the south to 'Parklane' in the north, another piece lies in 'Stonyfeld' between the feoffee's land in the east and the land of John atte Strate in the west, extending from 'Arnoldeslane' in the north to 'Parklane' in the south, another piece lies in 'le Pondfeld' between the feoffee's land in the north and the pond of the lord of Edmonton in the south, extending from the land of Richard Goldyng in the west to 'Pondlane' in the east, and of 1 acre of meadow in 'Holfloteschot', half of which lies between the meadow of William de Anesty in the east and the meadow of William Nel in the west, extending from the meadow of St Giles in the south to the River Lea in the north, and the other half lies between the meadows of the feoffee in the east, of John atte

Strate in the west, of the hospital of St Giles in the south and the River Lea in the north.

754 [*f. 64r*] Release in perpetuity by the same Richard Amys with warranty without date made to the same William of the same land and meadow.

755 Release in perpetuity by Nicholas de Normanby and Margery his wife who was formerly [wife] of Richard Amys senior without warranty made in London, 4 February 1321, to William de Causton of the same land and meadow.

756 Release in perpetuity by Isabel who was wife of William le Casiere without warranty made in London, 8 May 1321, to William de Causton of all lands and tenements in Edmonton which were once held by the said William le Casiere.

757 Charter of Thomas le Rowe in fee simple with warranty made at Edmonton, 10 May 1321, to John de Assherugge of $\frac{1}{2}$ acre of meadow in Edmonton lying between the meadow formerly of Roger Spyrk and the meadow of the prior of Holy Trinity, London, extending from the meadow of William le Vikere to 'le Roundmade'.

758 Release by John Somery of Enfield without warranty made in London, 9 April 1322, to William de Causton of 4d rent from the meadow of the same William lying in 'Enfeldesmerssh' which Robert Pyphurst, goldsmith of London, had granted to the same William.

759 Release in perpetuity by John Hemmyng of Edmonton without warranty made at Edmonton, 5 May 1322, to William de Causton of 4d rent from 1 acre of meadow which the said William holds in Edmonton marsh.
Witnesses: William de Anesty, John atte Ford, John Marsh (*de Marisco*), John de Strate, John de Myles and others.
[Hatfield Deeds 110/14]

760 Charter of William de Anesty in fee simple with warranty made at Edmonton, 12 May 1322, to William de Causton of one grove in Edmonton lying between the grove of the feoffee in the south and the grove of Richard Durant of Enfield in the north and between the groves of the prior of Christchurch [Holy Trinity],

London, and of the feoffee in the west and the grove once held
by Geoffrey de Say in the east.

761 Another charter of William de Anesty of the same date and
concerning the same grove, namely $4\frac{1}{2}$ acres of wood in Edmonton.

762 [*f. 64v*] Charter of John Feverel and Amice his wife in fee simple
with warranty made at Edmonton, 16 June 1322, to William de
Causton of a 5 acre grove in Edmonton called 'Palmereslond'
lying between the land of John Tubbe in the north and the land
and wood of William de Causton in the south.

763 Letter made in London, 5 July 1322, by which Reginald Fox
received of William de Causton 100s to trade with to the profit
of the said William and to render account when requested.

764 Charter of Reginald Fox in fee simple with warranty made at
Edmonton, 6 July 1322, to William de Causton of the wood
called 'Gonneldhegges' with adjacent arable land in Edmonton,
which William le Keu, son of Henry, had granted to the donor
by the charter above.
[Cf. **617**.]

765 Another version of the same charter.

766 Indenture made 7 July 1322[1] affirming that if William de Causton
does not surrender the said wood and land within the next 20
years then the said letter of receipt [763] will be cancelled.

1 MS: 16 Edward II (8 July 1322–7 July 1323), in error for 15 Edward II or
because the regnal year of Edward II was deemed to begin on 7 July. Cf. **1147**.

767 Release in perpetuity by Nicholas son of John Marsh made at
Edmonton, 19 August 1319, to William de Causton of all his
share in the rent, lands and tenements contained in the charter
above [**738**].

768 Release in perpetuity of William Hereward with warranty made
at Edmonton, 17 August 1322, to William de Causton of 1 acre
of land in Edmonton in the field called 'Russhefeld' which he
has of the gift of Ralph Hereward and lies between the land of
the said William de Causton in the north, extending from the

land of Nicholas Brest in the west to the land of the said William Causton in the west (*sic*).

769 Charter of Edmund de Wyndesore in fee simple with warranty made at Edmonton, 24 January 1323, to William de Causton of a grove in Edmonton lying between the groves of Robert Marny in the east and of the said William in the west and the grove of the prioress of Clerkenwell in the south and 'Arnoltestrate' in the north.

770 [*f. 65r*] Letter of attorney made by Edmund de Wyndesore at Edmonton, 26 January 1323, to Gilbert Lyf to deliver seisin according to the above charter.

771 Release in perpetuity by John Vincent son of Vincent le Webbe of Edmonton, 29 January 1323, to William de Causton of ½d rent issuing from the above grove which was held by Edmund de Wyndesore.

772 Charter of John Somery of Enfield in fee simple with warranty made at Enfield, 26 February 1323, to William de Causton of 12 perches of meadow in Enfield marsh between the donor's meadow in the south and the meadow of John Heroun in the north, extending from the ditch called 'Markedych' in the east to the meadow of Richard Durant in the west.

773 Charter of Thomas le Rowe in fee simple with warranty made at Edmonton, 26 August 1323, to William de Causton of 1 acre of meadow in Edmonton marsh between the feoffee's meadow in the south and the meadow of William de Furneys in the north, extending to the feoffee's land to the east and west.

774 Charter of John son of Walter Basse in fee simple with warranty, made at Edmonton, 18 January 1323, to William de Causton of one piece of land in Edmonton in the field called 'Russhefeld' between the land of Robert Haver in the south and that of the feoffee in the north, extending from his land in the east to the land of Nicholas (?)Bisze in the west.

775 Release in perpetuity by the same John Basse without warranty and date made to William de Causton of the same land.

776 Charter of John Somery of Enfield in fee simple with warranty made at Enfield, 29 April 1323, to William de Causton of ½ acre

and 12 perches of meadow in Edmonton marsh between the
donor's meadow in the south and the meadow in which the
donor had enfeoffed the feoffee in the north, extending to the
ditch called 'le Markdich' in the east and to the meadow of
Richard Durant in the west.

777 [f. 65v] Letter of attorney of Richard de Staundon made in
London, 11 March 1323, to Roger atte Lofte and Richard atte
Leye jointly and severally to deliver to William de Causton seisin
of ½ acre of meadow in Tottenham lying in the meadow called
'Yocstrid' between the meadow of William Turry in the north,
and the meadow formerly of Laurence Eggepol in the south,
extending from the meadow formerly Ralph le Blund in the east
to the stream called 'Wildemereslake' in the west.

778 Charter of the same Richard de Staundon in fee simple with
warranty made at Tottenham on the same day to William de
Causton of the said ½ acre of meadow.

779 Charter of William de Anesty in fee simple with warranty made
at Edmonton, 1 August 1323, to William de Causton of ½ acre of
meadow in Edmonton marsh between the meadow formerly of
William atte Forde in the north and the meadow of Thomas le
Rowe in the south extending from the donor's meadow in the
east to the meadow of Stephen de Abyndon in the west.

780 Charter of the same William de Anesty in fee simple with
warranty made at Edmonton, 22 September 1323, to William de
Causton of 1 acre of meadow in Edmonton marsh between the
meadows of the feoffee in the east and the meadow of Thomas
le Rowe, the meadow of John Cook (*Coci*), and the meadow of
William de Forde in the west, extending from the meadow called
'Holmesmade' in the south to 'Shaddesmade' in the north.

781 Charter of John Page in fee simple with warranty made at
Edmonton, 12 March 1324, to William de Causton of a piece of
meadow in Edmonton marsh which the donor acquired of Roger
King of Tottenham lying between the feoffee's land, formerly of
John le Bourse, in the north and the meadow of Isabel Vescy in
the south, extending from the meadow of the nuns of Clerkenwell
in the west to the meadow of Geoffrey de Eyton in the east.

782 Charter of Christine who was the wife of John Statinmar in fee
simple with warranty made at Edmonton, 22 March 1324, to

William de Causton of the moiety of 1 acre, 1 rood, 7½ perches of land and a grove which she had acquired jointly with [*f. 66r*] her husband in Edmonton lying between the feoffee's land in the south and the donor's land in the north, extending to the land of Richard de Ypre in the east and to the highway called 'Palmer's Green' in the west.

783 Charter of Thomas de Anesty in fee simple with warranty made at Edmonton, 22 June 1324, to William de Causton of 8 acres of land in Edmonton which descended to the donor after the death of William his father, lying in the Hyde between the land formerly of William atte Forde in the south and the land of William Godhowe and Robert Smith (*Fabri*) in the north, extending from the land of Roger Depham in the east to the land formerly of William atte Forde called 'Wonacre' and the land of Geoffrey de Anesty and the land of Nicholas de Anesty in the west.

784 Another charter of the same date concerning the same land.

785 Release in perpetuity by the same of Thomas de Anesty without warranty made at Edmonton, 27 June 1324, to the same William de Causton of the same 8 acres of land.

786 Charter of John Page in fee simple with warranty made at Tottenham, 18 December 1324, of two pieces of meadow in Tottenham marsh, of which one lies between the meadow formerly of John Myre in the north and the meadow of John le Boun in the south extending from 'Batfordelake' in the west to 'Yokfordlake' in the east, and the other piece lies between the meadow of John le Landeslane in the south extending from the meadow of 'Yokfordlake' in the west to the lord's meadow (*pratum domini*) in the east.

787 Charter of Richard Horn, citizen and the fishmonger of London, in fee simple made at Edmonton, 4 February 1325, to William de Causton of 1½ acres of meadow which John son of Robert Gisors granted to the donor in Edmonton marsh lying in le 'Esthale' between the meadow of the abbot of Thorney in the east and the meadow of Robert de Holm in the west, extending from the River Lea in the north to Tottenham marsh in the south.

788 [*f. 66v*] Letter of attorney of the same Richard Horn made in London on the same day to Nicholas Horn, the donor's servant

(*valettum*), to deliver seisin of the aforesaid meadow according to the above charter.
[WAM 341]

789 Charter of Thomas de Anesty in fee simple with warranty made at Edmonton, 29 March 1325, to William de Causton of 1 acre and 1 rood of meadow in Edmonton marsh lying between the meadows of Maud de Anesty, the donor's mother, and William Sutton in the south and the meadow of William Causton in the north, extending from his meadow in the east to the meadow of Roger Depham in the west.

790 Letter of the same Thomas de Anesty made in London, 29 March 1325, to deliver seisin according to the aforesaid charter.

791 Release in perpetuity by Robert de Anesty son and heir of Thomas de Anesty with warranty without date made to William de Causton of all lands and tenements in Edmonton which the same Robert acquired of Maud formerly wife of William de Anesty and of Thomas her son.

792 Charter of Thomas de Anesty son and heir of William de Anesty of Edmonton in fee simple with warranty made in London, 6 May 1325, to William de Causton of 3 roods of land in Edmonton marsh lying in 'Longemad' between the meadow formerly of Peter de Edelmeton' in the south and the meadow formerly of William atte Forde in the north.
Witnesses: Thomas de Cavendyssh, John de Ayllesham, Roger de Cavendyssh, citizen and mercer, of London, John atte Merssh of Edmonton, John atte Castel, Edmund Pymme, John atte Strete, John Myles and many others.
[WAM 278]

793 Letter of attorney of the same Thomas made in London on the same day to deliver seisin according to the charter.

794 Charter of Maud who was wife of Richard le Rowe in fee simple with warranty made at Edmonton, 17 July 1325, to William de Causton of two pieces of land in Edmonton lying in 'Langheg', of which one lies between the land of the feoffee in the west and the land of Simon Aldrich in the east extending from the land of the prior of Holy Trinity, London, in the south to the land of Thomas Willyot in the north, and the other piece lies between the land of the said prior in the west and the land of Thomas

Wiliot in the east extending from the land of the said William to the land of William Laurence in the north.

Witnesses: John Marsh (*de Marisco*), John ate Castel, William le Vykere, John ate Strate, Edmund Pymme, Peter le Lorimer, John Myles and many others.

[WAM 249]

795 [*f. 67r*] Release of Thomas son of Richard le Rowe with warranty made at Edmonton, 29 July 1325, to William de Causton of the same two pieces of land.

Witnesses: as above.

[WAM 288]

796 Letter of attorney of Richard son of John Abel, knight, made in London, 5 August 1325, to Thomas Lambert his servant (*valettum*) to deliver to William de Causton seisin of one messuage and two shops in the parish of St Vedast in Westcheap, London, according to the charter made to him.

Witnesses: Hamo de Chigewell, mayor of London, John de Causton, Benedict de Folsham, sheriffs, Nicholas de Farndon, alderman of that ward, Richard de Shordich, Ralph de Blyth, William Pykerel, Hugh de Hereford, Andrew de Seccheford, Robert de Bristowe, Roger Clerk and others.

[WAM 320]

797 Charter of William Godhowe in fee simple with warranty made at Edmonton, 10 October 1325, to William de Causton of one piece of land in Edmonton lying in the Hyde between the land of Edmund Pymme in the south and the land of the feoffee, which was [formerly] of Walter Basse, in the north, extending from the wood of the same feoffee in the west to his land in the east.

Witnesses: John Marsh (*de Marisco*), William le Vykere, John atte Castel, John ate Strete, Edmund Pymme, John Myles, Peter le Lorimer and others.

[WAM 229]

798 Letter of attorney of William de Anesty made in London, 4 November 1325, to John Page to deliver to William de Causton seisin of that plot of arable land which the donor had of the gift of Thomas, brother of William de Anesty.

[WAM 314]

799 Acquittance of Thomas Bardolf, knight, made in London, 21

July 1325, acknowledging receipt from William de Causton by the hands of Robert de Benyngton, bailiff of Sir Thomas Bardolf, of 60s of the farm of all the meadow of the said Thomas in Edmonton leased to the said William for 30s annual rent, namely for the two years following this acquittance.
[WAM 324]

800 Charter of John Breton and Alice his wife in fee simple with warranty made at Edmonton, 2 July 1325, to William de Causton of $3\frac{1}{2}$ acres of meadow called le 'Roundemad' in Edmonton marsh lying between the meadow of the said William and 'le Manemed' in the south, extending from the meadow called 'Claricegore' and from the meadow of the feoffee in the east to the meadow called 'Shipolshot' in the west.
Witnesses: John atte Merssh, John atte Castel, William le Vikere, John atte Strate, Edmund Pymme, Peter le Lorimer, John Miles and many others.
[WAM 253]

801 Letter of attorney of the same John Breton and Alice made at Edmonton on the same day to William de Boxstede to deliver seisin according to the aforesaid charter.

802 Indenture made in London, 21 July[1] 1325, [*f. 67v*] by which Thomas Bardolf, knight, leased to William de Causton the whole meadow of the same Thomas in Edmonton, to be held from 29 September next for 6 years at an annual rent of 30s. And the said William will not dig or make any destruction of the same during the above term.
Witnesses: John atte Mersh, John atte Castel, William le Viker, John atte Strate, Edmund Pimme of Edmonton and others.
[WAM 315]

1 MS: 1 July.

803 Release in perpetuity by William son of William de Anesty with warranty without date to William de Causton of all that plot of land which Thomas, brother of William de Anesty, granted to the said William de Causton in Edmonton lying between the land formerly of William atte Forde in the south and the land of the said William de Causton in the north.
Witnesses: John atte Mersch, William le Vycare, John atte Strate, Edmund Pymme, John Miles, Peter le Lorimer and others.

[Date: *c.* 1325.]
[WAM 321]

804 Release by Robert de Acton of Edmonton without date made to William de Causton of 6d rent issuing from a certain portion of land which the said William holds in Edmonton and which was formerly of John Nicol lying near Palmer's Green between the lands of the said William de Causton to the north and south and extending from his land in the west to the grove formerly of William de Anesty in the east.

805 Charter of John Somery son of the late John Somery in fee simple with warranty made at Enfield, 20 September 1326, to William de Causton of $\frac{1}{2}$ acre of meadow and 10 perches of meadow in Enfield marsh lying between the meadow of the said William in the north and the donor's meadow in the south, and extending from the meadow of Richard Durant in the west to the meadow of 'Clingfordesmerssh' in the east.

806 Indenture made at Enfield, 21 September 1326, affirming that if the same John Somery should pay to the said William de Causton in London 20s within one year from 29 September following then the above charter conferring seisin will be cancelled.

807 Another part of the same indenture.

808 Lease made by Agnes who was wife of John Somery of Enfield, 2 October 1326, to William de Causton of 1 rood of meadow which she held in dower in 'Mariscode', Enfield, lying between the meadow of the said William in the north and the meadow of Richard Durant [*f. 68r*] in the south, to be held for the life of the lessor.

809 Release in perpetuity by Stephen son and heir of John Myre, late citizen and draper of London, without warranty and date made to William de Causton of all the rent which the same William used to pay to Stephen's father and to Stephen himself for the lands and tenements which he held in Edmonton and Tottenham.

810 Release in perpetuity by Thomas le Rowe with warranty without date made to William de Causton of 1 acre of meadow in Edmonton marsh of the gift of the said Thomas lying between

the meadow of the said William in the south and the meadow
of William Fourneys in the north.

811 Release in perpetuity of John Somery son of John Somery of
Enfield without warranty made in London, 11 April 1327, to
William de Causton of $\frac{1}{2}$ acre of meadow and 10 perches of
meadow in Enfield marsh which the said John granted to the
said William on the conditions that appear in the charter above
[**805**] and the indenture which follows it [**806**].

812 Charter of John de Mountchaysy of Waltham in fee simple with
warranty made at Tottenham, 12 March 1327, to William de
Causton of the whole tenement with houses built upon it in
Tottenham in which Roger atte Lofte enfeoffed the donor, which
is situated between the tenement which belonged to John Ekepol
in the north and the tenement of the said Roger atte Lofte in
the south, extending from a road (*regia*) in the east to the tenement
formerly of the said John Ekepol in the west.
Witnesses: Robert atte Fen, Hugh Clerk, Anselm de Hatfeld,
Roger atte Lofte, John de Notiere, John Clerk and many others.
[WAM 239]

813 Charter of John Patryk in fee simple with warranty made at
Edmonton, 26 August 1316, to William de Causton, citizen and
mercer of London, of all that grove in Edmonton between the
grove of the prior and convent of Holy Trinity, London, and the
grove of William de Anesty in the north and the donor's land
called 'Wolfrichlond' in the south, extending from the grove
called 'Salonelane' in the east to the donor's land in the west,
and of a path (*semitam*), 12 feet wide, in 'Wolfricheslond' leading
from the said grove to the highway.
Witnesses: William atte Ford, William de Anesty, John atte Merssh,
Robert de Acton, William le Vykere, John de Chastel, John de
Strate, and many others.
[WAM 280]

814 [*f. 68v*] Release in perpetuity of the aforesaid John Patryk without
warranty made at Edmonton, 28 July 1322, to William de
Causton, citizen and mercer of London, of all lands and groves,
rents and tenements in Edmonton which the same William had
of the gift of the said John.

815 Charter of John Patryk in fee simple made at Edmonton, 27
October 1315, to William de Causton of $\frac{1}{2}$ mark rent to be

received from all the donor's lands and tenements in Edmonton with licence to distrain.

816 Charter of John Patrik son of Ralph Patrik in fee simple with warranty made at Edmonton, 9 December 1315, to William de Causton of a grove in Edmonton which the donor had by hereditary succession after his father, lying between the land called 'Wolfricheslond' in the south and the groves of William de Anesty and the prior of Holy Trinity, London, in the north, extending from the donor's land in the west to the grove called 'Salonelane' in the east.

817 Charter of John Patrik in fee simple with warranty made at Edmonton, 7 September 1343,[1] to William de Causton of an enclosed croft in Edmonton lying in the place called 'Alvene-bregge' between the land formerly of Agnes Hoppere in the east and the highway leading to Winchmore Hill in the west, and 1 rood of land in the field called 'Lovedayeslond'.

1 Vigil of the nativity of the Blessed Virgin Mary, 17 Edward III.

818 Charter of John Patrik in fee simple with warranty made at Edmonton, 5 December 1320, to William de Causton of the land called 'Wolfricheslond' lying between the grove which the said William previously had of the grant of the donor in the north and the highway leading from Enfield wood to London in the south, extending from the feoffee's road leading to his grove in the west to the grove called 'Salonelane' in the east.
Witnesses: William de Anesty, John atte Mersch, William le Vykere, John de Strete, Thomas William and others.
[WAM 319]

819 Charter of John Patrik in fee simple with warranty made at Edmonton, 27 October 1315, to William de Causton of 8d rent arising from the messuage and 2 acres of land which Richard Saleman then held in Edmonton.

820 Part of a fine levied at Westminster, 27 January 1339, whereby John de Chilterne and Maud his wife granted (*reddiderunt*) [*f. 69r*] two tofts, 86 acres of land, 12 acres of pasture, 16 acres of wood, 3s 4d rent in Edmonton to William de Causton in fee simple with warranty.
[*Feet of Fines, Lond. & Middx.* i, 114]

821 Release in perpetuity of John son of John Patryk made at Edmonton, 5 December 1320, to William de Causton of a grove in Edmonton in which the said releasor had enfeoffed the said William.

822 Indenture made at Edmonton, 6 December 1320, whereby John Patrik leased to William de Causton the land called 'Wolfricheslond' from Christmas 1320 for one year on condition that if he did not pay to the said William £6 10s, and if the same William paid to him 10s, then the land would remain to William in fee according to the force of the charter which he had thereof.
Witnesses: William de Anesty, John Marsh, William le Fiker, John de Strate, John de Castell and others.
[WAM 345]

823 Charter of John Patrik in fee simple with warranty made at Edmonton, 18 October 1314, to William de Causton of 3 acres of meadow in Edmonton, of which 2 acres lie between the meadow of Thomas le Rowe in the north and the meadow of the feoffee in the south, and the third lies in 'Chilpolsot' between the meadow of the prior of St John of Clerkenwell in the south and the meadow of Robert North (*Aquilon*) in the north.
Witnesses: William de la Ford, John de la Ford, William de Anesti, Robert de Actone, John Marsh, William le Fiker, John Castle, Ralph Clerk and others.
[WAM 250]

824 Charter of John Patrik in fee simple with warranty made at Edmonton, 16 August 1310, to William de Causton of 2 acres of land in Edmonton in which John Denteyt enfeoffed the donor, lying in the field called 'Bordureshfeldes' between the land formerly of John Bytok to the south and north, and of 5 acres of land lying in the field called 'Russhefeldes' between the land formerly of John Marsh and the water called 'Cherchebrok' which the said John Denteyt had granted to the donor.

825 Letter of sale of John Patrik made at Edmonton, 22 April 1322, to William de Causton of all his chattels in his tenement of Edmonton.

826 Deed of John Patrik made at Edmonton, 4 March 1315, by which the said John bound himself to acquit William de Causton [*f. 69v*] of all arrears of rent from 7 acres of land held of Isabel

Bardolf in which the said John had enfeoffed him.

827 Release in perpetuity by John son of Philip Patrik made at Edmonton, 19 August 1339, to William de Causton of all that tenement which was [formerly] of the said Philip, in which Thomas Horn, chaplain, had enfeoffed the said feoffee, which tenement is situated between the wood of the feoffee and the land formerly of Thomas William in the north, and the wood formerly of Philip Wilghby and the wood of the prioress and nuns of St Helen, London, and the land of Ralph Cowe in the south, extending from Southgate in the west to the field called 'Taillesfeld' in the east.
Witnesses: Edmund Pymme, Thomas de Anesty, Thomas le . . ., John . . .
[WAM 251]

828 Release in perpetuity of John son of John Patrik of Edmonton without warranty, made 20 April 1322 to William de Causton, citizen and mercer of London, of all lands and tenements in Edmonton in which the said releasor had enfeoffed him.
Witnesses: William de Anesty, John atte Mersh, John atte Ford, John atte Castel, Philip Patrik and others.
[WAM 338]

829 Bond of John Patrik made in London, 2 December 1314, to William de Causton of 13s 4d to be paid 2 February following.
[WAM 335, French]

830 Release in perpetuity by John son of John Patrik of Edmonton with warranty made at Edmonton, Friday before the feast of the apostles Philip and James [30 April 1322],[1] to William de Causton of that messuage, land and meadow in Edmonton in which the said John Patrik had enfeoffed the said William.
Witnesses: William de Anesty, John atte Mersh, John atte Forde, John atte Castel, Philip Patrik, Thomas William and others.
[WAM 340]

  1 MS: Friday after the feast of the apostles Philip and James [7 May].

831 Charter of John Patrik in fee simple with warranty made at Edmonton, 25 July 1322, to William de Causton of 7d rent issuing from a croft in Edmonton called 'Bullokespightel' which was formerly of John atte Hegge lying between the field formerly of William atte Forde called 'Jonesfeld Gilberd' in the east and the

highway in the west.
Witnesses: John atte Merssh, William atte Ford, William le Vykere, John Castle, John atte Strete and many others.
[WAM 342]

832 Acquittance of Isabel and Maud daughters of John atte Merssh made in London, [*f. 70r*] 28 May 1327, acknowledging that they had received 4s of William de Causton between Michaelmas last and Michaelmas next for the land called 'Fulbertesfeld', leased to the said William by them in fee at a rent of 8s according to the charter [**740**], and afterwards a moiety of the land was remitted to the said William by charter [**747**].
Witnesses: John de Dalling, John de Aylesham, John de Colewell, Thomas de Cavendissh and Roger Cavendissh, citizens and mercers of London, and others.
[WAM 343]

833 Release in perpetuity by John son of Richard Amys, late fishmonger of London, with warranty made in London to William de Causton of the whole meadow in Edmonton in which Richard Amys, brother of the said John, enfeoffed William.
Witnesses: Richard de Schordich, Richard Denys, Ralph de Blithe, Richard Coterel and William de Mymmes, citizens of London, John Clerk and many others.
[WAM 336]

834 Charter of Roger atte Lofte of Tottenham in fee simple with warranty made at Tottenham, 25 June 1327, to William de Causton of a piece of curtilage in Tottenham which the donor had acquired of John Egepol lying between the land of Robert atte Fen in the north and the garden of the donor in the south, extending from the tenement of the said William in the west, where it measures $1\frac{1}{2}$ perches and 4 feet in width, to the land of Robert atte Fen in the east, where it measures 1 perch and 4 feet in width.

835 Release in perpetuity by John atte Merssh made in London, 11 July 1327, to William de Causton of 12d rent issuing from a tenement in Tottenham contained in charter [**812**].
Witnesses: Robert atte Fen, Hugh Clerk, Anselm de Hatfeld, Roger atte Lofte of Tottenham, John de Aylesham, John de Dalling, Roger de Cavendish, mercers of London, John Clerk and many others.
[WAM 275]

836 Release in perpetuity by Robert one of the sons of John Marsh (*de Marisco*) with warranty made in London, 9 January 1328, to Nicholas his brother of 17s rent and the lands and tenements in Edmonton from which the same rent issued, [which were] previously leased to William de Causton as appears in charter [**738**].
Witnesses: John de Dalling, John de Aylesham and John de Colewell, citizens of London, Robert de Actone, Edmund Pymme, and Peter le Lorimer of Edmonton and others.
[WAM 240]

837 Release in perpetuity by the same Nicholas son of John atte Merssh with warranty made in London on the same day to William de Causton of all his share of the aforesaid lands and tenements.

838 Release in perpetuity by Margaret who was wife of Robert de Acton Squyler without warranty made in London, 19 January 1328, [*f. 70v*] to William de Causton of all the lands and tenements which the said Robert had granted to William in Edmonton.
Witnesses: John de Dalling, John de Aylesham, Thomas de Cavendissh and Roger de Cavendissh, citizens and mercers of London, John Marsh (*de Marisco*), John Castle (*de Castro*), William Viker, John de Strate, Edmund Pymme of Edmonton, John Clerk.
[WAM 260]

839 Letter of John son of John Marsh (*de Marisco*) made at Edmonton, 5 June 1328, containing that he bound himself and his heirs to acquit William de Causton his heirs and assigns against the chief lords of the fee and anyone else regarding all things for which they might be distrained pertaining to the lands and tenements in Edmonton which William had acquired of Nicholas, William and Robert, brothers, and Isabel and Maud, sisters of the said John.
Witnesses: John Castle (*de Castro*), Edmund Pymme, John de Strete, Peter le Lorimer, Thomas Williot, Thomas le Rowe, of Edmonton and others.
[WAM 323]

840 Charter of Nicholas son of John Marsh in fee simple with warranty made in London, 4 December 1328, to William de Causton of all lands and tenements in Edmonton which he had inherited after the death of William Marsh his brother, either by purchase from Robert his brother or from John his father jointly with Robert.

Witnesses: John de Dalling, John de Aylesham, John de Colewell, Roger de Wanlok, citizens and mercers of London, John Castle, John Marsh, John de Strate, Peter Lorimer, Thomas le Rowe of Edmonton, John Clerk and many others.

[WAM 245]

841 Letter of John son of Stephen de Colewell made in London, 27 January 1329, containing that he received from William de Causton, Laurence le Longe and Geoffrey le Palmere, executors of the will of Edith le Palmere, all muniments touching the lands and tenements of the same John in Edmonton and that he remitted (*remisit*) to the same executors all personal actions.

842 Release in perpetuity of Joan daughter of Adam Musters, called le Plastrer, of London and Edith Basyng his wife with warranty made in London, 28 March 1329, to William de Causton of the grove calle 'Gunnildesheg' in Edmonton in which Reginald Fox enfeoffed William and which the said Adam and Edith formerly acquired jointly from Robert de Lodine, clerk.

843 Indenture made at Edmonton, 11 December 1315, affirming that if John Patrik pay to William de Causton £10 at Christmas one year hence, a grove in Edmonton which descended to the said John after the death of Ralph his father, and which the same John granted to William according to his charter, will revert to the said John notwithstanding the said charter, and William de Causton will for the said term receive from the grove 2,000 faggots of the better sort (*de melioribus*) called 'baueyn', otherwise it will remain to the said William in fee.

Witnesses: William atte Ford, John atte Ford, William de Anesty, Robert de Acton, John atte Mersch, William le Vykere, John de la Strate and others.

[WAM 337]

844 [*f. 71r*] Indenture made at Edmonton, 6 December 1320, by which John Patryk leased to William de Causton the land called 'Wolfrichlond' lying between the grove of the said William in the north and the highway leading from Enfield wood towards London in the south, to be held for one year on condition that if the lessor pay to the lessee £6 10s the lessee's interest will cease, but if not the lessee may pay to the lessor 10s and hold that land in fee according to the charter which he has thereof.

Witnesses: William de Anesti, John Marsh, William le Fikere, John ate Strate, John Castle and others.
[WAM 262]

845 Charter of Philip Patrik son of Ralph Patryk in fee simple with warranty made at Edmonton, 6 April 1322, to William de Causton of ½ mark rent to be received by him and his heirs in perpetuity of all the donor's lands and tenements in Edmonton without licence to distrain.
Witnesses: William de Anesty, John atte Mersh, John atte Ford, John atte Castel, John Patrik, Thomas William and others.
[WAM 328]

846 Charter of John Patrik in fee simple with warranty made at Edmonton, 23 April 1322, to William de Causton of all the donor's tenement and land in Edmonton, except a plot of land recently enclosed, lying between the highway called 'Chirchewey' and the said messuage.
Witnesses: [William] de Anesty, John atte Mersh, John atte Ford, John atte Castel, Philip Patrik, Thomas William and others.
[WAM 333]

847 Release in perpetuity by John son and heir of John Patryk without warranty made in Edmonton, 8 November 1316, to William Causton in another grove which the said John his father leased to William.
Witnesses: William atte Forde, John atte Forde, John atte Merssh, John atte Castel, John atte Strete, Roger atte Slo and others.
[WAM 330]

848 Charter of Richard son of John Patrik of Edmonton in fee simple with warranty made in London, 3 September 1316, to William de Causton of a house with a curtilage situated in Edmonton between the land of John le Rede in the west and the messuage of Robert le Webbe in the east, and of one croft of land and wood in the same vill between the land and grove of the feoffee in the west and the land of John le Rede in the east, extending from the road leading to 'Aremholte'[1] in the north to the wood of the nuns of Clerkenwell in the south.
Witnesses: Richard de Wylehale, John Marsh, John Castle, William le Fiker, Edmund Pymme, John ate Strate and others.
[WAM 331]

1 MS: 'Bremholte'.

849 Release in perpetuity by John Patrik of Edmonton without warranty made at Edmonton, 4 December 1314, to William de Causton of all lands and tenements in which he had enfeoffed the said William, and which he had previously acquired of John Denteyt.

Witnesses: William atte Ford, John atte Ford, John atte Mersch, John de la Strete, John [Gisors] and others.

[WAM 344]

850 Release in perpetuity by John son of John Patrik of Edmonton without warranty made at Edmonton, 12 December 1320, to William de Causton of a piece of land in Edmonton called 'Wolfricheslond' which the said John Patrik his father formerly granted to the said William.

851 Charter of John son of Ralph Patrik of Edmonton in fee simple with warranty made at Edmonton, 6 April 1322, to William de Causton of all the donor's land in Edmonton except one messuage and a plot of enclosed land lying between the road called 'Cherchewey' and the said messuage.

Witnesses: William de Anesty, John atte Mersh, John atte Ford, John atte Castel, Philip P[atrik], Thomas William.

[WAM 241]

852 Indenture made at Edmonton, 11 December 1315, whereby if John Patrik of Edmonton pay to William de Causton £10 at Christmas 1316 at his house in London henceforth a grove in Edmonton which descended to the said John after the death of Ralph his father will revert to him, notwithstanding the charter William has thereof.

853 Charter of William de la Forde in fee simple with warranty without date made to William de Causton, citizen and mercer of London, of ½ acre of land in Edmonton, lying in the field called Colegrove between the land of the said William in the east and the land of William de Anesty in the west, extending from the land called 'Hokfeld' in the south to the land of Richard Spyrk in the north, to be held of the chief lords of the fee by ½d pa.

Witnesses: John atte Forth, Robert de Acton, John atte Merssch, John atte Castel, John ate Strate, William le Fikere, William Clerk and others.

[Date: *temp*. Edward II.]

[WAM 322]

854 Duplicate charter of William de la Forde in fee simple with warranty made at Edmonton, 2 May 1312, to the said William de Causton of 9 acres 1 rood of land in Edmonton, of which one piece lies in the field called 'Langhegg' between the land of Robert de Anesty and the land formerly of Richard le Roche, extending from the land of the said Richard to the road leading from 'Stynkendelonde' to 'Tothenhamstrate', another lies between the land of Roger le Kyng and the land of Thomas Wiliot extending from the land of the said Richard le Roche to 'le Grenedich', the third piece lies between the land of the said Roger le Kyng and the land formerly of Diamand de Anesty extending from the land of the said Diamand to 'la Grenedich', the fourth lies between the land formerly of the said Diamand and the donor's land extending from the land formerly of Walter[1] to the land formerly of the said Diamand, the fifth piece lies between the land of William de Anesty on either side extending from the donor's land to the land of William Laurence, the sixth lies between the land of the prior of Holy Trinity, London, and the land of Thomas Roghe extending from the land of the said prior to the land of Roger Aldred, and the seventh [f. 72r] between the land of Thomas Wilyet on either side extending from a pasture, also granted by the same charter, to 'le Fordestrate', and of $1\frac{1}{2}$ acres $1\frac{1}{2}$ roods of pasture lying between the water called 'Smalebreggewater' and the land formerly of William Pymme, extending [from] the land of the said Thomas Wilyet to the land formerly of William Pymme.
Witnesses: John de la Ford, John Marsh, Gilbert de Actone, Ralph le Clerk, John Castle, Robert de Anesty, Edmund Pymme, John FitzJohn, John Tebaud of Tottenham, Roger de Solio, Hugh de Heydene, clerk, and others.
[WAM 257, 329]

1 Surname omitted.

855 A deed of William de la Forde made at Edmonton, 6 May 1312, containing that the said William is held to acquit and defend the land contained in the previous charter in return for payment by William de Causton of 1d *pa* to the chief lords of the fees.
Witnesses: John de la Forde [others missing].
[WAM 326, partly damaged]

856 Charter of John son of William de la Forde in fee simple with warranty made at Edmonton, 7 June 1312, to William de Causton of $\frac{1}{2}$ acre of meadow lying between the meadow of William, the donor's brother, in the south and the meadow of Robert del Fen in the north, extending from the east to the River Lea.

Witnesses: John atte Merssh, William Vikere, Robert de Actone, Ralph called 'le Clerk', William de Anesty, John Castle (*de Castello*), Ranulph Clerk and others.

[WAM 256]

857 Charter of the said John de la Forde in fee simple with warranty made at Edmonton, 23 July 1311, to William de Causton of 1 acre of meadow in Edmonton lying between the meadow of the prioress of Clerkenwell in the north and the meadow formerly of Reginald Pymme in the south, extending from the River Lea in the east to the meadow formerly of Philip de Wilghby, to be held by paying each year to the chief lords, John de la Forde his heirs and assigns, one red rose.

Witnesses: William de la Ford, Robert de Actone, Richard le Clerk of Edmonton, William de Anesty, John son of John atte Merssh, William Vikere, John Gysors, John atte Strete, Richard Clerk and others.

[WAM 316]

858 Charter of William atte Forde in fee simple with warranty made at Edmonton, 25 August 1312, to William de Causton of 1 acre of meadow in Edmonton marsh lying between the meadow of the feoffee in the south and the meadow of the hospital of St John in the north, extending from the River Lea in the east to the meadow called 'Chipolshot' in the west.

Witnesses: John atte Merssh, Robert de Actone, William le Vikere, John atte Strate, John atte Forde, Roger atte Sloth, Ralph Clerk and others.

[WAM 327]

859 Charter of John de Forde in fee simple with warranty made at Edmonton, 9 December 1313, to William de Causton of ½ acre in Edmonton marsh lying between the meadow of William atte Forde in the south and the meadow of Robert atte Forde in the north, extending from the land of John Marsh in the west to the meadow called 'le Roundemed' in the east.

Witnesses: William de Ford, William de Anesty, Robert de Actone, John Marsh, William le Fyker, John Castle, Edmund Pymme, Thomas le Rowe, John de Strate, William le Keu, John de Notingham and many others.

[WAM 242]

860 [*f. 72v*] Indenture made at Tottenham, 29 April 1323, whereby if John atte Merssh pay to William de Causton 15s in his house in the parish of St Matthew Friday Street, London, on 24 August next ½ acre of meadow will revert to the said John and a charter granting the meadow in fee simple to the said William will be held null, 5s having been paid by William to John to complete the above enfeoffment.

Witnesses: John FitzJohn, Robert atte Fen, Anselm de Hatfeld, Roger atte Lofte, John le Notiere, Hugh de Heyden and others. [WAM 279]

861 Charter of John Chilterne of co. Hertford in fee simple with warranty made at Edmonton, 3 March 1338, to William de Causton of all the lands and tenements once held by William Laurence in Edmonton which John atte Noke of Hanslope [Bucks.] and Joan his wife had granted to the donor.

Witnesses: John Marsh, Edmund Pymme, Thomas de Anesty, John de Strate, Thomas le Rowe, William le Keu, John de Notingham and others. [WAM 317]

862 Charter of John de Chilterne in fee simple with warranty made at Edmonton, 3 March 1338, to William de Causton of all the lands and tenements which descended to the donor by inheritance after the death of Adam de Chilterne his uncle and John, the son of the said Adam, in Edmonton, in which Robert de Anesty had once enfeoffed the said Adam and Helen his wife as appears below [**878**].

Witnesses: John Marsh, John Castle, Edmund Pymme, Thomas le Rowe, John de Strate, William le Keu, John de Notingham, and many others. [WAM 243]

863 Letter of John de Chilterne made on the same day whereby he appointed Edmund de Radclif his attorney to deliver seisin according to the said charter. [WAM 346]

864 Bond of John de Chilterne made in London, 3 March 1338, to William de Causton of £100 to be paid to the said William or his attorney in the tenement which he inhabits in the parish of St Pancras, London, at midsummer next. [WAM 332]

865 Indenture made in London, 4 March 1338, by which if the said
William de Causton and his heirs hold all the aforesaid tenements
according to the form of the charter [**862**] without hindrance
by the said John [Chilterne] or his heirs, and are discharged of
all statutes and recognizances, and the said John and his heirs
give warranty for the same, the bond will be held null.
[WAM 259]

866 Release in perpetuity by John [Chilterne] with warranty made
at Edmonton, 8 March 1338, to William de Causton of all the
aforesaid lands and tenements.
Witnesses: John Marsh, John Castle, Edmund Pymme, John atte
Strete of Edmonton, Roger atte Lofte, Ralph Dulay, John le
Keu, John le Notiere, John de Rudham, John Abraham, clerk,
of Tottenham and others.
[WAM 285]

867 Memorandum that the said John Chilterne had married Maud
who was kinswoman and heir to William atte Forde, of whom
mention has been made before, that is, granddaughter of the
William who purchased all the lands as is said above, and John
and Maud alienated all their lands which had descended to [*f.
73r*] Maud to William de Causton as will now appear.

868 Duplicate charter of John de Chilterne and Maud his wife in
fee simple with warranty made at Edmonton, 27 August 1338,
to William de Causton of 80 acres of land lying in Edmonton
in divers parcels in the fields called 'Honeyfeld' in Old Ford,
'Longheg', 'Hokfeld', 'Colgrove', 'Gilbertsfeld', 'Gilbertshawe',
'Baselifeld', 'Baselyhawe', in two crofts lying between the pasture
called 'Mannemedes' on the one side and the Hyde on the other,
and of all their land lying in the Hyde, except 2 pieces of land
called 'Claricedoles', and of all their land lying in 'Hokfeld', and
of 3 groves called 'Colegrave', 'Juddesgrave' and 'Gilbertsgrave',
and of a piece of land next to the field called 'le Honifeld' which
Robert de Anesty held, and of another piece of land called 'le
Tulvereshouses Hawe' lying between the highway in the north
and the land of the said William and the stream called 'Medesenge' in the south, and of all the pasture called 'Mawenemedes',
and of a piece of land lying in a field called 'Dedesapelton', with
all innings and appurtenances.
Witnesses: John Marsh, Edmund Pymme, Thomas de Anesty,
John de Strate, Thomas le Rowe, William le Keu, John de

Notingham and others.
[WAM 258, 306]

869 Another charter of John de Chilterne and Maud made on the same day to the aforesaid William of the aforesaid piece of land called 'Doddesappelton' in Edmonton.
Witnesses: Edmund Pymme, John atte ..., Thomas de Anesty, Thomas Rowe and others.
[WAM 306*, badly damaged]

870 Letter of the same John and Maud made on the same day appointing Edmund de Radclif to deliver seisin according to the aforesaid charter.
[WAM 163]

871 Duplicate release in perpetuity by John de Chilterne and Maud his wife with warranty made at Edmonton, 30 August 1338, to the said William de Causton of all the said lands and tenements and of all rents which the same William was accustomed to pay for them.
Witnesses: John Marsh, Edmund Pymme, Thomas de Anesty, John de Strate, Thomas le Rowe, William le Keu, John de Notingham and many others.
[WAM 174, 201]

872 Charter of the same John de Chilterne and Maud in fee simple with warranty at Edmonton, 17 November 1341, to the said Wiliam de Causton of all their lands and tenements, rents and services in Edmonton.
Witnesses: John de Willehale, John Marsh, John Castle, William le Vikere, William Pymme, William Cook (*Coco*), William le Smith, Richard atte Berwe, John Stoune, Henry Willyot and many others.
[WAM 204]

873 [*f. 73v*] Letter of the same of John and Maud made on the same day with warranty selling to William de Causton all their chattels in Edmonton.
[WAM 200]

874 Letter of the same John son of Edmund de Chilterne and Maud, of the same date, appointing Willam de Hales, citizen and armourer of London, or Edmund de Radclif their attorneys to

deliver seisin of the same tenements by form of the same charter.
[WAM 161]

875 Release in perpetuity by John de Chilterne and Maud his wife,
daughter of William atte Ford junior and heir of William atte
Ford senior her grandfather, with warranty made in London, 16
February 1344, to William de Causton of all his lands and
tenements in Edmonton and in the parish of Barnet in Middlesex,
and of the reversion of 1 acre of meadow which Helen who was
wife of Anselm de Totenham holds for life.
[WAM 197]

876 Bond of John de Chilterne made in London, 27 August 1338, to
William de Causton of £200 to be paid at Christmas next.

877 Indenture made in London, 29 August 1338, whereby if William
de Causton holds for himself and his heirs in perpetuity the lands
and tenements granted to him by the charters of John de
Chilterne and Maud his wife in Edmonton without hindrance of
the donors or their heirs, and [the lands] are kept without loss
through warranties and the tenements are discharged of all
statutes and recognizances, the aforesaid bond will be held null.

878 Part of a fine levied at Westminster, 8 July 1331, whereby Adam
de Chilterne and Helen his wife acknowledged a messuage, 40
acres of land, 1 acre of meadow, 4 acres of pasture, 2 acres of
wood, 20s rent with appurtenances in Edmonton to be the right
of Robert de Anesty as those which he had of their gift, and for
which recognizance the same Robert granted the aforesaid
tenements to the same Adam and Helen in fee tail, remaining
in default of issue to the right heirs of the same Adam without
warranty.
[WAM 193]
[*Feet of Fines, Lond. & Middx.* i, 109]

879 And memorandum that the said Adam and Helen died without
heirs of their bodies, for which reason the tenements remained
to John de Chilterne, kinsman and heir of the said Adam, who
then granted the same tenements to William de Causton as
appears above.

880 Letter of the same John de Chilterne made in London, 12
November 1341, containing [f. 74r] that he had received of
William de Causton 200 marks with which to trade to the profit
of the said William and to render account by payment with

interest at William's house in London at Christmas next.

881 Similiar letter of the same John de Chilterne made at Edmonton on the same day.

882 Bond of the same John de Chilterne made in London, 14 November 1341, to William de Causton of 200 marks to be paid at Christmas next.
[WAM 218]

883 Duplicate part of a fine levied at York, 21 June 1338, whereby John atte Noke of Hanslope and Joan his wife and John de Chilterne granted one messuage, 40 acres of land, 1 acre of meadow, 4 acres of pasture, 2 acres of wood and 20s rent in Edmonton to William de Causton in fee simple with warranty for themselves and the heirs of the same John de Chilterne. And for this fine the said William paid 100 marks.
[WAM 222, 222*]
[*Feet of Fines, Lond. & Middx.* i, 114]

884 Part of a fine levied at Westminster, 27 January 1339, whereby John de Chilterne and Maud his wife granted 2 tofts, 86 acres of land, 12 acres of pasture, 16 acres of wood, 3s 4d rent in Edmonton to William de Causton in fee simple with warranty for themselves and the heirs of the same John. And for this fine the said William paid 20 marks.
[WAM 188]
[*Feet of Fines, Lond. & Middx.* i, 114]

885 Indenture made at Edmonton, 13 November 1345, whereby William de Causton leased to Thomas Golde and Christine his wife, Edmund and Agnes their children, an enclosed piece of garden in Edmonton containing 1 rood and 1 daywork, lying between the donor's land in the east and the land of Geoffrey de Anesty in the west and extending from the donor's land in the north and the highway in the south, to be held for their lives at a rent of 2s *pa.*
Witnesses: William de Pymme, Thomas le Rowe, William le Lorimer, Nicholas Reyner, Henry le Lorimer and many others.
[WAM 196]

886 Indenture of Thomas William of Edmonton made in the same place, 17 December 1329, leasing to William de Causton a piece of grove lying between the grove of the same William and

Enfield wood in the north [*f. 74v*] and the land of the prior of
Holy Trinity, London, in the south and west, and the donor's
land in the east, to be held henceforth for 10 years and longer
in fee simple unless the said Thomas pay to him at the end of
the 10 years 40s at his home in London.
[WAM 202]

887 Charter of Geoffrey son of Roger le Kyng of Tottenham in fee
simple with warranty made at Edmonton, 14 December 1329, to
William de Causton of 1 acre of land in Edmonton lying in
'Langheg' between the land of Robert de Anesty to the south
and north and extending from the land of Richard Wyrehale in
the west to the land of Richard Basse in the east.
Witnesses: John Marsh, John Castle (*de Castro*), John atte Strate,
Edmund Welyot, Edmund Pymme, Thomas le Rouwe, Peter le
Lorymer and others.
[WAM 225]

888 Indenture made at Edmonton on the same day containing that
if the said Geoffrey pay to the said William 2 marks¹ in his home
in the parish of St Matthew Friday Street, London, at the end
of 4 years then the aforesaid land will revert to Geoffrey and
the above charter will be cancelled.
[WAM 230]

  1 MS: 4 marks.

889 Another part part of the same indenture.

890 Charter of Thomas William of Edmonton in fee simple with
warranty made at Edmonton, 17 December 1329, to William de
Causton of that piece of grove in Edmonton contained in the
above indenture [**886**].
Witnesses: Richard de Wylehale, John Marsh, John Castle,
William le Vikere, Edmund Pymme, Edmund Wylioht, John atte
Strate, ..., and many others.
[WAM 234]

891 Charter of Henry Goldynd in fee simple with warranty made at
Edmonton, 31 January 1330, to William de Causton of one croft
of land called 'Cockesfeld' in Edmonton lying between the
highway leading from 'Parkcrouche' to Enfield wood in the north
and the land formerly of William atte Forde in the south,
extending from the land of the said William atte Forde and John

atte Strate in the east to the land of William Arnold in the west. *Witnesses*: John Marsh, John Castle, William le Vikere, John atte Strate, Edmund Pymme, Edmund Weloyot, John Patrik and others.
[WAM 156]

892 Charter of William de Fourneys, citizen and pepperer of London, in fee simple with warranty made at Edmonton, 17 January 1331, to William de Causton of 4 acres of land in Edmonton, of which 3 acres lie in 'Barfeld' between the land of Richard Gisors in the south and the land of Robert Gulle in the north, extending from the land of John atte Strate in the west to the land of the donor, William Smith (*Fabri*) and Alice Prat in the east, and the fourth acre lies in the same field between the highway called 'Berfeldeslane' in the north and the land of Robert Gulle in the south, extending from the land of John atte Strate in the west to the land of Alice Prat in the east.
Witnesses: John Marsh, John Castle, William le Vikere, John atte Strate, Edmund Pymme, Edmund Welyot, Peter le Lorymer and others.
[WAM 237]

893 [*f. 75r*] Charter of Robert Gulle in fee simple with warranty made at Edmonton, 18 January 1331, to William de Causton of 1 acre of land in Edmonton in the field called 'Berfeld' between the land of the said William on either side to the south and north, extending from the land of John atte Strate in the west to the land of Alice Prat in the east.

894 Charter of Thomas William in fee simple with warranty made at Edmonton, 1 February 1331, to William de Causton of the whole of the donor's land and wood in Edmonton lying between Enfield wood and the grove of the feoffee, and the land formerly of William Patrik in the north and the land of the prior of Holy Trinity, London, in the south, extending from the grove of John Skyn, which he acquired of the same donor, in the east to the land of the said prior in the west.
Witnesses: John Marsh, Edmund Pymme, John Patrik, John le Reed, John Vincent, John Skin, and many others.
[WAM 199]

895 Letter of the same Thomas William made at Edmonton on the same day by which he is bound to William de Causton in 100s to be paid at midsummer next, to which payment he binds himself, his heirs and executors.

Witnesses: John Marsh (*du Mareis*), Edmund Pymme, Peter le Lorimer, John Patrik, John le Reed, John Vincent, and John Skyn.

[WAM 221, French]

896 Schedule attached to the same letter that if the said William de Causton and his heirs peacefully hold the land and wood contained in the charter [**894**] without rent or other impediment the said letter will be annulled.

[WAM 227]

897 Charter of Thomas William and Nicholas his son in fee simple with warranty made at Edmonton, 21 April 1331, to William de Causton of 3s rent to be received from all the donor's lands and tenements in Edmonton situated between the tenement of Richard atte Wode and Margery his wife in the east and the tenement of Godard¹ atte Wodegate in the west, extending from the land of Richard atte Wod in the north and the highway in the south, with licence to distrain.

Witnesses: John Marsh, John Castle, Edmund Pymme, Edmund Williot, John Patrik, John Vincent and John Skyn, John Clerk and many others.

[WAM 216]

    1 MS:Godefrid.

898 Charter of John de Notyngham and Joan his wife in fee simple with warranty made at Edmonton, 7 June 1331, to William de Causton of one croft of land called 'Aldewyk' lying between the land of William le Kene in the west and the land of Richard Spirk and John Assherugg in the east, and of one piece of land lying in Edmonton between the lane leading from the house of John Gissors to the water called Medesenge in the west and the land of William le Keu in the east, extending from the highway of 'Blakemanneswell' to 'Wiklane' in the north to the land formerly of William de Anesty in the south.

899 [*f. 75v*] Letter of John le Venour made at Edmonton, 25 May 1331, notifying that he received of William Causton £8 to trade with to the profit of the said William until 1 November following, on which day he promised to repay the said £8 with interest to the same William.

[WAM 235, French]

900 Indenture made in London, 26 May 1331, affirming that if William de Causton peacefully hold a pasture called 'Risshefeldes' in Edmonton lying between the field called 'Berghfeld' in the north and the pasture of John atte Merssh and the said William de Causton in the south, extending from the highway in the east to the pasture of the prior of Holy Trinity, London, and of the same William in the west, leased to him by John le Venour for 3 years, the said letter of account [of £8] will be held null.
Witnesses: John de Dalling, John de Aylesham, Nicholas atte Merssh, citizens and mercers of London, John de Louthe, clerk, and others.
[WAM 212, French]

901 Letter of John son of William le Venour made in London, 31 October 1331, notifying that he had received from William de Causton £10 to trade with to the profit of the said William until 29 September following, and then to repay to the said William the same £10 with the profit accruing under bond of distraint of goods.
Witnesses: Nicholas Marsh (*de Marisco*), Theobald de Caustone, Roger de Cavendish, and Edmund de Hemnale, citizens of London, John de Luda, clerk, and others.
[WAM 231]

902 Indenture of John le Venour made in London, 1 November 1331, leasing to William de Causton the pasture 'Russhefeld' for 6 years.
Witnesses: Nicholas Marsh, Theobald de Causton, Roger de Cavendissh and Edmund Hemenhale, citizens of London, John Castle, John Marsh, and Edmund Pymme of Edmonton, John Clerk and others.
[WAM 192]

903 Indenture of the same John le Venour made in London, 1 November 1331, leasing to the same William de Causton 17 acres of meadow called 'le Middelmerssh' in Edmonton lying in the marsh between the meadow of lord de Say in the south and the meadow of Roger de Depham in the north, extending from the meadows of John de Pulteneye and the master of the St John's hospital in the east to the tenement of John le Venour in the west, to be held for 4 years.

904 Another indenture of the same John made on the same day leasing the same meadow to the same William for 2 years.

Witnesses: Nicholas Marsh, Theobald de Caustone, Roger de Cavendish, Edmund de Hemnale, citizens of London, John Castle, John Marsh, Edmund Pymme of Edmonton, John Clerk and others.
[WAM 179]

905 Charter of John Assherugge, citizen and tanner of London, in fee simple with warranty made at Edmonton, 13 October 1331, to William de Causton of 2 crofts containing 6 acres of land in Edmonton lying between the grove of Edmund Pymme in the south and the highway leading to 'Blakemaneswell' in the north, extending from the highway called 'le Wykelane' in the east and the land of the feoffee in the west.
Witnesses: John Marsh, John Castle, Edmund Pymme, William le Keu, Edmund Williot, John de Notingham, ..., and others.
[WAM 166]

906 [*f. 76r*] Letter of attorney of the same John de Assherugge made on the same day to Richard Spyrk to deliver seisin to William de Causton of the aforesaid crofts by the said charter.
[WAM 194]

907 Release in perpetuity by Richard Spyrk without warranty made at Edmonton, 16 October 1331, to William de Causton of the aforesaid crofts in which John de Assheregge had enfeoffed the same William.
[WAM 172]

908 Release in perpetuity by Avice[1], who was the wife of John de Assheregge, with warranty on her part only, made in London, 9 December 1331, to William de Causton of the said crofts.
Witnesses: John de Dalling, John de A[ile]sham, Nicholas Marsh, John de Brecheford, Theobald de Causton, citizens of London, John Luda, clerk.
[WAM 198]

> 1 MS: Amice.

909 Charter of the same Avice[1] in fee simple with warranty made at Edmonton, 11 January 1332, to William de Causton of 1½ acres of meadow which were formerly of Beatrice Spirk in Edmonton lying between the meadow of Thomas Wiliot in the north and the meadow of John Godwyne in the south, extending from the meadow of William Pykard in the east to the meadow of Richard

Swonyld, which Richard Spirk had formerly granted to her and her husband.

Witnesses: John Marsh, John Castle, John de Strate, Edmund Pymme, Edmund Wyliot, William le Keu, Peter le Lorimer and others.

[WAM 203]

1 MS: Amice.

910 Letter of attorney of the same Avice made in London on the same day to Richard Spyrk to deliver seisin to the said William de Causton of the aforesaid meadow.

[WAM 186]

911 Charter of John le Venour in fee simple with warranty made at Edmonton, 20 January 1332, to William de Causton of one grove called 'Salenelane' lying in Edmonton between the wood of lord de Say in the east and the wood of the said William in the west, and extending from his grove in the north to the highway in the south.

Witnesses: John Marsh, John Castle, John de Strate, Edmund Pymme, Adam de Chilterne, John Vincent, John Patrik, John Clerk and others.

[WAM 195]

912 Indenture made at Edmonton, 13 January 1332, containing that if Avice who was wife of John Asshregge should pay to William de Causton 60s on 29 September following at his home in the parish of St Matthew Friday Street, London, then 1½ acres of meadow in Edmonton granted to the said William by charter [**909**] will revert to the same Avice, and the charter made will be held null.

Witnesses: John Marsh, [Edmund] Pymme, Edmund Wyliot, [others illegible].

[WAM 190, badly damaged]

913 Release in perpetuity by Isabel and Maud daughters of John Marsh with warranty made in London, 10 March 1332, to William de Causton of 16 acres of land leased to the same William by them as appears above [**740**].

Witnesses: Richard Denys and John de Brichesford, goldsmiths, John Dalling junior, Thomas de Cavendish, William de Elsing junior, John de Aylesham, Nicholas de Causton, Robert de Hakebourne, mercers, citizens of London, John de Luda, clerk,

and others.
[WAM 210]

914 [*f. 76v*] Release in perpetuity by Geoffrey son of Roger le Kyng of Tottenham with warranty made in London, 13 March 1332, to William de Causton of 1 acre of land in Edmonton in which the same Geoffrey enfeoffed William lying in 'Langehegg' between the land of Robert de Anesty to the north and south, extending from the land of the said Robert in the west to the land of John son of Walter Basse in the east, and descending to Geoffrey after the death of the said Roger.
Witnesses: Richard Denys and John de Bricheford, goldsmiths, John de Dalling, junior, Thomas de Cavendish, William de Elsing, junior, John de Aylesham, Nicholas de Causton and Robert de Hakebourn, citizens and mercers of London, John de Luda, clerk.
[WAM 158]

915 Release in perpetuity by John son of John Somery of Enfield with warranty, 6 April 1332, to William de Causton of a piece of meadow in Enfield containing $1\frac{1}{2}$ acres of land lying between the meadow of John Heroun in the north and the meadow of Richard Durant in the south, extending from the meadow of the said Richard in the west to the ditch called 'Markedich' in the east, in which the said father and John his son enfeoffed William.

916 Charter of Maud who was the wife of William de Anesty with warranty made at Edmonton, 4 May 1332, granting to William de Causton one piece of meadow called 'Roundemade' lying in Edmonton marsh between the meadow of the prior of Holy Trinity, London, in the north and the meadow of William Causton in the south, and extending from the meadow of William le Vikere in the east to the meadows of William de Forde, William Causton and Edmund Pymme in the west, to be held for the term of the life of the said Maud.
Witnesses: John Marsh, John Castle (*de Castello*), John de Strate, Edmund Pymme, Peter le Lorimer, Richard Spirk of Edmonton, John Clerk and others.
[WAM 159]

917 Release in perpetuity by Thomas son of William de Anesty with warranty made at Edmonton, 6 May 1332, to William de Causton of the above meadow whose reversion had previously belonged to the said Thomas.

Witnesses: John Marsh, John Castle, John de Strate, Edmund Pymme, Peter le Lorimer, and Richard Spirk of Edmonton, John Clerk and others.
[WAM 209]

918 Release in perpetuity by Constance who was the wife of William Reyner of Edmonton without warranty made, 27 January 1333, to William de Causton of all lands and tenements in Edmonton which were of the said William her husband.

919 Letter of Thomas Squyler of Edmonton made in London, 31 March 1333, acknowledging that he had received from William de Causton 10 marks with which to trade to the profit of the said William until 29 September following, and that he should then repay the said 10 marks with the profit accruing.

920 [*f. 77r*] Letter of John le Venour made in London, 27 March 1333, acknowledging that he had received from William de Causton £20 with which to trade to the profit of the said William until 29 September next, when he will pay to the said William the said £20 with the interest accruing.

921 Charter of Thomas Squiler,[1] son of Robert Squiler,[2] in fee simple with warranty made at Edmonton, 1 June 1333, to William de Causton of 2 acres of meadow in Edmonton marsh lying between the meadow of William de Causton in the south and the meadow of John and William Godwyn in the north, extending from the meadow of Mary Box and Richard Sabarn in the east to the meadow of William Vikere in the west.
Witnesses: John Marsh, John Castle, John de Strate, Edmund Pymme, Edmund Williot, John Clerk and others.
[WAM 207]

1 MS: Swyler.
2 MS: Sqyler

922 Charter of Thomas Squyler of Edmonton in fee simple with warranty made at Edmonton, 30 March 1333, to William Causton of $1\frac{1}{2}$ acres of pasture lying in Edmonton between the pasture called 'Melchimor' in the west and the pasture of Richard Gulle in the east, extending from the pasture of Adam Yarald in the north to 'Pymore lane' in the the south.
Witnesses: John atte Merssh, John Castle, William le Vikere, John atte Strate, Edmund Pymme, Edmund Welyot, William son of

John atte Strate, and others.
[WAM 224]

923 Indenture made at Edmonton, 2 June [1333], containing that if Thomas Squyler pay to William de Causton 100s in his house in the parish of St Pancras, near Soper Lane, London, before 15 May following the aforesaid 2 acres of land will revert to the said Thomas and the aforesaid charter [**921**] will be annulled. *Witnesses*: John Marsh, John Castle, John de Strate, Edmund Pymme and Edmund Williot, John Clerk and others.
[WAM 219]

924 Another part of the same indenture.
[WAM 206]

925 Release in perpetuity of the same Thomas son of Robert Squiler with warranty made in London, 5 October 1333, to William de Causton of the same 2 acres of meadow in which he had previously enfeoffed William.

926 Letter of Thomas son of Robert Squyler of Edmonton made in London, 5 October 1333, containing that he had received of William de Causton £10 with which to trade until 1 November following, when he will pay to the same William the said £10 with interest accruing.
[WAM 233]

927 [*f. 77v*] Letter of John le Venour of Edmonton made in London, 8 August 1334, containing that he had received of William de Causton £40 with which to trade until 29 September the following year when he will repay the said £40 with interest accruing.

928 Indenture made at Edmonton, 9 August 1334, containing that if John le Venour pay to William de Causton 24 marks on 29 September for 7 years that the said William might hold the field called 'Reshfeld'[1] with grazing-land called 'le Brache' in Edmonton in which he had enfeoffed William by charter, thenceforth William for his life and his executors for 15 years thereafter will pay to the said John 16s *pa*. And if the said John does not pay the said 24 marks, then William de Causton may hold the said tenement in fee simple without any rent.
Witnesses: John Marsh, John Castle, John de Strete, Robert de Anesty, Adam de Chilterne, Edmund Pymme, Thomas le Rowe

and others.
[WAM 187]

1 MS: 'Asshefeld'.

929 Charter of John le Venour of Edmonton in fee simple with warranty made at Edmonton, 9 August 1334, to William de Causton of the field called 'Rissefeld' with grazing-land called 'le Breche' in Edmonton lying between the field called 'le Berefeld' in the north and the field of John Marsh (*de Marisco*) called 'Caumberleynesfeld' in the south, extending from the highway to the land of the said William in the east and that of the prior of Holy Trinity, London, in the west.
Witnesses: John Marsh, John Castle, John de Strete, Robert de Anesti, Adam de Chiltren, Edmund Pymme, Thomas le Rowe and others.
[WAM 215]

930 Another part of the indenture [?**928**].

931 Charter of Richard Salman in fee simple with warranty made at Edmonton, 18 December 1334, to William de Causton of the whole part of the donor's hedge in a croft called 'Desiree' in Edmonton, and of $1\frac{1}{2}$ selions of the donor's land lying on the eastern side of the said hedge.
Witnesses: John Marsh, John de Strate, William Dalman, Richard Arnold, and others.
[WAM 232]

932 Charter of Edmund Wiliot of Edmonton in fee simple with warranty made at Edmonton, 11 August 1335, to William de Causton of 3 acres of meadow in Edmonton marsh between the meadow of Sir Henry de Beaumont (*Bello Monte*) in the north and the meadow of the feoffee in the south extending from the meadow of John de Pulteneye in the east to the meadow of John Wilehale in the west.
Witnesses: John de Williehale, John Marsh, John Castle, John de Strate, Edmund Pymme, Thomas le Rowe, William le Lorimer and others.
[WAM 238]

933 [*f. 78r*] Letter of the same Edmund Wiliot made in London, 19 August 1335, containing that he had received of William de Causton £112 with which to trade to the profit of the said

William until 29 September following, when he will pay to the said William the said £112 with interest accruing.

934 Release in perpetuity by the same Edmund Wiliot with warranty made in London, 20 August 1335, to William de Causton of the whole messuage with two adjacent crofts and of all lands lying in the fields of 'Langheg', 'Colegrove', the Hyde, 'Fordecroft', 'Bramblecroft', and 'Hokfeld' in Edmonton and of 3 acres of meadow in Edmonton marsh in which the same Edmund had enfeoffed William on divers occasions.
Witnesses: [as **935**.]
[WAM 176]

935 Release in perpetuity by Thomas Wiliot of South Mimms, father of the said Edmund, without warranty made in London, 20 August 1335, to William de Causton of all the aforesaid lands and tenements.
Witnesses: John de Dalling, John de Aylesham, Thomas Worstede, Nicholas of Greenwich (*de Grenwico*), Theobald de Caustone, Nicholas Marsh (*de Marisco*), Thomas de Cavenidish, John de Gartone, citizens of London, John de Luda, clerk.
[WAM 182]

936 Another release in perpetuity by the same Thomas without warranty made in London, 21 August 1335, to William de Causton of all the aforesaid lands and tenements.
Witnesses: John de Dalling, John de Aylesham, Nicholas Marsh, John de Garton, Theobald de Causton and others.
[WAM 217]

937 A similar release of the same Thomas.
Witnesses: John de Willehale, John Marsh, John Castle, John de Strate, Edmund Pymme, Thomas le Rowe, William le Lorimer.
[WAM 236]

938 Charter of Edmund Wiliot of Edmonton in fee simple with warranty made at Edmonton, 16 August 1335, to William de Causton of 10 acres of land and $1\frac{1}{2}$ acres of pasture in Edmonton which descended to him after the death of Emma wife of Thomas Wiliot, his mother, of which 2 acres lie in the field called 'Langheg' between the land of Roger Depham in the north and the land of the prior of Holy Trinity, London, John de Wilhale and John atte Hegge in the south extending from the land of Edmund Pymme and Thomas Rowe in the east and the land of

William de Causton in the west, and 1 acre and 1 rood lie in the same field between the land of Richard Basse in the north and the land of John atte Pole in the south extending from the land of Nicholas Reyner in the east to the road called 'Garsonesweye' in the west, and ½ acre lies in the same field between the land of John le Doul in the east and the land of Thomas le Rowe in the west extending from the garden of John Thebaut in the south to the land of Edmund Pymme in the north, and 1 rood lies in the same field between the land of the feoffee in the east and the land of Maud atte Fen in the west [*f. 78v*] extending from the ditch called 'le Grenedich' in the south to the land of Walter Lorymer in the north, and 1 rood lies in 'Colegrove' between the land of Edmund Pymme to the north and south extending from the land of William Causton in the west to the land of Reginald Conduit, and 2 acres lie in the Hyde, of which 1 acre lies between the land of Edmund Pymme to east and west extending from the land of John atte Pole in the north to the land of John Basse, and the other acre lies between the land of Alice Brisse in the north and the land of Alice le Hoppere in the south extending from the land of lord de Say in the east to the land of the same Alice Brisse in the west, and 1 acre and 1 rood lie in 'Fordescroft' between the land of Edmund Pymme in the east and the land of William Causton in the west extending from the pasture in the north to 'Fordestrate' in the south, and 1 acre and 1 rood lie in 'Bremblescroft' between the land of Edmund Pymme in the east and west extending from the messuage of the same Edmund Pymme in the south to the pasture of the feoffee in the north, and the aforesaid pasture lies between the land of William atte Forde and Robert Anesty in the north and the pasture of the feoffee in the south extending from the land formerly of William atte Forde in the east to the road called 'Penyacrebeche' in the west.

939 Charter of the same Edmund Wiliot in fee simple with warranty made at Edmonton, 18 August 1335, to William de Causton of one messuage and two adjacent crofts, of which one is called 'Horncroft' and the other 'Penyacre', and of all the donor's arable lands in 'Langheg', 'Colegrove', the Hyde, 'Fordecroft', 'Brembelcroft' and 'Hokfeld' in Edmonton, and of 3 acres of meadow in Edmonton marsh.
Witnesses: John Marsh, John Castle, John de Strate, Edmund Pymme, Thomas le Rowe, William le Lorimer and others.
[WAM 168]

940 Indenture made in London, 21 August 1335, containing that if William de Causton his heirs and assigns peacefully hold all the aforesaid tenements contained in the two previous charters according to the same form without any let or hindrance, and quit of all except 7½d rent, the aforesaid letter of account of £112 [**933**] will be cancelled.
Witnesses: John de Dalling, John de Dole, Thomas de Worsted, Nicholas of Greenwich (*de Grenewyco*), Theobald de Causton, Nicholas Marsh (*de Marisco*), Thomas de Cavendish, John de Garton, citizens of London, John de Luda, clerk, and others.
[WAM 178]

941 Charter of William Humfrey in fee simple with warranty made at Edmonton, 26 March 1336, to William de Causton of ½ acre of meadow in Edmonton marsh lying between the meadow of William Pykard and the meadow of Robert Bourdeyn, extending from the meadow of John atte Strate in the east to the meadow of the abbot of Walden.
Witnesses: John Marsh, William le Vikere, John atte Strate, John Castle, Edmund Pymme, William le Smith and others.
[WAM 162]

942 Charter of Thomas de Anesty in fee simple with warranty made at Edmonton, [*f. 79r*] 10 December 1336, to William de Causton of 3 roods of land in the field called 'Langheg' in Edmonton between the land of the feoffee in the south and north, extending from the land of John Basse in the east to the donor's land in the west.
Witnesses: John Marsh, John atte Strate, Edmund Pymme, Thomas le Rouwe, Walter le Lorymer and others.
[WAM 211]

943 Indenture made at the same place and on the same day containing that if Thomas de Anesty pay to the said William de Causton 24s within one year of the feast of Michaelmas next, the 3 roods of land aforesaid will revert to the said Thomas and the said charter be annulled. And if Thomas default on this payment in part or in whole, the whole land will remain to William in perpetuity and the said William will pay 6s to Thomas de Anesty who will deliver the part of the indenture remaining with him.
[WAM 223]

944 Another part of the same indenture.

945 Charter of John Bardolf, knight, lord of Wormegay [Norfolk], son and heir of Sir Thomas Bardolf, in fee simple with warranty made at Edmonton, 1 October 1337, to William Causton of all the donor's meadows lying in Edmonton marsh.
Witnesses: John Marsh (*du Mareis*), John Castle (*du Chastel*), William Vikere, Edmund Pymme, John de Strate, Thomas le Rowe, John atte Slo and several others.
[WAM 164, French]

946 Letter of attorney of John Bardolf, 1 October 1337, to Gilbert de Ethill, parson of the church of Cantley in the diocese of Norwich, to deliver seisin on the aforesaid charter.
[WAM 157, French]

947 Release in perpetuity by John Bardolf with warranty made at Edmonton, 22 October 1337, to William de Causton of all the said meadows.
Witnesses: John Marsh (*du Mareis*), John Castle (*du Chastel*), William Vykere, Edmund Pymme, John de Strate, Thomas le Rowe, John atte Slo and others.
[WAM 181, French]

948 Charter of Thomas Bonde son of John Bonde, late citizen and draper of London, in fee simple with warranty made at Edmonton, 31 December 1337, to William de Causton of 5 acres of land called 'Taillouresfeld' in Edmonton lying between the land of William le Kene in the east and the highway called 'Eldelane' in the west, extending from the land formerly of Richard le Wylehale in the north to the grove called 'Degelesbeche' in the south.
Witnesses: John Marsh (*de Marisco*), Edmund Pymme, Thomas de Anesty, John de Strate, Thomas le Rowe, [Richard de] Ipr[e], John Patrik, John Clerk and others.
[WAM 185]

949 Release in perpetuity by Sybil, who was wife of Geoffrey de Anesty without warranty made at Edmonton, 24 October 1338, to William de Causton of the whole messuage called 'Lyneshamstall' which Richard de Anesty son of the aforesaid Geoffrey granted to the said William, and which is situated between the grove of the said William in the east and the highway called 'Southstrete' in the west, extending from the grove of the aforesaid William de Causton to the north and south.
Witnesses: Edmund Pymme, Thomas de Anesty, Thomas le Rowe,

John de Notingham, John le Rowe, John Patrik and others.
[WAM 173]

950 [*f. 79v*] Another part of indenture [**736**].
[WAM 184]

951 Charter of Thomas de Anesty of Edmonton in fee simple with warranty made at Edmonton, 1 March 1338, to William de Causton of ½ acre of land in Edmonton lying in the field called 'Langheg' between the land formerly of Richard Wilehale in the west, extending from the land of Richard Hereward in the south to the land of John de Chilterne in the north.
Witnesses: John Marsh (*de Marisco*), Edmund Pymme, John de Strate, Thomas le Rowe, Richard de Ipre, John Patrik and others.
[WAM 171]

952 Indenture made in London, 2 March 1338, containing that if Thomas de Anesty pay to the said William 20s on 12 April then following in his house in the parish of St Pancras, London, the said ½ acre of land will revert to Thomas and the charter will be held void.
[*Witnesses*: as **951**]
[WAM 213, badly damaged]

953 Another part of the same indenture.

954 Charter of William Humfrey of Edmonton in fee simple with warranty made at Edmonton, 6 March 1339, to William de Causton of ½ acre of meadow lying in Edmonton meadow between the meadow of John de Pulteneye, knight, in the south and the meadow of Nicholas Pentecost in the north, extending from the meadow of John le Venour in the east to the meadow of Richard le Hale in the west.
Witnesses: John Marsh, John Castle, John atte Strate, Edmund Pymme, Thomas le Rouwe and others.
[WAM 167]

955 Release in perpetuity of Maud who was wife of Thomas Sqyler without warranty made in London, 15 May 1338, to William de Causton of 2 acres of meadow in Edmonton marsh, and of 1 acre of pasture in 'Pymor', which the said Thomas late husband of Maud granted to him.
Witnesses: John de Aillesham, Nicholas Marsh, Theobald de

Causton, William de la Panetrie, John Poleyn and others.
[WAM 191]

956 Charter of Henry Wykwane in fee simple with warranty made
at Edmonton, 13 September 1338, to William de Causton of a
messuage, curtilage, garden, field and grove in Edmonton lying
between the wood of the abbot of St Albans in the west and the
highway called Southgate in the east, extending from the wood
of the prioress of St Helen's, London, in the south to the highway
in the north, [*f. 80r*] and of one croft in the same vill called
'Taillesfeld' lying between the land formerly of Philip Patrik in
the west and the land formerly of John Vincent in the east, and
extending from the wood formerly of Philip Wilughby in the
south to the highway in the north, and of 8d rent to be raised
of the messuage which Gilbert Lif formerly held for life in the
same vill, and of the rent of a wreath of red roses (*capelli rosarum*)
from the messuage of Richard Albern.
Witnesses: John Marsh, John le Venour, Edmund Pymme, Thomas
le Rowe, Thomas de Anesty, John le Rede, John Patrik, and
others.
[WAM 183]

957 Release in perpetuity by Alice who was wife of William Brinkele,
late citizen of London, with warranty made at Edmonton, 16
September 1338, to the same William de Causton of the said
messuage, lands and rents.

958 Charter of John le Neuman son of William le Neuman in fee
simple with warranty made at Edmonton, 4 October 1338, to
William de Causton of a field called 'Finchfeld' which the donor
acquired of Henry Wykwane in Edmonton.
Witnesses: John Marsh, John le Venour, Edmund Pymme, Thomas
le Rowe, Thomas de Anesty, John le Rede, John Patrik and
others.
[WAM 165]

959 Release in perpetuity by Richard de Anesty, with terms of grant
and concession and with warranty made at Edmonton, 19
October 1338, to William de Causton of the whole messuage
called 'Lynehamstall' in Edmonton which Richard inherited after
the death of Geoffrey his father and is situated between the
grove of the said William in the east and Southgate in the west,
extending to the grove of the said William in the south and
north.

960 Letter of attorney of the same Richard de Anesty made in London, 19 October 1338, to Hugh de Hyngry of London, to deliver seisin to William de Causton of the said messuage.
[WAM 170]

961 Charter of Thomas Horn, chaplain, in fee simple with warranty made in London, 30 May 1339, to William de Causton of all the donor's tenement in Edmonton which was formerly of Philip Patrik situated between the wood of the said William and the land formerly of Thomas William in the north and the wood of Philip de Wyleby and that of the prioress of St Helen's, London, and the land of Ralph Cowe in the south, extending from Southgate in the west to 'Taillesfeld' in the east.

962 [*f. 80v*] Indenture made in London, 20 September 1339, containing that if William Humfrey pay to William de Causton 30s within two years of the feast of Michaelmas next, ½ acre of meadow in which he had enfeoffed William Causton will revert to the donor.
[WAM 214]

963 Indenture made in London, 11 November 1339, containing that [if] William de Causton, in his heirs and assigns hold peacefully in fee simple 13 acres of meadow in Edmonton marsh unencumbered by statute merchant or otherwise, which Thomas de Eyton had granted to him, a bond of £40 made by the said Thomas to William will be held null.

964 Charter of Thomas de Eyton in fee simple with warranty made at Edmonton, 10 November 1339, to William de Causton of 13 acres of land in Edmonton marsh which the donor acquired of Geoffrey de Eyton, clerk, his brother.
Witnesses: John Marsh, William le Vykere, John Castle, John de Strate, Thomas de Anesty, Edmund Pymme, Thomas le Rowe and others.
[WAM 177]

965 Bond of Thomas de Eyton made in London on the same day to William de Causton of £40 by reason of a true and pure loan, to be paid 29 September next.
[WAM 180]

966 Release in perpetuity of Geoffrey de Eyton son and heir of William de Eyton made in London, 15 November 1339, to

William de Causton of the aforesaid 13 acres of meadow which the said Willam de Causton acquired of Thomas de Eyton, the releasor's uncle.
Witnesses: John Marsh, William le Vikere, John Castle, John de Strate, Thomas de Anesty, Edmund Pymme, Thomas le Rowe and others.
[WAM 208]

967 Another charter of Thomas de Eyton, 11 November 1339, to William de Causton of the same 13 acres of meadow lying in the fee and meadow of Edmonton, of which 1 acre lies between the meadow which was of Isabella de Vescy in the north and the meadow formerly of William Laurentz in the south extending from the meadow of Richard Prichet in the west and the meadow of John le Doul in the east, 1 acre lies between the meadow of the master of the hospital of St John, London, in the north and that of John Doul in the south extending from the meadow formerly of Richard Cook (*Coci*) and from the meadow formerly of Agnes de Holmes, and ½ acre lies between the meadow formerly of Stephen de Abindon in the south and that formerly of Roger Casiere in the north extending from the meadow which was of Isabel de Vescy called 'le Eye' in the west to the meadow which was once of John Chaucer in the east, and 2 acres lie between the meadow formerly of Stephen de Abindon in the north and the meadow formerly of Richard de Wirhale in the south extending from the meadow of Isabella Vescy in the west to the meadow called 'Mymmemedowe', and 1½ acres lie between the meadow which was of Isabel de Vescy in the north and that formerly of Walter Crepyn in the south extending from the meadow of the same Isabel in the west to the River Lea in the east, and 2½ acres lie between the meadow of Thomas le Rowe in the south and that of the feoffee and Adam Yarild in the north extending from the meadow of John Marsh in the west to the River Lea in the east, and 1½ acres lie between the meadow of the master of the hospital of St John, London, in the south and the meadow formerly of Richard Wirhale in the north extending from the meadow called 'Chipolschot' in the west to the River Lea in the east, and 2 acres of meadow lie between the meadow formerly of Robert de Acton in the south and the meadow of Edmund Pymme in the north extending from the meadow of John Marsh in the west to the meadow formerly of William de Anesty in the east, and 1 acre of meadow lies between the meadow which was once of Richard Skyn in the south and the meadow formerly of Edmund de Totenhale in the north,

extending from 'la Leymedewe' to 'le Smalmedewe'.
Witnesses: John Marsh, William le Vikere, John Castle, John de Strate, Thomas de Anesty, Edmund Pymme, Thomas le Rowe and others.
[WAM 169]

968 Indenture made in London, 15 September 1340, containing that if William Humfray pay to William de Causton 30s within two years of the feast of Michaelmas next, $\frac{1}{2}$ acre of meadow in Edmonton marsh which he had granted the said William de Causton will revert to the donor.
[WAM 160]

969 [*f. 81r*] Charter of Thomas de Anesty in fee simple with warranty made at Edmonton, 30 October 1340, to William de Causton of 3 acres of land in Edmonton in the field called 'Okfeld' between the land of the feoffee to east and west, extending from the pasture of the feoffee called 'Laurencelese' in the north to the land of Richard le Pottere in the south.
Witnesses: John Marsh, John de Strate, Edmund Pymme, John le Keu, Thomas le Rowe, William le Keu, Richard le Pottere and others.
[WAM 220]

970 Indenture made in London, 3 November 1340, that if Thomas de Anesty pay to William de Causton 7 marks on 29 September next the charter concerning the said 3 acres of land will be annulled. If the said Thomas default on the payment he grants that the said William may pay to him 3 marks and that the charter will remain in force.
[WAM 226]

971 Duplicate part of a fine levied at Westminster, 21 January 1342, whereby John le Venour and Juliana his wife acknowledged 50 acres of land, 2 acres of meadow, 5 acres of pasture, $1\frac{1}{2}$ acres of wood and 20d rent in Edmonton to be the right of William de Causton as those which they granted to him, to be held in fee simple with warranty for themselves and the heirs of the said John. And William paid to John and Juliana 100 marks.
[WAM 102, 137]
[*Feet of Fines, Lond. & Middx.* i, 118]

972 Charter of John le Bourser in fee simple with warranty made at Edmonton, Monday after the feast of the apostles Philip and

James 15 Edward II (3 May 1322),[1] to William de Causton of 3 roods of meadow in Edmonton marsh between the meadow of John Page in the south and the meadow of the prior of Holy Trinity, London, in the north.

Witnesses: William de Anesty, John atte Forde, John atte Mersch, William le Vykere, John Castel, John Myles and others.

[WAM 136]

1 MS: 15 Edward III.

973 Charter of Sybil who was wife of Geoffrey de Anesty and Richard son and heir of the same Geoffrey in fee simple with warranty made at Edmonton, 28 May 1341, to William de Causton of ½ acre of land in Edmonton lying in the Hyde between the land and grove of the said William to the east and west and extending from his lands to the north and south, and of one piece of enclosed land lying at Southgate in the same vill between the land of the feoffee in the north and the highway in the south, extending from the messuage of the same William in the east to the land formerly of Richard le Bakere in the west.

974 Charter of John le Venour and Juliana his wife in fee simple with warranty made at Edmonton, 5 September 1341, to William de Causton of the field called 'Risshefeld', one croft of land, [*f. 81v*] and a pasture called la Brache in Edmonton lying between 'Berghfeld' in the north and the field of John atte Merssh in the south, extending from the highway in the west to the lands of the said William, the prior of Holy Trinity, London, and 'Thurstoneslond' in the west, and of 1 acre and 3 roods of meadow in Edmonton marsh, of which 1 acre lies between the meadow of John de Beaumont (*Bellomonte*), knight, in the south and the meadow of Geoffrey de Say, knight, called 'le Wal' in the north, extending from the meadow of William Pykard in the east to the meadow of Richard in le Hale in the west, and 3 roods lie in the same marsh between the meadow of Maud atte Strate in the east and the meadow of Robert atte Grene, Sir John de Beaumont and John Chichely in the west, extending from 'le Wal' in the north to the meadow of the feoffee in the south, and of 1½ acres of grove called 'Salonelane' lying in the same vill between the grove of lord de Say in the west and that of the feoffee in the west, and of 20d arising from the croft of the prior of Holy Trinity, London, called 'la Brache' in the same vill, lying between the lands of William de Causton to the north and the south and extending from his land in the east to

'Thurstoneslond' in the west.
Witnesses: John Marsh, John Castle, William le Vikere, John de Strete, William Pymme, Thomas le Rowe, William le Keu and others.
[WAM 129]

975 Letter of John le Venour made in London, 5 September 1341, containing that he had received of William de Causton £40 with which to trade to the profit of the same William until 31 March next and binding him to repay the said sum with interest accruing.
[WAM 133]

976 Indenture made in London, 27 September 1341, that if William Humfray pay to William de Causton 30s within two years of the feast of Michaelmas next, $\frac{1}{2}$ acre of meadow which he had granted to William de Causton will revert to the donor.
[WAM 131]

977 Release in perpetuity by Isabel who was wife of Thomas de Anesty without warranty made in London, 4 September 1342, to William de Causton of all lands which the same William had of the gift of the said Thomas.
Witnesses: John de Eillesham, John de Dallyngg, Nicholas Marsh, John de Garton, William de Panetrie, mercers of London.
[WAM 130]

978 Release in perpetuity by Isabel who was wife of Robert Gulle without warranty made in London, 9 October 1342, to William Causton of all lands which the said William has of the gift of the aforesaid Robert.
[WAM 6]

979 [*f. 82r*] Indenture made in London, 29 September 1343, that if William Humfray pay to William de Causton 30s within 2 years in his house in London the charter of feoffment made to William Causton of $\frac{1}{2}$ acre of meadow in Edmonton marsh will be cancelled.
[WAM 125]

980 Duplicate part of a fine levied at Westminster, 20 October 1343, and afterwards on 3 November 1346, whereby John de Chilterne and Maud his wife acknowledged one messuage, three tofts, $140\frac{1}{2}$ acres of land, 15 acres of meadow, 38 acres of pasture, 60 acres

of wood, 56s rent in Edmonton to be the right of William de
Causton to be held in fee simple, and they granted to the said
William in fee simple the said rent with the homage and services
of Richard Bousser, Thomas Topfeld, Katherine Miles, Roger
de Depham, John atte Pole, Agnes le Forester, Henry Goldyng,
Margery Arnold, William le Vikere, John de Wyrhale, William
le Kene, William Pymme, Alice Basse, Katherine Germayn,
Thomas le Rowe, Alice Germayn, Richard Sabarn, Cecily
Denys, William Lound, John Stoune, Cecily Potewelle, Richard
atte Berewe, Juliana Gosselyn, William Baron, Maud atte Fen,
William atte Watre, John Stannop, Richard Neweman, John le
Portere, Richard Proudfot, bastard, William Saleman, John
Burdeyn, William le Keu, Richard le Webbe, Edmund Tirry
and Robert de Plesyngton for the tenements which they previously held of the said John and Maud in the same vill. And
likewise that 1 acre of meadow which Helen Auncels then held
for life of the inheritance of the said Maud will remain to the
said William in fee simple after the death of the said Helen, with
warranty from John and Maud and the heirs of John. And
William paid the donors £40.
[WAM 124]
[*Feet of Fines, Lond. & Middx.* i, 122]

981 Release in perpetuity by William Humfray with warranty made
in London, 17 December 1343, to William de Causton of two
halfacres of meadow in Edmonton marsh which he has of the
gift of the said William by two charters.
Witnesses: Nicholas Marsh, John de Dalygg, Theobald de Causton,
William de la Panetrie, William Caldecote, mercers, and others.
[WAM 100]

982 Release in perpetuity by Robert de Assherugge, son of John de
Assherugge without warranty made in London, 27 February
1346, to William de Causton of all the lands and meadows which
the same William had of the gift of John, father of the said
Robert, and Amice his wife in Edmonton.
Witnesses: Nicholas Marsh, William le Panetrie, John de Garton,
John de la Panetrie, William Depham and others.
[WAM 135]

983 [*f. 82v*] Release in perpetuity by John le Venour made in London,
19 May 1346, to William de Causton of 5s 6d rent which the
said William had formerly paid to John for the lands and
tenements held of him in Edmonton.

984 Charter of John de Sauston, citizen and mercer of London in fee simple with warranty made at Tottenham, 8 June 1346, to William de Causton of 2 acres of meadow which Walter son of Walter de Hernestede, late citizen and draper of London, had granted to the donor, lying in Tottenham marsh, called 'Yocford', between the meadow of Simon le Bounde in the north and the meadow of Richard Colyn of Newton in the south extending from the meadow formerly of Robert le Bruys in the east to the meadow of William atte Watre and the meadow of John son of Abraham in the west, and of 1 acre of meadow in Edmonton marsh lying between the meadow of William atte Forde in the south and that of John de Enefeld in the north, extending from the River Lea in the east to the meadow of John atte Merssh called 'Dunnemed' in the west.
Witnesses: Roger atte Lofte, John de Rudham, John atte Merssh, William Pymme, Thomas le Rowe and others.
[WAM 98]

985 Letter of attorney of the same John de Sauston made in London on the same day to deliver seisin according to this charter.

986 Indenture made in London, 28 April 1347, with warranty containing that William de Causton leased to William son of William le Smyth and Robert le Taillour all his arable lands in the field called 'Storkesnest' in Edmonton, to be held by them and their heirs from 29 September next for 6 years at an annual rent to the lessor of 9d for each acre.
Witnesses: John Marsh, John Castle, William le Vykere, William Strate and others.
[WAM 138]

987 Charter of William Pymme in fee simple with warranty made at Edmonton, 6 April 1349, to William de Causton of $\frac{1}{2}$ acre of meadow in Edmonton marsh lying in 'Longmede' between the meadows of the feoffee in the north and south.
Witnesses: John atte Merssh, Thomas de Oxendon, William atte Strate, William le Cook, Henry Lorimer and others.
[WAM 127]

988 Charter of Hugh de Braybrok of Enfield and William Pykard of Edmonton in fee simple with warranty made at Edmonton, 28 May 1346, to William de Causton of $\frac{1}{2}$ acre of meadow which the donors acquired of John atte Castel the younger, lying in Edmonton marsh between the meadow of Roger de Depham in

the south and the meadow of John atte More in the north, extending from 'Bluntdikesmad' to the west.
Witnesses: Thomas de Oxeneford, William Viker, William Salaman, John Golding, William Pimme, William Cook and others.
[WAM 123]

989 [*f. 83r*] Charter of William de Causton in fee simple with warranty made at Edmonton, 7 July 1354, to John atte Berne and John Organ, his apprentices, of all his lands and tenements in Edmonton, Tottenham and Enfield.
Witnesses: William Pymme, William Salman, William le Viker of Edmonton, John Huchon, Robert Hadham of Tottenham, Hugh Braybrok, John Thebaud of Enfield and others.
[WAM 8]

990 Letter of William de Causton in London on the same day, of the sale to John atte Berne and John Organ of all his goods and chattels in the same vills.

991 Letter of attorney of William de Causton made in London 6 July 1354 to John Broun to deiver to the said John atte Berne and John Organ seisin of the aforesaid lands and tenements.
[WAM 10]

992 Letter of Robert de Hadham made at Tottenham, 1 February 1354, transferring to John atte Berne and John Organ his services for the lands he holds of them in Edmonton, Enfield and Tottenham by virtue of the grant made to them by William de Causton of all his lands and services in the said vills.
[WAM 7, French]

993 Release in perpetuity by Christine who was wife of William de Causton made to John atte Berne and John Organ of all lands and tenements in Edmonton, Enfield and Tottenham which the said William de Causton had granted to them as aforesaid.
Witnesses: John Malweyn, John Wroth, Henry de Frowyk, Thomas de Frowyk, John de Durhem, Nicholas de Shordich, Nicholas atte Wyk, Henry Wikwane, Simon Bonde and others.
[WAM 122, French]

994 Charter of John atte Berne and John Organ in fee simple with warranty made in London, 6 March 1355, to Adam Fraunceys and Peter Favelore of all lands and tenements which were of the

said William de Causton in Edmonton, Enfield and Tottenham.
Witnesses: John Malwayn, John Wroth, Henry Wikwane, Simon
Bonde and others.
[WAM 126]

995 Letter of the same John atte Berne and John Organ made at
Edmonton, 12 March 1355, of the sale of all their goods, which
they had by purchase from William de Causton in Edmonton,
Enfield and Tottenham, to Adam Fraunceys and Peter Favelore.
With warranty.
[WAM 132, French]

996 Release in perpetuity of all actions real and personal made at
Edmonton, 15 [*f. 83v*] May 1355, by Hugh Braybrok, John
Goldyng, William Pymme and William Saleman to John atte
Berne, Christine who was wife of William de Causton, Adam
Fraunceys and Peter Favelore, of everything touching the lands,
goods or chattels which were of William de Causton in Edmon-
ton, Enfield and Tottenham and of all other things.
[WAM 24, French]

997 And memorandum that Peter Favelore died and the whole
[estate] accrued to the said Adam as survivor, as will appear
afterwards, but there immediately follow other charters which
state how Adam came by further tenements in those places by
purchase from other persons who had bought them in divers
ways, as will be shown by the charters themselves.

998 Charter of William, earl of Essex, in fee simple without warranty
and date made to Wolwyn le Sime of Edmonton of 1 virgate of
land and 5 acres of of meadow, of which 5 acres of land lie in
'Wythycroft', $4\frac{1}{2}$ acres lie in 'Thuryngredyng', $3\frac{1}{2}$ acres in the
Hyde, 3 acres in Pannaker, 2 acres in 'Langheg', and 5 acres on
the west side of the field called 'Aldaker', and the rest of the
land next to the wood at Southgate, and the 5 acres of meadow
[lie] in Edmonton marsh.
[Date: 1166 x 1189]

999 Charter of Roger Sone in fee simple with warranty without date
made to Agnes his daughter of part of his messuage in Edmonton
lying on the west side and containing in length from north to
south 3 perches, and in breadth from east to west 2 [perches],
to be held of the donor by service of one rose *pa*.
Witnesses: Robert Gizors, Richard Picot, Richard de Strata, Ralph

de la Berwe, Richard Humfrey, John le Burser, Stephen de Colewell.
[Date: *temp.* Henry III.]
[WAM 118]

1000 Charter of Roger Sone in fee simple without warranty and date[1] of his messuage and of all his land in Edmonton, to be held of the donor, and by due services to the chief lords.

> [1] Feoffee not mentioned.

1001 Indented charter of Agnes Sones in fee simple with warranty made at Edmonton, 23 May 1316, to Roger de Depham of a piece of arable land in Edmonton lying between the land formerly of Geoffrey atte Berewe to the north and the land of the feoffee and the donor's messuage to the south, [of which] one side abuts on the land of John Gisors to the east and the other on the highway to the west, by paying to the donor a quarter of wheat annually for life, for which the donor may distrain.
Witnesses: Richard de Wirhale, William atte Forde, John atte Forde, William de Furneys, William de Causton, Robert de Acton, John atte Merssh, William le Vykere, Robert atte Fen, Simon de Kelshell, clerk, and others.
[WAM 134]

1002 Charter of Ralph son of John Pycot, in fee simple with warranty made at [*f. 84r*] Edmonton, 11 June 1306, to Robert atte Fen and Katherine, daughter of the said Robert, of one croft of land lying in Edmonton between the land of Agnes Sones and the highway leading to the house formerly of John Blund, extending from the pasture of John Gisors in the east to the messuage of the said Agnes in the east, and of 2 acres of meadow in Edmonton marsh, of which 1 acre lies between the meadow of Robert le Squeler on the west side and the meadow called 'Longemad' on the east side, and $\frac{1}{2}$ acre lies between the meadow of Henry de Gloucester on the south side and the meadow of Roger Spirk on the north side, and $\frac{1}{2}$ acre lies between the meadow of John Saleman on one side and the meadow of Robert Gulle on the other, and of 6d rent to be raised of the tenement which the said Agnes Sones holds, lying between the aforesaid croft and the land of Geoffrey de Bergham, to be held at a rent of 10s.
Witnesses: William de Forde, John Marsh, William de Anesty, John de Ford, Geoffrey de Berg', Robert le Squeler, William le Fyker, John Gysors, John atte Strate, Nicholas Laur[ence],

William Laurence, Roger Spirk, William Clerk and others.
[WAM 109]

1003 Release in perpetuity by Robert atte Fen without warranty made at Tottenham, 16 December 1313, to Katherine his daughter of $1\frac{1}{2}$ acres of meadow in Edmonton of which 1 acre lies between the meadow of John Denteyth in the south and the meadow of John Hamyng in the north, extending from the meadow of Thomas le Rowe and from the meadow of Robert de Acton from the west to the meadow called 'Longemad' in the east, and $\frac{1}{2}$ acre lies between the meadow of Robert Gulle in the east and the meadow of John Saleman in the west, extending from the meadow called 'Bluntstikemad' in the south to the meadow of Robert de Acton.
Witnesses: John FitzJohn, Ralph de Lay, John le Barker, Roger de Sol[io], John Tebaud, John Stene and others.
[WAM 119]

1004 Release in perpetuity by Katherine daughter of Robert atte Fen made at Tottenham, 1 April 1314, to Robert atte Fen, father of the aforesaid Katherine, of one croft of land and $\frac{1}{2}$ acre of meadow and 6d rent in Edmonton, of which the croft is called 'Sounescroft'[1] and the meadow lies in Edmonton marsh between the meadow of Richard de Wilhale and the meadow fomerly of Roger Spyrk and the rent accrues from the messuage of Agnes Sones.
Witnesses: William de la Forde, John de la Forde, William de Anesty, Robert de Acton, John Marsh, John Castle of Edmonton, John FitzJohn, John Tebaud, Roger atte Loffte, Hugh de Heydon of Tottenham and others.
[WAM 152]

  [1] MS: 'Smythecroft'.

1005 Charter of Robert atte Fen in fee simple with warranty made at Edmonton, 25 January 1316, to Roger de Depham, clerk, of the land called 'Sonescroft' in Edmonton, contained in the preceding charter, extending in length from the tenement of Agnes Sones in the north to the meadow of John Gisors in the south, lying between the croft of Agnes Sones in the east and the highway in the west, and of 6d rent to be taken of the tenement of the said Agnes Sones.
Witnesses: Robert de Acton, John Marsh, William atte Forde, John Castle, John atte Strate, William Pykard, Edmund Pymme

and others.
[WAM 114]

1006 [*f. 84v*] Release in perpetuity by Katherine daughter of Robert atte Fen, with warranty made in London, 6 May 1317, to Roger de Depham in 'Sonescroft'.

1007 Charter of William del Holm in fee simple with warranty and acquittance, made in the year 38 Henry III (28 Oct. 1253–27 Oct. 1254) to Thomas son of Robert Forde of 1 acre of land in Edmonton which the donor purchased of Warin son of Ingulf, lying in the field called 'Honifeld' between the road and the land formerly of the said Warin, to be held of the donor by 4d *pa* for all service. Thomas paid the donor 10s.
Witnesses: Thomas Picot, William Picot, Laurence de Forda, John FitzJohn, Geoffrey Cook (*Coco*), Hugh Peverell, William son of Peter de Berga, Walter Clerk and others.
[WAM 97]

1008 Quitclaim to Walter le Moygne without date made by William son of William de la Forde of 60 marks which the said William acknowledged he owed Walter before the justices at Westminster.
[Date: *temp.* Edward I.]
Witnesses: John Marsh, Richard de Anesty, Ralph de la Berewe, Robert Gizors, Nicholas son of Laurence [de Forde], William Spirk, tailor.
[WAM 104]

1009 Charter of Geoffrey son of Robert de la Forde in fee simple with warranty and acquittance without date made to Hamo le Longe, fishmonger of London, of 1 acre of meadow in Edmonton marsh in 'Holfletessote'[1] between the meadow of Stephen de Colewelle and the meadow of Robert Smith (*Fabri*), the southern side of which abuts onto the River Lea, to be held of the donor for 4d *pa* for all service.
Witnesses: William de Forde, John Marsh, Ralph de la Berewe, Geoffrey de Laurence, Ralph Clerk, William le Vikere, John Gizors, Nicholas Laurence, John de la Strate, Richard Rowghe, Reginald Pymme, John de Claveringe, John Taylor (*Cissor*) and others.
[Date: *temp.* Edward I.]
[WAM 140]

[1] See above, **211**.

1010 Charter of Geoffrey de la Forde in fee simple with warranty and acquittance without date made to Hamo le Longe, fishmonger of London, and Maud his wife of a piece of enclosed land lying above the donor's messuage in 'Honyfeld' and of a certain plot of land 12 feet in width, extending above the donor's messuage from the highway leading to Winchmore Hill in the west to the aforesaid plot, to be held of the donor by 4d or by one pair of gloves valued at 4d for the donor's life, and afterwards by one rose for all service.

1011 Charter of Geoffrey de la Forde in fee tail with warranty and acquittance without date made to Hamo le Longe, fishmonger, and Maud his wife of a piece of land in Edmonton called 'Helberescroft' lying between the land of John Goldyng in the east and the highway in the west, extending from the land of John Goldyng in the south to his land in the north, to be held of the donor by 2d *pa* for all service.

1012 Charter of Roger de Askwode, citizen and girdler of London, in fee simple with warranty and defeasance made at Edmonton, 27 February 1329, to Maud atte Forde who was wife of Hamo Long, [*f. 85r*] fishmonger of London, of all his lands in Edmonton which Maud had granted to the donor to be held of the chief lords of the fee by due services.

1013 Release in perpetuity by Roger Askwode made at Edmonton, 26 September 1329, to Maud who was wife of Hamo Fishmonger of London, of all the above lands and tenements.

1014 Charter of Thomas son and heir of Robert le Squyler of Edmonton in fee simple with warranty made at Edmonton, 3 September 1329, to William le Vikere junior of one enclosed croft containing 10 acres called 'Churchefeld' in Edmonton which the said Robert had acquired from William de Wyncestre, lying between the land of William Hereward, the lord's villein, in the north and the lane called 'le Churchestride' in the south.

1015 Release in perpetuity by William le Vikere junior of Edmonton made without warranty, 8 October 1329, to Thomas son and heir of Robert de Akton of the said croft called 'Cherchefeld' which Robert had acquired from William de Wyncestre as above.

1016 Charter of Thomas son of Robert de Acton of Edmonton with warranty made at Edmonton, 5 November 1329, to Roger de

Depham of the croft called 'Chircesfeld' in Edmonton lying between the land which Margery, the donor's mother, held for life in the east and 'Sayeslane' in the west, extending from the street called 'Abboteslane' in the south to the land of William Hereward in the north, and of the reversion of one third of the same croft which the donor's mother then held in dower.

1017 Indenture of Roger de Depham made at Edmonton, 11 November 1329, containing that if Thomas son of Robert de Acton pay to the said Roger £10 on 29 September 1336 in London, then the said charter concerning the croft and reversion will be held null.

1018 [*f. 85v*] Release in perpetuity by Thomas son of Robert de Acton, with warranty made at Edmonton, 17 October 1333, to Roger de Depham of the aforesaid piece of land called 'Cherchefeld'.

1019 Similar release of the said Thomas with warranty made in London, 27 October 1333, to Roger de Depham of the aforesaid piece of land called 'Cherchefeld'.

1020 Letter patent of Margaret who was wife of the aforesaid Robert de Acton made at Edmonton, 25 October 1333, acknowledging the right of Roger de Depham upon grant of the reversion of the said third [of the croft] made to Roger by the said Thomas [her son].

1021 Release in perpetuity by Maud who was wife of Thomas Squyler without warranty made in London, 10 May 1338, to Roger de Depham and Margery his wife of all lands which the same Roger and Margery, or one of them, hold of the gift of the aforesaid Thomas late husband of the said Maud.

1022 Release in perpetuity by Maud who was wife of Thomas Squyler of Edmonton without warranty made at Edmonton, 19 October 1338, to Thomas Phelipe of Baldock of all the tenements which the said Thomas Phelipe acquired of the husband of the releasor in Edmonton.

1023 Charter of Thomas Phelipe in fee simple with warranty made at Edmonton, 13 January 1341, to William of St Neots (*de Sancto Neoto*), vicar of Ashwell [Herts.], of all tenements in Edmonton in which Thomas Squyler enfeoffed the donor.

1024 Letter of Thomas Phelipe made in London, 11 January 1341, appointing John Phelipot of Ashwell to deliver to [William of St Neots] the said vicar seisin of the tenements contained in the previous charter.

1025 Charter of William of St Neots, parson of the church of Waresley [Hunts.], made at Edmonton, 20 February 1342, to Robert de Plesyngton and Helen his wife of one messuage and two gardens in Edmonton.

1026 Acquittance of Thomas de Eston made in London, 26 February 1342, acknowledging receipt from Robert de Plesyngton of 20s in part payment of 7 marks in which the same Robert was bound to William of St Neots.

1027 [f. 86r] Indenture of Robert de Plesyngton made at Edmonton, 21 July 1342, containing that the said Robert leased at that time to Margaret who was wife of Robert le Squyler the principal chamber of the messuage which he had purchased of William of St Neots by the above charter [**1025**], with adjoining garden, and one small chamber opposite the first, to be held of the donor for the life of the same Margaret for 12d *pa.*

1028 Charter of Peter le Squyler son of Robert le Squyler in fee at Edmonton, 26 January 1344, to William Bernewell of 2 acres of land in Edmonton lying in 'Berefeld' between the land of William Strete in the north and the land of William Smyth in the south, abutting on to the land of William Strete in the east and the land of John le Venour in the west.

1029 Release in perpetuity by Peter son of Robert Squyler with warranty made at Edmonton, 1 May 1345, to William de Berne-well of the aforesaid 2 acres of land whereof the same Peter enfeoffed the same William.

1030 Charter of William de Bernewell in fee simple with warranty made at Edmonton, 9 July 1346, to Robert de Plesyngton of the said 2 acres of land in 'Berefeld' within the same boundaries contained in charter [**1028**].

1031 Release in perpetuity by John Amys son of Richard de Colewell with the warranty of the releasor made at Edmonton, 4 October 1327, to Margery de Acton lately wife of Robert de Acton of one messuage with curtilage in Edmonton which the releasor claimed to belong to him by inheritance after the death of Richard his brother, presuming (*supponens*) that he had earlier enfeoffed the said Margery thereof.

1032 Indenture of Thomas son of Robert Squyler of Edmonton made at Edmonton, 6 October 1330, to Margery who was wife of the aforesaid Robert of a cellar with chamber above on the north side of the messuage of the said Margery, of the tenement formerly of Richard Colewell, and of one adjacent cottage and garden acquired lately of William Clerk, [and] of certain parcels of land mentioned above in charter[1].

> [1] MS blank.

1033 [*f. 86v*] Charter of Stephen, son of Richard Claper of Edmonton, in fee simple with warranty and acquittance without date made to Saher Clerk and Maud his wife and Juliana their daughter of that grove in Edmonton which was formerly of Richard Claper, the donor's father, lying between the donor's land and the road leading to the gate of Enfield park called 'Southwodegate', extending from the donor's land in the east to the road leading to the grange of prior of Holy Trinity, London, to be held of the donor for 4d *pa* for all service.

1034 Part of a fine levied on 25 November 1271 by which Henry de Oxonia and Sabina his wife acknowledged one messuage and 1 acre of land and 1 acre of wood, which is the grove mentioned above, to be the right of Stephen Claper and they granted and released them to him for themselves and the heirs of Sabina, and Saher Clerk granted warranty to the said Stephen for the wood.
[*Feet of Fines, Lond. & Middx.* i, 48]

1035 Charter of John Claper of Edmonton with warranty made in Edmonton, 19 January 1334, to Roger de Depham of one piece of wood adjoining the wood of the said Roger in Edmonton, and of 6 feet surrounding the wood to enclose it, and of 6 feet for the enclosure of another wood in the same place.

1036 Charter of Jordan de Oxehale and Margery his wife in fee simple with warranty without date made to William son of Richard of Edmonton of 3 roods of land in Edmonton lying in the fields called 'Bultelereslane' between the water called 'Medesenge' in the south and the land of Richard Pymme in the north, one side of which abuts on to the path leading to 'Fordestrate' in the west and another on to the road called 'Saresmeswey' in the east, to be held of the donor by an annual rent of $\frac{1}{2}$d for all service.

1037 Indenture of John Marsh, made 25 December 1318, to William Fourneys of his whole messuage and all his lands and tenements in Edmonton and of the rent accruing from them, to be held for four years.

1038 [*f. 87r*] Charter of Philip le Nieuman of Edmonton in fee simple with warranty made at Edmonton, 27 April 1316, to William de Fourneys of 1 acre of enclosed land in 'Berefeld' between the highway called 'Berefeldeslane' in the north and the land of Robert Gulle in the south, extending from the land of John del Strete in the west to the land of Alice Prat in the east.

1039 Charter of Oger le Casiere of Edmonton in fee simple with warranty made at Edmonton, 30 September 1316, to William Fourneys of 3 acres of enclosed land in Edmonton lying between the land of Richard Gisors in the south and the land of Richard Godard in the north, extending from the land of John atte Strete in the west to the land of the feoffee, William Smith (*Fabri*) and Alice Sprot in the east.

1040 Charter of Thomas Tirry son of John Tirry, then dead, in fee simple with warranty and acquittance without date made to John Baldewyne, son of Richard Baldewyne, of one messuage in Tottenham situated between the messuage of John Dymor and the messuage formerly of Ralph le Bruere, extending on the west side to the highway and in the east to the land of John son of John son of Peter, to be held of the donor by $\frac{1}{2}$d *pa* and by 12d *pa* to be paid to John Baliol, chief lord.

1041 Indenture, made 1 November 1288, containing that Thomas Tirry of Tottenham granted to John Chyngford, clerk, all his messuage in Tottenham situated between the messuage of John Dymor and the messuage formerly of Ralph le Bruere, to be held of the donor for the life of the feoffee and that of Alice Inecestre, his wife, for 4d *pa* and 12d to John Baliol, chief lord of the fee.

1042 Charter of John Baldewyn in fee simple with warranty made at Tottenham, 12 May 1317, to William de Fourneys, citizen and pepperer of London, of the whole of the abovesaid messuage, presuming that (*supponend' quod*) Thomas Tirry enfeoffed the donor thereof as appears in charter [**1040**].

1043 Charter of the same William Fourneys in fee simple with warranty made at Edmonton, 3 January 1319, to Thomas de Enefeld of one messuage, 80 acres of land, 6 acres of meadow and 2 acres of pasture in Edmonton in which Robert de Acton enfeoffed the donor.

1044 [*f. 87v*] Charter of Walter de Gloucestre made at Uley [Glos.], 7 June 1308, to William le Venour, the donor's brother, and Sybil his wife of the donor's manor of Edmonton which he had of the gift of the said William to be held for the term of William's life.

1045 Indenture, made 29 September 1315, containing that William le Venour and Sybil his wife leased all their lands and tenements in Edmonton to William de Fourneys, to be held of the donor and the heirs of his wife for 20 years with reversion to them after that term.

1046 Copy of a fine made at Westminster, 27 November 1315, whereby William Venour and Sybil his wife granted seven messuages, 1 carucate of land, 40 acres of meadow, 13 acres of pasture, 1 acre of wood, 11s rent, which William son of William de Patrikdale de Fourneys holds for 20 years of the said William Venour and Sybil, to remain after that term to John their son and Juliana, daughter of the said William Fourneys, in fee tail at an annual rent to William and Sybil of 20 marks with reversion to the donors and the heirs of Sybil in default of issue.
[*Feet of Fines, Lond. & Middx.* i, 90]

1047 And memorandum that the same tenements are contained in the indenture immediately preceding [**1045**] and in the fine which follows [**1048**], and that William Fourneys and William Patrikdale are the same person.

1048 Part of a fine made, 27 November 1315, whereby the aforesaid William le Venour and Sibyl his wife granted the tenements contained in the last indenture to John son of William le Venour and Juliana daughter of William de Fourneys to hold in fee tail after the said term of 20 years at an annual rent of 20 marks to the donor for the life of Sybil with reversion to Sybil and her heirs in default of issue.
[*Feet of Fines, Lond. & Middx.* i, 90]

1049 And memorandum that William le Venour and Sybil had issue, John, called the elder, to whom the tenements which are contained in the fine immediately above were granted, and William the younger. After the death of William Venour and Sybil, the reversion was reserved to descend through Sybil to John, as son and heir, who then released [his right] with warranty to the possession of Roger Depham and died without issue, by which warranty William the younger was barred.

1050 [*f. 88r*] Indenture made in London, 29 January 1316, containing that William de Fourneys granted to pay annually to William Venour and Sybil his wife 20 marks for all lands and tenements which he holds for the term of 20 years in Edmonton and of which the said William Venour and Sybil granted the reversion after the said term to John their son and Juliana his wife to hold in fee tail, and the said William and Sybil granted that if the aforesaid tenements were restored (*recuperata*) to the said John and Juliana then the said William Fourneys would be discharged of the foregoing rent.

1051 Another indenture made in London, 30 November 1315, of the same tenor as the preceding.

1052 Indenture, made 25 December 1323, containing that John Marsh leased to William de Fourneys, citizen of London, all the lands and tenements which William son of John son of Peter of Tottenham leased to the said John Marsh in Tottenham, to be held for $5\frac{1}{2}$ years at a rent of 40s *pa*, on condition that if the said William son of John died within the term then William Fourneys would be discharged of the rent.

1053 Charter of Robert de Acton of Edmonton in fee simple with warranty made at Edmonton, 25 January 1316, to William de Fourneys, citizen of London, of one messuage, 80 acres of land, 6 acres of meadow, $2\frac{1}{2}$ acres of pasture, 11d rent in Edmonton, namely from all the donor's tenements on the eastern side of the highway leading from Tottenham to Cheshunt.

1054 Release in perpetuity by Thomas son of Roger de Wynton with warranty made at Edmonton, 28 October 1332, to William de Fourneys of the whole messuage and 22 acres of land in Edmonton in which Robert Sqyler of Acton had enfeoffed the said William.

1055 Writing of William le Venour made at Edmonton, 1 June 1326, surrendering to William de Fourneys all the lands and tenements which Robert de Acton had previously granted the said William Fourneys and which the feoffee later leased to William Venour for life by indenture [now] cancelled, and wholly releasing to the same William Fourneys his right in the said tenements.

1056 [*f. 88v*] Release in perpetuity by Margaret daughter and heir of Nicholas del Strete of Edmonton made in that place, 6 April 1316, to William de Fourneys of $\frac{1}{2}$d rent issuing from a tenement in Edmonton in which Robert Sqwyler enfeoffed the said William and which Richard Pycot, Margaret's uncle, once held, and of the tenement itself, and of all the tenements which John le Bourser fomerly held in the same vill.

1057 Writing of Geoffrey de Say made at Edmonton, 10 July 1316, granting William de Fourneys permission to erect a wall along the highway opposite the messuage he had acquired from Robert de Acton in Edmonton, extending from the north side of the messuage to the west side of the same, and that its edge (*extremitas*) will be at all points (*ubique*) 12 feet from the ditch of the same William.

1058 Charter of Thomas son of Roger de Wynton in fee simple with warranty made at Edmonton, 19 May 1332, to William de Fourneys of one toft, 50 acres of land, 6 acres of meadow and $1\frac{1}{2}$ acres of pasture in Edmonton.

1059 Release in perpetuity by the aforesaid Thomas son of Roger without warranty made at Edmonton, 21 June 1332, to William de Fourneys of the land contained in the previous charter.

1060 Charter of John le Venour in fee simple with warranty made at Edmonton, 18 September 1335, to Roger de Depham and Margaret his wife of 4 pieces of land lying in Edmonton, of which one lies between 'Colewelleslane' in the north and the stream called 'Hakebrok' in the south, and two pieces lie together between the land lately of Robert Bourdeyn in the north and 'Bourserslane' in the south, and the fourth piece lies between the land of the feoffee in the west and the highway in the north and east and is called 'Jopesfeld'.

1061 Charter of John le Venour in fee simple with warranty made at Edmonton, 12 June 1337, to Roger de Depham and Margaret his wife of three pieces of land and two gardens, of which one piece is called 'Litelcolwell' and lies between the highway called 'Colewelleslane' in the south and the land formerly of Geoffrey atte Berewe in the north, another piece with adjoining garden lies between the said road in the south and the land formerly of the said Geoffrey in the north, and the third piece and another garden lie between the land of Roger Depham in the east, the highway in the west and the tenements lately of Stephen Gardiner in the south.

1062 [*f. 89r*] Charter of John le Venour and Juliana his wife with warranty made at Edmonton, 27 March 1342, to Roger de Depham and Margaret his wife and the heirs of Roger, of one garden and two adjoining pieces of land called 'Humfreyesfeldes' lying between the land of John Castle (*de Castello*) in the north and the land lately of William Sabarn in the south, and of $5\frac{1}{2}$ acres of meadow in 'Middelmerssh', of which $3\frac{1}{2}$ acres lie between the meadow of lord Geoffrey de Say and the meadow of the said Roger in the north and the meadow of the master of the hospital St Giles in the south, and 2 acres lie between the same Roger's meadow in the north and the donor's meadow in the south.

1063 Charter of John Venour in fee simple with warranty made at Edmonton, 6 November 1345, to Roger de Depham and Margaret his wife and the heirs of Roger of 2 acres of land and 3 acres of meadow in Edmonton, of which 2 acres lie between the pasture formerly of Geoffrey atte Berewe in the south and the land of William le Vikere in the north, extending in the west to the garden lately of John Gisors and in the east to the donor's pasture, and 3 acres of meadow lie in Edmonton marsh between the meadow of Roger de Depham in the north and the donor's meadow in south.

1064 Charter of John Venour in fee simple with warranty made at Edmonton, 20 January 1346, to Roger de Depham and Margaret his wife and the heirs of Roger of 2 acres of meadow in Edmonton marsh, in 'Middelmerssh', between the meadow of Thomas de Salesbury in the south and the meadow of the said Roger in the north.

1065 Charter of John le Venour in fee simple with warranty without date made to Roger de Depham and Margaret his wife and the heirs of Roger of 1 acre of meadow in Edmonton marsh between the meadow of the said Roger in the north and the donor's meadow in the south.

1066 Duplicate part of a fine levied, 14 April 1342, whereby John le Venour and Juliana his wife granted three gardens, 32 acres of land and $5\frac{1}{2}$ acres of meadow to Roger de Depham and Margaret his wife and the heirs of Roger in fee with warranty.
[*Feet of Fines, Lond. & Middx.* i, 118]

1067 Charter of John le Venour with warranty made at Edmonton, 10 April 1346, to Roger de Depham and Margaret his wife of 4 acres of meadow in Edmonton marsh called 'Middelmerssh' between the meadow of Thomas de Salesbury in the north and the donor's meadow in the south.

1068 [*f. 89v*] Statute merchant made 23 January 1345 by John le Venour to Roger de Depham of £40 to be paid on 10 April next.

1069 Another statute made 16 September 1345 by John le Venour to Roger de Depham of £20 to be paid at Christmas next.

1070 Valuation of goods and extent of the lands of John le Venour which he had in Edmonton on 23 January 1345, on which day he made the first statute above, made by virtue of the said statute by writ of the lord king.

1071 Another valuation of goods and extent of lands of the said John made by virtue of the same statute and memorandum that this valuation exceeds the first.

1072 Release in perpetuity by John le Venour with warranty made at Edmonton, 17 September 1346, and enrolled *in banco* for Michaelmas term 1353 in the first rotulet of charters, to Roger de Depham of all lands and tenements of the same John in Edmonton assessed before and delivered to the said Roger by virtue of the above statutes.
Witnesses: Nicholas Hotot, John le Neve, Roger Hotot, Robert de Hatfeld, Salamon Faunt, John de Yonge and others.
[PRO CP40/371 Enrolled Deeds rot. 1d]

1073 Letter patent of the mayor of London,[1] made 22 October 1352, containing the aforesaid release word for word and witnessing that the said John acknowledged it to be his deed of surrender (*cognovit illam fore factum suum*).

[1] Adam Fraunceys.

1074 Then Robert de Plesyngton and Helen his wife purchased all the lands and tenements of the said John le Venour not delivered by extent and the reversion of the tenements which had been assessed by fine as though no release had been made, as will appear. And Robert de Plesyngton died and Helen married Gilbert de Haydok and they granted their interest by another fine to Henry de Walton.

1075 Indenture of John le Venour of Edmonton with warranty made 8 July 1332 to Alice, daughter of John atte Merssh, of a part of a messuage called 'Smytheshamstal' and of 3 acres of land in the field called 'Joppesfeld' between the land of the donor and the land of William Vikere, extending on one side to the street called 'Joppesgrove' and on the other side to the land of William Fourneys called 'Boursesfeld'.

1076 [*f. 90r*] Release in perpetuity of all right of the said Alice daughter of John atte Merssh with warranty for the term of her life made at Edmonton, 3 November 1335, to John le Venour of the aforesaid 3 acres of land in which he enfeoffed her for life as appears above [**1075**].

1077 Indenture of the said Alice made at Edmonton, 3 March 1344, to William Smith (*Fabro*) of the aforesaid part of the messuage called 'Smythamstall' contained in the charter [**1075**], to be held for the life of the same Alice by payment of 3s 4d *pa.*

1078 Charter of John le Venour in fee simple with warranty made at Edmonton, 18 June 1346, to Robert Plesyngton of all the land called 'Smythescroft' and of the reversion of one messuage which the said Alice atte Merssh holds for life of the lease of the donor, to be held in fee after her death.

1079 Indenture of Robert de Plesyngton made at Edmonton, 18 June 1346, containing that if the said John le Venour pay to Robert £10 on 29 September next, and if the same Robert peacefully hold the aforesaid land up to that date, then the previous charter will be held null.

1080 Letter of John Venour made on the same day appointing attorneys to deliver seisin according to the said charter.

1081 Another letter addressed to other persons to deliver seisin of the tenements as in the said charter and made on the same day.

1082 Charter of John le Venour of Edmonton in fee simple with warranty made at Edmonton, 25 April 1344, to Robert de Plesyngton of 2 acres of meadow in Edmonton lying together in the meadow called 'Middelmerssh' between the meadow of Roger de Depham in the north and the meadow of the donor in the south, extending from the meadow of the hospital of St John in the east to the donor's garden in the west.

1083 Charter of Edmund atte Forde in fee simple with warranty made at Edmonton, 29 May 1345, to Robert de Plesyngton of the whole croft called 'Shepcotescroft' lying next to 'Enfield wood' opposite the land of Richard Proutfot in Edmonton.

1084 [*f. 90v*] Indenture of Robert de Plesyngton made on the same day containing that if Edmund atte Forde pay to Robert 12s [*pa*] henceforth for 3 years the previous charter will be null and void (*vacua*), otherwise it will remain in force on condition that the said Robert pay to Edmund 40s.

1085 Release in perpetuity by Edmund atte Forde, 9 June 1348, to Robert de Plesynton of the aforesaid land called 'Shepecotescroft' contained above in charter [**1083**].

1086 Charter of Richard Arnold in fee simple with warranty made at Edmonton, 20 May 1336, to Simon le Meleward of Ugley [Essex], called Saman, of 1 acre of land in Edmonton called 'Pondfeld' between the land of William de Causton in the east and the land of the donor in the west, extending on the north side to 'Sayes Pond' and in the south to the land of William de Causton.

1087 Charter of the said Simon in fee simple with warranty made at Edmonton, 15 November 1338, to Thomas de Gisors of the aforesaid acre of land.

1088 Charter of Thomas Gisors in fee simple with warranty made at Edmonton, 16 May 1344, to Robert de Plesynton of the same acre of land.

1089 Release in perpetuity by William Saleman with warranty made at Edmonton, 9 May 1344, to Robert de Plesyngton of 17d rent issuing from the lands of the feoffee called 'Frenchefeld' in Edmonton.

1090 Charter of Richard Prat in fee simple with warranty made at Edmonton, 18 February 1342, to Robert de Plesyngton of 1 acre and 1 rood of land in Edmonton lying in 'Berghfeld' between the land of the said Robert which he had of William Smyth [and] 'Berghlane'.

1091 Charter of Richard Jordan in fee simple with warranty made at Edmonton, 22 June 1343, to Robert de Plesyngton of $3\frac{1}{2}$ acres of land and wood in Edmonton lying between Enfield forest and the wood of William Causton.

1092 [*f.91r*] Charter of Alexander Chigwell and Christine his wife in fee simple with warranty made at Enfield, 26 May 1342, to Robert de Plesyngton and Helen his wife and the heirs of Robert of 1 acre and 1 rood of land and a moiety of one messuage and garden in Edmonton which Alice Sharp had granted to the donors, lying between the land of William Smyth in the west and the land of John atte Merssh in the east, and the south side abuts on to the aforesaid messuage and the north [side] abuts on to the land of John atte Merssh.

1093 Charter of William Smyth in fee simple without warranty made at Edmonton, 12 November 1346, to Robert de Plesyngton of the messuage called 'Smytherhamstal' in Edmonton which the donor acquired of Alice atte Merssh as appears above in the charter [**1077**].

1094 Letter of Alexander de Chigwell and Christine his wife made 26 May 1342 appointing attorneys to deliver to Robert de Plesyngton and his wife seisin of the tenements contained in charter [**1092**].

1095 Charter of Alice Sharp of Edmonton in fee simple with warranty made at Edmonton in Easter week (12–19 April) 1338, to Alexander de Chigwell and Christine his wife of the whole part of her messuage in Edmonton, formerly of John Sharp her father, and of 2 pieces of land, of which one lies between the land of William Smyth in the west and the land of John atte Merssh in the east [continues as in charter **1092**] and the other piece lies between the land of Sir John Beaumont (*Beaumond*), the east side extending to the lane leading from the manor of the said John to the stream called the 'Medesenge'.

1096 Copy of a fine made 2 June 1342, whereby Alexander Chigewell, tailor, and Christine his wife granted 2½ acres of land, a moiety of one messuage and garden in Edmonton to Robert de Plesyngton in fee with warranty.
[*Feet of Fines, Lond. & Middx.* i, 117–8]

1097 Copy of a fine made 27 October 1341, whereby William le Smyth of 'Heghestrate' in Edmonton and Agnes his wife granted 1 acre of land in Edmonton to Robert de Plesyngton in fee with warranty.
[*Feet of Fines, Lond. & Middx.* i, 117]

1098 Copy of a fine made 25 June 1344, whereby Thomas son of William de Anesty [*f. 91v*] of Edmonton granted to Robert de Plesyngton and Helen his wife and the heirs of Robert two messuages and gardens, 80 acres of land, 8 acres of meadow, 10 acres of pasture and 16 acres of wood with appurtenances in Edmonton, which Maud who was wife of William de Anesty and several other tenants named in the fine hold separately of the grantor's inheritance for the life of Maud, to be held by the feoffees after the death of Maud, with warranty.

1099 Duplicate part of a fine levied 12 November 1346 between Robert de Plesyngton and Helen his wife, plaintiffs, and Robert son of Thomas son of William de Anesty, defendant, and afterwards on 17 June 1352, after the death of the said Robert and Robert, the grant and record (*concessio et recorda*) made between Gilbert de Haydok and the said Helen, now his wife, and Alice, sister and heir of Robert son of Thomas, whereby the defendant, Robert son of Thomas, granted to the plaintiffs, Robert and Helen, 33s rent which several tenants named in the fine used to pay him, and the reversion of two messuages and gardens, 100 acres and 1 rood of land, 6 acres of meadow, 16 acres of pastures and 20 acres of wood after the death of Maud who was wife of William de Anesty, to be held by Robert and Helen and the heirs of Robert de Plesyngton with warranty.
[*Feet of Fines, Lond. & Middx.* i, 130]

1100 Indenture made in London, 29 September 1339, containing that William de Fourneys, citizen of London, leased to Robert de Plesyngton all his lands and tenements in Edmonton except the chamber beyond the gate and the cellar below, to be held for a term of 9 years at a rent of 4½ marks *pa*.

1101 Release in perpetuity by William de Fourneys made in London, 15 February 1340, to Robert de Plesyngton and Helen his wife of one messuage, two adjacent gardens, with a grange and other buildings enclosed within the same messuage, and of 32 acres of land [and] 2 acres of pasture in Edmonton which the said William had previously leased to the said Robert for 9 years.

1102 Release in perpetuity by Thomas son of William Fourneys with warranty made in London, 19 February 1340, and enrolled in the Hilary term in the same year *in banco* in the first rotulet, to Robert de Plesyngton and Helen his wife of one messuage, two adjacent gardens and the other lands contained in the previous release.
[PRO CP40/321 Enrolled Deeds rot. 1d]

1103 [*f. 92r*] Release in perpetuity of personal and real actions by Thomas son of William Fourneys made in London, 19 February 1340, to Robert de Plesyngton his heirs and executors.

1104 Writing of William de Fourneys made in London, 18 February [1340], granting to Robert de Plesington all his goods in the messuage in Edmonton which Robert has for the donor's life.

1105 Part of a fine made, 9 February 1342, whereby William of Saint Neots, parson of the church of Waresley [Hunts.], granted to Robert de Plesyngton one messuage and two gardens in fee with warranty.
[*Feet of Fines, Lond. & Middx.* i, 118]

1106 Copy of a fine levied 21 April 1325[1] whereby Thomas de Enefeld of London, pepperer, granted to William de Fourneys and Cecily his wife one messuage, 80 acres of land, 6 acres of meadow and 2 acres of pasture in Edmonton which he had of the gift of the said William, to be held by the feoffees for life and after their death successively by each of those written below in fee tail, namely Thomas, William, Phyllis and Joan, children of William Fourneys, with remainder to the right heirs of the said William.
[PRO CP25(1) 149/52 no. 330]

[1] MS: quindene Easter 18 Edward III (for 18 Edward II).

1107 Part of a fine levied 10 April 1345 whereby John Dunle and Joan his wife, who was one of the daughters of William Fourneys, release all their right in one messuage, 30 acres of land and 2

acres of pasture in Edmonton to Robert de Plesyngton and Helen his wife and the heirs of Robert with warranty.
[*Feet of Fines, Lond. & Middx.* i, 120]

1108 Copy of a fine levied 21 May 1340 whereby John Barge and Phyllis his wife the other daughter of William de Fourneys, released all their right of one messuage, two gardens, 30 acres of land and 2 acres of pasture in Edmonton to Robert de Plesynton in fee with warranty.
[*Feet of Fines, Lond. & Middx.* i, 116]

1109 Charter of Robert, son of Thomas de Anesty, in fee simple with warranty [made] at Holborn in the parish of St Andrew, London, to Robert de Plesynton of the reversion of 60 acres of land, 4 acres of meadow, 8 acres of wood and 5 acres of pasture in Edmonton which Maud who was wife of William de Anesty [*f. 92v*] holds for life, and of the reversion of 20 acres of land in Edmonton which Isabel, the grantor's mother, holds by inheritance.

1110 Indenture made at Edmonton, 26 February 1346, containing that Maud lately wife of William de Anesty attorned to Robert de Plesinton for all the tenements which she held for life, of which the same Robert acquired the reversion by fine, and that she leased to the same Robert divers parcels of the said tenements to be held at farm for the term of her life, and that he released to the same Maud the suit of waste (*accionem vasti*) in the same tenements brought previously.

1111 Indenture made at Edmonton, 27 February 1346, containing that Robert de Plesyngton leased to John de Anesty an acre of land in Edmonton lying between the land formerly of John Taillour to the south and north, extending against the tenement of the same John de Anesty in the west, to be held for the life of the same John de Anesty for an annual rent of $\frac{1}{2}$lb of cumin.

1112 Acquittance of Robert son and heir of Thomas de Anesty made in London, 27 October 1346, containing that the same Robert received of Robert de Plesyngton by divers hands certain sums of money for the reversion of all lands and tenements in Edmonton which Maud de Anesty and Isabel, mother of the said Robert, hold in severalty (*separatim*) for life.

1113 Release by William son of William de Anesty with warranty made at Edmonton, 9 March 1348, to Robert de Plesyngton of one piece of land in Edmonton called 'Sygorshawe' lying next to the land of the prior of Christchurch, London, called 'Sygescroft'.

1114 Release in perpetuity by William de Anesty with warranty made at Edmonton, 12 June 1348, to Robert de Plesynton of 2s rent issuing from a croft in Edmonton lying next to Enfield wood, which was formerly of Richard Jordan.

1115 Indenture of Robert de Plesynton made at Edmonton, 7 December 1343, containing that if John Patrik pay to the said Robert 40s at Michaelmas and Christmas next, then one croft of land and wood in East Barnet lying next to Enfield forest [*f. 93r*] between the land of Henry Wikewane in the west and the lane called 'Barnetlane' in the east, in which the said John had previously enfeoffed Robert, will revert to him.

1116 Release in perpetuity by John son and heir of John Patrik made in London, 12 October 1343, to his father of the croft in East Barnet mentioned above.

1117 Release in perpetuity by Richard son of William and John son of John Patrik made in London, 1 December 1343, of the above croft.

1118 Another part of indenture [**1115**].

1119 Release in perpetuity by John Patrik with warranty made at Edmonton, 25 July 1344, to Robert de Plesyngton of the said croft.

1120 Indented charter of John son of Edmund de Chilterne in fee tail with warranty and acquittance made at Edmonton, 4 April 1335, to John son of Ralph Patrik of the whole tenement which Godard atte Wodegate once held of William atte Forde in Edmonton together with the croft mentioned above.

1121 Release in perpetuity by Thomas son and heir of William de Anesty with warranty made at Edmonton, 1 March 1332, to William de Anesty his brother of that piece of grove called 'Gysorsgrove' in Edmonton which Maud, mother of the said Thomas, leased to the same William.

1122 Copy of a fine levied 12 November 1346 whereby John le Venour of Edmonton granted to Robert de Plesyngton and Helen his wife one messuage, two gardens, 133 acres of land, 14 acres of meadow and 15 acres of pasture in Edmonton, after Roger de Depham had received from these lands £60 due to him and acknowledged by statute merchant, to be held for the lives of Robert and Helen and thereafter to remain in succession to each of the following and their male issue, if the first die without such heir, namely John son [f. 93v] of Robert and Helen, the other male issue of Robert, Alice daughter of the same Robert, Helen, Margaret and Isabel her sisters, John de Plesyngton, brother of Robert, Adam and Henry his brothers, and Richard Caterhale in fee tail. And [of] 18d rent issuing from the tenement of John de Merssh and Alice his wife, John Mabbe and Thomas le Blount in Edmonton, and of one knight's fee in Sawbridgeworth to the said Robert de Plesyngton and Helen his wife and the heirs of Robert, saving the reversion of all the residue in default of issue to John le Venour.

1123 And Robert de Plesyngton died and Helen married Gilbert [Haydok], and they granted all their estate by fine to Sir Henry de Walton, but before this grant was made, Adam brother of Robert, to whom the remainder was entailed by fine after the death of certain other persons named in the fine above, granted the reversion of the same tenements to the said Sir Henry by fine as appears below.

1124 Duplicate part of a fine levied 1 July 1350 and afterwards recorded on 13 October 1351 whereby Adam de Plesyngton granted to Henry de Walton [archdeacon of Richmond] one messuage, three tofts, 20 acres of land, 6 acres of pasture, 23 acres of wood and 3s rent in Edmonton, East Barnet and Enfield, and granted the reversion of $3\frac{1}{2}$ messuages, 140 acres of land, 10 acres of meadow, 24 acres of pasture and 34s rent in the aforesaid vills and $\frac{1}{6}$ knight's fee in Sawbridgeworth, to be held by the said Henry after the death of Helen wife of Gilbert Haydok in fee simple with warranty.
[*Feet of Fines, Lond. & Middx.* i, 228]

1125 Copy of a fine levied 9 February 1351 whereby Gilbert Haydok and Helen his wife granted to Henry de Walton one messuage, 30 acres of land and 2 acres of meadow in Edmonton, East Barnet and Sawbridgeworth in fee with warranty, and three messuages, 3 tofts, 97 acres of land, 6 acres of meadow, 14 acres of pasture, 4 [*recte* 24] acres of wood, 38s rent, half of one

[messuage] and one knight's fee in the said vills for the life of Helen with warranty.
[*Feet of Fines, Lond. & Middx.* i, 228]

1126 Duplicate part of a fine[1] levied 9 February [*f. 94r*] 1351 whereby Gilbert Haydok and Helen his wife granted to Henry de Walton one messuage, 30 acres of land and 2 acres of pasture in Edmonton in fee with warranty and released all their right in three messuages, 3 tofts, 97 acres of land, 6 acres of meadow, 14 acres of pasture, 24 acres of wood and 28s [*recte* 38s] rent, half of one messuage in Edmonton and $\frac{1}{6}$ knight's fee in East Barnet and Sawbridgeworth, to be held by the said Henry for the life of Helen with warranty.

[1] Presumably a duplicate of the above, despite slight variations in the transcription.

1127 Duplicate part of a fine levied 20 January 1352 and afterwards recorded on 22 April 1352 whereby Gilbert Haydok and Helen his wife granted to Henry de Walton, in fee with warranty for the life of Helen, one messuage, 133 acres of land, 14 acres of meadow, 12 acres of pasture in Edmonton which were to revert to Helen for life, after Roger de Depham, to whom the tenements were delivered in execution of the aforesaid statute,[1] raised from them £60.
[*Feet of Fines, Lond. & Middx.* i, 228]

[1] Above, **1122**.

1128 Release in perpetuity by John de Plesyngton with warranty made at Preston in the first week of Lent 1342[1] to Henry de Walton of all the tenements contained in the above fine [**1127**] and enrolled at Preston in the court of the duke of Lancaster on Wednesday in the said week.

[1] Ash Wednesday = 13 February.

1129 Release in perpetuity by Adam de Plesyngton with warranty made at Preston in the above week to Henry Walton of the same tenements contained in the release titled [**1128**].

1130 Charter of Henry Walton in fee simple without warranty made in London, 3 December 1351, to Roger de Depham of all his lands and tenements in Edmonton and Enfield.

1131 Letter patent of Henry de Walton made in London, 3 December 1351, appointing John Claveryng, his attorney, to deliver to Roger de Depham seisin of the tenements contained in the previous charter.

1132 Release in perpetuity by Henry de Walton, [archdeacon of Richmond], without warranty made, [*f. 94v*] 12 May 1352, to Roger de Depham of all lands and tenements lately of John le Venour in Edmonton and of all lands and tenements in which the said Henry had previously enfeoffed the said Roger.
Witnesses: Richard de Kelleshull, knight, Henry de Grene, John Lovekyn, William de Welde, Simon de Dolsely, John Not, Adam Fraunceys, Nicholas Hotot and others.
[WAM 103]

1133 Release in perpetuity by John Ive of Ellington without warranty and date made to John son of John Marsh of lands and tenements in Edmonton whereof he sued (*implicitavit*) the said John Marsh before the justices of the bench, 6 Edward II (1312–13). Also quitclaim to Nicholas, William and Robert, sons of John Marsh, and Maud, Alice and Katherine, their sisters, of all the lands and tenements for which he sued them before the same justices in the said year.
Witnesses: William de Anstey, William le Viker, Robert de Acton, Richard Duraunt, Giles Herberd, John de la Paneterye, John de Maundevill senior, John de Maundevill junior and others.
[WAM 205]

1134 Acquittance of John de Charleton, citizen of London, made at Westminster, 18 November 1342, to John atte Merssh of Edmonton of £20 which was acknowledged in Chancery by the said John atte Merssh to be due to him.

1135 Charter of John atte Merssh of Edmonton and Alice his wife in fee simple with warranty made at Edmonton, 3 October 1328, to Roger de Depham and Margaret his wife of a plot of land in Edmonton between the tenement formerly of John Sharp and the donor's land in the south and the land of Amice Broun and that formerly of Geoffrey atte Barewe in the north, extending eastwards to the meadow of the said Roger called 'Plottesmedwe' and westwards to the highway.
Witnesses: Richard de Wirhale, John le Venour, John Castle, Edmund Pymme, John atte Strete, William le Vykere, John le Vykere, William le Smyth, Hugh de Heydene and others.
[WAM 120]

1136 Charter of John atte Merssh and Alice his wife in fee simple with

warranty made at Edmonton, 3 October 1328, to Roger de Depham and Margaret his wife of 5 acres of land in Edmonton, [continues as in **1135**].
[*Witnesses*: As **1135**.]
[WAM 144]

1137 Charter of John atte Merssh in fee simple with warranty made at Edmonton, 10 March 1349, to Roger de Depham and Margaret his wife of a piece of land in Edmonton between the donor's meadow in the east and the land of the feoffee in the west and north.
Witnesses: John le Wyrhale, John Castle, William atte Strete, John le Smyth, Thomas le Rowe and others.
[WAM 154]

1138 Indenture of John atte Merssh, 4 October 1328, in which he granted to Roger de Depham 13 acres of land in Edmonton between the donor's land in the south and the land in which the donor had previously enfeoffed [*f. 95r*] the said Roger and his wife in the north, and between the donor's meadow in the east and the tenement formerly of John Sharp in the west, to be held for 12 years at a payment of 6s 6d *pa* to the donor, his heirs and assigns with warranty.
[*Witnesses*: As **1135**.]
[WAM 142]

1139 Release in perpetuity by John atte Merssh with warranty[1] made in London, 12 December 1330, to Roger de Depham of 6 acres of land in Edmonton leased to the feoffee by the said John for a term of years lying between the land also leased to the feoffee by the same John in the east and the tenement formerly of John Sharp in the west, the releasor's land in the south and the land of the feoffee and his wife in the north in which the releasor enfeoffed them.
Witnesses: Richard de Wyrehal, John le Venour, John Castle, Edmund Pymme, John atte Strate, William le Vykere, John le Vykere, William le Smyth, John of St Edmunds (*de Sancto Edmundo*), Thomas de Cantuar', John le Herwardstok, John de Shirbourne of London and others.
[WAM 141]

[1] MS: without warranty.

1140 Grant of Amice Broun with warranty made at Edmonton, 15

October 1329, to Roger de Depham of 2 acres of land in Edmonton in the field called 'Querndonesfeld' between the land of Roger de Depham in the south and the land formerly of Ralph [atte Berwe] in the north, extending to the land of the said Roger in the east and to the highway called 'le Grenestrate' in the west, to be held for the life of the donor for a sum of money in hand for the next four years, and thereafter for 12d *pa*. *Witnesses*: Richard de Wyrhale, John atte Merssh, John Castle, William le Vikere, John atte Strete and others. [WAM 111]

1141 Release in perpetuity by John atte Merssh with warranty made at Edmonton, 9 March, 1349, to Roger de Depham of the aforesaid 2 acres of land leased by the said Amice to Roger for her life.

1142 Letter of Henry Lorymer made at Edmonton, 10 April 1340, containing that if John Patrik pay to him 2s 8d within 3 years of 29 September next, a croft in Edmonton lying next to 'Alvenebregge' in which he enfeoffed the said Henry by his charter would be returned to John and the charter annulled.

1143 Charter of William son of Robert de Forde in fee simple with warranty without date made to Ralph son of John Patrik (*Paterici*) of a croft of land called 'Ruweputel' with adjacent grove to the west lying between the grove of the said Ralph and the land of Stephen son of William, to be held of the donor by service of 2d *pa*.

1144 Charter of John Denteyth' in fee simple with warranty made at Edmonton, 15 February 1314, to John [*f. 95v*] Patryk of one messuage [with] adjacent croft between the water called 'Medesenge' and the land of Walter Basse, and of one piece of land in Colegrave between the land of Richard de Wylhale and the land formerly of Nicholas Laurence, and of a piece of land in the Hyde between the land of William Godhowe and the land which Richard Proutfot holds of Geoffrey de Say, and of 2 acres of land in the field called 'Brodrisshefeld' between the land formerly of John Bytok on either side, and of all that land called 'Russhefeldes' lying between the land of John Marsh and the water called 'Chichebrok', and of 3 acres of meadow in Edmonton marsh of which 1 acre lies in 'Chipolshote' between the meadow of the prior of St John in the south and the meadow lately of Robert North (*Aquilon'*) in the north and 2 acres lie between the

meadow of Thomas le Rowe in the north and the meadow of William Causton in the south.
Witnesses: William de la Forde, John de la Forde, William de Anesti, Robert de Anesti, Robert de Actone, John Marsh, William le Fiker, John Castle and others.
[WAM 155]

1145 Charter of Thomas Picot in fee simple with warranty and acquittance without date made to John Sharp of 2 acres of land lying between the land of Thomas Pycot in the north and the land of John Faulkner (*Falconarii*) in the south, extending on the east side to the road leading to the messuage formerly of the feoffee and in the west to the land of Richard son of Reyner, to be held of the donor by 12d *pa.*
Witnesses: John Blund, William de la Forde, Robert Gizors, Richard Picot, Richard de Anesty, William Picot, Richard de la Brace, William Marsh, John Clerk and others.
[Date: *temp.* Henry III.]
[WAM 107]

1146 Charter of John Proudomme in fee simple with warranty and acquittance without date made to John Sharp of Edmonton, in return for a fine of 10s, of an acre of land lying between the land of Ralph le Berewe and the land of John le Hunteporte extending from the field called 'Berhfeld' from the west to the land of John le Hunteporte in the east, to be held of the donor by one clove of garlic *pa* and due services to the chief lords, viz. 4d.
Witnesses: Geoffrey de Querendon, Robert Gisors, John le Burg', Richard Street (*de Strata*), Richard Humfrey, Geoffrey son of Laurence Ford (*de Forda*), and Nicholas his brother, Stephen de Colewell and others.
[Date: *temp.* Henry III.]
[WAM 106]

1147 Charter of Simon Flemyng of Great Munden [Herts.] in fee simple with warranty made at Edmonton, 7 July 1325,[1] to William, younger son of Oger le Casiere, of 1 acre of land lying in 'Haggefeld' between the land of Hamo Fishmonger (*Piscenarii*) in the south and north, extending on the eastern side to the field called 'Lyncsfeld' [and] in the west to the land once held by John Hammyng of Geoffrey de Say.
Witnesses: Richard de Wylehale, John Marsh, John Castle, Robert de Actone, Adam de Chitren, Edmund Pymme, John Patric,

clerk, and others
[WAM 99]

¹ 'Translation of the Blessed Thomas, bishop and martyr of Canterbury, in the beginning of the 19th year of the reign of Edward II.' 7 July is generally considered to be the last day of the regnal year for Edward II's reign, but the use of *incipiente* must indicate 1325 rather than 1326.

1148 Charter of the said William son of Oger in fee simple with warranty made at Edmonton, 13 March 1330, to Michael de Knightbregge of the aforesaid acre of land contained in the last charter.
Witnesses: Richard de Wilehale, John Marsh, John Castle, John Street (*de Strata*), Adam de Chiltrene, Edmund Pymme and others.
[WAM 121]

1149 Release in perpetuity by Robert Aleyse without warranty made at Edmonton, 6 September 1330, to Michael de Knyghtbregge of the aforesaid acre of land.
Witnesses: John le Venour, John Marsh, John Castle, William le Vikere, John Street (*de Strata*), William Smith (*Fabro*), Robert le Neweman, Oger le Casyere and others.
[WAM 150]

1150 [*f. 96r*] Charter of Nicholas de Knyghtebregge in fee simple with warranty made at Edmonton, 31 December 1331, to Robert le Taillor of Edmonton of the aforementioned acre of land which descended to the donor after the death of Michael his uncle.

1151 Charter of Robert le Taillour in fee simple with warranty at Edmonton, 6 May 1333, to Roger de Depham and Margaret his wife of the same acre of land.
Witnesses: John le Venour, John atte Mersh, John Castle, Richard de Wyrehale, John atte Strate, William le Vikere, Edmund Pymme, Robert de Anesty and others.
[WAM 145]

1152 Charter of Richard son of John atte Heygate in fee simple with warranty made at Edmonton, 5 October 1298, to Richard Prat and Alice his wife for their service and for a fine of 100s of all the donor's tenements in Edmonton.
Witnesses: William Ford (*de Forda*), John Ford, John Marsh, William le Vikere, John Gysors, Richard le Ken, Nicholas Laurence, John atte Strate, Ralph Clerk and others.
[WAM 116]

1153 Charter of Alice Prat and Richard her son in fee simple with warranty made at Edmonton, 1 April 1330, to Roger de Depham and Margaret his wife of a messuage with adjacent croft in Edmonton between the land formerly of Geoffrey atte Berewe in the east and 'Grenestrete' in the west, extending to 'Heygatelane' in the south and the land of William Vikere.
Witnesses: John atte Merssh, William le Vikere, John atte Castel, John atte Strate, William Smith (*Fabro*), Robert Gulle and others.
[WAM 151]

1154 Charter of Peter Lorimer of Edmonton in fee simple with warranty made at Edmonton, 5 January 1298 to Roger le Kyng of Tottenham of a piece of land in Edmonton lying in 'Langheg' between the land of the prior of Holy Trinity, London, in the south and the land of John son of Stephen of Tottenham in the north, extending east and west to the land of the said prior, to be held of the chief lords of the fee for due services, namely 4d *pa.* And the feoffee paid 40s in fine.
Witnesses: William atte Forde, John Marsh, Ralph atte Berewe, Ralph Clerk, William le Vykere, Robert atte Fen, Hugh de Heydene, clerk, and others.
[WAM 147]

1155 Charter of Roger Spirk of Edmonton in fee simple with warranty made at Edmonton, 19 March 1303, to Roger le Kyng of Tottenham of one piece of land in Edmonton lying in 'Langheg' between the land of Richard le Rowe and the land of Juliana daughter of Geoffrey Laurence, extending in the east to the land of John Tebaud.
Witnesses: William de la Forde, John de la Forde, John Marsh, Geoffrey de la Berwe, Nicholas Laurence, Richard Cook (*Coco*) of Edmonton, John Tebaud, Anselm de Hatfeud, John atte Watere of Tottenham, Hugh de Heydene, clerk, and others.
[WAM 117]

1156 [*f. 96v*] Charter of Geoffrey Kyng of Tottenham in fee simple with warranty made at Edmonton, 15 March 1331, to Roger de Depham of 2 pieces of land in Edmonton lying in 'Langheg', of which one piece lies between the land of Helen Laurence in the south and the land of Thomas le Rowe in the north, extending to the land of John Tebaud in the east and the land of Richard de Wirhale in the west, and another piece lies between the land of the prior of Holy Trinity, London, in the south and the land of John Stephene in the north, extending to the land of the said

prior in the east and the land of John le Keu in the west.
Witnesses: John atte Merssh, John atte Castel, John le Venour,
John atte Strete, William le Vykere, John le Vykere, William le
Smyth, Hugh de Heydene and others.
[WAM 143]

1157 Release in perpetuity by John Denteyt without warranty made
at Edmonton, 5 May 1314, to Richard de Wilehale of a piece of
land lying in a field called 'Colegrave' between the land in which
the releasor had enfeoffed John Patrik and the land of William
de Anesty.
Witnesses: William de la Forde, John de la Forde, William de
Anesty, Robert de Acton, John Marsh, William le Fiker and
others.
[WAM 139]

1158 Charter of John son of Richard de Wyrhall in fee simple with
warranty made in London, 4 May 1340, to Roger de Depham
and Margaret his wife and the heirs of Roger of $1\frac{1}{2}$ acres of
meadow lying in Edmonton marsh between the meadow of
William de Causton in the south and the meadow of Richard
Sebarn in the north, extending to the meadow of John le Venour
in the west.
Witnesses: John le Venour, John atte Merssh, John atte Castell,
William Vyker, John atte Strete and others.
[WAM 4]

1159 Charter of John de Wilhale in fee simple with warranty made at
Edmonton, 1 December 1340, to Roger de Depham and Margaret
his wife and the heirs of the said Roger, of 4 acres of meadow
and 2 acres of land in Edmonton, of which 2 acres of meadow
lie in Edmonton marsh near 'le Botstake' of Chingford, $\frac{1}{2}$ acre of
land lies in 'Chipolschot' between the meadow of John atte Pole
in the north and the meadow of the said Roger in the south,
another $\frac{1}{2}$ acre of meadow lies between the meadow of John de
Chilterne in the east and the the meadow of John Mayheu in
the west, and 2 acres of land lie in 'Okefeld' between the land
formerly of John Miles and that formerly of Geoffrey de Anesty.
Witnesses: John le Venour, John Marsh (*le Mareys*), John Castle,
William le Vyker, John atte [?Strate], ...
[WAM 153, part damaged]

1160 Release in perpetuity by Simon Bonde without warranty made
in London, 8 May 1349, to Roger de Depham of all lands and

meadows which the same Roger holds in Edmonton of the grant of John de Wilhale late the husband of Joan, now wife of the said Simon.

1161 [*f. 97r*] Release in perpetuity by William Pykerel made in London, 5 October 1344, to Roger de Depham of a third part of 2 acres of land in Edmonton in a field called 'Okfeld' which belonged to Alice, now the releasor's wife, as dower by gift of Richard de Wilhale her former husband.
[WAM 105]

1162 Letter of John de Wilhale made at Edmonton, 1 December 1340, assigning in his place John Marsh to deliver seisin to Roger de Depham and Margaret his wife of the tenements contained in the charter [**1159**].
[WAM 149]

1163 Another letter of John son of Richard de Wilhale assigning John Marsh to deliver seisin to Roger de Depham and Margaret of the tenements contained in the charter [**1158**] and of the same date [4 May 1340].

1164 Charter of Henry Goldyng in fee simple with warranty made at Edmonton, 16 May 1334, to Roger de Depham and Margaret his wife of a piece of land in Edmonton lying between the lane called 'Hemmyngeswodegate' in the north and the land of William atte Forde in the south.

1165 Letter of John Cok[1] of Exeter, clerk, made in London, 6 August 1335, containing that he sold to Roger de Depham all the corn growing on the lands formerly of John le Venour, previously granted to Robert de Taunton, clerk.
[WAM 146]

   [1] MS: Cook.

1166 Recognizance of Thomas le Rowe made to Roger de Depham in Chancery, 7 May 1331, of £40 to be paid 13 October next.
[*CCR 1330–3*, 311.]

1167 Charter of William le Vikere of Edmonton in fee simple with warranty made in that place, 20 September 1310, to John his son of a piece of land called 'Blakelond' in Edmonton lying in the field called the Hyde between the land of Geoffrey de Say and that of William de Forde, extending in the west to the land of

William le Casiere and in the east to the land of John de Forde.
Witnesses: William de Forde ... John Marsh, John de Forde,
Ralph Clerk ... Robert de Acton, Thomas de Anesty, John
Patrik, William Clerk.
[WAM 281, badly damaged]

1168 Release in perpetuity by John le Vikere of Edmonton with
warranty made in London to Roger de Depham of 'le Blakelond'
in the Hyde in Edmonton which the releasor had previously
leased to the said Roger for a term of years.
Witnesses: ... Hamond, William de Elsyng, Thomas de Cantuar',
John de Herewardstok, William de Braghyng, ... de Depham
and others.
[WAM 115, partly torn]

1169 [*f. 97v*] Indented charter of Richard called le Keu of Edmonton
and Agnes his wife, lately wife of Ralph atte Berewe, in fee tail
with warranty and acquittance made at Edmonton, 14 February
1276, to James of St Edmunds (*de Sancto Edmundo*) and Margaret
his wife, lately wife of Geoffrey atte Berewe, and Christine,
daughter and heir of the same Geoffrey, and the heirs of Christine
of all lands and tenements of the dower or purchase of the said
Agnes with her first husband in Edmonton, to be held of the
donor at a rent of 8 marks *pa* for the life of Agnes and by due
services to the chief lords.
Witnesses: William atte Forde, John Marsh, Ralph Clerk, Robert
de Actone, John Gisors, William le Vikere and others.
[WAM 108]

1170 Charter of Richard le Ken of Edmonton and Agnes his wife in
fee tail with warranty and acquittance made at Edmonton, 14
February 1276,[1] to James of St Edmunds (*Sancto Edmundo*) and
Margaret his wife and Christine, daughter and heir of Geoffrey
atte Berewe, and the heirs of Christine of all lands and tenements
purchased by Agnes and Ralph atte Bergh her first husband in
Edmonton.

  [1] MS: 5 Edward I (for 4 Edward I, see below).

1171 Letter of Richard le Keu and Agnes of the same date[1] appointing
in their place William de Anesty to deliver seisin according to
the charter [**1169**].

Witnesses: William atte Forde, John Marsh, Ralph Clerk, John Gisors, William le Vikere, Robert de Actone and others.
[WAM 113]

¹ Original charter: the feast of St Valentine, 4 Edward I.

1172 Release in perpetuity by the said Richard le Keu and Agnes made 18 February 1276 to the said James of St Edmunds, Margaret, Christine and her heirs of all the above.
Witnesses: William atte Forde, John Marsh, John atte Forde, Robert de Actone, John Gisors, John atte Strate and others.
[WAM 101]

1173 Letter of Geoffrey atte Bergh made at Edmonton, 6 December 1308, attorning in his place John atte Strate to deliver to Simon de Kelshull seisin of one messuage, 6 pieces of land and three pieces of meadow in Edmonton.¹
Witnesses: John Marsh, Robert de Acton, William le Viker, John Gysors, John Castle, William Clerk and others.
[WAM 148]

¹ See **1179**.

1174 Release in perpetuity by John son of Warin Quyntyn of Newport with warranty made at Edmonton, 17 October 1312, to Margaret atte Berewe of 34s 4d rent in Edmonton which the releasor used to receive of the tenement formerly held by Geoffrey atte Berewe, late husband of the said Margaret.
Witnesses: Richard de Wyrhalle, William atte Forde, John atte Merssh, John de Gysors of Edmonton, John Castle of the same, John atte Strate, Ellis of Suffolk, Richard Durant, Robert de Asshele, Richard de Kelleshull, Thomas Wylliet, Roger de Depham and others.
[WAM 112]

1175 Letter of Geoffrey de Bergh made at Edmonton, 5 December 1308, appointing John Marsh to deliver seisin to Simon de Kelshull of 20 acres of land and one piece of meadow in Edmonton.
Witnesses: Robert de Acketone, William le Vikere, Ralph Clerk, John Gysors, William Clerk and others.
[WAM 57]

1176 [*f. 98r*] Indenture made 25 October 1309, containing that if Geoffrey de Say deliver (*amiserit*) custody of Christine daughter and heir of Geoffrey de la Berewe to John Quyntyn, by whom he was sued at an inquest of the jury of the neighbourhood (*per iurationem patrie*) in the king's court, the said Geoffrey de Say will be held to pay to Margaret, who was the wife of Geoffrey Berewe and to whom he had sold the wardship and marriage of Christine, 20 marks with damages which he had received from her for the wardship, and Margaret would then be deemed to have returned the wardship to Geoffrey de Say.

Witnesses: John de la Chambre, clerk, Roger de Depham, John de Hardingham and others.

[WAM 32, French]

1177 Letter of Geoffrey de Say without date containing that he sold to the said Margaret for 20 marks the wardship and marriage of Christine daughter and heir of Geoffrey de la Berewe.

Witnesses: William de la Forde, John his brother, Robert del Fen, Robert de Acton, Ralph le Clerk and others.

[WAM 18, French]

1178 Acquittance of Geoffrey de Say made at Edmonton, 21 October 1309, made to Margaret, who was wife of Geoffrey de la Berewe, and Richard le Keu and John atte Hegueweye of 20 marks received from them for the said wardship.

[WAM 74, French]

1179 Charter of Geoffrey atte Berewe in fee simple with warranty made at Edmonton, 6 December 1308, to Simon de Kelshull of one messuage situated next to 'Heigatesbregge' between the road called 'Querndoneslane' and the donor's tenement, and of six pieces of land in Edmonton, of which one lies between 'Grenedich' and the meadow formerly of Anselm Knotte and is called 'Southfeld', another piece is called 'Northfeld' enclosed on all sides, a third called the field of Thomas Godard lies in Colewell between the land of John de Colewell and the tenement of Agnes Sones, and a fourth lies in Colewell between the land of Adam Yarild and the land of William Amys, and the fifth piece lies in Colewell between the lands of John Castle and Richard le Sumter, and the sixth piece also lies in Colewell between the lands of John Castle and John Colewell, and of three pieces of meadow in Edmonton lying between the meadow of William le Venour and the donor's tenements called 'le Amb[er]landes'. Letter of attorney to deliver seisin on this charter appears above [**1173**].

Witnesses: William de Forde, John Marsh, William de Anesty, John de Forde, William le Vikere, Ralph Clerk, Robert de Actone, John Gysors, John Castle, Nicholas Laurence, Roger

Spirk, William Clerk and others.
[WAM 73]

1180 Indented charter of Simon de Kelleshull made at Edmonton, 14
January 1309, to Margaret who was wife of the said Geoffrey
atte Bergh of all the tenements contained in the previous charter,
to be held for the life of the same Margaret and after her death
to remain to Christine daughter of the aforesaid Geoffrey in fee
simple.
Witnesses: William de la Forde, John Marsh, John de la Forde,
Robert le Despenser, John atte Strate and others.
[WAM 36]

1181 Another part of the previous indenture.

1182 [*f. 98v*] Charter of Christine daughter of Geoffrey atte Bergh of
Edmonton made in London, 24 July 1322, to Roger de Depham
and Margaret his wife for life of all the lands and tenements which
they then held in Edmonton which had previously belonged to
Geoffrey atte Berewe, Christine's father.

1183 Acquittance of John Quyntyn made in the house of James of St
Edmunds (*Sancto Edmundo*) in London, 9 July 1311, of 103s received
from the said James and Margaret his wife in payment of all
arrears due to him for certain lands held of the same John, of
whom they held the wardship after the death of Geoffrey de
Berewe, first husband of Margaret.
[WAM 20]

1184 Release in perpetuity by John son of Warin Quyntein of Newport
made at Edmonton, 20 July 1308, to Margaret atte Berewe of
34s 4d rent in Edmonton which she used to receive from all the
lands and tenements which Geoffrey de Berewe, her late husband,
held of the same John in Edmonton.
Witnesses: Richard de Wyrehale, Ellis of Suffolk, John atte Merssh,
Thomas Wylhet, Robert Assele, Roger Depham, Richard de
Keleshull and others.
[WAM 54]

1185 Charter of John son of Waryn Quyntyn of Newport in fee simple
made at Edmonton, 16 October 1312, to Margaret atte Berewe
formerly wife of Geoffrey atte Berewe of 34s 4d rent contained
in the above release [**1184**].
Witnesses: Richard de Wyrhale, William atte Forde, John atte

Merssh, John de Gysors of Edmonton, John Castle of the same, John atte Strate, Ellis of Suffolk, Richard Durant, Robert de Asshele, Thomas de Wylliet, Richard de Kelleshull, Roger de Depham and others.
[WAM 30]

1186 Charter of Geoffrey de la Berewe in fee simple with warranty, made at Edmonton, 5 December 1308, to Simon de Kelleshull of 20 acres of land in Edmonton, of which 10 acres lie in 'Nortfeld' between the land of William le Vikere and the donor's land, and the other 10 acres lie in 'Thesonitefeld' between 'la Grenedich' and the donor's land, and of one piece of meadow called 'la Exelase' between the land of William le Venour and the donor's land, of which mention was made above [**1179**].
Witnesses: John Marsh, William de Forde, William de Anesty, John de Forde, Robert de Aiketone, William le Fyker, Ralph Clerk, John Gysors, John atte Strate, Richard Cook (*Coco*), William Laurence, William Clerk and others.
[WAM 69]

1187 Charter of John de la Forde in fee simple with warranty and acquittance without date made to John le Taillour of the croft of land contained in [**323**], to be held of the donor by 12d *pa* for all service.
Witnesses: William de la Forde, Richard de Anesty, John Marsh, Ralph atte Berewe, Geoffrey Laurence, Nicholas Laurence and others.
[Date: before 5 March 1318.]
[WAM 5]

1188 Indenture made 29 September 1268 containing that Thomas de la Forde leased to Ralph de la Berewe two-thirds of a tenement formerly of Ralph de Querndon except a wood, reliefs and heriots on condition that the lessee will manure 3 acres of land each year within his term and maintain the houses of the tenement in the same condition as he received them or better, to be held from this date for 3 years at a rent of 9 marks *pa*.
Witnesses: Thomas Picot, Richard Picot, William Picot, Robert Gysors, Geoffrey de la Forde, John (?)Thermyge.
[WAM 64]

1189 [*f. 99r*] Charter of Alice daughter of William Cole in fee simple with warranty and acquittance without date made to Adam Cole her brother of a messuage in the parish of St Leonard, Stratford, which the donor bought of William Tucheit, to be held of the donor by rent of $\frac{1}{2}$d *pa* and 4d to be paid to the chief lords of the fee for all service.

Witnesses: Alan Lebaud, Hamo de Bedesunt, Adam de Beddern', Hugh de Belebarbe, Simon le Brun, William son of Peter, Robert de la Funtayne, Alex Clerk and others.

[Date: *temp*. Henry III.]

[WAM 70]

1190 Charter of Salamon Butcher (*Carnificis*) in fee simple with warranty without date made to John son of John Cross (*de Cruce*) of 1 acre of land in 'Godthywescroft' lying between the donor's land in the west and the land of John Blundy in the east, extending to the land of Thurstan Salamon in the south and in the north to the land of Querndon, and the said John paid 36s in fine. To be held of the donor at a rent of 2d *pa* saving foreign service.

Witnesses: John Blund, Thomas Picoth, William Ford (*de Fordia*), Laurence Ford (*de Fordia*), Roger le Burser, Geoffrey son of Idonia, Richard Picot, John son of Agnes, Alan de Waleden, John Hereberd, Geoffrey Preacher (*predicatore*), Godard Haubry and others.

[Date: *temp*. Henry III.]

[WAM 50]

1191 Charter of Richard de Wrotham in fee simple with warranty and acquittance without date made to Thomas Pycot of all the land called 'Forde' in Wrotham [Kent] and of 1 perch of land which is in the fee of Addington [Kent], to be held of the donor by one pair of gold spurs or 12d and by due services to the chief lords of the fee.

1192 Indenture made 3 July 1330 containing that if Walter Lorymer peacefully hold one piece of pasture in Edmonton called 'Soutlase' for 8 years from 29 September 1330 then the charter of feoffment made thereof to the said Walter by John atte Merssh will be held null.

Witnesses: John le Venour, John Castle, John Street (*de Strata*), Edmund Pymme, John Cook (*Coco*), Peter le Lorymer and others.

[WAM 33]

1193 Indenture made 29 September 1249 containing that Margery More (*de Mora*) leased to John son of John Marsh all her land with houses in Edmonton, to be held from this date for 9 years, which land John will cultivate and improve as much as possible within the said term. And the lessor will receive one third of the fruits arising thereof each year within the prescribed term. The houses are to be maintained and returned in the same condition as they were received. If the lessor wishes to sell the houses within the term, they will be offered first to the lessee. With warranty and acquittance.

Witnesses: William Ford (*de Forda*), Thomas Picot, John FitzJohn, Laurence Ford (*de Forda*), Geoffrey Marsh, Richard Picot, William Picot, Robert de Gisors, Richard Lif and others.

[WAM 68]

1194 Indenture made at Edmonton, 8 November 1329, containing that if John Marsh pay to Walter Lorymer and Edmund atte Slow 50s within one year from Christmas next and if Walter and Edmund hold the whole pasture called 'Pykoteslase' and all the pasture called 'le Westfeld' in Edmonton until the end of that time, the charter made thereof to the said Walter and Edmund will be held null.

Witnesses: John Castle (*de Castro*), Edmund Pymme, John de Stre[te], ... Wyliot, Thomas le Rowe of Edmonton and others.

[WAM 14, much mutilated]

1195 Charter of John Marsh with warranty made at Edmonton, 16 March 1349, made to John, Nicholas and Henry, the donor's sons, of one piece of garden called 'Pykotestenement' and another piece of garden called 'Newegardyn', to be held for their lives for due and customary service.

Witnesses: William Pymme, William atte Strate, Richard de Godestre, William le Cook, Henry le Lorymer and Walter le Lorymer of Edmonton and others.

[WAM 17]

1196 [*f. 99v*] Charter of Robert de Acton in fee simple with warranty made at Edmonton, 1 February 1324, to Stephen de Asshewey, knight, of all lands and tenements which the feoffee leased to the donor in Edmonton.

Witnesses: Richard de Wyllehalle, William de Anesty, Edmund Pymme, John Castle, John Marsh, Robert atte Fen, Hugh de Hedene, John de Strate, Robert de Anesty.

[WAM 62]

1197 Release in perpetuity by Robert de Acton made at Edmonton with warranty, 16 February 1324, to Stephen de Asshewy, knight, of all lands and tenements contained in the previous charter.

Witnesses: Matthew de Essex, William de Anesty, Hugh de Heydene, John Gysors of Edmonton, Edmund Pymme, John de Wattone and others.
[WAM 43]

1198 Charter of Stephen Asshwy in fee simple with warranty made at Edmonton, 2 March 1324, to Roger de Depham and Margaret his wife of all lands and tenements which the donor had in Edmonton.
Witnesses: Richard de Willehale, William de Causton, John Marsh, John Castle, Edmund Pymme, John atte Strete, William le Vykere, John de Gysors, Robert de Anesty, Robert atte Fen, Matthew de Essex, John de Hardyngham and others.
[WAM 9]

1199 Release in perpetuity by Stephen de Asshwy, knight, with warranty made at Edmonton, 8 March 1324, to Roger de Depham and Margaret his wife of all lands and tenements contained in the previous charter.
Witnesses: John de Grantham, Adam de Sarum, Richard But, Matthew de Essex, Gregory de Norton, John de Hardyngham, William de Elsynge, Thomas de Cantuar', John de Shirebourne, clerk, and others.
[WAM 89]

1200 Letter of Stephen de Asshewy made in London, 2 March 1324, assigning John de Watton to deliver to Roger de Depham and Margaret seisin of the tenements contained the previous charter.

1201 Release in perpetuity of Margaret who was wife of Stephen de Asshewy made in London, 28 February 1343, to Roger de Depham and Margaret his wife of the same lands and tenements.
[WAM 82]

1202 Part of a fine levied, 25 June 1317, containing that Philip de Farnham granted two-thirds of a messuage, toft, 120 acres of land, 15 acres of meadow, 12 acres of pasture and 23s rent in Edmonton to John atte Merssh and Alice his wife and heir, together with the reversion of the third part of the said tenements, which Isabel who was wife of John atte Merssh the elder holds in dower.
[WAM 22]
[*Feet of Fines, Lond. & Middx.* i, 94–5]

1203 Release in perpetuity by Thomas son of Roger de Wynchestre with warranty made in London, 17 September 1333, to Roger de Depham and Margaret of two pieces of land and one piece of meadow.

1204 [*f. 100r*] Indenture made in London, 12 March 1337, containing that John de Chilterne leased to Roger de Depham all lands lying in 'Honifeld' at Old Ford, 'Longheg', the inning of 'Hokfeld', the inning of 'Colgrove', 'Gilbertesfeld', 'Gilberteshawe, 'Baselyfeld', 'Baselyhaw', in 2 crofts lying between the pasture called 'Mannemedes' and the field called the Hyde, and all the land lying in the Hyde except two pieces called 'Claricedoles' and all the pasture called 'la Mannemede', to be held from 29 September next for 3 years at an annual rent of 5 marks.
[WAM 47]

1205 Charter of Denise daughter and heir of William atte Merssh in fee simple with warranty made in London, 22 June 1349, to Roger de Depham of all the donor's lands and tenements in Edmonton.
Witnesses: Roger Houtot, Robert de Hathfeld, Salamon le Faunt, William Fossard, John le Clerk, William le Vykere, Robert le Vykere, John Goldyng and others.
[WAM 63]

1206 Letter of Denise, daughter and heir of William atte Merssh, made 22 June 1349, assigning John de Claverynge to deliver to Roger de Depham seisin of all the tenements of the said William in Edmonton made by charter of feoffment.
[WAM 84]

1207 Indenture made in London, 29 September 1340, containing that Roger de Depham leased to John Broun 4 acres and 1 rood of land in Edmonton, of which 1 acre and 3 roods lie between the land of William Pikard in the south and the highway in the north, $1\frac{1}{2}$ acres lie between the highway in the south and the land of William Vikere in the north, and another acre lies in the field called 'Godynesscroft', which John le Vikere granted to the lessor, to be held for 6 years at an annual payment to the lessor of 7s.

1208 Letter of Henry Lorimer made at Edmonton, 22 January 1344, assigning John atte Merssh to deliver to Richard Godfreye seisin of 1 acre of land in 'Barrefeld', also to put Geoffrey Pymme in seisin of 1 acre of land in 'Langheg', lying between the land of

John Stevene and William Lorymer, and Alice, daughter of Henry, in seisin of a moiety of a tenement formerly of John Hereward, which the donor had of the gift and feoffment of Peter de Lorimer his father.
[WAM 1]

1209 Charter of William Peverel in fee simple with warranty without date made to Richard son of Ralph of 4 acres of land in Edmonton of which 2 acres lie in the croft next to the messuage of the abbot of Walden, and $\frac{1}{2}$ acre lies in 'Churchefeld' next to the land formerly of Roger Herebert extending eastwards, and 1 acre of land which was of Ellis Clerk lies in the same field extending northwards, and $\frac{1}{2}$ acre lies in 'Langheg' between the land which was of Stannar' and the land which was of Nicholas Dul, extending to the north and south, to be held of the donor at an annual rent of 8d for all service. And the feoffee paid 40s in fine.
Witnesses: Ralph de Hayrun, Pycot Marsh, Thomas his son, Robert de Ford, Robert [Silvern], William son of Geoffrey, John son of Walter, Richard Burser, Richard de Gisors, Peter de Berg, William Daniel, John son of Richard, John Clerk and others.
[Date: (?)early 13th cent.]
[WAM 12]

1210 [*f. 100v*] Indenture made 2 February 1283 whereby Richard Bunde and Helen his wife leased with warranty to Walter Lippe a tenement with buildings on it situated between the tenement of Nicholas de Solar' and the tenement of William de Egepol in Tottenham, of which one side abuts on the land of William de Egepol in the east, the other on the highway in the west, to be held for 100 years. And the lessee paid 6 marks for the grant.
Witnesses: Laurence Subet, William de Derneford, Walter Bunde, John Pyket, John Tebaud, John Clerk, William le Notiere, William de Beyford, Richard de Solar', William Egepol and others.
[WAM 28]

1211 Release in perpetuity by Maud formerly wife of William de Anesty made at Edmonton, 20 May 1341, to Thomas her son of 2 pieces of enclosed land in Edmonton called 'Sparewelond' and 'Littel Pyrie', and of 3 acres of land in ploughland called 'la Wyke' in Edmonton [and] in headlands (*forreris*) next to the hedges of the said land, and a shepherd's cottage which the releasor held for life by virtue of joint feoffment with her husband.
Witnesses: John Castle, John atte Merssh, Robert de Plesyngton,

William le Viker, Richard de Ypres, John le Taillour and others.
[WAM 78]

1212 Charter of Thomas de Anesty in fee simple with warranty made
at Edmonton, 30 June 1341, to William le Cook of the pieces of
land and the house mentioned above.
Witnesses: John Castle, John Marsh, John le Venour, William le
Viker, John atte Strate, Thomas le Rowe and others.
[WAM 58]

1213 Indenture, made 25 December 1280, whereby Christine daughter
of John Forester (*Forestarii*) leased with warranty to Augustine
Allewele 1 acre of land in 'Chirchefeld' next to the highway
leading to the manor-house (*curia*) of Edmonton, to be held from
this day for 5 years.
Witnesses: John Marsh, William Idoyne, Robert Gizors, William
le Kadde, Richard Smith (*Fabro*), Robert Taylor (*Cissore*).
[WAM 37]

1214 Charter of Robert son of Richard de Anesty in fee simple with
warranty made at Edmonton, 5 June 1333, to Roger de Depham
and Margaret his wife of 5 acres of land in Edmonton in the
field called 'Austynesfeld' lying between the land formerly of
William atte Forde in the north and the land formerly of William
del Holm in the south, extending to the land once held by John
atte Forde in the east and the road called 'Scotteslane', in which
land Hamo le Fisshere had enfeoffed the donor.

1215 Charter of William son of Philip de Cheshunt in fee simple with
warranty made at Edmonton, 17 January 1297, to Sir Philip de
Wileghby of a plot of pasture called 'Conlese' lying in Tottenham
between the land of the feoffee in the east and the north and the
donor's land in the west and south, to be held of the chief lords.

1216 Charter of Hamo le Fishmongere in fee simple, with warranty,
made at Edmonton, 28 October [*f. 101r*] 1325, to Robert son of
Richard de Anesty of 5 acres contained in the charter above
[**1214**], which John Taylor (*Cissor*) had granted to the donor.

1217 Charter of Laurence atte Forde in fee simple without warranty
and date made to Walter [MS blank][1] of 1 acre of land lying in
the field called 'Risshefeld' between the land of Nicholas Hereward and the land of John Hereward, extending in the east to
the land of William Hereward and to the land of William Godho

in the west. And the said Walter paid 1 mark.

Witnesses: Thomas Picot, William de Forde, William Picot, Ralph Picot, Richard de Wadeam, Peter Spirc, Wahere Clerk and others.

[Date: *temp*. Henry III.]

[WAM 34]

¹ The surname is also omitted in the original charter.

1218 Release in perpetuity by Thomas son and heir of William de Anesty with warranty made at Edmonton, 6 December 1333, to William de Anesty his brother of that plot of land in Edmonton lying next to the grove called 'Gisorsgrave', namely between the grove in the north and the land of John de Oxenden and that of Maud de Anesty in the south, extending in the east to the land of the same Maud and to the land of William atte Ford in the west, which land descended to the said Thomas after the death of William his father.

1219 Deed of John le Vikere of Edmonton made in London, 3 October 1341, granting to Roger de Depham 5s annual farm for the term of 6 years from William le Gardiner for the tenement lying at 'Thurstanesfeld' which the donor had leased to William for the same term and for the said annual farm.

[WAM 88]

1220 Charter of William de Fourneys in fee simple with warranty made at Edmonton, 6 May 1333, to Roger de Depham and Margaret his wife of two pieces of land in Edmonton, of which 1 acre lies between 'Bourserslane' in the south and 'Colewelleslane' in the north, extending to the land of John le Venour and the messuage of John Mabbe in the east, and the other lies between 'Bourserslane' in the south and the land of John le Venour in the north, extending to the first piece in the east and to the land of John le Venour and the land formerly of Robert Burdeyn in the west.

Witnesses: John le Venour, John atte Merssh, John Castle, Richard Wyrhale, John atte Strete, William le Vikere, Edmund Pymme, Robert de Anesty and others.

[WAM 53]

1221 Release in perpetuity by John son and heir of William de Fourneys with warranty made in London, 7 October 1351, to Roger de Depham of all lands and tenements in Edmonton in

which the said William de Fourneys had enfeoffed him.
Witnesses: Nicholas Houetot, Robert de Hatfeld, Salamon Fant, William Fossard, John le Clerk and others.
[WAM 2]

1222 Charter of William de Fourneys in fee simple with warranty made at Edmonton, 10 September 1333, to Roger de Depham and Margaret his wife of one piece of meadow in Edmonton acquired of Thomas de Ware, stockfishmonger, lying next to the meadow of William de Causton in the south, extending to the meadow formerly of Geoffrey atte Berewe in the west, and of 4d rent accruing from 1 acre of meadow which William de Causton holds.
Witnesses: John atte Merssh, John atte Castel, William le Vikere, Robert de Anesty, Edmund Wyliot, John atte Strate, Adam Chilterne and others.
[WAM 76]

1223 Letter of Thomas son of Maud de Anesty made at Edmonton, 30 June 1341, appointing in his place John de Roiston, clerk, to deliver to William le Cook seisin of the two pieces of land contained in the charter [**1212**].
[WAM 61]

1224 Release in perpetuity by Alice daughter of Thomas de Anesty without warranty made at Edmonton, 19 January 1351, to Isabel her mother of all lands and tenements contained in the previous letter and in charter [**1212**].
Witnesses: Nicholas Punge, William le Fruter, John Ingram, and others.
[WAM 87]

1225 Charter of Isabel lately wife of Thomas de Anesty in fee simple with warranty made at Edmonton, 27 September 1352, to Roger de Depham of all the lands contained in the previous release and of 12d rent belonging to the donor as dower, [issuing] from a piece of land in the hands of the said Roger.
Witnesses: John atte Pole, Henry Wikerwane, William Pymme, William Vikere, William Salman, John Goldyng and others.
[WAM 15]

1226 Charter of John Broun of Edmonton in fee simple with warranty without date made to Ralph Park (*de Parco*) of a curtilage in Edmonton lying between the messuage of John Humfrey in the

north and the messuage of Maud Humfrey in the east, extending
westwards and southwards to the street called 'le Hallestrete', to
be held of the chief lords.

1227 Release in perpetuity of Thomas son and heir of William de
Fourneys with warranty made in London, 25 October 1342, to
Roger de Depham and Margaret his wife of all lands and
tenements in Edmonton in which the said William de Fourneys
his father had enfeoffed them.
Witnesses: Thomas de Cantuar', William de Braghyng, Robert de
Hatfeld, John le Neve the elder, John Morice, John le Yonge
and others.
[WAM 35]

1228 Release in perpetuity by Alice daughter of Thomas de Anesty
with warranty made at London, 8 December 1332, [*f. 102r*] to
Roger de Depham of all lands and tenements which he holds in
Edmonton and especially [those] of the gift of Isabel who was
wife of Thomas de Anesty.
Witnesses: Nicholas Hotot, Roger Hotot, Salamon Faunt, William
Pymme, William Salman and others.
[WAM 72]

1229 Letter made at Edmonton, 6 February 1335, concerning a piece
of land lying in a field called 'Pykotesfeld', between the land of
William Vikere in the west and the land formerly of Richard
Proutfot in the east, extending from the highway which leads
from the messuage of Edmund called Barker (*Berkarii*) to Enfield
wood in the north to the land of Roger Depham in the south,
leased by John de Chilterne at farm to Richard atte Park and
Agnes his wife, to be held from Michaelmas next for 12 years at
an annual rent of 16d.
Witnesses: Roger de Depham, John Castle, John Marsh, William
le Viker, Robert de Anesty and others.
[WAM 38]

1230 Indenture of John de Chilterne made at Edmonton, 13 April
1336, leasing to Richard de Eyton and Alice his wife a piece of
land in Edmonton between the land of William le Keu in the
east and the land formerly of Roger Aldred in the west, extending
from the land formerly of Richard de Wilhale in the north to
the land formerly of Reginald le Conduit, to be held at farm for
12 years at an annual rent of 16d.
Witnesses: John Marsh, John Castle, William le Vikere, John atte

Strate, John le Venour and others.
[WAM 77]

1231 Indented charter in fee tail with warranty made at Edmonton, 25 January 1337, of one messuage with houses built on it and a garden and one adjacent croft, enclosed by hedges and ditches, lying at Winchmore Hill between the land formerly of Ralph Gladewyne in the east and the land of Richard Proutfot in the west, extending from the land of the prior of Holy Trinity, London, called 'Marldesfeld' in the north to the lane leading from Enfield wood to Winchmore Hill in the south, granted by John de Chilterne to John de Clare and Maud his wife to be held of the donor by service of 3s *pa*.
Witnesses: John atte Merssch, John atte Castel, William le Viker, Edmund Pymme, John atte Strate, Thomas le Rowe, William le Smyth and others.
[WAM 90]

1232 Indenture of John de Chilterne made at Edmonton, 24 March 1337, leasing at farm to Richard de Ipres 2 acres of land in Edmonton lying in 'Hokfeld' between the land of Thomas de Anesty and the land now of the lessor but formerly of William Laurence, to be held from 25 March next for 10 years at an annual rent of 20d.[1]
[WAM 25]

   [1] MS: 20s.

1233 Indented charter made at Edmonton, 2 January 1340, of an acre of land in Edmonton called 'Longacre' lying between the land of Cecily Potwell in the north and the land of Agnes le Hoppere in the south, extending from the land called 'Louedayeslond' in the east to the street [*f. 102v*] leading to Palmer's Green in the west, granted by the said John de Chilterne and Maud his wife to Henry le Forester of Enfield in fee tail at a rent of 6d *pa* and payment of heriot and relief when the time comes, and the feoffee is not permitted to make waste.
Witnesses: John Castle, John Marsh, John atte Strate and others.
[WAM 75]

1234 Indenture made at Edmonton, 22 September 1337, of all the lands and tenements which descended to John de Chilterne after the death of Adam his uncle except 5 roods of land, rents and escheats leased by the same John at farm to Thomas son of

William de Anesty, to be held with warranty from Michaelmas next for one year at a rent of 40s. And Thomas grants that John and his heirs are permitted at the end of the term to fallow and plough without challenge of Thomas, his heirs or executors. And the said Thomas will maintain the houses in the condition in which they were received or better.
[WAM 92]

1235 And memorandum that John de Chilterne alienated all his lands, as it seems, to William de Causton as appears before by the fine [**883**].

1236 Charter of Thomas de Upton in fee simple with warranty made in London, 6 May 1337, to Roger de Depham and Margaret his wife of one piece of land in Edmonton marsh lying between the meadow formerly of Hugh Skyn in the east and the meadow formerly of Geoffrey atte Berewe in the west.
Witnesses: John Marsh, John Castle, John le Venour, John atte Strate, William le Smyth and others.

1237 Letter of attorney of the same Thomas de Upton made on the same day to John de Pelham to deliver seisin according to the said charter.
[WAM 56]

1238 Charter of John le Longe and Idonia his wife in fee simple with warranty made at Edmonton, 23 November 1335, to the same Roger de Depham, clerk, of 6 acres of meadow in Edmonton, in which John le Blound, late citizen of London, enfeoffed the donor, and of all the meadow which was once of Ralph atte Berewe in which the said John Blund also enfeoffed the donor.
Witnesses: John de Acton, John Marsh, John atte Strete, John atte Castel, John Tebaud, John de Depham, John de Hardingham, William atte Forde, William de Anesty, Walter Crepyn, Robert atte Fen and others.
[WAM 85]

1239 Duplicate part of a fine made at Westminster, 20 January 1336, whereby John Longe of Germany and Idonia his wife acknowledged the above meadow, namely 7 acres of meadow in Edmonton, to be the right of Roger de Depham to be held in fee simple with warranty. And Roger paid 60s to John and Idonia.

[WAM 94, 95]
[*Feet of Fines, Lond. & Middx.* i, 91]

1240 [*f. 103r*] Charter of John de la Chambre, clerk, in fee simple with
warranty made at Enfield, 27 June 1327, to the same Roger de
Depham of the 6 acres of land in Enfield lying in 'Melnemerssh'
by 'Halmeneys' to the north and 'Scodymad' to the south and
the meadows formerly of Bartholomew Absolon and Henry de
Enefeld to the west and east.
Witnesses: Richard Duraunt, John Heyron, Roger de Hakeneye,
John de la Panetrie, John atte Merssh, Robert atte Fen, Hugh
de Heydene, John of St Edmunds (*Sancto Edmundo*), John de
Hardyngham, clerk, John de Shirebourne, clerk, and others.
[WAM 67]

1241 Letter of the same John de la Chambre, made on the same day
to Edmund de Wymondham to deliver seisin on the aforesaid
charter.
[WAM 80]

1242 Charter of Roger le Kyng of Tottenham in fee simple with
warranty made at Edmonton, 6 December 1328, of 1 acre of
land in Edmonton lying in the Hyde between the land of John
le Vikere to the south and north.
Witnesses: Richard de Wyrhale, John Castle, John atte Merssh,
William le Vikere, John atte Strete, Hugh de Heydene, William
le Barber and others.
[WAM 21]

1243 Letter of the same Roger le Kyng made on the same day to
Geoffrey le Kyng to deliver seisin according to the same charter.

1244 Charter of Geoffrey le Kyng of Tottenham with warranty made
at Edmonton, 27 April 1330, to Roger de Depham of a piece of
land in Edmonton lying in 'Langheg' between the land of William
de Causton in the east and the land of the prior of Holy Trinity,
London, in the west, extending to 'Grenedich' in the south and
the land of Robert de Anesty the elder in the north.
Witnesses: [John] Castle, Edmund Pymme, Robert de [?Anesty],
William Vicare, John atte Strete and others.
[WAM 334, fragment]

1245 Release in perpetuity by Geoffrey le Kyng with warranty made
in London, 21 October 1330, to Roger de Depham of the same

land.

Witnesses: … of Saint Edmunds (*de Sancto Edmundo*), William de Camerwell, Edmund Cosyn, Thomas de Kent, William …aled…, [John] de Shirbourne and others.

[WAM 83, damaged]

1246 Charter of Stephen de Abyndon, citizen of London, in fee simple with warranty made in London, 21 October 1330, to the same Roger de Depham of 1 acre of meadow in Enfield lying between the land of John le Bohun in the east and the land of John de Enefeld in the west, extending from the land of John de Enefeld in the south to the land of the abbot of Thorney in the north.

Witnesses: Richard Duraunt, Richard Payn, Ralph Baldewyn, John Castle, John atte Merssh, John atte Strete, Edmund Pymme and others.

[WAM 29]

1247 Letter of the same Stephen made on the same day to Richard de Kelleshull to deliver seisin on the aforesaid charter.

[WAM 39]

1248 [*f. 103v*] Charter of Thomas le Rowe in fee simple with warranty made at Edmonton, 16 June 1331, to Roger de Depham and Margaret his wife of half an acre of meadow in Edmonton lying between the meadow of the prior of Holy Trinity, London, in the south and the meadow of William de Causton in the north, extending from the meadow of William le Vikere called 'Claricegore' in the east to the meadow of the same William called 'Roundemad' in the west.

Witnesses: Richard de Wyrhale, Adam de Chilterne, John Marsh, William le Vikere, John Castle, Richard de Anesty, John atte Strate, Edmund Pymme and others.

[WAM 13]

1249 Charter of Thomas le Rowe in fee simple with warranty made at Edmonton on the same day to Roger de Depham and Margaret his wife of one piece of land in Edmonton lying in the field called 'Langheg' between the land of the said Roger in the south and that of Edmund Pymme in the north, extending from the land of the said Edmund in the east to that of the prior of Holy Trinity, London, in the west.

Witnesses: [as **1248**]

[WAM 23]

1250 Letter of Maud who was wife of Hamo le Fisshemongere made in London, 17 October 1332, to Roger de Depham of all her goods in Edmonton.
[WAM 48]

1251 Letter of the same Maud made 18 October 1332 to Nicholas Hetot to deliver to Roger de Depham and Margaret seisin of all their lands and tenements in Edmonton.
[WAM 49]

1252 Charter of Thomas son of William de Anesty in fee simple with warranty made in London, 20 November 1334, to Roger de Depham and Margaret his wife of 1 acre of meadow between the meadow of John de Mockyng in the south and the meadow formerly of Nicholas Laurence and John atte Pole in the north. *Witnesses*: Gilbert de Furneys, John Marsh, John Castle, John atte Strete, Edmund Pymme, William le Smyth and others.
[WAM 66]

1253 Letter of the same Thomas son of William Anesty made on the same day to Richard Prat to deliver seisin according to the said charter.
[WAM 43]

1254 Release in perpetuity by Maud who was wife of William de Anesty without warranty made in London, 2 November 1334, to the same Roger de Depham and Margaret his wife of the same acre of meadow.
Witnesses: Thomas de Cantuar', Robert de Hatfeld, William de Braughyngg, William Faunt, John de Neve and others.
[WAM 31]

1255 Letter of Roger de Depham made in London, 11 March 1347, to Edward Chamberleyn, clerk, Richard son of [*f. 104r*] Richard de Kelleshull, John Ponde, Ralph Chamberleyn and John de Claveryng, of all his interest in the lands and tenements which were of John le Venour and delivered to him by statute merchant until he should raise £60 from them.
[WAM 19]

1256 Charter of Adam Fraunceys and Peter Favelore in fee simple with warranty made at Edmonton, 28 March 1355, to Roger de Depham of 6 acres of meadow in Edmonton called 'Dykemad' lying between the meadow of the same Roger in the east and

the land of the same Roger in the west, and of 7 acres of meadow in Edmonton called 'Longemed' lying between the meadow formerly of Simon Swanlond in the south and the meadow of Robert le Smyth in the north, and of 5 acres of meadow also called 'Longmed' lying between the meadow formerly of Robert le Smyth in the south and that of the prioress of Clerkenwell in the north, and of $4\frac{1}{2}$ acres and 1 rood of meadow called 'le Hod' lying next to the meadow of Richard le Heir in the south and the meadow called 'Smalemedes' in the north, and of 8 acres of wood lying near Palmer's Green, between the 'Stonhardeslond' and 'Sweyneslond' in the south and the land called 'Storkeslond' in the north, and of 8 acres of land lying between the highway in the south and the land of Henry Goldyng and William Baron the younger in the north, and of $1\frac{1}{2}$ acres [of land] lying near the tenement of Roger de Depham which was lately of Robert Squyler in the north and the highway in the east.
Witnesses: Henry de Frowyk, Nicholas de Shordych, John atte Pole, William le Vikere, William Salman, John Goldyng, William Pymme and others.
[WAM 16]

1257 Letter of the same Adam Fraunceys and Peter Favelore made in London, 28 March 1355, to Gregory Favelore to deliver to the same Roger seisin of the said land, meadow and wood.
[WAM 46]

1258 Charter of Thomas de Salesbury, knight, in fee simple with warranty made at Edmonton, 13 June 1355, to Roger de Depham, of 1 acre of meadow lying in 'le Middelmerssh' in Edmonton, between the meadow of the feoffee in the south and the north, in exchange for 1 acre of meadow in Edmonton marsh between the meadow of John atte Pole in the north.
Witnesses: John atte Pole, William le Vikere, William Salman, John Goldyng, William Pymme and others.
[WAM 71]

1259 Letter of Thomas de Salesbury made on the same day to Robert Antoigne to deliver seisin to the same Roger.
[WAM 81]

1260 Memorandum that the said Roger survived Margaret his wife and then alienated all his land in the ensuing manner.
[**1261**, **1265**, **1266**, **1268–70** are the six charters originally inscribed on f. 36]

1261 Charter of Roger de Depham in fee simple with warranty made in London, 7 January¹ 1358, under his seal and the seal [*f. 104v*] of the mayoralty of London to Thomas de Langeton, John Pitee, chaplains, and Salamon Howe of Barkway of all his lands and tenements in the vills of Great and Little Chishill in the counties of Essex, Hertford and Cambridge. John Lovekyn, mayor of London, had the said seal appended at the personal request of Roger.

Witnesses: Henry Pycard, Adam Fraunceys, John de Stodeye, William de Welde, Simon de Benyngton, citizens of London, Roger Gerard, John Beauchamp, Warin Martyn, John Lyne and others.

[WAM 41]

¹ MS: 7 June.

1262 Letter of the same Roger, made in London on the same day, to John Bilnail of Chishill to deliver seisin.

1263 Letter of Roger de Depham, made in London on the same day, of all his goods and chattels in the same vills, granted to the same Thomas, John and Salamon.

1264 Charter of the same Roger de Depham in fee simple with warranty made in London, 29 December 1358, to Thomas de Langton and John Pytee, chaplains, of all his lands and tenements in Edmonton, Enfield and Tottenham.

Witnesses: Henry Pycard, William de Welde, John Wroth, Simon de Benyngton, citizens of London, Henry de Frowyk, Nicholas atte Wyke, William Salman, Hugh Braybrok, William Pymme, William Vykere, William Pycard and others.

[WAM 52]

1265 Letter of the same Roger made on the same day of all his goods and chattels granted in Edmonton to the same Thomas and John.

[WAM 44]

1266 Letter of the same Roger made 29 December 1358 to John de Barton to deliver seisin of the said lands and tenements.

[WAM 65]

1267 And memorandum that Thomas de Langton died, whereupon the whole accrued to John Pytee who granted all in the ensuing manner.

1268 Charter of the said John Pytee in fee simple[1] made at Edmonton, 20 May 1361, to Gilbert Chaumpeneys, Henry de Bureford and John de Barton of all the aforesaid lands and tenements in Edmonton which were of John atte Merssh which Roger Depham had granted to the donor jointly with Thomas de Langeton.
Witnesses: John de la Pole, William Salman, John Golddyng, John Claveryng and others.
[WAM 59]

> [1] MS: with warranty.

1269 Letter of John Pytee made at Edmonton on the same day to John de Claveryng to deliver seisin according to the said charter.
[WAM 86]

1270 Charter of James de Bereford, knight, in fee simple with warranty made at Edmonton, 19 June 1351, to Adam Fraunceys and Peter Favelore of $13\frac{1}{2}$ acres of meadow in Edmonton between the meadow of Richard Asshwy [*f. 105r*] in the south and the meadow of the prior of Holy Trinity, London, in the north, and of 5 acres of meadow lying in Edmonton, between the meadows of lord de Say in the south and the hospital of St Giles in the the north, and of 2 acres of meadow lying in Enfield between the meadow of the prior of the hospital of St Mary Bishopsgate in the south and the meadow formerly of Geoffrey Scrope in the north, and of 2 acres of meadow lying in Enfield between the meadow of the prioress of Cheshunt in the south and that of John Goldbetere in the north, and 13 acres of wood lying in Edmonton between the street called Southgate (*le Southstrate*) in the north and the wood of the prioress of Clerkenwell in the west.
Witnesses: Simon Bounde, William Saleman, William Vikere, Robert de Hadham, Hugh de Braybrok and others.
[WAM 40]

1271 Part of a fine levied 31 May 1359 whereby Thomas de Langeton and John Pitee, chaplains, granted two messuages, 236 acres of land, 63 acres of meadow, 21 acres of pasture, and 50s rent in Edmonton to Adam Fraunceys, citizen of London, for life and after his death to Adam Fraunceys the younger of London in fee tail, and if he dies without issue to Robert Fraunceys in fee tail, and then to the right heirs of the said Adam without warranty. [*Feet of Fines, Lond. & Middx.* i, 137.]

1272 Release in perpetuity of William Vikere the elder of Edmonton without warranty made 10 July 1360 to Adam Fraunceys of all lands and tenements in Edmonton in which Thomas de Langeton and John Pytee enfeoffed the said Adam.
Witnesses: Hugh de Braybrook, John de Goldyng, William Salman, William Pymme, John Claveryng and others.
[WAM 79]

1273 Charter of Thomas de Langeton and John Pytee of Chishill, chaplains, in fee simple with warranty made at Edmonton, 12 June 1359, to Adam Fraunccys and Peter Favelore of a messuage called 'Hamondes' with 82 acres of land $4\frac{1}{2}$ acres of meadow and other profits pertaining to the said tenement in the same vill, and of a messuage called 'Anestyes' with 63 acres of land, 1 acre of meadow 11 acres of pasture and all profits pertaining to the said tenement, and of a messuage called 'Heghames' with 29 acres of land, 13 acres of pasture and all profits pertaining.
Witnesses: Henry Frowyk, John Wroth, Hugh Braybrook, William Salman, John ..., [William] Vikere and others.
[WAM 27]

1274 Memorandum that Peter Favelore died, whereby everything accrued to the said Adam who made further grants as will appear below.

1275 Charter of Adam Fraunceys in fee simple with warranty made at Edmonton, 20 May 1361, to Gilbert Chaumpeneys, Henry de Burforde and John de Barton of all lands and tenements formerly [*f. 105v*] of William de Causton which he and Peter Favelore had received of John atte Berne and John Organ in Edmonton, Enfield and Tottenham, and of all lands and tenements in Edmonton which he acquired jointly with the said Peter of Thomas de Langeton and John Pytee.
Witnesses: John Wroth, Henry Frowyk, Thomas Frowyk, Hugh Braybrook, William Salman, John Goldyng, William Vikere and others.
[WAM 55]

1276 Letter of the same Adam Fraunceys made at Edmonton on the same day of the sale of all his goods on these lands and tenements to the same Gilbert Chaumpeneys, Henry de Burford and John

Barton.
[WAM 11]

1277 Chirograph of William de Say made in London, 28 October 1361, and enrolled on the dorse of the Close Rolls for November 1361, granting to Gilbert Chaumpeneys and John Barton all lands and tenements which they held of him in Edmonton, Enfield and Tottenham, to be held of the donor and his heirs by fealty and rent of ¼d *pa*. And the donor is bound to acquit the same tenants against others who previously held the tenements of him by many other services.
[WAM 26]
[*CCR 1360–4*, 290]

1278 Chirograph of the same William de Say made in London, 28 October 1361, and enrolled in the said form, granting to Adam Fraunceys, citizen of London, two messuages, 236 acres of land of meadow, 21 acres of pasture and 50s rent in Edmonton which the same Adam holds for life of the donor, on condition that after the death of the feoffee the said tenements will remain to Adam Fraunceys of London, junior, and his heirs, thereafter to Robert Fraunceys of London and his heirs with remainder to the right heirs of Adam Fraunceys, citizen, to be held of the donor and his heirs by fealty and rent of ½d *pa*, and they are bound to acquit the said tenants against all higher lords.
[*CCR 1360–4*, 290]

1279 Indenture of William de Say made at Edmonton, 2 October 1361, to Adam Fraunceys, citizen of London, of his manor of Edmonton to be held for 22 years at a rent to William and his heirs after the first 12 years of 40 marks *pa*. And Adam is permitted to make waste without hindrance.
[WAM 93]

1280 [*f. 106r*] Recognizance made before the mayor of the Staple of Westminster, 3 March 1362, by William de Say that he is bound to Adam Fraunceys in £1000 sterling to be paid at Michaelmas next.
[WAM 28057]

1281 Indenture made in London on the same day containing that if Adam Fraunceys, citizen of London, hold the manor of Edmonton in peace for the term of 22 years according to the form of the indenture [**1279**], and if by the lessor's death the said Adam is removed from the manor by the king or otherwise, then provided certain other conditions on the part of the lessor's heirs are kept the foregoing recognizance will be invalidated.

1282 [*f. 106v*] Pleas of the Crown [held] before John de Berewyk and his fellow justices in eyre at Stonecross in Co. Middlesex, 25 November 1294.
Half-hundred of Edmonton comes [represented] by twelve jurors. Concerning liberties, the jurors said that William de Say claimed to have view of frankpledge, the exaction of compensation for breaking the assize of bread and ale, *tumbrellum, furcas, weif* and free warren in the manor of Edmonton, by what warrant they know not.[1] Afterwards the said William de Say came and said that King Henry III had granted to William de Say his father and his heirs, of whom he is one, free warren in all the lands of his manors of Sawbridgeworth and Edmonton by his charter which he produced and which bore witness to this. And he said that he had use of this from the time that the same charter was made, and the jurors bore witness to this on oath. And in this respect the said William [was granted] *sine die* etc. And with regard to the view of frankpledge and his other liberties he said that all his ancestors and he himself had use of them from time beyond memory in his said manor and he contests the inquest. And John de Mutford, who was suing on behalf of the king, likewise. And the jurors elected for this occasion said on oath that the said William and all his ancestors had use of these liberties on their manor of Edmonton from time beyond memory without any temporal break. And so [he was granted] *sine die* saving the right of the king etc.

[1] PRO JUST1/544 rot. 63 to this point.

1283 Charter of Henry III granting to William de Say and his heirs free warren in all the demesne lands of their manors of Sawbridgeworth and Edmonton and forbidding anyone to enter that warren to hunt there or to take anything which pertains to the warren without the will and licence of the same William and his heirs upon forfeiture of £10.
Witnesses: W. bishop of Norwich, E. le Bigot, earl of Norfolk, Hugh de Vynonu', Paulinus Peyrur', John de Lexinton, Roger de Thurkilby, William de Cheidney, Geoffrey de Childewyk and others.
Norwich, 22 March 1245.
[*Calendar of Charter Rolls* i, 282]

1284 [f. 109v] Assize to examine whether John Virly unjustly and without judgement disseised William Parchemener, William Edy, Thomas Fermoy, John Gloucester, John Gourney, William Sondes and William Broune of their free tenement in Harefield [Middx.]. And the plaintiffs sued in their own persons that the defendant disseised them of one messuage and 60 acres of land, 10 acres of meadow and 40 acres of pasture with appurtenances. And John Virley solemnly [?denied] the accusation. And the assize was held, Friday three weeks of Easter 1447, and found that the plaintiffs were seised of the said tenements, [holding] them as free until the defendant disseised them thereof unjustly, without judgement and by force of arms. And damages were assessed from the time of the disseisin to the holding of the said assize, net of costs, at 40s, and costs at 26s 8d, which damages were made threefold according to the form of the statute for this kind of disseisin, made by force of arms, and [the assize] settled upon £10. It was therefore decided that the plaintiffs should recover against the said John Virley their seisin of the said tenements and damages of £10. And the same John Virley was charged (*capiatur*) etc.

1285 [f. 112v] [Margin.] Eyworth nowe my Lo[rd] Andersons.
Final concord made at Westminster, 13 October 1341, between Edward le Despencer and Anne his wife, plaintiffs, represented by Thomas Thwaite, and John de Purley and Joan his wife, defendants, whereby the defendants granted to the plaintiffs two messuages, 104 acres of land, 12 acres of meadow, 2 acres of pasture and 10s rent with appurtenances in Eyworth, to be held by them and their heirs by the services pertair.ing to the said tenements with remainder to the right heirs of Edward. And for this fine the said Edward and Anne paid 100 marks.
[PRO CP25(1) 4/56 no. 25]

[Scribal note in English.] Lambert of Weston made ixchaunge of Eyworth for other lyvelode that was steward of Londe with Edward Spenser.

1286 [Separate folio bound in with cartulary.] Copy of the proceedings of the court of King's Bench held at Westminster, 11 November 1369, in which Adam Fraunceys, citizen of London, fearing oppression through the coincidence of his name and surname with that of two men indicted on charges of theft committed in 1342 in Hothersall [Lancs.], Bradley upon Colne and Airedale [West Yorks.], and subsequently outlawed at York on 28 June

1350, produced in court a writ of *supersedeas* from the king accepting that Adam Fraunceys, citizen of London, was neither of these two outlaws, which the said Adam was prepared to prove by ways and means acceptable to the court, and commanding the justices to stay proceedings taken against Adam Fraunceys, citizen of London, on account of this coincidence of name, and to revoke and annul any such process, dated Westminster, 10 November 1369. And the court duly considered the accusations made in the original hearing at York, and reviewed the records of the proceedings of outlawry taken there, and decided that there was insufficient evidence against one of the original accused, called simply (*tantum*) Adam Fraunceys, to uphold the sentence of outlawry against him, but that the sentence passed against the other, called Adam Fraunceys of Ribchester, should remain in force. And the court ordered that no further proceedings should be taken against Adam Fraunceys, citizen of London, nor against the first of those outlawed, but that the sheriff of Lancashire should pursue Adam Fraunceys of Ribchester, if he still survived, and that the escheator of the same county should inquire with all diligence into his goods and chattels.

[PRO KB27/435 Rex rot. 26]

INDEX OF PERSONS AND PLACES

Page references are in Roman type. References to numbered entries in the Calendar are in italics preceded by *P* for Pyel cartulary and *F* for Braunceys cartulary. As in the text, only the modern version of place-names appears in the index (field names are not included), while for personal names the principal variations of spelling are given, with Latin and French forms in italics and round brackets. 'Son of' is given in round brackets when it is likely to be part of the surname or is in some instances omitted in the text. Cross-references are made where necessary, but Latinised surnames and their French equivalents are only given if they appear in unmodernised form in the text. Members of families, or persons with the same surname, are generally listed in alphabetical order, wives and parents taking precedence over children. Members of the gentry or nobility are listed chronologically.

Akton *see* Acton
Amerose, Alice de *P1*
Amice, Israel 84, 92
Amys, Richard, cit. Lond., fishmonger
F685, 753, 755, 833
Margery, wife of *F755*; *see also* Normanby, Nicholas de
John, son of *F833*
Richard, son of *F753–4, 833*
John, of Haveringham, cit. Lond. *F418, 617–20*
William, son of Geoffrey Marsh, cit. Lond., fishmonger *F404, 408, 613–16, 666–7, 685–8, 690, 692, 695, 697, 709, 1179*
Julia, wife of *F615*
Agnes, mother of *F685*; *see also* Colewell
Edmund, son of *F615*
John, son of *F615*
Anderson, Edmund, lord chief justice Common Pleas 83–4, 93, *F1285*
Andrew, Andreu, John 20
Richard *F171*
Emma, wife of *F171*
Anesty, Anesti, Anasty, capital messuage *F489*
Geoffrey de *F491, 675, 783, 885, 949, 959, 973, 1159*
Sybil, wife of *F675, 949, 973*
Richard, son of *F949, 959–60, 973*
John de (*fl. c.* 1250) *F572*
John de (*fl.* 1346) *F1111*
Malyne de *F473*
Nicholas de *F783*
Richard de *F224–6, 238, 255, 261, 273, 280, 284–5, 363, 395, 599, 648, 663–4, 673, 675, 1008, 1145, 1187, 1214, 1216, 1248*
Diamand, wife of *F226, 284–5, 338, 406, 622, 663, 672, 854*
Richard, son of *F672, 674*
Robert, son of *F675, 1214, 1216, 1220, 1222, 1229*
Robert de *F264, 699, 854, 862, 868, 878, 887, 914, 928–9, 938, 1144, 1151, 1196, 1198, 1244*
William de *F289, 386, 426, 487, 496, 562, 670, 673, 674, 689, 699, 729, 732, 745, 753, 759–61, 779–80, 783, 791, 798, 803–4, 813, 816, 818, 822–3, 828, 830, 843–6, 851, 856–7, 859, 898, 916–17, 967, 972, 1002, 1004, 1098–9, 1109–10, 1113, 1121, 1133,*

1144, 1157, 1171, 1179, 1186, 1196–7, 1211, 1218, 1234, 1238, 1252–4
Maud, wife of *F320, 490, 673, 789, 791, 916, 1098–9, 1109–10, 1112, 1121, 1211, 1218, 1223, 1254*
Margery, mother of *F386*
Thomas, son of *F320, 406, 484, 486, 492, 783, 785, 789–93, 798, 803, 827, 861, 868–9, 871, 917, 942–3, 948–9, 951–2, 956, 958, 964, 966–7, 969–70, 977, 1098, 1109, 1112, 1121, 1167, 1211–12, 1218, 1223–5, 1228, 1232, 1234, 1252–3*
Isabel, wife of 54n., *F320, 492, 977, 1109, 1112, 1224–5, 1228*
Alice, daughter of *F320, 1099, 1224, 1228*
Maud, daughter of *F320*
Robert, son of *F492, 791, 1099, 1109, 1112*
Thomas, son of *F320*
William, son of *F470, 674–5, 798, 803, 1113–14, 1121*
Anketil, Anketill, Anketel, John, cit. Lond., woolmonger 58, 61, 63, 66, 67, 71, 72, 86, *P4–7, 21, 37–40, 42–4*
Agnes, widow of *P5, 7, 21*
Nicholas, kinsman of *P5, 7, 21, 44, 148*
Ankus, John *P173*
Antoigne, Robert *F1259*
Antwerp 55
Arderne, Robert de *P45*
Giles, son of *P45, 47*
William de *P151*
Armurer *see* Bailiff
Arnold, Margery *F980*
Richard *F931, 1086*
Simon *P253*
William *F891*
Assheburn, Thomas, friar 32
Ashton, Aschton, Asschton, Asshton, John de, kt 44, *P93, 95, 111*
Elizabeth (Isabel), wife of *P160–3, 179, 189, 190–1, 231, 247*
Ashwell (Herts.) *F1024*
vicar of *see* St Neots, William of
Asketyn, Robert, cit. Lond. *F429, 438*
Askwode, Roger, cit. Lond., girdler *F1012–13*
Asshcle, Assèle, Robert de *F1174, 1184–5*
Assherugge, Assheregge, John, cit. Lond., tanner *F654, 656–61, 757, 898, 905–8, 912, 982*

Childewyk, Geoffrey de *F1283*
Chilterne, Chiltren, Chiltrene, Chitren,
  Adam de *F479–80, 862, 878–9, 911,
    928–9, 1147–8, 1222, 1234, 1248*
    Helen, wife of *F479, 862, 878–9*
    John son of *F480, 862*
  Edmund de *F392, 475–7, 480, 874, 1120*
    John, son of 53, 54n. *F475–7, 480, 820,
      861–77, 879–84, 951, 980, 1120,
      1159, 1204, 1229–35*
    Maud, wife of *F475–6, 820, 867–75,
      877, 884, 980, 1233*
  Richard *F479*
Chingford (Essex) *F1159*
Chircheman, John, cit. Lond., grocer 66n.
Chiriton, Walter 65, 66, 71, 72, 73, *P235*
Chishill (Cambs.) *F1262, 1273; see also* Great,
  Little Chishill
Chitren *see* Chilterne
Chivaler, Geoffrey le *F298*
Chobham, Chabham, Thomas de 49, *F25,
  51–9*
  Margaret, wife of *F61*
Chobhams, manor of *see* West Ham
Christchurch *see* London, Holy Trinity
Church (*de Ecclesia*), Henry *F262*
  Robert *F267*
Chygwelle *see* Chigwell
Chyngford, Chyngeford, Bartinus de *F625*
  John, clerk *F293, 1041*
    Alice Incestre, wife of *F1041*
Claper, John *F261–2, 1035*
  Richard *F261–2, 1033*
    John, son of *F449*
    Stephen, son of *F1033–4*
  Nicholas le *F428, 540, 733*
Clare, Avice de *F271*
  John de *1231*
    Maud, wife of *1231, 1233*
  Ralph de *F199*
    Joan, daughter of *F199*
    Maud, daughter of *F199*
Clarel, Robert *F145*
  Alice, wife of *F145*
Clarence, duke of 79
  Philippa daughter of 79–80
Clavering, Claveryng, John de 56, *F1009,
  1131, 1206, 1255, 1268–9, 1272*
Clay, Walter *F465, 604, 749*
Cleeve (Som.), abbot of 11
Clerk, Alexander *F1189*
  Ellis *F1209*
  Hugh *F812, 835*

John *F273, 812, 833, 835, 838, 840, 897,
  902, 904, 911, 916–17, 921, 923, 948,
  1145, 1205, 1210, 1221*
Ralph *F181, 280, 286, 288–9, 351, 406,
  670, 686, 688, 823, 854, 856, 858,
  1009, 1152, 1154, 1167, 1169, 1171,
  1175, 1177, 1179, 1186*
Ranulph *F856*
Richard, of Edmonton *F857*
Richard *F258, 857*
Roger *F796*
Saher *F234, 236–9, 248–9, 261–2, 272,
  280, 327, 1033–4*
  Maud, wife of *F1033*
  Juliana, daughter of *F1033*
Thomas *F381*
Wahere *F1217*
Walter *F1007*
William *F254, 406, 853, 1002, 1032, 1167,
  1173, 1175, 1179, 1186*
William, of Rothwell (Northants.) *P53,
  200–1, 220*
Clerkenwell, prioress and nuns of *F237,
  359, 418, 541, 570, 617, 670, 769, 781,
  848, 857, 1256, 1270*
  St John of, prior of *F823*
Clervaux family 78
  Richard 78n.
Clove, Roger de *P156*
Clyve, John *P253–4*
Cnotte *see* Knotte
Cobbes, Maud *F240*
Coffrer, Salamon le *P7*
Cokes, Maud le *F735*
Cokham, John *F507–8*
Cokke, Peter atte *P24*
Cole, Alan *F218*
  Roger *F72*
  William *F1189*
    Adam, son of, cit. Lond. *F242–5, 275,
      379, 441, 1189*
    Alice, daughter *F1189*
Coleville, Geoffrey de *F569*
Colewelle, Agnes de *F211, 312, 332, 453, 575*
  Geoffrey *F431*
  John de, cit. Lond., mercer *F435, 832,
    836, 840, 1179*
  Richard de *F422, 431, 1031–2*
  John Amys, son of *F1031, 1179; see also*
    Amys
    Richard, brother of *1031*
  Stephen de *F269, 435, 530–5, 537–9, 613,
    666, 719, 841, 999, 1009, 1146*

Geoffrey, son of *F207–17, 219–26, 263, 249–50, 255–6, 263, 342, 352, 388, 440, 1009–11, 1188*

  Emma, wife of *F222–3*

  Leven, wife of *F219*

John, son of *F196, 362, 436, 546*

Richard, son of *F227–9, 232*

Thomas, son of *F211–12, 230–1, 233–4, 236, 245–6, 1007, 1188*

  John, son of *F212*

  William, son of *F1143*

Thomas *F232, 235, 237–8, 240, 249, 250, 261, 347, 509*

William 53, *F199, 205, 207, 234, 236, 238–9, 243, 248–9, 261–2, 264, 266, 270–3, 275, 280–1, 285, 288–90, 295, 303, 312, 321–2, 324–34, 337, 339–41, 343, 346, 348, 350–61, 363–4, 366–7, 370–1, 375–6, 379–80, 382–3, 385, 387–8, 406–7, 422, 424, 426, 453, 475, 524, 545, 553, 562, 572, 574, 581–91, 601, 622, 649, 662, 670, 674–5, 685, 689, 692, 694, 709, 729, 732, 736, 739, 745, 779–80, 783, 792, 803, 813, 823, 831, 843, 847, 849, 853–9, 867, 875, 891, 916, 938, 984, 1001–2, 1004–5, 1008–9, 1120, 1144–5, 1152–3, 1157, 1164, 1167, 1169, 1171–2, 1174, 1177, 1179–80, 1185–7, 1190, 1193, 1214, 1217–18, 1238*

  Cecily, wife of *F358, 380, 583*

  Alice, mother of *F376, 542, 549–50, 560*

  Alice, daughter of *F389*

  John, son of *F223, 336, 347, 426*

  Thomas, brother of *F338, 406, 622*

  Thomas, son of *F378–9*

  William, son of *F334, 341, 345, 377, 383–5, 585, 856, 867, 875, 1008*

  Lorence, wife of *F349*

  Maud, daughter of *F349*

Walter *F237*

Forester (*Forestarius*), Agnes le *F980*

Henry le *F1233*

John *F1213*

  Christine, daughter of *F1213*

Nicholas *F158*

Robert le *F373, 671*

Robert, of Cransley *P79*

  Margery, wife of *P79*

  Hugh, son of *P79*

  Juliana, daughter *P79*

  Thomas, son of *P79*

Forster, Walter, skinner 16

Forth *see* Ford

Fossard, William *F1205, 1221*

Fountain (*de Fonte*), Funtayne, Christine *F308*

  John *F215, 342*

  Robert de la *F1189*

Fox, Christine *P219*

  Reginald 53, *F418, 617, 619, 763–4, 842*

  Vincent *F255, 257*

FRAUNCEYS, ADAM, cit. & mayor of Lond. *P1–4, 6, 8–12, 14–18, 20–5, 26, 28–30, 32–4, 36–7, 41–4, 59–62, 87, 93–9, 111, 124, 126, 132–3, 151–3, 160, 213–15, 223, 245, 247, F1, 21–5, 46, 55–61, 69, 102, 106–7, 129–34, 143–4, 147, 158–61, 163–8, 170–2, 175, 994–7, 1073, 1132, 1256–7, 1261, 1270–6, 1278–81, 1286*

associates 15–21

attitude to London 13–14, 22

in Bruges 6–7

cartulary of 1, 77, 79, 81–6, 89, 92–3

civic career 13–15

commercial activity 5, 7–8

land acquisition 48–50, 52–64, 66–7, 69–72, 73–4

loans and credit 9–12, 15, 16, 26, 66–7, 97

mayor of the Staple of Westminster *P148, 159*

member of parliament 13, 15, 18

origins 3–6

piety 21–2, 70–2, 74

relations with the Crown 7, 21

  Agnes, wife of 3, 19, 58n. 69, 81, 83, *F21–2, 60*

  Adam, father of 3

  Constance, mother of 3

  Adam, son of, kt 3, 20, 22, 55, 56, 58n., 69, 70, 82, 83, 89, *F22, 60, 1271, 1278*

    Margaret, first wife of 22

    Agnes, daughter of 83

    Joan, daughter of 3

    Maud, daughter of 3

  Maud, daughter of, countess of Salisbury 3, 9, 20, 21, 22, 56

  Robert, son of 3, 49, 55, *F22, 60, 1271, 1278*

  Thomas, son of 3

Adam, of Buckenham 4n.

Adam, master of leper hospital at Eye 4n.

FRAUNCEYS, ADAM—*cont*
  Adam, accused of assault at Lechlade
    4n.
  Adam, of Minety 4n.
  Adam, of Ribchester 6, *F1286*
  Adam, felon of Yorks. 6, *F1286*
  Adam, son of Thomas 4n.
  Ellis, cit. Lond., mercer 4, 5, 15, 20, 50,
    55
  John, accused of assault at Lechlade 4n.
  Juliana, of Buckenham 4n.
  Richard, cit. Lond., mercer 19
  Robert of Buckenham 4n.
  Simon, cit. & mayor of Lond. 3, 4, 5, 8,
    10, 15, 16, 17, 20, 26, 33, 56n., 57n.,
    P21–3, 87, 97, 123
    Maud, wife of 15
    John, son of 5
    Thomas, son of 5
  William, of Tathewell 4
    John, son of 4
    Ellis, son of 4
    Richard, son of, cit. Lond. 4
Freman, Thomas *P140*
  William 40, 43, *P60, 92, 104, 122, 140,
    166, 179, 199, 200, 219, 220*
Frere, William *F216–7, 341, 365, 536, 553,
  625-6, 630, 632*
  Alice, wife of *F630*
  Katherine, daughter of *F330*
Frereman, John *P253*
  Richard, clerk of Bedford *P253*
Freth, Henry atte *P23*
Frost, John *P3*
Frowyk, Henry 70, *F993 1256, 1264, 1273,
  1275*
  Thomas *F993, 1275*
Fruter, William le *F1224*
Fubert, William, son of *F191*
Fulham, Adam *F62*
  Thomas de *P23*
Fulle, Robert le *F722*
Fullere, John le *F463*
Funtayne *see* Fountain
Furneys, Fourneys, Gilbert de *F1252*
  John, cit. Lond., draper 19, 59, 61
    Katherine, wife of 19, 59; *see also*
    Bovyndon
  William de, *alias* Patrikdale, cit. Lond.,
    pepperer *F292, 773, 810, 892, 1001,
    1037–9, 1042–3, 1045–8, 1050, 1052–
    9, 1075, 1100-3, 1104, 1106–8, 1220–
    2, 1227*

Cecily, wife of *F1106*
Joan, daughter of *F1106–7*; *see also*
  Dunle
John, son of *F1221*
Juliana, daughter of *F1046, 1048*; *see
  also* Venour
Phyllis, daughter of *F1106, 1108*
Thomas, son of *1102–3, 1106, 1227*
William, son of *F1046, 1106*
Fyker *see* Vikere

Galeys, John *F158*
Galicia 26, 87, *P58*
  shrine of St James de Compostella in
    28
Gardiner, Stephen *F1061*
  William le *F1219*
Gargate, Ralph *F181*
Garlekemongere, Adam, mayor of Nor-
  thampton 28, *P7, 82*
  John 27–8, 30, *P7, 82, 116*
  Richard 28, *P82, 116*
Garton, Gartone, John de, cit. Lond.,
  mercer 16, 18n., *F457, 935–6, 940, 977,
  982*
  Thomas de, cit. Lond. 18
    Hugh, father of 18n.
    Idonia, wife of 18
    Thomas, son of 18
Gate, Ronbert atte *F150*
Gattone, Hamo de, kt *F243*
Gaunt, John of, duke of Lancaster 4, 31,
  46
Gayton, John le, esq. *P81*
Gedyngton, John *P233*
Gege, Geg, Robert le *F390, 564, 566–7*
Geoffrey, Geffrey, John *P130*
  William (son of) *F241, 249, 251, 253, 258,
  271, 1209*
Gerald, king's chamberlain *F176*
  Henry, son of *F176–7, 182*
  Warin, son of *F177*
Gerard, Juliana *P180*
  Roger *F1261*
Geri *F181*
Germany *F1239*
Germayn, Katherine *F980*
  Alice *F980*
Gerton, William de *F145*
Gesors *see* Gisors
Gilbert, Gilherd, John *F199, 351, 386, 544*
Giles, Gyles, John *P181, 229*
Gisors, Gysors, Gesors, Gizors, John *F289,*

Loddington (Northants.), lord of *see* Alderby
Lodebury *see* Lothebury
Lodine, Lodne, Robert de, clerk *F432, 842*
Lofte, Loffte, Roger atte *F276, 365, 417, 470, 698, 718, 777, 812, 834–5, 860, 866, 984, 1004*
Lofwyk, Lufwyk, John de *P48, 157*
  Oliver de *P196*; *see also* Duffyn
  William de, parson of Aldwincle (Northants.) *P45, 49*
Loketon, Richard *F646*
  Amice, wife of *F646*; *see also* Humphrey
Lolymer, Nicholas *67, P6, 7*
Lomb, Richard *P151*
  Agnes, wife of *P151*
  Thomas *P196*
London *13–15, 16, 17–18, 28, 55, 85, F9, 11, 20, 23, 44, 60–1, 79, 82, 87, 97–8, 100–1, 112, 115, 119–20, 132, 153–4, 156, 165, 176–8, 237, 294, 318, 321, 323, 373, 398–9, 401, 408, 418, 424, 428, 432, 451, 474, 497, 501–2, 509, 515, 519–21, 525, 532, 554, 588, 592, 595, 618–9, 640, 654, 656, 670, 681–3, 690, 697, 703, 715, 733, 745, 747, 755–6, 758, 763, 777, 788, 790, 792–3, 796, 798–9, 802, 806, 811, 818, 829, 832–3, 835–8, 840–2, 844, 852, 864–5, 875–7, 880–1, 886, 910, 913, 920, 925, 933–6, 940, 952, 955, 960–3, 965–6, 968, 970, 975–9, 981–3, 985–6, 990–1, 994, 1006, 1017, 1019, 1021, 1024, 1026, 1050–1, 1100–3, 1104, 1112, 1116–17, 1130–1, 1139, 1158, 1160–1, 1168, 1182–3, 1201, 1203–4, 1207, 1219, 1227–9, 1236, 1245–6, 1252, 1254–5, 1261–4, 1281*
  Aldersgate *F294*n.
  Aldgate *81, F294*n.
  Bishopsgate *F294*n.
  bishop of *14, F158, 294*
  citizens and merchants of *4, 5, 6, 9, 10, 21, 28, 29, 51–2, 70, 85*
  convents, hospitals etc.
    Austin Friars *8, 63*
    Holy Trinity, Christchurch *F234, 339–40, 402, 626, 632, 654, 664, 721,728, 733, 757, 760, 794, 813, 816, 854, 886, 894, 900, 916, 929, 938, 972, 974, 1033, 1113, 1154, 1156, 1231, 1244, 1248–9, 1270*
      prior of *F310, 343, 356, 370, 383, 428, 509, 527, 540, 547, 553, 558*; *see also*

    Nicholas; Watton, Stephen
    hospital of St Bartholomew *P1, 3, F552*
    hospital of St Giles *F236, 647, 753, 1062, 1270*
    hospital of St John of Jerusalem *11, F239, 449, 542, 550, 858, 967, 1082, 1144*
      master of *F903*
      prior of *see* Thame, Philip de
    hospital of St Mary without Bishopsgate *P27, F1270*
      prior of *50*; *see also* James; Swyft, William
    hospital of St Thomas Acon *60, F64*
    St Helen's Bishopsgate *21, 35, 56–7, 62–3, 68, 70, P1, 3, 126, F670, 695, 827, 956, 961*
      prioress of *F374, 454, 611*; *see also* Margery; Wynton, Eleanor de
  diocese of *26*
  Fresh Wharf, Billingsgate *64*
  Guildhall *14, 69, P20*
    college of *55, 69, 70*
  mayor of the Staple of *P178*
  parishes and churches:
    All Hallows Barking *66, P7*
    All Hallows Bread Street *P5, 7, 9*
    All Hallows Honey Lane *59, 60*
    All Hallows Staining *P20*
    All Hallows the Less Thames Street *59, 66*
    St Andrew Holborn *64, 66, F1109*
    St Bartholomew the Less Broad Street *63, 65, 73*
    St Benedict Gracechurch *F615*
    St Botolph Aldgate *4*
    St Bride Fleet Street *66, 73*
    St Christopher in the Stocks *61*
    St Clement Eastcheap *73*
    St Dunstan in the East *64*
    St Ethelburga Bishopsgate *61, 62*
    St Giles without Cripplegate *P7*
    St Helen Bishopsgate *50, 51*n., *62, 69, 70, P1, 3, 29, 34, 36*
    St James Garlickhithe *66*
    St John Walbrook *51*n.
    St Lawrence Jewry *58, 59, 68*
    St Margaret Lothbury *65*
    St Martin le Grand *P44*
    St Martin without Ludgate *64*
    St Martin Outwich *62, 66*
    St Martin Vintry *18*
    St Mary Abchurch *66*
    St Mary at Hill Thames Street *18*

London—*cont*
 parishes and churches—*cont*
  St Mary Magdalene Milk Street 60,
   P5, 7, 9
  St Mary Matfelon *F65*
  St Mary Wolnoth 61
  St Mary, Woolchurch 19, *P44*
  St Matthew Friday Street *F726, 729,*
   860, 888, 912
   parson of *see* Staunton, Nicholas de
  St Michael Cornhill 20
  St Michael le Querne 63, *P7*
  St Mildred Poultry 58, *P5, 7, 20–1*
  St Nicholas Acon 66
  St Olave Jewry 65
  St Pancras 50 *F864, 923, 952*
  St Peter Broad Street 62
  St Stephen Coleman Street 64, 65
  St Vedast Westcheap *F796*
 property of Fraunceys and Pyel in 57–
  74, 86, 89
 property market in 61–2, 62n. 68–9, 73
  for charitable endowment 70–1, 74
 Servat's Tower 58
 Stocks Market 61
 streets and wards:
  Bartholomew Lane 66, 72
  Bearbinder Lane 61
  Beech Lane 64
  Berewards Lane *P7*
  Bishopsgate 58, 62
  Bread Street 66, 72, *P10, 21, 40, 43–4*
  Bridge 18
  Broad Street 30, 35, 58, 62, 63, 67, 71,
   72
   (Threadneedle St) 72
   (Throgmorton St) 65, 72
  Bucklersbury 58–9
  Candlewick Street 16, 18, 61, 63, *P13*
  Castle Baynard 30
  Chancellor's Lane *P5, 7, 44*
  Cheap 21, 58, 59, 69, *P21, 40, 43–4*
  Cheapside 58, 59, 60–1, 62, 64, 65
  Coleman Street 68, 64, 72
  Cornhill 58, 62, 66, 67
  Crooked Lane 16, 18, 63
  Dowgate 69n.
  Farringdon without *P40*
  Fenchurch Street 63, *P20*
  Finch Lane 20
  Fleet Street *P40, F532*
  Gracechurch Street 63, 66, 67
  Holborn *P40*

 Honey Lane 19, 59, 60, 64
 Ironmonger Lane 59
 Lombard Street 61, 66
 Lothbury 64, 72
 Ludgate *F532*
 Milk Street, 59
 Mincing Lane 63, 72, *P20*
 Monkwell Street 69
 Old Jewry 64
 Pancras Lane 58, 59
 Poultry 58, 59, 60, 61, 62n., 63, 65,
  67, 68, 69, 70, *Pg–10, 12, 22, 43,*
  44
 St Clement's Lane *P13*
 St Lawrence Lane 59, 69
 St Swithin's Lane 61
 Sise Lane 58
 Soper Lane 60, 64, 65, 69, *F923*
 Thames Street 64
 Walbrook 61, 62n.
 Westcheap 60
London, Walter de *F606*
Longe, Hamo le, cit. Lond., fishmonger
 F1009–13
 Maud, wife of *F1010–13*
 John le *F430, 1238–9*
 Idonia, wife of *F430, 1238–9*
 Laurence le *F841*
Longuevill, Richard *P82*
Lorchoun, John, armourer *P7*
Lord, Loord, John, rector of Harpole *P205,*
 229
 Gilbert *P53, 74–6, 219*
 Walter le *F288*
 William 34, *P53, 93, 122, 130, 136, 147,*
  154, 160, 171, 181, 189, 205–6, 213–
  14, 220
Lorifer, Simon *P114, 119, 232*
Lorimare, Alexander *F735*
Lorimer, Lorymer, Peter le *F794, 797, 800,*
 803, 836, 839–40, 887, 892, 895,
 899, 916–17, 1154, 1192, 1208
 Henry, son of *F372, 487–9, 885, 987,*
  1142, 1208
 Alice, daughter of *F1208*
 Walter *F938, 942, 1191–2, 1194*
 William le *F885, 932, 937, 939, 1208*
Lothebury, Lodebury, Richard de *F274,*
 524
 Richard son of *F524*
Lound, William *F980*
Louthe (*Luda*), John de, clerk *F900–1, 908,*
 913, 935

Shordich, Shordych, Schordich, John *F1*, *7–14*
  Helen, wife of *1*, *7–12*
  Nicholas de 97, *F24*, *993*, *1256*
    Alice, wife of *F24*
  Richard de *F796*, *833*
Shyn, Robert *F425*
Shyre *see* Shire
Sibson (Hunts.) *P49*
Siccor, Walter *F253*
Sigar *F176*
Silvern, Robert *F253*, *1209*
Silveston, Nicholas de *F161*
Sime, John le *F624*
  Wolwyn le *F998*
Simeon *see* Symeon
Simon, Henry (son of) *P121*, *146*, *183*, *186*, *205–6*
  Richard *P70*
    Ismanis, daughter of *P70*
Skin, Skyn, Hugh *F401*, *1236*
  John *F894–5*, *897*
  Richard, *F496*, *967*
  Robert *F633*, *647*
Skipwyth, William de 97
Skynnere, William *F43*
Slipton (Northants.) 37, *P107*
Slo *see* Sloth
Slonhard, John *F540*
Sloth, Slo, Alice de la *F392*
  John atte *F945*, *947*
  Roger atte *F736*, *739*, *847*, *858*
Slow, Edmund atte *F1194*
Smale, Robert le *F243*
Smalwode, William *F385*
Smart, Geoffrey *F144*
  John, son of *F144*
Smelt, Richard *P223*
Smith (*Faber*), Smyth, Edmund *F197*
  John le *F164*, *236*, *264*, *290*, *309*, *547*, *580*, *1137*
    Helen, wife of *F164*
  Maurice *F670*
  Philip *F215–7*, *336*, *341*, *382*
  Richard *F1213*
  Robert *F344*, *347*, *700*, *783*, *1009*, *1256*
  Roger *F362*
    Elizabeth, daughter of *F362*
  Thomas *P63–4*
  William le *F290*, *404*, *408*, *422*, *431*, *563*, *690*, *727*, *872*, *892*, *941*, *986*, *1028*, *1039*, *1077*, *1090*, *1092–3*, *1095*, *1097*,

1135, *1139*, *1149*, *1153*, *1156*, *1231*, *1236*, *1252*
  Agnes, wife of *1097*
  William, son of *F986*
  William, of Hardingstone (Northants.) *P118*
Solar' *see* Solers
Sole (*de Solio*), Nicholas *F293*
  Robert *F289*
  Roger *F412*, *577*, *713*, *854*, *1003*
Solers (*de Solar*') Nicholas *F1210*
  Richard *F1210*
Solio *see* Sole
Somery, John *F758*, *772*, *776*, *805*, *808*, *811*, *915*
  Agnes, wife of *F808*
  John, son of *F805–6*, *811*, *915*
Sompter, Thomas *P229*
Sondes, William *F1284*
Sone, Sones, James le *F199*, *205*
  Roger *F999–1000*
    Agnes, daughter of *F999*, *1001–2*, *1004–5*, *1179*
Sotiers, Christine *F398*
Souche *see* Zouche
South Mimms (Herts.) 59, *F935*
Southgate, 'Southwodegate' (Middx.) *F333*, *484*, *491*, *611*, *695*, *733*, *827*, *956*, *959*, *961*, *973*, *998*, *1033*, *1270*
Southous, Walter 33
Southwark 56, 57, *P15*, *19*, *F27*, *636*
Southwell (Notts.) 25, 88
Spayne, John *P228*
Spencer, John le (?= Despenser) *F750*
Spenser *see* Despenser
Sperke *see* Spirk
Spicer, Spycer, Robert, bailiff of Northampton *P116*, *233*
Spigurnel, Hugh, clerk *P207*
  John *P207*
Spir, Robert *F158*
Spirk, Spyrk, Spirck, Spirc, Spyrc, Sperke, Sprik, Beatrice *F909*
  Peter *F237*, *267*, *447*, *1217*
    William, son of *F447*
  Richard *F346*, *355*, *395*, *655–5*, *661*, *665*, *728*, *757*, *898*, *906–7*, *909*, *910*
  Robert *F1002*
  Roger *F280*, *325*, *346*, *355*, *395*, *402*, *523*, *531–3*, *538*, *592*, *599*, *654–5*, *659*, *1002*, *1004*, *1155*, *1179*
  William, tailor *F210*, *255*, *273*, *280*, *436*, *546*, *549*, *551*, *554*, *599*, *664*, *1008*

INDEX OF SUBJECTS

References in italics are to numbered entries in the Calendar, preceded by *P* for Pyel cartulary and *F* for Fraunceys cartulary.